Preparing for t

REGENTS EXAMINATION

Integrated

ALGEBRA 1

Richard J. Andres, Ph.D.
Retired Mathematics Teacher and SAT Instructor
Jericho High School
Jericho, New York

Joyce Bernstein, Ed.D.
Curriculum Associate for Mathematics
East Williston Union Free School District
Old Westbury, New York

AMSCO SCHOOL PUBLICATIONS, INC.

315 Hudson Street, New York, N.Y. 10013

Dedication

In remembrance of Edward P. Keenan, our Amsco mentor.

Special thanks to Peg and Marc for their encouragement,
patience, and understanding.

Reviewers

Sal Sutera
  Teacher of Mathematics
  New Utrecht High School
  Brooklyn, New York

Steven J. Balasiano
  Assistant Principal Mathematics
  Canarsie High School
  Brooklyn, NY

Compositor and Text Design: Monotype, LLC
Cover Design by Meghan J. Shupe
Cover Art by Image Source

Brief portions of this book were adapted from the following Amsco publications:

Amsco's Preparing for the ACT Mathematics and Science Reasoning

Amsco's Preparing for the SAT Mathematics, Second Edition

Florida: Preparing for FCAT Mathematics Grade 10

Michigan: Preparing for the MEAP/HST in Mathematics

Preparing for the Georgia High School Graduation Test: Mathematics

Please visit our Web site at:
  www.amscopub.com

Regents Examinations included: 6/11, 8/11, 1/12, 6/12

Additional Practice Examinations can be found at Amsco's eLearning site:
  amscoelearning.com.

When ordering this book, please specify either **R 037 W** or
PREPARING FOR THE REGENTS EXAMINATION: INTEGRATED ALGEBRA 1

ISBN 978-1-56765-587-2

Contents

Chapter 6: Ratio and Proportion   126

Chapter 7: Foundations of Geometry   145

---

*8th Grade May–June Topic

---

*8th Grade May–June Topic

*8th Grade May–June Topic

Chapter 15: Probability   371

Chapter 16: Statistics   392

Getting Started

About This Book

New York State has laid out a three-year, three Regents Examination series for high school mathematics. The first examination is the Integrated Algebra Regents. This book is intended to help you review the content described for the Integrated Algebra Regents in the New York State Core Curriculum for Mathematics. *Preparing for the Regents Examination Integrated Algebra 1* contains reviews with Model Problems, Practice, Chapter Reviews, and Cumulative Reviews to help you study for the Integrated Algebra Regents. These practice problems incorporate both content and problem-solving situations similar to Regents questions.

Students should take the Grade 8 Diagnostic Assessment on pages 3–5. This will assess students' mastery of pre-algebra topics that serve as the foundation for a student of algebra. The Analysis Table on page 8 maps each question to the New York State Mathematics Grade 8 Performance Indicator and the chapters in this book where the topic is reviewed.

Test-Taking Strategies

General Strategies

- <u>Become familiar with the directions and format of the test ahead of time.</u> There will be both multiple-choice and extended response questions where you must show the steps you used to solve a problem, including formulas, diagrams, graphs, charts, and so on, where appropriate.
- <u>Pace yourself.</u> You have three hours to complete the examination. Do not race to answer every question immediately. On the other hand, do not linger over any question too long. Keep in mind that you will need more time to complete the extended response questions than to complete the multiple-choice questions.
- <u>Speed comes from practice.</u> The more you practice, the faster you will become and the more comfortable you will be with the material. Practice as often as you can.
- <u>Keep track of your place on the answer sheet.</u> This way you can mark each successive answer easily. If you find yourself bogged down, skip the problem and move on to the next. Return to the problem later. Do not leave any answer

spaces blank. There is no penality for guessing. Make a note in the margin of the test booklet so that you can locate the skipped problem easily. Be careful when you skip a problem. Be sure to leave the answer line blank that corresponds to the question you skipped. When you return later to the skipped problem, find some reasonable response even if you must guess.

- <u>Be cautious about wild guessing on the extended response questions.</u> Remember that guess and check solutions require at least three guesses, selected in a logical way.

Specific Strategies

- <u>Always scan the answer choices</u> before beginning to work on a multiple-choice question. This will help you to focus on the kind of answer that is required. Are you looking for fractions, decimals, percents, integers, squares, cubes, and so on? Eliminate choices that clearly do not answer the question asked.
- <u>Do not assume that your answer is correct just because it appears among the choices.</u> The wrong choices are usually there because they represent common student errors. After you find an answer, always reread the problem to make sure you have chosen the answer to the question that is asked, not the question you have in your mind.
- <u>Sub-in.</u> To sub-in means to substitute. You can sub-in friendly numbers for the variables to find a pattern and determine the solution to the problem.
- <u>Backfill.</u> If a problem is simple enough and you want to avoid doing the more complex algebra, or if a problem presents a phrase such as $x = ?$, then just fill in the answer choices that are given in the problem until you find the one that works.
- <u>Do the math.</u> This is the ultimate strategy. Don't go wild searching in your mind for tricks, gimmicks, or math magic to solve every problem. Most of the time the best way to get the right answer is to do the math and solve the problem.

Grade 8 Diagnostic Assessment

Based on the New York State Mathematics Standards 2005 revised July 2009

1 Simplify the following expression: $4(x + 5)$

2 Simplify the following expression: $(4x^2 + 3x - 7) - (2x - 6)$

3 Simplify the following expression: $4rs(3r^2s + 2rs + 3rs^2)$

4 Write an algebraic expression that is the same as "ten less than half a number."

5 What is $3d^3 - 6d^2$ divided by $3d$?

6 Graph the solution set for the following inequality: $-z - 2 < -3z + 2$

7 Solve the following inequality for t: $0.2t + 0.3t \leq -2t - 3$

8 Solve the following inequality for s: $-0.5s \geq 2s + 1$

9 Central School District provides bus transportation to any student who lives more than 1.5 miles from school. Write an inequality that shows the distance from school for which bus transportation is *not* provided and graph the inequality.

10 In the diagram below, $\overleftrightarrow{PQ}$ is parallel to $\overleftrightarrow{LM}$ and line l is a transversal. What is the measure of angle 2?

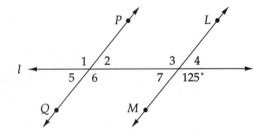

11 Factor $x^2 - 3x - 28$.

12 Identify the domain and range of the relation given below, which shows the amount of weight Marc lost on a diet.

Week #	1	2	3	4	5	6
Pounds Lost	2	2	1	1.5	1.5	2

13 Rewrite the relation shown as ordered pairs and explain whether this relation is a function.

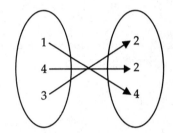

14 The following table represents a relation. Determine whether this relation is a function and explain your reasoning.

x	-2	-1	0	1	2
y	4	2	0	1	4

15 Construct a line segment congruent to line segment l below.

16 Construct an angle congruent to angle A below.

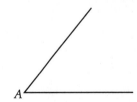

17 Construct the perpendicular bisector of segment $\overline{MN}$.

18 Construct the angle bisector of angle B.

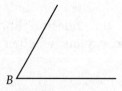

19 The graph below shows the cost of a taxicab ride in Springfield.

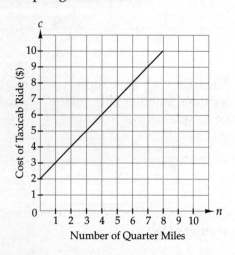

Number of Quarter Miles

a State the slope of the graph.

b State the y-intercept of the graph.

c Explain how the cost of a taxicab ride is determined.

20 The graph below shows Harry's bike ride home from school. He stopped at the library along the way. How long did he spend at the library? Explain your answer.

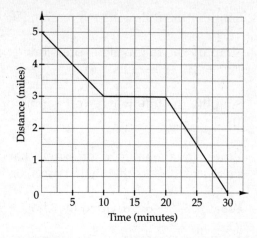

21 The equation of a line l is $y = -3x - 2$. Graph the line l.

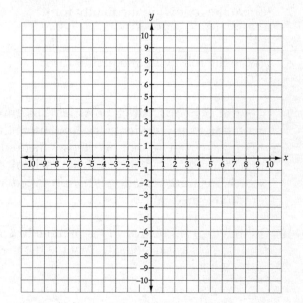

22 Solve the following system of equations graphically:

$y = -2x - 1$

$y = x + 5$

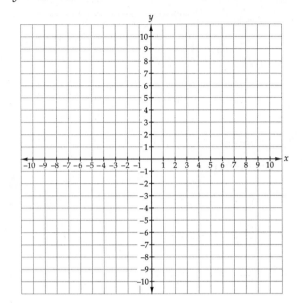

23 For any quadratic equation, what is the greatest power of x?

24 If $y = 4x^2 + 4x + 1$, what is the smallest value of y?

25 Graph the function represented in the table below.

x	y
-3	18
-2	8
-1	2
0	0
1	2
2	8
3	18

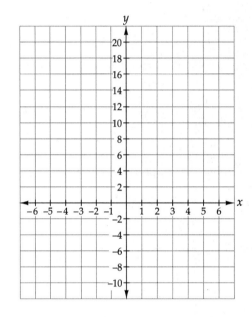

Grade 8 Diagnostic Assessment
Answer Key

1 $4(x + 5) = 4x + 20$

2 $(4x^2 + 3x - 7) - (2x - 6)$
Distribute the $-$ sign:
$4x^2 + 3x - 7 - 2x - {}^-6$
$4x^2 + 3x - 7 - 2x + 6$
$4x^2 + x - 1$

3 $4rs(3r^2s + 2rs + 3rs^2) = 12r^3s^2 + 8r^2s^2 + 12r^2s^3$

4 $\dfrac{n}{2} - 10$

5 $\dfrac{3d^3 - 6d^2}{3d} = d^2 - 2d$

6
$$-z - 2 < -3z + 2$$
$$\underline{+3z + 2 \qquad +3z + 2}$$
$$\frac{2z}{2} < \frac{4}{2}$$
$$z < 2$$

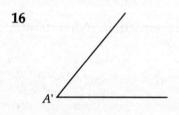

(number line from -5 to 5, open circle at 2, shaded to the left)

7
$$0.2t + 0.3t \le -2t - 3$$
$$0.5t \le -2t - 3$$
$$\underline{+2t \qquad\quad +2t}$$
$$\frac{2.5t}{2.5} \le \frac{-3}{2.5}$$
$$t \le -1.2$$

8
$$-0.5s \ge 2s + 1$$
$$\underline{-2s \qquad -2s}$$
$$\frac{-2.5s}{-2.5} \ge \frac{1}{-2.5}$$
$$s \le -0.4$$

9 $x \le 1.5$ (number line from -2 to 2, closed circle at 1.5, shaded to the left)

10 $180° - 125° = 55°$

11 $x^2 - 3x - 28 = (x + 4)(x - 7)$

12   Domain: {1, 2, 3, 4, 5, 6}
Range: {1, 1.5, 2}

13   {(1, 4), (4, 2), (3, 2)}   Relation is a function.

14   Relation is a function.

15 l' ——————————

16

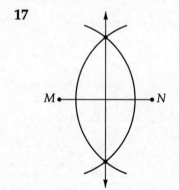

A'

17

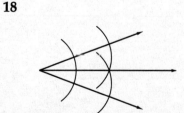

M N

18

19 a Slope = 1

b y-intercept = 2

c The cost of a taxicab ride is $2 dollars plus $1 for every additional quarter mile.

20 Harry spent 10 minutes at the library.

21

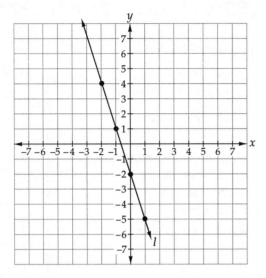

22

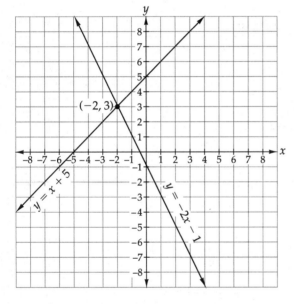

23 For any quadratic equation, the greatest power of x is 2.

24 Find the turning point for $y = 4x^2 + 4x + 1$.

$$x = \frac{-b}{2a}$$

$$x = \frac{-4}{2(4)} = -\frac{1}{2}$$

$$y = 4\left(-\frac{1}{2}\right)^2 + 4\left(-\frac{1}{2}\right) + 1 = 0$$

Therefore, the smallest value of y is 0.

25

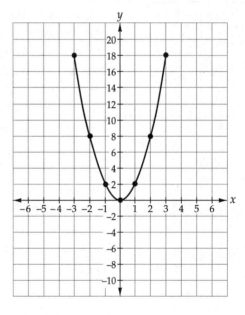

Grade 8 Diagnostic Assessment Analysis Table

Question	Performance Indicator Number	Performance Indicator	Chapter	Pages
1, 3	8.A.6	Multiply and divide monomials	5	103
2	8.A.7	Add and subtract polynomials (integer coefficients)	5	99
4	8.A.1	Translate verbal sentences into algebraic inequalities	3	63, 64
5	8.A.9	Divide a polynomial by a monomial (integer coefficients)	5	120
6	8.A.13	Solve multi-step inequalities and graph the solution set on a number line	4	89–96
7, 8	8.A.14	Solve linear inequalities by combining like terms, using the distributive property, or moving variables to one side of the inequality (include multiplication and division of inequalities by a negative number)	4	89–96
9	8.G.19	Graph the solution set of an inequality on a number line	4	89–96
10	8.A.4	Determine angle pair relationship when given two parallel lines cut by a transversal	7	152
11	8.A.11	Factor a trinomial into the form ax^2+bx+c; $a=1$ and c having no more than 3 sets of factors	11	278
12	8.A.17	Define and use correct terminology when referring to a function (domain and range)	9	207–210
13, 14	8.A.18	Determine if a relation is a function	9	237–242
15, 16, 17, 18	8.G.0	Construct the following using a straight edge and compass: segment congruent to a segment, angle congruent to an angle, perpendicular bisector, angle bisector	7	154–158
19, 20	8.G.13	Determine the slope of a line from a graph and explain the meaning of the slope as a constant rate of change	9	216–219, 222–227, 237–242
	8.G.14	Determine the y-intercept of a line from a graph and be able to explain the y-intercept		
	8.A.3	Describe a situation involving relationships that matches a given graph		
21	8.G.17	Graph a line from an equation in slope-intercept form	9	222–227
22	8.G.18	Solve systems of equations graphically (only linear, integral solutions, $y = mx + b$, no vertical/horizontal lines)	9	237–242
23, 24, 25	8.G.21	Recognize the characteristics of quadratics in tables, equations, and situations	13	307–315

Problem Solving

Steps in Problem Solving

A **problem** is defined as a situation that can be resolved if certain questions are answered. **Problem solving** is the process used to answer these questions. Problem solving often takes place in four steps: (1) Read and think about the problem. (2) Explore it. (3) Solve it. (4) Look back at it.

Step 1: Read and Think About the Problem

- To begin, look for the question or questions that must be answered to solve the problem.
- Identify the given facts.
- Be sure that you understand the vocabulary involved in the problem.
- Then check the given information. Is enough information given to solve the problem? Is more information given than you actually need?
- Think about the form of the answer. For example, will it be a measurement? If so, what will the unit of measure be? Make an estimate of the answer. This will help you recognize the answer when you see it.

Step 2: Explore the Problem

- Use tables, charts, and diagrams to organize the given information.
- Identify any questions and answers that will lead you to the solution.
- Decide on a strategy for reaching the solution. (Several strategies are described in this Introduction.)
- Choose the methods you need for your strategy.

Step 3: Solve the Problem

- Choose the operations you need for your strategy.
- Make an estimate, if appropriate.
- If a precise calculation is needed, try to choose the best method of finding the answer: mental computation, paper and pencil, or a calculator.

Step 4: Look Back at the Problem

- Is your answer reasonable? Does it answer the question asked? If not, work backward to find your mistake.
- Is your answer in the appropriate form? If the answer is a measurement, does the unit of measure make sense?
- Is your answer close to your estimate?
- If there is a mathematical check you can use, do the check.

Strategies for Problem Solving

In solving many problems, it is important to have a **strategy**—a plan or method for attacking the problem and finding the answer. You can also think of a strategy as a useful tool. Practice in using a variety of problem-solving tools will help you decide which strategy or strategies will be appropriate for solving a particular problem. Practice will also help you discover which strategies are easiest for you to understand and apply.

Drawing a Diagram   A diagram is a visual display, and its purpose is to organize information. This can be very helpful in problem solving.

MODEL PROBLEMS

1 Eight baseball teams are competing for a league championship. A team is eliminated when it loses a game. How many games must be played to determine the winner?

SOLUTION

Draw a diagram.

The standard diagram for an elimination tournament looks like this:

Answer: You find the answer by counting the number of blank lines, which represent games to be played. The diagram shows that 7 games are needed to determine the winner.

2 There are 32 students in a science class. Twelve of these students belong to the Math Club, 20 students belong to the Chemistry Club, and 9 students belong to both. How many students in the science class belong to neither the Math Club nor the Chemistry Club?

SOLUTION

Draw a diagram. A problem like this can be solved using a Venn diagram. A **Venn diagram** usually consists of circles within a rectangle. The rectangle represents the "universe"—the set of all the things being considered. The circles represent subsets of the universe. Intersections of the circles represent elements that are members of more than one subset. A Venn diagram can be a useful tool for counting the number of members of a set when sets overlap, that is, when members are in two or more sets at the same time.

In this case, use overlapping circles and begin with the number of students that belong to both clubs. Then use this number to determine how many belong to only the Math Club and how many belong to only the Chemistry Club.

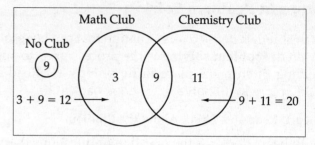

Add the numbers in the diagram (3 + 9 + 11 = 23). Thus there are 23 students in both clubs. The difference (32 − 23 = 9) means that there are 9 students who do not belong to either club.

3 The distance between two cities, M and N, is 300 miles. The distance between cities N and O is 500 miles. Which could be the distance between cities O and M?
(1) 100 miles
(2) 500 miles
(3) 850 miles
(4) 1,000 miles

SOLUTION

Draw a picture.

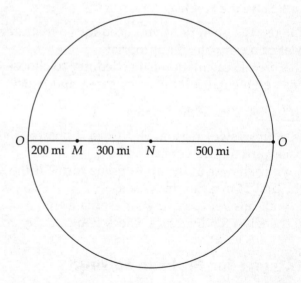

Point O can lie anywhere on the circle with N as its center. The distance from N to O, or the radius of the circle, is 500 miles, so the distance from M to O could be at most 800 miles. The smallest possible distance from M to O is 200 miles. The only answer choice between 200 miles and 800 miles is 500 miles.

Answer: (2) 500 miles

 **Practice**

Draw a diagram to solve each problem. Explain your reasoning.

1 Lupe started a pep club. On Monday, she got 2 friends to join. On Tuesday, each of these friends got 2 more people to join. On Wednesday, each person who joined on Tuesday got 2 more people to join. If this pattern continues, how many people (including Lupe) are in the club by the end of Saturday?

2 The numbers 1, 4, 9, and 16 are called squares. Find the tenth square and its pattern.

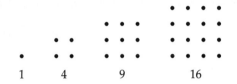

1   4   9   16

3 A string ensemble has 15 members. If 4 members play the cello and 9 members play the violin, but 4 members play neither of those instruments, how many members play both the violin and the cello?

4 Bus routes connect these cities: Ashton and Denby, Denby and Beacon, Elkton and Crestwood, Beacon and Crestwood, and Denby and Elkton. How many ways are there to travel from Elkton to Beacon? What are they?

5 In a middle school with 600 students, 100 are in the band, 70 are in the orchestra, and 12 are in both the band and the orchestra. How many students are not in either the band or the orchestra?

Using Tables and Lists Like a diagram, a table or a list is a visual display. In a table, data are arranged in rows and columns.

 MODEL PROBLEMS

1 The problem above about the 8-team tournament can also be solved by using a table. If 8 teams are competing for a championship, and a team is eliminated when it loses a game, how many games are needed to determine the winner?

SOLUTION

Set up a table to show the following information: 8 teams play 4 games, resulting in 4 winners and 4 losers. The 4 winners then play 2 games, resulting in 2 winners and 2 losers. These 2 winners play one game, which determines the final winner.

Teams	Games	Winners	Losers
8	4	4	4
4	2	2	2
2	1	1	1

The answer is found by adding up the numbers in the column headed "Games." The table shows that 7 games are needed.

2 Ann, Bryan, Carla, Don, and Ernesto have applied for three job openings at the library. What are all the possible groups of three that could be hired?

SOLUTION

Make a list of groups of 3 students using their initials. Note that in this situation the group ABC is the same as ACB, BCA, CAB, and so on.

ABC	ACD	BCD	CDE
ABD	ACE	BCE	
ABE	ADE	BDE	

Answer: There are 10 possible groups of 3 students.

Problem Solving **11**

Use a table or a list to solve each problem. Explain your reasoning.

1 How many triangles are in the figure?

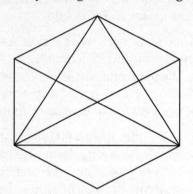

2 How many different ways can you make change for a quarter using pennies, nickels, and dimes?

3 Mr. Jenkins has 50 feet of fencing to enclose a rectangular pen. What will the length and the width have to be to give the pen the largest possible area if only whole feet are used?

4 Hot dogs come in packages of 8. Hot-dog rolls come in packages of 6. What is the least number of packages of hot dogs and hot-dog rolls needed to have the same number of hot dogs and rolls?

Working Backward   In **working backward**, we start with a given result and then go back, step by step, to the beginning.

Often, working backward involves thinking what operation (or operations) we would have used to get the given result, and then using the *opposite* operation (or operations) to find the original number.

 MODEL PROBLEMS

1 If we multiply a number by 6, subtract 357, and then divide by 9, the result is 237. Find the original number.

SOLUTION

To solve a problem like this, we can work backward. We start with the result (237) and reverse our steps to get to the original number.

$237 \times 9 = 2{,}133$	Multiply, the opposite of dividing.
$2{,}133 + 357 = 2{,}490$	Add, the opposite of subtracting.
$2{,}490 \div 6 = 415$	Divide, the opposite of multiplying.

Answer: 415

ALTERNATIVE SOLUTION

This problem can also be solved algebraically. Let the original number be n. Then solve the equation:

$$\frac{6n - 357}{9} = 237$$

2 Helen, Ira, Jan, and Ken shared a box of pens. Helen took half. Ira took half of what was left. Jan took a third of what was left. Ken took the remaining 6 pens. How many pens were in the box?

SOLUTION

Work backward.

Ken took 6 pens. This was two-thirds of n, if n is what was left after Ira took his pens. $6 = \frac{2}{3}n$, so $n = 9$.

If there were 9 pens left after Ira took half, there were 18 before he picked. Similarly, if there were 18 pens after Helen took half, there were 36 pens in the box to start.

3 Mr. James spent $32,500 for a sports car. This amount was 30 percent more than the sticker price. The manufacturer sets its sticker price at 150 percent of the production cost. How much did it cost to produce Mr. James's car?

SOLUTION

- Start at the end. Mr. James buys the car for $32,500, which is 30 percent more than the sticker price.
- To find the sticker price, go back one step. Let S be the sticker price. Think: "30 percent more than S" means 100 percent of S plus 30 percent of S, or 130 percent. Change this to its decimal equivalent, 1.30. Then:

$$1.30S = \$32,500$$

$$S = \$32,500 \div 1.30 = \$25,000$$

- To find the production cost, go back another step. Let P be the production cost. Sticker price S is 150 percent of P. Change 150 percent to its decimal equivalent, 1.50. Then:

$$1.50P = \$25,000$$

$$P = \$25,000 \div 1.50 = \$16,666.66\ldots, \text{ or approximately } \$16,667$$

Answer: It cost $16,667 to produce the car.

 ## Practice

1 Marcia's school starts at 8:30 A.M. Marcia must make three stops before she gets to school. It takes 15 minutes to get to her first stop from her house, 30 minutes to get to the second stop from the first stop, 30 minutes to get to the third stop from the second stop, and 30 minutes to get to school from the third stop. She spends 2 minutes at each stop. What is the latest time Maria can leave home to get to school on time? Solve by working backward. Explain your answer.

2 The price tag below shows that the price of a CD player is reduced for the second time. The current price, $39.20, represents an additional 20 percent discount after a 30 percent discount. What was the original price?

3 Three years ago, Mrs. Canada bought a new car. The first year the car lost 20 percent of its value. For each of the next 2 years it lost 10 percent of its remaining value. Its current value is $25,920. How much did Mrs. Canada pay for the car when it was new?

4 A football team gained 7 yards, lost 5 yards, gained 6 yards, then lost 3 yards. The team is now at its 30-yard line. From what line did the team start?

Guessing and Checking An effective procedure for solving some problems is to **guess and check**. When you use this strategy, you guess an answer and then check to see if it is correct. Use your first guess and the result of that guess to make better guesses until you find the correct answer. Remember that even if you find the right answer on the first guess, you must show all work for *at least three guesses*.

MODEL PROBLEMS

1 If $5x + 6 = 61$, find the value of x.

SOLUTION

Use guessing and checking. Guess a value of x. Substitute that value in the given equation and then evaluate the equation. If your guess gives a result greater than 61, try a lower value for x. If your guess gives a result smaller than 61, try a higher value for x. Keep guessing, substituting, and evaluating until you get the correct value.

Guesses may vary. Here is one example.

Guess	Check: $5x + 6 = 61$	Result
8	$(5 \cdot 8) + 6 = 40 + 6 = 46$	46 is too low. Try a greater value for x.
10	$(5 \cdot 10) + 6 = 50 + 6 = 56$	56 is still too low. Try a greater value for x.
11	$(5 \cdot 11) + 6 = 55 + 6 = 61$ ✓	Therefore the value of x is 11.

Answer: $x = 11$

2 There are 31 students in a math class. There are 5 more girls than boys. How many boys are there?

SOLUTION

Use guessing and checking. Guess the number of girls and the number of boys. (Remember that the number of boys must be 5 less than the number of girls.)

Add these numbers. If the sum is 31, your guesses were correct. *You must still show two other guesses.* If the sum is less than 31, guess again, using greater numbers, and then add again. If the sum is more than 31, use smaller numbers on your next guess. Keep guessing and checking until you get the right answer.

Guesses may vary. Here is one example.

Guess	Check	Result
15 girls, 10 boys	$15 + 10 = 25$	25 is too low. Try greater numbers of boys and girls.
20 girls, 15 boys	$20 + 15 = 35$	35 is too high. Try numbers less than 20 and 15 but more than 15 and 10 (the first guess).
18 girls, 13 boys	$18 + 13 = 31$ ✓	Right.

Answer: There are 18 girls and 13 boys.

Solve by guessing and checking.

1 What two consecutive numbers add up to 39?

2 An Internet provider is hiring 1,500 new workers. Of the new hires, there will be 250 more computer programmers than salespeople. How many computer programmers will be hired?

3 Chandler Used Car Company sells more recreational vehicles than regular automobiles. Last week Chandler sold 60 units. If the number of recreational vehicles sold is multiplied by the number of regular automobiles sold, the product is 779. How many recreational vehicles were sold?

4 Arrange the numbers −4, −5, 3, 2, 6, and 7 so that the sum of the numbers on each side of the triangle is 4.

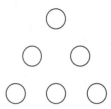

5 Arrange the numbers from 1 to 9 in the **magic square** so that the sum of each row, each column, and each diagonal is 15.

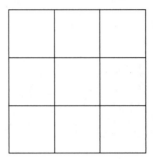

Finding a Pattern To solve a problem, we sometimes need to **find a pattern** in a given sequence of numbers. Each number in the sequence is called a **term**. Each term has a position in the sequence: first, second, third, and so on. Most patterns can be found by comparing a few terms to determine their relationship to one another. This gives us a rule for the relationship between consecutive terms so that the successive terms in the sequence can be found.

One way to find a pattern is to ask the following four questions, in order:

- Is the second term greater or less than the first term?
- What is the difference between the first term and the second?
- Is the difference the same between each term and the next term? If not, what is the pattern of the differences?
- What operation or operations can be performed on the first term to get the second term? This operation or combination of operations is the rule for the pattern.

MODEL PROBLEMS

1 What is the next number in the sequence 3, 8, 13, 18, 23, . . . ? Give a rule for finding other terms.

SOLUTION

To find a pattern, answer the four questions.

- The second term is greater than the first term.
- The difference between the first term and the second term is $8 - 3 = 5$.
- The difference, 5, is the same between consecutive terms:

  $$13 - 8 = 5 \qquad 18 - 13 = 5 \qquad 23 - 18 = 5$$

- To get from the first term to the second term, the operation is addition: add 5.

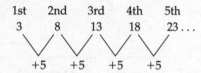

Answer: To get the next term after 23, add 5: $23 + 5 = 28$. The next term is 28.

The rule is: 5 added to each term gives the next term.

2 What is the next number in the sequence 1, 4, 9, 16, 25, 36, . . . ? Give a rule for finding other terms.

SOLUTION

Find a pattern.

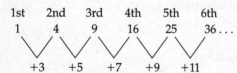

As shown above, the numbers added to each term are odd and increase by 2.

Therefore, the next term can be found by adding $11 + 2$, or 13, to 36.

Answer: To get the next term, add: $36 + 13 = 49$. The next term is 49.

The rule is: To find successive terms of the sequence, add positive odd numbers that increase by 2 each time.

ALTERNATIVE SOLUTION

The rule for this type of pattern can also be shown using multiplication.

1st	2nd	3rd	4th	5th	6th
1	4	9	16	25	36 . . .
1×1	2×2	3×3	4×4	5×5	6×6
1^2	2^2	3^2	4^2	5^2	6^2

Answer: The sequence is the perfect squares, in increasing order. Therefore the next term is the next perfect square: $7 \times 7 = 7^2 = 49$.

The rule is: Find the sequence of perfect squares in increasing order.

3 A store clerk is making a pyramid display of soup cans. The bottom row consists of 10 cans. Then, going upward, the next row has 9 cans, the next 8, and so on. To complete the pyramid, how many cases of soup should the clerk bring from the warehouse if each case contains 12 cans?

SOLUTION

Find a pattern.

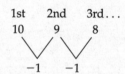

The rule for finding the next term is: subtract 1. There will be 10 rows. Apply the rule to find the numbers in the pattern.

$$10 + 9 + 8 + 7 + 6 + 5 + 4 + 3 + 2 + 1 = 55$$

To calculate the number of cases needed, divide: $55 \div 12 = 4\frac{7}{12}$. Assume that the clerk can bring only whole cases from the warehouse.

Answer: The clerk must bring 5 cases.

 **Practice**

1 For each sequence state the rule and give the next term.

a 9, 13, 17, 21, ...

b 1, 5, 8, 1, 5, ...

c 12, 17, 22, 27, ...

d 26, 24, 22, 20, ...

e 2, 5, 11, 23, ...

f 3, 6, 3, 6, ...

Solve each problem by finding a pattern. Explain your reasoning.

2 John is job hunting. He is 25 years old, and his goal is to be earning $40,000 a year by the time he is 35. He sees a job advertised that pays $24,000 per year now, with a raise of $1,000 each year. If John gets this job, will he reach his goal?

3 Paula received $1 for her first birthday, $2 for her second birthday, $4 for her third birthday, and $8 for her fourth birthday. At this rate, how much money will she have received in all after she celebrates her ninth birthday?

4 Mary bought a used car 2 years ago for $30,000. This model **depreciates** (loses value) at the following rate: $1,000 the first year; $2,000 the second year; $3,000 the third year, and so on. How much will the car be worth 5 years from now?

5 When a ball is dropped from a height of 64 inches, it bounces back half the original height. If it continues to bounce in this manner, what is the total distance that it will have traveled when it hits the ground for the fifth time?

Solving a Simpler Problem We can often solve a difficult problem more easily if we first solve a simpler problem. One way to do this is to use easier numbers. Using simpler numbers helps us to focus on the operations needed to solve the problem. Another way is to break a long problem into smaller parts.

 MODEL PROBLEMS

1 Find the sum of the series
2 + 4 + 6 + 8 + ... + 996 + 998 + 1,000

SOLUTION

Solve a simpler problem, the sum of the series
2 + 4 + 6 + 8 + 10 + 12:

$$2 + 4 + 6 + 8 + 10 + 12$$
$$\underline{14}$$
$$14$$
$$14$$

The sum of each *pair* is 14. There are 6 members of the series, so there are 3 pairs.

Therefore, the sum is 3 × 14 = 42.

Use this technique to solve the given problem:

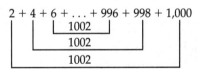

Now the sum of each pair is 1,002. There are 500 even numbers from 2 to 1,000, so there are 250 pairs. To find the sum, multiply:

250 × 1,002 = 250,500

2 Ballpoint pens are on sale at 3 for $1.29. Mr. Miller needs 100 pens for his department. How much will the pens cost?

SOLUTION

Break this problem into two simpler parts. First, find the cost of 1 pen, called the unit price. To do this, divide:

$1.29 ÷ 3 = $0.43

Next, multiply the unit price by 100:

$0.43 × 100 = $43

Answer: The pens will cost $43.

3 A cookbook recommends roasting a chicken $\frac{1}{2}$ hour per pound at 375°. How much time is needed to roast a $4\frac{1}{2}$-pound chicken?

SOLUTION

Solve a simpler problem. Suppose that the recommendation was 1 hour per pound. Then the solution is easy: $1 \cdot 4\frac{1}{2} = 4\frac{1}{2}$ hours. The operation used is multiplication. Since the given recommendation is $\frac{1}{2}$ hour, you need to multiply $4\frac{1}{2}$ by $\frac{1}{2}$.

$$\frac{1}{2} \cdot 4\frac{1}{2} = \frac{1}{2} \cdot \frac{9}{2} = \frac{9}{4} = 2\frac{1}{4}$$

Answer: $2\frac{1}{4}$ hours

ALTERNATIVE SOLUTION

There is another way to solve this problem. Suppose that the chicken weighs only 4 pounds. Then $\frac{1}{2} \cdot 4 = 2$ (half of 4 is 2). So to solve the real problem, use the same operation: multiply by $\frac{1}{2}$. The calculations are the same as in the first solution.

Sometimes unnecessary information is given. In this case the temperature, 375°, is not needed to solve the problem.

 Practice

Answer each question by solving a simpler problem. Explain your reasoning.

1 Find the sum of this series:

22, 24 , . . . , 68, 70

2 A "going out of business" sale offers folding chairs for $120 a dozen. Mrs. Smith needs to buy chairs for her catering service. How much will she pay for 18 chairs?

3 There are 1,500 students in the senior class at DeWitt Clinton High School. For a class trip, 25 percent of them will go to Washington, D.C. How many buses will be needed to get them there if each bus holds 47 passengers?

4 A 6-pack of 10-ounce bottles of spring water costs $4.80. A $1\frac{1}{2}$-gallon bottle of the same brand costs $5.75. Which is the better buy? (1 gallon = 128 ounces)

5 A recipe calls for $\frac{3}{4}$ cup of bread stuffing for each pound of turkey. If $9\frac{3}{8}$ cups of stuffing are needed, how much does the turkey weigh?

 ## PROBLEM-SOLVING REVIEW

Solve each problem. Explain the strategy you use.

1 A number is a two-digit multiple of 11. The product of the digits is a perfect square and a perfect cube. Find the number.

2 Ten chairs are placed along the four walls of a room so that each of the walls has the same number of chairs. Show how this can be done.

3 How many numbers are in this set?

2, 5, 8, 11, 14, . . . , 683

4 a Find the missing sums.

1	1
1 + 3	4
1 + 3 + 5	?
1 + 3 + 5 + 7	?
1 + 3 + 5 + 7 + 9	?

b Predict how many odd whole numbers you would have to add to obtain a sum of 169. Explain your reasoning.

5 A dog weighs 12 pounds plus half its weight. How much does the dog weigh?

6 Find the ones (or units) digit in 9^{28}.

7 In a dart game, three darts are thrown. All the darts hit the target. What scores are possible?

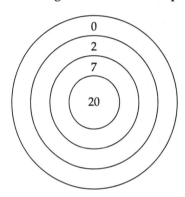

8 A recycling committee was paid $0.14 per pound for $87\frac{1}{2}$ pounds of newspaper and $0.32 per pound for $43\frac{3}{4}$ pounds of aluminum cans. How much money did the committee receive?

9 Maya wants to pin four photographs onto her office bulletin board. What is the least number of pins she will need if a pin goes through every corner of every photograph?

10 The area of a rectangular garden is 40.5 square feet. The garden is twice as long as it is wide. What are the dimensions of the garden?

CHAPTER 1

Numeration

Sets of Real Numbers

A **set** is a collection of distinct elements that can be listed within braces { }.

- A set with no elements is known as the **empty set** or the **null set** and can be written as $\varnothing$ or { }.
- A set with a specific number of elements such as {1, 2, 3, 4, 5} is a **finite set**. If the set is very large, three dots (…) can be used to show "and so on in the same pattern." So {1, 2, 3, …, 98, 99, 100} is the set of counting numbers from 1 to 100.
- A set that has no last element and continues indefinitely, like {1, 2, 3, 4, …}, is an **infinite set**.

Counting numbers, or **natural numbers**, are {1, 2, 3, …} and can be represented on a number line with an arrow to show that the set continues without end.

Whole numbers are the counting numbers and 0, {0, 1, 2, 3, …}. The whole numbers can also be shown on a number line.

Integers consist of the whole numbers and their negatives, or opposites. {…, −3, −2, −1, 0, 1, 2, 3, …}. Zero is its own opposite.

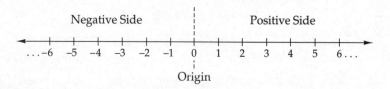

The letters *a* and *b* here are variables. A variable is a letter or symbol that takes the place of a specific unknown quantity.

Rational numbers consist of all numbers that can be expressed as quotients of two integers, $\frac{a}{b}$, where b, the denominator, does not equal zero. Every rational number can be represented as a terminating decimal or a repeating decimal.

Terminating decimals, such as 0.25 or −1.00, are rational numbers that have a finite number of nonzero digits to the right of the decimal point. The number 0.25 can also be written 0.25000000000…, but the extra zeros do not tell us anything more about the number. All integers are terminating decimals. For example, −1.00 equals −1.

Repeating decimals, such as −0.333… or 5.7321321321…, are rational numbers. These decimals have an infinite number of nonzero digits to the right of the decimal point in a repeating pattern. The number −0.333… has an infinite number of 3s, and in the number 5.7321321321… the pattern 321 repeats forever. Repeating decimals can be written with a horizontal bar over the digits that define the pattern. The two numbers above can be written as $-0.\overline{3}$ and $5.7\overline{321}$. Note that in the latter number, the bar does not extend over the 7, because the 7 does not repeat.

Irrational numbers are decimal numbers that neither repeat nor terminate. They cannot be expressed as fractions with integers for the numerator and denominator. For example, π (π = 3.1415926…) and some radicals (such as $\sqrt{2}$ = 1.41421…) are irrational numbers.

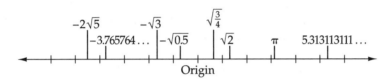

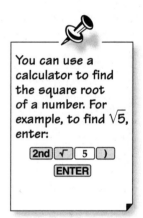

You can use a calculator to find the square root of a number. For example, to find $\sqrt{5}$, enter:

[2nd] [√] [5] [)]
[ENTER]

The set of **real numbers** consists of the elements in the set of rational numbers combined with the elements in the set of irrational numbers. The number line is a graphic representation of the set of real numbers. Every real number corresponds to a point on this number line.

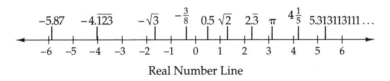

Real Number Line

The relationships between the various sets of numbers are shown in the diagram below. The set of natural numbers falls inside the set of whole numbers, the set of whole numbers is inside the set of integers, and so on. The shaded area has no numbers in it, because every real number is either rational or irrational.

Sets of Numbers

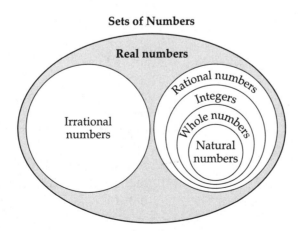

Guidelines for displaying answers

1   If a specific form is not required, such as a radical ($\sqrt{5}$) or fraction $\left(\dfrac{3}{7}\right)$ or

decimal to the nearest tenth (61.3), then answers may be left in any equivalent form, such as $\sqrt{48}$ or $4\sqrt{3}$ or 6.92820323. This information is especially important when answering the extended response questions.

2   Rounding in the *middle* of a problem should not happen; rounding should be done only when the final answer is reached. Instead of rounding common repeating decimals such as 0.666. . . , use the fraction menu item under the MATH key in the graphing calculator to convert to a fraction, $\dfrac{2}{3}$.

3   Lastly, π is an irrational number; it is not $\dfrac{22}{7}$ or 3.14. These are simply useful approximations. And unless otherwise specified, the $\boxed{\pi}$ key on a calculator should be used in computations.

 MODEL PROBLEM

List the numbers in the set {89, 3, 458, 0.89, 0, −3} that are natural numbers.

SOLUTION

The natural numbers are {1, 2, 3,…}. This set would include 89, 3, and 458 from the original set. Zero and −3 are integers, not natural numbers, and 0.89 is a rational number.

Answer: {89, 3, 458}

 Practice

---

1   The set of two-digit natural numbers is:
   (1)   finite
   (2)   infinite
   (3)   empty
   (4)   unclear

2   Name the number assigned to point *G* in this line.

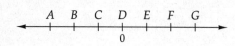

   (1)   −3
   (2)   0
   (3)   2
   (4)   3

3   What is the best sequence of names to identify the elements of this set?

$$\{-8, 7, 0.202202220\ldots, 0.\overline{4}\}$$

   (1)   integer, natural, real, irrational
   (2)   integer, whole, irrational, real
   (3)   integer, irrational, integer, rational
   (4)   integer, real, whole, rational

4   What is the best sequence of names to identify this set of numbers?

$$\left\{1\dfrac{3}{5}, -10, 0.5\overline{1}, \pi, 17\right\}$$

   (1)   rational, integer, irrational, irrational, natural
   (2)   rational, irrational, rational, irrational, whole
   (3)   rational, real, rational, real, natural
   (4)   real, integer, irrational, irrational, natural

Exercises 5–14: Identify each number as either a rational or an irrational number.

5 0.17

6 0.17171717…

7 0.172222…

8 0.17117111711117…

9 $\sqrt{52}$

10 π

11 0

12 $\frac{21}{3}$

13 −5.35

14 $7.\overline{17}$

15 List the elements in the set of the nonnegative integers.

16 Is 0 an irrational number? Explain your answer.

17 How can every whole number be written in the form $\frac{a}{b}$, $b \neq 0$?

18 True or false? Any fraction made up of two natural numbers is a rational number. Explain your answer.

Absolute Value

In operations with signed numbers, **absolute value** is important. This is the value of a number when we ignore the positive or negative sign. Another way to think of absolute value is that it is a number's distance from zero on the number line, in either direction. The absolute value of any number n is written $|n|$ and is always positive.

Opposites are any two numbers equidistant from zero on the number line in different directions. For any real number n, its opposite is $-n$. An opposite is also called an **additive inverse**.

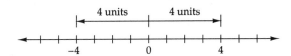

Symbols of Inequality

When two numbers are not equal, the relationship between them can be expressed in various ways in a form of an **inequality**.

Symbol	Example	Read
>	9 > 6	9 is greater than 6.
<	2 < 5	2 is less than 5.
≥	7 ≥ 3	7 is greater than or equal to 3.
≤	4 ≤ 8	4 is less than or equal to 8.
≠	5 ≠ 1	5 is not equal to 1.

MODEL PROBLEMS

What is the absolute value of each number? **SOLUTIONS**

1 $|35|$ 35

2 $|20 - 25|$ $|-5| = 5$

3 $|-6|$ 6

What is the opposite of each number?

4 -6.08 6.08

5 $\dfrac{86}{91}$ $-\dfrac{86}{91}$

6 $3,000,000$ $-3,000,000$

> The absolute value of zero is zero:
> $$|0| = 0$$
> Zero is its own opposite:
> $$-0 = 0$$

Practice

1 Which statement is true?

   (1) $7 > |7|$

   (2) $|-5| < 5$

   (3) $|-8| > -2$

   (4) $|-4| < 0$

2 On this number line, A is the opposite of E. What is the value of C?

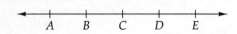

   (1)   0
   (2)   1
   (3)   2
   (4)   3

3 Evaluate: $|-5| - |2|$

   (1) -7
   (2) -3
   (3)   3
   (4)   7

4 $|10 - 2| - |3 + 1| + |-3| =$

   (1)   7
   (2)   4
   (3) -4
   (4) -7

Exercises 5–15: Evaluate.

5 $|-7|$

6 $-|6|$

7 $-|-6|$

8 $2|3|$

9 $2|-3|$

10 $-4|4|$

11 $-4|-4|$

12 $4 + |-2|$

13 $4 - |-2|$

14 $|4 - 7|$

15 $-|6 \bullet 2|$

16 On the number line below, the length of each interval is 2 units and point B is the opposite of point F. What is the value of point G? Explain.

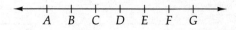

Exercises 17–20: Replace each ? with the symbol that makes the statement true: =, >, or <.

17 $|-6|$? -6

18 $|-8|$? $|6|$

19 $|-6|$? $|6|$

20 $-|-11|$? 11

The Order of Real Numbers

Whenever we compare two real numbers x and y, only *one* of the following can apply:

- $x < y$ or "x is less than y" if x is to the left of y on a number line.

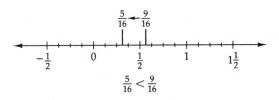

$$\frac{5}{16} < \frac{9}{16}$$

- $x > y$ or "x is greater than y" if x is to the right of y.

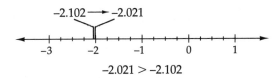

$$-2.021 > -2.102$$

- $x = y$ or "x is equal to y" if x is the same point as y.

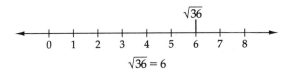

$$\sqrt{36} = 6$$

A number sentence with two *greater than* or two *less than* symbols can be used to show where on a number line some quantity may fall. For example, "the square root of 5 is somewhere between 2 and 3" can be written $2 < \sqrt{5} < 3$.

To Compare Decimal Numbers

- Line them up so that the decimal points are in a column.
- Add zeros to the end of the numbers so they are all the same length.
- Compare the numbers as if they were integers, ignoring the decimal points.

 MODEL PROBLEM

Put the numbers 1.05, 0.159, 1.5, 0.5 and 0.51 in order from least to greatest.

SOLUTION

Line up the numbers	Make numbers the same length.	Order numbers as if they were integers.
1.05	1.050	0.159
0.159	0.159	0.500
1.5	1.500	0.510
0.5	0.500	1.050
0.51	0.510	1.500

Answer: The numbers in order from least to greatest are 0.159, 0.5, 0.51, 1.05, 1.5.

To Compare Fractions

- Find a common multiple of the denominators.
- Build up fractions so they all have the common multiple for a denominator.
- Compare the numerators.

MODEL PROBLEMS

1 Which is greater, $\frac{3}{5}$ or $\frac{4}{7}$?

SOLUTION

$$\frac{3}{5} = \frac{3 \times 7}{5 \times 7} = \frac{21}{35} \qquad \frac{4}{7} = \frac{4 \times 5}{7 \times 5} = \frac{20}{35}$$

Since $21 > 20$, then $\frac{21}{35} > \frac{20}{35}$ and $\frac{3}{5} > \frac{4}{7}$.

2 If $\frac{1}{2} < \frac{x}{10} < \frac{4}{5}$, then what is the set of possible integer values for x?

SOLUTION

Express all fractions with the same common denominator. Thus, $\frac{1}{2} = \frac{5}{10}$ and $\frac{4}{5} = \frac{8}{10}$. Now, rewrite the original problem with these equivalent fractions: $\frac{5}{10} < \frac{x}{10} < \frac{8}{10}$.

Since either $\frac{6}{10}$ or $\frac{7}{10}$ could replace $\frac{x}{10}$, the possible integer values for x are 6 and 7.

Answer: $\{6, 7\}$

3 Which is smaller, $\frac{7}{8}$ or $\frac{4}{5}$?

SOLUTION

Use a calculator.

$$\frac{7}{8} = 7 \div 8 = 0.875$$

$$\frac{4}{5} = 4 \div 5 = 0.8$$

Since $0.8 < 0.875$, then $\frac{4}{5} < \frac{7}{8}$.

> You can also use a calculator to write each fraction as a decimal. Divide the numerator by the denominator, then compare.
>
> Or use the fraction menu item.

 Practice

---

1 Which irrational number lies between 0.122 and 0.123?

   (1) 0.1211311141111…
   (2) 0.12133113311133…
   (3) 0.122333…
   (4) 0.123212343212345…

2 Ann agrees to sell her CD player to the person who makes the best offer. Sally offers $550, Mitsi offers $499.98, Doug offers $549.75, and Jean offers $432. To whom should Ann sell the CD player?

   (1) Mitsi
   (2) Sally
   (3) Jean
   (4) Doug

3 The intervals on this number line are equal and the locations of 0 and 1 are shown.

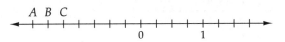

Point C is:

(1) $\dfrac{3}{4}$

(2) $-\dfrac{3}{4}$

(3) $1\dfrac{1}{4}$

(4) $-1\dfrac{1}{4}$

4 Between what two points on this number line is $-1.4141141114\ldots$ located?

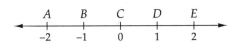

(1) A and B

(2) B and C

(3) C and D

(4) D and E

5 Which statement is *false*?

(1) $-3 < 9$

(2) $-4 < -12$

(3) $-7 < -3 < 5$

(4) $9 > 0 > -4$

Exercises 6 and 7: Order each set of numbers from least to greatest.

6 $\dfrac{78}{13}, 5\dfrac{5}{6}, \dfrac{1,430}{1,690}, \dfrac{250}{60}$

7 0.12, 0.112, 0.2, 0.21, 0.022

8 What is one possible integer value of k for which $\dfrac{1}{4} < \dfrac{k}{10} < \dfrac{1}{3}$ is true?

9 Is there a greatest negative integer? Explain your answer.

10 Is there a natural number that is closest to zero on the number line? Explain your answer.

11 Is there a positive real number that is closest to zero on the number line? Explain your answer.

12 How many natural numbers are in the set of integers between -3 and 4, inclusive?

13 Draw a standard horizontal number line. Show points for 0 and 1 and any other integers that may help you as guides. Graph these three numbers on your line: {1.69, $-0.91\overline{6}$, 1, $1.9\overline{6}$}.

14 Danisha is thinking of a fraction. She challenges you to guess what it is. She tells you that the numerator and the denominator add up to 100 and the fraction is equivalent to $\dfrac{1}{3}$. What is the fraction?

Converting Between Percents, Fractions, and Decimals

Percent (%) means *out of 100*. Thus, 5% = 5 out of 100 = 5 hundredths = $\dfrac{5}{100}$ = 0.05.

Although you can use your calculator, memorizing common equivalents will help you to find solutions to problems faster.

Fraction	$\dfrac{1}{10}$	$\dfrac{1}{8}$	$\dfrac{1}{5}$	$\dfrac{1}{4}$	$\dfrac{1}{3}$	$\dfrac{1}{2}$	$\dfrac{2}{3}$	$\dfrac{3}{4}$
Decimal	0.1	0.125	0.2	0.25	$0.\overline{3}$	0.5	$0.\overline{6}$	0.75
Percent	10%	$12\dfrac{1}{2}\%$	20%	25%	$33\dfrac{1}{3}\%$	50%	$66\dfrac{2}{3}\%$	75%

Converting To or From a Percent

Operation	Procedure	Examples
Change a percent to a decimal	Divide the number by 100.	$14\% = \dfrac{14}{100} = 0.14$ $5.6\% = \dfrac{5.6}{100} = \dfrac{56}{1{,}000} = 0.056$ $145\% = \dfrac{145}{100} = 1.45$
Change a decimal to a percent	Multiply the number by 100.	$0.315 = 0.315 \times 100 = 31.5\%$ $2.35 = 2.35 \times 100 = 235\%$
Change a percent to a fraction or a mixed number	Write the percent as a fraction in hundredths. Reduce the fraction if possible.	$6\% = \dfrac{6}{100} = \dfrac{3}{50}$ $375\% = \dfrac{375}{100} = 3\dfrac{75}{100} = 3\dfrac{3}{4}$
Change a fraction or a mixed number to a percent	Use a calculator: First divide the numerator by the denominator. Then change the decimal to a percent.	Change $4\dfrac{5}{8}$ to a percent. Enter 5 ÷ 8 Display 0.625 So, $0.625 = 62.5\%$ Thus, $4\dfrac{5}{8} = 4.625 = 462.5\%$

To change a terminating decimal to a fraction, just read the decimal using place-value vocabulary, write it in fraction form, and reduce if necessary. (The denominator of the fraction before reducing always has the same number of zeros as the number of decimal places in the terminating decimal.) For example: $12.44 = 12$ and 44 hundredths $= 12\dfrac{44}{100} = 12\dfrac{11}{25}$.

Changing a Repeating Decimal to a Fraction

Procedure: Steps	Example: 0.066666 . . . (or $0.0\overline{6}$)	Example: 0.73232 . . . (or $0.7\overline{32}$)
1. How many digits repeat?	1 digit (6) repeats	2 digits (32) repeat
2. Write a power of 10 with as many zeros as repeating digits.	1 digit → 1 zero → 10	2 digits → 2 zeros → 100
3. Multiply the decimal by this power of 10.	$0.0\overline{6} \times 10 = 0.\overline{6}$	$0.7\overline{32} \times 100 = 73.2323 \ldots$
4. Subtract the original decimal from this product.	$\begin{array}{r} 0.66666\ldots \\ -0.06666\ldots \\ \hline 0.6 \end{array}$	$\begin{array}{r} 73.23232\ldots \\ -0.73232\ldots \\ \hline 72.5 \end{array}$
5. Subtract 1 from the power of 10 you used in step 2	$10 - 1 = 9$	$100 - 1 = 99$
6. Write a fraction. $\dfrac{\text{difference from step 4}}{\text{difference from step 5}}$	$\dfrac{0.6}{9}$	$\dfrac{72.5}{99}$
7. Simplify the fraction.	$\dfrac{0.6}{9} = \dfrac{6}{90} = \dfrac{1}{15}$	$\dfrac{72.5}{99} = \dfrac{725}{990} = \dfrac{145}{198}$

When you work with irrational numbers, especially when you use a calculator, it is important to **estimate** or find a rational approximation for the number. This will help you to judge whether your answer is reasonable.

To round a decimal number, look at the digit to the right of the place you are rounding to. If that number is 5 or greater, add 1 to the last digit you are keeping. If the number is 4 or less, drop off the extra digits without adding.

Examples: 3.47 to the nearest tenth is 3.5.
1.965 to the nearest hundredth is 1.97.
462 to the nearest ten is 460.

 MODEL PROBLEMS

1 Change $9\frac{1}{2}\%$ to a fraction and a decimal.

SOLUTION

Since $9\frac{1}{2}\% = 9.5\%$, then $9.5\% = \frac{9.5}{100} = \frac{95}{1,000} = 0.095$

$\frac{95}{1,000}$ can be reduced to $\frac{19}{200}$.

Answer: $\frac{19}{200}$ and 0.095

2 Round $\pi = 3.14159265\ldots$ to the nearest hundredth and the nearest thousandth.

SOLUTION

To the right of the hundredths place is a 1, which is less than 4, so drop off the remaining digits. Thus, π to the nearest hundredth is 3.14. To the right of the thousandths place is a 5, which is 5 or greater, so add 1 to the last digit before dropping the remaining digits. Thus, π to the nearest thousandth is 3.142.

 Practice

1 Which fraction represents 0.3%?

(1) $\frac{3}{10}$

(3) $\frac{3}{1,000}$

(2) $\frac{3}{100}$

(4) $\frac{1}{300}$

2 0.4% is the same as 1 out of every:

(1) 100

(3) 250 $\frac{.4}{1000} = \frac{1}{250}$

(2) 125

(4) 1,000

3 $\frac{5}{4}$ is equal to:

(1) $1\frac{1}{4}\%$

(2) 25%

(3) 80%

(4) 125%

4 Find a fraction that names the same rational number as 0.3232 . . .

(1) $\frac{32}{100}$

(3) $\frac{10}{33}$

(2) $\frac{32}{99}$

(4) $\frac{32}{10}$

5 0.005 is equal to:

(1) $\frac{1}{2}\%$

(2) 5%

(3) 50%

(4) $\frac{1}{200}\%$

6 Write $\dfrac{5}{12}$ as a repeating decimal.

    (1) 0.4160

    (2) $0.\overline{416}$

    (3) $0.41\overline{6}$

    (4) $0.0\overline{416}$

Exercises 7−9: Write each number in the form $\dfrac{a}{b}$ where a and b are integers and $b \neq 0$.

7 0.7777…

8 0.31

9 24%

Exercises 10−12: Write each number in decimal form. Round to the nearest thousandth, if necessary.

10 135.9%

11 $\dfrac{5}{3}$

12 $\dfrac{1}{5}$%

Exercises 13−15: Write each number as a percent.

13 $-4\dfrac{1}{5}$

14 0.8

15 2.3

16 Find a rational approximation for $-\sqrt{21}$ to the nearest hundredth.

17 Find a rational approximation for $\sqrt{5}$ to the nearest thousandth.

18 Write the decimal form for each number: $\dfrac{4}{9}$, $\dfrac{4}{99}$, $\dfrac{4}{90}$

19 Put the following numbers in order from least to greatest:

$\dfrac{5}{6}$, $\dfrac{1}{5}$, $\dfrac{13}{11}$, 1.2, 1.02, $\dfrac{10}{3}$

20 Of 3.14, $\dfrac{22}{7}$, and $3\dfrac{14}{99}$, which is the best approximation of π? Explain your reasoning.

1 Which of the following numbers is *not* an integer?

    (1) -15

    (2) $\sqrt{64}$

    ~~(3)~~ $\dfrac{-3}{4}$

    (4) 0

2 Which of the following statements is true?

    (1) $-5.4 > -5\dfrac{1}{3}$

    ~~(2)~~ $-5.4 < -5\dfrac{1}{3}$

    (3) $-5.4 > 5\dfrac{1}{3}$

    (4) $5.4 < 5\dfrac{1}{3}$

3 Which of the following sets of numbers is arranged in order, beginning with the smallest?

    (1) $42.4\%, \dfrac{21}{50}, 0.425, \dfrac{266}{625}$ 0.424

    (2) $\dfrac{266}{625}, 0.425, \dfrac{21}{50}, 42.4\%$ 0.4256

    (3) $\dfrac{21}{50}, \dfrac{266}{625}, 0.425, 42.4\%$ $0.42 \mid 0.4256$

    ~~(4)~~ $\dfrac{21}{50}, 42.4\%, 0.425, \dfrac{266}{625}$ $0.42 \mid 0.424$

4 What is the correct sequence of words to identify this set of numbers?

$$\left\{0.8\overline{3},\ 0,\ -\dfrac{18}{3},\ \sqrt{215}\right\}$$

    (1) natural, real, integer, irrational

    ~~(2)~~ rational, whole, integer, irrational

    (3) irrational, rational, whole, irrational

    (4) irrational, irrational, integer, irrational

5 The set of negative even integers between -3 and 4 has how many elements? ~~0~~ 1

6 The set of nonnegative integers between -3 and 10 has how many elements? $\mathbb{N}$ 10

7 Express $9.2\overline{4}$ as a mixed number. ~~231/25~~ $9\dfrac{24}{100}$

8 What is the positive difference between 40% of 100 and 4% of 100? $40 - 4 = 36$

9 In the set {0.1, 0.01, ⟨0.11⟩, 0.011}, which decimal has the greatest value?

Exercises 10−12: Write each expression as a decimal.

10 $6\dfrac{66}{1,000}$ ~~0.396~~ 6.066

11 $\dfrac{1}{4} + 0.202 + \dfrac{1}{5}$ $0.25 + 0.202 + 0.2 = 0.652$

12 $5\dfrac{1}{4}\%$ ~~0.0125~~ ~~5.25~~ ~~5.0~~ $.0525$

Exercises 13−15: Write each number as a percent.

13 0.06 6%

14 $4\dfrac{3}{5}$ ~~23%~~ ~~41.6%~~ 460%

15 10 ~~10%~~ 1000%

Exercises 16−20: Indicate whether each statement is true or false. If a statement is false, change the symbol of equality or inequality to make it true.

16 $0.12131213121312... > 0.12123123412345...$ *True*

17 $-5.335 \not> -5\dfrac{3}{8}$ *vs.* $-5.335 > -5.375$

18 $0.5 \neq 0.\overline{5}$

19 $-5.6 > -5.9$ *True*

20 $\pi \neq 3.14$ ~~*True*~~ *approximate*

CHAPTER 2

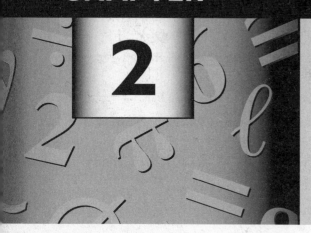

Operations With Real Numbers

Fundamental Operations

The four basic **arithmetic operations** are **addition** (+), **subtraction** (−), **multiplication** (×), and **division** (÷). Multiplication can be indicated in several ways:

$$a \times b \qquad a \bullet b \qquad (a)(b) \qquad a(b) \qquad ab$$

Division can be indicated as:

$$a \div b \qquad \frac{a}{b} \qquad b\overline{)a} \qquad a/b$$

Addition, subtraction, multiplication, and division are called **binary operations** because they are performed on two numbers at a time. (The prefix *bi-* means "two".) When we perform a binary operation, we replace any two members of a set—such as the set of real numbers—with exactly one member, or one answer.

Other operations include **powers** and **roots**. Raising a number to a power is a type of multiplication, and extracting a root is related to division.

Properties of Operations

The following table summarizes important properties of arithmetic operations.

Property	Meaning	Examples
Commutative property of addition or multiplication	The order of the numbers does NOT affect the sum or the product.	$5 + 8 = 8 + 5 = 13$ $\frac{2}{3} + \frac{1}{4} = \frac{1}{4} + \frac{2}{3} = \frac{11}{12}$ $7 \bullet 4 = 4 \bullet 7 = 28$ $3(11) = 11(3) = 33$
Associative property of addition or multiplication	The way the numbers are paired does NOT affect the sum or the product.	$(1 + 2) + 3 = 1 + (2 + 3) = 6$ $\left(\frac{1}{2} \times \frac{1}{3}\right)\frac{1}{5} = \frac{1}{2}\left(\frac{1}{3} \times \frac{1}{5}\right) = \frac{1}{30}$ $(1 \times 3)(4) = 1(3 \times 4) = 12$

(continued)

Property	Meaning	Examples
Distributive property	Multiplication can be distributed over addition or subtraction.	$2 \times (3 + 5) = (2 \times 3) + (2 \times 5) = 16$ $7 \times (4 - 1) = (7 \times 4) - (7 \times 1) = 21$
Additive identity	When zero is added to or subtracted from any number, the number remains unchanged.	$18 + 0 = 18$ $18 - 0 = 18$ $0 + 25 = 25$ $25 - 0 = 25$
Additive inverse	The sum of a number and its additive inverse (also called its **opposite**) is zero.	4 and -4 are additive inverses: $4 + (-4) = 0$ $\frac{3}{4}$ and $-\frac{3}{4}$ are additive inverses: $\frac{3}{4} + \left(-\frac{3}{4}\right) = 0$
Multiplicative identity	Any number multiplied by 1 remains unchanged.	$1 \times 15 = 15$ $-7 \times 1 = -7$
Multiplicative inverse or **reciprocal**	The product of any number and its multiplicative inverse (its reciprocal) is 1.	5 and $\frac{1}{5}$ are multiplicative inverses: $5 \times \frac{1}{5} = 1$
Zero product property	The product of zero and any number is zero.	$-8 \times 0 = 0$ $\pi \times 0 = 0$

Note: A number and its reciprocal are either both positive or both negative. For example:

$$6 \times \frac{1}{6} = 1 \qquad \frac{3}{5} \times \frac{5}{3} = 1 \qquad \left(-\frac{1}{6}\right)(-6) = 1 \qquad \left(-\frac{3}{5}\right)\left(-\frac{5}{3}\right) = 1$$

Zero has *no* reciprocal, because $\frac{n}{0}$ is undefined.

MODEL PROBLEMS

For $-\frac{2}{3}$, name the following:

SOLUTIONS

1 Additive inverse $\qquad$ $\frac{2}{3}$, because $-\frac{2}{3} + \frac{2}{3} = 0$

2 Multiplicative identity $\qquad$ 1, because 1 is the multiplicative identity for any number

3 Reciprocal $\qquad$ $-\frac{3}{2}$ or $-1\frac{1}{2}$, because $\left(-\frac{2}{3}\right)\left(-\frac{3}{2}\right) = 1$

4 Additive identity $\qquad$ 0, because 0 is the additive identity for any number

5 Multiplicative inverse $\qquad$ $-\frac{3}{2}$, because the multiplicative inverse is the reciprocal, found above

 **Practice**

1 The additive inverse of -8 is

(1) $-\dfrac{1}{8}$

(2) 0

(3) $\dfrac{1}{8}$

(4) 8

2 The reciprocal of $\dfrac{1}{5}$ is

(1) -5

(2) $-\dfrac{1}{5}$

(3) $\dfrac{1}{25}$

(4) 5

3 Which statement illustrates the zero product property?

(1) $\dfrac{0}{n} \cdot \dfrac{n}{0} = 1$

(2) $n^0 = 0$

(3) $0n = 0$

(4) $0 - n = -n$

4 Which statement illustrates the distributive property?

(1) $a(b + c) = ab + ac$

(2) $a + b + c = c + b + a$

(3) If $ab = c$, then $a = \dfrac{c}{b}$.

(4) $1 \cdot abc = abc$

5 A binary operation is so called because it

(1) yields exactly two answers

(2) is performed on two members of a set

(3) is performed on members of two different sets

(4) is a two-step operation

6 *Opposite* means the same as

(1) additive inverse

(2) additive identity

(3) reciprocal

(4) zero product

Exercises 7–17: Identify the property illustrated by each statement.

commutative   associative
distributive   additive identity
additive inverse   multiplicative identity
multiplicative inverse

7 $-6(10) = 10(-6)$

8 $1(64) = 64$

9 $6 + 10 = 10 + 6$

10 $6 + 0 = 6$

11 $6 + (10 + 8) = (6 + 10) + 8$

12 $3(4 \times 5) = (3 \times 4) \times 5$

13 $6 \times 8 = 8 \times 6$

14 $6(3 + 4) = (6 \times 3) + (6 \times 4)$

15 $-84 + 84 = 0$

16 $7(31 - 13) = (7 \times 31) - (7 \times 13)$

17 $\dfrac{p}{q} \cdot \dfrac{q}{p} = 1$

18 The number 1 is its own multiplicative inverse. Name another number with this property.

19 Which integer has *no* multiplicative inverse?

20 Which number is its own additive inverse?

Closure

If we perform an operation on any number in a set with itself or with any other member of the set and the result is always still in that set, then the set is **closed** under that operation. Here are examples of **closure**:

- For any integers a and b, the sum $a + b$ is an integer.
- For any integers a and b, the difference $a - b$ is an integer.
- For any integers a and b, the product ab is an integer.

Therefore, the integers are closed under addition, subtraction, and multiplication.

However, a set is not closed under an operation if the result is *not always* in the set. For example:

- For all integers a and b, the quotient $a \div b$ is *not* always an integer. For instance, when $a = 5$ and $b = 2$, the quotient $5 \div 2 = 2\frac{1}{2}$, which is *not* an integer.
- Therefore, the integers are *not* closed under division.

Thus we can say that the integers are closed only for the binary operations of addition, subtraction, and multiplication.

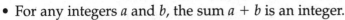 **MODEL PROBLEM**

The set $A = \{-1, 0, 1\}$ is closed under which operation?

(1) addition

(2) subtraction

(3) multiplication

(4) none of the above

SOLUTION

Test each answer option:

(1) Since $1 + 1 = 2$ and 2 is not in set A, this set is NOT closed under addition.

(2) Since $1 - (-1) = 1 + 1 = 2$, the set is NOT closed under subtraction.

(3) Since the product of any number in this set with itself or any other member is only -1, 0, or 1, the set is closed under multiplication.

(4) Since the set is closed under multiplication, this option is obviously false.

Braces { } indicate a set.

Answer: (3)

  Practice

1 The set $\{0, 1\}$ is closed under

(1) multiplication
(2) division
(3) addition
(4) all of the above

2 Which set is closed under division?

(1) {natural numbers}
(2) {whole numbers}
(3) {rational numbers}
(4) none of the above

3 The set {rational numbers} is *not* closed under

    (1) multiplication
    (2) subtraction
    (3) extraction of square root
    (4) squaring

4 How many of these sets are closed under the given operation?

    {0, 2, 4, 6, …} under addition
    {0, 1, 2, …} under subtraction
    {0, 1, 2} under multiplication
    {0, 1} under extraction of square root

    (1) exactly one   (3) exactly three
    (2) exactly two   (4) all four

Excercises 5–10: Match each set with the operation or operations under which it is closed. An answer may be used more than once or not at all.

Set	Closed Under …
5 {0}	(a) Addition
	(b) Squaring
6 {2, 4, 16, 256, …}	(c) Addition, multiplication, and squaring
7 {… , −3, −2, −1}	(d) Addition, subtraction, multiplication, and squaring
8 {… , −21, −14, −7, 0, 7, 14, 21, …}	(e) Multiplication, division, and squaring
9 $\left\{\dfrac{1}{3}, \dfrac{1}{9}, \dfrac{1}{27}, \dfrac{1}{81}, \dots\right\}$	(f) Multiplication and squaring
10 $\left\{\dots, \dfrac{1}{8}, \dfrac{1}{4}, \dfrac{1}{2}, 1, 2, 4, 8, \dots\right\}$	

Factors and Multiples

The **factors** of a positive number are all the natural numbers that can be divided evenly into that number. For example, the factors of 12 are 1, 2, 3, 4, 6, and 12. Each of these factors divides 12 with no remainder. Since 12 is divisible by 4, 12 is a **multiple** of 4.

A **prime number** is a number greater than 1 that has exactly two different natural numbers as factors: the number 1 and itself. For example, 13 is a prime number. The factors of 13 are 1 and 13, since only $1 \times 13 = 13$. The set of prime numbers from 1 to 25 is {2, 3, 5, 7, 11, 13, 17, 19, 23}.

A **composite number** is a natural number greater than 1 that has more than two factors. The number 12 is a composite number. Its set of six factors is {1, 2, 3, 4, 6, 12}.

A composite number written as the product of its prime factors is called the **prime factorization** of the number. For example, the prime factorization of 60 can be found by using a **factor tree**.

The number 2 is the first prime and is the only even prime number.

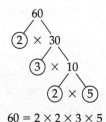

$$60 = 2 \times 2 \times 3 \times 5$$

The **greatest common factor (GCF)** of two or more numbers is the largest number that is a factor of each of the given numbers. For example, 4 is the greatest common factor of 8 and 12 because 4 is the largest number that will divide evenly into both 8 and 12.

To Find the GCF

- Write the prime factorization of each number.
- Select the common factors, the factors that appear in both prime factorizations. If a factor appears twice in each prime factorization, select it twice.
- Find the product of the common factors.

 MODEL PROBLEM

Find the GCF of 24 and 60.

SOLUTION

Prime factorization of 24 = 4 • 6 = 2 • 2 • 2 • 3

Prime factorization of 60 = 4 • 15 = 2 • 2 • 3 • 5

The common factors are 2, 2, and 3, so the GCF is 2 • 2 • 3 = 12.

The **least common multiple (LCM)** of two or more numbers is the smallest number that is a multiple of each of the given numbers. For example, 24 is the least common multiple of 8 and 12 because $8 \times 3 = 24$ and $12 \times 2 = 24$.

To Find the LCM

- List the multiples of each given number until a common multiple appears.
- Find the lowest multiple that appears in all the lists.

 MODEL PROBLEM

Find the LCM of 9, 18, and 24.

SOLUTION

List the multiples of each number:

Multiples of 9: 9, 18, 27, 36, 45, 54, 63, <u>72</u>, 81, 90, 99, …

Multiples of 18: 18, 36, 54, <u>72</u>, 90, …

Multiples of 24: 24, 48, <u>72</u>, 96, 120, …

The LCM of 9, 18, and 24 is 72.

1 Which of the following is the prime factor-ization of 144?

   (1) 1×144
   (2) $9 \times 4 \times 2 \times 2$
   (3) $3 \times 4 \times 3 \times 4$
   (4) $2 \times 2 \times 2 \times 2 \times 3 \times 3$

2 Which statement is true for any natural number x?

   (1) If x is divisible by 70, then it is divisible by 12.
   (2) If x is divisible by 70, then it is divisible by 14.
   (3) If x is divisible by 70, then it is divisible by 16.
   (4) If x is divisible by 70, then it is divisible by 18.

3 $3 \times 3 \times 5 \times y$ could be the prime factorization for which number?

   (1) 11   (3) 135
   (2) 30   (4) 335

4 If a movie house gives *one* free ticket to every 60th customer and *two* free tickets to every 160th customer, what customer will be the first to get *three* free tickets?

   (1) 220th   (3) 480th
   (2) 360th   (4) 960th

5 What is the least common multiple of natural numbers m and n, if m and n are both prime numbers?

   (1) m (3) $m + n$
   (2) n (4) mn

6 If an integer N is found on the number line between 40 and 100, inclusive, then how many possible integer values of N are divisible by 4?

   (1) 25
   (2) 21
   (3) 16
   (4) 10

Exercises 7–11: Factor if possible. If the number cannot be factored, state that it is prime.

7 2

8 9

9 11

10 60

11 108

12 Find the greatest common factor of 20 and 63.

13 Find the greatest common factor of 60 and 144.

14 Find the least common multiple of 6, 8, and 9.

15 If set R contains only factors of 32 and set M contains only factors of 24, then what is one number that is contained in set R but *not* in set M?

Order of Operations

To **evaluate** or **simplify** a mathematical expression means to carry out the indicated operations as far as possible. In evaluating, it is necessary to follow these rules for the **order of operations**.

- First, simplify any expression within **grouping symbols**: parentheses ( ), brackets [ ], and braces { }. A fraction bar $\frac{m}{n}$ also serves as a grouping symbol. For example, $\frac{x+4}{2}$ means $\frac{(x+4)}{2}$. When grouping symbols appear within other grouping symbols, work from the inside out.

> To remember order of operations, use the catchword PEMDAS:
> <u>P</u>arentheses
> <u>E</u>xponents (and roots)
> <u>M</u>ultiply and <u>D</u>ivide
> <u>A</u>dd and <u>S</u>ubtract

- Second, evaluate
  - (i) powers, which are expressions with exponents.
    Example: $5^2 = 5 \cdot 5 = 25$
  - (ii) roots, which are expressions with radicals.
    Example: $\sqrt{25} = \sqrt{5 \cdot 5} = 5$
- Third, multiply and divide in order from left to right.
- Last, add and subtract in order from left to right.

Braces { } are a grouping symbol and also symbolize a set. Notice the context, and don't confuse the two uses!

MODEL PROBLEMS

Simplify each expression.

SOLUTIONS

1 $10 + 8 \div 2$

Division comes first: $10 + 8 \div 2 = 10 + 4$
Addition comes next: $10 + 4 = 14$

Answer: 14

2 $4^2 + 10 \cdot 3 \div 5 - 10$

Evaluate exponents: $4^2 + 10 \cdot 3 \div 5 - 10 = 16 + 10 \cdot 3 \div 5 - 10$
Multiply and divide in order from left to right:
$16 + 10 \cdot 3 \div 5 - 10 = 16 + 30 \div 5 - 10 = 16 + 6 - 10$
Add and subtract in order from left to right: $16 + 6 - 10 = 22 - 10 = 12$

Answer: 12

3 $5(2^3 + 4) \div \sqrt{36} - 4$

$5(2^3 + 4) \div \sqrt{36} - 4 = 5(2^3 + 4) \div \sqrt{6 \cdot 6} - 4$
$= 5(8 + 4) \div 6 - 4$
$= 5(12) \div 6 - 4$
$= 60 \div 6 - 4$
$= 10 - 4 = 6$

Answer: 6

Practice

1 $(21 - 7) \times (15 - 7) - 4 \times 3 =$

   (1) 50   (3) 100
   (2) 75   (4) 125

Exercises 2–4: Which choice demonstrates the correct way to evaluate the given statement?

2 $6 + 4 \cdot 8 - 3$

   (1) $(6 + 4) \cdot (8 - 3)$
   (2) $[6 + (4 \cdot 8)] - 3$
   (3) $[(6 + 4) \cdot 8] - 3$
   (4) $6 + [4 \cdot (8 - 3)]$

3 $2^3 + 16 \div 4 + 4$

   (1) $[2^3 + 16] \div (4 + 4)$
   (2) $[(2^3 + 16) \div 4] + 4$
   (3) $2^3 + [16 \div (4 + 4)]$
   (4) $2^3 + [(16 \div 4) + 4]$

4 $6^2 - 2^2 + 5$

   (1) $(6 - 2)^2 + 5$
   (2) $[(6 \cdot 2) - (2 \cdot 2)] + 5$
   (3) $[(6^2) - (2^2)] + 5$
   (4) $6^2 - [(2^2) + 5]$

Exercises 5–20: Evaluate using the order of operations.

5 $16 - 2 \bullet 3$

6 $9 - 3 \bullet 5$

7 $3 + 4 \bullet 2$

8 $7 \bullet 5 - 4 + 3$

9 $-2 \bullet 3^2 + 20$

10 $7 \bullet 5 - 4 \bullet 3 + 2$

11 $20 - 5(5 - 1)$

12 $5 \bullet 10 \div 5 + 2 \bullet 5$

13 $40 - 10^2$

14 $15 - 10 \div 5 \bullet 2 + 4$

15 $-5[7 - 2(-3)]$

16 $18 \div 2 \bullet 3$

17 $3^2(2 - 3) + 5\sqrt{4}$

18 $2 \bullet 3^2 \div 3\sqrt{4}$

19 $(6 - 4)^2 (6 - 4^2)$

20 $\dfrac{7(3 + 1) - 2}{5 \bullet 2 + 2}$

Operations With Signed Numbers

Signed numbers (see Chapter 1) are positive (+) and negative (−) numbers. On a horizontal number line, positive numbers are to the right of zero and negative numbers are to the left of zero. On a vertical number line, positive numbers are above zero and negative numbers are below zero.

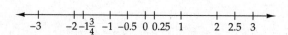

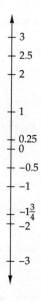

Remember:

- The positive sign + is "understood" and need not be written. Thus *positive three* or +3 can be written simply as 3. When *no* sign is written, a number is always positive.
- The negative sign − must always be written. Thus *negative three* is always written −3.

Adding and Subtracting Signed Numbers

To add and subtract with positive and negative numbers, follow the rules below.

Rules for Addition of Signed Numbers

- To add numbers with *like signs*: Add the absolute values. The sum has the same sign as the given numbers (the addends).

  Examples: $+3 + 2 = +5$ and $-3 + (-2) = -5$.

- To add numbers with *unlike signs*: Subtract the smaller absolute value from the larger absolute value. The sum has the sign of the number with the larger absolute value.

  Example: Add $+3 + (-5)$. First step: $5 - 3 = 2$. Next step: Since −5 has a larger absolute value than +3, the sum is negative, −2. Answer: $+3 + (-5) = -2$.

MODEL PROBLEMS

1 $7 + (-4) = ?$

2 $-7 + 4 = ?$

3 $-3 + 7 + 5 + 3 + (-8) = ?$

SOLUTIONS

1 $7 + (-4) = 3$

2 $-7 + 4 = -3$

3 An expression such as $-3 + 7 + 5 + 3 + (-8)$ can be computed by grouping the positive and negative integers separately. When opposites appear, they can also be grouped:

$-3 + 7 + 5 + 3 + (-8) = (7 + 5 + 3) + [-3 + (-8)] = 15 + (-11) = 4$

$-3 + 7 + 5 + 3 + (-8) = (7 + 5) + (-3 + 3) + (-8) = 12 + 0 + (-8) = 4$

Rules for Subtraction of Signed Numbers

- Subtracting a number is the same as adding its opposite.
  Example: $2 - 5 = 2 + (-5)$.
- Therefore, to subtract signed numbers, change the number being subtracted to its opposite, and then follow the rules for addition: $2 - 5 = 2 + (-5) = -3$.

MODEL PROBLEMS

1 $8 - (-3) = ?$

SOLUTION

$8 - (-3) = 8 + 3 = 11$

Check: $11 + (-3) = 8$

2 $-6 - 5 = ?$

SOLUTION

$-6 - 5 = -6 + (-5) = -11$

Check: $-11 + 5 = -6$

3 A diver is 10 meters below the ocean surface. What is the new depth if the diver descends 2 meters lower?

SOLUTION

Model this situation using a number line:

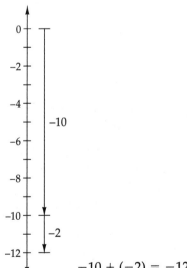

$-10 + (-2) = -12$

Answer: The diver's new depth is 12 meters.

1 $1,364 - 1,200 - 64 + 100 =$

  (1) 100
  (2) 150
  (3) 200
  (4) 250

2 If m and p are positive integers, which expression *must* be negative?

  (1) $m - p$
  (2) $p - m$
  (3) $-(m - p)$
  (4) $-(m + p)$

3 If m and p are negative integers, which expression *must* be positive?

  (1) $m - p$
  (2) $p - m$
  (3) $-(m - p)$
  (4) $-(m + p)$

4 $-20 + 14 + (-16) =$

  (1) -40
  (2) -22
  (3) -18
  (4) 18

5 An airplane is flying at an altitude of 6,000 feet. Find its new altitude:

  a after it first ascends 2,500 feet
  b after it then descends 1,500 feet

6 A credit card balance is \$452.18. Find the new balance after these things happen: two items costing \$26.45 and \$15.90 are returned; three items costing \$3.17, \$16.42, and \$57.71 are purchased; and a payment of \$100 is made.

7 The temperature is $-6°F$. Find the new temperature:

  a if it falls 12°
  b if it rises 10°

8 Mercury freezes at $-39°C$ and boils at $360°C$. Find the difference between these two temperatures.

9 Here is the yardage for six plays by a football team: 4 yards, -3 yards, 9 yards, -5 yards, 13 yards, 6 yards. What was the total yardage?

10 Perform the operation $-7 + 4$, modeling it on a number line.

Multiplying and Dividing Signed Numbers

Below are the rules for multiplication and division with positive and negative numbers.

Rules for Multiplication of Signed Numbers

To multiply two signed numbers, multiply the absolute values.
  Then, to give a sign to the product, do the following:

- The product of two *positive* numbers is *positive*. Example: $+2 \bullet (+5) = +10$.
- The product of two *negative* numbers is *positive*. Example: $(-2) \bullet (-5) = +10$.
- The product of one *positive* number and one *negative* number is *negative*.
  Examples: $+2 \bullet (-5) = -10$ and $(-2) \bullet (+5) = -10$.

> If two signs are the same, the sign of the product is positive.
>
> If two signs are different, the sign of the product is negative.

MODEL PROBLEMS

SOLUTIONS

1 $13 \cdot (-25)$

The two signs are different, so the product is negative: -325

2 $-6 \cdot (-4)$

The two signs are the same, so the product is positive: 24

3 $183 \cdot (-206)$

The two signs are different, so the product is negative: $-37{,}698$

4 $(-x)(y)$

The two signs are different, so the product is negative: $-xy$

5 The temperature drops 3° each hour for 4 hours. How much does it fall?

$-3 \cdot (+4) = -12$

Answer: The temperature falls 12°.

Rules for Division of Signed Numbers

To divide signed numbers, divide the absolute values.
   To give a sign to the quotient, do the following:

If two signs are the same, the quotient is positive.

If two signs are different, the quotient is negative.

- The quotient of two *positive* numbers is *positive*. Example: $(+10) \div (+2) = +5$.
- The quotient of two *negative* numbers is *positive*. Example: $(-10) \div (-2) = +5$.
- The quotient of one *positive* number and one *negative* number is *negative*.
   Examples: $+10 \div (-2) = -5$ and $(-10) \div (+2) = -5$.

 MODEL PROBLEMS

Divide:

SOLUTIONS

1 $-12 \div 2$

The two signs are different, so the quotient is negative: -6

2 $-12 \div (-2)$

The two signs are the same, so the quotient is positive: 6

3 $26 \div (-13)$

The two signs are different, so the quotient is negative: -2

 Practice

1 Which expression does *not* equal -5?

   (1) $-5 + (8 \times 2) - (2 \times 8)$
   (2) $3 + [2 \times (-4)]$
   (3) $3 + [5 \times (-2)] + 8$
   (4) $[17 \times (-2)] + (14 \times 2) + 1$

2 If a is positive integer and b is a negative integer, which expression *must* be positive?

   (1) $a - b$
   (2) $a + b$
   (3) $a \times b$
   (4) $a \div b$

3 If pq is a negative integer, which expression *must* be positive?

(1) $-3p^2q^2$
(2) $-4pq$
(3) $p + q^2$
(4) pq^2

4 Given: mx is a negative integer. Which *must* also be a negative integer?

(1) $(-m)(x)$

(2) $\dfrac{m}{x}$

(3) $m - x$
(4) $-m - x$

5 Given: r is a positive integer and s is a negative integer. Which value is largest?

(1) $r + s$
(2) $r - s$
(3) rs

(4) $\dfrac{s}{r}$

6 Given: kx, ky, and xy are positive integers. Which statement *must* be true of k, x, and y?

(1) Exactly two of them are negative.
(2) They are all positive.
(3) They are all negative.
(4) They are either all positive or all negative.

Exercises 7–14: Perform the indicated operations.

7 $2^3 \div (-4) - 2(2 - 5)$

8 $|4(-3)| - |-5|$

9 $3^2 + (-7) - (2^3 - 3)$

10 $12 \div 2 - 4^2 - (-3^2)$

11 $-5 + 3(-6) \div 2 - 1$

12 $8 + \dfrac{12 - 4}{2^2 + 4} - 3$

13 $(-5 \times 2) + [6 \div (-2)] + 5$

14 $(2.5 \times 14) - 30 + [2 \times 5 \div (-2)]$

15 From Monday through Friday, Geri worked for 27 hours earning $7 per hour and for 8 hours earning $9 per hour. How much did she have left if she spent $3 per day for bus fare and $3.50 a day for lunch?

Exercises 16–20: Is each statement true or false? If a statement is false, give a counterexample.

16 $|n - m|$ is positive.

17 The difference of two positive numbers is always a positive number.

18 The sum of two negative numbers is never a positive number.

19 The product of a positive number and a negative number is sometimes a positive number.

20 The quotient of two negative numbers is always a positive number.

Operations With Fractions

Adding and Subtracting Fractions

Fractions can be added and subtracted if the denominators are the same (**like**). When the denominators are *not* the same (**unlike**), the two fractions are first written with a common denominator and then added or subtracted. Follow these steps:

- Add or subtract the numerators. The common denominator remains the same.
- Simplify the result if possible.

MODEL PROBLEMS

Find each sum:

1 $\dfrac{1}{8} + \dfrac{3}{8}$

2 $\dfrac{8}{15} + \dfrac{7}{9}$ $\dfrac{72}{135} + \dfrac{105}{135} = \dfrac{177}{135}$

SOLUTION

$\dfrac{1}{8} + \dfrac{3}{8} = \dfrac{1+3}{8} = \dfrac{4}{8} = \dfrac{1}{2}$

SOLUTION

Step 1. Write the two fractions with 45 as their common denominator (since 45 is the LCM of 15 and 9):

$\dfrac{8}{15} \cdot \dfrac{3}{3} = \dfrac{24}{45}$ and $\dfrac{7}{9} \cdot \dfrac{5}{5} = \dfrac{35}{45}$

Step 2. Add the new numerators. The common denominator stays the same:

$\dfrac{24}{45} + \dfrac{35}{45} = \dfrac{24+35}{45} = \dfrac{59}{45}$

Step 3. Simplify the answer:

$\dfrac{59}{45} = 1\dfrac{14}{45}$

To add or subtract positive and negative fractions, follow the rules for addition and subtraction of signed numbers.

 MODEL PROBLEMS

SOLUTIONS

1 $-3\dfrac{4}{5} + \left(-2\dfrac{3}{5}\right)$

$-3\dfrac{4}{5} + \left(-2\dfrac{3}{5}\right) = -\dfrac{19}{5} + \left(-\dfrac{13}{5}\right) = -\dfrac{32}{5} = -6\dfrac{2}{5}$

Or: $-3\dfrac{4}{5} + \left(-2\dfrac{3}{5}\right) = -5\dfrac{7}{5} = -6\dfrac{2}{5}$

2 $\dfrac{5}{8} + \left(\dfrac{-7}{8}\right)$

$\dfrac{5}{8} + \left(\dfrac{-7}{8}\right) = \dfrac{-2}{8} = -\dfrac{1}{4}$

3 $\dfrac{3}{10} - \dfrac{7}{15}$

$\dfrac{3}{10} - \dfrac{7}{15} = \dfrac{9}{30} - \dfrac{14}{30} = \dfrac{-5}{30} = \dfrac{-1}{6}$

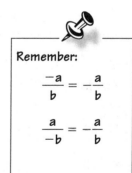

Remember:

$\dfrac{-a}{b} = -\dfrac{a}{b}$

$\dfrac{a}{-b} = -\dfrac{a}{b}$

SOLUTIONS

4 $6\frac{3}{7} - \left(-4\frac{2}{3}\right)$

Add the opposite of $-4\frac{2}{3}$:

$$6\frac{3}{7} - \left(-4\frac{2}{3}\right) = 6\frac{3}{7} + 4\frac{2}{3}$$

Now we use a common denominator, 21, to get:

$$6\frac{9}{21} + 4\frac{14}{21} = 10\frac{23}{21} = 11\frac{2}{21}$$

5 $3\frac{7}{8} + \left(-5\frac{5}{6}\right)$

Use a common denominator, 24, to get:

$$3\frac{7}{8} + \left(-5\frac{5}{6}\right) = 3\frac{21}{24} + \left(-5\frac{20}{24}\right)$$

Next, subtract the smaller absolute value from the larger absolute value:

$$5\frac{20}{24} = 4\frac{44}{24} \text{ so } 5\frac{20}{24} - 3\frac{21}{24} = 4\frac{44}{24} - 3\frac{21}{24} = 1\frac{23}{24}$$

The negative number has the larger absolute value, so give the sum a negative sign:

$$-1\frac{23}{24}$$

Answer: $3\frac{7}{8} + \left(-5\frac{5}{6}\right) = -1\frac{23}{24}$

 Practice

---

1 Acme Shipping charges $6 a pound for packages. You have 3 packages to send, weighing $\frac{3}{5}$ pound, $1\frac{4}{15}$ pounds, and $\frac{23}{30}$ pound. How much will you pay Acme?

(1) $15
(2) $15.80
(3) $16
(4) $16.20

2 You buy $2\frac{1}{2}$ pounds of apples, $\frac{3}{4}$ pound of bananas, $1\frac{2}{5}$ pounds of peaches, and $5\frac{7}{10}$ pounds of watermelon. What is the total weight, in pounds?

(1) $9\frac{1}{2}$

(2) $10\frac{5}{8}$

(3) $10\frac{7}{20}$

(4) $11\frac{13}{30}$

3 You need a rope at least 8 feet long. You have four shorter ropes, of the following lengths:

Rope A = $4\frac{2}{3}$ feet	Rope B = $4\frac{2}{5}$ feet
Rope C = $3\frac{3}{4}$ feet	Rope D = $3\frac{2}{3}$ feet

You can tie two or more of these ropes together, but each time you tie you lose $\frac{1}{4}$ foot. Which combination will *not* give you a piece at least 8 feet long?

(1) A and C
(2) B and C
(3) A and D
(4) A, B, and C

4 Which expression does *not* equal 1?

(1) $\frac{1}{2} + \frac{3}{12} + \frac{9}{36}$

(2) $\frac{2}{3} + \frac{2}{6}$

(3) $\frac{3}{8} + \frac{20}{24} - \frac{1}{6}$

(4) $\frac{13}{7} - \frac{12}{14}$

5 Milly, Tilly, Lilly, and Billy are sharing a pizza that has been cut into 8 equal slices. Milly eats 2 slices, Tilly eats 1, Lilly eats 3. What fraction of the pie is left for Billy?

(1) $\frac{3}{8}$

(2) $\frac{1}{2}$

(3) $\frac{1}{8}$

(4) $\frac{1}{4}$

Exercises 6–8: Perform the indicated operation.

6 $10 + \left(-4\frac{1}{3}\right)$

7 $8\frac{2}{3} - \left(-1\frac{1}{4}\right)$

8 $2\frac{1}{8} - 3\frac{5}{6}$

9 On a test, $\frac{1}{4}$ of a class earned A's and $\frac{1}{3}$ earned B's. What part of the class earned either an A or a B?

10 A share of stock gained $\frac{1}{2}$ point, then lost $1\frac{1}{4}$ points, and then gained $2\frac{1}{8}$ points. Find the overall change in its value.

Multiplying and Dividing Fractions

To multiply fractions:

- Find the product of the numerators and the product of the denominators.
- Then simplify the result if possible.

For example:

$$\frac{1}{3} \cdot \frac{2}{3} = \frac{1 \cdot 2}{3 \cdot 3} = \frac{2}{9}$$

$$\frac{2}{3} \cdot \frac{3}{4} = \frac{2 \cdot 3}{3 \cdot 4} = \frac{6}{12} = \frac{1}{2}$$

$$\frac{1}{2} \cdot \frac{2}{5} = \frac{1 \cdot 2}{2 \cdot 5} = \frac{2}{10} = \frac{1}{5}$$

To perform operations with mixed numbers, we often need to write them as improper fractions.

To divide fractions:

- Multiply by the reciprocal of the divisor.
- Simplify the result if possible.

For example:

$$\frac{1}{4} \div \frac{3}{4} = \frac{1}{4} \bullet \frac{4}{3} = \frac{4}{12} = \frac{1}{3}$$

$$\frac{5}{6} \div \frac{3}{8} = \frac{5}{6} \bullet \frac{8}{3} = \frac{40}{18} = \frac{20}{9} = 2\frac{2}{9}$$

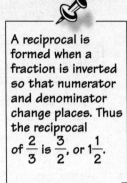

A reciprocal is formed when a fraction is inverted so that numerator and denominator change places. Thus the reciprocal of $\frac{2}{3}$ is $\frac{3}{2}$, or $1\frac{1}{2}$.

To multiply or divide positive and negative fractions, follow the rules for multiplication and division of signed numbers.

MODEL PROBLEMS

Perform the indicated operation.   SOLUTIONS

1   $\dfrac{-2}{15} \bullet \dfrac{10}{11}$

$\dfrac{-2}{15} \bullet \dfrac{10}{11} = \dfrac{-20}{165} = \dfrac{-4}{33}$

2   $-2\dfrac{4}{7} \bullet \left(-1\dfrac{5}{16}\right)$

$-2\dfrac{4}{7} \bullet \left(-1\dfrac{5}{16}\right) = -\dfrac{18}{7} \bullet \left(-\dfrac{21}{16}\right) = \dfrac{378}{112} = 3\dfrac{42}{112} = 3\dfrac{3}{8}$

3   $\dfrac{91}{9} \bullet \dfrac{51}{14}$

$\dfrac{91}{9} \bullet \dfrac{51}{14} = \dfrac{4641}{126} = \dfrac{221}{6} = 36\dfrac{5}{6}$

4   $\dfrac{15}{16} \div \dfrac{3}{20}$

$\dfrac{15}{16} \div \dfrac{3}{20} = \dfrac{15}{16} \bullet \dfrac{20}{3} = \dfrac{300}{48} = 6\dfrac{12}{48} = 6\dfrac{1}{4}$

5   $-2\dfrac{3}{4} \div 5\dfrac{5}{6}$

$-2\dfrac{3}{4} \div 5\dfrac{5}{6} = \dfrac{-11}{4} \div \dfrac{35}{6} = -\dfrac{11}{4} \bullet \dfrac{6}{35} = -\dfrac{66}{140} = -\dfrac{33}{70}$

6   $-\dfrac{75}{44} \div -\dfrac{3}{4}$

$-\dfrac{75}{44} \div -\dfrac{3}{4} = -\dfrac{75}{44} \bullet -\dfrac{4}{3} = \dfrac{300}{132} = \dfrac{25}{11} = 2\dfrac{3}{11}$

7   $\dfrac{9}{20} + \dfrac{22}{7} \bullet \dfrac{7}{9}$

$\dfrac{9}{20} + \dfrac{22}{7} \bullet \dfrac{7}{9} = \dfrac{9}{20} + \dfrac{154}{63} = \dfrac{9}{20} + \dfrac{22}{9} = \dfrac{81}{180} + \dfrac{440}{180} = \dfrac{521}{180} = 2\dfrac{161}{180}$

8   $10 \div \dfrac{1}{90} - \dfrac{5}{8}$

$10 \div \dfrac{1}{90} - \dfrac{5}{8} = \dfrac{10}{1} \bullet \dfrac{90}{1} - \dfrac{5}{8} = \dfrac{900}{1} - \dfrac{5}{8} = 899\dfrac{3}{8}$

Verbal problems often involve operations with fractions. The next model problems are examples.

MODEL PROBLEMS

1 Leo buys $\frac{3}{4}$ pound of ham at $5 a pound, $3\frac{1}{2}$ pounds of cheese at $3 a pound, and $\frac{1}{2}$ pound of salami at $6 a pound. How much change does he get from a $20 bill?

SOLUTION

To find the cost of each item, multiply:

$$\frac{3}{4} \times \$5 = \frac{\$15}{4} = \$3.75$$

$$3\frac{1}{2} \times \$3 = \frac{7}{2} \times \$3 = \frac{\$21}{2} = \$10.50$$

$$\frac{1}{2} \times \$6 = \$3$$

To find total cost, add: $3.75 + $10.50 + $3 = $17.25

To find the change, subtract: $20 − $17.25 = $2.75

Answer: He will get $2.75 change.

2 You have a piece of wood $5\frac{1}{4}$ feet long. If you cut it into 7 equal pieces, what will be the length of each piece?

SOLUTION

Divide $5\frac{1}{4}$ by 7:

$$5\frac{1}{4} \div 7 = \frac{21}{4} \div 7 = \frac{21}{4} \times \frac{1}{7} = \frac{21}{28} = \frac{3}{4}$$

Answer: Each piece will be $\frac{3}{4}$ foot long. (Or: 9 inches long.)

3 Julio finds $\frac{3}{4}$ of an apple pie on the kitchen table and eats $\frac{1}{3}$ of it. How much of the pie is left?

SOLUTION

Step 1. To calculate how much of the whole pie he ate, multiply:

$$\frac{1}{3} \times \frac{3}{4} = \frac{3}{12} = \frac{1}{4}$$

Step 2. To calculate how much pie is left, subtract:

$$\frac{3}{4} - \frac{1}{4} = \frac{2}{4} = \frac{1}{2}$$

Answer: Half of the pie is left.

 # Practice

1 Pat runs $\frac{2}{3}$ mile. Matt runs one-third as far. What distance does Matt run, in miles?

(1) $\frac{1}{9}$

(2) $\frac{2}{9}$

(3) $\frac{1}{3}$

(4) 2

2 Bernie's cousin weighs four-fifths as much as Bernie. If Bernie's weight is 135 pounds, what is his cousin's weight?

(1) 168.75 pounds
(2) 162 pounds
(3) 108 pounds
(4) 101.25 pounds

3 $\dfrac{2}{5} + \left(\dfrac{25}{9} \div \dfrac{1}{3} \right) =$

    (1) $\dfrac{3}{10}$

    (2) $\dfrac{13}{25}$

    (3) $3\dfrac{1}{3}$

    (4) $8\dfrac{11}{15}$

4 A college math professor has to grade 160 exams. He gives $\dfrac{1}{2}$ of the exams to his assistant to grade. Then the assistant gives $\dfrac{1}{4}$ of her exams to a graduate student to grade. How many exams does the graduate student get?

    (1) 20
    (2) 40
    (3) 60
    (4) 70

5 $n \bullet \dfrac{1}{3} \div \dfrac{3}{4} =$

    (1) $\dfrac{n}{4}$

    (2) $\dfrac{n}{3}$

    (3) $\dfrac{3n}{4}$

    (4) $\dfrac{4n}{9}$

6 Which procedure gives the same result as multiplying by $\dfrac{3}{4}$ and then dividing by $\dfrac{3}{8}$?

    (1) dividing by 2
    (2) multiplying by 2
    (3) dividing by 32
    (4) multiplying by $\dfrac{9}{32}$

7 If $\dfrac{3}{4}$ pound of pot roast is recommended per serving, how much should you buy to serve 6 people?

8 To multiply $\dfrac{1}{2} \bullet \dfrac{2}{3}$, Ricky did this:

$$\dfrac{1}{2} \bullet \dfrac{2}{3} = \dfrac{3}{6} \bullet \dfrac{4}{6} = \dfrac{12}{6} = 2$$

Is Ricky's work correct or incorrect? Explain your answer, referring specifically to the rules for operations with fractions. If you think he was *incorrect*, redo the problem correctly.

Exercises 9–20: Perform the indicated operations and give each answer in simplest form

9 $\dfrac{3}{8} \times \dfrac{4}{5}$

10 $3\dfrac{1}{2} \times 1\dfrac{3}{4}$

11 $4 \times 2\dfrac{2}{3}$

12 $\dfrac{3}{4} \div \dfrac{5}{8}$

13 $\dfrac{1}{3} + \dfrac{2}{5} \bullet 10$

14 $\left(\dfrac{2}{3} \right)^2$

15 $\left(\dfrac{1}{2} \right)^3$

16 $\left(\dfrac{1}{3} \right)\left(\dfrac{-4}{5} \right)\left(\dfrac{3}{8} \right)$

17 $\left(-2\dfrac{1}{2} \right)\left(\dfrac{-1}{3} \right)\left(-2\dfrac{1}{4} \right)$

18 $\left(\dfrac{3}{4} \right)^2 - \left(\dfrac{1}{2} \right)^3 + \dfrac{3}{4}$

19 $\dfrac{3}{8} \div \left(\dfrac{5}{6} + \dfrac{2}{3} \right)$

20 $\dfrac{5}{7} \div \dfrac{15}{3} \times \dfrac{11}{13}$

Operations With Decimals

Operations with decimals are often used in solving verbal problems. The following model problems are examples.

 MODEL PROBLEMS

1 Janet spent $30.38 for fabric that cost $2.48 per yard. How many yards did she buy?

SOLUTION

Divide: $30.38 ÷ $2.48 = 12.25

Answer: She bought 12.25 or $12\frac{1}{4}$ yards.

2 If steak costs $4.95 a pound, and Mrs. Waters buys a 3-pound steak, how much change will she get from a $50 bill?

SOLUTION

Step 1. To find total cost, multiply:
$4.95 × 3 = $14.85

Step 2. To find her change, subtract:
$50 − $14.85 = $35.15

Answer: She will get $35.15 in change.

 Practice

1 Yesterday the high temperature was 92.6°F and the low was 77.8°F. What was the difference between the high and the low?

   (1) 16.6°
   (2) 14.8°
   (3) 14.4°
   (4) 13.8°

2 A carpenter has fifty 1.5-inch nails and fifty 0.75-inch nails. If all these nails were lined up end to end, what would the length be?

   (1) 112.5 inches
   (2) 115 inches
   (3) 117.5 inches
   (4) 119 inches

3 Garrett weighed 170 pounds. By dieting and exercising, he lost 0.8 pound a week for 5 weeks. How much did he weigh after the 5 weeks?

   (1) 164 pounds
   (2) 165 pounds
   (3) 166 pounds
   (4) 167 pounds

4 An **odometer** registers miles driven. The odometer on Alyssa's car now reads 2,004.7. What will it read after she drives the following distances?

Day	Miles
Monday	5.6
Tuesday	10.4
Wednesday	7.8
Thursday	11.2
Friday	22.7

   (1) 2,006.2
   (2) 2,045.6
   (3) 2,062.4
   (4) 2,074.7

5 On a 3-day trip, the Lemoine family drove 125.5 miles the first day, 80.4 miles the second day, and 95.7 miles the third day. What was the total distance?

   (1) 3,016 miles
   (2) 301.6 miles
   (3) 300.16 miles
   (4) 3.016 miles

Exercises 6–12: Perform the indicated operations with pencil and paper. Show your work.

6 $9.2 - 2.6$

7 2.8×5.9

8 2.4×0.08

9 0.7×0.6

10 $31.76 \div 4$

11 $0.24\overline{)3.948}$

12 $3.573 + 0.00065 + 240 + 6.2$

13 You read 0.15 of a book on Monday and 0.6 of it on Tuesday. How much of the book do you have left to read?

14 A laundry charges $9.50 for the first 12 shirts and $0.55 for each additional shirt. How much will it cost to launder 31 shirts?

15 A library is constructing some new shelves: 4 shelves each 2.75 meters long, and 3 shelves each 3.25 meters long. Will 20 meters of board be just enough, more than enough, or not enough to make all the shelves? If 20 meters is *not* the exact amount required, how much more or less will be needed?

Operations With Exponents

A **power** is the value indicated by a **base** with an **exponent**:

$$\text{Base}^{\text{Exponent}}$$

We say that the exponent *raises the base to a power*. For example:

$$10^2 \qquad 4^3 \qquad m^n$$

In 10^2, the base is 10, the exponent is 2, and the exponent raises the base to the second power. The expression is read *ten to the second power* or *ten squared*. In 4^3, the base is 4, the exponent is 3, and the exponent raises the base to the third power. This expression is read *four to the third power* or *four cubed*. In m^n the base is m and the exponent is n, and the expression is read *m to the nth power*.

An exponent may be positive, negative, or zero:

- A *positive* whole-number exponent tells us how many times the base is used as a factor. In 10^2, for instance, 10 is used as a factor 2 times. In 4^3, 4 is used as a factor 3 times. In m^n, m is used as a factor n times:

$$10^2 = 10 \bullet 10 = 100 \qquad 4^3 = 4 \bullet 4 \bullet 4 = 64 \qquad m^n = m \bullet m \bullet m \bullet m \ldots$$

- A *negative* exponent can be written as a unit fraction with a positive exponent in the denominator:

$$10^{-2} = \frac{1}{10^2} = \frac{1}{100} \qquad 4^{-3} = \frac{1}{4^3} = \frac{1}{64} \qquad m^{-n} = \frac{1}{m^n}$$

- The exponent *zero* has a special meaning. Any number to the zero power equals 1:

$$10^0 = 1 \qquad 4^0 = 1 \qquad 1{,}000{,}000{,}000{,}000^0 = 1 \qquad m^0 = 1$$

- The exponent 1 has a special meaning. Any number to the first power equals itself:

$$10^1 = 10 \qquad 4^1 = 4 \qquad 1{,}000{,}000{,}000{,}000^1 = 1{,}000{,}000{,}000{,}000 \qquad m^1 = m$$

- The number 1 to any power equals 1:

$$1^0 = 1 \qquad 1^1 = 1 \qquad 1^{153} = 1 \qquad 1^n = 1 \qquad 1^{-n} = \frac{1}{1^n} = \frac{1}{1} = 1$$

Remember:
$x^1 = x$
$x^0 = 1, x \neq 0$
$x^{-n} = \frac{1}{x^n}$
$1^n = 1$

Rules for Operations on Terms with Exponents

Operation	Rule	Examples
Addition and subtraction $x^n + x^m = x^n + x^m$ $x^n - x^m = x^n - x^m$	Like bases with unlike exponents *cannot* be added or subtracted unless they can be evaluated first.	$2^2 + 2^3 = 4 + 8 = 12$ $3^3 - 3^2 = 27 - 9 = 18$ $a^2 + a^3 = a^2 + a^3$ $a^3 - a^2 = a^3 - a^2$
Multiplication $x^n \bullet x^m = x^{n+m}$	To multiply powers of like bases, add the exponents.	$3^4 \times 3^5 = 3^9$ $a^2 \bullet a^3 = a^{2+3} = a^5$ $a^{-4} \bullet a^5 = a^{-4+5} = a^1 = a$
Division $\dfrac{x^n}{x^m} = x^{n-m}, x \neq 0$	To divide powers of like bases, subtract the exponent of the divisor from the exponent of the dividend.	$\dfrac{4^7}{4^5} = 4^{7-5} = 4^2$ $\dfrac{a^5}{a^2} = a^{5-2} = a^3$ $\dfrac{a^3}{a^8} = a^{3-8} = a^{-5} = \dfrac{1}{a^5}$
Raising a power to a power $(x^m)^n = x^{mn}$	To raise a term with an exponent to some power, multiply the exponents.	$(5^2)^3 = 5^{2 \times 3} = 5^6$ $(a^4)^3 = a^{4 \bullet 3} = a^{12}$
Raising a fraction to a power $\left(\dfrac{x}{y}\right)^n = \dfrac{x^n}{y^n}$	To raise a fraction to a power, raise the numerator and the denominator to that power.	$\left(\dfrac{3}{5}\right)^2 = \dfrac{3^2}{5^2} = \dfrac{9}{25}$ $\left(\dfrac{a}{b}\right)^7 = \dfrac{a^7}{b^7}$
Raising a product to a power $(xy)^n = x^n y^n$	To raise a product to a power, raise each factor to that power.	$(5 \bullet 2)^3 = 5^3 \bullet 2^3 = 1{,}000$ $(4a)^2 = 4^2 \bullet a^2 = 16a^2$ $(ab)^5 = a^5 b^5$

Here are some useful points to remember about working with negative bases:

- $-x^n$ means $-(x^n)$. For example: $-3^2 = -(3^2) = -9$ and $-3x^2 = -3(x^2)$
- $(-x)^n$ means $(-x)(-x)(-x) \ldots$ For example: $(-3)^2 = (-3)(-3) = 9$
- When a negative base is raised to an *even* power, the result becomes positive: $(-2)^4 = (-2)(-2)(-2)(-2) = +16$
- When a negative base is raised to an *odd* power, the result remains negative: $(-2)^3 = (-2)(-2)(-2) = -8$

MODEL PROBLEMS

Perform each operation.

SOLUTIONS

1 $p^0 + p^1 + p^2 + p^5 + 1^p =$

$1 + p^1 + p^2 + p^5 + 1 = p + p^2 + p^5 + 2$

2 $5^6 \bullet 5^{-3} =$

$5^{6+(-3)} = 5^{6-3} = 5^3 = 125$

3 $4^3 \div 4^5 =$

$4^{3-5} = 4^{-2} = \dfrac{1}{4^2} = \dfrac{1}{16}$

4 $(10^4)^{-1} =$

$10^{(4)(-1)} = 10^{-4} = \dfrac{1}{10^4} = \dfrac{1}{10{,}000}$

5 $\left(\dfrac{3p}{2q}\right)^2 =$

$\dfrac{3p \bullet 3p}{2q \bullet 2q} = \dfrac{9p^2}{4q^2}$ Or: $\dfrac{3^2 p^2}{2^2 q^2} = \dfrac{9p^2}{4q^2}$

6 $(4p)^3 =$

$4^3 \bullet p^3 = 64p^3$

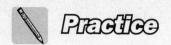

1 What is the product of 75^3 and 75^7?

   (1) 75^{10}
   (2) 75^{21}
   (3) 150^{10}
   (4) 150^{21}

2 Which expression is equal to 10,000?

   (1) 100^3
   (2) $(5^4)(2^4)$
   (3) $(10^2)(50^2)$
   (4) $(2)(250^2)$

3 Which expression is *not* equal to the other three?

   (1) $x^2 \bullet x^4$
   (2) $(x^2)^4$
   (3) $x^{-2} \bullet x^8$
   (4) $\dfrac{x^{10}}{x^4}$

4 Which expression is *not* equal to the other three?

   (1) 2^6
   (2) $32(2)^0$
   (3) $2^5 + 2^5$
   (4) $(-2)^6$

5 Which statement is *false*?

   (1) $4^0 = 6^0$
   (2) $3^4 = 9^2$
   (3) $3 \bullet 2^0 = 1$
   (4) $(4^2)^3 = (4^3)^2$

6 If $5^k \times 5^3 = 5^6$, what is the value of k?

   (1) 2   (3) 9
   (2) 3   (4) 18

Exercises 7–13: Find each value.

7 $4^3 - 4^2$

8 $4^{-3} + 4^{-2}$

9 $4^3 \bullet 4^2$

10 $4^3 \div 4^2$

11 $3^0 + 6^0$

12 $2^{-1} - 3^{-1}$

13 $(-6)^2$

Exercises 14–18: Simplify.

14 $x^5 \bullet x^{-3}$

15 $(x^3y^3)^3$

16 $(4x^3)(3x)^2$

17 $\dfrac{x^2}{x^6}$

18 $\left(\dfrac{x^2}{y}\right)^2$

19 Explain why

   a $x^2 \bullet x^3 \neq (x^2)^3$

   b $-4^2 \neq (-4)^2$

20 Find the value of x that makes each statement true:

   a $(3^3)^{5x} = 3^{30}$

   b $5^{28} = 5^{3x} \bullet 5^7$

   c $(6^4 \bullet 6^x) = 6^{24}$

Sets, Set Notation, Unions, and Intersections

Sets and Set Notation

A **set** is any collection of objects, people, or things that are carefully defined, such as {American coins}, {one-digit prime numbers}, {even numbers}, {baseball players on a team}, or {0, 1, 2, 3, 4, 5, 6, 7, 8, 9}.

    Each object in the set is called a **member** or an **element** of the set.

The members of a set can be placed in brackets as a *list* or *roster* of elements, as in {2, 4, 6, 8, 10} or as a *rule*, as in {the positive odd integers less than 100}. Specifying a set within brackets by a list, roster, or rule should clearly identify the members of the set.

Here are three examples of identical sets that are given by a roster (a list) and by a rule:

1 {2, 3, 5, 7} and {one-digit prime numbers}

2 {i, m, p, s} and {the letters of the word Mississippi}
   Note: The letters are not repeated.

3 {California, Oregon, Washington, Alaska, Hawaii} and {states of the U.S. that touch the Pacific Ocean}

Using the symbol ∈ to mean "is a *member* of" or "is an *element* of" and ∉ to mean "is *not a member* of" or "is *not an element* of," we can write that 6 ∉ {odd whole numbers}, 7 ∉ {multiples of 10}, 19 ∈ {prime numbers}, and $\frac{1}{2}$ ∈ {multiples of $\frac{1}{4}$}.

A set is **finite** if the process of counting the elements comes to an end. For example, the finite set of two-digit integers can be written as {10, 11, 12, . . . , 99}. A finite set is also defined as a set containing a specific number of elements.

A set is **infinite** if the process of counting the elements never comes to an end. The infinite set of whole numbers can be written as {0, 1, 2, 3, . . .} with the three dots indicating that the roster continues without end.

The **empty set** written as the symbol ∅ or with empty braces { } is a set that contains no numbers. For example, the set of integers between 7 and 8 is ∅ or { }.

If A = {0, 1, 2}, then any set that contains *only* the elements from set A is said to be a **subset** of set A. For example, the following are subsets of set A: {0}, {1}, {2}, {0, 1}, {0, 2}, {1, 2}, {0, 1, 2}, and ∅, the empty set.

Notes: (1) The set {0, 1, 2} is called the **improper subset**, but it is, nonetheless, a subset. (2) The empty set, ∅, is a subset of all sets except itself.

Examples: Identify each statement as true or false.

    1 {2, 3, 5} is a subset of {1, 2, 3, 4, 5, 6}
    2 {0, 3} is a subset of {1, 2, 3, 4}
    3 {Maine} is a subset of {the New England states}
    4 {college students} is a subset of {people studying calculus}
    5 {0} is a subset of {0}
    6 {0, 1, 2, 3, . . . , 9} is a subset of {all digits}
    7 {rational numbers} is a subset of {the real numbers}
    8 {integers} is a subset of {whole numbers}
    9 {odd integers} is a subset of {all prime numbers}
    10 {triangles} is a subset of {polygons}

Solutions
1 T   2 F   3 T   4 F   5 T   6 T   7 T   8 F   9 F   10 T

Union, Intersection, Complement, and Venn Diagrams

The **intersection** of two sets consists of the elements they have *in common*.

For example, if A = {2, 4, 6, 8, 10} and B = {3, 4, 5, 6, 7, 8}, the intersection of these sets would be a third set C = {4, 6, 8}.

Using the symbol ∩ for intersection, we can write
$A \cap B = C$ or $\{2, 4, 6, 8, 10\} \cap \{3, 4, 5, 6, 7, 8\} = \{4, 6, 8\}$.

Obviously, set C is a subset of both sets A and B. However, when two sets have no elements in common, the sets are said to be **disjoint** and the intersection is Ø, the empty set.

The **union** of two sets consists of *all of the elements of both sets* with no common elements listed more than once. For example, if $A = \{3, 5, 7\}$ and $B = \{a, b, c, 5, 7, 9\}$, the union of these sets would be a third set $G = \{3, 5, 7, 9, a, b, c\}$. Note that 5 and 7 are not listed twice.

Using the symbol ∪ for union, we can write $A \cup B = G$ or $\{3, 5, 7\} \cup \{a, b, c, 5, 7, 9\} = \{3, 5, 7, a, b, c\}$.

Example: If $A = \{$odd integers$\}$ and $B = \{$even integers$\}$, then $A \cap B = $ Ø and $A \cup B = \{$integers$\}$

Sets, subsets, and operations with sets can be illustrated by **Venn diagrams**. Venn diagrams are usually pictured as sections of a plane such as circles, ellipses, and rectangles.

The *intersection* of two sets A and B usually looks like this, with the common area shaded:

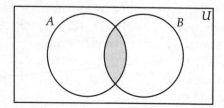

The rectangle containing the two overlapping circles is called the **universal set**, **U**, which (while not always drawn) is the set of all possible replacements for the items under discussion. In *algebra*, the universal set is usually the set of real numbers. In *geometry*, the universal set could be the set of all points in a plane.

The *union* of two sets A and B usually looks like this:

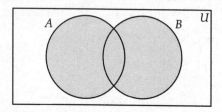

Example: If $U = \{$all nonnegative integers less than 12$\}$,
        $N = \{$all even natural numbers less than 11$\}$, and
        $P = \{$all one-digit prime numbers$\}$,

then the typical Venn diagram illustrating this data would be the following:

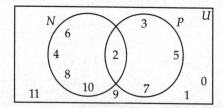

The **complement** of a set is the set of elements in the universe U that are not in the given set. The symbol of the complement is a bar over the letter: the complement of A would be $\bar{A}$.

For example, if U represents all the students in math class and A represents all the students who passed the midterm exam, then the complement, $\bar{A}$, represents all the students who did not pass the test.

Example: If $U = \{1, 2, 3, 4, 5, 6, 7, 8, 9, 10\}$ and $R = \{2, 4, 6, 8, 10\}$, then $\bar{R} = \{1, 3, 5, 7, 9\}$

 MODEL PROBLEMS

1 If P is the set of positive even integers and M is the set of multiples of 10, which of the following sets has no members in common with either set P or set M?

   (1) $\{-27, -7, -4, 7, 14\}$
   (2) $\{-24, -20, 8, 10, 15\}$
   (3) $\{-24, -7, 5, 7, 14\}$
   (4) $\{-24, -8, 5, 7, 15\}$

SOLUTION

Since set $P = \{2, 4, 6, 8, 10, 12, \ldots\}$ and set $M = \{\ldots -20, -10, 0, 10, 20, \ldots\}$, only choice (4) has no members in either P or M.

Answer: (4)

2 If P is the set of positive even integers and M is the set of multiples of 10, which of the following sets is the *intersection* of sets P and M?

   (1) $\{10, 20, 30, \ldots\}$
   (2) $\{\ldots -20, -10, 0, 10, 20, \ldots\}$
   (3) $\{0, 2, 4, 6, 8, \ldots\}$
   (4) $\{\ldots -30, -20, -10, 0, 2, 4, 6, 8, 10, \ldots\}$

SOLUTION

The intersection must be positive multiplies of 10.

Answer: (1)

3 There are 18 boys in the class: 6 play football, 5 play baseball, and 3 play on both teams. How many boys are *not* on either team?

SOLUTION

Using a Venn diagram, where F stands for football and B for baseball, you can see the numerical relationship of the boys on the teams. By filling in the overlapping region first with the 3, which represents the number of boys who play on both teams, we see that 3 boys play only football and 2 boys play only baseball.

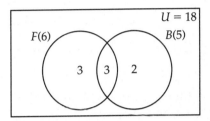

By adding the numbers in the circles, $3 + 3 + 2$, the actual number of boys playing sports is 8. Therefore, $18 - 8 = 10$ boys who do not play on either team.

Answer: 10

4 Of the 25 students who play in the band, 12 play the drums, 7 play the trumpet, and 11 play neither drums nor trumpet. How many students play *both* drums and trumpet?

SOLUTION

Use a Venn diagram and the fact that there are $25 - 11 = 14$ students who play drums, trumpet, or both. But $12 + 7 = 19$, so the difference is $19 - 14 = 5$ students must play both.

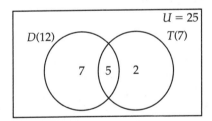

Answer: 5

5 If $U = \{a, b, c, d, e, f, g, h, i, j\}$, $A = \{b, c, d, f, h\}$, and $B = \{a, c, d, g\}$, find the following:

   a $A \cap B$ **c** $A \cup B$
   b $\bar{B}$ **d** $\bar{A}$

SOLUTION

   a $\{c, d\}$ **c** $\{a, b, c, d, f, g, h\}$
   b $\{b, e, f, h, i, j\}$ **d** $\{a, e, g, i, j\}$

1 $A = \{0, 2, 3, 6, 9, 10\}$
$B = \{1, 2, 3, 4, 5, 6, 8\}$
$C = \{1, 3, 6, 7, 8, 9\}$

If set D contains only those numbers that belong to exactly two of the sets shown above, how many numbers does set D contain?

(1) 2
(2) 3
(3) 4
(4) 5

2 If $N = \{$natural numbers$\}$ and $I = \{$Integers$\}$, then $N \cap I$ is which of the following?

(1) {prime numbers}
(2) {whole numbers}
(3) {natural numbers}
(4) {positive real numbers}

3
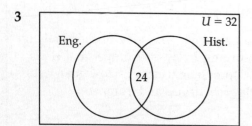

The Venn diagram above illustrates *some* of the following facts: of the 32 students in the class, 28 passed the English test, 26 passed the history exam, and 24 passed both. How many students did not pass either English or history?

(1) 2
(2) 4
(3) 6
(4) 8

4 If set G contains 4 elements and set M contains 3 elements, what could be the least number of elements in $G \cup M$?

(1) 1
(2) 3
(3) 4
(4) 7

5 Club M has 11 members and Club R has 18. If a total of 24 people belong to the two clubs, how many people belong to *both* clubs?

(1) 5
(2) 6
(3) 7
(4) 29

Exercises 6 and 7: What is the union and intersection of each of the following pairs of sets?

6 $A = \{$prime numbers less than 10$\}$
$B = \{$nonnegative integers less than 10$\}$

7 $N = \{$natural numbers less than 13$\}$
$G = \{$factors of 12$\}$

8 **a** Using the sets in exercise 7, if the universal set $U = \{$integers from 0 to 12$\}$, then what is $\overline{N}$ and $\overline{G}$?
  b Using the sets in exercise 6, if the universal set $U = \{$integers from 0 to 10$\}$, then what is $\overline{A}$ and $\overline{B}$?

9 Using your answers for exercise 8, what is $\overline{A} \cap \overline{G}$?

10 If $U = \{$whole numbers less than or equal to 12$\}$, $P = \{$prime numbers less than 12$\}$, and $N = \{$all odd natural numbers less than 12$\}$, find the following:

  a List the elements of each set U, P, and N
  b $P \cup N$
  c $P \cap N$
  d $\overline{P}$
  e $\overline{N}$
  f $\overline{P} \cap \overline{N}$

Graphing Number Pairs

The **Cartesian coordinate system** provides an easy way to locate points on a plane, which is a two-dimensional surface. It consists of a coordinate grid separated by a horizontal number line called the x-axis and a vertical number line called the y-axis. The intersection of these number lines is called the **origin**. The two axes divide the grid into four **quadrants**, numbered I to IV counterclockwise.

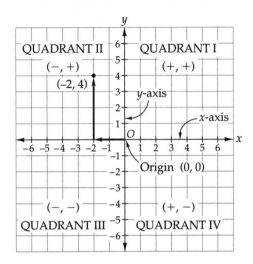

Every point on the grid can be identified with two numbers called **coordinates**:

- The first number is the x-**coordinate** (or **abscissa**). This is the distance from the origin horizontally to the point on the x-axis to the left or right of the origin.
- The second number is the y-**coordinate** (or **ordinate**). This is the distance from the origin vertically to the point on the y-axis above or below the origin.
- The sign of the coordinate (+ or −) indicates the direction in which to move; "+" means to the right (for x) or up (for y), and "−" means to the left (for x) or down (for y). The absolute value of each coordinate indicates the distance.
- For any point, the coordinates are written (x, y). When in this form, they are called an ordered pair. The coordinates of the origin are $(0, 0)$
- On the graph above, point $(-2, 4)$ has an x-coordinate of -2 and a y-coordinate of 4, which places it in quadrant II. To *graph* or *plot* the point, start at the origin and move 2 units left and 4 units up. Place a dot at the point and indicate the graph of $(-2, 4)$. **Order** is important because the point $(-2, 4)$, is *not* the same as the point $(4, -2)$, which can be found 4 units to the right and 2 units down, in quadrant IV.
- The correct signs for coordinates in each quadrant are shown in parentheses.

Note: On the Regents Examination, all graphs you draw must be labeled. The x-axis and y-axis must be labeled and the scale (1, 2, 3, . . . ; 2, 4, 6, . . .) must be indicated.

Given the points $A(-3, -2)$, $B(1, 5)$, and $C(4, -2)$, plot the ordered pairs, connect the dots, and find the area of the figure.

SOLUTION

In the figure shown, the points are plotted and connected. The horizontal distance (or the base of the triangle) from A to C is 7 units. The vertical distance (or height of the triangle) from point B to the base, point D $(1, -2)$, is also 7 units.

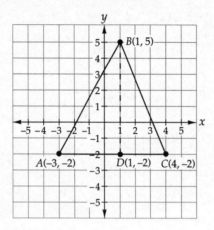

Since the area of a triangle is $\frac{1}{2}bh$,

$$\text{Area} = \frac{1}{2}(7)(7) = \frac{1}{2}(49) = 24.5$$

 Practice

1 State the coordinates on the graph of each lettered point.

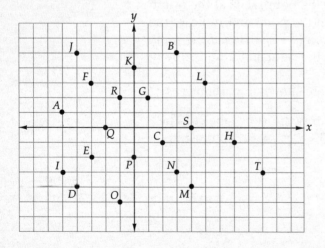

2 Locate these points and identify the quadrants they are in.

Note: Points found on the x- or y-axis are not in any quadrant. They are simply axis points.

$A(-1, 7)$	$B(4, 8)$	$C(6, 0)$	$D(3, 5)$
$E(0, 9)$	$F(-4, -4)$	$G(8, -3)$	$H(-3, 0)$
$I(-2, -5)$	$J(0, -7)$	$K(1, 2)$	$L(0, 0)$
$M(0, 8)$	$N(6, -6)$	$P(-3, -8)$	

3 Plot the given points, connect them, and find the area of the triangle formed.

$A(-4, -3)$, $B(-2, 3)$, and $C(3, -3)$

4 Plot the given points and find the perimeter and area of the square formed.

$A(-3, 3)$, $B(4, 3)$, $C(4, -4)$, and $D(-3, -4)$

5 Plot the given points and find the area of the square formed.

$A(-4, -3)$, $B(-4, 3)$, $C(2, 3)$, and $D(2, -3)$

6 If the coordinates of $\triangle ABC$ are $A(12, 0)$, $B(0, 18)$, and $C(16, 0)$, what is the area of this triangle?

7 Plot and connect the following points: $A(-5, -1)$, $B(-3, 3)$, $C(5, 3)$, and $D(7, -1)$. What is the area of the figured formed?

8 What is the area of the pentagon with the following vertices: $A(-2, -2)$, $B(-2, 3)$, $C(1, 6)$, $D(4, 3)$, and $E(4, -2)$?

9 What is the area of the closed figure with the following points: $A(-7, -3)$, $B(-4, 2)$, $C(4, 2)$, and $D(7, -3)$? What is the name of this figure?

10 If the given points $A(-4, -1)$, $B(-2, 6)$, $C(3, -1)$, and $D(-1, 2)$ are connected in this order, A, B, C, D, and A, what is the area of the concave quadrilateral formed?

 CHAPTER REVIEW

$(-15)(-5) = 75$

1 What is the opposite of $|(-10 - 5)(-10 + 5)|$?

  (1) -75
  (2) -50
  (3) 50
  (4) 75

2 The product of two integers, -1 and -8, is 8. If each integer is increased by 1, what is the new product?

  (1) 18
  (2) 14
  (3) 0
  (4) -18

3 The toll on a bridge is \$2 for a car and driver and \$0.75 for each additional passenger. If the toll for Marigold's car was \$4.25, how many people were riding in it?

  (1) 2
  (2) 3
  (3) 4
  (4) 5

$\frac{4.25}{.2}$

4 $2^3 \cdot 4^3 =$

  (1) 2^9
  (2) 2^{18}
  (3) 8^6
  (4) 8^9

5 The number 0.006 is 100 times as large as which of the following numbers?

  (1) 0.6
  (2) 0.06
  (3) 0.0006
  (4) 0.00006

6 If $x = 10$, then which of the following represents 7,005?

  (1) $70x + 5$
  (2) $7x^2 + 5$
  (3) $7x^3 + 5$
  (4) $7x^4 + 5$

7 Which of the following is an equivalent form of $a + a(a + a)$? $(2a + 2a)$

  (1) $4a$
  (2) $a^2 + 2a$
  (3) $2a^2 + a$
  (4) $2a^2 + 2a$

8 If $U = \{1, 2, 3, 4, 5, 6, 7\}$, $A = \{6, 7\}$, and $B = \{3, 5, 7\}$, then $\overline{A} \cap \overline{B}$ is

  (1) $\{1, 2, 3, 4, 5\}$
  (2) $\{1, 2, 4, 6\}$
  (3) $\{1, 2, 4\}$
  (4) $\{1, 2, 3, 4, 5, 6\}$

9 What property is illustrated by $(3 + 5)6 = 6(5 + 3)$?

  (1) Commutative property of multiplication
  (2) Commutative property of addition
  (3) Associative property of addition
  (4) Both properties (1) and (2) above

$1-10$ $16-29$

10 Match each equation with the property it illustrates.

Equations	Properties
(1) $3 + (4 + 5) = (3 + 4) + 5$ *e*	(a) Commutative property of multiplication
(2) $5 \times 3 = 3 \times 5$ *a*	(b) Additive identity
(3) $8 \times 11 + 8 \times 9 = 8 \times 20$ *F*	(c) Multiplicative inverse (reciprocal)
(4) $d + 0 = 0 + d = d$ *B*	(d) Commutative property of addition
(5) integer + integer = integer *B G*	(e) Associative property of addition
(6) $1 \cdot t = t \cdot 1 = t$ *H*	(f) Distributive property
(7) $\left(\dfrac{1}{x}\right)\left(\dfrac{x}{1}\right) = 1$ *C*	(g) Closure
(8) $x + 7 = 7 + x$ *d*	(h) Multiplicative identity

11 In football, a team needs 10 yards to make a first down. Suppose that in three plays, your team gains 6 yards, then loses 2 yards, then gains 7 yards. What was the total yardage, and did the team make a first down?

   a Calculate the yardage using signed numbers.
   b Show the situation on a number line.

12 Find the least common multiple of 3, 8, 9, and 12.

13 Find the least possible multiple of 4 that is greater than 25.

14 Two bells ring in a constant pattern. One bell rings every 6 minutes and another bell rings every 8 minutes. If Bob makes a note of the first time the bells sound together, after how many minutes will the bells ring together again?

15

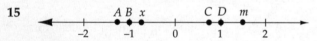

When the coordinate of x is multiplied by the coordinate of m, the result could be represented by which of the lettered points A, B, C, or D in the number line above?

Exercises 16–29: Simplify, using the order of operations.

16 $10 + 15 \div 5$ $= 13$

17 $12 - 6 \div 3$ $= +10$

18 $3 \times 4 + 8 \div 2 - 6 \div 2$ $12 + 4 - 3 = 19$

19 $10 - 48 \div 3 \times 8 + 6$ $= 124\ -12$

20 $72 \div 6 - 2 \times 3$ $= 6$

21 $10 - 4[3 - 2(15 \div 3)]$ $= 8\ 38$

22 $[60 \div (2 \times 3)] \div 10$ $= 1$

23 $\dfrac{(18 \div 3) + 6}{18 \div (6 \div 3)}$ $\dfrac{12}{9}$

24 $-42.5 - 2(3^2 - 4.7)(-5)$ 0.5

25 $(|4 - 3| - |2 - 5|) \div -2$ $(-2) \div (-2) = 1$

26 $\dfrac{15 \div 3 + 3 \cdot 7}{2(5 + 1) + 1}$ $\dfrac{26}{13} = 2$

27 $(16 - 4 + 8 \div 2) \div 4 \times 5$ $= 20$

28 $\dfrac{1}{4}(8 \div 2 \times 4) \div (8 \times 4 \div 2)$ $4 \div 16 = 1/4$

29 $\dfrac{1 + 33 \div 3 + 12 \times 3}{3 \times 3 - 3 \div 3 + 4}$ $\dfrac{48}{12} = 4$

30 If the coordinates $A(0, 0)$, $B(0, 10)$, $C(10, 16)$, and $D(10, 0)$ are joined,

   a what is the area of the figure formed?
   b what is the name of the figure?
   c If there is more than one way to find the area, explain at least two methods and name one formula that could be used.

Now, turn to page 422 and take the Cumulative Review test for Chapters 1–2. This will help you monitor your progress and keep all your skills sharp.

Algebraic Operations and Reasoning

The Language of Algebra

Any situation in which one or more numbers are unknown can be made into an algebra problem. When an algebra problem is presented in words, part of the job of solving the problem is to rewrite the information using algebraic expressions. **Algebraic expressions** contain numbers, variables, and symbols for the operations. **Algebraic equations** are statements containing two algebraic expressions joined with a sign of equality. **Algebraic inequalities** contain two algebraic expressions joined with a sign of inequality.

Use the following table to help translate key phrases into mathematical symbols.

Key Words	Symbol	English and Algebra Translations
Signs of Operations		
sum, add, increase, more than, plus, increased by, greater, exceeded by, and	$+$	f increased by 10 $f + 10$ the sum of x and 9 $x + 9$
difference, subtract, take away, minus, decrease, fewer, less, less than, decreased by, diminished by	$-$	4 less than y $y - 4$ 32 fewer CDs than Abdul's $A - 32$
multiply, of, product, times	$\times$	the product of 4 and t $4 \times t$ or $4t$ One-half of the pumpkin weighs 3 pounds. $\frac{1}{2}p = 3$
divide, quotient, into, for, per, divided by	$\div$	500 divided into 4 parts $500 \div 4$ Sue cut a 24-inch board into 8 pieces. $24 \div 8$

(continued)

Key Words	Symbol	English and Algebra Translations
Sign of Equality		
equals, is equivalent to, is the result of, is	$=$	Twice a number plus 4 is 14. $2n + 4 = 14$
Signs of Inequality		
is greater than, is more, has more	$>$	x is greater than 5. $x > 5$
is less than, is fewer, has fewer	$<$	Pauline and Fredrica together have fewer books than Vicki. $P + F < V$
is greater than or equal to, is at least, has at least	$\geq$	The program was at least 4 hours long. $p \geq 4$
is less than or equal to, is at most, has at most	$\leq$	The bank is at most 1.5 miles away. $b \leq 1.5$
is not equal to, is not the same as, cannot equal, does not equal	$\neq$	Today is not the third of the month. $d \neq 3$

Points to Remember

- Before you translate a problem situation into an algebraic expression, be sure you understand what the situation means.
- Define each variable you create with an equals sign.
- When there are two or more unknown quantities, you may need to represent only one of them with a letter variable. Try to express the other unknown quantities in terms of that letter if possible.
- Often, translation assumes that you know certain relationships about money, measurement, or time. If a relationship is not clear to you, you should try making a chart or table of the situation before translating it into an algebraic expression.

 MODEL PROBLEMS

1 If x = Luke's age and $x + 6$ = Nancy's age in years, write an equation for each of the following statements:

  a The sum of Luke's and Nancy's ages is less than 30 years.

SOLUTION

$x + (x + 6) < 30$

  b Three times Luke's age equals twice Nancy's age.

SOLUTION

$3x = 2(x + 6)$

  c The difference between Nancy's age in 10 years and twice Luke's present age is 4 years.

SOLUTION

$[(x + 6) + 10] - 2x = 4$

2 When 8 is subtracted from 3 times a number, the result is 19. Which of the following equations represents this statement?

(1) $8 - 3x = 19$
(2) $3x - 8 = 19$
(3) $3(x - 8) = 19$
(4) $3(8 - x) = 19$

SOLUTION

Let x = the number.

Then "3 times a number" = $3x$.

"8 is subtracted from 3 times a number" = $3x - 8$.

"The result is" translates into an equal sign. Thus, $3x - 8 = 19$.

Answer: (2)

3 Jonas has 20 coins, all nickels and dimes, that have a total value of $1.25. If n represents the number of nickels, which algebraic equation represents this situation?

(1) $20n = 125$
(2) $5n = 1.25$
(3) $5n + 10(20 - n) = 125$
(4) $5n + 10n - 20 = 125$

SOLUTION

Let the number of nickels = n.

Then the value of the nickels at five cents per nickel = $5n$.

Since Jonas has 20 coins in all, the number of dimes he has is 20 minus the number of nickels. Thus, the number of dimes = $20 - n$.

The value of the dimes at 10 cents per dime = $10(20 - n)$.

The total amount of money is the sum of the values of the nickels and the dimes. Thus, Jonas's total = $5n + 10(20 - n)$. If the total value is $1.25, then $5n + 10(20 - n) = 125$ cents.

Answer: (3)

When you are solving coin problems like this, work in cents so that decimal operations are not required.

 Practice

1 Eight years ago, Clyde was 7 years old. Which equation is true if C represents Clyde's age now?

(1) $8 + C = 7$
(2) $7 + C = 8$
(3) $8 - 7 = C$
(4) $C - 8 = 7$

2 Which of the following represents the total cost of x shirts bought at a cost of $(x + 5)$ dollars each?

(1) $(x + 5)$ dollars
(2) $x + (x + 5)$ dollars
(3) $x(x + 5)$ dollars
(4) $x^2 + 5$ dollars

3 If a batch of holiday cookies requires 3 cups of flour, how many cups of flour would be used in baking m batches of cookies?

(1) $m + 3$
(2) $m - 3$
(3) $\dfrac{m}{3}$
(4) $3m$

4 If y represents the tens digit and x the units digit of a two-digit number, then the number is represented by

(1) $y + x$ (3) $10x + y$
(2) yx (4) $10y + x$

5 George is 15 years old. He is one-third as old as his father. Which equation is true if g represents George's father's age?

(1) $3g = 15$
(2) $g + 3 = 15$
(3) $\dfrac{1}{3}g = 15$
(4) $g - 3 = 15$

Exercises 6–10: Match each statement on the left to the correct open sentence on the right.

6 The square of a number is greater than one-tenth of the number.

7 A number is greater than twice the number decreased by 10.

8 Twice a number is less than the number and 10.

9 Maria is at least 10 years older than Nadine.

10 A number is ten less than a second number

(a) $n > 2n - 10$

(b) $n = m - 10$

(c) $m \geq n + 10$

(d) $n^2 > \dfrac{n}{10}$

(e) $2n < n + 10$

(f) $n^3 > \dfrac{1}{10}n^2$

Exercises 11–19: Represent each situation with an algebraic equation.

11 Four times a number is nine more than the number.

12 Todd's weight is 16 pounds more than three times his son's weight, w.

13 A number squared, increased by 15, is the same as the square of 1 more than the number.

14 Twice Jacqueline's age is the same as her father's age.

15 The quotient of p divided by r, decreased by the product of p and r, is 5.

16 In 20 years, Tracy's age will be 5 years greater than twice her current age.

17 Jack worked 6 hours on Friday and $x + 2$ hours on Saturday at a constant rate of pay. He earned $92.

18 If b baseball cards were divided equally among 3 people, each person would receive 25 cards less than if the b baseball cards were divided equally between 2 people.

19 From the product of $3x - 2$ and $4x + 3$ subtract double the square of $(2x - 5)$ to get 0.

20 Genna has $12.50 in pennies, dimes, and half-dollars in her piggy bank. She has 5 times as many dimes as half-dollars and 5 times as many pennies as dimes.

a If Genna has h half-dollars, write an expression for the number of dimes and pennies that she has.

b Using these expressions, write an equation showing that the total value of all Genna's coins is $12.50.

Evaluating Algebraic Expressions

The group of values that can be substituted for a variable in an algebraic expression is known as the **domain** or **replacement set**. For example, let $6x$ represent the number of soda cans in a certain number, x, of six-packs. Here, x can be replaced by any counting number, so the replacement set for x is {0, 1, 2, 3, …}. To find the number of sodas in three six-packs, we would let $x = 3$ and substitute 3 in the expression, getting 6×3, or 18. Substituting numbers for variables to find a value for an expression is called **evaluating** the expression.

To Evaluate an Algebraic Expression

- Substitute the given values for the letters (or variables).
- Simplify by using the order of operations.

Some expressions with variables located in the denominator of a fraction or in a radicand ($\sqrt{}$) have limits on their replacement sets due to the properties of fractions and radicals. Since division by zero is impossible, a fraction is undefine when its denominator equals 0. Thus, the fraction $\dfrac{x}{x + 7}$ is undefined when $x = -7$. In this case the domain of $\dfrac{x}{x + 7}$ cannot include -7.

The domain is important in functions. See Chapter 9.

Since the square root of a negative number is not real, an algebraic expression with a negative radicand cannot be evaluated as a real number. Thus $2\sqrt{7 - x}$ is not a real number when $7 - x$ is negative. In this case the domain cannot include any real numbers greater than 7.

MODEL PROBLEMS

1 Evaluate $a - b(a - x)^2$ if $a = -1$, $b = -2$, and $x = 3$.

SOLUTION

$$-1 - (-2)[(-1) - 3)]^2$$
$$-1 + 2[-4]^2$$
$$-1 + 2[16]$$
$$-1 + 32 = 31$$

2 If d is an odd integer and e is an even integer, which of the following is an odd integer?

(1) $2d + e$ (3) $de + d$
(2) $2d + 2e$ (4) $3e + 3d + 1$

SOLUTION

The best method to solve a problem involving sets of numbers is to substitute an element from each set. Substitute any even number for e, like 2, and any odd number for d, like 3. Then we have

(1) $2d + e = 2 \times 3 + 2 = 8$
(2) $2d + 2e = 2 \times 3 + 2 \times 2 = 10$
(3) $de + d = 3 \times 2 + 3 = 9$
(4) $3e + 3d + 1 = 3 \times 2 + 3 \times 3 + 1 = 16$

Answer: (3)

3 Which of these values will make the algebraic fraction $\dfrac{2x + 3}{2x - 3}$ undefined?

(1) 2
(2) 3
(3) $\dfrac{2}{3}$
④ $\dfrac{3}{2}$

$2x - 3 = 0$
$2x = 3$
$x = \dfrac{3}{2}$

SOLUTION

Substitute the values for x in the denominator to see which would make the denominator equal zero.

(1) $2(2) - 3 = 1$
(2) $2(3) - 3 = 3$
(3) $2\left(\dfrac{2}{3}\right) - 3 = \dfrac{4}{3} - 3 = \dfrac{4}{3} - \dfrac{9}{3} = -\dfrac{5}{3}$
(4) $2\left(\dfrac{3}{2}\right) - 3 = 0$

Answer: (4)

4 Using the domain {0, 2, 4}, find the solution set of the open sentence $x + 8 = 12$.

SOLUTION

Replace x in the open sentence with each number from the domain {0, 2, 4} and check the truth value:

Let $x = 0$. Then $0 + 8 = 12$ is false.
Let $x = 2$. Then $2 + 8 = 12$ is false.
Let $x = 4$. Then $4 + 8 = 12$ is true.

The domain element 4 is the only replacement value that makes the open sentence true.

Answer: {4}

5 Using the domain {1, 2, 3, 4} find the solution set of the open sentence $3k \leq 9$.

K = (1,2)
K = (1, 2, 3)

SOLUTION

Replace k in the open sentence with each number from the domain {1, 2, 3, 4} and check the truth value:

Let $k = 1$. Then $3(1) \leq 9$ or $3 \leq 9$ is true.
Let $k = 2$. Then $3(2) \leq 9$ or $6 \leq 9$ is true.
Let $k = 3$. Then $3(3) \leq 9$ or $9 \leq 9$ is true.
Let $k = 4$. Then $3(4) \leq 9$ or $12 \leq 9$ is false.

The domain elements 1, 2, and 3 make the open sentence true.

Answer: {1, 2, 3}

 Practice

---

1 Find the value of $a - (b - c)$ when $a = -3$, $b = 4$, and $c = -5$.

-3   4
-3 - (4+5)

(1) -12 (3) -2
(2) -4 (4) 6

2 Find the value of $ab + ac$ when $a = -3$, $b = 4$, and $c = -5$.

(1) 27 (3) -3
(2) 3 (4) -27

(-3)(4)
-12 + 15 = 3
(-3)(-5)

3 If $x + 3$ is an even integer, which of the following is not an even integer?

(1) $2x + 2$ (3) $x - 3$
(2) $2x + 3$ (4) $3x - .1$

4 Which of the fractional expressions has a value greater than 1 if K is an integer greater than 1?

(1) $\dfrac{K}{1 + K}$ (3) $\dfrac{K + 1}{K}$

(2) $\dfrac{1}{1 - K}$ (4) $\dfrac{K}{1 - K}$

5 If e is an even integer and d is an odd integer, which of the following is an even integer?

(1) $2d^2 + 3e$ (3) $3e^2 + d$
(2) $de + d^2$ (4) $d^2 + 3e$

6 If a and b are prime numbers greater than 2, which of the following expressions must be odd?

(1) $a + b - 2$ (3) $ab + 1$
(2) $ab - 1$ (4) $ab + 2$

Exercises 7–16: Find the numerical value of each expression. Use $w = 4$, $x = -2$, $y = 3$, and $z = -6$.

7 $w + 5$

8 $\dfrac{w + x}{2}$

9 $\dfrac{wxz}{3}$

10 $4x^2$

11 $0.25wy$

12 $\dfrac{1}{2}xy + \dfrac{1}{3}wz$

13 $x(y + z)$

14 $x + yz$

15 $(2x - 3z)^2$

16 $(2x)^2 - (3z)^2$

17 If $m = -3$, then what does $-2m^3$ equal?

18 If $a = \dfrac{2}{3}$, and $b = -\dfrac{3}{2}$, then what is the value of $a^3 + b^2$?

19 If $x = 3$ and $y = -3$, find the value of $x^3 + y^3$.

20 If $r = s = -5$, then what is the value of $r(r + s) - s(r - s)$?

21 What value of r will make $\dfrac{2}{(r - 4)^2}$ undefined?

22 For what values of x will $\dfrac{3(x - 3)^3}{3x}$ be undefined?

23 If $a = 1$ and $b = -20$, find the value of $\dfrac{-a + a^2 + 4b}{4}$.

24 Given that $s = 4$ and $t = -3$, evaluate the expression $(s^3 - t^3 + s)(t^2 + t)$.

25 If $r = 4$, $p = -1$, and $q = 2$, evaluate $\dfrac{(rp)^2 - pq + 3}{(r - p + q)^2}$.

26 What is the value of $3x^2 - 3x - 3$ as x takes each one of the three following values? Show your work clearly.

   a -1
   b 0
   c 1

Exercises 27–31: Using the domain $\{-4, -2, 0, 2, 4\}$, find the solution set for each of the following.

27 $p + 4 = 0$

28 $7 - z = 2$

29 $2k - 4 = -2$

30 $\dfrac{c}{4} = c$

31 $3v + 3 < 15$

Exercises 32–35: Let $x = 3$ and $y = 4$. Fill in each blank in the four statements below with "less than," "equal to," or "greater than."

32 The value of $\dfrac{x}{y - 1}$ is _____ the value of $\dfrac{x}{y}$.

33 The value of $\dfrac{x - 2}{y - 2}$ is _____ the value of $\dfrac{x}{y}$.

34 The value of $\dfrac{x^2 - 1}{2y}$ is _____ the value of $\dfrac{x}{y}$.

35 The value of $\dfrac{x^2}{y^2}$ is _____ the value of $\dfrac{x}{y}$.

Algebraic Terms and Vocabulary

A **term** is an algebraic expression written with numbers, variables, or both and using multiplication, division, or both. A term that has no variables is often called a **constant**. Examples: 5, x, cd, $6mx$, $\dfrac{4x^2y}{-3m^3}$ are all terms. Of these, 5 is a constant.

The **numerical coefficient** of a term is the numerical part of the term. If no numerical coefficient is written, then it is understood to be 1. The numerical coefficient of $6mx$ is 6, the numerical coefficient of $\dfrac{4x^2y}{-3m^3}$ is $-\dfrac{4}{3}$, and the numerical coefficient of cd is 1.

If a **term** contains more than one variable or a numerical coefficient and one or more variables, each number and variable and all combinations of products of the number and variables are called **factors** of the term. The factors of $6ab$ are 1, 2, 3, 6, a, $2a$, $3a$, $6a$, b, $2b$, $3b$, $6b$, ab, $2ab$, $3ab$, and $6ab$.

A number that can be expressed by means of a base and an exponent is called a **power**. A power is a term or a factor of a term that can be written as the product of equal factors. The **base** is one of the equal factors. The exponent is the number of times the base is used as a factor.

$4^3 = (4)(4)(4)$:	base $= 4$	exponent $= 3$	power $= 4^3 = 64$
$10w^2$:	base $= w$	exponent $= 2$	power $= w^2$
$c(ab)^2$:	base $= ab$	exponent $= 2$	power $= (ab)^2$
$6j$:	base $= j$	exponent $= 1$	power $= j^1$ or j
$-x^2$	base $= x$	exponent $= 2$	power $= x^2$

 Practice

1 Name the factors of $4mn$.

2 Name the factors of $8m^2$.

3 Name the numerical coefficient of x: $\dfrac{x+2}{3}$ $\dfrac{1}{3}x$

4 Name the numerical coefficient of x: $6 - 4x$

5 Name the base, exponent, and power: $9(a + b)^3$

6 Name the base, exponent, and power: $\dfrac{-3m^2}{4}$

7 Write using exponents: $2g\pi g\pi$

8 Write using exponents: $5(x + y)(x + y)(x + y)$

9 Name the coefficient, the base, and the exponent: $7(bx)^2$

10 Name the coefficient, the base, and the exponent: $-b^4$

Literal Equations and Formulas

Algebraic expressions have no specific value until values are substituted for each variable. Algebraic equations made of algebraic expressions cannot be called true or false until values are chosen from the domain for each variable.

The set of numbers from the domain that makes the equation true is called the **solution set** or the **roots** of the equation.

An equation with more than one variable is called a **literal equation**. For example, $x + y = r$ and $3m = 2n + 1$ are literal equations. A **formula** is a literal equation that expresses a rule about a real-world relationship. For instance, $d = rt$ is a formula comparing distance to rate and time.

For some problems in the Regents Examination, you may be given a formula. For others, you may be asked to remember a formula or develop one from the problem situation. You may then be given information about all but one of the variables. In all three types of problems, you must then solve for the unknown variable's value.

Solving for Unknown Variables in Literal Equations and Formulas

• Write the equation.
• Substitute the known values of the variables.
• Simplify and solve for the value of the remaining variable.
• State the answer with the correct label.

MODEL PROBLEMS

1 The formula used to convert from degrees Celsius to degrees Fahrenheit is $F = 1.8C + 32$. The temperature in Montreal is reported at 24°C. Convert that temperature to degrees Fahrenheit.

SOLUTION

Write the formula.	$F = 1.8C + 32$
Substitute known values.	$F = 1.8(24) + 32$
Simplify and solve for F.	$F = 75.2$
Write the answer with the correct label.	$F = 75.2°F$

2 Simple interest is calculated using the formula $I = prt$, where I = simple interest, p = principal, r = annual rate of interest expressed as a decimal or fraction, t = time in years. Compute the simple interest if the initial principal is $1,000 invested for 3 years at 6% interest.

SOLUTION

Write the formula.	$I = prt$
Substitute known values.	$I = (1,000)(0.06)(3)$
Solve for the variable I.	$I = 60(3) = 180$
Write the answer with the correct label.	$I = \$180$

3 If a slug that has been traveling 1 inch per hour has covered a distance of 24 inches, how long has it been moving?

SOLUTION

This relationship is described by the formula $d = rt$.	$d = rt$
Substitute known values.	24 in. = (1 in./h)t
Solve for the variable t.	$t = \dfrac{24 \text{ in.}}{1 \text{ in./h}}$
Answer with the correct label.	$t = 24$ hours or 1 day

 Practice

1 The centripetal force, F, of a rotating object equals the mass, m, multiplied by the square of its velocity, v, divided by the radius, r, of its path. This formula can be written

(1) $F = m + \left(\dfrac{v}{r}\right)^2$

(2) $F = \dfrac{(mv)^2}{r}$

(3) $F = \dfrac{m + v^2}{r}$

(4) $F = \dfrac{mv^2}{r}$

2 To find the cost of two quarts of milk and three small packages of cream cheese if each quart of milk costs $1.50 and each package of cream cheese costs $0.89, which formula would you use?

(1) $C = m + c$, where $m = 1.5$ and $c = 0.89$

(2) $C = 3m + 2c$, where $m = 1.5$ and $c = 0.89$

(3) $C = 2m + 3c$, where $m = 1.5$ and $c = 0.89$

(4) $C = 2m \cdot 3c$, where $m = 1.5$ and $c = 0.89$

3 Find the number of miles traveled by Mrs. Smith if she drove 40 miles per hour for $\frac{3}{4}$ hour and 65 miles per hour for $3\frac{1}{2}$ hours.

(1) 485 miles

(2) $332\frac{1}{2}$ miles

(3) $257\frac{1}{2}$ miles

(4) $109\frac{1}{4}$ miles

4 If $S = \frac{rm - a}{r - 1}$, what is the value of S when $r = 3$, $m = 15$, and $a = 5$?

(1) 10
(2) 15
(3) 20
(4) 25

5 Find the value of A if $A = \pi dh + \frac{1}{2}\pi d^2$ and $\pi = 3.14$, $h = 7$ centimeters, and $d = 10$ centimeters.

(1) $A = 476.99$ cm^2
(2) $A = 376.8$ cm^2
(3) $A = 230.5$ cm^2
(4) $A = 219.8$ cm^2

6 The formula used to convert from degrees Fahrenheit to degrees Celcius is $C = \frac{5}{9}(F - 32)$. Find the Celsius temperature rounded to the nearest degree when the Fahrenheit temperature is 86 degrees.

(1) 16°C
(2) 30°C
(3) 48°C
(4) 51°C

7 Write a formula for the cost C in dollars for renting a movie if the cost is $4 for the first 2 days and $1.50 for each additional day.

8 Sales tax is 8%. If the price paid for an item is P, write a formula that can be used to find N, the price of the item before tax.

9 $C = 7N$ is a formula that can be used to find the cost (C) of any number of articles (N) that sell for $7 each.

a How will the cost of 9 articles compare to the cost of 3 articles?
b If N is doubled, what happens to C?

10 The formula for the volume of a sphere is $V = \frac{4}{3}\pi r^3$. Find the value of V in terms of π when $r = 3$ centimeters.

11 If $S = \frac{a}{1 + r}$, find the value of S when $a = 12$ and $r = 7$.

12 A car travels at a constant rate of 60 miles per hour. How long will it take to travel 105 miles?

Exercises 13–15: Find the value of d in the formula $d = b^2 - 4ac$, if possible.

13 $a = 3$, $b = 2$, and $c = -\frac{1}{2}$

14 $a = 3$, $b = 4$, and $c = -2$

15 $a = 4$, $b = 3$, and $c = -2$

Exercises 16–19: Find the value of an investment (A) if the value is given by the formula $A = p + prt$.

16 $p = \$600$, $r = 3\%$, and $t = 2$ years

17 $p = \$4,000$, $r = 5\%$, and $t = 8$ years

18 $p = \$1,250$, $r = 4\%$, and $t = 2\frac{1}{4}$ years

19 $p = \$3,500$, $r = 2\%$, and $t = 4.5$ years

20 The thickness of each piece of a certain kind of paper is 0.01 cm. The paper is used in the printing of a book. Each outside cover of the book is 0.2 cm. and the book has 350 pages.

a Write a formula for the thickness of the book in meters.
b Use your formula to express the width of shelf space in meters needed to hold 50 books standing upright.

1 The distance in feet, S, an object will fall equals the product of 16 and the time, t, squared, in seconds. $S =$

   (1) $16t^2$
   (2) $16 + t^2$
   (3) $16t$
   (4) $\dfrac{16}{t^2}$

2 Christine is renting a bicycle at the boardwalk. She must leave a $25 deposit. When she returns the bike she will get a refund on her deposit and she will be charged $5 per hour or part of an hour. If she keeps her bicycle for 3 hours and 15 minutes, how much does she spend?

   (1) $15
   (2) $20
   (3) $40
   (4) $45

Exercises 3–6: Use mathematical symbols to translate the verbal phrases into algebraic language.

3 A number diminished by 6 $x - 6$

4 Twice the product of a and b $2 \times (a+b)$

5 k decreased by twice j $k - 2j$

6 3 times a number, increased by 7 $3x + 7$

Exercises 7–10: Represent each answer in algebraic language, using the variables mentioned in the problem.

7 A movie ticket cost $8.25. Represent the cost of x tickets.

8 Georgette bought 2 more sweaters than Danielle. If Danielle bought s sweaters, how many did Georgette buy?

9 Kevin weighed p pounds. After a workout in the gym, he lost m pounds. How much did Kevin weigh after his workout?

10 Gabby is twice as tall as Vincent. If Vincent is x inches tall, how tall is Gabby?

Exercises 11–14: For each given term, name the coefficient, the base, and the exponent.

11 x $1, x, 1$

12 $4k^2$ $4, k, 2$

13 $-(gh)^3$ $-1, gh, 3$

14 jk^6 $1, k, 6$

15 If $x = 10$ and $y = 3$, then what is the value of $(2x + 7) + y$?

$(2(10) + 7) + 3$
$(20 + 7) + 3$
$27 + 3 = 30$

16 Using the domain $\{-1, 0, 1\}$, find the solution set of the open sentence $x + 1 = 1$.

17 Using the domain $\{1, 2, 3, 4, 5, 6\}$, find the solution set of the open sentence $x - 6 = 1$.

18 Using the domain $\{-5, -4, -3, -2, -1, 0\}$, find the solution set of the open sentence $x + 1 > 0$.

19 Using the domain $\{-3, -2, -1, 0, 1, 2, 3\}$, find the solution set of the open sentence $-3x < 0$.

20 What is the product of all one-digit prime numbers?

21 At the local town swimming pool, family membership is $10 dollars per car for a parking pass plus $20 per family member. The cost for a family of n people with c cars is therefore $10c + 20n$. Determine the cost for a family of 5 people with 2 cars.

22 Write a formula that expresses the volume of a cone as one-third the product of π, the square of the radius of the base, and the height of the cone.

23 The cost C of a taxi ride m miles long is $4.50 plus $2.50 for each mile. Write the formula for C in terms of m.

24 The relationship between the velocity of an object, the time it is in motion, and the distance it travels is $d = vt$. If an object travels 120 meters in 40 seconds, what is the velocity of the object in meters per second?

25 Of the 300 students attending an anti-bullying rally, 40 students had been physically bullied, 185 students had been verbally bullied, and 105 had not been bullied. How many students had been both physically and verbally bullied?

Now turn to page 424 and take the Cumulative Review test for Chapters 1–3. This will help you monitor your progress and keep all your skills sharp.

3-6 11-15

CHAPTER 4

First-Degree Equations and Inequalities in One Variable

Solving Linear Equations

An equation is an open sentence that states that two algebraic expressions are equal. The equation is called **linear** if the variables on either side of the equals sign have at most a greatest integral exponent value, or degree, of 1. An equation with more than one variable is called a **literal equation**. A **formula** is a literal equation

that expresses a rule about a real world relationship. For instance $F = \frac{9}{5}C + 32$ is

a formula comparing temperature measures in degrees Fahrenheit and degrees Celcius. You may be given a formula with information about all but one of the variables. You may be asked to solve for the unknown variable.

The process of finding the solution for the unknown variable is called solving the equation or solving the open sentence. The value of the unknown variable that makes the open sentence true is called the root of the open sentence.

An equation is like a balanced scale. To keep the equation in balance, *any change made on one side must also be made on the other side.* To solve an equation, you must manipulate the left and right expressions of the equation so that the variable is left alone on one side. This is done by performing opposite or inverse operations to "unwrap" the variable.

A number without a variable, such as 7, has a degree of zero, because $7x^0 = 7 \cdot 1 = 7$.

- If an equation is true for only some values of the variable or variables, it is called a **conditional equation**. Thus, $8x = 16$ is a conditional equation because it is true only when $x = 2$.
- If an equation is true for all possible values of the variable or variables, it is called an **identity**. $4x + 2x = 6x$ is an identity, since any number replacing x will make the equation true.
- If no possible values of the variable or variables make the equation true, it is called the **contradiction**. $1 + x = x$ is a contradiction, since no value of x will make it true.

Once we have a solution, we must test that solution in the equation. This is called checking. **Checking** involves two steps:

- First, the solution must be substituted for the variable *in the original equation.*
- Second, each side of the equation must be simplified. If the two sides of the equation are the same, then the solution is correct.

Solving Equations of the Form $x + a = b$

To undo the addition of a number, add its opposite to both sides of the equation. This is the same as subtracting the number from both sides.

MODEL PROBLEMS

1 Solve the equation $x - 7 = 2$.

SOLUTION

Write the equation.

Add the opposite of -7 to both sides. Arrange in columns and add.

$$
\begin{array}{rcr}
x - 7 = & 2 \\
+ 7 = & + 7 \\
\hline
x \quad = & 9
\end{array}
$$

Check. $x - 7 = 2 \rightarrow 9 - 7 = 2\ \checkmark$

Answer: $x = 9$

2 Solve the equation $5 + x = 20$.

SOLUTION

Write the equation.

Add the opposite of 5 to both sides.

$$
\begin{array}{rcr}
5 + x = & 20 \\
- 5 \quad = & - 5 \\
\hline
x = & 15
\end{array}
$$

Check. $5 + x = 20 \rightarrow 5 + 15 = 20\ \checkmark$

Answer: $x = 15$

 Practice

---

1 If $x + 4\dfrac{3}{4} = 7$, then $x =$

   (1) $11\dfrac{3}{4}$

   (2) $3\dfrac{3}{4}$

   (3) $2\dfrac{3}{4}$

   (4) $2\dfrac{1}{4}$

2 If $9 = x + 2$, then $x =$

   (1) -7
   (2) 7
   (3) 11
   (4) 18

3 If $x - 2.5 = -6$, then $x =$

   (1) -8.5
   (2) -3.5
   (3) 3.5
   (4) 8.5

4 If $x - \$1.25 = \$4.90$, then $x =$

    (1) $3.65
    (2) $3.92
    (3) $6.13
    (4) $6.15

5 To solve $1.4 = x + 8.2$, what number should you add to both sides of the equation?

Exercises 6–10: Solve for the variable.

6 $x - 8 = 12$

7 $x + 5\frac{1}{2} = 3$

8 $x - 1.6 = -3.8$

9 $2 = k + 0.4$

10 $x - \frac{1}{8} = 2\frac{3}{8}$

Solving Equations of the Form $ax = b$

To undo multiplication by a number, do the opposite. That is, divide by that number or multiply by its reciprocal. Remember that the process of multiplying by the reciprocal is the same as dividing by the number.

    Consider the equation $3x = 21$. Note that on one side of the equation, x is multiplied by 3. The solution is found by dividing each side of the equation by 3. Multiplying by the reciprocal is another method that can be used to find the solution. Both methods are shown below.

Note: Proportion and conversion problems are equations of the form $ax = b$. For example, the proportion $\dfrac{x\text{ feet}}{30\text{ yards}} = \dfrac{3\text{ feet}}{1\text{ yard}}$ is similar to $\dfrac{1}{30}x = 3$. Proportions with x in the denominator can be inverted. Thus $\dfrac{30\text{ yards}}{x\text{ feet}} = \dfrac{1\text{ yard}}{3\text{ feet}}$ has the same solution as $\dfrac{x\text{ feet}}{30\text{ yards}} = \dfrac{3\text{ feet}}{1\text{ yard}}$.

 MODEL PROBLEMS

1 Solve $12x = 36$ for x.

SOLUTION

Write the equation.

$$12x = 36$$

Divide both sides by 12.

$$\frac{12x}{12} = \frac{36}{12}$$

Simplify.

$$x = 3$$

Check. $12x = 36 \rightarrow 12(3) = 36$ ✓

Answer: $x = 3$

2 Solve the equation $\frac{x}{4} = -5$ for x.

SOLUTION

Write the equation.

$$\frac{x}{4} = -5$$

The opposite of division by 4 is multiplication by 4.

$$(4)\frac{x}{4} = (4)(-5)$$

Simplify each side.

$$x = -20$$

Check. $\frac{x}{4} = -5 \rightarrow \frac{-20}{4} = -5 \checkmark$

Answer: $x = -20$

A term containing a fractional coefficient may be written as a fraction.

$$\frac{1}{4}x = \frac{x}{4}$$

$$\frac{3}{4}x = \frac{3x}{4}$$

3 Solve $0.01x = 7$ for x.

SOLUTION

Write the equation.

$$0.01x = 7$$

Rewrite the equation.

$$\frac{1}{100}x = 7$$

Multiply both sides by 100.

$$(100)\frac{1}{100}x = 7(100)$$

Simplify.

$$x = 700$$

Check. $0.01x = 7 \rightarrow 0.01(700) = 7 \checkmark$

Answer: $x = 700$

 Practice

1 A piece of imported cheese costs \$4.77. If the piece weighs $\frac{9}{10}$ of a pound, solve the eqution $\$4.77 = \frac{9}{10}x$ to find how much the cheese costs per pound.

(1) \$3.87
(2) \$4.29
(3) \$5.30
(4) \$5.67

2 How long does it take for a car traveling at 45 miles per hour to cover 225 miles?

(1) 265 minutes
(2) 5 hours
(3) 3 hours
(4) 2 hours

3 On a map, 1 inch represents 50 miles. If two cities are 275 miles apart, how many inches apart are they on the map?

(1) 13.75 inches
(2) 5.5 inches
(3) 3.25 inches
(4) 2.25 inches

4 If a bus travels 152 miles in 4 hours, how long will it take the bus to travel 342 miles at the same rate?

    (1)   6.25 hours
    (2)   9 hours
    (3)   13 hours
    (4)   47.5 hours

Exercises 5–15: Solve for the variable and check.

5 $\dfrac{a}{5} = -6$

6 $0.7m = -1.4$

7 $\dfrac{3}{4}x = -27$

8 $-12x = -60$

9 $18 = -2x$

10 $0.06m = 12$

11 $6x = 3$

12 $\dfrac{1}{4}x = 3$

13 $3 = \dfrac{1}{9}x$

14 $\dfrac{2}{3}x = 8$

15 $-0.02x = 6.4$

Solving Equations of the Form $ax + b = c$

On the Regents Examination, the solution of equations will usually require more than one operation. In general, in order to "unwrap" or solve multiple-step equations, the operations should be done in reverse order: for equations of the form $ax + b = c$, it is easier to undo the addition first and then undo the multiplication.

 MODEL PROBLEMS

1   Solve $-6x + 4 = 34$ for x and check.

SOLUTION

Write the equation.	$-6x + 4 = 34$
Add the opposite of 4 to each side.	$\underline{\ -4 = -4}$
	$-6x = 30$
Divide each side by -6.	$\dfrac{-6x}{-6} = \dfrac{30}{-6}$
Simplify.	$x = -5$
Check.	$-6x + 4 = 34$
	$-6(-5) + 4 = 34$
	$30 + 4 = 34$
	$34 = 34 ✓$

Answer: $x = -5$

2 Solve: $\dfrac{2}{7}x + \dfrac{4}{7} = 2$

SOLUTION

Multiply every term by the common denominator, 7.

$$7 \cdot \dfrac{2}{7}x + 7 \cdot \dfrac{4}{7} = 7 \cdot 2$$

> To solve problems with fractional coefficients, it is often easier to multiply both sides of the equation by the least common multiple, thereby eliminating all the fractions.

Simplify. Now there are no fractions.

$$2x + 4 = 14$$

Add -4 to each side.

$$\underline{\quad -4 = -4\quad}$$

$$2x \quad = 10$$

Divide by 2.

$$\dfrac{2x}{2} = \dfrac{10}{2}$$

Simplify.

$$x = 5$$

Check.

$$\dfrac{2(5)}{7} + \dfrac{4}{7} = 2$$

$$\dfrac{10}{7} + \dfrac{4}{7} = 2$$

$$\dfrac{14}{7} = 2 \checkmark$$

Answer: $x = 5$

3 Solve the equation $\dfrac{5x}{6} + \dfrac{1}{3} = \dfrac{5}{12}$.

SOLUTION

Eliminate fractions by multiplying each term by 12 (LCD of 6, 3, and 12).

$$12 \cdot \dfrac{5x}{6} + 12 \cdot \dfrac{1}{3} = 12 \cdot \dfrac{5}{12}$$

Simplify.

$$10x + 4 = 5$$

Add -4 to each side.

$$\underline{\quad -4 = -4\quad}$$

Simplify.

$$10x \quad = 1$$

Divide each side by 10.

$$x = \dfrac{1}{10}$$

Check.

$$\dfrac{5\left(\dfrac{1}{10}\right)}{6} + \dfrac{1}{3} = \dfrac{5}{12}$$

$$\dfrac{\left(\dfrac{1}{2}\right)}{6} + \dfrac{1}{3} = \dfrac{5}{12}$$

$$\dfrac{1}{12} + \dfrac{1}{3} = \dfrac{5}{12}$$

$$\dfrac{1}{12} + \dfrac{4}{12} = \dfrac{5}{12} \checkmark$$

(With calculator)

$$\dfrac{5(0.1)}{6} + \dfrac{1}{3} = \dfrac{5}{12}$$

$$\dfrac{0.5}{6} + \dfrac{1}{3} = \dfrac{5}{12}$$

$$0.08\overline{3} + 0.\overline{3} = \dfrac{5}{12}$$

$$0.41\overline{6} = \dfrac{5}{12} \checkmark$$

Answer: $x = \dfrac{1}{10}$

1 Solve: $7x + 5 = 33$

$7x = 28$
$\frac{7}{7} \quad \frac{28}{7}$
$x = 4$

   (1) $x = 4$

   (2) $x = 5\frac{1}{5}$

   (3) $x = 5\frac{3}{7}$

   (4) $x = 8$

2 Which choice is the solution to $8 = 3x - 4$?

   (1) $x = 1\frac{1}{3}$

   (2) $x = 4$

   (3) $x = 12$

   (4) $x = 36$

3 If $v = V + gt$, what is the value of t when $v = 116$, $V = 20$, and $g = 32$?

   (1) 3,732

   (2) 96

   (3) 64

   (4) 3

4 Which choice is *not* a step you would take to solve the equation $4 - \frac{x}{2} = 0$?

   (1) Add -4 to both sides of the equation.
   (2) Divide both sides by -2.
   (3) Multiply each term by -2.
   (4) Subtract 4 from both sides.

5 To solve $10 - 2x = 18$, what number should you add to both sides of the equation for the first step? For the second step, what number should you divide by?

6 Ms. Healy asked her class to solve the equation $10 + \frac{x}{3} = 23$. Maria multiplied both sides of the equation by 3, then subtracted 10 from both sides. Leon divided both sides of the equation by $\frac{1}{3}$, then subtracted 30 from both sides. Which student was correct? What mistake did the other student make?

Exercises 7–11: Solve for the variable and check.

7 $5y - 7 = 15$

8 $4 - 2x = 14$

9 $\frac{1}{4}m + 5 = -3$

10 $\frac{3}{4}c - 8 = 4$

11 $5x + 6 = 81$

12 A business had $1,395 in sales and $261 in expenses. How much did each of the three partners receive if they divided the profits evenly?

Solving Equations With Like Terms

To solve equations with like terms, move all like terms to the same side of the equals sign and combine them. When many terms are involved, the best method is to simplify both sides of the equation before solving.

Note: In the model problems on page 81, the step of checking has been left for the student to complete.

MODEL PROBLEMS

1   Solve for x: $7x - 8 = 10 + 4x$

SOLUTION

Write the equation. $7x - 8 = 10 + 4x$

Add 8 to each side. $\underline{+ 8 = + 8}$

                             $7x = 18 + 4x$

Add $-4x$ to each side. $\underline{- 4x = - 4x}$

                             $3x = 18$

Divide both sides by 3. $x = 6$

Answer: $x = 6$

2   Willis, Bryan, and Franklin together inherited their aunt's horses after the five oldest mares were sold. The ratio of horses they received, in order, is $1:2:5$. How many horses did each man get if there were originally 101 horses?

SOLUTION

Define all unknowns with one variable, the number of horses in one share, or h.

Willis $= h$ horses
Bryan $= 2h$ horses
Franklin $= 5h$ horses

Write an equation for the original number of horses.

$h + 2h + 5h + 5 = 101$

Combine like terms. $8h + 5 = 101$

Add -5 to each side. $\underline{ - 5 = - 5}$

                             $8h = 96$

Divide both sides by 8. $\dfrac{8h}{8} = \dfrac{96}{8}$

                             $h = 12$

Answer: Willis received 12 horses, Bryan received 24 horses, and Franklin received 60 horses.

3   Solve $x + 0.04x = 832$ for x.

SOLUTION

Write the equation. $x + 0.04x = 832$

Combine like terms. $1.04x = 832$

Divide each side by 1.04 $\dfrac{1.04x}{1.04} = \dfrac{832}{1.04}$

Answer: $x = 800$ $x = 800$

4   Neil's telephone service costs \$25 per month plus \$0.15 for each local call. There is an additional charge for long-distance calls. Last month, Neil's telephone bill was \$31.50. His long-distance charge was \$2. How many local calls did he make?

SOLUTION

Let n = number of local calls

Write an equation. $25 + 0.15n + 2 = 31.50$

Combine like terms. $27 + 0.15n = 31.50$

Add -27 to each side. $\underline{-27 = - 27}$

                           $0.15n = 4.5$

Divide both sides by 0.15. $\dfrac{0.15n}{0.15} = \dfrac{4.5}{0.15}$

                           $n = 30$

Answer: Neil made 30 local calls.

 Practice

1   If $6x - 4 = 20 - 2x$, then $x =$

(1) 6
(2) 4
(3) 3
(4) 2

$8x - 4 = 20$

$8x = 24$

$x = 3$

2   If $5x - 2 = 28 - x$, then $x =$

(1) 6
(2) 5
(3) 4
(4) 3

$6x - 2 = 28$

$6x = 30$

$x = 5$

3 If $8x - 4 + 7 = 6x + x + 9$, then $x =$

    (1) 6
    (2) 4
    (3) 2
    (4) 0

4 At a school fund-raising drive, $350 was collected for washing sedans, coupes, and sport-utility vehicles. The cost of a wash for any type of vehicle was $2. Twice as many coupes were washed as sedans. Four times as many sport-utility vehicles were washed as sedans. How many coupes were washed?

    (1) 175
    (2) 100
    (3) 50
    (4) 25

Exercises 5–18: Solve for the variable and check.

5 $\dfrac{5}{6}x - \dfrac{1}{6}x = 10$

6 $\dfrac{7}{8}x - \dfrac{1}{8}x = 9$

7 $5x = 15 + 2x$

8 $4x + 6 = 6x$

9 $a - 0.04a = 240$

10 $3x + 10 = 8x$

11 $6x + 3x - 4 = 32$

12 $5x + 2 = 8x - 7$

13 $3x + 5x - x = 56$

14 $9x - 12 = 7x - 6$

15 $5a + 3 = 15 + 2a$

16 $3a - a = a + 8$

17 $7x - 8 - 2x = 64 - 3x$

18 $7x + 6 = 8 - x - 2$

19 Three cousins belong to a school basketball team. The ratio of their field goals in the championship game was 3 to 3 to 4. The total number of field goals made by the cousins was 30. Determine the number made by each cousin. Explain your answer.

20 Three less than a certain number is 12 less than twice the number. Write an equation and solve to find the number.

Solving Equations With Parentheses and Rational Expressions

- To solve equations with parentheses, first use the distributive property to remove the parentheses, then solve as before.
- To solve equations with rational expressions, multiply each term in the equation by the LCD (the least common denominator).
- If the equation is set up like a proportion, then cross multiply, set the two products as equal, and solve.

Note: The step of checking has been left for the student to complete in model problems 4 and 5 on pages 84 and 85.

MODEL PROBLEMS

1 The train stations in New York and Boston are 220 miles apart. A train left New York for Boston at 8:00 A.M. traveling at 65 mph. An hour later, an express train left Boston for New York traveling at 90 mph. At what time did they pass each other?

SOLUTION

When the trains meet, the total distance traveled is the same as the distance between cities, 220 miles. Let t represent the time the express train was traveling and $t + 1$ represent the travel time of the other train.

Use $d = rt$.	$90t + 65(t + 1) = 220$
Remove parentheses.	$90t + 65t + 65 = 220$
Combine like terms.	$155t + 65 = 220$
Add -65 to both sides.	$\underline{-65 \quad -65}$
	$155t \quad = 155$
Solve.	$t \quad = \quad 1$

Check. $90t + 65(t + 1) = 210 \rightarrow 90 + 65(2) = 90 + 130 = 220$ ✓

Answer: The trains passed after the express train had been traveling for one hour, which was at 10:00 A.M.

2 Solve and check: $\dfrac{4a + 3}{3} - \dfrac{7a - 1}{4} = 5$

SOLUTION

Write the equation.	$\dfrac{4a + 3}{3} - \dfrac{7a - 1}{4} = 5$
Multiply each term by the LCD, 12.	$\overset{4}{\cancel{12}}\left(\dfrac{4a + 3}{\cancel{3}}\right) - \overset{3}{\cancel{12}}\left(\dfrac{7a - 1}{\cancel{4}}\right) = 12 \bullet 5$
Multiply.	$16a + 12 - 21a + 3 = \quad 60$
Simplify.	$-5a + 15 = \quad 60$
Subtract 15 from both sides.	$\underline{- 15 = -15}$
	$-5a \quad = \quad 45$
Divide by -5.	$a \quad = \quad -9$

Check. $\dfrac{4a + 3}{3} - \dfrac{7a - 1}{4} = 5 \rightarrow \dfrac{4(-9) + 3}{3} - \dfrac{7(-9) - 1}{4} = \dfrac{-33}{3} - \dfrac{-64}{4} = -11 + 16 = 5$ ✓

Answer: $a = -9$

3 Solve $\dfrac{2}{3x} + \dfrac{1}{4} = \dfrac{11}{6x} - \dfrac{1}{3}$ for x and check.

SOLUTION

Write the equation.

$$\dfrac{2}{3x} + \dfrac{1}{4} = \dfrac{11}{6x} - \dfrac{1}{3}$$

Multiply every term by the LCD, $12x$.

$$\overset{4}{\cancel{12x}} \cdot \dfrac{2}{\cancel{3x}} + \overset{3}{\cancel{12x}} \cdot \dfrac{1}{\cancel{4}} = \overset{2}{\cancel{12x}} \cdot \dfrac{11}{\cancel{6x}} - \overset{4}{\cancel{12x}} \cdot \dfrac{1}{\cancel{3}}$$

Simplify.

$$4 \cdot 2 + 3x \cdot 1 = 2 \cdot 11 - 4x \cdot 1$$

$$8 + 3x = 22 - 4x$$

Add -8 to each side.

$$\dfrac{-8 \qquad\quad = -8}{}$$

$$3x = 14 - 4x$$

Add $4x$ to each side.

$$\dfrac{+4x = \qquad +4x}{}$$

$$7x = 14$$

Divide each side by 7.

$$\dfrac{7x}{7} = \dfrac{14}{7}$$

Simplify.

$$x = 2$$

Check.

$$\dfrac{2}{3(2)} + \dfrac{1}{4} = \dfrac{11}{6(2)} - \dfrac{1}{3}$$

$$\dfrac{2}{6} + \dfrac{1}{4} = \dfrac{11}{12} - \dfrac{1}{3}$$

$$\dfrac{4}{12} + \dfrac{3}{12} = \dfrac{11}{12} - \dfrac{4}{12}$$

$$\dfrac{7}{12} = \dfrac{7}{12} \checkmark$$

Answer: $x = 2$

4 Solve $\dfrac{4x}{9} = \dfrac{2(x + 4)}{3}$.

SOLUTION

Write the equation.

$$\dfrac{4x}{9} = \dfrac{2(x + 4)}{3}$$

Use the distributive property.

$$\dfrac{4x}{9} = \dfrac{2x + 8}{3}$$

Cross multiply.

$$12x = 9(2x + 8)$$

Use the distributive property.

$$12x = 18x + 72$$

Subtract $18x$ from both sides.

$$\dfrac{-18x = -18x}{}$$

$$-6x = 72$$

Divide both sides by -6.

$$\dfrac{-6x}{-6} = \dfrac{72}{-6}$$

Simplify.

$$x = -12$$

Answer: $x = -12$

5 In a group of four consecutive, positive, even integers, the product of the first and the last integers equals the square of the second. Find the integers.

SOLUTION

Consecutive integers can be represented algebraically with one variable. The set $\{x, x + 1, x + 2\}$ is a set of consecutive integers. To represent a set of four consecutive even integers, use $\{x, x + 2, x + 4, x + 6\}$ where x can be any even integer. If x is odd, this same set would represent consecutive odd integers.

Define variables.	first number $= x$ second number $= x + 2$ third number $= x + 4$ last number $= x + 6$
Write the equation.	$x(x + 6) = (x + 2)(x + 2)$ $x(x + 6) = x(x + 2) + 2(x + 2)$
Distribute.	$x^2 + 6x = x^2 + 4x + 4$
Add $-x^2$ to both sides.	$\underline{-x^2 \qquad = -x^2}$ $6x = \qquad 4x + 4$
Add $-4x$ to both sides.	$\underline{-4x = \qquad -4x}$ $2x = \qquad 4$
Divide both sides by 2.	$x = \qquad 2$

Answer: The numbers are 2, 4, 6, and 8.

 Practice

1 Solve $5x - (x + 3) = 7 + 2(x + 2)$ for x.

   (1) 3
   (2) 4
   (3) 6
   (4) 7

Handwritten work:
$5x - x - 3 = 7 + 2x + 4$
$4x - 3 = 7 + 2x + 4$
$4x = 10 + 2x + 4$
$2x = 14$
$x = 7$

2 Solve $3x + 2(50 - x) = 110$ for x.

   (1) 5
   (2) 10
   (3) 15
   (4) 105

3 $\dfrac{x - 5}{10} = \dfrac{x + 4}{4}$

   (1) -40
   (2) -10
   (3) 10
   (4) 40

4 $\dfrac{5}{10x} + \dfrac{1}{3} = \dfrac{3}{5x} + \dfrac{2}{5}$

   (1) $-\dfrac{3}{2}$

   (2) $-\dfrac{2}{3}$

   (3) $\dfrac{2}{3}$

   (4) $\dfrac{3}{2}$

5 A cash register has 5 times as many quarters as nickels, 2 fewer dimes than nickels, and 30 pennies. All together, the cash register contains $8.50 in change. How many nickels are in the cash register?

(1) 4 nickels
(2) 5 nickels
(3) 6 nickels
(4) 30 nickels

Exercises 6–18: Solve for the variable. Assume that no denominator is equal to zero.

6 $18 - (a - 4) = 9 + (a + 3)$

7 $2x(3x + 1) = 3x(2x + 1) - 2$

8 $(a - 1) - (a + 2) - (a - 3) = a$

9 $\dfrac{x}{5} = \dfrac{x - 3}{2}$ $2x = 5x - 15$

$-3x = 15$

$\cancel{3x}$ $x = 5$

10 $\dfrac{x + 2}{4} = \dfrac{x}{2}$

11 $\dfrac{4x + 5}{6} = \dfrac{7}{2}$

12 $\dfrac{x - 3}{2} = \dfrac{x + 4}{6}$

13 $\dfrac{8}{3x} = \dfrac{4}{4x - 5}$

14 $\dfrac{2x - 3}{4} - \dfrac{x - 2}{3} = 2$

15 $\dfrac{x}{3} - \dfrac{3x}{4} = 5 - \dfrac{5x}{6}$

16 $\dfrac{9}{x} + \dfrac{3}{x} = 4$

17 $\dfrac{17}{2x} - \dfrac{5}{2x} = 12$

18 $1 + \dfrac{1}{2n} + \dfrac{2}{3n} = \dfrac{13}{6n}$

19 Of four consecutive even numbers, 4 times the smallest minus twice the largest is 4. Find the smallest number.

20 The sum of five consecutive integers equals 5.5 times the middle integer. Find the integers.

Solving Literal Equations and Formulas for Unknown Variables

Simple literal equations can be solved using the same methods as illustrated in all the preceding examples. When an equation has more than one variable, we can solve for any variable using these methods, treating the other variables like constants.

To Find the Value of a Variable from a Literal Equation or Formula

- Write the equation.
- Substitute the known values of the variables.
- Simplify and solve for the value of the remaining variables.
- State the answer with correct label.

MODEL PROBLEMS

1 Solve for R in $I = \dfrac{E}{R}$.

SOLUTION

Write the equation. $I = \dfrac{E}{R}$ Divide both sides by I. $\dfrac{RI}{I} = \dfrac{E}{I}$

Multiply both sides by R $R \bullet I = \dfrac{E}{R} \bullet R$ $R = \dfrac{E}{I}$
to eliminate the fraction.

$RI = E$

2   Solve the equation $a + c = b - a$ for a.

SOLUTION

Write the equation. $a + c = b - a$

Combine the a terms.

$$\underline{+a \quad\quad = \quad + a}$$
$$2a + c = b$$

Isolate the a.

$$\underline{- c = \quad\quad - c}$$
$$2a = b - c$$
$$\frac{2a}{2} = \frac{b - c}{2}$$
$$a = \frac{b - c}{2}$$

3   Solve the equation $m(n + r) = s$ for n.

SOLUTION

Write the equation. $m(n + r) = s$

Use the distributive property. $mn + mr = s$

Add $-mr$ to both sides.

$$\underline{-mr = \quad\quad - mr}$$
$$mn = s - mr$$

Divide both sides by m. $\dfrac{mn}{m} = \dfrac{s - mr}{m}$

Simplify. $n = \dfrac{s - mr}{m}$

Answer: $n = \dfrac{s - mr}{m}$ or $\dfrac{s}{m} - r$

4   Solve for p in $A = p + prt$.

SOLUTION

Write the equation. $A = p + prt$

Use the distributive property. $A = p(1 + rt)$

Divide both sides by $(1 + rt)$. $\dfrac{A}{(1 + rt)} = \dfrac{p(1 + rt)}{(1 + rt)}$

Simplify. $\dfrac{A}{(1 + rt)} = p$

Answer: $p = \dfrac{A}{1 + rt}$

5   The area of a rectangle is 48 square inches. If the length l of the rectangle is 8 inches, find the width w to the nearest inch. The formula for the area of a rectangle is $A = lw$.

SOLUTION

$$A = lw$$

Substitute 48 for A and 8 for l. $48 = 8w$

Divide both sides by 8. $\dfrac{\overset{6}{\cancel{48}}}{\cancel{8}} = \dfrac{8w}{\cancel{8}}$

$$w = 6 \text{ inches}$$

Check: $A = lw$

$$48 \overset{?}{=} 8 \times 6$$
$$48 = 48$$

6   The area of a rhombus-shaped garden is 25 yd². A straight path connecting two opposite vertices is 5 yards. The formula for the area of a rhombus is $A = \dfrac{d_1 d_2}{2}$ where d_1 and d_2 are the diagonals of the rhombus. Find the length of the straight path connecting the other two vertices.

SOLUTION

Both paths are diagonals of the rhombus.

$$A = \frac{d_1 d_2}{2}$$

Substitute 25 for A and 5 for d_1. $25 = \dfrac{5d_2}{2}$

Multiply both sides by 2. $25 \times 2 = \dfrac{5d_2}{\cancel{2}} \times \cancel{2}$

$$50 = 5d_2$$

Divide both sides by 5. $\dfrac{\overset{10}{\cancel{50}}}{\cancel{5}_1} = \dfrac{5d_2}{\cancel{5}}$

$$d_2 = 10 \text{ yards}$$

Check: $A = \dfrac{d_1 d_2}{2}$

$$25 \overset{?}{=} \frac{5 \times 10}{2}$$
$$25 = 25$$

1 Solve the volume formula, $V = lwh$ for h.

   (1) $h = Vlw$

   (2) $h = V - lw$

   (3) $h = V + lw$

   ~~(4)~~ $h = \dfrac{V}{lw}$

2 Solve $c = ax + b$ for x.

   ~~(1)~~ $x = \dfrac{c - b}{a}$

   (2) $x = ca - b$

   (3) $x = \dfrac{cb}{a}$

   (4) $x = a(c - b)$

3 Solve for x in the equation $\dfrac{ax}{b} = \dfrac{bx}{a}$. Assume that a and b are not equal and do not equal zero.

   (1) $x = \dfrac{a^2}{b^2}$

   (2) $x = 0$

   (3) x can equal any real number as the equation is an identity.

   (4) x has no answer as the equation is a contradiction.

4 Solve the equation $p(q + r) = 1$ for q.

   (1) $q = 1 - p - r$

   (2) $q = \dfrac{1}{p + r}$

   (3) $q = \dfrac{1 - pr}{p}$

   (4) $q = \dfrac{1 - p}{r}$

Exercises 5–13: Solve for x.

5 $ax = 7$

6 $mx = g$

7 $2a + x = 6$

8 $ax + n = m$

9 $nx = 4j - 5x$

10 $R = \dfrac{a(x + b)}{3}$

11 $5x - 8a = 3x + 7a$

12 $\dfrac{1}{x} - \dfrac{1}{a} = \dfrac{1}{b}$

13 $\dfrac{ax}{c} - b = \dfrac{c}{b}$

Exercises 14–19: Solve for the indicated variable.

14 $B = \dfrac{P}{R}$ for R

15 $S = \dfrac{\pi r^2 A}{90}$ for A

16 $S = c + g$ for g

17 $R = \dfrac{gs}{g + s}$ for g

18 $fx - gx = h$ for x

19 $2x = ax + 7$ for x

20 The formula for the total amount of money owed on a long-term loan is $A = p + prt$.

   a Solve for t (time in years).

   b Find t when p (principal) = \$7,400, A (total amount) is \$9,176, and r (rate) is 8%.

21 The length of a rectangle is 4 centimeters longer than the width. The perimeter of the rectangle is 72 centimeters. Find the length and width of the rectangle.

22 The length of each side of a square is 2 inches less than the length of the side of an equilateral triangle. The perimeters of the two shapes are the same. Find the lengths of the sides of each figure.

23 When Lillian emptied her wallet, she had 14 coins, all quarters, dimes, and nickels. She had twice as many dimes as quarters and twice as many nickels as dimes. All together, the value of the coins was \$1.30. How many quarters did she have? How many dimes? How many nickels?

24 Barbara babysat for 8 hours. Copy the table below and fill in the spaces using the answers to **a** through **c.**

	Hours	Salary per Hour	Salary Earned
Before Midnight			
After Midnight			

    a If x is the total number of hours Barbara worked before midnight, express, in terms of x, the number of hours she worked after midnight.

    b Barbara earns $8.00 an hour before midnight. Express, in terms of x, her earnings before midnight.

    c Barbara earns $10.50 an hour after midnight. Express, in terms of x, her earnings after midnight.

    d Last Saturday Barbara earned $74. How many hours did she work before midnight? How many hours did she work after midnight?

25 Cereal is sold in rectangular solid–shaped boxes. The formula for the volume of a rectangular solid is $V = lwh$, where V is the volume, l is the length of the base, w is the width of the base, and h is the height. Solve the formula for the width of the base.

Linear Inequalities in One Variable

An **inequality** consists of two or more expressions joined by a sign of inequality. The **signs of inequality** are < (less than), > (greater than), ≤ (less than or equal to), ≥ (greater than or equal to), and ≠ (not equal to).

A **linear inequality in one variable** is an inequality of the first degree that contains only one variable. Examples of linear inequalities in one variable are $x - 2 > 2x$ and $5x + 2 \neq 4$.

Unless a restriction is stated, the domain of any inequality is the real number line. The solution set is the set of all numbers in the domain that make the inequality true. This set can be represented on a number line.

An open circle marking a value on the number line indicates that the number is *not* included in the solution set.

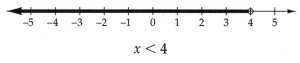

$$x < 4$$

A closed circle marking a value on the number line indicates that the number *is* included in the solution set.

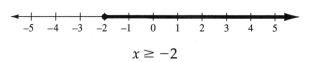

$$x \geq -2$$

Compound inequalities joined with *and* can be combined.
"2 < y and y ≤ 4" is the same as 2 < y ≤ 4.
There is no shortcut for phrases with *or*.

A **compound inequality** is formed by joining two inequalities with *and* or *or*. Examples of compound inequalities are "*x* is greater than 3 *or* less than 0" ($x > 3$ or $x < 0$) and "2 is less than *y* *and* *y* is less than or equal to 4" ($2 < y$ and $y \leq 4$).

Compound inequalities can also be written using the symbol $\wedge$ for *and*, and the symbol $\vee$ for *or*. For example, ($x < 5$) *and* ($x \geq -2$), can be written as ($x < 5$) $\wedge$ ($x \geq -2$), as well as $-2 \leq x < 5$. This compound inequality containing *and* is true only *if both inequalities are true*. The graph of this compound inequality is the *intersection* of the graphs of the two inequalities. Thus,

($x < 5$) means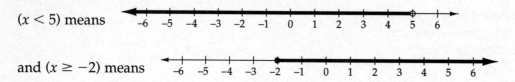

and ($x \geq -2$) means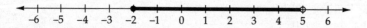

The overlap or *intersection* of the two sets represented by ($x < 5$) $\wedge$ ($x \geq -2$) is

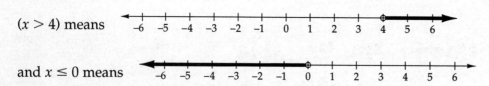

A compound inequality using an *or* statement, such as ($x > 4$) or ($x \leq 0$), can be written as ($x > 4$) $\vee$ ($x \leq 0$). There is no shorter notation. This compound inequality containing the word *or* is true *if one or more of the inequalities is true*. The graph of this compound inequality is the *union* of the graphs of the two inequalities. Thus,

($x > 4$) means

and $x \leq 0$ means

The *union* of the two sets represented by ($x > 4$) $\vee$ ($x \leq 0$) is

An easy way to remember the symbol $\wedge$ for *and* is that it looks like an A without the crossbar.

Properties of Inequalities

In each case below, assume that a, b, and c are real numbers.

Property	Description	Examples
Comparison or order property of numbers	For all numbers a and b, exactly one of the following statements is true: $a < b$, $a = b$, or $a > b$.	For 2 and 3, only $2 < 3$ is true.
Addition property of inequality	If $a > b$, then $a + c > b + c$.	$4 > 1$, so $4 + 2 > 1 + 2$ $6 > 3$
	If $a < b$, then $a + c < b + c$.	$-3 < 1$, so $-3 + 5 < 1 + 5$ $-2 < 6$
Subtraction property of inequality	If $a > b$, then $a - c > b - c$.	$2 > -5$, so $2 - 4 > -5 - 4$ $-2 > -9$
	If $a < b$, then $a - c < b - c$.	$0 < 3$, so $0 - 4 < 3 - 4$ $-4 < -1$
Multiplication property of inequality	If $a > b$ and c is positive ($c > 0$), then $ca > cb$.	$3 > 1$, so $2 \bullet 3 > 2 \bullet 1$ $6 > 2$
	If $a < b$ and c is positive ($c > 0$), then $ca < cb$.	$5 < 6$, so $3 \times 5 < 3 \times 6$ $15 < 18$
	If $a > b$ and c is negative ($c < 0$), then $ca < cb$.	$9 > 4$, so $-1 \times 9 < -1 \times 4$ $-9 < -4$
	If $a < b$ and c is negative ($c < 0$), then $ca > cb$.	$3 < 8$, so $-3 \times 3 > -3 \times 8$ $-9 > -24$
Division property of inequality	If c is positive ($c > 0$) and $a > b$, then $\dfrac{a}{c} > \dfrac{b}{c}$.	$12 > 6$, so $\dfrac{12}{3} > \dfrac{6}{3}$ $4 > 2$
	If c is positive ($c > 0$) and $a < b$, then $\dfrac{a}{c} < \dfrac{b}{c}$.	$4 < 8$, so $\dfrac{4}{2} < \dfrac{8}{2}$ $2 < 4$
	If c is negative ($c < 0$) and $a > b$, then $\dfrac{a}{c} < \dfrac{b}{c}$.	$3 > 2$, so $\dfrac{3}{-1} < \dfrac{2}{-1}$ $-3 < -2$
	If c is negative ($c < 0$) and $a < b$, then $\dfrac{a}{c} > \dfrac{b}{c}$.	$3 < 6$, so $\dfrac{3}{-3} > \dfrac{6}{-3}$ $-1 > -2$
Transitive property of inequality	For all numbers a, b, and c: If $a < b$ and $b < c$, then $a < c$ and, similarly If $a > b$ and $b > c$, then $a > c$	If $4 < 5$ and $5 < 7$, then $4 < 7$ Also, if $3 > 1$ and $1 > -5$, then $3 > -5$

To solve an inequality, follow the same steps that apply to solving equations, with one very important exception: *When you multiply or divide by a negative number, you must change the direction of the inequality.*

Therefore $-3x > 3$, when divided by -3, becomes $x < -1$.

To check the answer for an inequality, substitute a number from the graph of the solution set.

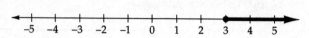

MODEL PROBLEMS

1 Solve and graph $x + 3 \geq 6$.

SOLUTION

$$x + 3 \geq 6$$
$$x + 3 - 3 \geq 6 - 3$$
$$x \geq 3$$

2 Solve and graph $1 - 4x < 13$.

SOLUTION

$$1 - 4x < 13$$
$$1 - 1 - 4x < 13 - 1$$
$$-4x < 12$$

$$\frac{-4x}{-4} > \frac{12}{-4} \qquad \textit{Note the change in the inequality!}$$

$$x > -3$$

3 Solve the inequality $\dfrac{2x}{5} - \dfrac{x}{2} > \dfrac{9}{10}$, and graph the solution set.

SOLUTION

The LCD of 5, 2, and 10 is 10.

$$10\left(\frac{2x}{5} - \frac{x}{2}\right) > 10\left(\frac{9}{10}\right)$$

$$4x - 5x > 9$$

$$-x > 9$$

$$(-1)(-x) < (-1)9 \qquad \textit{Note the change in the inequality!}$$

$$x < -9$$

4 Graph the following:

SOLUTIONS

a $x \neq 1$

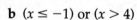

All real numbers except 1 are included in the solution set.

b $(x \leq -1)$ or $(x > 4)$

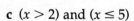

The word *or* means that the solution set is all the values that satisfy at least one of the inequalities.

c $(x > 2)$ and $(x \leq 5)$

The word *and* means that the solution set is all the values that satisfy both inequalities.

5 Solve and graph the following:

 a $(2 \le y + 5) \wedge (y + 5 < 9)$

 b $(3 + x \le -2) \vee (5 + x \ge 5)$

SOLUTIONS

 a $2 \le y + 5$ and $y + 5 < 9$

   $2 - 5 \le y$ and $y < 9 - 5$

   $-3 \le y$ and $y < 4$

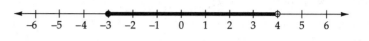

 b $3 + x \le -2$ or $5 + x \ge 5$

   $x \le -2 - 3$ or $x \ge 5 - 5$

   $x \le -5$ or $x \ge 0$

6 Write a compound inequality for the solution set graphed below.

 Note: This is a compound inequality that contains another compound inequality.

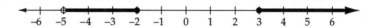

SOLUTION

The graph to the left is an *and* inequality, while the graph to the right is part of an *or* inequality. Therefore, the statement is $(-5 < x \le -2)$ or $(x \ge 3)$.

Answer: $(-5 < x \le -2) \vee (x \ge 3)$

7 The members of a school booster club are creating buttons for sale at basketball games. The machine to make the buttons costs $45. The material needed to make each button costs 20 cents. The buttons will be sold for $1 each. How many buttons must be sold to make a profit of at least $100?

SOLUTION

Let number of buttons sold $= b$.

Then the income from sales $= \$1.00(b)$, or simply b dollars.

The expense of making buttons $= 0.20b$ dollars.

The total expenses $= 45 + 0.2b$ dollars.

Profit is equal to the income from sales minus the expenses. $\qquad b - (45 + 0.2b) \ge 100$
Profit is at least $100.

Distribute -1 over the parentheses. $\qquad\qquad\qquad\qquad b - 45 - 0.2b \ge 100$

Combine like terms. $\qquad\qquad\qquad\qquad\qquad\qquad\qquad 0.8b - 45 \ge 100$

Add 45 to both sides. $\qquad\qquad\qquad\qquad\qquad\qquad\qquad 0.8b \ge 145$

Divide both sides by 0.8. $\qquad\qquad\qquad\qquad\qquad\qquad b \ge \dfrac{145}{0.8}$

$\qquad\qquad\qquad\qquad\qquad\qquad\qquad\qquad\qquad\qquad\qquad b \ge 181.25$

Replace 181.25 with the nearest greater whole number, $\qquad b \ge 182$
since they cannot sell pieces of buttons.

Answer: They must sell at least 182 buttons to make a profit of at least $100.

1 Which of the following is a member of the solution set of $-6 < x \le -1$?

(1) -7 (3) -1

(2) -6 (4) 3

2 Which inequality is represented by this graph?

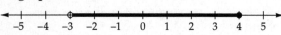

(1) $4 \le x < -3$

(2) $-3 \le x \le 4$

(3) $-3 < x \le 4$

(4) $-3 \le x < 4$

3 Which graph represents the solution set of $2x > 6$?

(1) 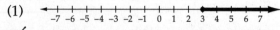

(2) 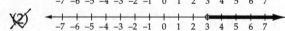

(3) 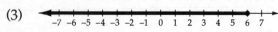

(4) 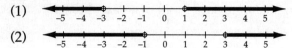

4 Which graph shows the solution to $(x < 3)$ and $(x > -1)$?

(1)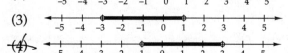

(2)

(3)

(4)

5 Which of the following inequalities represents the graph below?

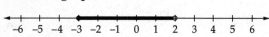

(1) $-3 > x > 3$

(2) $-3 \le x < 2$

(3) $-3 < x \le 2$

(4) $3 \le x < -2$

6 Find the solution set for $\frac{1}{2}x + 4 \ge 4$ if the domain or replacement set for x is $\{-2, 0, 2, 3\}$.

(1) $\{-2, 0\}$ (3) $\{2, 3\}$

(2) $\{0\}$ (4) $\{0, 2, 3\}$

7 The solution set of $-5(x - 4) + 3x > -16$ is

(1) $x > 18$

(2) $x > -6$

(3) $x < 6$

(4) $x < 18$

8 Choose a variable and write an inequality that could be used to solve each problem. Then solve the problem.

  a A number decreased by -5 is at least 10.

  b The sum of a number and -4 is no smaller than 18.

  c Twice a number is greater than three times the number added to 10.

  d Five times a number is at most 40.

  e The sum of five times a number and 8 is less than three times that number.

  f A number increased by 3 is at most 7.

  g A number increased by -7 is at least 11.

  h The opposite of 7 times a number is less than 140.

  i If the area of a square with side s is at least 64 square feet, what could be the possible values of s?

  j The product of 3 and a number is no more than the sum of 8 and three times the number.

Exercises 9–15: Solve each inequality and graph the solution set.

9 $x - 3 > 1$

10 $4j + 1 \ge 25$

11 $1.5 - 3x \ne -4.5$

12 $21 - 5x \le 36$

13 $4x + 3 > 3x - 7$

14 $6x - 7 \ge 2x + 25$

15 $3(x + 2) + 11 > 20$

Exercises 16–25: Graph each compound inequality on a number line. (Where necessary, simplify first and then solve and graph.)

16 $-2 \le x < 3$

17 $-4 < x - 2 \le 3$

18 $(c \geq -1)$ or $(c < -4)$

19 $(2x > 8) \vee (-3x > -6)$

20 $(x + 3 \geq 7) \wedge (3x < 15)$

21 $(x < -2) \vee (x > 4)$

22 $-3 < x + 2 < 7$

23 $(2y + 4 > 0)$ and $(y < 1)$

24 $2 + x \leq 2$ and $2 + x \geq 4$

25 $(9 - 4j > 17)$ or $(2j + 1 > 1)$

26 If the replacement set for x is $\{-4, -3, -2, -1, 0, 1, 2, 3, 4\}$, what is the solution set for $-2x > 6$?

27 If the domain for x is $\{-2, -1, 0, 1, 2, 3, 4\}$, what is the solution set (or range) of answers for $3x - 1 > 5$?

28 What are the integer values in the solution set of $3 \leq x < 7$?

29 Find the whole number that makes the following sentence true when substituted for x: $(3x > 6)$ and $(x < 4)$.

Exercises 30–36: Write the compound inequality for each solution set graphed below.

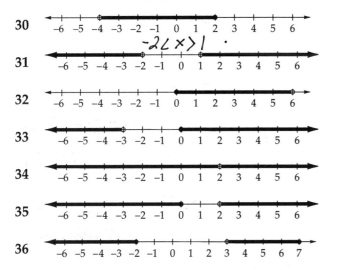

37 If x, $x + 1$, and $x + 2$ are three consecutive integers, write the inequality given in the three sentences below. Then solve each inequality.

  a The sum of two consecutive integers is less than or equal to 9.

  b The sum of three consecutive integers is greater than 20.

  c The sum of three consecutive integers is less than -6.

38 As a waiter at a restaurant, Dave earns $8 an hour plus tips. If he made $35 in tips and his total earnings were less than $80, how many hours could he have worked? Write an inequality that would help solve this problem.

39 At an amusement park, Kendra pays $15 to enter and $0.50 for each ride or game. If she doesn't want to spend more than $25, write an inequality that would tell her the number of tickets she could purchase. Solve the inequality.

40 Jeff and Jermaine go ice-skating. Jeff has to rent skates at $3.50 a pair, while Jermaine has brought her own skates. Every hour of skating costs each of them $2.00. Jeff can spend at most $12, while Jermaine can spend at most $9. Write an inequality for Jeff and for Jermaine that would describe how many hours Jeff and Jermaine can each skate. Solve the inequalities and determine how much longer Jermaine can skate than Jeff.

41 In the figure below, rectangle $ABCD$ has a perimeter that is at most 44 feet. Write an inequality that models the condition. Solve the inequality.

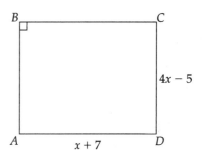

42 The product of two numbers is no greater than 90. If one of the numbers is -10, what is the other number? Write an inequality that can be used to find the other number, and identify the smallest integer for which it is true.

43 An empty mailing carton weighs 3 pounds. The weight of each small antique wooden box is 2 pounds. For shipping purposes, the packed carton must weigh at least 10 pounds and no more than 22 pounds. What is the acceptable number of antique boxes that can be packed in the carton?

44 Andrew used vocabulary lists to practice for the SAT. He studied for 5 days, each day increasing the number of new words he knew by 5. After 5 days, he believed that he knew at least 75 new words. What is the smallest number of words he knew on the first day?

45 Joyce must move a shipment of books from the lobby to the fifth floor. The sign in the elevator says, "Maximum weight: 1,000 pounds." Each box of books weighs 60 pounds.

  a Find the maximum number of boxes the elevator can lift.

  b If Joyce, who weighs 115 pounds, must ride up with the boxes, then what is the maximum number of boxes she can put in the elevator?

CHAPTER REVIEW

1 A ride in a taxi costs $3.50 plus $0.35 for every fourth of a mile traveled. If Sam travels x miles, then which of the following algebraic expressions represents the cost of the trip?

  (1) $3.50 + $1.40x$
  (2) $3.50 + $0.35x$
  (3) $3.85x$
  (4) $0.35 + $3.50x$

2 Mr. Schmidtmann took 55 minutes to drive into the city and back. He took 5 minutes less for the return trip than for the drive into the city. How long did his return trip take?

  (1) 20 minutes
  (2) 25 minutes
  (3) 30 minutes
  (4) 35 minutes

3 Which inequality is equivalent to $5x - 5 > 15$?

  (1) $x > 4$ $5x > 20$
  (2) $x < 4$ $x > 4$
  (3) $x > \dfrac{1}{4}$
  (4) $x < \dfrac{1}{4}$

4 Which inequality is equivalent to $4 - 4x > 16$?

  (1) $x > -3$ $-4x > 12$
  (2) $x > 3$
  (3) $x < -3$ $x < -3$
  (4) $x < 3$

Exercises 5–15: Solve for the variable.

5 $\dfrac{7}{12}x = 3\dfrac{1}{2}$

6 $\dfrac{5}{8}n = 55$ $n = 88$

7 $7 = 3x - 8$ $15 = 3x \quad x = 5$

8 $3x - 4 = 14$ $3x = 18 \quad x = 6$

9 $x + 0.02x = 510$ $x = 500 \quad 550$

10 $\dfrac{2}{3}m + 7 = 27$ $\dfrac{2}{3}m = 20 \quad m = 30$

11 $5(x + 2) = 6 + 3(2x - 1)$ $-x = -13 \quad x = 13$
     $5x + 10 = 6 + 6x - 3 \quad x = 7$

12 $\dfrac{3x - 5}{2} + \dfrac{5x + 1}{4} = 2x$ $x = 9/10 \quad x = 4\frac{1}{2}$

13 $\dfrac{x}{2} + \dfrac{x}{3} - \dfrac{x}{4} = 21$ $x = \frac{1}{2}$

14 $5m - 8 + 4m = 5 - (3m + 13)$ $m = 0 \;\; \frac{0}{12}$

15 $20 - (8 + x) - (x - 1) = 39$ -13

Exercises 16–23: Evaluate.

16 If $l = 25$, $n = 8$, $d = 3$, and $l = a + (n - 1)d$, find the value of a. $a = -2 \quad a = 4$

17 If $A = p + prt$, and $A = 77$, $p = 70$, and $r = 0.02$, what is the value of t?

p96-7 # 3,4,26-16, 24-26   39A5, 40u

18 Using the formula $C = \dfrac{5}{9}(F - 32)$, find the value of C if $F = 14$.

19 If $A = p + prt$, and $A = 250$, $r = 0.05$, and $t = 5$, what is the value of p?

20 The sum of the angles of any triangle is $180°$. In $\triangle ABC$, $\angle A$ is twice $\angle C$, and $\angle B$ is 10 degrees more than $\angle A$. What is the degree measure of each angle?

21 The volume, V, of a right circular cone is 7,700 cu in. If $V = \dfrac{1}{3}\pi r^2 h$, the radius is 35, and $\pi = \dfrac{22}{7}$, then what is the value of the height, h?

22 The formula for the volume of a sphere is $V = \dfrac{4}{3}\pi r^3$. If r is the radius of the sphere, what is the volume of a sphere, *to the nearest hundredth*, with a diameter of 6?

23 If the replacement set (the domain) for x is $\{-3, -2, -1, 0, 1, 2, 3\}$, write the solution set for $-3x < 0$.

Exercises 24–34: In each literal equation solve for x.

24 $a + x = 2$ $a = 2 - x$ $x = 2 - a$

25 $mx = 1$ $x = 1/m$

26 $ax - m = 2m - 10$ $a = \dfrac{3m - 10}{x}$ $x = \dfrac{3m - 10}{a}$

27 $6ab + 3ax = 3ac$

28 $ax = am - at$

29 $7dx - 2d = 3dx + 6d$

30 $\dfrac{ax}{c} = b$

31 $5(x + a) = -2(2x + 3a)$

32 $b(x - b) = d(x - d)$

33 $\dfrac{5 + a}{2}x = m$

34 $ab(d + x) = x$

Exercises 35–37: Solve for x and graph the solution set.

35 $6 - 4x > 8 + 5x$

36 $0.5(3 - 8x) < 10(1 - 0.5x)$

37 $\dfrac{x}{2} - \dfrac{x}{6} \le \dfrac{7}{3}$

38 Replace each ? with one $<$, $>$, or $=$.

   a 4^2 ? 2^4

   b 5^2 ? 2^5

   c 2^{-3} ? 3^{-2}

   d 1^8 ? 1^{-3}

   e 3^7 ? $3 \bullet 3^6$

   f $2x$? $2(x + 1)$

   g $7(m + 3)$? $7m + 3$

   h $|-1|$? -3

   i $3 + (-4)$? $6 + (-10)$

   j -9 ? $7 + (-16)$

   k $|1 + (-1)|$? $|1| + |-1|$

   l $|-4 + (-7)|$? $|-4| + |-7|$

   m $(-2)^2$? $-(2)^2$

39 For the following compound inequalities, graph the solution set. (Where necessary, simplify first and then solve.)

   a $x \ge -3$ and $x < 4$

   b $(x \ge -1) \vee (x < -4)$

   c $-1 < x + 2 < 5$

   d $(2a + 7 \le 1) \wedge (a + 12 > 2 - a)$

   e $(-5 + x \le -4) \vee (x \le 4)$

   f $(x \le 1) \wedge (x > 3)$

40 Solve each inequality. Graph the solution set on a number line. $x > 4$

   a $x + 6 > 10$

   b $\dfrac{x}{3} \le 1$

   c $\dfrac{x}{2} \ge -1$

   d $2 > -3 + x$

41 In the figure below, if rectangle *ABCD* has the given dimensions, write the algebraic expression for

a   the perimeter

b   the area

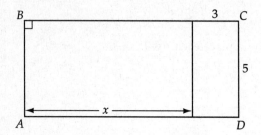

42 The number of girls on a committee was supposed to be more than three times the number of boys. If 15 girls are on the committee, how many possible values are there for the number of boys?

43 A sugar donut has 110 more calories than twice the number of calories in a slice of brown bread. Together they contain at least 194 calories. What is the smallest possible number of calories in the slice of bread?

44 If the area of the rectangle in the figure below is at least 55 square inches, what are the possible values of *x*? Write an inequality that can be used to solve this problem. Solve the inequality.

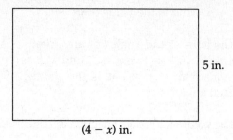

45 The sophomore class is planning to sell school mascot puppets to help cover the cost of a class trip. A local supplier will charge $76.25 for the design and $2.25 for each puppet ordered. The class plans to sell the puppets for $5. How many puppets must be sold to earn at least $2,000?

Now turn to page 426 and take the Cumulative Review test for Chapters 1–4. This will help you monitor your progress and keep all your skills sharp.

Operations With Algebraic Expressions

Adding and Subtracting Algebraic Expressions

A **term** is an algebraic expression written with numbers, variables, or both and using multiplication, division, or both. A term that has no variables is often called a **constant**. Examples: 5, x, cd, $6mx$, $\dfrac{4x^2y}{-3m^3}$ are all terms. Of these, 5 is a constant.

An algebraic expression of exactly one term is called a **monomial**. Examples of monomials include 7, a, and $2x^2$.

Like terms contain the *same variables* with corresponding variables having the *same exponents*. Terms are separated by plus (+) and minus (−) signs. Examples: $7x^3y^4$ and x^3y^4 are like terms; 5 and 100 are like terms. Y and X are not like terms; n and n^3 are not like terms.

Since algebraic expressions themselves represent numbers, they can be added, subtracted, multiplied, and divided. When algebraic expressions are added or subtracted, they can be combined only if they have like terms.

To Add or Subtract Monomials With Like Terms

- Use the distributive property and the rules of signed numbers to add or subtract the coefficients of each term.
- Write this sum with the variable part from the terms.

 MODEL PROBLEMS

SOLUTIONS

1 Add $-2x^3$ and $5x^3$.

$$-2x^3 + 5x^3 = (-2 + 5)x^3 = 3x^3$$

2 Subtract $7mn^2$ from $4mn^2$.

$$4mn^2 - 7mn^2 = (4 - 7)mn^2 = -3mn^2$$

An algebraic expression of one or more unlike terms is a **polynomial**. **Binomials** are polynomials with *two* unlike terms. $7v + 9$ and $3x^2 - 8y$ are both binomials. **Trinomials** are polynomials with *three* unlike terms. $x^2 - 3x - 5$ and $3a^2bx - 5ax - 2ab$ are both trinomials.

A polynomial with one variable is said to be in **standard form** when it has no like terms and is written in order of descending exponents. For example, $4x + 9 - 5x^2 + 3x^3$ in standard form is $3x^3 - 5x^2 + 4x + 9$. When you are asked to **simplify** a polynomial, you should always write it in standard form.

When you are rearranging terms, keep signs with the terms to their right. Here, the $-$ moves with the $5x^2$.

To Add Polynomials

- Use the commutative property to rearrange the terms so like terms are beside each other.
- Combine like terms.

 MODEL PROBLEM

Add $-3x^2 + 4y$ and $5x^3 - 6x^2 - 3y$.

SOLUTION

$$(-3x^2 + 4y) + (5x^3 - 6x^2 - 3y)$$
$$= -3x^2 + 4y + 5x^3 - 6x^2 - 3y$$
$$= 5x^3 - 3x^2 - 6x^2 + 4y - 3y$$
$$= 5x^3 + (-3 - 6)x^2 + (4 - 3)y$$
$$= 5x^3 - 9x^2 + 1y$$
$$= 5x^3 - 9x^2 + y$$

To Subtract Polynomials

- Change the sign of every term in the subtracted polynomial and remove parentheses.
- Combine like terms.

 MODEL PROBLEM

Subtract $9x^2 - 5x$ from $-4x^2 - 8x$.

SOLUTION

First, rewrite the problem to show the subtraction as $(-4x^2 - 8x) - (9x^2 - 5x)$. Change the signs in the subtracted polynomial and remove the parentheses.

$(-4x^2 - 8x) - (9x^2 - 5x)$ Check.

$= -4x^2 - 8x - 9x^2 + 5x$ $(-13x^2 - 3x) + (9x^2 - 5x)$

$= -4x^2 - 9x^2 - 8x + 5x$ $= (-13x^2 + 9x^2) + (-3x - 5x)$

$= (-4 - 9)x^2 + (-8 + 5)x$ $= -4x^2 - 8x$

$= -13x^2 - 3x$

Changing signs is like multiplying each term inside the second parentheses by -1.

1 Simplify $(7x + 6x) - 12x$.

   (1) x
   (2) $2x$
   (3) x^2
   (4) 1

2 Simplify $m - [2 - (2 - m)]$.

   (1) -4
   (2) 0
   (3) $2m - 2$
   (4) $2m$

3 Find the sum of $-3x^2 - 4xy + 2y^2$ and $-x^2 + 5xy - 8y^2$. $-x^2 + 5xy - 8y^2$

   (1) $-2x^2 + xy - 6y^2$ $-4x^2 + xy - 6y^2$
   (2) $-4x^2 + xy - 6y^2$
   (3) $-4x^2 - 9xy - 6y^2$
   (4) $-2x^2 - 9xy + 10y^2$

4 What is the result when $4x + 6$ is subtracted from $8x + 6$? $8x + 6$

   (1) $12x + 12$
   (2) $12x$
   (3) $4x + 6$
   (4) $4x$

5 Simplify $5x - 3y - 7x + y$.

6 What is the result when $10x - 7$ is subtracted from $9x - 15$?

7 What is the result when $3 - 2x$ is subtracted from the sum of $x + 3$ and $5 - x$?

8 Add $2x - 3x^2 - 7$, $3 - 5x - 5x^2$, and $2x^2 + 12 + x - x^2$.

9 Find the sum of $4x^2 - 6x - 3$ and $3x^2 - 5x + 7$.

10 From $16x^2 + 25y + 12z$ subtract $16x^2 - 5y + 8z$.

Exercises 11–17: Remove parentheses and find each sum or difference.

11 $(x^2 + 3x + 1) + (2x^2 - x - 2)$

12 $(-3x^2 + 4x - 8) + (4x^2 + 5x - 11)$

13 $(4x^2 - 4) + (x^2 - x + 4)$

14 $(-3x^2 + 6x + 1) - (4x^2 + 7x - 3)$

15 $(x^2 - x - 9) - (-2x^2 + x + 4)$

16 $(x^2 + 2x - 3) - (x^2 - 4)$

17 $(x^3 - 3x^2 + 2x + 5) - (-5x^3 + x^2 + 3x - 2)$

18 What polynomial will produce the sum $6x^2 - x + 2$ when added to $4x^2 - 6x + 3$?

Exercises 19–26: Use the distributive property, remove the parentheses, and solve each of the following equations.

19 $13x - (x + 21) = 39$

20 $3a - (5 - 2a) = 35$

21 $7x - (x^2 - x - 9) = 17 - x^2$

22 $19m - (1 - 2m - m^2) = 20 + m^2$

23 $10 - (x + 6) - 2 = -5x + 9 - (-5x + 3)$

24 $0.5a + (a - 1) - (0.2a + 10) = 0.2a - (0.2a - 28)$

25 $2x - [5x - (6x + 2)] = 14 - x$

26 $7x - [x - (2x + 8)] = 3x - 7$

Exercises 27–30: If a taxi ride costs d dollars a mile for the first 5 miles and $d + n$ dollars for each additional mile, write an expression that describes the cost, in dollars, to ride each of the following distances. Combine like terms in your answers.

27 5 miles

28 6 miles

29 7 miles

30 8 miles

Multiplying Powers With Like Bases

When multiplying powers with like bases, count the number of times that the base is used as a factor or simply add the exponents.

Rules for Operations on Terms with Exponents

Operation	Rule	Examples
Addition and subtraction $x^n + x^m = x^n + x^m$ $x^n - x^m = x^n - x^m$	Like bases with unlike exponents *cannot* be added or subtracted unless they can be evaluated first.	$2^2 + 2^3 = 4 + 8 = 12$ $3^3 - 3^2 = 27 - 9 = 18$ $a^2 + a^3 = a^2 + a^3$ $a^3 - a^2 = a^3 - a^2$
Multiplication $x^n \cdot x^m = x^{n+m}$	To multiply powers of like bases, add the exponents.	$3^4 \times 3^5 = 3^9$ $a^2 \cdot a^3 = a^{2+3} = a^5$ $a^{-4} \cdot a^5 = a^{-4+5} = a^1 = a$
Division $\dfrac{x^n}{x^m} = x^{n-m}, x \neq 0$	To divide powers of like bases, subtract the exponent of the divisor from the exponent of the dividend.	$\dfrac{4^7}{4^5} = 4^{7-5} = 4^2$ $\dfrac{a^5}{a^2} = a^{5-2} = a^3$ $\dfrac{a^3}{a^8} = a^{3-8} = a^{-5} = \dfrac{1}{a^5}$
Raising a power to a power $(x^m)^n = x^{mn}$	To raise a term with an exponent to some power, multiply the exponents.	$(5^2)^3 = 5^{2 \times 3} = 5^6$ $(a^4)^3 = a^{4 \cdot 3} = a^{12}$
Raising a fraction to a power $\left(\dfrac{x}{y}\right)^n = \dfrac{x^n}{y^n}$	To raise a fraction to a power, raise the numerator and the denominator to that power.	$\left(\dfrac{3}{5}\right)^2 = \dfrac{3^2}{5^2} = \dfrac{9}{25}$ $\left(\dfrac{a}{b}\right)^7 = \dfrac{a^7}{b^7}$
Raising a product to a power $(xy)^n = x^n y^n$	To raise a product to a power, raise each factor to that power.	$(5 \cdot 2)^3 = 5^3 \cdot 2^3 = 1,000$ $(4a)^2 = 4^2 \cdot a^2 = 16a^2$ $(ab)^5 = a^5 b^5$

MODEL PROBLEMS

SOLUTIONS

1 $y^{106} \cdot y^{14}$ $y^{106+14} = y^{120}$

2 $b \cdot b^4 \cdot b^{10}$ $b^{1+4+10} = b^{15}$

3 $(10^5)(10^6)$ $10^{5+6} = 10^{11}$

To Find Powers of a Power

- Raise the numerical coefficient to the indicated power.
- Follow the rule for signs in multiplication.
- Multiply the exponents of the give literal factors by the power.
- If any give term is a fraction, raise both the numerator and the denominator to the indicated power.

MODEL PROBLEMS

SOLUTIONS

1	$(3a^2xy^3)^2$	$3^2a^4x^2y^6 = 9a^4x^2y^6$
2	$(-3xy^4)^2$	$(-3)^2x^2y^8 = 9x^2y^8$
3	$(4bx^2)^3$	$4^3b^3x^6 = 64b^3x^6$
4	$(-3m^4)^3$	$(-3)^3m^{12} = -27m^{12}$
5	$(-2c^3x)^4$	$(-2)^4c^{12}x^4 = 16c^{12}x^4$
6	$(-2x^2a)^5$	$(-2)^5x^{10}a^5 = -32x^{10}a^5$
7	$\left(\dfrac{2}{3}a^2b^3\right)^2$	$\left(\dfrac{2^2}{3^2}\right)a^4b^6 = \dfrac{4}{9}a^4b^6$
8	$(0.3a^3x^5)^2$	$0.3^2a^6x^{10} = 0.09a^6x^{10}$
9	$\left(\dfrac{x^2m}{5a^2b^5}\right)^2$	$\dfrac{x^4m^2}{25a^4b^{10}}$

 Practice

Simplify the following.

1   $(3ab^3)^2 = 9a^2b^6$

2   $(-3x^2y^3)^2 = 9x^4y^6$

3   $(am^4x)^3 = a^3m^{12}x^3$

4   $(-x^3)^3 = -x^9$

5   $(-2m^3x)^4$

6   $(5a^3b^{10})^2$

7   $(-5x^4)^2$

8   $(-3a^2x^5)^3$

9   $(4a^5x^4)^3$

10   $(2x^4y^6)^5$

11   $(-0.5ab^4)^2$

12   $(-3x^2y^4)^5$

13   $\left(\dfrac{1}{3}a^4b^5\right)^5$

14   $(-0.3x^2)^3$

15   $\left(\dfrac{3}{5}ab^3x^2\right)^2$

16   $\left(\dfrac{4ab^2}{-5c^3}\right)^2$

17   $\left(\dfrac{-3x^2y^4}{2a^2}\right)^2$

18   $(abc)^x$

19   $(a^xb^x)^m$

20   $(6x^2y^b)^a$

Remember:
$x^a \cdot x^b = x^{a+b}$

Multiplying a Monomial by a Monomial

To Find the Product of Monomials

- Multiply the numerical coefficients using the rule of signs for multiplication.
- Multiply variables of the same base by adding the exponents.
- Multiply these two products together.

MODEL PROBLEMS

1 Multiply $-4a^2b^3$ and $3a^3b$.

SOLUTION

$(-4a^2b^3)(3a^3b)$

$= (-4 \cdot 3)(a^2 \cdot a^3 \cdot b^3 \cdot b^1)$

$= -12a^5b^4$

2 Simplify: $(3x^a)^2(4x^b)$

SOLUTION

$(3x^a)^2(4x^b) = 3^2x^{2a} \cdot 4x^b = (9 \cdot 4)(x^{2a} \cdot x^b) = 36x^{2a+b}$

 Practice

For Exercises 1–30: Simplify

1 $5x^2 \cdot 2x^4 = 10x^6$

2 $(-3a^3)(-4x^2)\ 12a^3x^2$

3 $(5a^3)(-4a^7)\ -20b^{10}$

4 $(-8r^4)(2r^3)$

5 $(-3ab^2c^2)(2a^2bc^3)$

6 $(-4x^5y)(x^7y)$

7 $(-x^2)(-1)$

8 $(2xb^2)(5b^4)$

9 $-a^b(a^{3b})(a^n)(a^{4n})$

10 $-5x^{10}(20x^{20})$

11 $-6a^3b^2(8a^2b^5)$

12 $\left(\dfrac{1}{4}x^4y^2\right)(2x^3y^5)$

13 $(-x)^3(-2x)^5$

14 $(8a)(-2a^x)$

15 $(2y^a)(-7y^{3a})$

16 $(5a^3)(2a^2)^3$

17 $(-x^2)(3xy^2)$

18 $(5a^n)^2(3xy^2)$

19 $(-4m^{t+2})(5m^{2t})^2$

20 $(-xyz)^2(-4x^4)^2$

21 $(3xy)^3(-2x^2)^3(-x^2y)^3$

22 $(7x^2y^3z^4)^2(-2x^4y^3z^2)^3$

23 $\left(\dfrac{1}{2}a^2b^3\right)^3\left(-\dfrac{2}{3}a^4b^5\right)^2$

24 $(5x^2y^3z)(2xy^2z^4)(-xyz)$

25 $2am(-mr^2)^3(-3a^2r^2)$

26 $(-2x^2y)^3 + (3x^3)(5xy)^3$

27 $(-2a)(-3ab)^3 + (3a)^2(ab)^2(-6b)$

28 $(2x)^2(-25x^4) + (-4x^4)(-x)^2 + (-10x^3)^2$

29 $x^a(x^b)(x^c) + 3x^ax^bx^c - 2x^ax^bx^c$

30 $(-3ax^2)(3ax^3)(ax)^2 + (-2ax)^2(ax^4)(4ax)$

31 Represent the distance an airplane flies in 8 hours at the rate of $75x$ miles an hour.

32 If the length of a rectangle is $5a^2$ and the width is $7ab^2$, what is the area of the rectangle?

33 Find the area of a square if a side is $12k$.

34 What is the volume of a rectangular solid with a length of $10n$, a width of $3n$, and a height of $\dfrac{1}{6}n$?

35 What is the cost of $5m$ dozen golf balls at $3m^2$ dollars per dozen?

Multiplying a Polynomial by a Monomial

To Find the Product of a Polynomial and a Monomial

- First use the distributive property, where $a(b + c) = ab + ac$, to remove parentheses.
- After multiplying each term of the polynomial by the monomial, simplify the product sums, if possible.

 MODEL PROBLEMS

SOLUTIONS

1 $-6(2a^2 - 3a + 1)$

$= -6(2a^2) + (-6)(-3a) + (-6)(1)$

$= -12a^2 + 18a - 6$

2 $3a^2b(a^2 - 2ab - 3b^2)$

$= 3a^2b(a^2) + 3a^2b(-2ab) + 3a^2b(-3b^2)$

$= 3a^4b - 6a^3b^2 - 9a^2b^3$

 Practice

Exercises 1–29: Simplify.

1 $5(3b + 1)$

2 $8(3x - 4)$

3 $-3(5w + 6)$

4 $-4(-5x - 1)$

5 $7(-2x^2 - 4x)$

6 $x^2(3x^3 - 5)$

7 $5x(3x^2 + 2)$ $15x^3 + 10x$

8 $a(a^2 - 2ab + b^2)$

9 $-x^2(5x^2 - x + 3)$

10 $-3a^2(a^2 - 6a + 9)$

11 $-3x^4(-4x^2 - 3x + 2)$ $12x^6 + 9x^5 - 6x^4$

12 $ax(6x - a)$

13 $4xy(5x^2 - 7y^2)$

14 $-x(-x^2 - x)$

15 $-a^2n(-a^2n - 5)$

16 $2y^a(3y^b - y^3)$

17 $\frac{1}{2}b(4b^2 - 8b + 16)$

18 $a(a^x - 3)$

19 $x^a(5x^{3a} - x)$

20 $-n^x(2n^x - 3n^4)$

21 $xy(3x^2 + 6xy - 4y^2)$

22 $-5a^3(2a^2 - 3a - 1)$

23 $2x^2y(x^2 - 3xy - 2y^2)$

24 $5x^{4a}(3x^{2a} + x^a + x)$

25 $a^2b(a^3b - 4a^2b^2 - 5ab^3)$

26 $-4a^2x(5a^2 - ax - 5x^2)$

27 $-\frac{1}{3}ab(9a^2 - 6ab - 18b^2)$

28 $\frac{2}{5}m^3(10m^3 - 5m^2 - 20m + 5)$

29 $0.4a(0.5a^2 - 0.3a - 0.1a^3)$

30 Multiply $x^5 + 2x^4 - 3x^3 + x^2 - x + 1$ by $3x^2$.

Multiple Operations, Grouping Symbols, and Removing Nested Parentheses

In the case of $5x^2 - 3x(5x + x + 4) + (2x)^2$, the process of simplifying requires that we follow an *operations rule*: work first with **P**arentheses, then **E**xponents, then **M**ultiplications and **D**ivisions (as they appear when reading from left to right), and, lastly do the **A**dditions and **S**ubtractions (as they appear, also when reading from left to right). A simple pneumonic (or memory device) for recalling the correct order of operations is the word **PEMDAS** which takes each of the capital letters above and puts them together to make a word.

 MODEL PROBLEMS

1 Simplify $5x^2 - 3x(5x + x + 4) + (2x)^2$.

SOLUTION

Simplify in the parentheses first.	$5x^2 - 3x(6x + 4) + (2x)^2$
Apply the exponent in the last term.	$5x^2 - 3x(6x + 4) + 4x^2$
Remove parentheses using distributive property.	$5x^2 - 18x^2 - 12x + 4x^2$
Combine like terms.	$-9x^2 - 12x$

2 Simplify $b^2 - 4[2b - 3(b - 5)]$

SOLUTION

Simplify in the inner parentheses first.	$b^2 - 4[2b - 3b + 15]$
Simplify within the brackets.	$b^2 - 4[-b + 15]$
Remove brackets using distributive property.	$b^2 + 4b - 60$

Notes: (1) In the first model problem, the quantity $(5x + x + 4)$ is thought of being immediately preceded by the coefficient $-3x$ and not by the term $5x^2$.

(2) In some problems such as $4x + (2x - 5)$ and $3m - (2x - 5)$, the quantity $(2x - 5)$ is understood as being immediately preceded $+1$ and -1, respectively, and not by $4x$ or $3m$. Thus, the parentheses are removed by multiplying each term in the parentheses by either $+1$ or -1.

 Practice

Simplify.

1 $-5(4x - 3) + 6x - 4$

2 $4 + 7(m - 3) + 3m$

3 $9 - 4(3c + 10) - 10$

4 $8b - b(2b - 1)$

5 $4x - 3x(5x - 6) + 8x^2$

6 $9x + 4 - (2x - 6)$

7 $4x^2 - 3x - (4x - 9x^2) + (3x)^2$

8 $-a - 4[2a - (3x - 5)]$

9 $x + 3(x - 2) - (x - 1) - 1$

10 $x - (x^2 - x - 6) - (x^2 - 6x + 5)$

11 $2x - [3x + 8 + 2(3 - 5x)]$

12 $3x + [2x - 3(5 - 4x)]$

13 $2 + 3[5x - 3(4y + x)]$

14 $-7x [5(2x - y) - (3x + 2y)]$

15 $-2[5 + 2(2x - 1)]$

16 $2x - [-3x - (3x + 4) + 5]$

17 $5[3a - 4(a - 2)]$

18 $\frac{x}{2}[2a - (x - 1)a]$

19 $2a - [-2(x - 1(a - 1) - 1)]$

20 $5 - x[x - x[(x - 1) - x] - x]$

Multiplying Polynomials by Polynomials

When we multiply polynomials, each term of one polynomial must multiply each term of the other polynomial. There are three methods for multiplying polynomials: **distributive property**, **columns**, and the **FOIL method**. The FOIL method can be used only to multiply two binomials.

To Use the Distributive Property for Multiplying Polynomials

• Distribute the first polynomial over the terms of the second.
• Solve as before.

 MODEL PROBLEMS

1 Multiply: $(x + 2)(x + 3)$

SOLUTION

Distribute $(x + 2)$ over x and 3.

Distribute x over the first $(x + 2)$ and 3 over the second.

Combine like terms.

$(x + 2)(x + 3)$
$= (x + 2)x + (x + 2)3$
$= x^2 + 2x + 3x + 6$
$= x^2 + 5x + 6$

2 $(2x - 3)(3x^2 - 5x + 4)$

SOLUTION

$(2x - 3)(3x^2 - 5x + 4)$
$= (2x - 3)3x^2 + (2x - 3)(-5x) + (2x - 3)4$
$= 6x^3 - 9x^2 - 10x^2 + 15x + 8x - 12$
$= 6x^3 - 19x^2 + 23x - 12$

Note: The distributive property can also be used this way: Distribute the first term to each term in the second parentheses and then the second term to each term in the second parentheses.

3 $(x + 4)(2x - 3)$

SOLUTION

$(x + 4)(2x - 3)$
$= x(2x) + x(-3) + 4(2x) + 4(-3)$
$= 2x^2 - 3x + 8x - 12$
$= 2x^2 + 5x - 12$

To Use Columns for Multiplying Polynomials

- Set up the multiplication in columns of like terms.
- Multiply as you would large whole numbers.

 MODEL PROBLEMS

1 Multiply $x^2 + 2$ and $x + 3$.

SOLUTION

Set up columns of like terms.
Multiply:

  3 times $(x^2 + 2)$

  x times $(x^2 + 2)$

Add the products in columns:

$$
\begin{array}{r}
x^2 \ + 0x \ + 2 \\
\times \quad\quad x \ + 3 \\
\hline
3x^2 \ + 0x \ + 6 \\
x^3 + 0x^2 \ + 2x \quad\quad \\
\hline
x^3 + 3x^2 \ + 2x \ + 6
\end{array}
$$

2 Multiply $3x^2 - 5x + 4$ and $2x - 3$.

SOLUTION

$$
\begin{array}{r}
3x^2 \ - 5x \ + 4 \\
\times \quad\quad 2x \ - 3 \\
\hline
- \ 9x^2 \ + 15x \ - 12 \\
6x^3 \ - 10x^2 \ + 8x \quad\quad \\
\hline
6x^3 \ - 19x^2 \ + 23x \ - 12
\end{array}
$$

To Use the FOIL Method for Multiplying Binomials

- F   Multiply the first terms.
- O   Multiply the outer terms.
- I   Multiply the inner terms.
- L   Multiply the last terms.
- Combine any like terms.

FOIL stands for First, Outer, Inner, Last.

 MODEL PROBLEMS

1 $(x + 3)(x + 4)$

SOLUTION

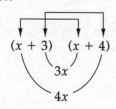

$$x^2 \ + \ 7x \ + \ 12$$

product of   sum of   product of
first terms inner and last terms
$x \bullet x$ outer $3 \bullet 4$
$3x + 4x$

2 $(2a - 3)(5a + 2)$

SOLUTION

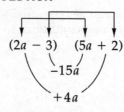

$$10a^2 \ - \ 11a \ - \ 6$$

Exercises 1–25: Find the product.

1 $(x + 4)(x - 3)$

2 $(a + 5)(a + 6)$

3 $(b - 7)(b - 4)$

4 $(x + 3)(x + 3)$

5 $(x + 8)^2$

6 $(c - 2)^2$

7 $(x + y)(x + y)$

8 $(a - b)(a - b)$

9 $(2x - 6)(4x + 3)$

10 $(3x + 5)(x - 1)$

11 $(2x + 3)(5x + 5)$

12 $(3ax - 2)(ax - 5)$

13 $(2x + 3d)(4x + d)$

14 $(x^2 + x)(x + 1)$

15 $(3x^2 + 2)(x + 5)$

16 $(a + b)(a + x)$

17 $(2x^2 + 5)(x - 1)$

18 $(x - 1)(x^2 - 2x + 1)$

19 $(8ab + x)(3ab + x)$

20 $(2x^2 - 3x)(x - 1)$

21 $(x + 1)(x^2 + 2x + 1)$

22 $(x + 3)^3$

23 $(a - b)(a^2 + 2ab + b^2)$

24 $(x + 3)(5x^2 + 3x - 2)$

25 $(2x - 5)(x^3 - 2x^2 - x + 3)$

Exercises 26–30: Simplify

26 $x(x - 2) + (x + 2)^2$

27 $7a^3 + a(a - 3)^2$

28 $10x^2 - (3x + 1)(3x - 1)$

29 $5m^2 - 2(m + 1)(m + 1) + 4$

30 $(x + 1)^2 - (x - 1)^2$

Exercises 31–35: Write an algebraic expression that represents the answer. Express the answer as a polynomial in simplest form.

31 If the length of a square measures $3x - 2$, express the *area* of the square as a polynomial.

32 If the sides of a rectangle are $4x + 9$ and $x - 8$, express the *area* of the rectangle as a polynomial.

33 If the edge of a cube is $x - 1$, express the *volume* of the cube as a polynomial.

34 If three consecutive integers are represented as x, $x + 1$, and $x + 2$, write the product of those three integers as a polynomial in simplest form.

35 A truck travels at the average rate of $10x + 25$ miles per hour.

   a Represent the distance traveled in $x + 5$ hours.

   b If $x = 4$, how fast does the truck travel?

   c If $x = 4$, how far does the truck travel in $x + 5$ hours?

Special Products of Binomials

Certain binomial products appear so often that you should know them on sight. They are useful to have memorized when you are factoring quadratic equations.

Product of a Sum and a Difference: $(x + y)(x - y) = x^2 - y^2$

Distributive Method	Column Method	FOIL Method
Distribute the first term, x, to each term in the second parentheses. Then distribute the second term, y, to each term in the second parentheses. $(x + y)(x - y)$ $= x(x - y) + y(x - y)$ $= x^2 - xy + yx - y^2$ $= x^2 - y^2$	Solution to $(x + y)(x - y)$: $\quad x + y$ $\times \quad\quad x - y$ $\overline{ - xy - y^2}$ $\underline{+ \; x^2 + xy }$ $x^2 -y^2$	**F** Multiply the first terms: $\quad (x)(x) = x^2$ **O** Multiply the outer terms: $\quad (x)(-y) = -xy$ **I** Multiply the inner terms: $\quad (y)(x) = yx$ **L** Multiply the last terms: $\quad (y)(-y) = -y^2$ Product: $\quad x^2 - xy + yx - y^2 = x^2 - y^2$

Square of a Binomial: $(x + y)^2 = x^2 + 2xy + y^2$ and $(x - y)^2 = x^2 - 2xy + y^2$

Distributive Method	Column Method	FOIL Method
To find the first term, square the first term of the binomial: $\quad x^2$ To find the middle term, double the product of the two terms of the binomial: $\quad 2xy$ or $-2xy$ To find the third term, square the second term of the binomial: $\quad (y)(y) = y^2$ or $(-y)(-y) = y^2$ Products: $(x + y)^2 = (x + y)(x + y)$ $\quad\quad = x^2 + 2xy + y^2$ $(x - y)^2 = (x - y)(x - y)$ $\quad\quad = x^2 - 2xy + y^2$	Solution to $(x + y)^2$: $\quad x + y$ $\times \quad\quad x + y$ $\overline{ xy + y^2}$ $\underline{+ \; x^2 + \; xy }$ $x^2 + 2xy + y^2$ Solution to $(x - y)^2$: $\quad x - y$ $\times \quad\quad x - y$ $\overline{ -xy + y^2}$ $\underline{+ \; x^2 \; - \; xy }$ $x^2 - 2xy + y^2$	$(x + y)^2$ or $(x - y)^2$ **F** Multiply the first terms: $\quad (x)(x) = x^2$ **O** Multiply the outer terms: $\quad (x)(y) = xy$ or $(x)(-y) = -xy$ **I** Multiply the inner terms: $\quad (y)(x) = yx$ or $(-y)(x) = -yx$ **L** Multiply the last terms: $\quad (y)(y) = y^2$ or $(-y)(-y) = y^2$ Products: $(x + y)^2 = x^2 + xy + yx + y^2$ $\quad\quad = x^2 + 2xy + y^2$ $(x - y)^2 = x^2 - xy - yx + y^2$ $\quad\quad = x^2 - 2xy + y^2$

MODEL PROBLEMS

SOLUTIONS

1 $(2m - 1)(2m + 1)$

Substitute $2m$ for x and 1 for y in the expression $x^2 - y^2$.

$(2m)^2 - (1)^2 = 4m^2 - 1$

2 $(3y + 2)(3y + 2)$

Substitute $3y$ for x and 2 for y in the expression $x^2 + 2xy + y^2$.

$(3y)^2 + 2(3y)(2) + (2)^2 = 9y^2 + 12y + 4$

3 $(5x - 6)(5x - 6)$

Substitute $5x$ for x and 6 for y in the expression $x^2 - 2xy + y^2$.

$(5x)^2 - 2(5x)(6) + (6)^2 = 25x^2 - 60x + 36$

When you square a binomial, the first and third terms are always positive. The sign of the middle term is the same as the sign between the terms of the given binomial.

1 Which is the simplified form of $(x + 10)(x - 10)$?

   (1) $x^2 + 20x + 100$
   (2) $x^2 + 10x + 100$
   (3) $x^2 - 100$
   (4) $x^2 - 10x + 100$

2 Simplify $(2m + 3)^2$.

   (1) $2m^2 + 6m + 9$
   (2) $2m^2 + 12m + 9$
   (3) $4m^2 + 9$
   (4) $4m^2 + 12m + 9$

3 Simplify: $\left(\dfrac{2}{3}v - 2\right)\left(\dfrac{2}{3}v - 2\right)$

   (1) $\dfrac{2}{3}v^2 - 4v + 4$

   (2) $\dfrac{4}{9}v^2 - \dfrac{8}{3}v + 4$

   (3) $\dfrac{4}{9}v^2 - \dfrac{4}{3}v + 4$

   (4) $\dfrac{4}{9}v^2 + \dfrac{4}{3}v - 4$

4 Find the product of $(1.2a + 0.3b)$ and $(1.2a - 0.3b)$.

   (1) $0.0144a^2 - 7.2ab + 0.09b^2$
   (2) $1.2a^2 + 0.3b^2$
   (3) $1.44a^2 - 0.09b^2$
   (4) $1.44a^2 + 7.2ab - 0.9b^2$

Exercises 5–12: Multiply the expressions and simplify the result.

5 $(mx + 2)(mx + 2)$

6 $(3x - 3)(3x - 3)$

7 $(12c + 4)(12c - 4)$

8 $(13x + 30)(13x - 30)$

9 $(0.4a - 0.02)^2$

10 $\left(\dfrac{3}{4} + \dfrac{1}{3}x\right)\left(\dfrac{3}{4} - \dfrac{1}{3}x\right)$

11 $(2.1g - 3)(2.1g + 3)$

12 $2x(3x + 1)^2$

Dividing Powers (Positive, Zero, and Negative) That Have the Same Base

When dividing powers that have the same base, remember the following rules:

(1) $\dfrac{x}{x} = 1$ and $\dfrac{x^a}{x^a} = x^{a-a} = x^0 = 1$ (**Note:** $x \neq 0$)

   Any number (except 0) to the zero power equals 1. 0^0 is undefined. $100^0 = 1$, $4^0 = 1$, and $12,345^0 = 1$.

(2) $\dfrac{x^a}{x^b} = x^{a-b}$ and thus, $\dfrac{x^5}{x^3} = x^{5-3} = x^2$

(3) Similarly

   (a) $\dfrac{10^7}{10^2} = 10^{7-2} = 10^5$

   (b) $\dfrac{10^4}{10^0} = 10^{4-0} = 10^4$ or $\dfrac{10^4}{10^0} = \dfrac{10^4}{1} = 10^4$

Practice

Leave the answers in simplest exponential form.

1 $\dfrac{a^{16}}{a^4}$

2 $\dfrac{m^5}{m}$

3 $\dfrac{x^w}{x^2}$ (where $w > 2$)

4 $\dfrac{5^9}{5^3}$

5 $\dfrac{7^y}{7^x}$ (where $x < y$)

6 $\dfrac{y^x}{y}$ (where $x > 1$)

7 $\dfrac{4^a}{4^b}$ (where $a > b$)

8 $\dfrac{5^3 \bullet 5^7}{5^2}$

9 $\dfrac{10^8 \bullet 10^3}{10^0 \bullet 10 \bullet 10^{10}}$

10 $\dfrac{10^{10} \bullet 10^a}{(10^2)^5 \bullet 10^a}$

Using Negative Exponents

Rules and reminders:

(1) $\dfrac{x^a}{x^b} = x^{a-b}$ and $\dfrac{x^3}{x^7} = x^{3-7} = x^{-4}$

(2) Similarly, $\dfrac{x^3}{x^7} = \dfrac{x^3}{x^3 \bullet x^4} = \dfrac{1}{x^4}$

(3) Thus, $x^{-4} = \dfrac{1}{x^4}$ and, in general, $x^{-n} = \dfrac{1}{x^n}$

(4) The number 1 to any power equals 1.

$\quad 1^0 = 1 \qquad 1^1 = 1 \qquad 1^{234} = 1 \qquad 1^n = 1 \qquad 1^{-n} = \dfrac{1}{1^n} = \dfrac{1}{1} = 1$

MODEL PROBLEMS

Perform each operation. Compute the values.

1 $3^7 \bullet 3^{-4}$

2 $a^{-2} \bullet b^{-4}$

3 $3^4 \bullet 3^{-4} \bullet 3^0$

4 $\dfrac{1}{3^{-2}} + (10^3)^{-1}$

5 $(-5)^0 - 5^{-2}$

6 $(a^{-4})^{-3} + (a^2)^6$

SOLUTIONS

$3^{7 + (-4)} = 3^3 = 27$

$\dfrac{1}{a^2} \bullet \dfrac{1}{b^4}$

$3^{4 + (-4)} \bullet 1 = 3^0 \bullet 1 = 1 \bullet 1 = 1$

$3^2 + 10^{3(-1)} = 9 + 10^{-3} = 9 + \dfrac{1}{10^3} = 9\dfrac{1}{1,000}$

$1 - \dfrac{1}{5^2} = 1 - \dfrac{1}{25} = \dfrac{25}{25} - \dfrac{1}{25} = \dfrac{24}{25}$

$a^{12} + a^{12} = 2a^{12}$

7 $(x^{-3})^2 \cdot (y^6)^{-1}$

$x^{-6} \cdot y^{-6} = \dfrac{1}{x^6} \cdot \dfrac{1}{y^6}$ or $\dfrac{1}{(xy)^6}$

8 $\left(\dfrac{3}{4}\right)^{-2}\left(\dfrac{x}{y}\right)^{-5}$

$\left(\dfrac{4}{3}\right)^2\left(\dfrac{y}{x}\right)^5 = \left(\dfrac{16}{9}\right)\left(\dfrac{y^5}{x^5}\right) = \dfrac{16y^5}{9x^5}$

9 $(x - y)^{-2}$

$\dfrac{1}{(x-y)^2}$ or $\dfrac{1}{x^2 - 2xy + y^2}$

10 $\left(\dfrac{2x^{-4}y}{3x^{-3}y^{-2}z}\right)^2$

$\dfrac{2^2x^{-8}y^2}{3^2x^{-6}y^{-4}z^2} = \dfrac{4x^6y^4y^2}{9x^8z^2} = \dfrac{4y^6}{9x^2z^2}$

 Practice

Exercises 1–24: Simplify. Write the variable answers with positive exponents.

1 $5^{-3} \cdot 5^5$

2 $-3b^{-3}$

3 $7 \cdot 10^{-3}$

4 $\dfrac{9}{10^{-2}}$

5 $\dfrac{5}{a^{-2}b^{-2}}$

6 $2^{-\frac{1}{2}} \cdot 2^{\frac{5}{2}} \cdot 2^0$

7 $\dfrac{xy^{-4}}{x^{-2}y}$

8 $\left(\dfrac{1}{4}\right)^{-2} + \left(\dfrac{1}{2}\right)^3$

9 $\left(\dfrac{2}{3}\right)^{-3}\left(\dfrac{3}{2}\right)^{-2}$

10 $\left(\left(x^{-1}\right)^{-2}\right)^{-3}$

11 $2 \cdot 3^{-1} \cdot 6^2 \cdot 12^{-1}$

12 $\dfrac{2^2 \cdot 2^{-2} \cdot 2^4}{2^{-1} \cdot 2^0 \cdot 2^{-3}}$

13 $\left(\dfrac{3}{4}\right)^0 \cdot \left(\dfrac{3}{4}\right)^{-1} \cdot \left(\dfrac{3}{4}\right)$

14 $3x^{-8}y^2 \cdot 5x^3y^{-3}$

15 $\left(2a^{-3}\right)^{-4} + \left(4x^{-4}\right)^{-2}$

16 $\dfrac{36x^4a^2}{9x^{-1}a^5}$

17 $\dfrac{(a + b)^{-6}}{(a + b)^{-7}}$

18 $\dfrac{16x^3y^{-5}}{4x^{-1}y^2}$

19 $\dfrac{x^{2a+1}}{x^{a-1}}$

20 $\dfrac{8a^{-8}x^{-12}}{2a^{-2}x^{-6}}$

21 $\dfrac{(a^2b^{-1})^3}{(a^3b^2)^2}$

22 $\dfrac{(a^{-2}x^4)^{-6}}{(a^4x^{-8})^3}$

23 When $x = 5$, what is the value of $5x^0 - (5x)^0 + 5x^{-1}$?

Exercises 24–28: Find the value of x that makes each statement true.

24 $3^x \cdot 3^4 = 3^{12}$

25 $3^{-2} \cdot 3^x = 3^6$

26 $3^x \cdot 3^x = 3^{16}$

27 $3^x \cdot 3^{x-1} = 3^7$

28 $\dfrac{3^{-3}}{3^x} = 3^4$

Scientific Notation and Significant Digits

In working with very large or very small numbers, it is often easier to write the numbers in scientific notation. **Scientific notation** is the product of two factors: (a decimal greater than or equal to 1 but less than 10) × (an integer power of 10), or $a \times 10^n$. An example of scientific notation is 8.3×10^4.

To raise a number to a given power use the ∧ key on a graphing calculator.

$7^2 \to 7 \boxed{\wedge} 3 = 343$

Powers of 10

10^4	10,000
10^3	1,000
10^2	100
10^1	10
10^0	1
10^{-1}	0.1
10^{-2}	0.01
10^{-3}	0.001
10^{-4}	0.0001

Note: (a) For *positive* powers of 10, the number of zeros following the 1 is the same as the exponent of 10. 10^3 has 3 zeros and equals 1,000.

(b) For *negative* powers of 10, the number of decimal places is the same as the absolute value of the exponent. 10^{-3} has 3 decimal places and equals 0.001.

To Write a Standard Number Greater Than 10 in Scientific Notation

• Move the decimal point to make the number a decimal between 1 and 10.
• Count how many places you moved the decimal point to the left.
• Write the number of places the decimal moved as the exponent.

MODEL PROBLEMS

1 Write 21,400 in scientific notation.

SOLUTION

21,400. =   2.14   × 10^4
↑   ↑   ↑
Move the decimal point   number between 1 and 10   4th power of 10
4 places to the left.

2 Write this product in scientific notation: $(2.7 \times 10^4) \times (5 \times 10^7)$

SOLUTION

Use the commutative property to regroup. $(2.7 \times 5) \times (10^4 \times 10^7)$

Multiply the elements in the two groupings. 13.5×10^{11}

Rewrite in scientific notation as. $1.35 \times 10 \times 10^{11} = 1.35 \times 10^{12}$

To Write a Standard Number Between 0 and 1 in Scientific Notation

- Move the decimal point to make the number a decimal between 1 and 10.
- Count how many places you moved the decimal point to the right.
- Write the negative of the number of places the decimal moved as the exponent.

 MODEL PROBLEM

Write 0.0000034 in scientific notation.

SOLUTION

0.0000034 =

↑
Move the decimal point
6 places to the **right**.

$3.4 \times$

↑
number between 1 and 10

10^{-6}

↑
negative **6th** power of 10

Note: In scientific notation, if a number is greater than or equal to 10, the exponent of the power of 10 is positive. If a number is greater than or equal to 1 but less than 10, the exponent of the power of 10 is zero. If a number is between 0 and 1, the exponent of the power of 10 is negative.

To change a number in scientific notation to standard form, multiply.

To Multiply by a Power of 10

- To multiply a decimal by a positive power of 10, move the decimal point one place to the right for each power of 10.

  $5.68 \times 10 = 56.8$

  $5.68 \times 10^2 = 568$

  $5.68 \times 10^3 = 5680$ ← add zero as a placeholder

- To multiply a decimal by a negative power of 10, move the decimal point one place to the left for each power of 10.

  $87.25 \times 10^{-1} = 8.725$

  $87.25 \times 10^{-2} = 0.8725$

  $87.25 \times 10^{-3} = 0.08725$ ← add zero as a placeholder

 MODEL PROBLEM

Between what two integers does 3.445×10^2 lie?

(1) 3 and 4
(2) 33 and 34
(3) 34 and 35
(4) 344 and 345

SOLUTION

Convert the number from scientific notation into standard form.

$3.445 \times 10^2 = 344.5$

344.5 lies between 344 and 345.

Answer: (4)

1 Find the expression with the smallest value.

   (1) 5^0
   (2) 1^5
   (3) 0^{10}
   (4) 10^{-1}

2 Express 5.46×10^0 in standard form.

   (1) 546
   (2) 54.6
   (3) 5.46
   (4) 0.546

3 Express 9.19×10^{-5} in standard form.

   (1) 0.0000919
   (2) 0.00000919
   (3) 0.00919
   (4) 919,000

4 In scientific notation 3,450,000 is equal to

   (1) 34.5×10^5
   (2) 345×10^4
   (3) 3.45×10^6
   (4) 3450×10^3

5 Which of the following represents a number between 0.01 and 0.001?

   (1) 3.7×10^0
   (2) 3.7×10^{-1}
   (3) 3.7×10^{-2}
   (4) 3.7×10^{-3}

6 Between what two integers does 4.23×10^{-5} lie?

   (1) 1 and 2
   (2) 0 and 1
   (3) −4 and −5
   (4) −5 and −6

Exercises 7–11: Write in standard decimal form.

7 3.76×10^5

8 4.5×10^{-3}

9 3.9×10^{-2}

10 7.0×10^6

11 6.88×10^{-1}

Exercises 12–21: Write in scientific notation.

12 198,000,000

13 0.006

14 56,200

15 0.0008722

16 $\dfrac{2}{125}$

17 7,255,000,000,000

18 8,040,000,000

19 0.00019

20 0.000000002

21 30.232×10^6

Exercises 22–26: Express the measurement in scientific notation.

22 The distance from the sun to Pluto is about six billion kilometers.

23 The sun is approximately 93 million miles from Earth.

24 The width of a virus is 0.0000001 meter.

25 A diode in a microchip measures 0.00025 centimeter thick.

26 The wavelength of a long X-ray is 0.000001 cm.

Exercises 27–35: Simplify and express each product or division in scientific notation.

27 $(5.9 \times 10^4) \times (3.7 \times 10^5)$

28 $(8.1 \times 10^{13}) \times (4.8 \times 10^{16})$

29 $(4.3 \times 10^{-3}) \times (1.6 \times 10^8)$

30 $(3.2 \times 10^{-3}) \times (2.2 \times 10^{-4})$

31 $(4.8 \times 10^{12}) \div (3.2 \times 10^6)$

32 $(5.6 \times 10^{15}) \div (2.5 \times 10^5)$

33 $63,000,000 \times 3,700,000$

34 $0.000025 \times 0.000000005$

35 $300,000,000 \div 250,000$

Significant Digits

When a measurement is written in scientific notation, such as in 3.41×10^3, the **significant digits** are found in the first factor, 3.41. The numbers 1, 2, 3, 4, 5, 6, 7, 8, and 9 are always considered significant digits and so are any zeros placed between any two of them. Thus, 2.305 contains three decimal places and four significant digits and 80.401 has five significant digits. However, zeros placed to the left or before any of the digits 1 to 9 inclusive are not significant, as in 0.000507 and 0.49. The decimal 0.000507 contains three significant digits: 5, 0, and 7; 0.49 has two significant digits: 4 and 9. Also, while the number $\frac{4}{5} = 0.8000$, and has four decimal places, there is really only one significant digit, 8, because the number can be expressed exactly as 0.8.

Consider the number 14,567. It has five significant digits. If the number is rounded to the nearest thousand, then it is written as 15,000 and contains only two significant digits, 1 and 5. However, if we count out exactly $15,000 in thousands (with no hundreds, tens, or single dollars), then there are five significant digits. Thus, when a measurement is given by an integer that ends in zeros, such as 300, we cannot tell without additional information which, if any, of the final zeros are significant. For example:

If 300 feet is written as 3×10^2, it is accurate to the nearest hundred feet.
If 300 feet is written as 3.0×10^2, it is accurate to the nearest ten feet.
If 300 feet is written as 3.00×10^2, it is accurate to the nearest foot.

In mathematical computations the results should never have more significant digits than the item that has the fewest significant digits. For example, if the length and width of a rectangle are 75.63 feet and 25.37 feet, respectively, with four significant digits each, then the area equals $75.63 \times 25.37 = 1,918.7331$ square feet. But the answer can be written most accurately only after rounding as 1,919 to four significant digits. Similarly, if we multiply 5.602 by 10.3, the answer 57.7006 can be written accurately to only three significant digits as 57.7, since the number 10.3 has only three significant digits.

 MODEL PROBLEMS

1 Identify the number significant digits in each given number.

SOLUTION

Number	Number of Significant Digits	Answer Underlined
0.0609	3	0.0609
7.005	4	7.005
7.80	2	7.80
7,800	2	7,800
67,000 (to the nearest hundred)	3	67,000

2 **a** Round the number 0.002608 to 3 significant digits.
    b Write the result in scientific notation.

SOLUTION

  a 0.00261
  b 2.61×10^{-3}

Exercises 1–10: Find the number of significant digits.

1 57,306

2 448,000

3 0.1204

4 0.003103

5 0.7000

6 6.01×10^3

7 30,003,000

8 0.00061

9 305.03

10 0.0812×10^{-2}

Exercises 11–15: Round each number to three significant digits and then write the result in scientific notation.

11 0.04109

12 350,800

13 56,770

14 7.066

15 12,345,000,000

Dividing Algebraic Expressions by a Monomial

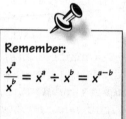

Remember:
$$\frac{x^a}{x^b} = x^a \div x^b = x^{a-b}$$

Dividing a Monomial by a Monomial

The rules for division follow from the fact that division is the inverse operation of multiplication.

To Divide a Monomial by Another Monomial

- Divide the numerical coefficients, using the law of signs for division.
- Divide the variable factors that have the same base using the laws of exponents, subtracting the exponent in the denominator from the exponent in the numerator.
- Simplify by multiplying the quotients that remain.
- Check the answer by multiplying.

MODEL PROBLEMS

SOLUTIONS

1 $\dfrac{24x^5}{-3x^2}$

$= \dfrac{24}{-3} \bullet \dfrac{x^5}{x^2} = \dfrac{8}{-1} \bullet x^{5-2} = -8x^3$

Check: $(-3x^2) \times (-8x^3) = 24x^5$

2 $\dfrac{-8a^3b^2}{8a^3b}$

$= \dfrac{-8}{8} \bullet \dfrac{a^3}{a^3} \bullet \dfrac{b^2}{b} = (-1)(1)b = -b$

Check: $(8a^3b)(-b) = -8a^3b^2$

SOLUTIONS

3 $\dfrac{36x^2b^5}{-12x^4b^4}$ $\qquad\qquad$ $-3x^{2-4}b^{5-4} = -3x^{-2}b$ or $\dfrac{-3b}{x^2}$

4 $\dfrac{a(a^2 + 1)}{a} - (a^2 + 1)^0$ $\qquad$ $(a^2 + 1) - (a^2 + 1)^0 = a^2 + 1 - 1 = a^2$

5 $\dfrac{(-2a^3b^2x^4)^2}{16a^6b^4x^8}$ $\qquad\qquad$ $\dfrac{4a^6b^4x^8}{16a^6b^4x^8} = \dfrac{4}{16} = \dfrac{1}{4}$

Note: Don't forget! Any expression (except zero) divided by itself is 1.

 $\mathcal{Practice}$

Exercises 1–30: Simplify. Express all answers with positive exponents.

1 $\dfrac{8x^5}{-2x^2}$

2 $\dfrac{12a^3b^2c}{4ab^2}$

3 $\dfrac{x^4y^5z^2}{x^2y^3z}$

4 $\dfrac{-0.08a^3x^2y^4}{0.2axy^2}$

5 $\dfrac{a^4b^3c^7}{a^3c^4}$

6 $\dfrac{21a^3b^2}{-7}$

7 $\dfrac{8x^3y^2}{-1}$

8 $\dfrac{-18r^4c^2}{-3rc}$

9 $\dfrac{-48a^4b^3c}{-8a^2c}$

10 $\dfrac{-44a^5x^4y}{11a^2x}$

11 $\dfrac{-100a^4d^2t}{0.25ad^2t}$

12 $\dfrac{0.6a^7x^2}{0.2a^2x}$

13 $\dfrac{a^m}{a^n}$ (when $m > n$)

14 $\dfrac{2^{6x}}{2^{4x}}$

15 $\dfrac{-45x^{a+5}}{9x^3}$

16 $\dfrac{48a^4x}{6x^3}$

17 $\dfrac{45a^2z^0}{-5a^4z}$

18 $\dfrac{32(xy)^m z}{8x^m y^m}$

19 $\dfrac{30xy^2}{-10x^2y^3}$

20 $\dfrac{-40a^2b}{-40ab^2}$

21 $\dfrac{-6a^{10}m^4}{-30a^7m^5}$

22 $\dfrac{4x^m y^m}{x^m y^k}$ (when $m > k$)

23 $\dfrac{15a^3(x - y)^5}{30a^4(x - y)^4}$

24 $\dfrac{a^0b^n}{a^x a}$

25 $\dfrac{4(x^2)^3(y^4)^2}{2(x^2)^2(y^2)^4}$

26 $\dfrac{-(8)^2 x^{3a} \pi^4}{2x^{2a} \pi}$

27 $\dfrac{12a^{3x} b^{2y} c^z}{8a^3 b^2 c}$

28 $\dfrac{-9x^{3a}}{-3x^{a+3}}$

29 $\dfrac{(-5)(x^{2a})^2 y^{4b-1}}{25x^{4a-1} y^{4b}}$

30 $\dfrac{x^2(1-x^2)}{x^2} - (y^2)^0$

Dividing a Polynomial by a Monomial

In general, for all real numbers a and b, and all nonzero real numbers, c,
$\dfrac{a+b}{c} = \dfrac{a}{c} + \dfrac{b}{c}$ and $\dfrac{a-b}{c} = \dfrac{a}{c} - \dfrac{b}{c}$.

To Divide a Polynomial by a Monomial

- Divide each term of the polynomial by the monomial, using the distributive property.
- Combine the quotients with correct signs.
- Check by multiplying.

 MODEL PROBLEMS

SOLUTIONS

1 $\dfrac{6m^2 - m}{-m}$

$= \dfrac{6m^2}{-m} + \left(\dfrac{-m}{-m}\right) = -6m^{(2-1)} + 1 = -6m + 1$

Check: $-m(-6m+1) = 6m^2 - m$

2 $\dfrac{9x^5 - 6x^3}{3x^2}$

$= \dfrac{9x^5}{3x^2} + \left(\dfrac{-6x^3}{3x^2}\right) = 3x^3 - 2x$

Check: $3x^2(3x^3 - 2x) = (9x^5 - 6x^3)$

3 $\dfrac{4a^2x - 8ax + 12ax^2}{4ax}$

$= \dfrac{4a^2x}{4ax} - \dfrac{8ax}{4ax} + \dfrac{12ax^2}{4ax} = a - 2 + 3x$

Check: $4ax(a - 2 + 3x) = 4a^2x - 8ax + 12ax^2$

 Practice

1 Simplify: $\dfrac{6x^2 + 12x^3}{-6x^2}$

(1) $1 - 2x$
(2) $-1 - 2x$
(3) $-x + 2x^2$
(4) $2x - 1$

2 Simplify: $\dfrac{a^5x - 2a^4x^2 + a^3x^3}{a^2x}$

(1) $a^5x - 2a^2x + a^3x^3$
(2) $a^3x - 2a^2x^2 + ax^3$
(3) $a^3 - 2a^2x + ax^2$
(4) $a^2 - 2a^2x + ax$

Exercises 3–20: Simplify the following expressions by dividing by the monomial or constant.

3 $\dfrac{p + prt}{p}$

4 $\dfrac{5x^4 + 3x^2}{x^2}$

5 $\dfrac{4a^2 - a}{-a}$

6 $\dfrac{8x^3 - 6xy}{2x}$

7 $\dfrac{12x^2 - 18xy + 24y^2}{6}$

8 $\dfrac{4a^2 + 3b^2 - c^2}{-1}$

9 $\dfrac{c^2d - cd^2}{cd}$

10 $\dfrac{\pi r^2 h + 4\pi rh}{\pi rh}$

11 $\dfrac{5x^3 - 4x^2 - 2x}{-x}$

12 $\dfrac{24x^3 - 12x^2 + 15x}{3x}$

13 $\dfrac{8x^3 - 14x^2 + 2x}{-2x}$

14 $\dfrac{10a^3b^3 - 5a^2b^2 + 15ab}{5ab}$

15 $\dfrac{-x^3 + 5x^4 - 6x^5}{-x^3}$

16 $\dfrac{x^a + x^y + x}{x}$

17 $\dfrac{6x^8 - 8x^6 - 2x^4}{2x^4}$

18 $\dfrac{9a^5b^3 - 27a^2b^2 + 6a^3b^5}{-3ab^2}$

19 $\dfrac{3.4a^8b^9c^{10} - 5.1a^6b^2c^8}{-1.7a^6b^2c^8}$

20 $\dfrac{5a^4 - 15a^3 + 45a^2 - 10a}{-5a}$

Dividing a Polynomial by a Binomial

Divide $x^2 - 5x + 6$ by $x - 3$.

Procedure

1 Set up a form of long division so that the polynomial is arranged in descending powers, leaving space for the missing terms (if any).

2 Divide the first term of the dividend (x^2) by the first term of the divisor (x). Write the answer as the first term of the quotient.

3 Multiply the entire divisor by the first term of the quotient. Write this product, ($x^2 - 3x$), under the dividend, keeping similar terms under each other.

4 Subtract this product from the dividend and bring down one or more terms as needed.

5 Repeat **steps 2, 3, and 4** until the remainder is no longer divisible. Thus, *divide* $-2x$ by x and the result is -2. *Multiply* the divisor by -2 and the result is $-2x + 6$. *Subtract* $-2x + 6$ and the remainder is 0.

Solution

$x - 3 \overline{) x^2 - 5x + 6}$

$\begin{array}{r} x \phantom{{}- 5x + 6} \\ x - 3 \overline{) x^2 - 5x + 6} \end{array}$

$\begin{array}{r} x \phantom{{}- 5x + 6} \\ x - 3 \overline{) x^2 - 5x + 6} \\ x^2 - 3x \phantom{{}+ 6} \end{array}$

$\begin{array}{r} x \phantom{{}- 5x + 6} \\ x - 3 \overline{) x^2 - 5x + 6} \\ x^2 - 3x \phantom{{}+ 6} \\ \hline -2x + 6 \end{array}$

$\begin{array}{r} x - 2 \\ x - 3 \overline{) x^2 - 5x + 6} \\ x^2 - 3x \phantom{{}+ 6} \\ \hline -2x + 6 \\ -2x + 6 \\ \hline \end{array}$

To check the answer, multiply the quotient $(x - 2)$ by the divisor $(x - 3)$. The result should be the dividend: $x^2 - 5x + 6$. Thus, $(x - 2)(x - 3) = x(x - 3) + [-2(x - 3)]$ $= x^2 - 3x + (-2x) + 6 = x^2 - 5x + 6$.

Note: Since there is no remainder, both of these binomials, $(x - 2)$ and $(x - 3)$, are called factors of the polynomial $x^2 - 5x + 6$.

MODEL PROBLEMS

1 Divide $-11x + 3x^2 - 20$ by $x - 5$ and check.

SOLUTION

Note the order of terms. First rearrange and then divide.

$$\begin{array}{r} 3x + 4 \\ x - 5 \overline{)3x^2 - 11x - 20} \\ \underline{3x^2 - 15x} \\ 4x - 20 \\ \underline{4x - 20} \end{array}$$

Check $\begin{array}{r} 3x + 4 \\ \underline{x - 5} \\ 3x^2 + 4x \\ \underline{-15x - 20} \\ 3x^2 - 11x - 20 \end{array}$

2 Divide $x^3 + 5x^2 + 7x + 2$ by $x + 2$ and check.

SOLUTION

$$\begin{array}{r} x^2 + 3x + 1 \\ x + 2 \overline{)x^3 + 5x^2 + 7x + 2} \\ \underline{x^3 + 2x^2} \\ 3x^2 + 7x \\ \underline{3x^2 + 6x} \\ x + 2 \\ \underline{x + 2} \end{array}$$

Check $\begin{array}{r} x^2 + 3x + 1 \\ \underline{x + 2} \\ x^3 + 3x^2 + x \\ \underline{2x^2 + 6x + 2} \\ x^3 + 5x^2 + 7x + 2 \end{array}$

Note: Observe how the steps used in the division procedure are parallel to the steps used in the usual long division process.

3 Divide $a^3 - 8$ by $a - 2$ and check.

SOLUTION

Note the placeholders, $0a^2$ and $0a$.

$$\begin{array}{r} a^2 + 2a + 4 \\ a - 2 \overline{)a^3 + 0a^2 + 0a - 8} \\ \underline{a^3 - 2a^2} \\ 2a^2 + 0a \\ \underline{2a^2 - 4a} \\ +4a - 8 \\ \underline{+4a - 8} \end{array}$$

Check $\begin{array}{r} a^2 + 2a + 4 \\ \underline{a - 2} \\ a^3 + 2a^2 + 4a \\ \underline{-2a^2 - 4a - 8} \\ a^3 \qquad\qquad -8 \end{array}$

4 Divide $x^2 - 2xy + y^2$ by $x - y$ and check.

SOLUTION

$$
\begin{array}{r}
x - y \\
x - y \overline{)x^2 - 2xy + y^2} \\
\underline{x^2 - xy} \\
-xy + y^2 \\
\underline{-xy + y^2}
\end{array}
$$

Check
$$
\begin{array}{r}
x - y \\
\underline{x - y} \\
x^2 - xy \\
\underline{-xy + y^2} \\
x^2 - 2xy + y^2
\end{array}
$$

5 Division with a remainder

Divide $x^2 + 9$ by $x + 3$ and check.

$$
\begin{array}{r}
x - 3 + \dfrac{18}{x + 3} \\
x + 3 \overline{)x^2 + 0x + 9} \\
\underline{x^2 + 3x} \\
-3x + 9 \\
\underline{-3x - 9} \\
+18
\end{array}
$$

Check
$$
\begin{array}{r}
x - 3 \\
\underline{x + 3} \\
x^2 - 3x \\
\underline{-3x - 9} \\
x^2 \qquad -9
\end{array}
$$

Add remainder
$$
\begin{array}{r}
+18 \\
\hline
x^2 \qquad + 9
\end{array}
$$

 Practice

Exercises 1–20: Divide and check.

1 $x^2 + 5x + 6$ by $x + 3$

2 $x^2 + 3x + 2$ by $x + 1$

3 $x^2 - 13x + 42$ by $x - 6$

4 $x^2 - 5x - 7$ by $x + 1$

5 $3x^2 - 13x - 10$ by $x - 5$

6 $3x^2 + 14x + 8$ by $x + 4$

7 $x^2 - 5x - 6$ by $x + 1$

8 $3x^2 - 8x + 4$ by $3x - 2$

9 $4x^2 - 12x + 9$ by $2x - 3$

10 $2x^2 - 8$ by $x - 2$

11 $x^3 - 3x + 5$ by $x + 2$

12 $x^2 - 7x - 9$ by $x + 1$

13 $2a^2 + 11a - 18$ by $2a - 3$

14 $x^3 - x^2 - 7x - 2$ by $x + 2$

15 $x^3 - 7x^2 + 14x - 20$ by $x - 5$

16 $a^3 - 4a^2 - a + 4$ by $a^2 - 1$

17 $10x^2 + 7x - 12$ by $2x + 3$

18 $25x^2 - 81$ by $5x + 9$

19 $2x^3 - 5x^2 + 21x - 14$ by $2x - 3$

20 $x^3 - 3x^2 - 7x - 15$ by $x^2 + 2x + 3$

21 If one factor of $a^3 + 1$ is $a + 1$, what is the other factor?

22 If one factor of $x^3 - 1$ is $x - 1$, what is the other factor?

23 If the length of a rectangle is $x - 5$ and the area is $x^2 + 2x - 35$, then what is the *width* of the rectangle?

24 If the length of a rectangle is $2x - 3$ and the area is $4x^2 - 12x + 9$, then what is the *perimeter* of the rectangle?

25 If the width of a rectangle is $2x + y$ and the area is $6x^2 - xy - 2y^2$, then what is the *perimeter* of the rectangle?

1 If Dr. Beck has a *weekly* income of x dollars and his average *monthly* expenses are m dollars, which of the following algebraic expressions represents the amount of money he saves in one year?

(1) $12(4x - 12m)$
(2) $52m - 12x$
(3) $52x - 12m$
(4) $12m - 12x$

2 Evaluate each of the following.

a 4^{-2} 0.0625
b 10^{-3} 0.001
c 2×10^{-2} 0.02
d -10^{-2} -0.01
e $(-8)^2$ 64
f -8^2 -64
g $\left(-\dfrac{1}{4}\right)^{-3}$
h $(-4)^{-3}$
i $7^0 + 7^{-2} \times 7$
j $-1^4 \times (-1)^5$

3 Simplify and express the following with positive exponents.

a $5^2 \times 5^7$ 3.814697266 $\times 10^{12}$ 5^9
b $(8^2)^3$ 262144 8^6
c $(10 \times 10^3)^2$
d x^{-3}
e $3a^{-2}$
f $a^{-1}b^2$
g $\dfrac{4x^3}{y^{-2}}$
h $\dfrac{15x^{-1}}{3x^{-2}}$
i $(3x^{-4})^2$
j $(xy)^4 \div (xy)^3 \times (0.2)^{-3}$

4 Write the following in standard decimal notation.

a 5×10^3 5000
b 5.07×10^{-4} 0.000507
c 8.9×10^5
d 1.003×10^{-3}

5 Identify the number of significant digits in each number and then write the given number in scientific notation.

a 17,900
b 0.00005
c 24,090,000
d 0.00000382

Exercises 6–8: For each problem, complete the operation, then

a Write the result in standard decimal notation.
b Write the answer in scientific notation.

6 $(4.8 \times 10^3) \times (3.5 \times 10^{-7})$

7 $(5 \times 10^{-8}) \times (4.1 \times 10^6)$

8 $\dfrac{40.59 \times 10^2}{3.3 \times 10^{-3}}$

Exercises 9–41: Simplify each expression.

9 $7ax - ax$ = 6ax

10 $2x^2 - 8a^2 + 5x^2 - 4ax - 3a^2 + 4a^2 - 5ax$ $7x^2 - 7a^2 - 9ax$

11 $3a - 4 - (-2a^2 - a)$ 6a-4

12 $7x^2 - 3x + 5 - (7x^2 - 5x - 5)$ $2x+10$

13 $(mr)(mr)(-m)$ $-mr^2m - m^3r^2$

14 $(-x)^2(x^2y)(-y)^3$ $-x^4y^4$

15 $-3(x - y)$ $-3x+3y$

16 $x(a + b - 1)$ $ax+bx-x$

17 $4x(x - 1)$ $4x^2-4x$

18 $x^3(x^4y - 2z)$ $x^7y - 2x^3z$

19 $3a^2(b - k - 1)$ $3a^2b - 3a^2k - 3a^2$

20 $0.5ab(-8a + 2b + 5)$

21 $\pi r^2(h - 4r + 1)$

22 $10^a(10^b + 10^c)$

23 $(-3x^2y^5)^2$

24 $(-2a^2b^2)^3 + (4a^3b^3)^2$

25 $(x + 2)^2$ x^2+4 ⟶

26 $(x - 2y)^2$

27 $(3x + 7)^2$

28 $(3x - 7)(3x + 7)$ $9x^2-49$

29 $3x - 7(3x + 7)$

30 $(2n + 3)(n^2 - 4n - 1)$

31 $\dfrac{36a^3b^2}{-9a^2b}$ -4ab

32 $\dfrac{7a^3b^2c^5}{-28a^2b^2c^2}$ $\dfrac{ab^3}{4}$ $\dfrac{ac^3}{4}$

33 $\dfrac{10x^{3a}}{2x^a}$ $5x^{2a}$

34 $\dfrac{2x^2 + 4x}{x}$ $2x + 4$ ...

35 $\dfrac{\pi r^2 - 2\pi r}{\pi r}$ $r - 2$

36 $\dfrac{2a^4 - 3a^3 - 4a^2}{-a^2}$ $-2a^2 + 3a + 4$

37 $\dfrac{x^2 + 7x - 8}{x + 8}$

38 $\dfrac{a^2 - 5a - 36}{a + 4}$

39 $6b + 2b(-3b + 2) + 5b^2$

40 $a^2 - (a - 5)(a + 2)$

41 $10x - 7x(2x - 4) + (x - 5)(x + 2)$

42 What polynomial must be added to $a^2 - 3a + 8$ to obtain the sum $3a^2 + 5a - 9$?

43 What is the value of x if $10 \cdot 10x = 10^{-3}$?

44 $49x^{12}y^7$ is how many times $(-7x^9y^5)$?

45 The perimeter of a rectangle is $10a + 8$ and the length is $4a + 7$.

  a What is the algebraic expression for the width of the rectangle?

  b What is the area of the rectangle in simplest form?

Now turn to page 428 and take the Cumulative Review test for Chapters 1–5. This will help you monitor your progress and keep all your skills sharp.

(handwritten work)

$* \;(x+2)^2$

$(x+2)(x+2)$

$x^2 + 2x + 2x + 4$

$x^2 + 4x + 4$

$4^{-1} = 1/4$

$E(2 A\text{-}F, 3 AB, 4 AB, 9\text{-}19, 25, 28, 31\text{-}36$

CHAPTER 6

Ratio and Proportion

Ratios and Rates

A **ratio** is a comparison of two numbers—called its **terms**—by division. Ratios can be written in several ways. For example, if your school has 4 freshmen to every 3 sophomores, the ratio can be written as:

4 to 3   4 : 3 $\frac{4}{3}$

The order of the terms is important. When a fraction is used, the numerator is the term before *to* or the colon. The denominator is the term after *to* or the colon.

For calculations involving ratios, the fraction form is most useful. Ratios in fraction form are usually simplified, or "reduced," to lowest terms. Equivalent fractions are equivalent ratios (see "Using Proportions," below).

A **continued ratio** has more than two terms, in a definite order. For example, if the ratio of *a* to *b* to *c* is 2 : 3 : 5, then $\frac{a}{b} = \frac{2}{3}, \frac{b}{c} = \frac{3}{5}$, and $\frac{a}{c} = \frac{2}{5}$.

In general, we use the word *ratio* for a comparison of *like* terms, such as freshmen and sophomores. If the terms are measurements, the unit of measure must be the same. For example, in a ratio of time *h* spent doing homework to time *t* spent watching television, *h* and *t* should both be in minutes or both be in hours.

A ratio that compares *unlike* terms is called a **rate**. Familiar examples of rates are 55 miles per hour (speed, which compares distance and time) and $10 per hour (pay, which compares money and time). A **unit rate** is a rate written with a denominator of 1. When a given rate has some other denominator, you can find the unit rate by simplifying. For instance:

$$\frac{125 \text{ miles}}{2 \text{ hours}} = \frac{125}{2} = 62.5 = \frac{62.5}{1} \text{ miles per hour}$$

Unless a problem states otherwise, "rate" generally means unit rate.

Many real-life problems involve unit prices. A **unit price** is a rate: the rate of cost, or price, per 1 unit of measure, such as $1 per pound. To find the unit price, divide the total cost by the number of units.

MODEL PROBLEMS

1 Carol's favorite radio station plays 6 new hit songs and 4 oldies every hour. Write a comparison using three ratio notations.

SOLUTION

This problem does not specify order of terms, so we can write the ratio of hits to oldies or oldies to hits.

Words	6 hits to 4 oldies	4 oldies to 6 hits
Colon	6 hits : 4 oldies	4 oldies : 6 hits
Fraction	$\dfrac{6 \text{ hits}}{4 \text{ oldies}} = \dfrac{3 \text{ hits}}{2 \text{ oldies}}$	$\dfrac{4 \text{ oldies}}{6 \text{ hits}} = \dfrac{2 \text{ oldies}}{3 \text{ hits}}$

2 Write a ratio comparing 8 hours to 3 days.

SOLUTION

To make the unit of measure the same, we can convert days to hours or hours to days. (Note that this problem specifies order of terms.)

Converting 3 Days to Hours	Converting 8 Hours to Days
Step 1. There are 24 hours in a day, so multiply: $3 \times 24 \text{ hours} = 72 \text{ hours}$	Step 1. In this case we divide by 24: $8 \text{ hours} \div 24 = \dfrac{8}{24} \text{ day} = \dfrac{1}{3} \text{ day}$
Step 2. Set up the ratio: $\dfrac{8 \text{ hours}}{3 \text{ days}} = \dfrac{8 \text{ hours}}{72 \text{ hours}} = \dfrac{1}{9}$	Step 2. Write the ratio and simplify. $\dfrac{1}{3} \text{ day to 3 days} = \dfrac{1}{3} \div 3 = \dfrac{1}{3} \bullet \dfrac{1}{3} = \dfrac{1}{9}$

3 Your car can go 100 miles on 3 gallons of gasoline. What is the unit rate?

SOLUTION

$$\frac{100 \text{ miles}}{3 \text{ gallons}} = \frac{100}{3} = 33.\overline{3} = \frac{33.\overline{3}}{1}$$

Answer: The rate is $33.\overline{3}$ $\left(\text{or } 33\dfrac{1}{3}\right)$ miles per gallon.

4 You earn $54 for 4 hours of work. What is the unit rate?

SOLUTION

$$\frac{\$54}{4 \text{ hours}} = \frac{54}{4} = 13.5 = \frac{13.5}{1}$$

Answer: The rate is $13.50 per hour.

> Money is often rounded to the nearest cent.

5 Which costs less per ounce: 12 ounces of Oatsies for $2.79 or 17.2 ounces of Kornsies for $3.33?

SOLUTION

Find the unit price—the rate per 1 ounce—of each cereal and see which is less:

$$\text{unit price of Oatsies} = \frac{\text{total cost}}{\text{number of units}} = \frac{\$2.79}{12} = \$0.2325, \text{ rounded to 23 cents}$$

$$\text{unit price of Kornsies} = \frac{\text{total cost}}{\text{number of units}} = \frac{\$3.33}{17.2} = \$0.1936, \text{ rounded to 19 cents}$$

Answer: Kornsies costs less.

1. John F. Kennedy High School is collecting waste metal and paper for recycling. Five classes bring in the following amounts. Which two classes brought in the same ratio of bags of metal to bags of paper?

Class	Number of bags	
	Metal	Paper
Ms. Ginty's	4	6
Ms. Greenberg's	7	3
Mr. Rondone's	2	3
Mr. Scott's	3	2
Mr. Stanley's	4	3

   (1) Mr. Scott's and Mr. Rondone's
   (2) Ms. Ginty's and Mr. Stanley's
   (3) Mr. Scott's and Mr. Stanley's
   (4) Ms. Ginty's and Mr. Rondone's

2. A candy dish contains p peppermints, s spearmints, and b butterscotch candies. Write an expression for the ratio of spearmints to total number of candies.

   (1) $s : (p + s + b)$
   (2) $s : (p + b)$
   (3) $(p + s + b) : 3$
   (4) $s : b$

3. On each floor of a building, the ratio of offices to windows to doors is $25 : 55 : 33$. What is the ratio of doors to windows?

   (1) 11 to 5   (3) 3 to 5
   (2) 11 to 10 (4) 5 to 3

4. Write a ratio comparing 4 feet to 2 yards.

   (1) $4 : 2$ (3) $12 : 2$
   (2) $4 : 6$ (4) $12 : 6$

5. Every working day, Angela commutes 35 minutes each way. If she works 7 hours, what is the ratio of her total travel time to her time at work?

   (1) $\dfrac{5}{1}$ (3) $\dfrac{10}{1}$
   (2) $\dfrac{1}{6}$ (4) $\dfrac{1}{12}$

6. A school has 500 books for every 25 students. Express this as a unit rate.

   (1) 20 books per student
   (2) 20 students per book
   (3) 500 books per student
   (4) 1 student per 25 books

7. Write two other notations for "7 to 10."

8. A soccer team played 32 games and won 20. Find the ratio and simplify:

   a games won to games lost
   b games won to total number of games

9. A baseball team played 5 games and scored a different number of runs in each game: 3, 4, 1, 0, 5. Express this as a rate.

10. A secretary keyboards a 500-word document in 12 minutes. How many words per minute can he type?

11. Arriving in Freedonia, you cash a $100 traveler's check and get 912.35 freedons (the local currency). What is the exchange rate for:

    a dollars to freedons
    b freedons to dollars

12. Cindy watched a music channel for an hour and a half and counted 5 commercial breaks. She then watched a movie on network TV for 3 hours and counted 13 commercial breaks. Which channel had a higher rate of commercial breaks per hour, and what was its rate?

13. Write as a ratio in simplest form: 750 milliliters to 2 liters.

14. Which costs *more* per ounce: 13.5 ounces of Wheatsies for $3.09 or 20 ounces for $3.99?

15. Which costs *less* per cup: 3 cups of yogurt for $2 or 5 cups for $3?

Using Proportions

A **proportion** is a statement that two ratios are equal, or **proportional**. Proportions may be written in several ways. For example:

$$\frac{4}{5} = \frac{8}{10}$$

$$4 : 5 = 8 : 10$$

Four is to five as eight is to ten.
Four-fifths is proportional to eight-tenths.

There is a simple test to determine whether or not two ratios are proportional:

- Two ratios written with colons are equal if and only if the product of the **means** equals the product of the **extremes**:

```
    ┌── Extremes ──┐
    ↓              ↓
  4 : 5    =    8 : 10
      ↑          ↑
      └─ Means ──┘
```

$5 \cdot 8 = 40$ and $4 \cdot 10 = 40$

- Two ratios in fraction form are equal if and only if their **cross products** are equal:

$$\frac{4}{5} \diagdown\diagup \frac{8}{10}$$

$4 \cdot 10 = 40$ and $5 \cdot 8 = 40$

As with ratios, it is often most useful to express proportions as fractions when calculations are necessary. A proportion in fraction form has four terms: a numerator and a denominator for each of two fractions. Proportion problems often involve finding one missing term, or value, when the other three terms are known.

Since cross products are equal, we can use **cross multiplication** to find the missing value in a proportion:

Note: When cross multiplying, try to keep the cross product with the variable on the left side of the equal sign.

Many kinds of verbal problems can be solved by setting up a proportion.

These include problems about scale models and drawings.

For algebraic solutions to proportion problems, see Chapter 4.

MODEL PROBLEMS

Problems 1–3: In each proportion, find the value of the missing term.

1 $\dfrac{2}{5} = \dfrac{4}{x}$

SOLUTION

Cross multiply: $2 \bullet x = 5 \bullet 4$

Divide: $x = \dfrac{20}{2} = 10$

Answer: $x = 10$

2 $4 : 5 = s : 15$

SOLUTION

Rewrite in fraction form and cross multiply.

$\dfrac{4}{5} = \dfrac{s}{15}$

Cross multiply: $5 \bullet s = 4 \bullet 15$

Divide: $s = \dfrac{60}{5} = 12$

Answer: $s = 12$

3 r is to 6 as 3 is to 2

SOLUTION

Rewrite in fractional form and cross multiply.

$\dfrac{r}{6} = \dfrac{3}{2}$

Cross multiply: $2 \bullet r = 3 \bullet 6$

Divide: $r = \dfrac{18}{2} = 9$

Answer: $r = 9$

4 A map has a scale of 1 inch = 60 miles. If two cities are 93 miles apart, what is the distance between them on the map to the nearest tenth of an inch?

SOLUTION

Set up a proportion: $\dfrac{1 \text{ inch}}{60 \text{ miles}} = \dfrac{x \text{ inches}}{93 \text{ miles}}$

Cross multiply: $60 \bullet x = 93 \bullet 1$

Divide: $x = \dfrac{93}{60} = 1.55$

Answer: The distance on the map is 1.6 inches.

5 A builder uses 20 bricks to cover 3 square feet of wall. How many square feet can be covered with 2,090 bricks?

SOLUTION

Set up a proportion, being sure to write each ratio in the same way. Here, we use the rate of bricks to square feet:

$$\dfrac{20 \text{ bricks}}{3 \text{ square feet}} = \dfrac{2,090 \text{ bricks}}{x \text{ square feet}}$$

Or:

$\dfrac{20}{3} = \dfrac{2,090}{x}$ where x = square feet to be covered with 2,090 bricks

Cross multiply: $20 \bullet x = 3 \bullet 2,090$

Divide: $x = \dfrac{6,270}{20} = 313.5$

Answer: 2,090 bricks will cover 313.5 square feet.

ALTERNATIVE SOLUTIONS

There is more than one way to set up a proportion. Here, our proportion could also be:

$$\dfrac{20}{2,090} = \dfrac{3}{x} \text{ or } \dfrac{3}{20} = \dfrac{x}{2,090} \text{ or } \dfrac{2,090}{20} = \dfrac{x}{3}$$

6 A child's fire truck has two gear belts, one in front and one in back. When the front belt turns 5 times, the rear belt turns 8 times. If the front belt turns 800 times, how many times does the rear belt turn?

SOLUTION

Set up a proportion:

$$\dfrac{5 \text{ front turns}}{8 \text{ rear turns}} = \dfrac{800 \text{ front turns}}{x \text{ rear turns}} \text{ or } \dfrac{5}{8} = \dfrac{800}{x}$$

Cross multiply: $5 \bullet x = 8 \bullet 800$

Divide: $x = \dfrac{6,400}{5} = 1,280$

Answer: The rear belt turns 1,280 times.

7 The numerator of a fraction is 6 less than the denominator of the fraction. The value of the fraction is $\frac{2}{3}$. Find the original fraction.

SOLUTION

Let x = the denominator of the original fraction.

Let $x - 6$ = the numerator of the original fraction.

Then $\frac{x - 6}{x} = \frac{2}{3}$.

Cross Multiply: $3(x - 6) = 2x$

$$
\begin{array}{rcl}
3x - 3(6) &=& 2x \\
3x - 18 &=& 2x \\
-2x &=& -2x \\
\hline
x - 18 &=& 0 \\
+ 18 &=& +18 \\
\hline
x &=& 18 \text{ (denominator)} \\
x - 6 &=& 12 \text{ (numerator)}
\end{array}
$$

Therefore, the fraction is $\frac{12}{18}$. The check for this problem is to make sure $\frac{12}{18} = \frac{2}{3}$. You could reduce $\frac{12}{18}$ to simplest terms or check that the product of the means equals the product of the extremes.

Answer: $\frac{12}{18}$

Practice

1 $\frac{6}{p} = \frac{36}{24}$. Solve for p.

(1) $p = 1\frac{1}{2}$

(2) $p = 4$

(3) $p = 9$

(4) $p = 144$

2 $3 : x = 2 : 3$. Solve for x.

(1) $\frac{2}{3}$ 　　　　(3) 3

(2) 2 　　　　(4) $\frac{9}{2}$

3 In one county in New York state, the ratio of Eagle Scouts to Boy Scouts is 1 : 4. If the number of Boy Scouts is 2,400, what is the number of Eagle Scouts?

(1) 38,400 　　(3) 2,400

(2) 9,600 　　　(4) 600

4 Which proportion is equivalent to $y : 7 = 5 : 3$?

(1) $y : 3 = 5 : 7$
(2) $y : 3 = 7 : 5$
(3) $5 : y = 3 : 7$
(4) $5 : y = 7 : 3$

5 According to the directions on the box, $1\frac{1}{3}$ cups of pancake mix and 1 cup water will make enough pancakes for 2 people. How many cups of mix are needed to make pancakes for 5 people?

(1) $1\frac{7}{8}$ 　　　(3) $3\frac{1}{3}$

(2) $2\frac{2}{3}$ 　　　(4) $3\frac{1}{2}$

6 At a book sale, 6 books cost $13. At that rate, how many books could you buy for $32.50?

(1) 15 　　　(3) 19

(2) 17 　　　(4) 23

7 $\dfrac{100 \text{ fleas}}{16 \text{ dogs}} = \dfrac{25 \text{ dogs}}{4 \text{ fleas}}$

    a Explain what is wrong with this proportion.

    b Rewrite it correctly.

8 The wingspan of a jet plane is 22.5 meters. If a model of the plane is built to a scale of 1 centimeter = 3 meters, what is the wingspan of the model?

9 The ratio of boys to girls in a school band is 4 : 3. There are 21 girls in the band. How many members does the band have?

10 In 2 weeks, a family drinks 3 gallons of milk. How many gallons will this family drink in 9 weeks?

11 If $\dfrac{2}{3}$ of a bucket is filled in 1 minute, how much *more* time will it take to fill the whole bucket?

12 You are making a cookie recipe that calls for 2 cups of flour and 4 eggs. You have $6\dfrac{1}{2}$ cups of flour, and you want to use it all up. How many eggs will you use?

13 A theater has 1,500 seats. One night, 9 out of every 10 seats were filled. How many people attended that night?

14 The tax bill for a house with an assessed value of $75,620 is $847. At the same rate, find the tax (to the nearest dollar) for a house with an assessed value of $110,000.

15 On a bus, 2 adults can ride for the same price as 3 children. If 1 adult ticket costs $48, what is the price of a child's ticket?

16 The denominator of a fraction exceeds the numerator by 4. If 2 is subtracted from the numerator of the original fraction and the denominator is left unchanged, the resulting fraction is equal to $\dfrac{1}{2}$. Find the original fraction.

Changing Units of Measure

Sometimes problems appear in real life for which dimensions, time, or other measures are given in more than one unit of measure. For example, dimensions of a yard may be given in feet and inches. Time may be given in hours and minutes. It is easier to work with this information if we adjust the measure information so that only one unit is used. The process we use is referred to as **dimensional analysis**. We know that if we multiply a quantity by 1, we have not changed the value of the quantity. If a fraction is formed for which the numerator and denominator are equal, the value of the fraction is 1. For example, 12 inches = 1 foot. The measures are equal. Thus, $\dfrac{12 \text{ inches}}{1 \text{ foot}} = \dfrac{1 \text{ foot}}{1 \text{ foot}} = 1$. To change 18 inches to an appropriate number of feet, we multiply $\dfrac{18 \text{ inches}}{1} \times \dfrac{1 \text{ foot}}{12 \text{ inches}}$. Note that the unit fraction is written so that the inch labels cancel:

$$\dfrac{\overset{3}{\cancel{18 \text{ inches}}}}{1} \times \dfrac{1 \text{ foot}}{\underset{2}{\cancel{12 \text{ inches}}}} = \dfrac{3}{2} \text{ ft}$$

MODEL PROBLEM

Arvin wants to put a border made up of slate square tiles, each side 8 inches, around a rectangular garden that is 12 feet long and 8 feet wide. How many tiles does she need?

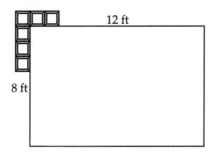

SOLUTION

If the dimensions of the garden are expressed in inches, we can find out how many tiles Arvin needs along each side. Then we will add 4 tiles, one for each corner.

$\dfrac{12 \text{ ft}}{1} \times \dfrac{12 \text{ in.}}{1 \text{ ft}} = 144$ inches. Then $\dfrac{144 \text{ inches}}{8 \text{ inches}} = 18$ tiles along each length.

$\dfrac{8 \text{ ft}}{1} \times \dfrac{12 \text{ in.}}{1 \text{ ft}} = 96$ inches. Then $\dfrac{96 \text{ inches}}{8 \text{ inches}} = 12$ tiles along each width.

Therefore, we need $2(18) + 2(12) + 4 = 64$ tiles

Answer: 64 tiles

 Practice

1   In Europe, the currency unit is one euro. If the exchange rate is 0.75 euro per dollar, how many euros did Michael get when he cashed in his $500 traveler's check?

2   The British pound is worth $1.70 in U.S. currency. Bridgette visited the United States and exchanged her British currency for U.S. currency. What is the value in U.S. currency of 1,250 British pounds?

3   Stanley traveled from Australia to Canada. The Australian dollar is worth $0.75 in U.S. currency. The Canadian dollar is worth $0.80 is U.S. currency. How many Canadian dollars did Stanley get for $3,000 Australian?

4   Change 40 miles per hour to feet per second. Round your answer to the nearest tenth. (5,280 feet = 1 mile)

5   Sasha wants to tile a wall panel that is 6 feet high and 2 feet 3 inches wide with square tiles that measure 9 inches on each side. The tiles cost $0.50 each. How much will she spend to tile the panel?

6   Wendy traveled 12 miles to school in 20 minutes. What was her speed in miles per hour?

Direct Variation

A teacher hands out a 25-question quiz with a note that each correct answer is worth 4 points. A table can be created to show the relation between the number of correct answers (x) and points earned (y).

x	1	2	3	...	25
y	4	8	12	...	100

Notice that in comparing the values of x and the corresponding values of y, the ratios, $\frac{y}{x}$, are all equivalent: $\frac{y}{x} = \frac{4}{1} = \frac{8}{2} = \frac{12}{3} = 4$. This relationship between the variables y and x is a **direct variation**. We say that y varies directly as x or that y is directly proportional to x. This constant ratio of $\frac{y}{x}$ is called the **constant of variation**, or k, and we can write the relation as an equation $y = kx$. The ratio of any set of (x_1, y_1) values is equal to the ratio of any other corresponding set of (x_2, y_2) values in the table. Thus, $\frac{y_1}{x_1} = \frac{y_2}{x_2}$.

It is necessary to indicate the order in which the variables are being compared. The constant of variation of y with respect to x is $\frac{y}{x} = \frac{4}{1}$, since y equals $4x$. The constant of variation of x with respect to y is $\frac{x}{y} = \frac{1}{4}$, since x equals $\frac{1}{4}y$. Note that the two constants are reciprocals.

Direct variation problems may be conveniently solved by proportion when we are not required to find the constant of variation. In many problems, however, finding the constant k is very useful information.

> Unless a problem states otherwise, assume that the constant of variation is the constant of the equation for y in terms of x.

Note: In direct variation...

... if x increases, y increases.

... if x decreases, y decreases.

... if x is multiplied by a number, y is multiplied by the same number.

... if x is divided by a number, y is divided by the same number.

MODEL PROBLEMS

1 If x varies directly as y and $x = 1.5$ when $y = 3.75$,

    a Find the constant of variation for x in terms of y.
    b Find the constant of variation for y in terms of x.

SOLUTION

    a Constant of variation $= \frac{x}{y} = \frac{1.5}{3.75} = 0.4 = \frac{2}{5}$

    b Constant of variation $= \frac{y}{x} = \frac{3.75}{1.5} = 2.5 = \frac{5}{2}$

2 The cost (C) of ground beef varies directly with the weight (W) of the package. Find the cost of 5 pounds of ground beef if 2 pounds cost $3.90.

SOLUTION

The constant of variation is $= \dfrac{\text{cost}}{\text{weight}} = \dfrac{3.90}{2}$.

METHOD 1

Using the proportion method:

$$\dfrac{3.90}{2} = \dfrac{C}{5}$$

Cross multiply.

$2C = 5(3.90)$

$2C = 19.50$

$\dfrac{2C}{2} = \dfrac{19.50}{2}$

$C = \$9.75$

METHOD 2

Using constant of variation:

$k = \dfrac{3.90}{2}$ (constant of variation)

$C = kW$

$C = \dfrac{3.90}{2} \cdot 5$

$C = 1.95(5)$

$C = \$9.75$

Answer: Five pounds of ground beef cost $9.75.

3 The table gives pairs of values for s and P, where s is the side of an equilateral triangle and P is the perimeter. The units of measure are the same.

s	1	2	3	4
P	3	6	9	12

a Express the relationship between s and P as a formula.
b Find the value of P when $s = 9$.
c Find the value of s when $P = 21$.

SOLUTION

a By examining the pattern, we find that $P = 3s$.

Answer: $P = 3s$

b $P = 3s$
$P = 3 \times 9$
$P = 27$

Answer: 27 units

c $P = 3s$
$21 = 3s$

$s = \dfrac{21}{3} = 7$

Answer: 7 units

4 Express each of the following relations as an equation using k as the constant of variation.

SOLUTIONS

a The cost (c) of a railroad ticket varies directly as the distance in miles (m) of the trip.

$c = km$

b The surface area (A) of a sphere varies directly as the square of its radius (r).

$A = kr^2$

c The volume of sphere (V) varies directly as the cube of its radius (r).

$V = kr^3$

d The velocity of sound (V) varies directly as the square root of the absolute temperature (t) of the air.

$V = k\sqrt{t}$

 Practice

1 Two quantities, A and h, vary directly. When $A = 18.75$, $h = 7.25$. Find the value of h rounded to the nearest hundredth when $A = 8.75$.

(1)   3.38
(2)   2.59
(3)   2.14
(4)   1.21

2 A car travels 4 miles in 5 minutes. What distance will the car cover in 33 minutes?

(1)   6.6 miles
(2)   8.25 miles
(3)   26.4 miles
(4)   41.25 miles

3 Paul set up a car wash to raise money for a school fund-raiser. He found that he needed 5 buckets of water for every 2 cars. If 35 cars were washed, how many buckets of water were used?

(1)   14 buckets
(2)   62.5 buckets
(3)   75 buckets
(4)   87.5 buckets

4 Andrea is making cookies from a recipe that calls for $2\frac{1}{2}$ cups of flour for a yield of 2 dozen cookies. How much flour will she need to make 5 dozen cookies?

(1) $5\frac{1}{5}$ cups

(2) $5\frac{1}{2}$ cups

(3)   6 cups

(4) $6\frac{1}{4}$ cups

Exercises 5–9: The table shows a relationship between two variables.

a Check the proportionality of the variables to see if the variation is direct.

b If the variation is direct, find the constant of variation and express the relationship between the variables as a formula.

5

X	2	3	4	5	6
Y	4	8	12	16	20

6

R	0.5	1	1.5	2	2.5
D	2	4	6	8	10

7

S	2	3	4	5	6
A	4	9	16	25	36

8

H	6.0	6.2	6.4	6.6	6.8
W	10	11	12	13	14

9

X	0	1	2	3	4
Y	2	3	4	5	6

10 In the following table, one variable varies directly as the other.

    a Find the missing numbers.

    b Write the formula that connects the variables.

H	1	2	?	7
d	5	?	25	35

11 In the following table, one variable varies directly as the other.

    a Find the missing numbers.

    b Write the formula that connects the variables.

D	4	8	?	22
S	6	?	15	33

12 Two quantities, x and y, vary directly. When $x = 4$, $y = 10$. Find the value of y when $x = 6$.

13 If x varies directly as y when $x_1 = 13$, $x_2 = 3$, and $y_1 = 7$, then what is the value of y_2?

14 If x varies directly with y and $x = 6$ when $y = 10$, what is the value of x when $y = 25$?

15 The perimeter of a garden is 80 feet. Its length and width are in the ratio of 3 to 1. Find the dimensions of the garden.

Applications of Percent

Percent (%) means *hundredths* or *out of 100* or *per 100*.

Problem situations that involve applying percents include sales tax, tips, commissions, grades, and percent of increase or decrease.

Computing With Percents

Three basic percent problems are:

- Find the given **percent** of a number. This amount is referred to as the **rate**. The percent is written as 6% or 0.06 or $\dfrac{6}{100}$.
- Find what **percentage**, or **part**, one number is of another number.
- Find what **base**, or **whole**, a given number is a percent of.

To compute with percents, we use the fraction or decimal equivalent (see Chapter 1). When we use fractions, we can solve percent problems by setting up the following proportion and solving for the unknown quantity—percent, part, or whole:

$$\frac{\text{part}}{\text{whole}} = \frac{\text{percent}}{100}$$

The next model problems are typical examples.

MODEL PROBLEMS

1 About 65 percent of a person's body weight is water. Find the weight of the water in the body of a 150-pound person.

This problem is asking: What is 65 percent of 150?

SOLUTION

Fraction Method	Decimal Method
Express 65 percent as a fraction: $\frac{65}{100}$. Think: 65 is the same part of 100 as x is of 150. Then the proportion is solved for percent: $\frac{\text{part}}{\text{whole}} = \frac{\text{percent}}{100}$　　$\frac{x}{150} = \frac{65}{100}$ Cross multiply: $150 \times 65 = 9{,}750$ Divide: $9{,}750 \div 100 = 97.5$	Convert 65 percent to a decimal: $65\% = \frac{65}{100} = 0.65$ Multiply: $0.65 \times 150 = 97.5$

Answer: 65 percent of 150 is 97.5. Therefore, the weight of the water is 97.5 pounds.

2 On a 20-question mathematics quiz, Cindy answered 18 questions correctly. What percent of the items did she answer correctly?

This problem is asking: 18 is what percent of 20?

SOLUTION

Fraction Method	Decimal Method
Think: x is the same part of 100 (the whole) as 18 is of 20. Then the proportion is solved for part: $\frac{\text{part}}{\text{whole}} = \frac{\text{percent}}{100}$　　$\frac{18}{20} = \frac{x}{100}$ Cross multiply: $100 \times 18 = 1{,}800$ Divide: $1{,}800 \div 20 = 90$	We are finding a part, so the answer will be in decimal form, to be converted to percent. Think: $18 = ? \bullet 20$ Divide: $18 \div 20 = 0.9$ Convert the quotient to a percent: $0.9 = \frac{9}{10} = \frac{90}{100} = 90$ percent

Answer: 18 is 90 percent of 20. Therefore, Cindy answered 90 percent of the questions correctly.

3 Ninety-five percent of a chorus performed in a concert. If 114 members performed, how many are in the chorus?

This problem is asking: 114 is 95 percent of what number?

SOLUTION

Fraction Method	Decimal Method
Think: 95 is the same part of 100 as 114 is of x. Then the proportion is solved for whole: $$\frac{\text{part}}{\text{whole}} = \frac{\text{percent}}{100} \qquad \frac{114}{x} = \frac{95}{100}$$ Cross multiply: $100 \cdot 114 = 11{,}400$ Divide: $11{,}400 \div 95 = 120$	Convert 95 percent to a decimal: $$95\% = \frac{95}{100} = 0.95$$ Think: $0.95 \cdot ? = 114$ Divide: $114 \div 0.95 = 120$

Answer: 114 is 95 percent of 120. Therefore, the chorus has 120 members.

Note: Percent problems can be solved algebraically using an equation of the form $ax = b$. (See Chapter 4.)

 Practice

1 Keith drove 259 miles of a 500-mile trip. His wife drove the rest of the way. What percent of the trip did his wife drive?

(1) 25.9%
(2) 48.2%
(3) 49.8%
(4) 51.8%

2 During a fund-raising drive, Kathy, Keri, and Kim raised $10, $15, and $25, respectively. What percent of this money did Kathy raise?

(1) 5%
(2) 10%
(3) 15%
(4) 20%

3 At a summer camp, there are 60 girls and 30 boys. Twenty percent of the girls and 40 percent of the boys passed the swimming test. What percent of the campers passed?

(1) 24%
(2) $26\frac{2}{3}\%$
(3) $36\frac{2}{3}\%$
(4) 54%

4 Stefan stopped for a drink of water when he had completed 60 percent of a jog. At that point, he had jogged 3 miles. What is the total distance he jogged?

(1) 2 miles
(2) 3 miles
(3) 4 miles
(4) 5 miles

5 Cassandra paid $35 for a shirt that originally cost $50. What percent of the original price did the shirt cost?

(1) 40%
(2) 65%
(3) 70%
(4) 85%

6 The sticker price of a car is $15,800. If the sales tax is 8 percent, what is the total cost?

(1) $15,808
(2) $17,064
(3) $17,500
(4) $18,000

7 After dieting, Devon weighed 180 pounds, which was 90 percent of his original weight. What was his original weight?

8 When a tank is 19 percent full, it contains 136.8 gallons. How much does the full tank hold?

9 Chris is 20 years old and Susan is 50 years old.

   a What percent of Susan's age is Chris?
   b What percent of Chris's age is Susan?

10 A play was attended by 1,071 people. This was 85 percent of the capacity of the auditorium. What is the capacity?

11 Jamila made 51 out of 72 free throws. Find the percentage of free throws made, to the nearest tenth of a percent.

12 A 40 percent discount on a sweater resulted in a saving of $14.40. Find the original price.

13 A bill for a meal is $10.38, including tax. Find the total cost if the customer leaves a 15 percent tip.

14 **Commission** is the amount of money earned for selling a product or service. It is usually a percent of total sales. If a sales representative is paid a monthly salary of $800 plus a 12 percent commission, find his or her income for a month when sales totaled $4,235.50.

15 A test has 125 items. Each correct answer earns 1 point, and 65 percent is a passing grade. If you get 42 answers *wrong*, will you pass? Show your work.

Percent of Increase and Decrease

Percent of increase and **percent of decrease** can be expressed as a ratio:

$$\frac{\text{change in value}}{\text{original value}} \cdot 100$$

Therefore:

$$\text{percent of increase} = \frac{\text{new value} - \text{original value}}{\text{original value}} \cdot 100$$

$$\text{percent of decrease} = \frac{\text{original value} - \text{new value}}{\text{original value}} \cdot 100$$

These formulas can be used to find percent of increase or decrease, original value, or new value when the other two terms are known.

 MODEL PROBLEMS

1 If the price of an accordion is marked down from $150 to $120, what is the percent of decrease?

SOLUTION

Percent of decrease is:

$$\left(\frac{\text{original value} - \text{new value}}{\text{original value}}\right) \cdot 100 = \left(\frac{150 - 120}{150}\right) \cdot 100 = \frac{30}{150} \cdot 100 = 20\%$$

2 If a stamp increases in value from $120 to $150, what is the percent of increase?

SOLUTION

Percent of increase is:

$$\left(\frac{\text{new value} - \text{original value}}{\text{original value}}\right) \cdot 100 = \left(\frac{150 - 120}{120}\right) \cdot 100 = \frac{30}{120} \cdot 100 = 25\%$$

Many real-world problems involve percent of increase and decrease. For example, a **markup** is a percent-of-increase situation, and a **discount** is a percent-of-decrease situation.

 Practice

---

1 If the cost of a No. 2 pencil has increased from 8 cents to 18 cents over the last 10 years, what was the percent of increase?

(1) 175%
(2) 125%
(3) 55.5%
(4) 44.4%

$$18-8 \longrightarrow \frac{10}{8} = 1.25$$
$$8 \qquad 125\%$$

2 You buy a $3.75 notebook for $3.30. What was the percent discount?

(1) 6.4%
(2) 12%
(3) 13.6%
(4) 45%

3 A MP3 player costs a store $270. If the markup is 23 percent, what is the selling price?

(1) $293
(2) $332.10
(3) $405
(4) $500

4 Shampoo is on sale: "BUY ONE AND GET THE SECOND AT HALF PRICE!" If you buy 2 bottles, what is the total discount?

(1) 25%   (3) 50%
(2) 30%   (4) 75%

5 The original price of a TV is $600. It goes on sale with a discount of 25 percent. Then, in a closeout sale, it is discounted 10 percent. What is its final selling price?

(1) $135   (3) $390
(2) $210   (4) $405

6 Ali's salary was cut 20 percent. Later, it was raised 20 percent. After the raise, his pay was:

(1) equal to his original salary
(2) less than it would have been if the raise had come before the cut
(3) 96 percent of his original salary
(4) 120 percent of his original salary

7 Describe what happens when a number is:
a increased by 100 percent
b decreased by 100 percent

8 Explain whether or not each of the following is possible:
a percent of increase greater than 100 percent
b percent of decrease greater than 100 percent

9 A jacket originally priced at $85 goes on sale for $49.99. What is the percent discount to the nearest percent?

10 The price of a train ticket rises from $15 to $18.30. What is the percent of increase to the nearest percent?

11 A school's enrollment decreases from 4,850 to 3,104. What is the percent of decrease?

12 A balloon ascends from 13,500 feet to 19,008 feet. Its altitude has increased by what percent?

13 What is the total cost of a $28.50 garden rake including an 8 percent sales tax?

14 During an autumn sale, an air conditioner that originally sold for $510 is discounted 25 percent.
a If you waited for this sale, how much did you save?
b What is the sale price of the air conditioner?

15 Felipe buys a computer for $2,000 and has it shipped to his home. The sales tax is 6.5 percent. The shipping charge is 8 percent of the pretax price.
a What is the total cost?
b How much would Felipe have saved if he had taken the computer home himself instead of shipping it?

Percent of Error

When we measure, we are sometimes limited by the accuracy of the tools we have or by the accuracy of the person who is actually measuring. The **error** is the absolute value of the difference between the two values. The **percent of error** is the ratio of the error to the true value, written as a percent:

Error = |actual measure − observed measure|

$$\text{Percent of error} = \frac{\text{error}}{\text{actual measure}} \times 100 \text{ or } \frac{|\text{actual measure} - \text{observed measure}|}{\text{actual measure}} \times 100$$

 MODEL PROBLEMS

1 Our bathroom scales are often inaccurate. We go to the doctor for a checkup and find a discrepancy. If you get a reading of 113 pounds on your bathroom scale and a reading of 111 pounds on the doctor's scale, what is the percent of error?

SOLUTION

$$\text{Percent of error} = \frac{|\text{actual measure} - \text{observed measure}|}{\text{actual measure}} \times 100$$

$$= \frac{|111 - 113|}{111} = \frac{2}{111} \approx 0.01801801802 \approx 1.80\%$$

2 Using the bathroom scale above, Chris weighed 150 pounds. What was his actual weight to the nearest pound?

SOLUTION

From the model problem above, we know that the percent error is approximately 1.80%.

$$\text{Percent of error} = \frac{|\text{actual measure} - \text{observed measure}|}{\text{actual measure}} \times 100$$

$1.80 \approx \dfrac{|w - 150|}{w} \times 100$ Multiply both sides by w

$\cancel{w}\dfrac{|w - 150|}{\cancel{w}} \times 100 \approx 1.80w$

We know $w - 150$ is negative. Therefore $150 - w$ is positive and $|w - 150| = 150 - w$.

$(150 - w) \times 100 \approx 1.80w$ Distribute

$100(150) - 100(w) \approx 1.80w$

$15{,}000 - 100w \approx 1.80w$

$+100w \approx +100w$

$\dfrac{15{,}000}{101.80} \approx \dfrac{10\cancel{1.80}w}{10\cancel{1.80}}$

$w \approx 147.347707$ Rounded to the nearest pound, $w \approx 147$ pounds.

1 In a physics experiment, the acceleration of gravity was found to be 9.5 meters per second squared. The accepted acceleration of gravity to this degree of accuracy is 9.8 meters per second squared. What is the approximate percent of error?

(1) 96.9%
(2) 3.16%
(3) 3.06%
(4) 1.03%

$$9.8 - 9.5 = .3$$
$$\frac{.3}{9.8}$$

Exercises 2 and 3: A car odometer measured the car's speed at 55 mph when the actual speed was 52 mph.

2 To the nearest tenth of a percent, what is the percent of error for this odometer?

3 If the actual speed was 45 mph, what would the odometer read?

Exercises 4 and 5: A scale measured an object as 45 kilograms when the actual weight is 50 kilograms.

4 To the nearest hundredth of a percent, what is the percent of error for this scale?

5 If the measured weight of an object is 20 kilograms, what is the actual weight to the nearest kilogram?

6 A student measured the volume of a 2-liter container to be 2.2 liters. What was the percent of error of the student's measurement to the nearest hundredth?

7 A scientist found the density of a metal to be 2.35 grams/cm^3. The accepted value for the density is 2.59 grams/cm^3. What is the percent of error in the student's measure to the nearest tenth?

8 Three students measured the density of a solution in a science lab. Their average value was 1.125 g/mL. The accepted value is 1.097 g/mL. What is the percent of error in the student's measure to the nearest tenth?

9 A census of the population undercounted a particular group by 2%. The number of people recorded for this group was 2,367. To the nearest whole number, how many members of this group should have been recorded?

10 An odometer measures the distance a vehicle travels. The odometer on Eric's car read 65,480 miles before he left Long Island. When he arrived at his cousin's house in Orange County, his odometer read 65,565 miles. The trip distance was actually 90 miles. On a trip from New York City to Albany, his odometer display changed from 66,450 miles to 66,620 miles. Assuming that the odometer is always incorrect by the same percentage, how far did he actually travel?

11 Harry was stopped on the New York State Thruway for driving at an excessive speed. The officer's radar recorder indicated a speed of 80 mph. Harry claimed that although he was driving too fast, his speedometer recorded a speed of 70 miles per hour. If the radar has a margin of error of ±3 mph, what is the minimum percent of error of Harry's speedometer?

Exercises 12–15: The temperature of Maddy's oven is always off by the same percent of error. She must set the oven temperature to 400° when she uses a recipe that calls for roasting at 375°. Finish the chart for Maddy so that she can easily convert from recipe temperature to displayed oven temperature. Round all temperatures to the *nearest 5 degrees*.

	Desired temperature	Setting on Maddy's oven
12	325	
13	350	
	375	400
14	400	
15	425	

CHAPTER REVIEW

Exercises 1 and 2: A speed of 50 miles per hour is equal to about 80 kilometers per hour.

1 Find the speed in kilometers per hour that equals 55 miles per hour to the nearest whole number.

2 Find the speed in miles per hour that equals 60 kilometers per hour to the nearest whole number.

3 The numerator of a fraction is 3 less than the denominator. The value of the fraction is $\frac{7}{8}$. Find the original fraction. 5/8 $\frac{x-3}{x} = \frac{7}{8}$ 8x = 8x -24/ x=24

4 The denominator of a fraction is 5 more than the numerator. The value of the fraction is $\frac{3}{4}$. Find the original fraction. 2\16 2⁴¹

5 The ratio of Democrats to Republicans to Independents in a town of 40,000 people is 9 to 7 to 4. Find the number of Independents in the town. 1600

✗6 The perimeter of a quadrilateral is 40 cm. If the sides are in a ratio of 7 : 6 : 4 : 3, find the length of each side of the quadrilateral. 14 : 12 : 8 : 6

7 Two numbers are in the ratio 2 : 3. The larger number exceeds the smaller number by 32. Find the numbers.

8 A cereal box contains 8 servings of cereal. If there are 125 calories per serving, how many calories are in half the box? 500

9 A recipe calls for 1.2 cups of flour for a dozen big cookies. How many cups of flour are needed to make three and a half dozen cookies? 4.2 cups

10 One U.S. dollar is worth 27 Russian rubles. A set of crystal costs $1,250 in the United States and 30,000 rubles in Russia. In which country is the crystal a better buy? Explain your answer.

11 If 1 in. = 2.54 cm, to the nearest hundredth, how many feet equal 1 meter?

12 How many 16 in. square stones are needed to make a straight path 300 ft long?

13 A class collected unwanted eyeglasses for a charity. The first week, 36 pairs of glasses were collected. The second week, 45 pairs of glasses were collected. What was the percent increase in collections? 25%

14 The junior class collected old shoes for a charity drive. They collected 30 pairs of shoes in September, 40 pairs of shoes in October, and 52 pairs of shoes in November. What was the percent increase in collections from September to October? What was the percent increase from October to November?

15 Rick made $20 washing cars in May. He made 20% more money in June. How much money did he make in June?

16 An odometer recorded speed below the actual reading with a 2.5% of error. To the nearest mph, what was the actual speed if the odometer displayed 65 mph?

17 A treadmill meter showed that Robin ran 3.25 miles. She really ran 3.40 miles. The meter showed 4.0 miles when Kevin ran. How many miles, to the nearest tenth, did Kevin actually run?

18 A backyard swimming pool with a capacity of 1,000 gallons of water contains 850 gallons of water. 17/20

  a Find the ratio of the number of gallons of water in the pool to its capacity.

  b What part of the pool is full? 85%

19 A sweatshirt that usually costs $39.95 is on sale at a 15 percent discount. The sales tax is 6 percent. Find to the *nearest cent*:

  a the amount of the discount 5.95

  b the new price 34

  c the total cost including tax 36.04

20 A green log is 50 percent water, by weight. As it ages, it dries out, until it is only 25 percent water. What is the percent decrease in water? Justify your answer with an example.

Now turn to page 430 and take the Cumulative Review test for Chapters 1–6. This will help you monitor your progress and keep all your skills sharp.

3, 5, 6, 8, 9, 13, 18, 19   9 : 7 : 4

9x + 7x + 4x = 40,000

20x = 40,000

x = 2000 x4 = 8000

Foundations of Geometry

Basic Elements

Geometry is a branch of mathematics concerned with the properties, position, measurement, and relationships of points, lines, angles, planes, and solids.

Points, Lines, and Planes

Most terms in mathematics are **defined** by referring to more basic terms that have already been defined. But as we go back to concepts that are more and more basic, we eventually come to a starting place where terms are **undefined**. In geometry, the point, the line, and the plane are undefined. The characteristics of these three concepts are described below.

- **Point**: A location in space. A point has *no* dimensions—no length, no width, no height. It has only position. We represent a point as a dot and usually name it with a capital letter, such as point P.

  $\bullet P$

- **Line**: An infinite set of points, with no endpoints. A **straight line**, which could be represented by a string stretched tight, extends endlessly in two opposite directions. (Unless otherwise described, lines are assumed to be straight.) A line has only one dimension, length. We can name a line by any two points on it. For example, if the two points are A and B, we have line AB or $\overleftrightarrow{AB}$. We can also name a line by a single lowercase letter: line ℓ.

  A **curved line** is a line of which no portion is straight.

- **Plane**: A set of points forming a flat surface that extends infinitely in all directions. A plane has two dimensions, length and width. It has *no* thickness.

All other terms in geometry are defined in terms of points, lines, and planes. Here are some key definitions.

- **Figure**: A point or a set of points.

- **Collinear points**: A set of points all lying on the same line. (Noncollinear points do not all lie on the same line.) Any two points are collinear.

- **Coplanar points**. A set of points all lying in the same plane. (Noncoplanar points do not all lie in the same plane.) Any three points are coplanar.

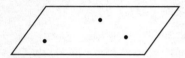

- **Ray**: Part of a line, consisting of one **endpoint** and all the points on one side of that endpoint. A ray is named by the endpoint and any other point. If the endpoint is A and the ray passes through B, we can refer to the figure as ray AB or $\overrightarrow{AB}$. (The endpoint is the first letter.) *Opposite rays* are on the same line that have a common endpoint but no other points in common.

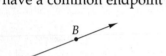

$\overleftrightarrow{AB}$: line

$\overrightarrow{AB}$: ray

$\overline{AB}$: line segment

AB: measure of a segment

- **Line segment**: Part of a line, consisting of two endpoints and all the points on the line between them. A line segment is named by its endpoints. If the endpoints are A and B, we have line segment AB or $\overline{AB}$, which we could also call $\overline{BA}$. (Either endpoint can be the first letter.) The measure—or measured length—of the segment is the distance between A and B and is written AB or BA.

- **Congruent line segments** have the same measure. The symbol for congruence is $\cong$. $\overline{AB} \cong \overline{CD}$ compares segments and indicates that they have the same length. $AB = CD$ compares the numerical measures of the segments and states that they are equal.

1 Which statement is true of ray *KL*?

   (1) It extends infinitely in both directions.
   (2) Its endpoint is *L*.
   (3) It contains exactly two points, *K* and *L*.
   (4) It is a portion of a line beginning with point *K*.

2 What does *FG* represent?

   (1) length of a line
   (2) length of a line segment
   (3) length of a ray
   (4) a plane

3 Which *must* be collinear?

   (1) points *A*, *B*, and *C*
   (2) points *A* and *C*
   (3) lines *LM* and *NO* when $\overline{LM} \cong \overline{NO}$
   (4) none of the above

4 We can measure the length of

   (1) point *X*
   (2) $\overleftrightarrow{XY}$
   (3) $\overline{XY}$
   (4) none of the above

Exercises 5–10: Draw each of the following.

5 Line segment *JK*

6 Ray *ZX*

7 Noncollinear points *Q*, *R*, *S*, *T*

8 Points *P* and *Q* on line *l*

9 Opposite rays $\overrightarrow{AB}$ and $\overrightarrow{AC}$

10 Curved line segment *OP*

Drawing reasonable sketches of geometric figures is a useful skill that gets easier with practice.

Angles

An **angle** ($\angle$) is formed by two rays that share an endpoint. The rays are called its **sides**, and the endpoint is called the **vertex**. We can also say that angles are formed by **interesecting lines**—lines that meet or cross. In this case the vertex is the point of intersection.

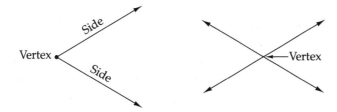

There are several ways to **name** an angle:

• By a capital letter that names its vertex, such as $\angle B$.

• By a lowercase letter or a number placed inside the angle, such as $\angle x$ or $\angle 1$.

- By three capital letters, such as ∠*ABC*. The middle letter is the vertex, and the other two letters name points on different rays (or lines), in either order: ∠*ABC* can also be named ∠*CBA*.

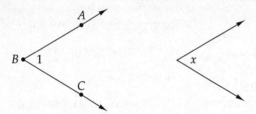

Angles are measured by **degrees** (°) and are classified by their measure. *The measure of angle ABC is 50 degrees* can be written m∠*ABC* = 50. **Congruent angles** are equal in measure. Above, ∠1 ≅ ∠*x*.

Classification of Angles

Angle	Defintion
Right angle	An angle of exactly 90°. The symbol for a right angle is a square at the vertex.
Acute angle	An angle less than 90°.
Obtuse angle	An angle greater than 90° but less than 180°.
Straight angle	An angle of exactly 180°. A straight angle is a line.
Reflex angle	An angle greater than 180° but less than 360°.

 MODEL PROBLEMS

1   Refer to the following angle:

a   Name this angle in four different ways.
b   Name its vertex and its sides.

SOLUTIONS

a   Four names for the angle:
    ∠1, ∠*S*, ∠*RST*, ∠*TSR*
b   Vertex: *S*. Sides: $\overrightarrow{SR}$ and $\overrightarrow{ST}$.

2 Refer to the illustration below:

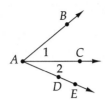

a Why is ∠A an incorrect name for any of the angles shown?

b Why is ∠EAD an incorrect name for ∠2?

c Give four correct names for ∠2.

SOLUTIONS

a All three angles have the same vertex, *A*. Therefore, the name ∠*A* does not identify any one of them.

b ∠*EAD* is an incorrect name for ∠2 because *D* and *E* are on the same side of the angle.

c Four names for ∠2 are: ∠*CAD*, ∠*CAE*, ∠*DAC*, ∠*EAC*.

 Practice

1 Choose the correct name or names for ∠1.

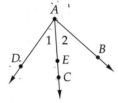

● ∠DAE ~~acute ∠EAD, ∠1, ∠CA~~
(2) ∠A and ∠DAE ~~No~~
(3) ∠CEA and ∠DAE
(4) ∠A, ∠CEA, and ∠DAE

2 In which case are points *X*, *Y*, and *Z* collinear?

(1) ∠*XYZ* is acute.
(2) ∠*XYZ* is a 90° angle.
(3) ∠*XYZ* is obtuse.
(4) ∠*XYZ* is a 180° angle.

3 The measure of a right angle is

(1) less than 90°
(2) at least 90°
(3) equal to 90°
(4) approximately 90°

4 An obtuse angle could be made up of

(1) a straight angle plus an acute angle
● three acute angles
(3) two smaller obtuse angles
(4) a smaller obtuse angle plus a right angle

Exercises 5 and 6: Refer to the illustration below.

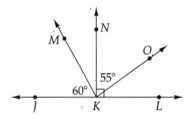

5 Name 5 acute angles, 2 obtuse angles, 2 right angles, 1 straight angle. ∠JKM, MKN, NKO, OKL. ∠OKJ, MKL. ∠NKL, NKJ. JKL

6 How many degrees does each of the following have: ∠*LKO*, ∠*MKN*, ∠*MKO*? 35° 30° 90° 85°

Exercises 7–10: Draw and label an angle to fit each description.

7 Acute angle *DEF*

8 Obtuse angle with sides $\overrightarrow{BR}$ and $\overrightarrow{BT}$

9 Right angle *V*

10 Reflex angle *GHI*

Line and Angle Relationships

The following table reviews important relationships of angles and lines.

Relationship	Description	Examples
Adjacent angles	Two angles having the same vertex and sharing one side.	 ∠1 and ∠2 are adjacent.
Complementary angles	Two angles, adjacent or nonadjacent, whose sum is 90°.	 ∠3 and ∠4 are complementary.
Supplementary angles	Two angles, adjacent or nonadjacent, whose sum is 180°.	 ∠5 and ∠6 are supplementary.
Congruent angles	Angles having the same measure.	 ∠7 and ∠8 are congruent; ∠7 ≅ ∠8.
Vertical angles	Opposite angles formed by intersecting lines. Vertical angles are congruent: their measures are equal.	 $x = y$ ∠x and ∠y are vertical angles.
Bisector	A line that divides a line segment or an angle into two equal (congruent) parts.	 If line CD bisects $\overline{AB}$, then $\overline{AO} \cong \overline{OB}$. If line FH bisects ∠EFG, then ∠$EFH \cong$ ∠HFG.

(continued)

Relationship	Description	Examples
Perpendicular (⊥) lines	Lines that form right angles.	 If line BC ⊥ line AC, then ∠C measures 90°.
Parallel (∥) lines	Lines that are the same perpendicular distance apart and do not intersect.	 $AB = CD$ If $AB = CD$, then line ℓ_1 ∥ line ℓ_2.
Transversal	A line that intersects two parallel lines.	 Transversal t crosses lines ℓ and m.
Corresponding angles	Angles in the same relative position when a transversal intersects two parallel lines. Corresponding angles are congruent.	 Corresponding angles: ∠1 and ∠5 ∠3 and ∠7 ∠2 and ∠6 ∠4 and ∠8
Alternate interior angles	Angles on opposite sides of a transversal, inside the two parallel lines. Alternate interior angles are congruent.	 Alternate interior angles: ∠4 and ∠6 ∠3 and ∠5
Alternate exterior angles	Angles on opposite sides of a transversal, outside the two parallel lines. Alternate exterior angles are congruent.	 Alternate exterior angles: ∠1 and ∠7 ∠2 and ∠8

Relationship	Description	Examples
Consecutive interior angles	Inside angles on the same side of a transversal. Consecutive interior angles are supplementary.	 Consecutive interior angles: ∠4 and ∠5 ∠3 and ∠6
Parallel lines cut by a transversal	Any pair of angles formed by the intersection of a transversal and two parallel lines are either congruent or supplementary. When parallel lines are cut by a perpendicular transversal, all angles formed are right angles.	 If line ℓ ∥ m, then: • Corresponding angles are congruent (for example, ∠1 ≅ ∠5). • Pairs of alternate interior and exterior angles are congruent (for example, ∠4 ≅ ∠6 and ∠1 ≅ ∠7). • Consecutive interior angles are supplementary (for example, ∠4 + ∠5 = 180°).

Note: In working with intersecting lines and transversals, remember that pairs of vertical angles are congruent and pairs of adjacent angles are supplementary.

MODEL PROBLEMS

1 If $\overleftrightarrow{AB} \parallel \overleftrightarrow{CD}$ and t is not perpendicular to them, which pair of angles are *not* congruent?

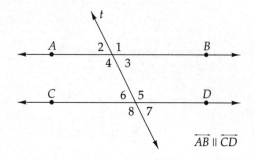

$\overrightarrow{AB} \parallel \overrightarrow{CD}$

(1) ∠1 and ∠4
(2) ∠2 and ∠7
(3) ∠6 and ∠3
(4) ∠3 and ∠5

SOLUTION

Consider each pair.

Choice (1): ∠1 ≅ ∠4 because they are vertical angles.

Choice (2): ∠2 ≅ ∠7 because they are alternate exterior angles.

Choice (3): ∠6 ≅ ∠3 because they are alternate interior angles.

Choice (4): ∠3 and ∠5 are same-side interior angles, so they are supplementary. Two supplementary angles are congruent only if each measures 90°, and that is impossible here, because t is not perpendicular to lines AB and CD.

Answer: (4)

2 Which are adjacent angles?
  (1) ∠2 and ∠3
  (2) ∠7 and ∠8
  (3) ∠4 and ∠5
  (4) ∠2 and ∠7

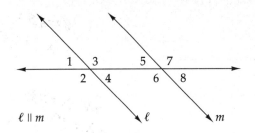

ℓ ∥ m

SOLUTION

Choice (2) is the answer, because ∠7 and ∠8 have the same vertex and a common side.

 Practice

1 Two parallel lines are cut by a nonperpendicular transversal. Which are *not* congruent?

  (1) same-side exterior angles
  (2) corresponding angles
  (3) alternate interior angles
  (4) alternate exterior angles

2 If m∠3 = 50, what is m∠8?

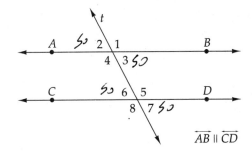

$\overrightarrow{AB} \parallel \overrightarrow{CD}$

  (1) 40
  (2) 50
  (3) 90
  (4) 130

3 In the figure below, if m∠8 = 120, what is m∠1?

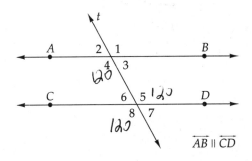

$\overrightarrow{AB} \parallel \overrightarrow{CD}$

  (1) 60
  (2) 120
  (3) 180
  (4) 300

4 In the figure below, if m∠6 = 60, what is m∠4?

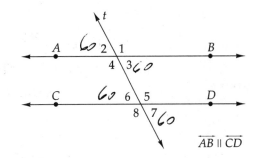

$\overrightarrow{AB} \parallel \overrightarrow{CD}$

  (1) 30
  (2) 60
  (3) 120
  (4) 180

5 Which choice lists all the angles that are supplementary to ∠13 in the figure below?

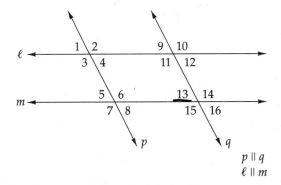

p ∥ q
ℓ ∥ m

  (1) ∠1, ∠4, ∠5, ∠8, ∠16
  (2) ∠2, ∠3, ∠6, ∠7, ∠10, ∠11, ∠14, ∠15
  (3) ∠1, ∠4, ∠5, ∠8, ∠9, ∠12, ∠16
  (4) ∠1, ∠2, ∠3, ∠4, ∠5, ∠6, ∠7, ∠8

Exercises 6–10: Find the value of *x*.

6

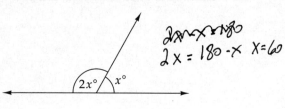

$180 - 25 =$
$X = 155°$

7

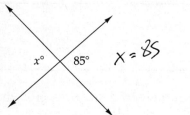

$2x + x = 180$
$2x = 180 - x \quad X = 60$

8

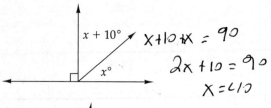

$X = 85$

9

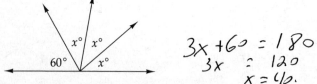

$X + 10 + X = 90$
$2x + 10 = 90$
$X = 40$

10

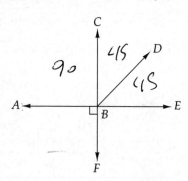

$3x + 60 = 180$
$3x = 120$
$X = 40.$

11 In the figure below, $\overline{BD}$ bisects $\angle CBE$. What is the measure of $\angle ABD$? $\_ 135 \ 135$

C
45
90
D
45
A
B
E

F

12 Draw lines ℓ_1, ℓ_2, and ℓ_3 if $\ell_1 \parallel \ell_2$ and $\ell_1 \perp \ell_3$.

13 If $\angle x$ and $\angle y$ are complementary, $\angle y$ and $\angle z$ are supplementary, and $m\angle x = 50$, what is $m\angle z$?

14 In the figure below, $\ell_1 \parallel \ell_2$. Fill in the missing angle values.

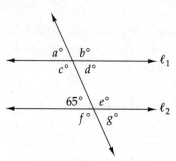

15 In the figure below, $\ell_1 \parallel \ell_2$ and $\ell_3 \parallel \ell_4$. What are the values of w, x, y, and z?

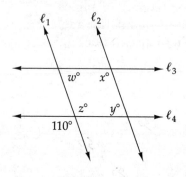

16 Find the indicated measures.

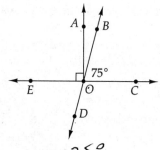

a $m\angle DOE$ ~~135°~~ $75°$
b $m\angle AOB$ $15°$
c $m\angle DOC$ $105°$

Geometric Constructions*

A **geometric construction** is a much more constrained process than simply drawing an object. When a figure is constructed, only two instruments are allowed: the compass and the straightedge. A **compass** is an adjustable V-shaped device used for drawing arcs and measuring distances. A **straightedge** has a straight edge without any ruler-type markings and is used only for drawing lines.

_____

*8th Grade May–June Topic

Constructing Congruent Figures and Angles

To Construct $\overline{CD}$ Congruent to $\overline{AB}$

- Using the straightedge, draw any segment longer than $\overline{AB}$ and mark point C near one end of the segment.
- On $\overline{AB}$, place the point the compass on A and the pencil point on B.
- Without changing the compass setting, place the point of the compass at C and draw an arc intersecting your line segment.
- Label the point of intersection D.
- $\overline{CD} \cong \overline{AB}$

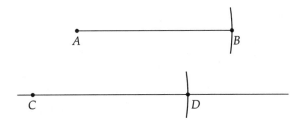

To Construct $\angle FED$ Congruent to $\angle ABC$

- Draw point E and draw a line segment through it with a straightedge.
- Place the point of the compass on B and draw an arc intersecting $\overline{BA}$ and $\overline{BC}$. Label the points of intersection G and H.
- Without changing the compass setting, place the point of the compass at E and draw an arc longer than $\overarc{GH}$ through your line segment. Label the point of intersection D.
- Place the point of the compass on H and the pencil point on G.
- Without changing the compass setting, place the point of the compass at D and make a second arc that intersects the first. Label the intersection F.
- Draw $\overrightarrow{EF}$ with the straightedge.
- $\angle FED \cong \angle ABC$

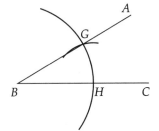 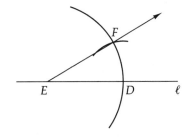

Exercises 1–3: Use only a compass and the figures below.

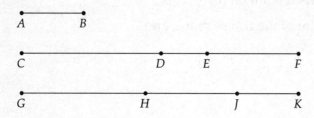

1 Which two line segments are congruent?

(1) $\overline{CD}$ and $\overline{GJ}$

(2) $\overline{CD}$ and $\overline{HK}$

(3) $\overline{EF}$ and $\overline{GH}$

(4) $\overline{EF}$ and $\overline{HJ}$

2 Which line segment is exactly twice as long as $\overline{AB}$?

(1) $\overline{CE}$

(2) $\overline{DF}$

(3) $\overline{GH}$

(4) $\overline{HK}$

3 Which line segment is exactly three times as long as $\overline{AB}$?

(1) $\overline{CE}$

(2) $\overline{DF}$

(3) $\overline{GJ}$

(4) $\overline{HK}$

4 Using a straightedge and a compass, which segment is congruent to the given segment $\overline{HJ}$?

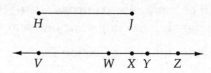

(1) $\overline{VW}$

(2) $\overline{VX}$

(3) $\overline{XZ}$

(4) $\overline{YZ}$

5 Draw a line segment and label it AB. Construct $\overline{AC}$ that is three times the length of $\overline{AB}$.

6 Construct $\angle RST$ congruent to $\angle MNO$.

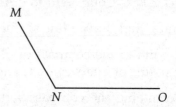

7 Construct $\overline{ST}$ so that $\overline{ST} \cong \overline{QR}$.

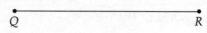

Constructing a Perpendicular Bisector and an Angle Bisector

To Construct the Perpendicular Bisector of $\overline{AB}$

- Open the compass so that the radius is more than half the length of $\overline{AB}$.

- Using point A as a center, draw one long arc through $\overline{AB}$.

- Using point B as a center, draw a second arc with the same radius through $\overline{AB}$ so that it intersects the first arc.

- Label one intersection of the two arcs C. Label the other intersection of the two arcs D.

- Use the straightedge to draw a line through C and D. This is $\overleftrightarrow{CD}$, the perpendicular bisector of $\overline{AB}$.

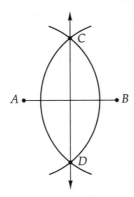

To Construct the Bisector of $\angle ABC$

- With B as the center, draw an arc that intersects $\overrightarrow{BA}$ at D and $\overrightarrow{BC}$ at E.

- With D and E as centers, draw intersecting arcs. The radii of these two arcs must be the same. Be certain that the radius is large enough to allow an intersection.

- Label the intersection F.

- Draw $\overrightarrow{BF}$, the angle bisector.

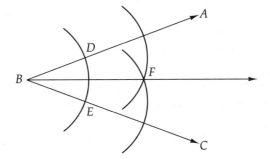

 Practice

---

1 The angle bisector of $\angle RST$ goes through which point?

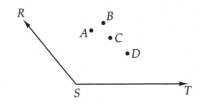

(1) A
(2) B
(3) C
(4) D

2 Which point lies on the angle bisector of $\angle MNO$?

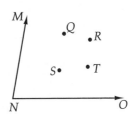

(1) Q
(2) R
(3) S
(4) T

3 Construct the perpendicular bisector of $\overline{MN}$. Find the point that lines on the perpendicular bisector of $\overline{MN}$.

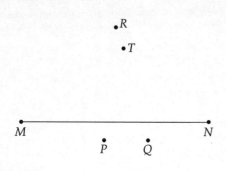

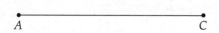

(1) Q
(2) P
(3) R
(4) T

4 Construct the perpendicular bisector of $\overline{AC}$.

A   C

5 Line segment CD is the perpendicular bisector of the line segment LM.

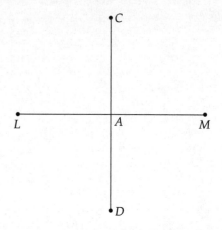

a Name two line segments that are perpendicular to each other.
b Name four angles that are right angles.
c Name two line segments that are congruent.

General Properties of Polygons

A **polygon** is a closed figure formed by three or more coplanar line segments joined at their endpoints. The line segments are the **sides** of the polygon, and the endpoints are its **vertices**. A polygon is named by the letters of its vertices, starting with any vertex and going in order in either direction: for instance, square $ABCD$.

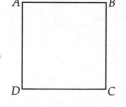

Polygons are classifed by number of sides. The table lists some common polygons:

Polygons

Number of sides	Name	Example
3	Triangle	
4	Quadrilateral	
5	Pentagon	

(continued)

Number of sides	Name	Example
6	Hexagon	
8	Octagon	
10	Decagon	
n	n-gon	16-gon

A **regular** polygon is both equilateral and equiangular: all its sides are congruent, and all its angles are congruent.

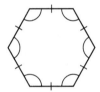

Remember: The symbols used in geometric drawings give information about lines and angles:

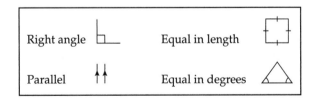

A **diagonal** of a polygon is a line segment connecting one vertex to any other nonconsecutive vertex.

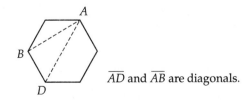

$\overline{AD}$ and $\overline{AB}$ are diagonals.

Interior angles of a polygon are inside it. In **convex polygons**, such as those in the table on pages 158–159, each interior angle measures less than 180°.

Exterior angles of polygons are formed by extending one of two adjacent sides. An exterior angle is supplementary to its adjacent interior angle. Shown below are interior and exterior angles of a regular pentagon, a regular hexagon, and a regular octagon.

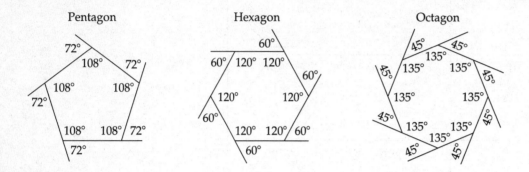

Pentagon   Hexagon   Octagon

All convex polygons have the following angle properties:

- The sum of the measures of the exterior angles is 360°. The measure of each exterior angle of a regular polygon with n sides is thus $\dfrac{360°}{n}$. The measure of each exterior angle of an equilateral (equiangular) triangle is thus $\dfrac{360°}{3} = 120°$.

  Note: The rule is true for a rectangle even though it is not a regular figure because all of its angles have the same measure. $\dfrac{360°}{4} = 90°$

- The sum of the measures of the interior angles of a polygon with n sides is $180°(n - 2)$. The measure of each interior angle of a regular polygon with n sides is thus $\dfrac{180°(n - 2)}{n}$. The measure of each interior angle of an equilateral triangle is thus $\dfrac{180°(3 - 2)}{3} = \dfrac{180°}{3} = 60°$.

MODEL PROBLEMS

1   Given a regular pentagon, find the following degree measures.

SOLUTIONS

a   Sum of the exterior angles.

360°. This is the sum of the exterior angles in any convex polygon.

b   Sum of the interior angles.

$180(n - 2) = 180(5 - 2) = 180 \cdot 3 = 540°$

c   An exterior angle.

$$\frac{360}{n} = \frac{360}{5} = 72°$$

d   An interior angle.

Use the formula:

$$\frac{180(n - 2)}{n} = \frac{180(5 - 2)}{5} = \frac{180 \cdot 3}{5} = 108°$$

Or find the supplement of the exterior angle found in **c**:

$180° - 72° = 108°$

2   How many sides does a regular polygon have if the measure of an exterior angle is 15°?

SOLUTION

Use the formula: measure of an exterior angle $= \dfrac{360}{n}$ where n = number of sides. Then:

$$15 = \frac{360}{n}$$

$15n = 360$

$n = 360 \div 15 = 24$

Answer: 24 sides

3   If the sum of the measures of the interior angles of a regular polygon is 1,080°, what is the measure of one exterior angle?

SOLUTION

First, find the number of sides, n, by using the formula for the sum of the angles.

$180(n - 2) = 1,080$

$$\frac{180(n - 2)}{180} = \frac{1,080}{180}$$

$n - 2 = 6$

$n = 8$

Next, use the formula for an exterior angle:

$$\frac{360}{n} = \frac{360}{8} = 45$$

Answer: 45°

1 A polygon is classified by its number of sides. This is the same as the number of

   (1) interior angles
   (2) vertices
   (3) both of the above
   (4) neither of the above

2 In a convex polygon, the measure of each interior angle is

   (1) greater than 180°
   (2) less than 180°
   (3) approximately 180°
   (4) at most 180°

3 A regular polygon is

   (1) equilateral but not necessarily equiangular
   (2) equiangular but not necessarily equilateral
   (3) both equilateral and equiangular
   (4) not necessarily equilateral or equiangular

4 In a polygon, a vertex is connected to any other nonadjacent vertex by

   (1) a side
   (2) an interior angle
   (3) an exterior angle
   (4) a diagonal

5 Pairs of interior and exterior angles in a polygon are

   (1) always equal
   (2) never equal
   (3) complementary
   (4) supplementary

6 How many sides does a regular polygon have if the measure of an exterior angle is 36°? $\frac{36°}{36} = 10$

7 What is the measure of an exterior angle of a square? 90

8 A STOP sign is a regular octagon. What is the measure of an interior angle? $\frac{360}{8} = 45$ $180 - 45 = 135$

9 The sum of the measures of the interior angles of a polygon is 1,440°. Name the polygon.

10 The Pentagon in Washington, D.C., is built in the shape of a regular pentagon. What is the sum of the measures of the interior angles? $180(n-2)$ $180(5-2)$ $180 \cdot 3 = 540$

11 What is the sum of the interior angles of a 20-gon?

12 If the sum of the interior angles of a regular polygon is 720°, what is the measure of one exterior angle?

13 If the sum of the degree measures of the angles of a polygon is 1,620, how many sides does the polygon have?

14 What is the measure of an exterior angle of a regular n-sided polygon if

   a $n = 4$?   d $n = 8$?
   b $n = 5$?   e $n = 10$?
   c $n = 6$?   f $n = 12$?

15 How many sides does a regular polygon have if each of its exterior angles has the following given measure?

   a 30
   b 45
   c 60
   d 72

16 If the sum of the interior angles of a polygon equals 24 right angles, how many sides are in the polygon?

17 How many straight angles are in the sum of the interior angles of a polygon

   a of 9 sides?
   b of 12 sides?
   c of 100 sides?

18 How many sides does a regular polygon have if its exterior angle equals the interior angle of an equilateral triangle?

19 How many sides does a regular polygon have if the sum of its interior angles equals twice the sum of its exterior angles?

20 How many sides does a polygon have if the sum of its interior angles is equal to three times the sum of the angles of a hexagon?

Triangles

Following are key definitions and facts about triangles.

- **Triangle** (△): A closed figure formed by three line segments.

- **Side**: One of the line segments making up the triangle.

- **Vertex**: A point where two sides of the triangle meet.

- **Interior angle**: An angle within the triangle. A triangle has three interior angles.

- **Exterior angle**: An angle formed outside the triangle by one side and the extension of the adjacent side.

- **Altitude**, or **height**: A line segment with one endpoint at any vertex of the triangle, extending to the line containing the opposite side and perpendicular to that side.

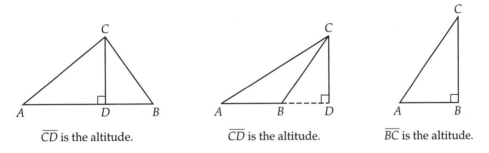

$\overline{CD}$ is the altitude. $\overline{CD}$ is the altitude. $\overline{BC}$ is the altitude.

- **Median**: A line segment with one endpoint at any vertex of the triangle, extending to the **midpoint** (middle) of the opposite side.

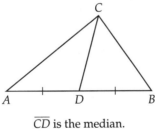

$\overline{CD}$ is the median.

- **Angle bisector**: A line segment with one endpoint at any vertex of the triangle, extending to the opposite side so that it bisects (evenly divides) the vertex angle.

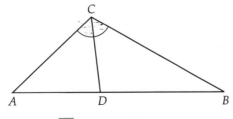

$\overline{CD}$ is the angle bisector.

For all triangles, the following statements are true. Note the examples and applications.

- *The sum of the measures of the interior angles is 180°.* This fact can be used to find the measure of an unknown angle.

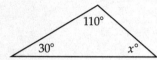

Add up all the angles. $x + 30 + 110 = 180$
Solve for x. $x + 140 = 180$
$x = 40$

- *The longest side is opposite the largest angle.* (Also, the largest angle is opposite the longest side.)

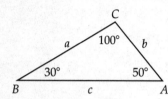

Since $\angle C$ is the largest angle, c is the longest side. The size order of the sides is:
$$b < a < c$$

- *The smallest angle is opposite the shortest side.* (Also, the shortest side is opposite the smallest angle.)

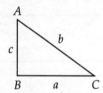

Since c is the shortest side, $\angle C$ is the smallest angle. The size order of the angles is:
$$m\angle C < m\angle A < m\angle B$$

- *An exterior angle of a triangle equals the sum of the measures of the two nonadjacent interior angles.*

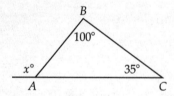

$\angle x$ is the exterior angle. $\angle B$ and $\angle C$ are the nonadjacent interior angles.
$$x = 100 + 35 = 135$$

- *The sum of any two sides of a triangle must be greater than the third side.*

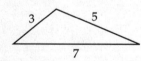

$3 + 5 > 7$
$5 + 7 > 3$
$3 + 7 > 5$

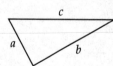

$a + b > c$
$b + c > a$
$a + c > b$

Also: *Any side of a triangle is greater than the difference of the other two sides.*

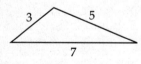

$3 > 7 - 5$
$5 > 7 - 3$
$7 > 5 - 3$

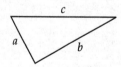

$a > c - b$
$b > c - a$
$c > b - a$

Therefore, where a, b, and c are sides:

$(a - b) < c < (a + b)$

A triangle can be classified by the number of its congruent (equal) sides or by its angles.

Classification of Triangles by Sides

Name	Description	Example
Scalene triangle	No two sides are equal. No two angles are equal.	
Isosceles triangle	Two sides, called the **legs**, are equal. The third side is the **base**. Two angles, called the **base angles**, are equal. The third angle, called the **vertex angle**, is opposite the base. Two sides of a triangle are equal if and only if the angles opposite these sides are equal. An altitude drawn from the vertex angle bisects the angle and the base.	
Equilateral triangle	All three sides are equal. Equilateral triangles are **equiangular**: all angles are equal and each angle = 60°.	

Classification of Triangles by Angles

Name	Description	Example
Acute triangle	All angles are acute. That is, each angle is less than 90°.	
Obtuse triangle	One angle is obtuse. That is, one angle is between 90° and 180°.	
Right triangle	One angle is a right (90°) angle. The side opposite the right angle is the **hypotenuse**. The other two sides are the **legs**. The **Pythagorean theorem** is true of all right triangles: $a^2 + b^2 = c^2$.	

The Pythagorean theorem is an important geometric relationship. It applies to every right triangle.

Pythagorean Theorem

- In a right triangle, the square of the hypotenuse c equals the sum of the squares of the legs a and b:

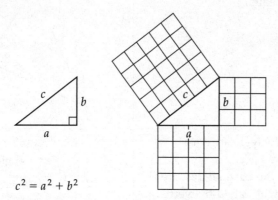

$$c^2 = a^2 + b^2$$

- Conversely, if the lengths of the sides of any triangle satisfy the Pythagorean theorem, that triangle is a right triangle.

- Any three whole numbers that satisfy the equation $c^2 = a^2 + b^2$ form a **Pythagorean triple**. For example:

  3, 4, 5   5, 12, 13   7, 24, 25   8, 15, 17

- Multiples of any set of triples are also triples. For example:

  3, 4, 5 $\rightarrow$ 6, 8, 10 $\rightarrow$ 15, 20, 25   …

The Pythagorean theorem is reviewed further in Chapter 8.

MODEL PROBLEMS

1 Classify each triangle by its sides and by its angles.

a

b

c

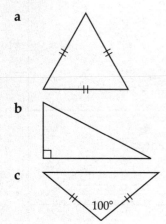

2 For any triangle, the sum of the measures of the interior angles is 180°. In $\triangle ABC$, $m\angle A = 52$ and $m\angle B = 16$. Classify $\triangle ABC$ as acute, right, or obtuse.

SOLUTION

To classify $\triangle ABC$, find the measure of the third angle by subtracting the two given angles from 180 degrees (the total):

$$m\angle C = 180 - (52 + 16) = 180 - 68 = 112$$

The third angle measures 112°, and an angle of 112° is obtuse. Therefore, $\triangle ABC$ is an obtuse triangle.

SOLUTIONS

   a   Equilateral, acute
   b   Scalene, right
   c   Isosceles, obtuse

3 Determine whether each set of lengths represents a right triangle:

SOLUTIONS

a 5, 6, 8 $8^2 = 64$ and $5^2 + 6^2 = 25 + 36 = 61$

$8^2 \neq 5^2 + 6^2$

Answer: No

b 30, 24, 18 $30^2 = 900$ and $24^2 + 18^2 = 576 + 324 = 900$

$30^2 = 24^2 + 18^2$

Answer: Yes

Practice

1 Which statement about triangles is true?

(1) If a triangle has two sides of equal length, it has two angles of equal measure.
(2) A triangle can have more than one right angle.
(3) A triangle always has one angle of at least 90°.
(4) The sum of the measures of the interior angles of a triangle is greater than 180°.

2 Which statement about the triangle below is *wrong*?

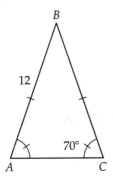

(1) $m\angle B = 40$
(2) $m\angle C + m\angle B = 100$
(3) $AB + BC = 24$
(4) $m\angle A = 70$

3 In the triangle below, if $m\angle A = 40$, what is the degree measure of the vertex angle?

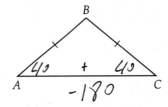

(1) 40
(2) 50
(3) 90
(4) 100

4 Which statement must be *false*?

(1) A scalene triangle has angles measuring 40°, 60°, and 80°.
(2) An acute triangle has angles measuring 60°, 60°, and 60°.
(3) An obtuse triangle has angles measuring 45°, 45°, and 90°.
(4) An isosceles triangle has angles measuring 45°, 45°, and 90°.

5 If the lengths of two sides of a triangle are 2 and 4, which is a possible length of the third side?

(1) 1
(2) 2
(3) 4
(4) 6

6 The direct distance between city A and city B is 400 miles. The direct distance between city B and city C is 500 miles. Which could be the direct distance between city C and city A?

   (1)   50 miles
   (2)   150 miles
   (3)   950 miles
   (4)   1,050 miles

7 If the ratio of the degree measures of a triangle is $3 : 4 : 11$, what is the degree measure of the smallest angle? *40*

8 In $\triangle ABC$ below, $\overline{AB}$ is extended to D, $\angle CBD$ is an exterior angle, m$\angle CBD = 130$, and m$\angle C = 90$. What is m$\angle CAB$?

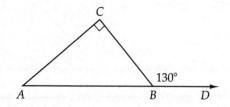

9 In $\triangle ABC$ below, $\overline{AB}$ is extended to point D, m$\angle A = 45$, and m$\angle C = 85$. What is m$\angle CBD$?

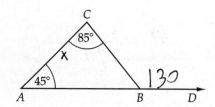

10 ABC and ABD below are isosceles triangles with m$\angle CAB = 45$ and m$\angle BDA = 50$. If $AB = AC$ and $AB = BD$, what is m$\angle CBD$?

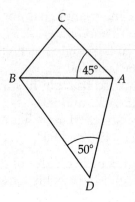

11 In the figure below, what is the value of x?

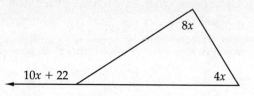

12 Find the length of $\overline{BC}$ in the figure below if $BD = 4$.

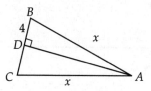

13 Explain why the altitude drawn from the vertex angle to the base of an isosceles triangle also bisects the vertex angle.

14 Richard says that he has measured a triangle and found two obtuse angles. Explain why he is wrong.

15 Find the values of x and y.

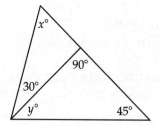

Exercises 16–20: Determine whether the lengths represent the sides of a right triangle:

16 $\sqrt{3}, \sqrt{5}, \sqrt{8}$

17 $4, 4, 4\sqrt{2}$

18 $4\sqrt{3}, 4, 8$

19 $5, 6, 8$ $5^2 + 6^2$ *no*

20 $6, 12, 17$

#7 $3x + 4x + 11x = 180°$
$18x = 180$
$x = 10 \quad 4(10)$

Quadrilaterals

A **quadrilateral** is a polygon with four sides. Figure *ABCD* is an example of a quadrilateral. Refer to *ABCD* as the parts of a quadrilateral are defined.

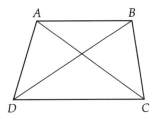

Parts of a Quadrilateral

- **Opposite sides** are sides that do not touch. $\overline{AB}$ and $\overline{CD}$ are opposite sides. $\overline{AD}$ and $\overline{BC}$ are opposite sides.

- **Opposite vertices** are vertices not connected by a side. *A* and *C* are opposite vertices, and *B* and *D* are opposite vertices.

- **Consecutive angles** are angles whose vertices are consecutive. That is, their vertices are next to each other, either clockwise or counterclockwise. In our example, consecutive angles are:

  $\angle ABC$ and $\angle BCD$ $\angle BCD$ and $\angle CDA$ $\angle CDA$ and $\angle DAB$ $\angle DAB$ and $\angle ABC$

- **Opposite angles** are angles whose vertices are not consecutive. $\angle ABC$ and $\angle CDA$ are opposite angles. $\angle BCD$ and $\angle DAB$ are opposite angles.

- **Diagonals** of a quadrilateral are line segments whose endpoints are pairs of opposite vertices. In our example, $\overline{AC}$ and $\overline{BD}$ are the diagonals.

- The **altitude**, or **height**, of a quadrilateral is a line segment extending from a vertex to the line containing the opposite side, and perpendicular to that side. In a rectangle or a square, the height is a side.

Some quadrilaterals have special names and properties. These include parallelograms, rectangles, rhombuses, squares, and trapezoids.

Special Quadrilaterals

Name	Properties
Parallelogram	Opposite sides are parallel: $AB \parallel CD$ and $BC \parallel AD$
	Opposite sides are congruent:
	$\quad AB \cong CD \qquad BC \cong AD$
	Opposite angles are congruent:
	$\quad \angle ABC \cong \angle CDA \qquad \angle BCD \cong \angle DAB$
	Consecutive angles are supplementary. For example:
	$\quad \mathrm{m}\angle ABC + \mathrm{m}\angle DAB = 180 \qquad \mathrm{m}\angle ABC + \mathrm{m}\angle BCD = 180$
	Diagonals bisect each other:
	$\quad AE \cong EC \qquad BE \cong ED$
	A diagonal forms two congruent triangles (triangles of the same size and shape).

(continued)

Name	Properties
Rectangle (figure: rectangle $GHIF$ with diagonals)	Parallelogram in which all angles are right angles: $m\angle FGH = m\angle GHI = m\angle HIF = m\angle IFG = 90$ Diagonals are congruent: $FH \cong GI$
Rhombus (figure: rhombus $KLMJ$ with diagonals)	Parallelogram in which all sides are congruent: $JK \cong KL \cong LM \cong MJ$ Diagonals are perpendicular: $JL \perp KM$ Diagonals bisect the angles of the rhombus: $\angle KJL \cong \angle MJL \qquad \angle JKM \cong \angle LKM$ $\angle KLJ \cong \angle MLJ \qquad \angle LMK \cong \angle JMK$
Square (figure: square $OPQN$ with diagonals)	Rhombus in which all angles are right angles: $m\angle NOP = m\angle OPQ = m\angle PQN = m\angle QNO = 90$ Also—Rectangle in which all sides are congruent: $NO \cong OP \cong PQ \cong QN$ Diagonals are equal and perpendicular: $NP \cong OQ \qquad NP \perp OQ$ Diagonals bisect the angles of the square.
Trapezoid (figure: trapezoid $STUR$)	Has only one pair of parallel sides, called the **bases**: $ST \parallel RU$ The nonparallel sides are the **legs**. If one leg is perpendicular to the bases ($m\angle R = m\angle S = 90$), then the figure is a **right trapezoid**.
Isosceles trapezoid (figure: isosceles trapezoid $WXYV$ with angles 3, 4, 1, 2)	Trapezoid with congruent legs: $VW \cong YX$ Diagonals are congruent: $VX \cong YW$ **Base angles** are congruent: $\angle 1 \cong \angle 2 \qquad \angle 3 \cong \angle 4$

The following chart categorizes special quadrilaterals. The correct or most appropriate name for a quadrilateral is usually the one that *gives the most information about it*—in other words, the most *specific* name.

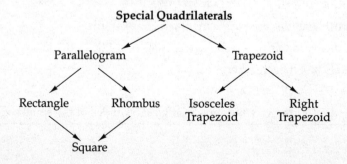

1 *BEST* is a parallelogram. Find m∠*ETS*, m∠*BTE*, and m∠*TEB*.

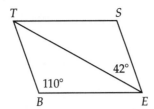

SOLUTION

Since ∠*S* and ∠*B* are opposite angles, m∠*S* = m∠*B* = 110.

The sum of the angles in △*ETS* = 180°, so:

m∠*ETS* = 180 − (110 + 42) = 180 − 152 = 28

Both ∠*BTS* and ∠*BES* are supplementary to both ∠*S* and ∠*B*. Thus:

m∠*BTS* = m∠*BES* = 180 − 110 = 70

Parts of each of these angles are already known:

m∠*BTS* = m∠*BTE* + m∠*ETS*	m∠*BES* = m∠*TEB* + m∠*TES*
70 = m∠*BTE* + 28	70 = m∠*TEB* + 42
m∠*BTE* = 70 − 28 = 42	m∠*TEB* = 70 − 42 = 28

Answer: m∠*ETS* = 28, m∠*BTE* = 42, m∠*TEB* = 28

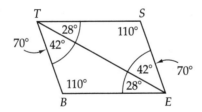

2 In rectangle *GROW*, how long is *RW*?

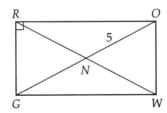

SOLUTION

A rectangle is a parallelogram, and the diagonals of a parallelogram bisect each other. Thus *ON* is half of *GO*, so length of *GO* is 10.

The diagonals of a rectangle are congruent. Therefore, length of *RW* is also 10.

Answer: 10 units

3 In rhombus *PINK*, the diagonals measure 6 units and 8 units. What is the length of a side?

SOLUTION

Diagonals of a rhombus are perpendicular to each other. Thus, they form 4 right triangles within the rhombus, and for each of these triangles the hypotenuse is a side of the rhombus:

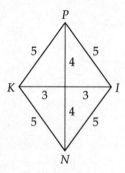

Diagonals of a rhombus bisect each other, so for each right triangle the legs are 3 units and 4 units.

Substitute these values in the Pythagorean theorem, where *c* is the hypotenuse and *a* and *b* are the legs:

$$c^2 = a^2 + b^2$$

$$c^2 = 3^2 + 4^2 = 9 + 16 = 25$$

$$c = \sqrt{25} = 5$$

Answer: 5 units

Shortcut: Recognize the Pythagorean triple 3, 4, 5.

4 The bases of an isosceles trapezoid measure 10 cm and 20 cm. The height (altitude) is 12 cm. How long are the legs?

SOLUTION

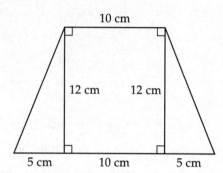

Because the legs are congruent, the shorter base must be centered over the larger base. Thus altitudes drawn from the upper vertices form a rectangle with sides of 10 cm and 12 cm.

The lower base is 10 cm longer than the upper base. This difference must be evenly divided to the left and right of the rectangle, so each leftover segment is 5 cm.

Thus two right triangles are formed with legs 5 cm and 12 cm, and hypotenuse *c* is a leg of the trapezoid.

Substitute these values in the Pythagorean theorem:

$$c^2 = a^2 + b^2$$

$$c^2 = 5^2 + 12^2 = 25 + 144 = 169$$

$$c = \sqrt{169} = 13$$

Answer: 13 cm

Shortcut: Recognize the Pythagorean triple 5, 12, 13.

 Practice

1 Which is *not* a correct name for this figure?

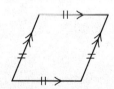

(1) polygon
(2) regular polygon
(3) parallelogram
(4) rhombus

2 Which statement is *false*?

(1) Every parallelogram is a quadrilateral.
(2) Every parallelogram is a rectangle.
(3) Every rhombus is a parallelogram.
(4) Every rectangle is a parallelogram.

3 Which polygons are always regular?

(A) equilateral triangle	(C) rectangle
(B) square	(D) rhombus

(1) A and B only
(2) A, B, and C only
(3) A, B, and D only
(4) A, B, C, and D

4 Identify the necessarily true statement or statements.

(A) A rhombus with right angles is a square.
(B) A rectangle is a square.
(C) A parallelogram with right angles is a square.

(1) A only
(2) B only
(3) C only
(4) A and C only

5 The bases of a trapezoid are

(1) the parallel sides
(2) the nonparallel sides
(3) always congruent
(4) always perpendicular to the legs

Exercises 6–9: Name the special quadrilateral that corresponds to each set of diagonals.

6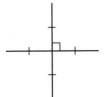

8

7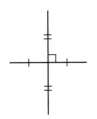

9

10 The shorter base of an isosceles trapezoid is 8 units, the longer base is 20 units, and each nonparallel side is 10 units. Find the altitude of the trapezoid.

11 Two congruent isosceles triangles are joined at their bases. Which special parallelogram is formed? Explain.

Exercises 12–15: Solve for x.

12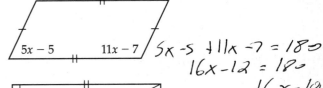

$5x - 5 + 11x - 7 = 180$
$16x - 12 = 180$
$16x = 192$
$x = 12$

13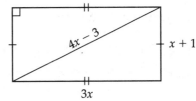

14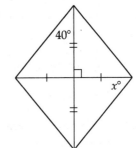

15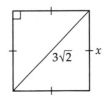

Circles

A **circle** (⊙) is the set of all points in a plane that are the same distance from a point called the **center**. A circle is named by its center: for example, ⊙C. Two or more circles with the same center are called **concentric circles**.

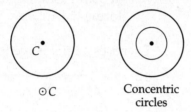

⊙C   Concentric circles

Here are some important definitions and relationships.

- **Chord**—A line segment with both endpoints on the circle.

- **Radius**—A line segment with one endpoint at the center of the circle and the other on the circle. The plural of *radius* is **radii**. Radius $r = \frac{1}{2}$ diameter d.

- **Diameter**—A chord that passes through the center of the circle. All diameters are chords, but only those chords that pass through the center are diameters. Diameter $d = 2r$.

- **Semicircle**—Half a circle. A diameter divides a circle into two semicircles.

- **Arc**—Part of a circle. An arc is identifed with the symbol ⌒.

- **Degrees of arc**—An arc (like an angle) can be measured in degrees. For example: $m\overset{\frown}{AB} = 90$. A full circle has 360°.

- **Central angle**—An angle formed by two radii. Its sides (the radii) **intercept** an arc. The vertex of a central angle is the center of the circle. The measure of a central angle equals the measure (degrees) of the intercepted arc.

- **Circumference**—The distance (length) around a circle.

Radii:	$\overline{OC}, \overline{OA}, \overline{OB}$
Diameter:	$\overline{AB}$
Chords:	$\overline{AB}, \overline{DE}$
Central angles:	$\angle AOC, \angle COB, \angle AOB$

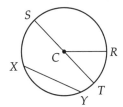

1   Draw a circle with center C. Then draw and label: radius CR; diameter ST; and chord $\overline{XY}$ that is not a diameter.

SOLUTION

2   Circle D has a radius of 6 centimeters. Locate each of these points inside, outside, or on the circle:

Point A is 7 centimeters from D.

Point B is 5 centimeters from D.

Point C is 6 centimeters from D.

SOLUTIONS

Point A is outside ⊙D.

Point B is inside ⊙D.

Point C is on ⊙D.

Practice

1   Which statement is *false*?

   (1)   Every diameter of a circle is a chord.
   (2)   The longest chord of any circle is a diameter.
   (3)   Every radius of a circle is a chord.
   (4)   A circle with a radius of 6 centimeters can have a chord of 10 centimeters.

2   Which statement is *not always* true?

   (1)   If the radius of a circle is 6 centimeters, its diameter is 12 centimeters.
   (2)   If point A is on ⊙C, only one radius of ⊙C contains point A.
   (3)   If points A and B are outside a circle, $\overline{AB}$ intersects the circle at two points.
   (4)   Every diameter of ⊙C contains point C.

3   In ⊙P, radius = 5 centimeters, PQ = 6 centimeters, and PR = 7 centimeters. Which statement is true?

   (1)   Points Q and R are inside the circle.
   (2)   Points Q and R are on the circle.
   (3)   Points Q and R are outside the circle.
   (4)   The distance between Q and R is 1 centimeter.

4   Points A and B are both inside ⊙C, and its radius = 6 centimeters. Which statement can *not* be true?

   (1)   AB = 14 centimeters
   (2)   AB = 8 centimeters
   (3)   AB = 6 centimeters
   (4)   AB = 4 centimeters

5   Concentric circles *always* have

   (1)   equal radii
   (2)   the same center
   (3)   equal circumferences
   (4)   all of the above

Exercises 6–9: Refer to the illustration (⊙C) and name the following.

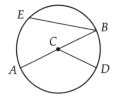

6   3 radii

7   1 diameter

8   2 chords

9   1 central angle

10   If the central angle of a circle measures 72°, what percent of the circle is included in the sector marked by the central angle?

Perimeter and Circumference

The **perimeter** (P) of a polygon, the distance around it, is the sum of the measures of its sides. Perimeter is expressed in linear units, such as inches, feet, and centimeters.

To find the perimeter of a polygon that is *not* regular or is not a rectangle, add the measures of all the sides. For example, the following figures are a scalene triangle and a general quadrilateral.

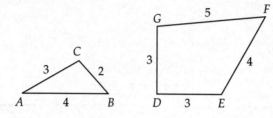

For the triangle: $P = 4 + 3 + 2 = 9$

For the quadrilateral: $P = 3 + 3 + 4 + 5 = 15$

To find the perimeter of a regular polygon or a rectangle, we can of course add as above, but formulas provide a faster method.

- In a **rectangle**, opposite sides are congruent. Two sides have a measure we call the **length** (l), and the other two sides have a measure we call the **width** (w). Thus the **formula for perimeter of a rectangle** is:

  $P = 2l + 2w$

To find the perimeter of a rectangle, substitute the measures for length and width in this formula. The rectangle below is an example:

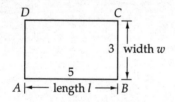

$P = 2l + 2w$

$P = 2(5) + 2(3) = 10 + 6$

$P = 16$

- A **regular polygon** (such as a square) is equilateral, so to find its its perimeter we multiply the measure of one side s by the number n of sides. Thus the **formula for perimeter of a regular n-sided polygon** is:

  $P = ns$

To find the perimeter of a regular polygon, substitute the measure of a side and the number of sides in this formula. The regular hexagon below is an example:

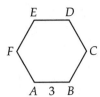

$P = ns$

$P = 6 \cdot 3$

$P = 18$

This equation also works for other equilateral polygons, such as a rhombus.

The **circumference** (C) of a circle, the distance around it, is measured in linear units and is found with a formula. In every circle, the ratio of the circumference C to the diameter d is a constant, called **pi** and represented by the symbol π:

$$\frac{C}{d} = \pi$$

Since the diameter is twice the radius r, this ratio can also be written:

$$\frac{C}{2r} = \pi$$

- Thus the **formula for the circumference of a circle** is:

    $C = \pi d$ or $C = 2\pi r$

Pi is an irrational number, 3.1415626 . . . , which is usually approximated as 3.14 or $\frac{22}{7}$.

> When you substitute a value for π, the calculation is approximate, so use the symbol $\approx$.

You will use the $\boxed{\pi}$ key on the calculator unless a problem specifies an approximation, such as 3.14 or $\frac{22}{7}$. Remember that π is an irrational number and is not equal to 3.14 or $\frac{22}{7}$. You will often be asked to leave your answer "in terms of π."

If you are asked to round the final answer, don't round intermediate values in the solution. The full power of the calculator should be used, saving rounding for the final step.

 MODEL PROBLEMS

1   A building has the shape of a regular decagon. The length of each outer wall is 7 meters. What is the perimeter of the building?

SOLUTION

Use the formula for perimeter of a regular polygon, $P = ns$, substituting 10 for n and 7 for s:

$P = ns$

$P = 10$ meters $\cdot$ 7

$P = 70$ meters

2 The circumference of a circle is 10 inches. Find its diameter to the nearest tenth of an inch.

SOLUTION

Use the formula $C = \pi d$ and solve for d. In this case, $C = 10$ inches, so:

10 inches $= \pi d$

$d = \dfrac{10}{\pi}$ inches Enter $10 \div \pi$ into the calculator. You will get $d = 3.183098862.\ldots$ This rounds to 3.2.

Answer: 3.2 inches.

3 Rhombus $ABCD$ has diagonals that measure 6 cm and 8 cm. Find the perimeter of the rhombus.

SOLUTION

Sketch the figure:

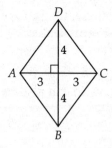

The diagonals of a rhombus are perpendicular to each other and bisect each other, so these diagonals form four congruent right triangles with legs that are 3 cm and 4 cm. We can use Pythagorean triples (3, 4, 5) to find that each hypotenuse measures 5 cm.

Then:

$P = ns$

$P = 4(5) = 20$

Answer: Perimeter is 20 cm.

 Practice

1 The perimeter of any polygon can be calculated as

  (1) $P =$ sum of the sides
  (2) $P = 2l + 2w$
  (3) $P = ns$ where s is a side and n is number of sides
  (4) all of the above

2 Pi (π) is the ratio of

  (1) the diameter of a circle to the circumference
  (2) the circumference to the diameter
  (3) the radius to the circumference
  (4) the circumference to the radius

3 You want to find the distance around a plane figure, given only one length. In which case is this impossible?

(1) circle
(2) square
(3) trapezoid
(4) equiangular triangle

4 When we use a value for π, the result of our calculations will always be

(1) exact
(2) approximate
(3) 3.14 or $\frac{22}{7}$
(4) a circumference

5 Given the circumference of a circle, you need to find the radius. Use

(1) $r = \pi d$
(2) $r = 2\pi d$
(3) $r = \dfrac{C}{2\pi}$
(4) $r = \dfrac{2\pi}{C}$

6 A rectangle has a width of 5 mm and a diagonal of 13 mm. Find the perimeter.

7 The base of an isosceles triangle is 8 cm. The height of the triangle is 3 cm. Find the perimeter.

8 The shorter diagonal of a rhombus measures 10, and the longer diagonal measures 24. Find the perimeter of the rhombus.

9 Each exterior angle of a regular polygon measures 36°. The perimeter is 140 cm. Find the length of a side.

10 A square banner for a school play shows a logo within a circle inscribed in the banner. The radius of the circle is 5 feet. Find the circumference of the circle and the perimeter of the banner.

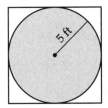

11 A circle is inscribed in a square. A side of the square is $2\sqrt{2}$. Find the circumference of the circle. Leave the answer in terms of π.

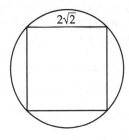

12 The radius of a circle is 6. Find the perimeter of a quartercircle. Leave the answer in terms of π.

13 The figure below is made up of two squares and two quartercircles. Find its perimeter.

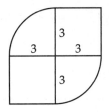

14 The swimming pool shown below has a semicircular shallow end. Find the perimeter of the pool.

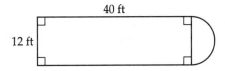

15 Find the perimeter of the shaded region.

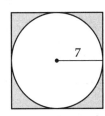

Area

The **area** (*A*) of a plane figure or surface is the number of square units (such as ft² or m²) in the region enclosed by the figure. Formulas used to find area are summarized in the table that follows.

Remember these definitions.

- **Base** (*b*): The **base of a polygon** is the side from which its height is measured.

  The **base of a triangle** is the side opposite any vertex.

  Bases of a trapezoid are a pair of parallel sides.

- **Height** (*h*): The **height of a triangle** is a perpendicular line segment connecting a vertex to the opposite base.

  The **height of a parallelogram or trapezoid** is a perpendicular line segment connecting its bases.

  Height is also called **altitude**.

- **Length** (*l*) and **width** (*w*): The base and height of a rectangle.

- **Side** (*s*): One of the line segments forming a regular polygon.

Formulas for Area

Figure	Formula	Example
Triangle	$A = \frac{1}{2} bh$	$A = \frac{1}{2} \times 10 \times 4 = 20$
Equilateral triangle	$A = \frac{s^2 \sqrt{3}}{4}$	$A = \frac{10^2 \sqrt{3}}{4} = \frac{100 \sqrt{3}}{4} = 25\sqrt{3}$
Parallelogram	$A = bh$	$A = 10 \times 3 = 30$

Formulas for Area (*continued*)

Figure	Formula	Example
Rectangle	$A = lw$	$A = 5 \times 3 = 15$
Rhombus	$A = \frac{1}{2}d_1 \times d_2$	$A = \frac{1}{2} \times 8 \times 6 = \frac{1}{2} \times 48 = 24$
Square	$A = s^2$	$A = 6^2 = 36$
Trapezoid	$A = \frac{1}{2}h(b_1 + b_2)$	$A = \frac{1}{2} \times 4(8 + 20) = 56$
Circle	$A = \pi r^2$	$A = \pi(3)^2 = 9\pi \approx 28.27$

Note: Problems involving area of a circle may specify a value for π $\left(3.14 \text{ or } \frac{22}{7}\right)$ or may say that the answer should be left in terms of π. A problem may also specify a degree of decimal accuracy.

MODEL PROBLEMS

1 Find the area of each figure.

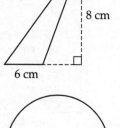

5 cm | 3 cm
10 cm

SOLUTIONS

Use the formula for area of a parallelogram $A = bh$. Height h is the dashed line.

$$A = (10)(3) = 30 \text{ cm}^2$$

Use the formula for area of a triangle $A = \frac{1}{2}bh$. Height h is the dashed line.

$$A = \frac{1}{2}(6)(8) = 24 \text{ cm}^2$$

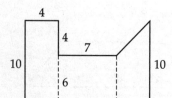

8 cm

6 cm

Use the formula for area of a circle $A = \pi r^2$.

$$A = \pi(4)^2 = 16\pi \text{ cm}^2 \qquad \text{(exact area)}$$
$$A \approx 16(3.14) \approx 50.24 \text{ cm}^2 \qquad \text{(approximate area)}$$

4 cm

2 Find the area of each region by dividing it as shown. Dimensions are in meters (m).

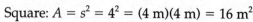

SOLUTIONS

Rectangle: $A = lw = (10 \text{ m})(4 \text{ m}) = 40 \text{ m}^2$

Rectangle: $A = lw = (7 \text{ m})(6 \text{ m}) = 42 \text{ m}^2$

Trapezoid:

$$A = \frac{1}{2}h(b_1 + b_2) = \frac{1}{2}[(4 \text{ m})(10 \text{ m} + 6 \text{ m})] = \frac{1}{2}(4 \text{ m} \cdot 16 \text{ m})$$
$$= \frac{1}{2}(64 \text{ m}^2) = 32 \text{ m}^2$$

Total area = $40 \text{ m}^2 + 42 \text{ m}^2 + 32 \text{ m}^2 = 114 \text{ m}^2$

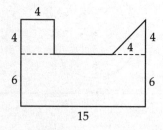

Square: $A = s^2 = 4^2 = (4 \text{ m})(4 \text{ m}) = 16 \text{ m}^2$

Rectangle: $A = lw = (6 \text{ m})(15 \text{ m}) = 90 \text{ m}^2$

Triangle: $A = \frac{1}{2}bh = \frac{1}{2}(4 \text{ m} \cdot 4 \text{ m}) = \frac{1}{2}(16 \text{ m}^2) = 8 \text{ m}^2$

Total area = $16 \text{ m}^2 + 90 \text{ m}^2 + 8 \text{ m}^2 = 114 \text{ m}^2$

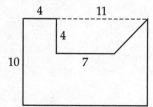

The quickest way to find total area is to *subtract* the area of the trapezoid from the area of the rectangle formed by the dashed line.

Rectangle: $A = lw = (15 \text{ m})(10 \text{ m}) = 150 \text{ m}^2$

Trapezoid:

$$A = \frac{1}{2}h(b_1 + b_2) = \frac{1}{2}[(4 \text{ m})(11 \text{ m} + 7 \text{ m})] = \frac{1}{2}(4 \text{ m} \cdot 18 \text{ m})$$
$$= \frac{1}{2}(72 \text{ m}^2) = 36 \text{ m}^2$$

Total area = $150 \text{ m}^2 - 36 \text{ m}^2 = 114 \text{ m}^2$

1 Which amount is *not* an application of area?

   (1) carpeting needed for a living room
   (2) extension cord needed to reach from an appliance to an outlet
   (3) sod needed for a lawn
   (4) laminate needed for a countertop

2 Parallelograms *A*, *B*, and *C* have the same area. Which has the greatest perimeter?

   (1) *A*
   (2) *B*
   (3) *C*
   (4) Their perimeters are equal.

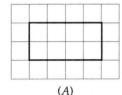 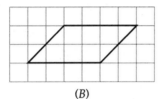

(*A*)   (*B*)

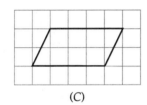

(*C*)

3 Which statement is *always* true?

   (1) Two rectangles with the same perimeter have the same area.
   (2) Two rectangles with the same area have the same perimeter.
   (3) Two quadrilaterals with the same area have congruent corresponding sides.
   (4) Two quadrilaterals with congruent corresponding sides and angles have the same area.

4 If the diameter of a circle is 10, then $A =$

   (1) 100π
   (2) 50π
   (3) 25π
   (4) 5π

5 Given the area of a circle, you need to find its radius. Use

   (1) $r = \sqrt{\dfrac{A}{\pi}}$

   (2) $r = \sqrt{\pi A}$

   (3) $r = \dfrac{A}{\pi}$

   (4) $r = \left(\dfrac{A}{\pi}\right)^2$

6 The perimeter of a square field is 12 centimeters. Find its area.

7 One rectangular yard has a length of 36 feet and a width of 24 feet. A second yard with the same area has a length of 32 feet. Find the width of the second yard.

8 One diagonal of a rhombus measures 6 feet, and the area of the rhombus is 48 square feet. Find the measure of the other diagonal.

9 To the nearest tenth of an inch, find the area of the patio below.

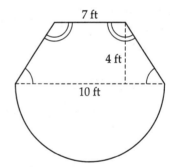

10 The height of a triangle is half as long as its base. The area of the triangle is 36 square inches. Find the base and height.

11 The bases of an isosceles trapezoid are 8 and 12. The bases are 2 units apart. Find the area of the trapezoid.

12 Ms. Green is planting a quarter-circle garden in her square yard. As shown below, one side of the yard is 30 feet long. What part of her yard will *not* be included in the garden? Give your answer to the nearest tenth of a square yard.

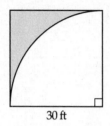

30 ft

13 In a regular polygon, the **apothem** is a perpendicular line segment from the center of the figure to a side. In the regular hexagon below, the apothem is 4 units and each side is $4\sqrt{3}$ units. Find the area of the hexagon in simplest radical form.

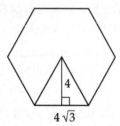

4

$4\sqrt{3}$

14 The floor plan below is made up of a parallelogram, a right triangle, and a trapezoid. Find the total area.

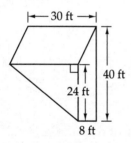

$\leftarrow$ 30 ft $\rightarrow$

40 ft

24 ft

8 ft

15 A 4-foot-wide sidewalk around an office building must be repaved. The building covers a rectangular space 100 feet by 50 feet. If repaving costs $0.50 per square foot, what is the total cost?

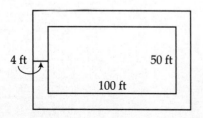

4 ft

50 ft

100 ft

16 On a basketball court, the center circle has a diameter of 4 feet. What is its area to the nearest tenth of a square foot?

17 A circle is inscribed in a square, as shown below. The area of the square is 36 square inches. To the nearest tenth of a square inch, what is the area of the shaded region?

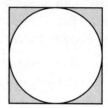

18 The target below consists of two concentric circles. The radius of one circle is 4 inches, and the radius of the other circle is 8 inches. To the nearest tenth of a square inch, what is the area of the shaded region?

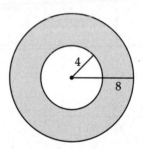

4

8

19 Using an overhead projector, a teacher displays a circular chart on a screen. By adjusting the focus, the teacher changes the radius of the circle from 3 feet to 4 feet. Find the percent increase in the area of the circle, to the nearest tenth of a percent.

20 The cost of making a cheese pizza is 4 cents per square inch. If Town Pizzeria sells a 9-inch-diameter pizza for $10, what is the profit made on each pizza?

Surface Area and Volume

For three-dimensional (solid) figures, we can find surface area and volume.

Surface Area

The **surface area** (SA) of a solid figure is the sum of the areas of all its surfaces, or faces. For figures that have a base or bases and a lateral surface or lateral faces, SA includes the base or bases. The **lateral area** (LA) of these figures does *not* include the base or bases—in other words, for such figures SA is lateral area plus the base or bases.

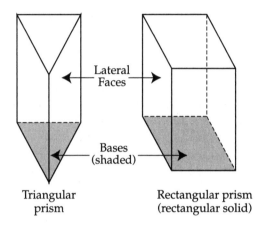

Surface Area of a Right Prism
A common example of a right prism is a rectangular prism. To understand how a rectangular prism is formed, consider this diagram:

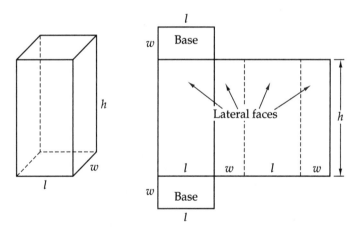

Lateral area LA of a right prism is the sum of the areas of the lateral faces. If the edges are laid out side by side, a rectangle is formed with the base equal to the perimeter of the base of the solid and the height equal to the height of the solid. Therefore, a **formula for lateral area of a right prism** with base perimeter P and height h is:

$$LA = Ph$$

Surface area SA of a prism is the sum of lateral area plus 2 times the area of the base. The area of the base, B, is found using the correct formula for the area of the polygon. Therefore, a **formula for surface area of a right prism** with lateral area LA and base area B is:

$$SA = LA + 2B$$

An alternative **formula for surface area of a rectangular prism** (rectangular solid) with length l, width w, and height h is:

$$SA = 2(lw + lh + hw)$$

A cube is defined by one measure, the length of an edge e. Area of each face is therefore e^2. Since there are six faces, we have this **formula for surface area of a cube**:

$$SA = 6e^2$$

Surface Area of a Right Circular Cylinder As the number of sides of a regular polygon increases, the polygon looks more and more like a circle. The lateral faces of a prism with such a polygon as a base look more and more like a single curved surface. When the base has an infinite number of sides, the result is a right circular cylinder. This cylinder has 2 congruent circular bases and a continuous curved edge that is perpendicular to both bases:

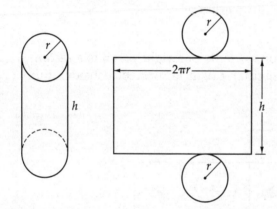

The **formula for lateral area of a right circular cylinder** with radius r and height h is:

$$LA = 2\pi rh \quad \text{or} \quad LA = Ch \text{ where } C \text{ is the circumference of the base}$$

The **formula for surface area of a right circular cylinder** is the sum of the lateral area and twice the base area:

$$SA = 2\pi rh + 2\pi r^2 \quad \text{or} \quad SA = Ch + 2B \text{ where } B \text{ is base area}$$

MODEL PROBLEMS

Find surface area for each figure.

SOLUTIONS

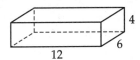

This is a rectangular solid, so, in square units:

$SA = 2(lw + lh + hw)$

$SA = 2[(12 \times 6) + (6 \times 4) + (4 \times 12)] = 2(72 + 24 + 48) = 288$

Use the formula for surface area of a cylinder:

$SA = 2\pi rh + 2\pi r^2$

$SA = (2 \bullet \pi \bullet 3 \bullet 10) + (2 \bullet \pi \bullet 3^2) = 60\pi + 18\pi = 78\pi$

$SA \approx 244.92 \approx 245$ square units

Volume

The amount of space enclosed by a three-dimensional figure is its **volume** (V). Volume is measured in cubic units, such as in.^{3} or cm^3. We can use the methods reviewed here to find the volume of certain prisms and cylinders.

Volume of a Right Prism or a Right Cylinder To find the volume of any right prism or right circular cylinder:

• Step 1. Express all the dimensions of the solid using the same linear unit of measure, such as inches, feet, or centimeters.

• Step 2. Find the area of one base. Call this area B.

• Step 3. Find the height h of the solid.

• Step 4. Use this **formula for volume of a right prism or circular cylinder:**

   $V = Bh$

Note also these alternative formulas:

• For the volume of a **rectangular solid** (a rectangular prism), with length l, width w, and height h, we can use the formula:

   $V = lwh$

• For the **volume of a cube** with edge e, we can use this formula:

   $V = e^3$

• For the volume of a **right circular cylinder** with radius r, we can use this formula:

   $V = \pi r^2 h$

MODEL PROBLEMS

1 A prism has a trapezoidal base with parallel sides measuring 12 inches and 8 inches. The parallel sides are 4 inches apart. The height of the trapezoidal prism is 6 inches. Find its volume.

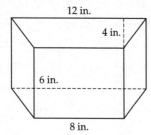

SOLUTION

First find the area B of a base of the prism, using the formula for area of a trapezoid:

$B = \dfrac{1}{2}h(b_1 + b_2)$ where b_1 and b_2 are bases of the trapezoid

$B = \dfrac{1}{2} \cdot 4$ in. $\cdot$ (12 in. + 8 in.) = 40 in.^{2}

Now use the formula for volume of a prism:

$V = Bh$

$V = (40$ in.$^2)(6$ in.$) = 240$ in.^{3}

Answer: Volume is 240 in.^{3}.

2 A juice can is a cylinder. The radius of the base is 2.5 centimeters, and the height of the can is 12 centimeters. Find the volume to the nearest cubic centimeter.

SOLUTION

Use the formula for volume of a cylinder, substituting the given values and using the π key on your calculator:

$V = \pi r^2 h$

$V = \pi(2.5$ cm$)^2(12$ cm$) \approx 235.2$ cm^3

Answer: Volume to the nearest cubic centimeter is 235 cm^3.

 ## Practice

---

1 If the surface area of a cube is 96 cm^2, what is the length of a side?

(1) 3 cm
(2) 4 cm
(3) 5 cm
(4) 6 cm

2 What is the surface area of this rectangular prism?

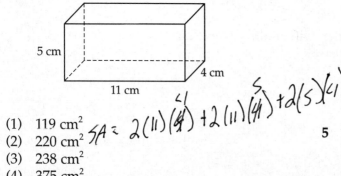

(1) 119 cm^2
(2) 220 cm^2
(3) 238 cm^2
(4) 375 cm^2

3 The height of a cylinder is 16, and the area of a base is 25π square units. In cubic units, the volume is

(1) 25π (3) 200π
(2) 50π (4) 400π

4

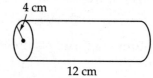

a Name the polygon.
b Find its lateral area.
c Find its surface area.
d Find its volume.

5 A right cylinder is 8 inches high. The circumference of the base is 6π inches. Find

a lateral area

b surface area

c volume

6 A cereal box is a rectangular prism 30 centimeters high. The sides of the base measure 8 centimeters and 25 centimeters. Find

    a lateral area

    b surface area

    c volume

7 A swimming pool is 8 feet deep, 25 feet long, and 12 feet wide. The water in it comes up to a level 2 feet below the top edge. Find the volume of water in the pool.

8 The volume of a rectangular prism is 54 cubic inches, and its height is 3 inches. Find the area of the base of the prism.

 CHAPTER REVIEW

1 A circle is divided into two semicircles by

    (1) a central angle

    (2) a radius

    (3) a diameter

    (4) an arc

2 Find the value of x in each drawing.

    a

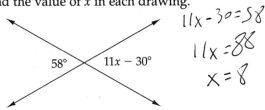

$11x - 30 = 58$
$11x = 88$
$x = 8$

    b

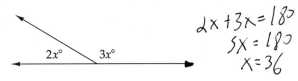

$2x + 3x = 180$
$5x = 180$
$x = 36$

    c

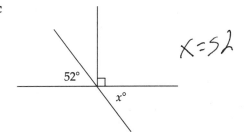

$x = 52$

    d

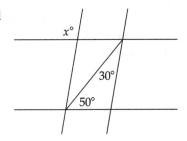

3 **a** In the figure below, x, y, and z are in the ratio $2 : 3 : 4$. Find the values of x, y, and z.

$2x + 3x + 4x = 180$
$9x = 180$
$x = 20$

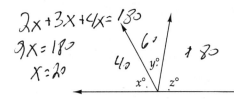

    b In the figure below, $\ell_1 \parallel \ell_2$ and x and y are in the ratio $1 : 2$. Find the values of x and y.

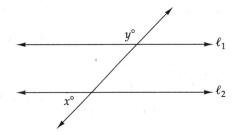

4 **a** In the figure below, $\ell_1 \parallel \ell_2$. Find the value of y.

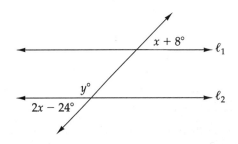

    b In the figure below, $\ell_1 \parallel \ell_2$. Find the value of x.

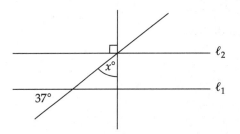

1, 2ABC, 3A, 7, 17, 19

5 In the figure below, $\ell_1 \perp \ell_2$ and $m = 80$. What is the value of $x - z$?

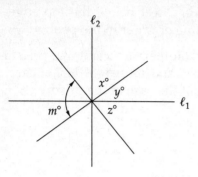

6 Lines ℓ_1, ℓ_2, and ℓ_3 intersect as shown below. What is the value of c in terms of a and b?

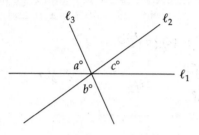

7 $\triangle ABC$ and $\triangle ABD$ below are isosceles triangles with $m\angle CAB = 30$ and $m\angle BDA = 45$. If $AB = AC$ and $AB = BD$, what is $m\angle CAD$?

$180 - 60 = C = 120°$

$A = 75°$

$m\angle CAD = 97.5$

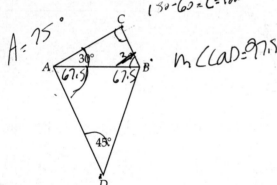

8 a Parallelogram *GAME* has a right angle. Explain why *GAME* is a rectangle.

b Parallelogram *CAKE* has four congruent angles. Explain why *CAKE* is a rectangle.

9 In parallelogram *SONG*, $SO = 2x + 4$, $ON = 3x - 6$, and $NG = 4x - 16$. Explain why *SONG* is a rhombus.

10 If the shorter diagonal, *KT*, of rhombus *KITE* is 5 and $m\angle KIT = 60$, find the length of a side of the rhombus.

11 If the length of a side of a rhombus is 8 and one of the angles measures 120, find the lengths of each of the diagonals.

12 In rhombus *GOLF*, diagonal *GL* is congruent to each of the sides. Find the measure of $\angle GOL$.

13 Find x and y in trapezoid *SODA* below.

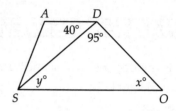

14 Find x and y in trapezoid *TRAP* below.

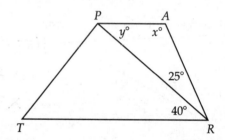

15 Find, w, x, y, and z in isosceles trapezoid *TALK* below.

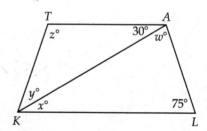

16 The dimensions of a room are 20 feet long, 12 feet wide, and 8 feet high. Gary wants to paint the walls and ceiling. What is the area, in square feet, of the surface Gary wants to paint?

17 Find the area of the garden shown below to the nearest square foot.

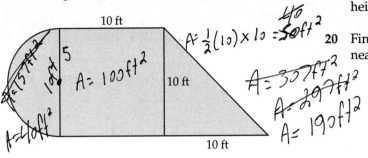

(handwritten notes) $A = \frac{1}{2}(10) \times 10 = 50 ft^2$

$A = 357 ft^2$
$A = 297 ft^2$
$A = 190 ft^2$

A = 100 ft²

10 ft

10 ft

10 ft

18 A right cylinder is 10 inches high and the radius of its base is 2 inches. Find the surface area to the nearest tenth of an inch.

19 The volume of a cylindrical storage tank is 100π m³ and the radius of the base is 5 m. Find the height of the tank. *(handwritten)* $h = 4/$

(handwritten) $V = \pi r^2 h$

20 Find the area of the shaded region, rounded to the nearest hundredth of an inch.

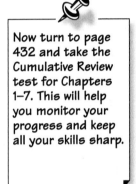

(handwritten work)

#19 $100\pi = \ell \times w \times h$

$100\pi \ell \times 25\pi \times h$

$100\pi = 7.85 \times 25\pi \times h$

$\dfrac{100\pi}{7.85 \times (25\pi)}$

616.53

$h = \dfrac{100\pi}{616.53}$

Now turn to page 432 and take the Cumulative Review test for Chapters 1–7. This will help you monitor your progress and keep all your skills sharp.

(handwritten)
Need to know
p153 #3
p154 #6
p162 #4
p168 #8
p188 #2

CHAPTER 8

Trigonometry of the Right Triangle

The Pythagorean Theorem

As reviewed in Chapter 7, the Pythagorean theorem states that in a right triangle, the sum of the squares of the legs equals the square of the hypotenuse, or $a^2 + b^2 = c^2$. Conversely, if the lengths of any triangle satisfy the Pythagorean theorem, then the triangle is a right triangle.

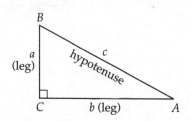

- Any three counting numbers that satisfy the equation $c^2 = a^2 + b^2$ form a **Pythagorean triple**. For example:

  3, 4, 5   5, 12, 13   7, 24, 25   8, 15, 17

- Multiples of any set of Pythagorean triples are also triples. For example:

  3, 4, 5   6, 8, 10   15, 20, 25

MODEL PROBLEMS

1 If the hypotenuse of a triangle is 4 inches more than one leg and 2 inches more than another, then what is the perimeter of the triangle?

SOLUTION

Let x represent the hypotenuse. Then the legs can be represented by $x - 2$ and $x - 4$.

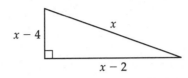

The Pythagorean theorem can help us find x.

Write the Pythagorean theorem.	$a^2 + b^2 = c^2$
Substitute.	$(x - 4)^2 + (x - 2)^2 = x^2$
Square each binomial.	$(x^2 - 8x + 16) + (x^2 - 4x + 4) = x^2$
Combine like terms.	$2x^2 - 12x + 20 = x^2$
Subtract x^2 from each side.	$x^2 - 12x + 20 = 0$
Factor.	$(x - 10)(x - 2) = 0$
Set each factor equal to zero and solve.	$(x - 10) = 0 \quad \text{or} \quad (x - 2) = 0$
	$x = 10 \quad \text{or} \quad x = 2$

Check: When $x = 2$, then $x - 4 = -2$. Since a length can never be negative, we must reject this value. When $x = 10$, then $x - 2 = 8$ and $x - 4 = 6$.

Add the sides. $10 + 8 + 6 = 24$

Answer: The perimeter is 24 inches.

2 To the nearest tenth of an inch, find the base of a rectangle whose diagonal is 25 inches and whose height is 16 inches.

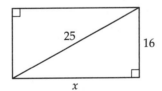

SOLUTION

Since the part of the triangle below the diagonal is a right triangle, we can use the Pythagorean theorem.

Write the Pythagorean theorem.	$a^2 + b^2 = c^2$
Substitute.	$16^2 + x^2 = 25^2$
Evaluate exponents.	$256 + x^2 = 625$
Simplify.	$x^2 = 625 - 256$
	$x^2 = 369$
	$x = \sqrt{369} \text{ or } 19.2$

Answer: The base to the nearest tenth is 19.2 inches long.

1 Which of the following are the sides of a right triangle?

(1) 1, 2, 3
(2) 1.5, 2, 2.5
(3) 3.5, 4.5, 5.5
(4) 5, 6, 7

2 Two college roommates, Henry and Harry, leave college at the same time. Henry travels south at 30 miles per hour and Harry travels west at 40 miles per hour. How far apart are they at the end of one hour?

(1) 50 miles
(2) 60 miles
(3) 70 miles
(4) 80 miles

3 The legs of one right triangle have a ratio of 5 : 12. If the hypotenuse is 65 feet in length, what is the length of the shorter leg?

(1) 63.88 feet
(2) 60 feet
(3) 25 feet
(4) 13 feet

4 A ladder 39 feet long leans against a building and reaches the bottom ledge of a window. If the foot of the ladder is 15 feet from the foot of the building, how high is the window ledge above the ground? (Hint: Buildings usually make right angles with the ground.)

(1) 24 feet
(2) 24.2 feet
(3) 36 feet
(4) 41.8 feet

Exercises 5–8: a and b represent the legs of a right triangle, and c represents the hypotenuse. Find the missing side. If the answer is not an integer, then find the answer both in simplest radical form and to the nearest tenth.

5 $a = 8, b = 15$

6 $a = 20, c = 25$

7 $a = 5, c = 15$

8 $b = 15, c = 17$

9 In an isosceles triangle, each of the equal sides is 26 centimeters long and the base is 20 centimeters long. Find the area. (Hint: First, draw the altitude to the base.)

10 If a right triangle has sides of lengths $x + 9$, $x + 2$, and $x + 10$, find the value of x.

11 If a rectangle has a diagonal of 20 feet and a side of 12 feet, find the perimeter and area of the rectangle.

12 If the base of an isosceles triangle is 12 inches and the altitude is 8 inches, what is the perimeter of the triangle?

Special Right Triangles

Any family of similar triangles has fixed ratios of sides. Two common triangles have ratios that are useful to memorize. These triangles are referred to by their angle measures: the 45°–45°–90° triangle and the 30°–60°–90° triangle.

The 45°–45°–90° Triangle A triangle with angle measures of 45°, 45°, and 90° is an isosceles right triangle. Since the triangle is isosceles, the ratio comparing the legs is 1 : 1. If we let a triangle have legs of length 1 and use the Pythagorean theorem, we find that the hypotenuse is $\sqrt{1^2 + 1^2}$ or $\sqrt{2}$. Therefore the ratio of sides for a 45°–45°–90° triangle is $1 : 1 : \sqrt{2}$.

45°–45°–90° Isosceles Right Triangle Relationships

- If you know the length of a leg, say x, you can find the hypotenuse by multiplying the leg by $\sqrt{2}$. Thus, $x\sqrt{2}$.

- If you know the length of the hypotenuse, say 8, you can find the legs by taking half the hypotenuse and multiplying by $\sqrt{2}$. Thus, $4\sqrt{2}$ and $4\sqrt{2}$.

- In all isosceles right triangles, the two legs have the same length.

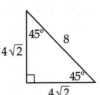

MODEL PROBLEMS

1 To the nearest tenth, find the distance from second base to home plate on a baseball diamond where the bases are 90 feet apart.

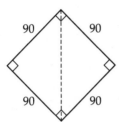

SOLUTION

The line from second base to home plate splits the field into two isosceles right triangles, with legs 90 feet long. The distance is simply $90 \times \sqrt{2}$ or approximately 127.3 feet.

2 If the hypotenuse of a right isosceles triangle is 10, find the exact length of the legs.

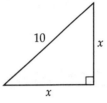

SOLUTION

To find the legs, simply divide 10 by $\sqrt{2}$.

$$\frac{10}{\sqrt{2}} = \frac{10}{\sqrt{2}} \cdot \frac{\sqrt{2}}{\sqrt{2}} = \frac{10\sqrt{2}}{2} = 5\sqrt{2}$$

The 30°–60°–90° Triangle A triangle with angle measures of 30°, 60°, and 90° has a ratio of sides of $1 : \sqrt{3} : 2$. This ratio is easy to verify using an equilateral triangle.

In the equilateral triangle shown, $AB = BC = AC = 10$.

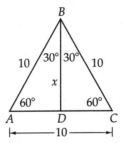

The altitude $\overline{BD}$ bisects the base so that $AD = DC = 5$. Using the Pythagorean theorem for triangle ABD, we can find BD:

$$(AD)^2 + (BD)^2 = (AB)^2$$
$$5^2 + (BD)^2 = 10^2$$
$$25 + (BD)^2 = 100$$
$$(BD)^2 = 75$$
$$BD = \sqrt{75} = \sqrt{25 \cdot 3} = 5\sqrt{3}$$

Therefore, the sides are, from shortest to longest, 5, 5√3, 10. These sides are in the ratio 1 : √3 : 2. Any triangle with this ratio of sides is a 30°–60°–90° triangle.

To Find the Lengths of the Sides of a 30°–60°–90° Triangle

- If you know the hypotenuse, say 8, divide by 2 to find the length of the leg opposite the 30° angle (the short leg), now 4. Multiply the short leg by √3, to find the long leg, 4√3.

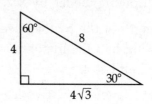

- If you know the short leg, say 7, then multiply by 2 to find the hypotenuse, 14. Multiply the short leg by √3 to find the leg opposite the 60° angle (the long leg), now 7√3.

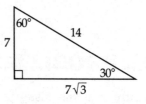

- If you know the long leg, say 2√3, divide by √3 to find the short leg, 2. Then double the short leg to find the hypotenuse, 4.

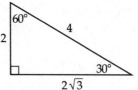

MODEL PROBLEMS

1 If the perimeter of equilateral triangle ABC is 27, what is the altitude BD rounded to the nearest tenth?

SOLUTION

Draw the situation.

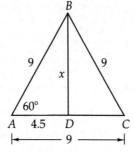

AC is one-third the perimeter.　　　　　　$AC = 27 \div 3 = 9$

AD is one-half of AC since $\overline{BD}$ bisects $\overline{AC}$.　　$AD = 9 \div 2 = 4.5$

BD is the long leg of $\triangle ABD$ and AD is the short leg.　$BD = AD \times \sqrt{3}$

$$BD = 4.5\sqrt{3} = 7.79422\ldots$$

Answer: $BD \approx 7.8$

2 If the width of a rectangle is 4 inches and the diagonal is 8 inches, what is the length of the rectangle in simplest radical form?

SOLUTION

Draw the situation.

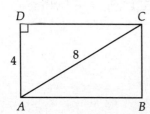

Examine the ratio $AC : AD$.

This ratio of sides for $\triangle ACD$ corresponds to the 30°–60°–90° relationship.

Find the length of CD.

$8 : 4 = 2 : 1$

AC is the hypotenuse, AD is the short leg, and CD must be the long leg.

$CD = AD \times \sqrt{3}$

$BD = 4\sqrt{3}$

Answer: The length of the rectangle is $4\sqrt{3}$.

 Practice

1 If the perimeter of a square is $8\sqrt{2}$, then what is the length of the diagonal?

(1) 8   (3) 4
(2) $4\sqrt{2}$ (4) 2

2 If the longest side of an isosceles right triangle is 12 feet long, how long are the other sides?

(1) $6\sqrt{2}$ feet and $6\sqrt{2}$ feet
(2) 6 feet and $6\sqrt{3}$ feet
(3) 6 feet and $6\sqrt{2}$ feet
(4) $4\sqrt{3}$ feet and $4\sqrt{3}$ feet

3 If the altitude of an equilateral triangle is $21\sqrt{3}$ inches, what is the perimeter of the triangle?

(1) 63 inches
(2) 99.4 inches
(3) 109.1 inches
(4) 126 inches

4 If the legs of a right triangle are $2\sqrt{3}$ and 6, what is the length of the hypotenuse?

(1) $4\sqrt{3}$
(2) $4\sqrt{6}$
(3) $6\sqrt{2}$
(4) 12

Exercises 5–10: $\triangle XYZ$ is a 30°–60°–90° triangle. The length of one side is given. Find the lengths of the other two sides in radical form.

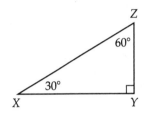

5 $YX = 36$ 8 $YZ = 4\sqrt{3}$
6 $YZ = 9$ 9 $YX = 27$
7 $ZX = 6\sqrt{3}$ 10 $ZX = 10$

Exercises 11–16: $\triangle ABC$ is a 45°–45°–90° triangle. The length of one side is given. Find the lengths of the other two sides in radical form.

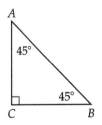

11 $AB = 12$ 14 $AB = 17$
12 $AC = 3\sqrt{2}$ 15 $BC = 10\sqrt{2}$
13 $BC = 4$ 16 $AB = 8\sqrt{3}$

Trigonometric Ratios

The ratio of the lengths of any two sides of a right triangle is called a **trigonometric ratio**. These ratios refer to right triangles only. The three most common ratios are **sine**, **cosine**, and **tangent**. Their abbreviations are *sin*, *cos*, and *tan*.

The following chart of definitions and formulas refers to the right triangle ABC where $\angle C = 90°$.

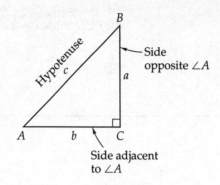

Definition	Formulas
The **sine** of an acute angle equals the length of the leg opposite the angle divided by the hypotenuse.	$\sin \angle A = \dfrac{\text{leg opposite } \angle A}{\text{hypotenuse}} = \dfrac{a}{c}$ $\sin \angle B = \dfrac{\text{leg opposite } \angle B}{\text{hypotenuse}} = \dfrac{b}{c}$
The **cosine** of an acute angle equals the length of the leg adjacent the angle divided by the hypotenuse.	$\cos \angle A = \dfrac{\text{leg adjacent to } \angle A}{\text{hypotenuse}} = \dfrac{b}{c}$ $\cos \angle B = \dfrac{\text{leg adjacent to } \angle B}{\text{hypotenuse}} = \dfrac{a}{c}$
The **tangent** of an acute angle equals the length of the leg opposite the angle divided by the leg adjacent to the angle.	$\tan \angle A = \dfrac{\text{leg opposite } \angle A}{\text{leg adjacent to } \angle A} = \dfrac{a}{b}$ $\tan \angle B = \dfrac{\text{leg opposite } \angle B}{\text{leg adjacent to } \angle B} = \dfrac{b}{a}$

Remember these with "SOH-CAH-TOA":

$Sin = \dfrac{Opp}{Hyp}$

$Cos = \dfrac{Adj}{Hyp}$

$Tan = \dfrac{Opp}{Adj}$

There are a number of formulas that show the relationships between the trigonometric functions. Use the table to verify these for yourself.

- $\sin \angle A = \cos \angle B$

- $\sin \angle B = \cos \angle A$

- $\tan \angle A = \dfrac{\sin \angle A}{\cos \angle A}$

- $\tan \angle B = \dfrac{\sin \angle B}{\cos \angle B}$

It is important to know that the value of the trigonometric ratio does not depend on the size of the right triangle. It depends only on the angle. To illustrate, consider three overlapping right triangles that share a common acute angle, $\angle A$. Since all three triangles are similar, the corresponding sides are proportional.

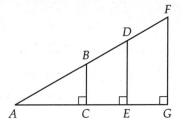

Therefore, $\dfrac{BC}{AB} = \dfrac{DE}{AD} = \dfrac{FG}{AF} = \sin \angle A$. This relationship is true for $\cos \angle A$ and $\tan \angle A$.

Note: When you use a calculator to find trigonometric functions, first be sure that the calculator is in degree mode. The **2nd** key will allow you to find angles when you know any trigonometric ratios of the triangle, usually found from the lengths of the sides.

We will use trigonometric ratios to find the missing measure of a side of a right triangle when we know the measure of one other side and we know the measure of one acute angle.

Inverse Trigonometric Functions

Sometimes we have information about two sides of a right triangle and need to find the measure of one of the acute angles. We will use the inverse trigonometric functions, $\sin^{-1}$, $\cos^{-1}$, and $\tan^{-1}$, found on the calculator by pressing **2nd** and then **SIN**, **COS**, or **TAN** respectively. These functions are called *arc sin*, *arc cos*, and *arc tan*.

- $\sin^{-1}(x)$ means the angle whose sine is x.
- $\cos^{-1}(x)$ means the angle whose cosine is x.
- $\tan^{-1}(x)$ means the angle whose tangent is x.

Note: When you use the calculator, make sure you are in DEGREE mode. Check by pressing **MODE**, highlighting DEGREE, and pressing **ENTER**.

 MODEL PROBLEM

A right triangle ABC has sides 5, 12, and 13. Find the sine, cosine, and tangent for $\angle A$ and $\angle B$, rounding your answers to the nearest ten thousandth. Find $\angle A$ and $\angle B$ to the nearest degree.

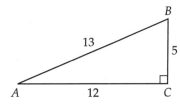

SOLUTION

$\sin \angle A = \dfrac{\text{opp}}{\text{hyp}} = \dfrac{5}{13} = 0.3846$ $\qquad$ $\sin \angle B = \dfrac{\text{opp}}{\text{hyp}} = \dfrac{12}{13} = 0.9231$

$\cos \angle A = \dfrac{\text{adj}}{\text{hyp}} = \dfrac{12}{13} = 0.9231$ $\qquad$ $\cos \angle B = \dfrac{\text{adj}}{\text{hyp}} = \dfrac{5}{13} = 0.3846$

$\tan \angle A = \dfrac{\text{opp}}{\text{adj}} = \dfrac{5}{12} = 0.4167$ $\qquad$ $\tan \angle B = \dfrac{\text{opp}}{\text{adj}} = \dfrac{12}{5} = 2.4000$

Using a calculator to work backward from any of these decimals, we find that $\angle A = 23°$ and $\angle B = 67°$ when rounded to the nearest degree. Since $23° + 67° + 90° = 180°$, our answer checks out.

1 Which equation is true?

   (1) $\sin 30° = \sin 60°$
   (2) $\sin 45° = \cos 45°$
   (3) $\tan 45° = \cos 45°$
   (4) $\sin 90° = \tan 60°$

2 Which statement about trigonometric ratios is true?

   (1) The sine of an angle decreases as the angle increases from 0° to 90°.
   (2) The cosine of an angle increases as the angle increases from 0° to 90°.
   (3) The cosine of an angle decreases as the angle increases from 0° to 90°.
   (4) The tangent of an angle decreases as the angle increases from 0° to 90°.

3 Which statement about trigonometric ratios is true?

   (1) The cosine of an angle is always less than or equal to 1.
   (2) The tangent of an angle is always less than or equal to 1.
   (3) The cosine of an angle is always greater than or equal to 1.
   (4) The tangent of an angle is always greater than or equal to 1.

4 If we know that $\tan \angle A = 0.75$ and the side adjacent to $\angle A$ is 12 units long, how long is the side opposite $\angle A$?

   (1) 85   (3) 16
   (2) 37   (4) 9

Exercises 5–12: Find the trigonometric function or the angle measure as indicated. Use $\triangle RAG$.

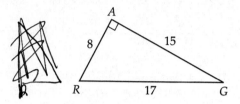

5 $\sin \angle R$ to the nearest hundredth

6 $\cos \angle R$ to the nearest hundredth

7 $\tan \angle R$ to the nearest hundredth

8 $\angle R$ to the nearest degree

9 $\sin \angle G$ to the nearest hundredth

10 $\cos \angle G$ to the nearest hundredth

11 $\tan \angle G$ to the nearest hundredth

12 $\angle G$ to the nearest degree

13 What angle has a tangent of 1?

14 What angle has a sine of $\dfrac{1}{2}$?

15 What angle has a tangent of $\sqrt{3}$?

Indirect Measure

Very often, it is necessary to find the measurement of a distance or of an angle in a situation where it is impossible to use a ruler or another measuring tool. The height of a tree, the distance across a lake, and the angle of elevation of the sun are examples of measurements that are difficult to find directly. These measurements can be obtained by imagining a right triangle in the situation and applying the principles of trigonometry.

    With trigonometry, if you know the length of one side of a right triangle, and either one more side or one of the acute angle, then you can find all the lengths and angle measures of the triangle.

To Solve for Parts of a Right Triangle Using Trigonometric Ratios

- Make a sketch of the triangle that contains the given information and label clearly what is given and what needs to be found.
- Decide which ratio connects the given information with the side or angle that needs to be found.
- Substitute the known information in this ratio.
- Solve for the unknown value.

In many triangle problems, the measured angle is referred to as an *angle of elevation* or *angle of depression*. An **angle of elevation** is the angle formed by a horizontal line and the upward line of sight to an object. An **angle of depression** is the angle formed by a horizontal line and the downward line of sight to an object. The measure of the angle of depression equals the measure of the angle of elevation as they are alternate interior angles.

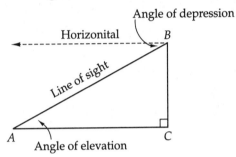

Finding a Length   When you need to find the length of the side of a right triangle, choose the trigonometric ratio that compares the side you seek with a side that is given. Once two sides are known, you can find the third side with the Pythagorean theorem instead of trigonometric ratios.

 MODEL PROBLEMS

1   An engineer wishes to estimate the height of a building. He knows that when he stands 225 feet from the base of the building, the angle of elevation to the roof is 18°. To the nearest foot, what is the approximate height of the building?

SOLUTION

Draw and label a right triangle clearly. From the 18° angle, the height of the building on the opposite side is x, and the distance of 225 feet is the adjacent side.

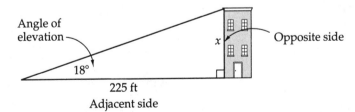

The tangent ratio involves the opposite and adjacent sides. $\tan 18° = \dfrac{x}{255}$

Using the calculator press, ⎡2⎤⎡2⎤⎡5⎤⎡TAN⎤⎡1⎤⎡8⎤ and ⎡ENTER⎤. $x = 255(\tan 18°)$
The calculator will show 73.10693165, which rounds to 73.

Answer: The building is about 73 feet tall.

2 From the top of a lighthouse 160 feet above sea level, the angle of depression to a boat at sea is 25°. To the nearest foot, what is the horizontal distance from the boat to the base of the lighthouse?

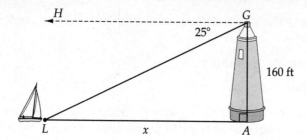

SOLUTION

The angle of depression, $\angle HGL$, is not inside the right triangle LAG.

Find $\angle LGA$, the angle complementary to $\angle HGL$.

$$\angle LGA = 90° - \angle HGL$$
$$\angle LGA = 90° - 25° = 65°$$

From $\angle LGA$, x is opposite and 160 is adjacent. We will use the tangent ratio.

$$\tan 65° = \frac{x}{160}$$

Using the calculator press, ⟨1⟩⟨6⟩⟨0⟩ [TAN] ⟨6⟩⟨5⟩ and [ENTER].
The calculator will show 343.1211073, which rounds to 343.

$$x = 160(\tan 65°)$$

Answer: The boat is about 343 feet from the base of the lighthouse.

Note: An alternate solution: Use the angle of elevation from the boat, which equals the angle of depression from the lighthouse, and proceed as in Model Problem 1.

Finding an Angle When you need to find an angle in a right triangle, you should use a trigonometric ratio that compares two known lengths. The decimal answer is converted to a degree measure using the [2nd] key. If one of the acute angles is already known, you can subtract it from 90° to find the other.

 MODEL PROBLEMS

1 In $\triangle ABC$, $AC = 10$ and $BC = 6$. Find $\angle A$ to the nearest degree.

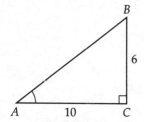

SOLUTION

$\overline{AC}$ is adjacent to $\angle A$ and $\overline{BC}$ is opposite $\angle A$. Therefore, we choose to use tangent of $\angle A$.

$$\tan \angle A = \frac{\text{opp}}{\text{adj}} = \frac{6}{10} = 0.6$$

Use the calculator to find the angle whose tangent is 0.6. Press [2nd] [TAN] ⟨.⟩⟨6⟩ and [ENTER]. The calculator will show 30.96375653, which rounds to 31.

Answer: $\angle A \approx 31°$

2 If a 20-foot ladder reaches 18 feet up a wall, what angle does the ladder make with the ground, to the nearest degree?

SOLUTION

Sketch the basic details of the situation.

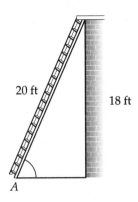

20 ft

18 ft

A

Since we are working with the hypotenuse and a side opposite our angle, we will use the sine ratio:

$$\sin \angle A = \frac{18}{20} = 0.9$$

Use the calculator to find the angle whose sine is 0.9. Press [2nd] [SIN] [.] [9] and [ENTER]. The calculator will show 64.15806724, which rounds to 64.

Answer: The ladder makes an angle of about 64° with the ground.

3 A pilot takes off at point A and ascends at a fixed angle with the level runway. If he flies a distance of 2,500 yards but covers only a ground distance of 2,200 yards, then what is his angle of ascent?

SOLUTION

Sketch the details of the situation.

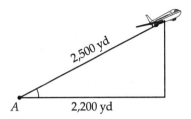

2,500 yd

A   2,200 yd

Since we are working with the hypotenuse and a side adjacent to our angle, we will use the cosine ratio:

$$\cos \angle A = \frac{2200}{2500} = 0.88$$

Use the calculator to find the angle whose cosine is 0.88. Press [2nd] [COS] [.] [8] [8] and [ENTER]. The calculator will show 28.35763658, which rounds to 28.

Answer: The plane is ascending at an angle of about 28°.

 Practice

---

1 In $\triangle ABC$, $AB = 5$ and $AC = 4$. What is the measure of $\angle A$ to the nearest degree?

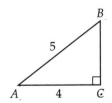

B

5

A   4   C

A

4

5

(1) 53°
(2) 51°
(3) 39°
(●) 37°

2 Wire braces are needed for the 80-foot ridge-pole of a circus tent. Each brace is supposed to make a 60° angle with the ground. Find, to the nearest foot, how long each brace should be.

(1) 46 feet
(2) 69 feet
(3) 92 feet
(4) 139 feet

3 At a point 40 feet from the foot of an oak tree, the angle of elevation to the top of the tree is 42°. Find the height of the tree to the nearest foot.

   (1) 54 feet
   (2) 44 feet
   (3) 36 feet
   (4) 30 feet

4 In a Rochester parking garage, the levels are 23 feet apart. Each up-ramp to the next level is 144 feet long. Find the measure of the angle of elevation of the incline for each ramp to the nearest tenth of a degree.

   (1) 9.2°
   (2) 9.1°
   (3) 8.1°
   (4) 3.9°

5 Since the distance across Smokey Swamp cannot be measured directly, Margaret (at point *M*) uses her knowledge of trigonometry. Using the accompanying diagram and the indicated measurements, find, to the nearest meter, the distance across the swamp.

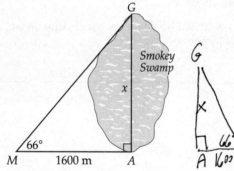

6 If the diagonal of a rectangular sundeck makes an angle of 67° with one side of the deck and the length of the diagonal is 24 feet, what are the dimensions, to the nearest foot, of the sundeck?

7 A ladder leaning against a house makes an angle of 70° with the ground. If the ladder is 25 feet long, find, to the nearest foot,

  a how far the foot of the ladder is from the base of the house

  b how high above the ground the ladder touches the house

8 At a certain time, the angle at the sun between Earth and Jupiter is 90°. The distance from Earth to the sun is 1 astronomical unit and the distance between Jupiter and the sun is 5 astronomical units. At this time, what is the angle separating the sun and Jupiter, when seen from Earth? Round your answer to the nearest degree.

9 An observer lying at the edge of a 200-foot cliff finds that the angle of depression out to a distant farmhouse is 40°. To the nearest foot, how far is the farmhouse from the foot of the cliff?

10 Ken Pollitt's distance from Jericho's water tower is 1,000 feet. If Ken is 6 feet tall and his eyes sight the top of the tower at an angle of 30°, what is the height of the tower?

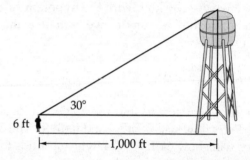

11 A kite is flying at the end of a taut 175-foot string. Patricia, who is 5 feet tall, holds the string, which reaches up into the air at an angle of 75° with the horizontal. Find, to the nearest foot, how high *above the ground* the kite is.

12 From the top of a Maine lighthouse 100 feet above sea level, the angles of depression of two lobster boats in line with the foot of the lighthouse are seen to be 18° and 32°. Find, to the nearest foot, the distance between the boats.

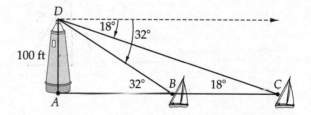

1 If a side of a square is 5, its diagonal is

(1) $5\sqrt{2}$

(2) $5\sqrt{3}$

(3) 10

(4) $10\sqrt{2}$

2 A pocket park is a rectangle 33 feet by 44 feet. If you walk diagonally across the park instead of along two adjacent sides, how many feet do you save?

(1) 11

(2) 22

● 55

(4) 77

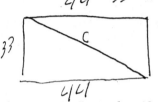

3 A rectangle has dimensions 5 cm by 12 cm. How many centimeters long is a diagonal of the rectangle?

(1) 12

(2) 13

(3) 17

(4) 30

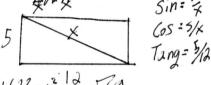

4 Elizabeth walked 4 km due east and then 7 km due north. Which of the following is the most reasonable answer for the distance between Elizabeth's start and endpoint?

(1) 6.5 km

(2) 8.1 km

(3) 9 km

(4) 11 km

5 An 8-foot ladder leaning against a wall reaches 6 feet up the wall. How far from the base of the wall is the bottom of the ladder?

(1) 2 ft

(2) 5.3 ft

(3) 6.2 ft

(4) 10 ft

6 A diagonal of a rectangle is 5 centimeters. The height is 1 centimeter more than the width. Find the perimeter.

7 A leg of an isosceles right triangle measures $8\sqrt{2}$. Find the length of the hypotenuse.

8 Each diagonal of a rectangle has a length of 10 yards. If one dimension of the rectangle is 6 yards, find the area.

9 The length of the hypotenuse of a 30°–60°–90° triangle is 40. In simplest radical form, what are the lengths of the legs?

10 In isosceles triangle ABC, legs $\overline{AB}$ and $\overline{CB}$ measure 30 cm and the base angles BAC and BCA measure 30°. Find the length of the altitude drawn from vertex B to base $\overline{AC}$.

11 A surveyor needs to find how far away he is from a 200-foot cliff. If the angle of inclination he makes with the top of the cliff is 28°, how far, to the *nearest foot*, is he from the bottom of the cliff?

12 The angle of elevation from a point 25 feet from the base of a tree on level ground to the top of the tree is 30°. Write an equation that can be used to find the height of the tree.

13 A 20-foot flagpole casts a 25-foot shadow at the same time that a telephone pole casts a 32-foot shadow. Find the height of the telephone pole to the nearest tenth of a foot.

14 At a point 43 feet from the base of a statue, the angle of elevation to the top is 52°. To the nearest tenth of a foot, how tall is the statue?

15 A 24-foot ladder, leaning against a house, reaches the bottom of a window that is 20 feet above the ground. To the nearest degree, find the angle the ladder makes with the house.

Now turn to page 434 and take the Cumulative Review test for Chapters 1–8. This will help you monitor your progress and keep all your skills sharp.

Functions and the Coordinate Plane

The **Cartesian coordinate system** provides an easy way to locate points on a plane, which is a two-dimensional surface. It consists of a coordinate grid separated by a horizontal number line called the x-axis and a vertical number line called the y-axis. The intersection of these number lines is called the **origin**. The two axes divide the grid into four **quadrants**, numbered I to IV counterclockwise.

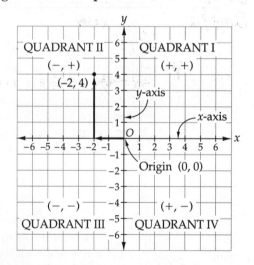

Every point on the grid can be identified with two numbers called **coordinates**:

- The first number is the x-**coordinate** (or **abscissa**). This is the distance from the origin horizontally to the point on the x-axis to the left or right of the origin.
- The second number is the y-**coordinate** (or **ordinate**). This is the distance from the origin vertically to the point on the y-axis above or below the origin.
- For any point, the coordinates are written (x, y). When in this form, they are called an **ordered pair**. Graphing of the ordered pair means placing a dot at the point on the coordinate plane that matches the ordered pair. This is called **plotting the point**. Recall that the coordinates of the origin are $(0, 0)$. The plotted point is found by moving left or right from the origin for the x-value and then, *from that place*, moving up or down for the y-value.
- On the graph above, point $(-2, 4)$ has an x-coordinate of -2 and a y-coordinate of 4.
- The correct signs for coordinates in each quadrant are shown in parentheses.

Relations and Functions*

A **relation** is any set of ordered pairs. The **domain** of the relation is the set of all the first elements of the ordered pair. The **range** of the relation is the set of all the second elements of the ordered pair. The **rule** for a relation describes the relationship between values of the domain and the range. A rule assigns or **maps** the values in the domain to the values in the range.

Relations with a limited number of ordered pairs can be expressed in many ways. Consider the following relation: The domain is the set of integers greater than 0 and less than 4, {1, 2, 3}. The range is the same set {1, 2, 3}. The rule for this relation maps odds to 1, evens to 2, and prime numbers to 3.

This relation can be expressed in several ways, including:

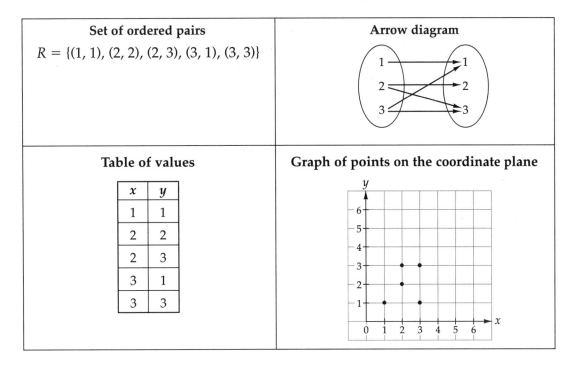

Set of ordered pairs	Arrow diagram
$R = \{(1, 1), (2, 2), (2, 3), (3, 1), (3, 3)\}$	

Table of values

x	y
1	1
2	2
2	3
3	1
3	3

Graph of points on the coordinate plane

If no set is specified for the domain, assume that the domain is the set of real numbers, or the entire *x*-axis. A relation with an infinite domain would have an infinite number of ordered pairs. Relations with infinite numbers of ordered pairs are usually expressed as algebraic rules or drawn as graphs.

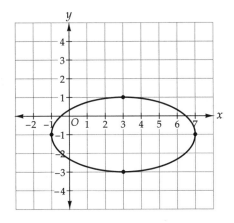

For the relation shown here, the graph indicates all values of *x* between −1 and 7. Therefore, the domain is the infinite set of real numbers such that $-1 \leq x \leq 7$. All values of *y* between −3 and 1 are shown in the graph, so the range is the infinite set of real numbers such that $-3 \leq y \leq 1$. The domain and range are infinite sets because a line has an infinite number of points.

*8th Grade May–June Topic

A **function** is a relation in which each element of the domain is paired with *one and only one* element of the range. In other words, no two ordered pairs have the same *x*-value.

Relations That Are Functions				Relations That Are Not Functions			

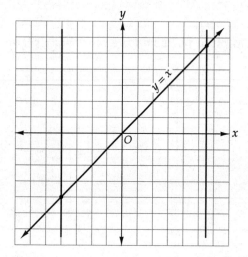

Vertical Line Test for Functions   A simple way to check whether a relation is a function is to look at its graph. If you draw a vertical line through any part of the domain, the line should intersect the graph of a function at one and only one point. If you can draw a vertical line that touches two or more points of the graph, the relation is *not* a function.

An example of a relation that is a function is $y = x$. Notice its graph.

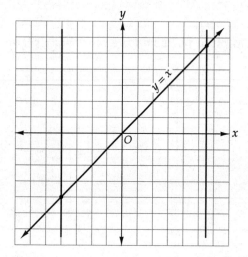

Compare the graph above with the graph of a circle. A vertical line can be drawn that intersects the circle at more than one point. The circle is not a function.

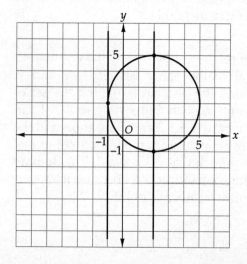

The domain is $\{-1 \le x \le 5\}$ and the range is $\{-1 \le y \le 5\}$.

1 If a relation has a rule $y = 2x$ and a domain of {2, 4, 6, 8}, identify the range.

    (1) {1, 2, 3, 4}
    (2) {2, 4, 6, 8}
    (3) {4, 8, 12, 16}
    (4) {(2, 4), (4, 8), (6, 12), (8, 16)}

2 Choose the rule for a relation that describes this table of values:

x	y
1	1
1	−1
2	2
2	−2

    (1) The first value is the absolute value of the second value.
    (2) The second value is the absolute value of the first value.
    (3) The first value is the opposite of the second value.
    (4) The second value is the opposite of the first value.

3 Choose the rule for a function that describes this table of values:

x	y
0	2
1	6
2	10
3	14

    (1) $y = x + 2$
    (2) $y = 4x + 2$
    (3) $y = 4x - 2$
    (4) $y = 6x - 2$

4 Which letter, when drawn on the coordinate plane, could represent a function?

    (1) W
    (2) X
    (3) Y
    (4) Z

5 Which of the following relations represents a function?

    (1) {(1, 1), (1, 2), (1, 3)}
    (2) {(2, 1), (1, 2), (2, 3)}
    (3) {(1, 1), (2, 1), (3, 1)}
    (4) {(1, 1), (2, 1), (2, 2)}

Exercises 6–10: State the domain and range for each relation and tell whether the relation is a function.

6 {(1,1), (2,4), (3,9)} $x = 1,2,3 \quad y = 1, 4, 9$

7 {(5,1), (6,2), (7,1)}

8

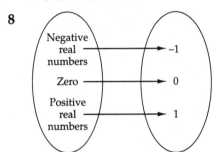

9

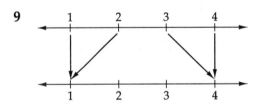

10

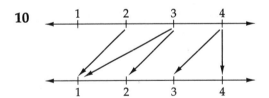

Exercises 11–15: Use the vertical line test to determine whether or not the graph represents a function.

11

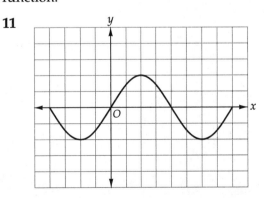

12

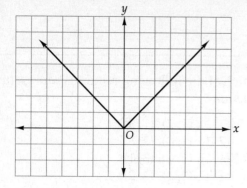

13

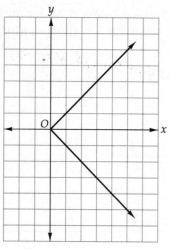

14

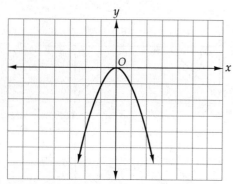

15

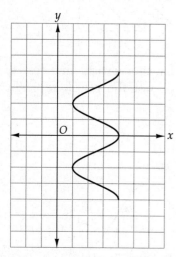

16 If the domain is {0, 2, 3} and the range is {1, 4}, list all the possible coordinate pairs. Is the resulting relation a function? Justify your answer.

17 If the domain for x is {all even integers}, what are three even integers in the range that satisfy the equation $3y + x = 8$? Write the set of three ordered pairs.

Exercises 18–20: For each of the following, identify completely the domain and range. Determine whether each relation is a function.

18

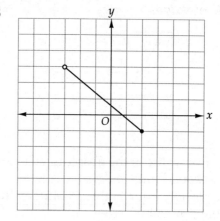

19

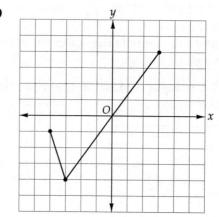

20

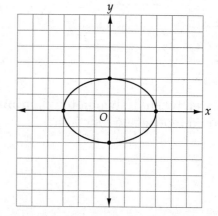

Graphing Linear Equations

A function that has a line as its graph is called a **linear function** and the equation of that function is called a *linear equation in two variables*. The standard form of a linear equation in two variables is $ax + by = c$ where a, b, and c are real numbers and a and b are *not both* equal to 0. For example, $2x + y = 4$, $x - 3y = 8$, $y = \frac{1}{3}$, and $-x + 4y = -5$ are linear equations in standard form. However, $4xy + 1 = 25$ is not a first-degree linear equation because the variables x and y are not separate terms.

The **solution set** of a linear equation is the set of all the ordered pairs (x, y) that make the algebraic sentence true. The **graph of a linear equation** is the graph of its solution set, which is always a straight line. Of course, a first-degree equation in two variables, such as $x + y = 10$, has an infinite number of pairs of values of x and y that satisfy it.

- *Every coordinate pair (x, y) that satisfies a given equation is a point that lies on the graph, and every point that lies on the graph has coordinates, or a number pair, (x, y), that satisfies the equation.*

To Graph a Linear Equation

- Solve the equation for y in terms of x.
- Find at least three points in the solution set by picking three convenient values for x and computing the corresponding values of y. (Although two points determine a straight line, we use a third point as a check.)
- Graph the three points determined by the ordered pairs (x, y).
- Draw a line through the three points. (If the three points are not in a straight line, there has been a mistake.)

You can also use a graphing calculator to graph a line. See the appendix.

MODEL PROBLEMS

1 Graph $x - y + 4 = 0$.

SOLUTION

Solve the equation for y: $y = x + 4$

Make a table using three values of x:

x	y
0	4
1	5
2	6

Plot these points and draw the line between them.

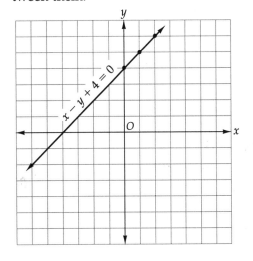

2 Explain why the point (2, 3) does or does not lie on the line $y = 4x - 3$.

SOLUTION

Substitute the coordinates of the point in the equation of the line.

$$y = 4x - 3$$
$$(3) = 4(2) - 3$$
$$3 = 8 - 3$$
$$3 \neq 5$$

If the coordinates of the point make the equation true, the point lies on the line.

Answer: Since the coordinates of the point are not a solution of the equation, the point does not lie on the line.

The graph of any linear equation of the form $ax + by = c$, where $a \neq 0$ and $b \neq 0$, eventually crosses both the x-axis and y-axis. The point at which the graph intersects an axis is called the **intercept**.

To Find the Intercepts of the Graph of an Equation

- For the x-intercept, substitute 0 for y in the given equation and solve for x.
- For the y-intercept, substitute 0 for x in the given equation and solve for y.

 MODEL PROBLEM

Find the x- and y-intercepts of $x - y + 4 = 0$.

SOLUTION

To find the x-intercept, replace y with 0. $x - 0 + 4 = 0$

Solve for x. $x = -4$

To find the y-intercept, replace x with 0. $0 - y + 4 = 0$

Solve for y. $y = 4$

Answer: The x-intercept is -4 and the y-intercept is 4.

 Practice

1 The abscissa for an ordered pair in the solution set of $x + 2y = 11$ is 3. Find the ordinate.

(1) 3
(2) 4
(3) 5
(4) 9

$3 + 2y = 11$
$2y = 8 \quad y = 11$

2 Which point lies on the graph of $y = x + 3$?

(1) $(-3, 0)$
(2) $(1, 3)$
(3) $(3, 9)$
(4) $(5, 9)$

3 Which line passes through the point $(2, -1)$?

(1) $2y - x = 0$ $2 - 2$
(2) $2x - y = 0$
(3) $3x - 2y = 8$
(4) $3x - 2y = 8$

4 Which line has a y-intercept of 2?

(1) $2 = x$
(2) $4 = x + y$
(3) $5 = x + 2y$
(4) $6 = x + 3y$

put in 0 for x

5 If the ordinate is -1 in the equation $4x - y = 9$, what is the abscissa?

6 If the abscissa is -2 in the equation $2x + 3y = -10$, what is the ordinate?

7 What is the ordinate of every point on the x-axis?

8 What is the abscissa of every point on the y-axis?

9 Write each of the following verbal sentences as an equation.

   a The ordinate is five less than the abscissa.

   b The abscissa is three less than twice the ordinate.

   c The ordinate is seven less than three times the abscissa.

10 Translate each of the given facts into an equation in two variables.

   a If x is the smaller number and y is the larger number, then the sum of twice the smaller and three times the larger is 73.

   b If a rectangle has a length of x and a width of y, then the perimeter is 64 inches.

   c If x is the amount of money invested at 4% and y is the amount of money invested at 7%, then the total interest income will be $450.

11 Determine whether or not each equation is a linear equation.

   a $4x - 3y = 16$

   b $y = x^2 + 8$

   c $\frac{1}{2}x = y + 5$

   d $xy = 20$

   e $2y - 4x = 0$

   f $3y - 2x - 6 = 0$

12 Find the coordinates of the point where the graph of each equation crosses

     (1) the x-axis

     (2) the y-axis

   a $2x + 3y = 18$

   b $5x - 2y - 30 = 0$

   c $5y = 9x$

   d $3x - 6y = 12$

   e $2x = 12 - 4y$

   f $y - x = 0$

Exercises 13–15: Which of the three given points, if any, lie on the given line?

13 $x + y = 7$ (2, 5) (−2, −5) (−3, 10)

14 $2x = y + 1$ (−1, −3) (0, 1) (2, 3)

15 $2x - y = 8$ (4, 0) (1, −7) (−2, − 12)

Exercises 16–19: Find the unknown coordinate of the point on the given line.

16 $x + y = 5$ $(x, 4)$ $x = 1$

17 $x - 2y = 8$ $(6, y)$ $y = -1$

18 $3y - 1 = x$ $(-3, y)$

19 $3x + 7 = 5y$ $(x, 5)$

Exercises 20–23: State whether the given line passes through the given point. Show your work.

20 $2y + x = 7$ (1, 3)   yes

21 $4x + y = 10$ (2, −2)

22 $2y = 3x - 5$ (−1, −4)

23 $y = -2x + 4$ (3, 10)

Exercises 24–30: Use each equation to create a table of ordered pairs. Graph the line using the ordered pairs in the table. State the y-intercept and the x-intercept.

24 $2x - y = 2$

25 $x - 2y = -6$

26 $2x + y = 0$

27 $3y = 6x - 6$

28 $y = 2x + 3$

29 $x + y = 12$

30 $4x = 12 - 2y$

31 Find the value of c so that the point (3, 2) will be on the line $2x - y = c$.

32 Find the value of m so that the line $y = mx - 5$ will pass through the point (−2, 3).

33 Find the value of c so that the line $2x + 3y = c$ will pass through the origin.

34 Without plotting, find a point on the graph of $y = 7x - 15$ whose ordinate is twice its abscissa.

35 Without plotting, find a point on the graph of $x + y = 21$ whose ordinate is three more than its abscissa.

Graphing a Line Parallel to an Axis

Horizontal and Vertical Lines

The graph of a first-degree equation in only one variable is either the x-axis, the y-axis, or a line parallel to one of the axes. Actually, we can think of these equations as linear equations in two variables by writing them in the form $y = 0x + n$ or $x = 0y + n$, where n is any real number.

In the graph below

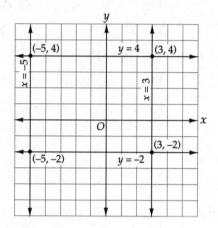

a the graph of $y = 0$ is the x-axis and the graph of $x = 0$ is the y-axis.

b the graphs of $y = 4$ and $y = -2$ are lines parallel to the x-axis, so that $(x, 4)$ is the ordered pair of any point on the line $y = 4$ and $(x, -2)$ is the ordered pair of any point on the line $y = -2$. Thus, $(-6, 4)$, $(0, 4)$, $(3, 4)$, $(9, 4)$, and $(89, 4)$ are some of the infinite pairs of points in the solution set for $y = 4$.

c the graphs of $x = 3$ and $x = -5$ are lines parallel to the y-axis, so that $(3, y)$ and $(-5, y)$ are the ordered pairs, respectively, of any point on the lines $x = 3$ and $x = -5$. Thus, $(3, -7)$, $(3, 0)$, $(3, 8)$, and $(3, 19)$ are some of the infinite pairs of points in the solution set for $x = 3$.

In general, the equation of a horizontal line is $y = b$, where b is a constant and where the **y-intercept** is b. Similarly, the equation of a vertical line is $x = a$, where a is a constant and where the **x-intercept** is a.

A function whose graph is a *horizontal line*, as in $y = b$, is called a **constant function**. The linear equation $x = a$ is constant, but it is *not a function* since the first element x has an infinite set of y-values in the range.

Lastly, the *intersection* (x, y) of lines parallel to the axes are constants of the two linear equations. Thus, in the graph above, the ordered pair $(3, 4)$ indicates the intersection of the two lines $x = 3$ and $y = 4$. Similarly, $(-5, -2)$ is the ordered pair found at the intersection of $x = -5$ and $y = -2$.

1 The equation of the y-axis is

  (1) $x = 0$ (3) $y = 0$
  (2) $x = y$ (4) $y = y$

2 Which equation describes the line in this graph?

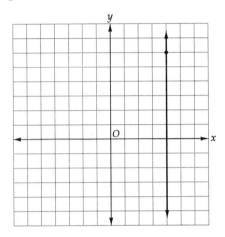

  ~~(1)~~ $x = 4$
  (2) $x = 6$
  (3) $y = 4$
  (4) $y = 6$

3 What is the x-intercept of $x = 7$?

  (1) 0
  (2) 1
  (3) 7
  (4) $x = 7$ has no x-intercept

4 Which equation has a graph that is parallel to the x-axis?

  (1) $x = 0$
  (2) $x = 25$
  (3) $x = 25 + y$
  (4) $x = 25 + y + x$

Exercises 5–12: Write the equation of each of the lines described below.

5 The line parallel to the y-axis and 5 units to the right of it $x = 5$

6 The line parallel to the x-axis and 4.5 units above it

7 The line parallel to the y-axis and 5 units to the left of it

8 The line parallel to the x-axis and 3 units below it

9 The line parallel to the line $y = 5$ and 4 units above it

10 The line parallel to the line $x = -3$ and 2 units to the left of it

11 The line containing all the points whose abscissas are 15

12 The line containing all the points whose ordinates are -7

13 Describe fully the graph of a line whose equation is

  a $y = 3$
  b $x = -2$
  c $x = 5$
  d $y = -4.5$
  e $x = 0$
  f $x = 3.5$
  g $y = 0$
  h $y = x$

Exercises 14–16: Is the line containing points A and B vertical or horizontal? Write an equation of the line.

14 $A(-2, 5)$ and $B(-2, 8)$

15 $A(-3, -6)$ and $B(10, -6)$

16 $A(3, 8)$ and $B(3, 0)$

Exercises 17–22: Graph each pair of equations and state the ordered pair (x, y) of the intersection.

17 $y = 2$ and $x = 3$

18 $x = -3$ and $y = -1$

19 $y = 0$ and $x = -1$

20 $x = 5$ and $y = -8$

21 the y-axis and $y = -8$

22 $x = -4$ and the x-axis

Exercises 23–26: Given the ordered pair (x, y) of an intersection of two lines parallel to the axes, state the equation of those two lines.

23 $(-3, 5)$

24 $(0, -11)$

25 $(2, -7)$

26 $(-5.5, 10)$

The Slope of a Line

The **slope** of a line is the ratio of the difference in y-values to the difference in x-values between any two points on the line. Thus,

$$\text{slope} = \frac{\text{difference in } y\text{-values}}{\text{difference in } x\text{-values}} \text{ or } \frac{\text{vertical change}}{\text{horizontal change}}$$

Sometimes the slope is shown as

$$\frac{\text{rise}}{\text{run}}$$

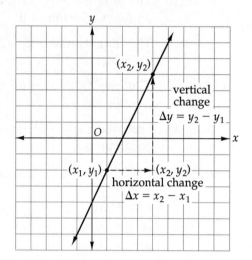

Mathematicians use the Greek letter Δ (delta) as a symbol for difference. Slope is usually symbolized by the letter m. Therefore, the formula for the slope of the line connecting points (x_1, y_1) and (x_2, y_2) is

$$m = \frac{\Delta y}{\Delta x} \text{ or } m = \frac{y_2 - y_1}{x_2 - x_1}$$

It makes no difference which points are labeled (x_1, y_1) and (x_2, y_2); the value of m will always be the same.

To find the Slope of a Line

- Choose any two points (x_1, y_1) and (x_2, y_2) on the line.
- Find the difference in y-values by subtracting y_1 from y_2.
- Find the difference in x-values by subtracting x_1 from x_2.
- Write the ratio: $\text{slope} = \dfrac{\text{difference in } y\text{-values}}{\text{difference in } x\text{-values}}$ as $m = \dfrac{y_2 - y_1}{x_2 - x_1}$ or $m = \dfrac{\Delta y}{\Delta x}$.

When graphing, express the slope as a fraction. This makes it easier to determine points on the graph. Thus, a slope of 7 is really:

$$\frac{7}{1}$$

Possible values of m

Value of m	Values of Δy and Δx	Appearance of Graph
positive	Δy and Δx have the same sign.	Line rises from left to right. /
negative	Δy and Δx have opposite signs.	Line falls from left to right. \
zero	$\Delta y = 0$	Line is horizontal. —
undefined	$\Delta x = 0$	Line is vertical.	

MODEL PROBLEMS

1 Draw the graph of $2x - y = 4$ and find the slope.

SOLUTION

Solve the equation for y.
$$-y = -2x + 4$$
$$y = 2x - 4$$

Create a table of values.

x	0	2	3
y	-4	0	2

Plot the points and draw the graph.

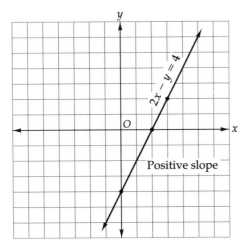

Choose points $(0, -4)$ as (x_1, y_1) and $(3, 2)$ as (x_2, y_2).

Then $m = \dfrac{\Delta y}{\Delta x} = \dfrac{y_2 - y_1}{x_2 - x_1} = \dfrac{2 - (-4)}{3 - 0} = \dfrac{6}{3} = \dfrac{2}{1} = 2$

Note: Slope can also be found in reverse order:
$$\dfrac{y_1 - y_2}{x_1 - x_2} = \dfrac{-4 - 2}{0 - 3} = \dfrac{-6}{-3} = \dfrac{2}{1} = 2$$

2 Draw the graph of $x + 2y = -4$ and find the slope.

SOLUTION

Solve the equation for y.
$$2y = -x - 4$$
$$y = -\dfrac{x}{2} - 2$$

Create a table of values.

x	-4	-2	0
y	0	-1	-2

Plot these points and draw the graph.

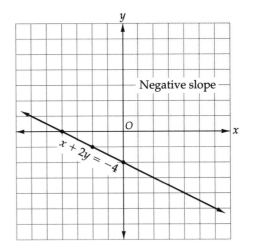

Choose points $(-4, 0)$ as (x_1, y_1) and $(0, -2)$ as (x_2, y_2). Then

$$m = \dfrac{\Delta y}{\Delta x} = \dfrac{y_2 - y_1}{x_2 - x_1} = \dfrac{-2 - 0}{0 - (-4)} = \dfrac{-2}{4} = \dfrac{-1}{2} \text{ or } -\dfrac{1}{2}$$

3 Draw the graph of $y = 3$ and find the slope.

SOLUTION

We have already discussed the idea that graphs of this type are parallel to the x-axis with y-intercept 3.

Draw the graph.

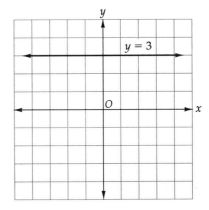

Notice that, since all y-values are the same, the change in y or Δy is 0. Thus, $m = \dfrac{\Delta y}{\Delta x} = \dfrac{0}{\Delta x} = 0$.

4 Draw the graph of $x = 1$ and find the slope.

SOLUTION

We have already discussed the idea that graphs of this type are parallel to the y-axis with x-intercept 1.

Draw the graph.

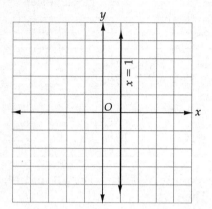

Notice that, since all x-values are the same, the change in x, or Δx, is 0, which means the denominator in the ratio $\frac{\Delta y}{\Delta x}$ is 0. Thus $\frac{\Delta y}{\Delta x} = \frac{\Delta y}{0}$. However, since division by zero is undefined, the slope is *undefined*.

All graphs of the form $y = b$ have zero slope.

The slope of all graphs of the form $x = a$ is undefined.

Reminders:

1 Since the slope of the line is constant, all segments of a line have the same slope. Thus, using any two points from the line must produce the same slope.

2 If a line is parallel to the y-axis, such as $x = 5$ or $x = -3$, the line is not a function and the slope of that vertical line is *undefined* or is said to have *no slope*. Also, the *vertical y-axis* itself has no slope.

 Practice

1 What is the slope of the line represented by this table of values?

x	y
-3	1
-2	3
-1	5

(1) -2 (3) 0.5
(2) -0.5 (4) 2

2 What is the slope of the line passing through $(0, 0)$ and $(-2, -5)$?

(1) -2.5 (3) 0.4
(2) -0.4 (4) 2.5

$\dfrac{-5 - 0}{-2 - 0} \quad \dfrac{-5}{-2} \quad \dfrac{}{}$

3 What is the slope of the line passing through $(5, -4)$ and $(-2, -1)$?

(1) -1 (3) $\dfrac{5}{3}$

(2) $-\dfrac{3}{7}$ (4) $\dfrac{5}{7}$

4 Which line has a slope of 5? The line passing through

(1) $(0, -5)$ and $(-5, 0)$
(2) $(0, 10)$ and $(2, 0)$
(3) $(0, -10)$ and $(2, 0)$
(4) $(0, 5)$ and $(5, 0)$

Exercises 5–8: Find the slope of the line represented by each table of values.

5

x	y
0	0
1	−1
2	−2

6

x	y
−5	1
−5	3
−5	5

7

x	y
1	4
2	4
3	4

8

x	y
−2	0
0	−2
2	−4

Exercises 9–18: Find the slope of the line passing through the following pairs of points. State whether the slope is positive, negative, zero, or undefined.

9 $(1, 1), (6, 7)$

10 $(2, −5), (4, 0)$

11 $(4, −3), (6, −5)$

12 $(−3, −5), (−2, −4)$

13 $(4, −7), (−7, 4)$

14 $(−1, 2), (−3, 6)$

15 $(6, −2), (7, −2)$

16 $(0, 0), (5, 5)$

17 $(4, 1), (1, 4)$

18 $(5, 3), (7, 3)$

Exercises 19–23: Graph the given point and use the given slope, m, to draw a line.

19 $(−2, 3); m = \dfrac{1}{3}$

20 $(1, 5); m = −\dfrac{2}{3}$

21 $(2, −4); m = \dfrac{2}{3}$

22 $(−4, −1); m = 3$

23 $(0, 0); m = −2$

24 Points $A(−2, 0)$, $B(0, 3)$, and $C(4, −3)$ are the vertices of triangle ABC. Find the slope of each side of the triangle.

25 Points $A(−2, −1)$, $B(4, 3)$, and $C(4, −1)$ are the vertices of right triangle ABC. Plot the points and draw the figure. Find the slope of each side of the triangle. What is the special relationship between the sides that form a right angle? What is the relationship between the slopes of side AC and side BC?

The Slopes of Parallel and Perpendicular Lines

If two lines in the coordinate plane have the *same slope* and *different y-intercepts*, or if they are vertical lines that have different *x*-intercepts, then the lines are **parallel**.

For example, the graphs of the following pairs of linear equations are *parallel*.

1 $y = 3x + 5$ and $y = 3x − 1$

The slope for both lines is 3 and the *y*-intercepts are 5 and −1.

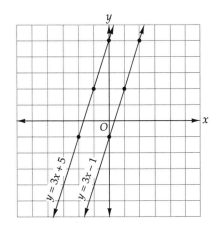

2 $y = \frac{2}{3}x - 2$ and $y = \frac{2}{3}x + 4$

The slope for both lines is $\frac{2}{3}$ and the

y-intercepts are -2 and 4.

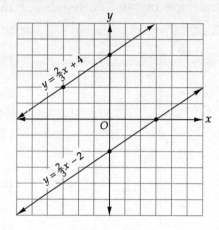

3 $y = -\frac{1}{3}x + 1$ and $y = -\frac{1}{3}x - 2$

The slope for both lines is $-\frac{1}{3}$ and

the y-intercepts are 1 and -2.

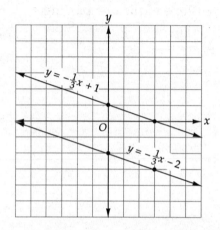

If two lines in the coordinate plane have slopes that are *negative reciprocals* of each other, then the two lines are **perpendicular**. The y-intercepts can be any real numbers. If two lines are *perpendicular*, then the product of their slopes is -1. For example, $\frac{3}{5} \bullet \left(-\frac{5}{3}\right) = -\frac{15}{15} = -1$. Exception: lines parallel to the x-axis (slope equal to 0) are perpendicular to the lines parallel to the y-axis (slope is undefined). The product is obviously not -1.

The graphs of the following pairs of linear equations are *perpendicular*.

1 $y = \frac{2}{3}x + 2$ and $y = -\frac{3}{2}x - 1$

The slopes are $\frac{2}{3}$ and $-\frac{3}{2}$.

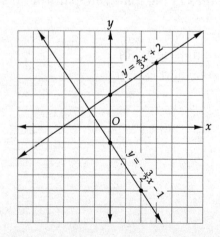

2 $y = -4x + 3$ and $y = \frac{1}{4}x + 1$

The slopes are -4 and $\frac{1}{4}$.

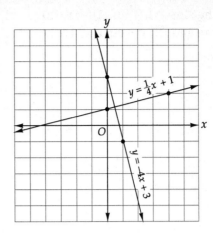

3 $y = x + 2$ and $y = -x + 2$

The slopes are 1 and -1.

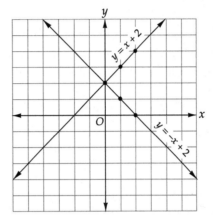

Note: In each case, to check that these are the correct graphs, find the x- and y-intercepts. That is, let $x = 0$, then solve for the y-intercept $(0, y)$ and for the x-intercept $(x, 0)$.

 Practice

Exercises 1–8: State whether the given lines are parallel, perpendicular, or neither. Solve for y if necessary.

1 $y = \frac{2}{3}x - 5$

$y = -\frac{2}{3}x + 5$

2 $y = 3x - 5$

$y = 3x + 7$

3 $y = 7$

$x = 6$

4 $y = 5x$

$y = -5x$

5 $4x - 5y = 20$

$15x + 12y = 60$

6 $3y + 5 = 14$

$y = -1$

7 $y = -\frac{1}{2}x - 1$

$x + 2y = -4$

8 $x + y = 9$

$y - x = 13$

Exercises 9–15: State the slope of a line that is (a) parallel to the given line and (b) perpendicular to the given line.

9 $y = 5x - 2$ ~~$5/1 \cdot 1/5$~~

10 $y = -2x + 7$

11 $y = -\dfrac{4}{3}x + 3$

12 $x - y = 6$

13 $4x + 6y = 12$

14 $x = 8$

15 $y = -3$

Using Slopes and Intercepts to Graph a Line

Every nonvertical line crosses the y-axis at one and only one point. The ordinate (y-value) of the point at which the line intersects the y-axis is called the **y-intercept of the line**. Since the abscissa (x-value) of any point on the y-axis is 0, we can easily find the y-intercept.

For example, if we substitute 0 for x in the equation $3x + 2y = 12$ and solve for y, we will get:

$$3(0) + 2y = 12$$
$$2y = 12$$
$$y = 6$$

Once again, if we substitute 0 for x in equation $y = -3x - 5$ and solve for y, we will get:

$$y = -3(0) - 5$$
$$y = -5$$

Lastly, consider the table of values for each of the three given graphs and their linear equations. The slopes and y-intercepts are easily found.

1 Equation: $y = 2x - 1$

x	0	1	2
y	−1	1	3

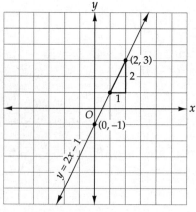

The slope is 2 or $\dfrac{2}{1}$ and the y-intercept is −1.

2 Equation: $y = -\dfrac{2}{3}x + 3$

x	−3	0	3
y	5	3	1

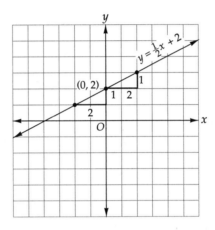

The slope is $-\dfrac{2}{3}$ and the y-intercept is 3.

3 Equation: $y = \dfrac{1}{2}x + 2$

x	−2	0	2
y	1	2	3

The slope is $\dfrac{1}{2}$ and the y-intercept is 2.

Slope-Intercept and Point-Slope Forms

Certain forms of a linear equation can provide enough information to easily graph the corresponding line.

Slope-Intercept Form   In several of the examples discussed in this and previous sections, the first step in graphing the equation was to solve the equation for y. You may have noticed that in each of these examples, the value of the slope happened to equal the coefficient of x, and the y-intercept equaled the numeric constant. These equalities are always true.

> If a linear equation is expressed in the form $y = mx + b$, then m represents the slope of the line and b represents the y-intercept. Thus, $y = mx + b$ is called the **slope-intercept form** of the equation.

For example, if $y = \dfrac{-2}{3}x + 4$, then the slope is $\dfrac{-2}{3}$ and the y-intercept is 4.

Conversely, if we are told that the slope of a line is $\dfrac{3}{4}$ and the y-intercept is -2,

then the equation of the line is $y = \dfrac{3}{4}x - 2$.

The slope-intercept form is the easiest form to use when a graph of the line is required. Using the last example, $y = \dfrac{3}{4}x - 2$, we can graph the y-intercept (-2), at the point $(0, -2)$. *Remember that b is the value of y where the graph crosses the y-axis.* To find a second point, use the slope, $m = \dfrac{3}{4}$. Remember that $\dfrac{3}{4} = \dfrac{\Delta y}{\Delta x}$. This means that when y changes $+3$, x changes $+4$. So starting at the y-intercept $(0, -2)$, the next point would be $(0 + 4, -2 + 3)$ or $(4, 1)$. Plot that point. We can repeat the procedure by adding 3 to y and 4 to x. The next point would then be $(8, 4)$. Plot that point and draw a line connecting the three points.

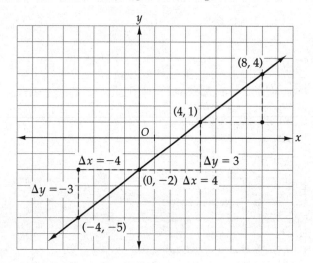

The slope-intercept form is the appropriate form for use with a graphing calculator.

Use $\boxed{Y=}$. Make sure the y-intercept is within your graphing window.

MODEL PROBLEMS

1 Find the slope and y-intercept of $4x + 3y = 3$.

SOLUTION

Solve for y.

$$4x + 3y = 3$$
$$3y = 3 - 4x$$
$$y = 1 - \dfrac{4}{3}x$$

Rewrite in slope-intercept form: $y = mx + b$.
$$y = -\dfrac{4}{3}x + 1$$

Answer: Slope $m = -\dfrac{4}{3}$ and y-intercept $b = 1$

2 Write the equation of a line in standard form if the slope is $-\dfrac{4}{5}$ and the y-intercept is 5.

SOLUTION

Begin with the slope-intercept form $y = mx + b$ and replace m with $-\dfrac{4}{5}$ and b with 5. Thus, $y = -\dfrac{4}{5}x + 5$. To change into standard form, add $\dfrac{4}{5}x$ to both sides.

Rewrite as $\dfrac{4}{5}x + y = 5$

Multiply every term by 5, so $4x + 5y = 25$

Answer: $4x + 5y = 25$

Point-Slope Form   Given the slope m of line l and the coordinates (x_1, y_1) of any point on the line, it is possible to write an equation for the line. Since the slope is the same for any two points on the line, we can let (x, y) represent another point on the line and write the slope as $m = \dfrac{y - y_1}{x - x_1}$. By cross multiplying we get $y - y_1 = m(x - x_1)$.

> If a line passes through the given point (x_1, y_1) and has slope m, the **point-slope form** of the equation of the line is $y - y_1 = m(x - x_1)$.

 MODEL PROBLEM

Given a line with point $P(4, 6)$ on the line and slope $m = 3$, write the correct linear equation in slope-intercept form.

SOLUTION

Substitute $(4, 6)$ in the slope equation $m = \dfrac{y - y_1}{x - x_1}$, and substitute 3 for m. $3 = \dfrac{y - 6}{x - 4}$

Multiply both sides by $x - 4$. $3(x - 4) = y - 6$

Remove parentheses. $3x - 12 = y - 6$

Rewrite the equation in slope-intercept form. $3x - 6 = y$

    or $y = 3x - 6$

 Practice

1   Which is the graph of $x + y = 5$?

(1)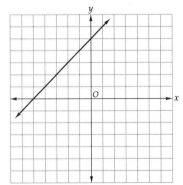

(3)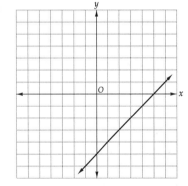

(2)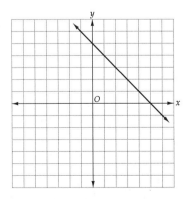

(4)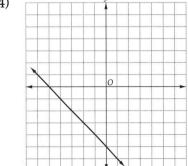

2 Which is the graph of $3y + 12x = 2$?

(1)

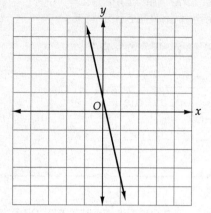

(2)

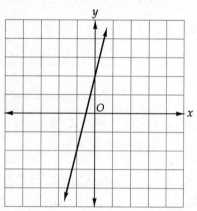

(3)

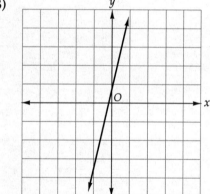

(4)

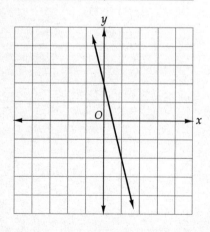

3 Which is the graph of $y - 3 = x - 5$?

(1)

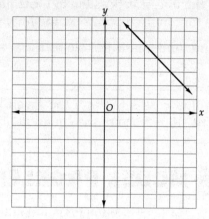

(2)

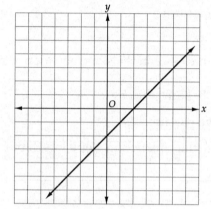

(3)

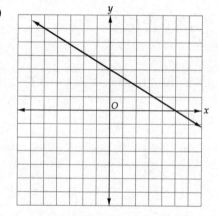

(4)

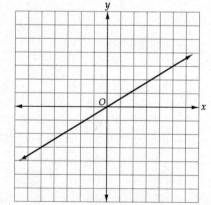

4 Which is the graph of $y - 2 = \frac{1}{3}(x - 3)$?

(1)
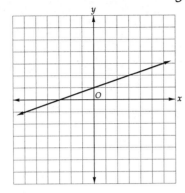

(3)
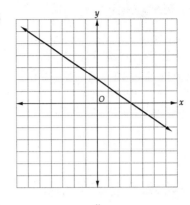

(2)
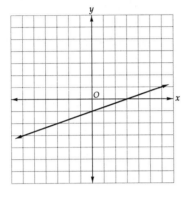

(4)
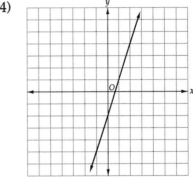

Exercises 5–12: Fill in the table.

	Equation	Solve for y	Slope	y-intercept
5	$2x + 2y = 6$			
6	$2x + 8y = 8$			
7	$3x - 3y = 12$			
8	$4x + 2y = 0$			
9	$10x + 7y = 7$			
10	$3x - y + 7 = 0$			
11	$-x + 3y = -9$			
12	$3y - 7 = 0$			

Exercises 13–16: Write an equation of the line whose slope and y-intercept are given, and graph the line.

13 Slope is 4 and y-intercept is 1. $y = 4x + 1$

14 Slope is $-\frac{1}{2}$ and y-intercept is 0.

15 Slope is -1 and y-intercept is 1. $y = -x + 1$

16 Slope is 0 and y-intercept is 6.

Exercises 17–20: Using the **point-slope form**, write an equation of the line with the given slope that passes through the given point. Transform the equation into the $y = mx + b$ form and graph.

17 $m = -2, (4, 2)$

18 $m = -\frac{1}{2}, (-4, -2)$

19 $m = \frac{2}{3}, (-3, 1)$

20 $m = \frac{3}{2}, (2, -2)$

Functional Notation and Direct Variation

Functional Notation

When we write the linear equation $y = 3x$, we are saying that y is a function of x.

If the symbol f stands for the word "function," then "y is a function of x" becomes $y = f(x)$ and, thus, $y = f(x) = 3x$. The notation $f(x)$ is read "f of x" or, sometimes, "f at x." The notation $f(x)$ *never* means the product of f and x.

Any letter may be used in functional notation, so that $g(x)$, $h(x)$, $F(x)$, etc., may each represent functions of x.

MODEL PROBLEMS

1 Evaluate the given function for $f(3)$, if $f(x) = x^2 - 5x$.

SOLUTION

Substitute 3 for the x-value:

$f(3) = 3^2 - 5(3) = 9 - 15 = -6$

Answer: -6

2 If $f(x) = 4x + 3$ and $f(x) = 23$, what is the value of x?

SOLUTION

Since, $f(x) = 23$, substitute 23 for $f(x)$ in the given equation $f(x) = 4x + 3$ and solve for x.

$23 = 4x + 3$

$20 = 4x$

$5 = x$

Answer: $x = 5$

Practice

1 If $f(x) = x^2 + 2x + 5$, what is the value of each of the following?

  a $f(10)$ 125   **e** $f(-1)$

  b $f(5)$ **f** $f(-2)$

  c $f(0)$ **g** $f\left(\dfrac{1}{2}\right)$

  d $f(1)$ **h** $f(-10)$

2 If $g(x) = 2x^3 - 1$, what is the value of each of the following?

  a $g(3)$ 53   **e** $g(-2)$

  b $g(2)$ **f** $g(1)$

  c $g(0)$ **g** $g\left(\dfrac{1}{2}\right)$

  d $g(-1)$ **h** $g(-3)$

3 If $f(x) = 4x + 3$ and $f(x) = 10$, what is the value of x?

4 If $f(x) = 2x + 7$ and $f(x) = -3$, then what is the value of x?

5 If $h(x) = x^2 + 4$ and $h(x) = 40$, find the value of x.

6 If $f(x) = 2x + 5$, then what is the value of $f(-9) - f(0)$?

7 If $f(x) = 20$ and $f(x) = 2x^2 - 80$, to the *nearest tenth*, what is the value of x?

8 If $m(x) = -6.7$ and $m(x) = x^2 - 2x - 6.7$, what are the values of x?

9 If $f(x) = 2x - 2$, what is the linear equation represented by $f(x - 1)$?

10 If $f(x) = x^2 + 5x$, what is the polynomial represented by $f(x + 2)$?

Direct Variation

There are several special cases of the linear function, $y = mx + b$ or $f(x) = mx + b$.

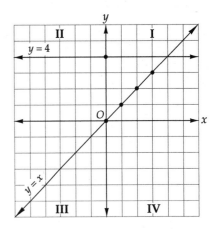

First, if $m = 0$, then we have the *constant function*, $y = 0x + b$ or $y = b$, which is graphed as a horizontal line, such as $y = 4$ in the figure on the right.

Second, if $m = 1$ and $b = 0$, then we have the *identity function*, $y = 1x + 0$ or $y = x$, as graphed in the figured on the right.

Third, and most important, if m is a nonzero constant and $b = 0$, then we have the function, $y = mx$, which is called a **direct variation**, and where m is called the *constant of variation*.

In Chapter 6, we discussed direct variation where k, rather than m, is the agreed symbol for the *constant of variation*. Thus, we will use $y = kx$ ($k \neq 0$) for direct variation. Lastly, the graph of every direct variation is a line that has a slope of $k = \dfrac{y}{x}$ and passes through the origin.

MODEL PROBLEMS

1 Determine whether the given table expresses a direct variation. Find the constant of variation and write the equation. Then graph the equation.

x	-6	-3	3	6	9
y	-4	-2	2	4	6

SOLUTION

In each case, the constant of variation, $\dfrac{y}{x}$, from $\dfrac{-4}{-6}$ to $\dfrac{6}{9}$, is $\dfrac{2}{3}$. Thus, the equation for $y = kx$ is $y = \dfrac{2}{3}x$ or $f(x) = \dfrac{2}{3}x$. All the given values lie on the graph of $y = \dfrac{2}{3}x$ and illustrate the direct variation.

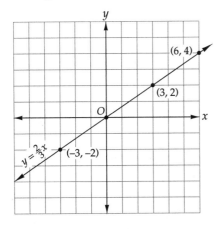

2 In the graph below, a straight line passes through the three indicated points.

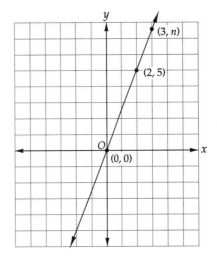

a Is this the graph of a direct variation?
b If it is, what is the constant of variation?
c What is the equation of the line?
d What is the value of n?

SOLUTION

a Since the y-intercept of this linear equation passes through the origin, this is a direct variation.

b The constant of variation, $y = \dfrac{y}{x} = \dfrac{5}{2}$.

c The equation of the line is $y = \dfrac{5}{2}x$ or $f(x) = \dfrac{5}{2}x$.

d Sub-in 3 for x and n for y and then solve. Thus, $n = \dfrac{5}{2} \cdot 3 = \dfrac{15}{2}$ or 7.5.

1 Determine which of the following equations express direct variation. State the constant of variation.

   a $y = 3x - 1$

   b $r = 4h$

   c $C = 2\pi r$

   d $y = 3x^2$

   e $\dfrac{3y}{x} = -9$

   f $\dfrac{x}{y} = -7$

   g $-2y = 8$

   h $\dfrac{y}{x} = \dfrac{3}{7}$

   i $-5y = -20x$

Exercises 2–6: Determine whether the given table expresses a direct variation. If it does, find the constant of variation. Write the equation in the form $y = kx$ and graph the equation using the given table of values.

2

x	2	4	5	6	8
y	−8	−16	−20	−24	−32

$K = -4$

3

x	−2	4	3	−1	5
y	−6	12	9	−3	15

4

x	2	4	6	8	10
y	4	6	10	16	24

5

x	5	10	15	20	25
y	1	2	3	4	5

6

x	−4	0	8	12	20
y	5	0	−10	−15	−25

Exercises 7–15: Set up proportions to express the direct variations involved and solve.

7 If the ABC Company paid a total dividend of $44 on 400 shares of its stock, how much of a dividend did it pay on 225 shares of stock?

8 Gas consumption is directly proportional to the distance traveled. If 21 gallons are used on a trip of 378 miles, then how far will the car travel on 7 gallons of gas?

9 If 7 cubic centimeters of blood contain 0.8 gram of hemoglobin, how many grams of hemoglobin can we expect to find in 9.8 cubic centimeters of blood?

10 If gasoline is used in an amount that varies directly as the time traveled, and if 3 gallons of gas are consumed in 1 hour and 15 minutes, how long (in hours and minutes) will 8 gallons of gas last?

11 If 24 square feet of a fabric weigh 50 ounces, what is the weight of a rectangular piece that is 12 feet long and 8 feet wide?

12 The distance from a lightning bolt is directly proportional to the time elapsed between seeing the lightning bolt and hearing the thunder. Thus, if you hear the thunder 7 seconds after you see the lightning bolt, then you are 1.5 miles away from the bolt. How far away is the bolt if you hear the thunder 2 seconds after you see the bolt?

13 A number, a, varies directly as the square of another number, m. If $a = 14$ when $m = 3$, what is the value of a when $m = 12$?

14 The distance necessary to stop a car varies directly as the *square* of its speed. If a car traveling 60 mph needs 144 feet to stop, what distance is required to stop a car going only 40 miles an hour? Give the answer in feet as well as in yards.

15 The amount of work done in a given time varies directly as the number of men employed.

   a Express this as a proportion.

   b If 18 men in 10 days can dig a 90-foot drainage ditch for water, how many men will be needed to dig a ditch 120 feet long in the same amount of time?

   c Draw the graph of a linear equation showing the relationship between the number of men and the number feet dug in 10 days.

Graphing First-Degree Inequalities in Two Variables

A line graphed in the coordinate plane divides the plane into two regions, called **half planes**. When the equation of the line is written in slope-intercept form or $y = mx + b$ form, the half plane *above* the line is the graph of $y > mx + b$ and the half plane *below* the line is the graph of $y < mx + b$. If a half-plane is to be included in a solution set, we show this by shading its entire region. The line itself, considered a **boundary line** (or plane divider), is drawn as a solid line when it is part of the solution set, and as a dashed line if it is not.

To Graph a Linear Inequality

- Graph the boundary line for the inequality by expressing the inequality as an equation in slope-intercept form or by creating a table of values.
  If the sign is $>$ or $<$, the boundary line will be broken or dashed.
  If the sign is $\geq$ or $\leq$, the boundary line will be solid.

- Shade the half plane of the inequality.

  Method 1: Select two points, one on each side of the boundary line, and substitute them into the inequality. Shade the half plane with the point that makes the inequality true.

  Method 2: Solve the inequality for y or for x.

    If the inequality begins with $y >$ or $y \geq$, shade the half plane *above* the boundary line. If the inequality begins with $y <$ or $y \leq$, shade the half-plane *below* the boundary line.

    If the inequality begins with $x >$ or $x \geq$, shade the half-plane to the *right* of the boundary line. If the inequality begins with $x <$ or $x \leq$, shade the half-plane to the *left* of the boundary line.

Note: If you solve without selecting points, check your answer by substituting the coordinates of a point in the given equation. The origin $(0, 0)$ is a point that is especially easy to use when determining on which side of a boundary line the graph is located.

 MODEL PROBLEMS

1 Graph $y > 2x + 1$ and $y < 2x + 1$.

SOLUTION

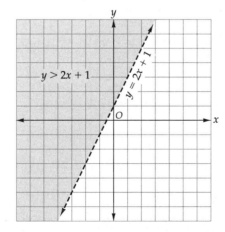

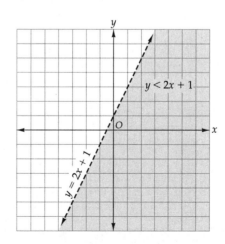

2 Graph $y \geq 2x + 1$ and check.

SOLUTION

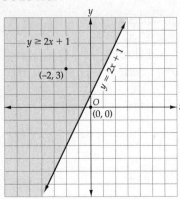

Check $(-2, 3)$ by substituting.

$$y \geq 2x + 1$$
$$3 \geq 2(-2) + 1$$
$$3 \geq -4 + 1$$
$$3 \geq -3 ✓$$

Check $(0, 0)$ from outside the solution set.

$$y \geq 2x + 1$$
$$0 \geq 2(0) + 1$$
$$0 \geq 0 + 1$$
$$0 \not\geq 1 \text{ (not in solution set) } ✓$$

3 Graph the inequality $x - 3y > 6$.

SOLUTION

Rewrite the inequality in $y = mx + b$ form:
$$x - 3y > 6$$
$$x - 6 > 3y \text{ or } 3y < x - 6$$
$$y < \frac{x}{3} - 2$$

Create a table of values for $y = \dfrac{x}{3} - 2$.

x	-3	0	3
y	-3	-2	-1

Graph the inequality.

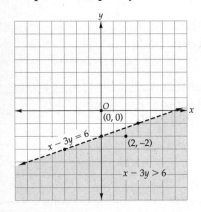

Check $(2, -2)$ by substituting.

$$x - 3y > 6$$
$$(2) - 3(-2) > 6$$
$$2 + 6 > 6$$
$$8 > 6 ✓$$

Check $(0, 0)$ from outside the solution set.

$$x - 3y > 6$$
$$(0) - 3(0) > 6$$
$$0 \not> 6 \text{ (not in solution set) } ✓$$

4 Graph $x > 3$ and $x \leq 3$ on separate coordinate planes.

SOLUTION

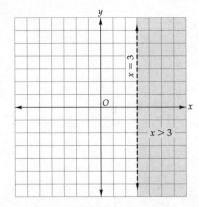

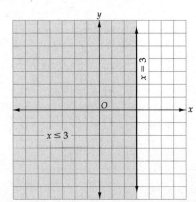

1 Which graph shows $y < 3x$?

(1)

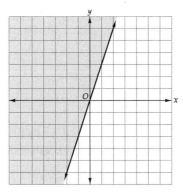

(2)

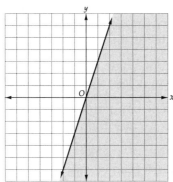

(3)

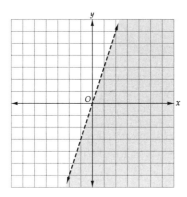

(4)

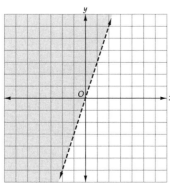

2 Which graph shows $y > -x - 1$?

(1)

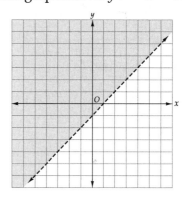

(2)

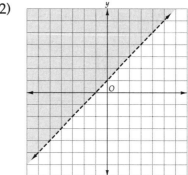

(3)

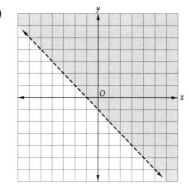

(4)

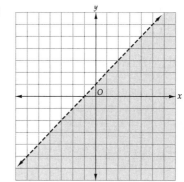

3 Which equation describes the shaded area of the graph?

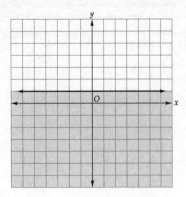

  (1) $y > 1$ **(3)** $y \leq 1$
  (2) $y < 1$ (4) $y \geq 1$

4 Which equation describes the shaded area of the graph?

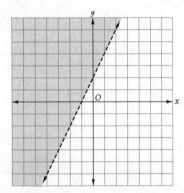

  (1) $y \leq \dfrac{1}{2}x + 2$

  (2) $y \geq -\dfrac{1}{2}x + 2$

  (3) $y < -2x + 2$

  (4) $y > 2x + 2$

Exercises 5–10: Solve for y. Graph each inequality in the coordinate plane.

5 $y \leq -2x$

6 $x + y \geq 1$

7 $2x + y > -4$

8 $2x - y < 3$

9 $x \leq 0$

10 $x < 1 + y + x$

Exercises 11–15: Write each verbal sentence as an open sentence and graph the inequality.

11 The ordinate of a point is greater than 2 less than the abscissa.

12 The sum of the abscissa and the ordinate of a point is greater than or equal to 4.

13 Twice the ordinate of a point decreased by the abscissa is less than or equal to -1.

14 The ordinate of a point decreased by half the abscissa is greater than 0.

15 The abscissa of a point decreased by the ordinate is less than or equal to 3.

Graphs Involving Absolute Value

The graph of the absolute value function $y = |x|$ can be found by setting up a table of values. For example,

x	-6	-4	-2	0	2	4	6
y	6	4	2	0	2	4	6

The graph of $y = |x|$ is a V-shaped union of two rays.

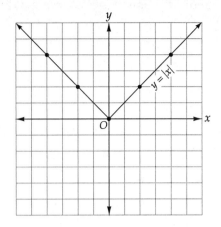

And the graph is symmetric with respect to the y-axis.

If we graph the three absolute value graphs $y = 2|x|$, $y = \frac{1}{2}|x|$, and $y = -|x|$ against the original $y = |x|$, we can see the effect clearly.

    a The graph of $y = 2|x|$ is *narrower* than $y = |x|$, and the slopes of the rays are 2 and -2.

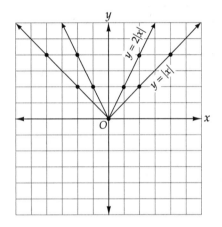

    b The graph of $y = \frac{1}{2}|x|$ is *wider* than $y = |x|$, and the slopes are $\frac{1}{2}$ and $-\frac{1}{2}$.

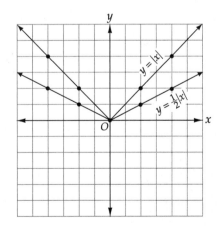

c The graph of $y = -|x|$ opens *downward* and has the same shape as $y = |x|$, with the vertex at the origin. Because the coefficient of $|x|$ is always negative here, the graph is an inverted V.

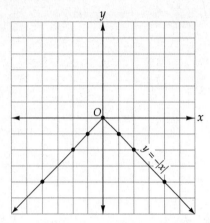

If we add or subtract constants from $|x|$, the graph moves *vertically*. The shape remains unchanged, as shown below in the graphs of $y = |x| + 4$ and $y = |x| - 2$ below. The vertex of $y = |x| + 4$ is $(0, 4)$ and the vertex of $y = |x| - 2$ is $(0, 2)$.

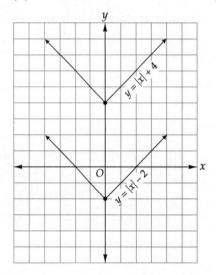

Lastly, if we add or subtract constants *inside* the absolute value sign, the graph slides *right* or *left* on the x-axis, as shown below in the graphs of $y = |x - 4|$ and $y = |x + 2|$.

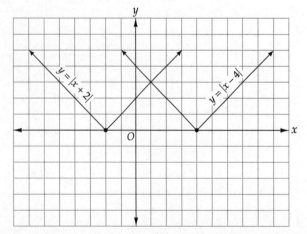

Note: Moving the graph $y = |x|$ by adding or subtracting constants *outside* or *inside* the absolute value sign is called a **translation**.

Exercises 1–3: Graph each of these in the coordinate plane.

1 $|y| = 3$

2 $|x - 2| = 1$

3 $|y + 3| = 1$

Exercises 4–15: Set up a table of values for x and y. Graph each function. Name the coordinate of the vertex.

4 $y = 2|x|$

5 $y = \frac{1}{4}|x|$

6 $y = |x| - 3$

7 $y = |x| + 2$

8 $y = |x + 3|$

9 $y = |x - 3|$

10 $y = -|x| + 2$

11 $y = |x| - 1$

12 $y = -|x + 2|$

13 $y = 3|x| + 1$

14 $y = |x + 1| + 2$

15 $y + 4 = |x + 5|$

Graphic Solutions of Real Situations

Graphs are used to represent relationships between two variables. They help us understand the relationships and often help us generalize beyond the data supplied. In functions, a value of y is assigned to each value of x. The primary relationship in a function is that the y-value depends on the x-value. For this reason, the x-axis is called the **independent axis** and the y-axis is called the **dependent axis**. The relationship can also be seen in terms of *slope*, as the rate of change between the *dependent* y-axis and the *independent* x-axis: $\frac{\text{dependent } \Delta y}{\text{independent } \Delta x}$.

Drawing the Graph of a Situation In dealing with real situations, it becomes necessary to think of the x-axis as some independent variable, such as time, and to think of the y-axis as a dependent variable, such as height or distance. Whenever it is clear that one variable depends on the other, the dependent variable should be the y and the independent variable should be the x. If a graph is comparing air pressure at different altitudes, then the pressure (y) depends on the altitude (x). But if a graph is charting a mountain climber's progress, then the altitude (y) depends on the time spent climbing (x).

It is important to label each axis of a graph you create.

Deluxe Limousine Service charges $2 for the initial pickup of a passenger and then $1 per mile. Make a graph of this situation.

SOLUTION

Note that the fee for the ride *depends* upon the number of miles traveled. Therefore, the fee will be represented by the variable y and distance will be represented by the variable x. The change per mile is the fraction that represents the change in price per change in miles traveled, or $\frac{\Delta y}{\Delta x}$, the slope, which equals $\frac{\$1}{1 \text{ mile}}$ or 1. The equation will then be $y = \$2 + \$1x$.

We can make a table of miles and fees for Deluxe Limousine Service. The label for the *x*-axis is *miles traveled* and the label for the *y*-axis is *taxi fee in dollars*.

Miles Traveled x	Taxi Fee in Dollars y
0	2
1	3
2	4

The graph starts where the number of miles traveled is 0. The fee at zero miles is $2. Thus the point (0, 2) is on the graph. A 1-mile trip costs $3 and a 2-mile trip costs $4. When we plot these points, we see a linear pattern. We can extend the graph in the first quadrant and we can read the fees for longer trips.

Answer:

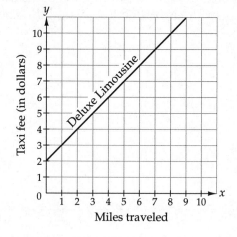

Note: The graph is in the first quadrant only. Why does the graph stop at the *y*-axis?

Reading the Graph of a Situation On any math exam, you may be given the graph of a situation and then asked various questions about the situation. When answering these questions, remember:

- Questions that involve rates (time per room painted, daily charge) or speeds (miles per hour, births per year) will usually require information about the slope.

- Questions that involve starting times, opening deposits, beginning locations, or similar **initial conditions** are usually asking questions about the *y*-intercept.

- Questions that start "When will…" or "How many…" usually provide a value for one variable and expect you to find the value for the other variable from the corresponding point on the graph.

MODEL PROBLEM

This graph represents the billing structure for Friendly Taxi. What is the initial pickup fee and charge per mile for this service?

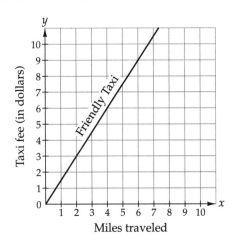

SOLUTION

The initial pickup fee is the charge before any driving is done, in other words when x is 0. The point on the graph with an x value of zero is the origin, $(0, 0)$. Therefore, the pickup fee is $0.

The charge per mile is the change in price per change in miles, or $\frac{\Delta y}{\Delta x}$, the slope. Two points on the line are $(0, 0)$ and $(2, 3)$, so $\frac{\Delta y}{\Delta x} = \frac{3 - 0}{2 - 0} = \frac{3 \text{ dollars}}{2 \text{ miles}} = 1.5$ dollars per mile.

Answer: There is no pickup fee, and the charge per mile is $1.50.

Situations Involving Graphs of Systems   When two equations are graphed on the same coordinate plane, many types of questions involve comparing the graphs.

- Questions that ask "When is situation A better/lower than situation B?" want you to find an inequality involving x that describes what part of the graph satisfies the situation. For example, the answer might be "When the time is longer than 5 days."
- Questions that ask "When are the values the same?" want you to find the coordinates of the point of intersection.
- Questions that ask about differences at specific values of x require you to subtract the y-value of one line from the other.

 MODEL PROBLEM

Deluxe Limousine Service charges $2 for the initial pickup of a passenger and then $1 per mile. By comparison, Friendly Taxi does not have an initial pickup charge but charges $1.50 per mile. Graph the fee schedule for Deluxe Limousine on the same coordinate plane as the graph for Friendly Taxi. Then answer the following questions:

   a For what length trips is it cheaper to use Friendly Taxi?

   b At what mileage is the cost the same for both services? What is the cost?

   c What is the difference in cost at the 6-mile mark?

SOLUTION

The graphs of the costs of each service were discussed earlier in this section. By graphing them on the same coordinate plane, you can answer the three questions.

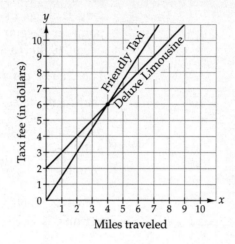

Miles traveled

Answers:

a The graph for Friendly Taxi is below the graph for Deluxe Limousine up to the 4-mile mark. So for trips under 4 miles long, it is cheaper to use Friendly Taxi.

b The lines intersect at (4, 6). So at 4 miles, the cost for both services is $6.

c At 6 miles, the graph shows the cost for Deluxe Limousine is $8 and the cost for Friendly Taxi is $9. The difference is $9 − $8 = $1.

 Practice

1 The graph represents the number of books read by Claire and Terry over a 4-week period. Who reads faster and by how much?

   (1) Claire reads 8 more books per week than Terry.
   (2) Claire reads 2 more books per week than Terry.
   (3) Claire reads 1 more book per week than Terry.
   (4) Claire reads twice as many books per week as Terry.

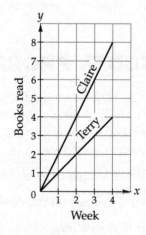

Week

2 Alyssa bicycled for 2 hours at 4 miles per hour. She stopped for one hour to visit a friend. She bicycled for another hour at 5 miles per hour. Which graph best represents Alyssa's trip if the horizontal axis is time and the vertical axis is distance?

(1)

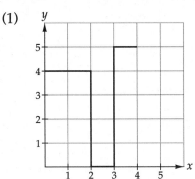

(2)

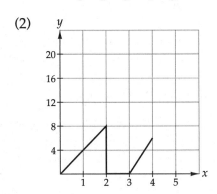

(3)

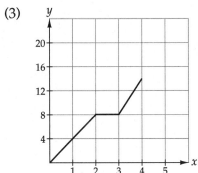

(4)

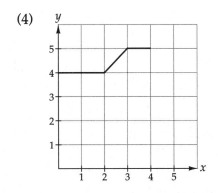

3 Both Janine and Fran used exercise equipment at their gym. Fran walked on a treadmill and Janine rode a stationary bicycle. Their times and calories burned are shown in the graph below. In calories burned per hour, how much faster was Janine than Fran?

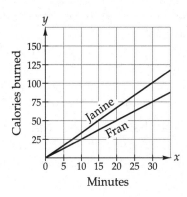

4 The figure below shows the cost of membership for two recreational clubs. For each club, the cost includes an initial fee to join the club plus a monthly charge.

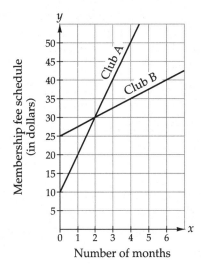

a What is the initial fee for Club A? For Club B?

b For which month will the total expenses be the same for both clubs? What is that total cost?

c What is the monthly charge for club A? For Club B?

5 Two different health clubs have the following rates. Sammy's Spa charges a flat fee of $350 a year for the use of the club, machines, the pool, and the classes. Shape Up! charges $150 a year for the use of the club, machines, and pool, plus $20 per exercise class.

   a Write an equation to represent each health club's yearly fees.

   b Graph each equation with appropriate labels for the axes.

   c Under what circumstances is it more economical to join Shape Up?

6 The graph below shows the relationship between the depreciated value (*v*) of a car (in thousands of dollars) and the passage of time (*t*).

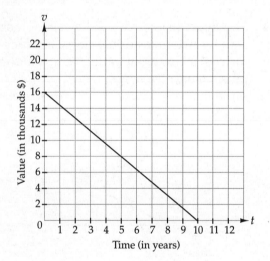

   a Write a linear equation to represent the depreciated value of the car.

   b Use that equation to find the value of the car after 4.5 years.

7 The graph below shows the relationship between the cost, *C*, (in thousands of dollars) of manufacturing DVD players and the number of DVD players produced, *N*.

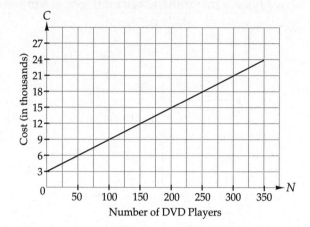

   a Write a linear equation to represent the cost of manufacturing the DVD players.

   b Use that equation to find the cost of manufacturing 300 DVD players.

8 George goes walking at noon at a rate of 3 miles an hour. At 2 P.M., Pete follows George on a bicycle at the rate of 5 miles an hour. The graph below shows both the time (in hours) and distance (in miles) of both George and Pete.

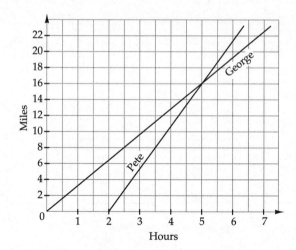

   a Write a linear equation to represent the distance traveled in terms of rate and time for each person.

   b After how many hours does Pete finally catch up to George?

   c After how many *more* hours will George be 8 miles behind Pete?

Exponential Functions: Growth and Decay

The graph of the exponential function $y = 2^x$ is shown below, along with a table that gives some of the values from this increasing function.

x	$y = 2^x$
-3	$2^{-3} = \dfrac{1}{2^3} = \dfrac{1}{8}$
-2	$2^{-2} = \dfrac{1}{2^2} = \dfrac{1}{4}$
-1	$2^{-1} = \dfrac{1}{2}$
0	$2^0 = 1$
1	$2^1 = 2$
2	$2^2 = 4$
3	$2^3 = 8$

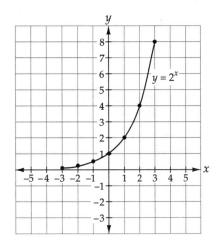

An exponential function can also illustrate a decrease, as with $y = \left(\dfrac{1}{2}\right)^x$. The graph of this decreasing function along with a table of values is given below.

x	$y = \left(\dfrac{1}{2}\right)^x$
-3	$\left(\dfrac{1}{2}\right)^{-3} = 2^3 = 8$
-2	$\left(\dfrac{1}{2}\right)^{-2} = 2^2 = 4$
-1	$\left(\dfrac{1}{2}\right)^{-1} = 2^1 = 2$
0	$\left(\dfrac{1}{2}\right)^0 = 1$
1	$\left(\dfrac{1}{2}\right)^1 = \dfrac{1}{2}$
2	$\left(\dfrac{1}{2}\right)^2 = \dfrac{1}{4}$
3	$\left(\dfrac{1}{2}\right)^3 = \dfrac{1}{8}$

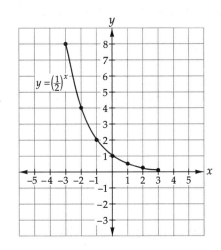

This concept of exponential growth and decay when applied to word problems, normally involve a quantity (some number) growing or decaying at a constant percentage over time. Typically, **exponential growth** focuses on populations, financial investments, or biological entities growing in size, while **exponential decay** is often found in the diminishing price of a product (as in the yearly loss of value of a car, called depreciation), the steady decrease in a population, or the radioactive decay of isotopes. Consider the following example.

EXAMPLE: If a population of 100 grows by 6% a year, how large will the population be in 20 years?

SOLUTION

While we could take the long route and multiply 100 by 0.06 and add that to 100, and take the result and again multiply by 0.06 and add that to the previous result. Or, still keeping to the long road, we could use this method:

Year 1 $100 \times 1.06 = 106$

Year 2 $100 \times 1.06 \times 1.06 = 100 \times (1.06)^2 = 112.36$

Year 3 $100 \times 1.06 \times 1.06 \times 1.06 = 100 \times (1.06)^3 = 119.10$

Etc.

However, by observing the pattern shown above, there is a shortcut, which is $100 \times (1.06)^{20} = 320.71$ or approximately 321 people.

In general, the formula for calculating *exponential growth* over a specific period of time, such as months, years, or decades, where the rate of growth is positive and the base for the exponent is greater than 1 (as in 1.06 in the example above), is:

original amount (dollars, population, etc.) $\times$ (1 + *growth rate*)$^{\text{(period of time or number of changes)}}$

Exponential decay, mathematically speaking, is the same as negative exponential growth. Instead of growing at a constant rate, the quantity *shrinks* at a constant rate. Exponential decay is a repeated percent decrease, so that the base of the exponent is less than 1. To calculate *exponential decay* we use the following:

original amount (dollars, population, etc.) $\times$ (1 − *decay rate*)$^{\text{(period of time or number of changes)}}$

Consider the following two formulas that are the most general forms of the exponential function, where a = original amount and b = the rate.

$y = a \cdot b^x$ represents **exponential growth** when $b > 1$
$y = a \cdot b^x$ represents **exponential decay** when $b < 1$

Note: In exponential decay, the *base* of the exponent is always less than 1.

1 The population of a town, which is now 6,000, increases 10% each year for five years.

   a To the nearest integer, what will be the total population after five years?

   b To the nearest integer, what will be the percent increase in population over the five years?

SOLUTION

Let P = the new total population
Let a = 6,000 (the original population)
Let b = 1 + 10% or (1 + 0.10)
Let x = 5, which is the number of years later.
Thus, to find P use the formula
$P = 6{,}000(1 + 0.10)^5$.
$P = 6{,}000(1.1)^5 = 6{,}000(1.61051) = 9{,}663.06$

   a Approximately 9,663 people.

   b Since the increase is 10% a year, then (1 + 0.10) to the 5th power should represent the percent increase over five years. Since $(1 + 0.10)^5 = 1.61$, the percent increase in the population is 61%

2 If the population of a town in 1920 was 1,000 and statistically seemed to *double* every 12 years, what should its expected population be in the year 2016?

SOLUTION

The starting number $1{,}000 = a$; the constant ratio (doubling) or base, $b = 2$; the number of times this should happen is the difference in years divided by 12, that is $\dfrac{2016 - 1920}{12} = \dfrac{96}{12} = 8$ times.

Therefore, $y = a \cdot b^x = 1{,}000(2^8) = 1{,}000(256) = 256{,}000$.

Answer: 256,000 people

3 A bank offers a savings account annual interest rate of 4.5% *compounded monthly*. The formula for simple compound interest is $A = p(1 + r)^t$, where A represents the final amount, p is the principal or original investment, and r is the annual rate. If $5,000 is placed in that account and no money is withdrawn, how much money (to the nearest dollar) would be in that account after two years?

SOLUTION

This is an exponential growth problem.

If the bank was providing only annual compounding, this problem would be very easy. We could just plug the numbers into the formula as follows:

$A = \$5{,}000 \times (1 + 0.045)^2 = \$5{,}460.13$

However, when we have *monthly compounding*, we must find the rate per month. First, divide the yearly rate by 12; $\dfrac{4.5\%}{12} = \dfrac{0.045}{12} = 0.00375$ per month. Second, since the compounding is occurring every month for two years, we must use 24 months as our exponent.

$A = \$5{,}000 \times (1 + 0.00375)^{24} = 5{,}000 \times (1.00375)^{24}$
$= \$5{,}469.9506 \approx \$5{,}470.$

Note: Over a two-year period, there is approximately a $10 difference between yearly compounding and monthly.

4 A piece of machinery that costs $8,000 depreciates each year by an amount equal to $\dfrac{1}{10}$ of its value at the beginning of the year. To the nearest dollar, how much will it be worth at the end of the fifth year?

SOLUTION

Since the machinery loses $\dfrac{1}{10}$ or 10% or 0.1 of its value each year, that means this is an exponential decay (depreciation) situation. The formula that models this situation is $V(\text{value}) = a(\text{cost}) \times b(\text{rate})^t$, where t is time in years. Since a is 8,000, b is (1 − 0.10), and the exponent is 5, by substitution, $V = 8{,}000 \times (1 - 0.10)^5 = 8{,}000 \times (0.9)^5 = \$4{,}723.92.$

Answer: $4,724, to the nearest dollar

5 The growth of a certain strain of bacteria is modeled by the equation $N = B(1 + r)^t$, where N represents the final number of bacteria, B is the initial number of bacteria, t is the time in hours, and r is the rate of growth per hour. After 11 hours, how many bacteria will there be if there were 8 to begin with and the rate of growth is 80%? Round your answer to the nearest hundred.

SOLUTION

Substitute 8 for B, 11 for t, and 0.8 for r in the equation:

$N = 8(1 + 0.8)^{11} = 8(1.8)^{11} = 8(642.684) = 5{,}141.5$

Answer: To the nearest hundred, there are 5,100 bacteria.

 Practice

---

1 On the same coordinate system and for the interval $-3 \le x \le 3$, sketch each graph (**a** to **d**) and compare the results. Make sure your answer includes the following:

  (i) What point is common to all the graphs?

  (ii) If the base is greater than 1, describe the direction of the curve.

  (iii) If the base is less than 1, describe the direction of the curve.

  a $y = 3^x$

  b $y = 4^x$

  c $y = \left(\dfrac{2}{3}\right)^x$

  d $y = \left(\dfrac{1}{3}\right)^x$

2 The cost of maintenance on an automobile increases each year by 8%. If Alberto paid $400 this year for maintenance for his car, what will the cost be (to the nearest dollar) seven years from now?

3 The population of a large herd of 6,000 buffalo increases at a rate of 20% each year. How close to *triple* its present size will the population of buffalo be in 6 years?

4 Depreciation (the decline in cash value) on a car can be determined by the formula $V = c(1 - r)^t$, where V represents the value of the car after t years, c is the original cost, and r is the rate of depreciation. If the car cost $25,000 when new and the rate of depreciation is 8%, what is value of the car after 4.5 years?

5 If the population of a town in 1850 was 250 and it increased by 60% every 25 years, what will the population be in the year 2025?

6 A used car was purchased in July 1999 for $12,900. If the car depreciates 14% of its value each year, what is the value of the car (to the nearest hundred dollars) in July 2003?

7 An Impressionist painting increases in value at an average rate of 9% a year. If the original cost of the painting to the Museum of Modern Art was $1,500, what was the value of the painting (to the nearest dollar) at the end of a 20-year holding period?

8 A beach ball loses 5% of its air every day. If the beach ball originally contained 4,000 cubic centimeters of air, how many cubic centimeters of air does it hold after 8 days? Give the answer to the nearest integer.

9 A ball rebounds one-half the distance that it falls. If the ball is dropped from a height of 512 feet, how high does it go on its 8th rebound?

10 The value of an early American coin increase in value at the rate of 6.5% annually. If the purchase price of the coin this year is $1,950, what is its value to the nearest dollar in 15 years?

1 Which graph does *not* represent a function?

(1)

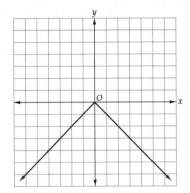

(2)

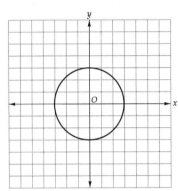

(3)

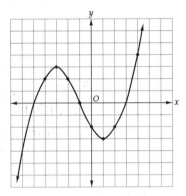

(4)

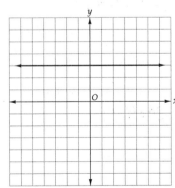

2 What is the slope of the line in the graph?

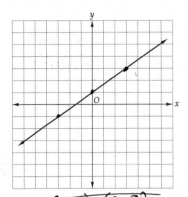

(1) $\frac{3}{2}$

(2) 1

(3) $\frac{2}{3}$

(4) $-\frac{2}{3}$

(handwritten) (0,1) (3,3)
$\frac{3-1}{}$
$(-3,-1)(3,3)$
$\frac{3+1}{3+3}$ $\frac{4}{6}$

3 If the point $A(x, -y)$ is in quadrant IV, then which of the following is correct?

(1) $x > 0, y > 0$
(2) $x > 0, y < 0$
(3) $x < 0, y > 0$
(4) $x < 0, y < 0$

4 Which point does *not* lie on the graph of $4x - y = 8$?

(1) $(0, -8)$
(2) $(2, 0)$
(3) $(1, -4)$
(4) $(-3, 4)$

(handwritten)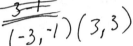
$4x-y=8$
$y=4x-8$

5 Which ordered pair is *not* in the solution set of $y > 3x - 3$?

(1) $(-1, -1)$
(2) $(0, -3)$
(3) $(1, 1)$
(4) $(-2, 2)$

6 If x varies directly as y and $x = 2.4$ when $y = 6$, which is a possible ordered pair for (x, y)?

(1) $(24, 6)$
(2) $(0.4, 1)$
(3) $(0.4, 2.5)$
(4) $(1, 2.4)$

(handwritten) ✱ 1,2,4,8,9,11,21,22
25,26,28A,29A

7 If $-|m| = m$, then which of the following is true?

    (1) $m = 0$
    (2) $m \leq 0$
    (3) $m \geq 0$
    (4) $m < 0$

8 Name the quadrant that contains each of the following:
$2(-,+)|(+,+)\ 1$
$3\ F(-)|(+,-)\ 4$

    a $(-4, 3)$ 2
    b $(3, -4)$ 4
    c $(3, 4)$ 1
    d $(-4, -3)$ 3

9 Find the ordinate of a point on the graph of $y = \frac{1}{2}x - 5$ if the abscissa is 12. $x=6$ $y=1$

10 What is the value of c so that the line $y = 5x + c$ will pass through the point $(3, 7)$?

11 Categorize the slope of the seven lines $(a–g)$ in the figure slope as positive, negative, zero, or undefined.

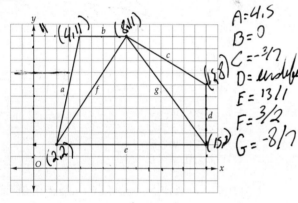

$A = 4.5$
$B = 0$
$C = -3/7$
$D = $ undefined
$E = 13/1$
$F = 3/2$
$G = -8/7$

12 What is the slope of the line representing the equation $x + 3y + 6 = 0$?

Exercises 13–16: Create a table of at least three value pairs for each equation. Graph the line using those ordered pairs. State the x- and y-intercepts.

13 $5y = 9x$

14 $2x - y = 4$

15 $3y = 2x + 1$

16 $12 - 4y = 2x$

Exercises 17–20: State the intersection point of each given pair of lines.

17 $x = 5, y = -3$

18 $x = -3, y = 7$

19 the x-axis and the y-axis

20 $x = -1, y = -4$

21 What is the slope of the line $y = 8$? 0

22 What is the slope of the line $x = -2$? undefined

23 If two points on line h are $(-2, 3)$ and $(4, -1)$ and two points on line k are $(1, 1)$ and $(3, 4)$, is it true that lines h and k are perpendicular? Support your conclusion.

24 The graph below illustrates a demand curve, where the demand, d, varies with the change in price, p, the independent variable.

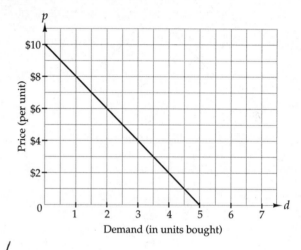

    a Write a linear equation to represent the relationship of price and demand.

    b Find the *demand* for the product when the price is $6.

Exercises 25–27: Examine each relation and determine (a) the domain, (b) the range, and (c) identify which relations are functions.
$D=(2,4)$ not a function
$R=(-4,-2,3)$

25 $\{(2, -2), (4, 3), (2, -4)\}$

26 $\{(-2, -2), (7, -6), (3, -6)\}$ $D=(-2,7,3)$ $R=(-2,6)$

27 $\{(-1, 4), (-2, 5), (-3, 5), (-4, 4)\}$ yes

28 If $f(x) = 3x - 2$, what is the value of

    a $f(-4)$ $3(-4)-2 = -14$
    b $f(0)$
    c $f(-1)$
    d $f(x - 1)$

29 If $g(x) = x^2 + 4$, what is the value of

    a $g(-2)$ $-2^2+4 = 8$
    b $g(0)$
    c $g(-1)$
    d $g(x + 1)$

30 If an investor deposits $8,000 into an account that earns 7% interest compounded semiannually, what is the value of the investment after 5 years? (Compound interest formula: $A = P(1 + r)^t$)

31 If line k is represented by the linear equation $y = 2x - 1$ and line r is represented by the linear equation $y = -\dfrac{2}{5}x + 2$

   a Identify the slope of line k and line r.

   b What are the x-intercept and y-intercept of line k and of line r?

   c Write a linear equation *parallel* to line k and another equation *parallel* to line r.

   d Write a linear equation *perpendicular* to line k and another equation *perpendicular* to line r.

   e If point $(10, y)$ lies on line k and point $(x, -3)$ lies on line r, what is the missing y-coordinate for line k and the missing x-coordinate for line r?

Exercises 32–40: Graph the following equations and inequalities.

32 $y = \dfrac{3}{2}x$

33 $y = -\dfrac{2}{3}x$

34 $x + 3y = 12$

35 $y = -\dfrac{1}{2}x + 3$

36 $3y - 9x > 6$

37 $2x - y \geq 6$

38 $y = |x| - 3$

39 $y = |x + 3|$

40 $y = |x - 3| - 3$

Now turn to page 437 and take the Cumulative Review test for Chapters 1–9. This will help you monitor your progress and keep all your skills sharp.

CHAPTER 10

Systems of Linear Functions

Writing Equations Using (a) the Slope and One Point, and (b) the Slope and Y-Intercept

In Chapter 9, we learned that sometimes partial information is enough for us to determine whether two lines are perpendicular or parallel. The slope of each line is enough for us to determine if the lines are parallel (same slopes) or perpendicular (negative reciprocal slopes).

We can use any one of the following to determine the equation of the line:

a) the slope m and one point (x, y)
b) the slope m and the y-intercept $(0, y)$
c) two points (x_1, y_2) and (x_2, y_2)
d) the y-intercept $(0, y)$ and any other point (x, y)

For part (a) of this section, recall that in Chapter 9, we learned how to graph a line when given the slope m and one point (x, y). We also learned how to write the linear equation with that information. For example, if the slope m is $\frac{2}{3}$ and the point (x, y) is $(6, -4)$, then simply substitute that information into $y = mx + b$ and solve for b. Thus, $-4 = \frac{2}{3}(6) + b$, and $-4 = 4 + b$, so $-8 = b$. The linear equation is now $y = \frac{2}{3}x - 8$.

For part (b) of this section, to write the linear equation of a line when given the slope m and the y-intercept $(0, y)$, we can substitute those values for m and b in the equation $y = mx + b$. For example, if $m = -2$ and the y-intercept is $(0, 5)$, then $y = -2x + 5$. We can also change the equation into the form $Ax + By = C$, where A, B, and C are integers.

MODEL PROBLEMS

1 If the slope $m = \dfrac{1}{3}$, and the y-intercept is $(0, -2)$, write the linear equation in the form $y = mx + b$ and then change the answer into $Ax + By = C$ form.

SOLUTION

Substitute the given data where $m = \dfrac{1}{3}$ and $b = -2$ into $y = mx + b$ so that the linear equation is $y = \dfrac{1}{3}x + (-2)$. To put the equation in the form $Ax + By = C$, just multiply each term by 3, so that A, B, and C are integers. We now have $3y = x - 6$ and $-x + 3y = -6$, so that $A = -1$, $B = 3$, and $C = -6$.

Note: If we multiply by -1, this last equation can also be written as $x - 3y = 6$, where $A = 1$, $B = -3$, and $C = 6$.

2 Write the equation of the line parallel to $2y = x + 3$ and passing through the point $(6, -2)$.

SOLUTION

First, solve for y. $y = \dfrac{1}{2}x + \dfrac{3}{2}$. Since the new line is parallel, it has the *same slope, $m = \dfrac{1}{2}$*. Using the point-slope method, $y - (-2) = \dfrac{1}{2}(x - 6)$ and $y + 2 = \dfrac{1}{2}x - 3$. Thus, $y = \dfrac{1}{2}x - 5$.

3 Write the equation of the line perpendicular to $3y = -2x - 3$ and passing through the point $(2, -1)$.

SOLUTION

First, solve for y. $y = -\dfrac{2}{3} - 1$. Since the new line is perpendicular, the slope is the *negative reciprocal* of $-\dfrac{2}{3}$, which is $\dfrac{3}{2}$. Again, using the point-slope method, $y - (-1) = \dfrac{3}{2}(x - 2)$ and $y + 1 = \dfrac{3}{2}x - 3$. Thus, $y = \dfrac{3}{2}x - 4$.

Practice

1 Which pair of lines are parallel?

    (1) $y = 4x - 9$ and $y + 4x = 3$
    (2) $y = 3x + 7$ and $y + 2 = 3(x - 5)$
    (3) $y = 2x$ and $2y = x - 9$
    (4) $y + x = 0$ and $y = x$

2 Which pair of lines are perpendicular?

    (1) $y = 4x - 9$ and $y - 4x = 3$
    (2) $y = 3x + 7$ and $y + 2 = 3(x - 5)$
    (3) $y = 2x$ and $2y = x - 9$
    (4) $y + x = 0$ and $y = x$

3 Which line passes through (2, 3) with a slope of −2?

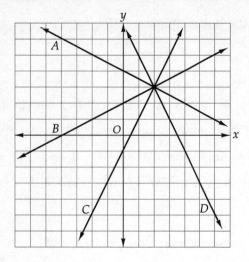

(1) line *A*   (3) line *C*
(2) line *B*   (4) line *D*

Exercises 4–9: State the slope and *y*-intercept for each equation.

4 $y = 3x - 2$

5 $2y = 5x - 6$

6 $3y - x = 12$

7 $2x + 3y = 0$

8 $5y - 4 = 0$

9 $5x - 3y + 6 = 0$

Exercises 10–15: Given the slope and a point, write the equation of a line in $y = mx + b$ form.

10 $m = 5$, *y*-intercept = (0, 3)

11 $m = -3$, $b = 5$

12 $m = -\dfrac{2}{3}$, $b = \dfrac{1}{2}$

13 $m = -\dfrac{1}{3}$, *y*-intercept = (0, 0)

14 $m = 0$, $b = 4$ $y = 4$

15 $m = \dfrac{3}{5}$, *y*-intercept = $\left(0, -\dfrac{1}{2}\right)$

Exercises 16–20: Given the slope and a point, write the equation of a line.

16 slope = $-\dfrac{2}{3}$; (−9, −1)

17 $m = 0$; (2, −5)

18 $m = 3$; (4, −2)

19 slope = $\dfrac{2}{5}$; (−5, −4)

20 slope = $-\dfrac{2}{3}$; (−1, 2)

Exercises 21–27: Write the equation for each line.

21 a line parallel to the *y*-axis and passing through the point (3, 5)

22 a line parallel to the *x*-axis and passing through the point (3, 5)

23 a line parallel to $3y - 4x = 6$ with $b = -3$

24 a line perpendicular to the line $y = -2x + 5$ and containing point (3, 1)

25 a line perpendicular to the line $y = \dfrac{3}{2}x - 2$ and containing the point (1, −4)

26 a line through the point (−1, −5) and perpendicular to the line $y = x$

27 a line through the point (2, 2) and perpendicular to the line $5x - 4y = 0$

Exercises 28–30: For each equation, (a) use the given coordinates (*x*, *y*) to find the value of *k*. (b) Substitute the value for *k* and find the *y*-intercept of the equation.

28 $y = 2x + k$ and $(x, y) = (-2, 1)$

29 $5x = 3y - k$ and $(x, y) = (4, 2)$

30 $4x + 3y = k$ and $(x, y) = (-1, -2)$

Writing Equations Using (c) Two Points, and (d) the *Y*-Intercept and a Point

For part (c) of this section, to find the equation of a line from two points, (x_1, y_1) and (x_2, y_2), there are two methods:

Method 1

- Use the two points to find slope *m* of the line.
- Use slope *m* and either one of the given points to substitute in the slope-intercept formula: $y = mx + b$.
- Solve for *b*, the *y*-intercept.
- Substitute the values for *m* and *b* in $y = mx + b$.

Method 2

- Use the two points to find slope *m* of the line.
- Then use slope *m* and either one of the given points to substitute in the point-slope formula: $y - y_1 = m(x - x_1)$
- Simplify and change into $y = mx + b$ form.
- Use the slope and the *y*-intercept to graph the equation.

 MODEL PROBLEM

Find the equation of the line that joins the points (1, 3) and (2, 5).

SOLUTION

METHOD 1 (Slope-Intercept)

Substitute and find slope *m*:

$$m = \frac{y_2 - y_1}{x_2 - x_1} = \frac{5 - 3}{2 - 1} = \frac{2}{1} \text{ or } 2$$

Now substitute 2 for slope *m*, and point (1, 3) for (*x, y*) in the slope-intercept formula $y = mx + b$. Solve for *b*:

$3 = 2(1) + b$, and $b = 1$

Once again, substitute 2 for *m*, and 1 for *b* in $y = mx + b$:

The equation of the line is $y = 2x + 1$.

Check by substituting the coordinates of one of the points for (*x, y*) in the equation of the line.

METHOD 2 (Point-Slope)

Substitute and find the slope *m*:

$$m = \frac{y_2 - y_1}{x_2 - x_1} = \frac{5 - 3}{2 - 1} = \frac{2}{1} \text{ or } 2$$

Now substitute 2 for slope *m* and point (1, 3) for (x_1, y_1) in the point-slope formula:

$$y - y_1 = m(x - x_1)$$
$$y - 3 = 2(x - 1)$$

If we had chosen the point (2, 5), then

$$y - y_1 = m(x - x_1)$$
$$y - 5 = 2(x - 2)$$

In fact, these are dependent lines; that is, they have the same graph. If we convert each equation to slope-intercept form, the result is the same equation.

$y - 3 = 2(x - 1)$	$y - 5 = 2(x - 2)$
$y - 3 = 2x - 2$	$y - 5 = 2x - 4$
$y = 2x + 1$	$y = 2x + 1$

For part (d) of this section, to find the equation of a line from the y-intercept $(0, y)$ and a point (x, y), there are two methods:

Method 1

- Use the two points to find the slope m of the line.
- Sub in the y-value of the intercept for b and the value for m in the equation $y = mx + b$.

Method 2

- Sub in the y-value of the intercept for b in the equation $y = mx + b$.
- Sub in the given coordinates for x and y in the equation $y = mx + b$.
- Solve the equation for the slope m.
- Rewrite the equation $y = mx + b$ and sub in the values for m and b.

 MODEL PROBLEM

Find the equation of the line if the y-intercept is $(0, 6)$ and the line passes through the point $(2, -4)$.

SOLUTION

METHOD 1

Use $(0, 6)$ and $(2, -4)$ and find the slope $m = \dfrac{6 - (-4)}{0 - 2} = \dfrac{10}{-2} = -5$.

Now sub in 6 for b and -5 for m so that $y = -5x + 6$.

METHOD 2

Use $y = mx + b$ and substitute 6 for b and $(2, -4)$ for (x, y) and solve for m.

$-4 = m(2) + 6,\ -10 = 2m,\ m = -5$

Now use $y = mx + b$ again and sub in 6 for b and -5 for m: $y = -5x + 6$.

 Practice

1 Which equation passes through $(3, -5)$ and $(-1, 3)$?

  (1) $y + 5 = x - 3$
  (2) $y = 2x + 1$
  (3) $y - 3 = -2(x + 1)$
  (4) $y = x + 2$

Exercises 2–5: Write an equation of the line that passes through the given points.

 2 $(1, 3)$ and $(-2, -6)$

 3 $(6, 1)$ and $(-4, -4)$

 4 $(4, 0)$ and $(2, -2)$

 5 $(7, 4)$ and $(1, 1)$

Exercises 6–15: Write the linear equation determined by the following pairs of points. Put your answer in $y = mx + b$ form and then $Ax + By = C$, where A, B, and C are integers.

 6 $(3, 5)$ and $(4, 7)$

 7 $(-2, 3)$ and $(1, 5)$

 8 $(2, 1)$ and $(3, 2)$

 9 $(5, -3)$ and $(0, 0)$

10 $(5, -7)$ and $(-3, 1)$

11 $(1, 5)$ and $(3, 5)$

12 $(5, 1)$ and $(-7, -11)$

13 $(-5, 1)$ and $(0, -2)$

14 $(2, 3)$ and $(2, 5)$

15 $(-1, -2)$ and $(2, 2)$

16 If the vertices of triangle *ABC* are located at $(2, -2)$, $(6, 4)$, and $(-4, 2)$, what are the slopes of the three lines that determine the triangle?

17 If the vertices of triangle *RST* are located at $(-4, 0)$, $(2, 3)$, and $(4, -1)$, what are the slopes of the three lines that determine the triangle?

Exercises 18–25: Write the linear equation determined by the following information.

18 *y*-intercept $(0, 3)$ and point $(1, 2)$

19 *y*-intercept $(0, -2)$ and point $(2, 5)$

20 $b = 5$ and point $(3, -2)$

21 $b = -4$ and point $(3, 1)$

22 *y*-intercept $(0, 0)$ and point $(-2, 5)$

23 *y*-intercept $(0, 4)$ and point $(-2, -2)$

24 $b = -3$ and point $(-1, -3)$

25 $b = -1$ and point $(3, 4)$

Writing Equations Using the X-Intercept and Y-Intercept

Using the *x*-intercept and *y*-intercept is simply another version of the conditions we studied in the previous section: using two points (x_1, y_1) and (x_2, y_2) to determine a linear equation.

If the *x*-intercept is $(x, 0)$ and the *y*-intercept is $(0, y)$, then these two points can be used to find the slope: $m = \dfrac{\Delta y}{\Delta x} = \dfrac{0 - y}{x - 0} = \dfrac{-y}{x}$.

For example, if the *x*-intercept is $(3, 0)$ or $x = 3$ and the *y*-intercept is $(0, -5)$ or $y = -5$, then $m = \dfrac{-y}{x} = \dfrac{-(-5)}{3} = \dfrac{5}{3}$. Since the *y*-intercept, -5, is also b, using the slope-intercept form, $y = mx + b$, the linear equation is $y = \dfrac{5}{3}x - 5$.

Of course, given an equation such as $2x + 3y = 4$, finding the *x*- and *y*-intercepts is easy. To find the *x*-intercept, substitute 0 for *y*. Thus, $2x + 3(0) = 4$, and $2x = 4$ and $x = 2$. To find the *y*-intercept, or *b*, substitute 0 for *x*. Thus, $2(0) + 3y = 4$, and $3y = 4$, and $y = b = \dfrac{4}{3}$.

 MODEL PROBLEMS

1 Write the equation of the line where the *x*-intercept is $(2, 0)$ and the *y*-intercept is $(0, -4)$.

SOLUTION

Since the intercepts are $(2, 0)$ and $(0, -4)$, the slope is $\dfrac{-y}{x} = \dfrac{-(-4)}{2} = 2$.

Now sub in -4 for *b* and 2 for the slope *m*. The equation is $y = 2x - 4$.

2 Write an equation of a line whose *x*-intercept is $\left(\dfrac{5}{2}, 0\right)$ and *y*-intercept is $(0, -5)$.

SOLUTION

Since the *x*-intercept is $\dfrac{5}{2}$ and the *y*-intercept is -5, the slope $\dfrac{-y}{x} = \dfrac{-(-5)}{\dfrac{5}{2}} = 5 \times \dfrac{2}{5} = 2$.

Now sub in -5 for *b* and 2 for the slope *m*. The equation is $y = 2x - 5$.

1 What are the x- and y intercepts of $x = 2$?

    (1) (2, 0) and (0, 2)
    (2) (2, 0) and (0, 0)
    (3) (2, 0) and no y-intercept
    (4) no x-intercept and (0, 2)

2 What are the x- and y-intercepts of $y = -3$?

    (1) (0, 0) and (0, -3)
    (2) no x-intercept and (0, -3)
    (3) (-3, 0) and (0, -3)
    (4) (-3, 0) and no y-intercept

Exercises 3–15: Find the x- and y-intercepts of the following equations.

3 $x + 2y = 2$

4 $3x - y = 9$

5 $2x - 5y = 20$

6 $2x + 3y = 12$

7 $5y = 2x - 15$

8 $y = \dfrac{3}{5}x + 5$

9 $y = 10$

10 $4y + 4 = 5x$

11 $y - 5 = -2x$

12 $8 - x = 2y$

13 $y = \dfrac{1}{4}x - 2$

14 $y = -\dfrac{2}{3}x + 3$

15 $3x + y - 3 = 0$

Exercises 16–25: Given the x- and y- intercepts, write the linear equation.

16   (2, 0) and (0, -6)

17 $\left(\dfrac{1}{2}, 0\right)$ and $\left(0, \dfrac{4}{3}\right)$

18   (4, 0) and (0, 1)

19   (3, 0) and $\left(0, -\dfrac{1}{2}\right)$

20   (-5, 0) and (0, -3)

21 $\left(\dfrac{2}{3}, 0\right)$ and $\left(0, \dfrac{1}{2}\right)$

22   (-1, 0) and (0, -6)

23   (-2, 0) and (0, -2)

24 $\left(-\dfrac{3}{4}, 0\right)$ and (0, -1)

25   (1, 0) and $\left(0, -\dfrac{2}{3}\right)$

Using Graphs to Solve Systems of Linear Equations

Systems of Linear Equations

Often, math problems will include information relating two variables without providing a value for either variable. To find a solution, we need two sets of information in the form of equations.

    Suppose that the perimeter of a rectangular vegetable patch is 12 feet and the length is twice the width. If we let x represent the width and y represent the length, we know that $2x + 2y = 12$, or $x + y = 6$. We also know that $y = 2x$. The two equations, $x + y = 6$, and $y = 2x$, are called a **system of simultaneous linear equations**. While neither equation alone is enough to find the dimensions of the rectangle, they can be solved together either graphically or algebraically.

In graphing simultaneous equations in the same coordinate plane, we must remember that

- each straight line graph is the solution set for one of the equations and
- every point on each graph represents the (x, y) values that satisfy the given equation

To Solve Simultaneous Linear Equations Graphically

- Draw the graph of each equation on the same coordinate plane.
- The coordinates of the point of intersection of the graphs are the required values of x and y.
- Check the solution in both original equations.

To find the dimensions of the vegetable patch, we graph the two equations on the same coordinate plane.

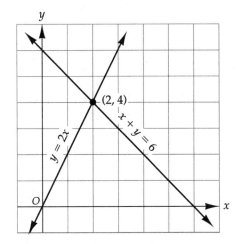

Check the solution $(2, 4)$ in both original equations:

$$x + y = 6 \qquad y = 2x$$
$$2 + 4 = 6 \qquad 4 = 2(2)$$
$$6 = 6 \checkmark \qquad 4 = 4 \checkmark$$

To graph the two linear equations above using a graphing calculator, follow the keystrokes listed below.

First graph the two linear equations by inputting the equations into Y_1 and Y_2:

[Y=] [2] [X, T, θ, n] [ENTER] [(-)] [X, T, θ, n] [+] [6] [GRAPH]

Then find the point of intersection:

[2nd] [CALC] [5] [ENTER]

Thus, two linear equations in a system can have

(1) exactly *one* solution
(2) *no* solution
(3) *infinitely many* solutions

In addition to the number of solutions, linear systems are classified as consistent, inconsistent, or dependent.

(1) If two distinct lines intersect, the values of x and y at that *one point* are the unique coordinates that make both equations true. This linear system is said to be **consistent**.

(2) If two distinct lines have the same slope but different *y*-intercepts, they are *parallel* and have *no point of intersection*. This linear system is said to be **inconsistent**.

(3) If the graph of two linear equations produces lines that *coincide*, the system has *infinitely many solutions*. In other words, every point on the line is a solution. This system of equations is called **dependent**.

An example of each these linear systems is illustrated below.

Consistent Equations

- Lines have different slopes.
- Lines intersect in exactly one point.

Check
Substitute the coordinates (2, 1) in each equation.

$y = -x + 3$ $y = x - 1$
$1 = -2 + 3$ $1 = 2 - 1$
$1 = 1$ (true) $1 = 1$ (true)

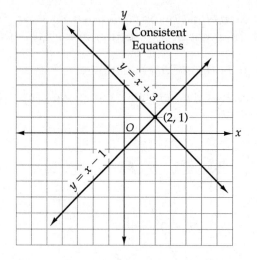

Inconsistent Equations

- Lines have the same slope but different *y*-intercepts.
- Lines are parallel and do not intersect.

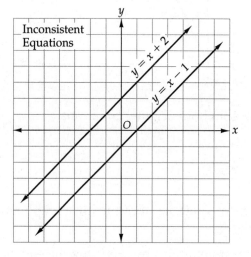

Dependent Equations

- Lines have the same slope and the same *y*-intercept.
- Lines are identical and share all points in common.

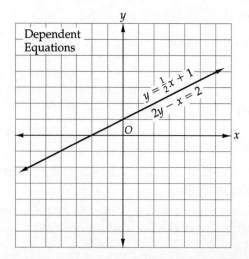

1

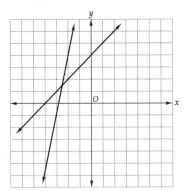

The system of equations represented by this graph is

(1) consistent
(2) inconsistent
(3) dependent
(4) codependent

2

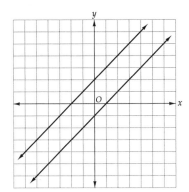

The system of equations represented by this graph is

(1) consistent
(2) inconsistent
(3) dependent
(4) codependent

3 The simultaneous solution to $y = 5$ and $y = 4x - 3$ is

(1) $(5, 17)$
(2) $(2, 5)$
(3) $(0, 5)$
(4) $\varnothing$, since the lines have different y-intercepts

4 The lines $y = 2x + 2$ and $y = 3x - 1$ intersect at point

(1) $(-3, -8)$
(2) $(-1, -4)$
(3) $(1, 4)$
(4) $(3, 8)$

Exercises 5–7: Identify each system of linear equations as consistent or inconsistent.

5

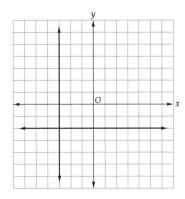

6

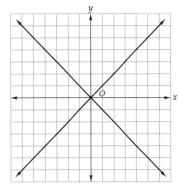

7

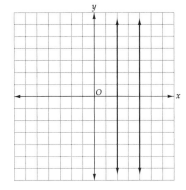

Exercises 8–21: (a) Solve each system graphically, (b) check, and (c) state whether each system is *consistent*, *inconsistent*, or *dependent*.

8 $x + y = 4$
$y = 3x$

9 $y = -x + 7$
$y = 2x + 1$

10 $x - y = 4$
$y = \dfrac{1}{2}x$

11 $-2x + y = 1$
    $-2x + y = 2$

12 $-2x + y = 1$
    $2y = 4x + 2$

13 $2x + y = 2$
    $y - x = 5$

14 $y - x = 2$
    $y - 2x - 2 = 0$

15 $x = 0$
    $y = -3$

16 $y = 3x - 3$
    $y - 3x - 1 = 0$

17 $x + y = 1$
    $-x + y = 1$

18 $y = \dfrac{1}{2}x + 4$
    $2y = x - 6$

19 $2y = 4x - 6$
    $4y + 12 = 8x$

20 $y = -3x$
    $2x + y + 2 = 0$

21 $y = -2x - 1$
    $x + y + 4 = 0$

Exercises 22–28: In the following problems, (a) write a systems of two first-degree equations involving the variables x and y that represent the conditions stated. (b) Solve the system graphically.

22 If the sum of two numbers is 13 and their difference is 7, what are the numbers?

23 The sum of two numbers is 8. If three times the first number is equal to the second number, find the numbers.

24 If five pencils and three erasers cost 65 cents, and three pencils and two erasers cost 40 cents, what is the cost of one pencil and one eraser?

25 If Robert has ten coins, all nickels and dimes, worth 70 cents, how many of each kind of coin does he have?

26 The difference between two numbers is 24 and the sum of those numbers is 48. What are the numbers?

27 The difference between two numbers is 4. If twice the larger number is equal to three times the smaller number increased by two, what are the numbers?

28 The perimeter of a rectangle is 18. If the length is twice the width, what are the dimensions of the rectangle?

Using Addition-Subtraction to Solve Systems of Linear Equations

Two or more linear equations with the same variables form a **system of linear equations**, sometimes called **simultaneous equations**. A **solution** to a system is any pair of values (x, y) that makes all equations true. For example, the pair $(2, 4)$ means $x = 2$ and $y = 4$. $(2, 4)$ is a solution to the system of equations $y = 2x$ and $y = x + 2$.

There are two methods for solving systems of equations algebraically: the **addition-subtraction method** and the **substitution method**. Remember, the solution to a system of equations means finding the value of *each* of the unknown variables.

To Solve Systems of Equations with the Addition-Subtraction Method

• If necessary, rewrite the equations in the form $Ax + By = C$. This is the **standard form** of a linear equation.
• Decide which variable you want to eliminate.
• Multiply one or both equations by constants, if necessary, so that the coefficients of the variable you want to eliminate are opposites.
• Set the equations up in columns. Align like terms.
• Add the columns. This will result in a single equation in one variable.

- Solve the resulting equation.
- Substitute the resulting value into either *original* equation.
- Solve the resulting equation.
- Check by substituting both values into *all original equations.*

Note: If both variables cancel out when the columns are added, the system of equations is either inconsistent (parallel lines) or dependent (lines that coincide), so that a single solution is not possible.

 MODEL PROBLEMS

1 Solve the system of equations $x + y = 8$ and $x - y = 2$.

SOLUTION

The equations are already in standard form, and the y terms are already opposites.

Set up the equations in columns.

$$x + y = 8$$
$$\underline{x - y = 2}$$

Add the columns.

$$2x = 10$$

Solve for x.

$$\frac{2x}{2} = \frac{10}{2}$$

$$x = 5$$

Substitute 5 for x in the first equation.

$$(5) + y = 8$$

Solve for y.

$$\underline{-5 \qquad = -5}$$
$$y = 3$$

Check. Substitute 5 for x and 3 for y in the original equations.

$$x + y = 8 \qquad\qquad x - y = 2$$
$$(5) + (3) = 8 \qquad\quad (5) - (3) = 2$$
$$8 = 8 \checkmark \qquad\qquad 2 = 2 \checkmark$$

Answer: (5, 3)

2 Find the solution of the system $x - 2y = 1$ and $x + y = 10$.

SOLUTION

The coefficients of x are the same.
Write the first equation.
Multiply each term by -1.
Simplify.
Set up the equations in columns and add.

$$x - 2y = 1$$
$$(-1)x + (-1)(-2y) = (-1)1$$
$$-x + 2y = -1$$
$$-x + 2y = -1$$
$$\underline{x + y = 10}$$
$$3y = 9$$

Solve.

$$y = 3$$

Replace y in either equation.

$$x + y = 10$$
$$x + 3 = 10$$
$$x = 7$$

Check by substituting 3 for y and 7 for x in both original equations.

$$x - 2y = 1 \qquad\qquad x + y = 10$$
$$7 - 2(3) = 1 \qquad\quad 7 + 3 = 10 \checkmark$$
$$7 - 6 = 1 \checkmark$$

Answer: $(x, y) = (7, 3)$

3 Solve the system $5x - 2y = 10$ and $2x + y = 31$.

SOLUTION

More work is involved to make the y coefficients cancel.

Write the second equation.	$2x + y = 31$
Multiply each term by 2.	$(2)2x + (2)y = (2)31$
Simplify.	$4x + 2y = 62$
Set up the equations in columns and add.	$5x - 2y = 10$
	$\underline{4x + 2y = 62}$
	$9x\quad\ \ = 72$
Solve.	$x\quad\ = 8$
Replace x in either equation.	$2x + y = 31$
	$2(8) + y = 31$
	$16 + y = 31$
	$y = 15$

Check by substituting 15 for y and 8 for x in both original equations.

$$5x - 2y = 10 \qquad\qquad 2x + y = 31$$
$$5(8) - 2(15) = 10 \qquad 2(8) + (15) = 31$$
$$40 - 30 = 10 \ \checkmark \qquad\quad 16 + 15 = 31 \ \checkmark$$

Answer: $(x, y) = (8, 15)$

4 Karlene invests \$3,900 at two different rates; 4% and 6%. If she receives a total of \$210 annual interest from her two investments, how much does she invest at each rate? Check your answers.

SOLUTION

Let x = amount invested at 4%. $0.04x$ = annual income from 4% investment.

Let y = amount invested at 6%. $0.06y$ = annual income from 6% investment.

Then, $x + y = 3{,}900$ and $0.04x + 0.06y = 210$.

Solve the system of equations.

More work is involved to make the x coefficients cancel.

Write the second equation.	$0.04x + 0.06y = 210$
Multiply each term by 100.	$(100)0.04x + (100)0.06y = (100)210$
Simplify.	(1) $4x + 6y = 21{,}000$
Write the first equation.	$x + y = 3{,}900$
Multiply each term by 4.	$(4)x + (4)y = (4)3{,}900$
Simplify.	(2) $4x + 4y = 15{,}600$
Set up the equations in columns and subtract equation #2 from #1.	$4x + 6y = 21{,}000$
	$\underline{-(4x + 4y = 15{,}600)}$
	$2y = 5{,}400$
Solve.	$y = 2{,}700$
Replace y in either equation.	$x + y = 3{,}900$
	$x + 2{,}700 = 3{,}900$
	$x = 1{,}200$

Check by substituting 2,700 for y and 1,200 for x in both original equations.

$$x + y = 3{,}900 \qquad\qquad\qquad 0.04x + 0.06y = 210$$
$$1{,}200 + 2{,}700 = 3{,}900 \qquad 0.04(1{,}200) + 0.06(2{,}700) = 210$$
$$3{,}900 = 3{,}900 \ \checkmark \qquad\qquad 48 + 162 = 210$$
$$210 = 210 \ \checkmark$$

Exercises 1–20: Find the ordered pair (x, y) that satisfies each system, and check.

1 $x + y = 5$
  $2x - y = 7$

2 $2x + 3y = 2$
  $4x + 3y = 3$

3 $x - 3y = 1$
  $2x + 3y = 20$

4 $4x - y = 8$
  $4x - 3y = 8$

5 $5x + y = 15$
  $3x + y = 11$

6 $2x - 5y = 7$
  $4x - 5y = 19$

7 $2x - 3y = -4$
  $2x + 5y = 12$

8 $-5x - 4y = 23$
  $2x - 4y = 2$

9 $6x + 2y = 18$
  $3x - 2y = 6$

10 $2x + y = 6$
  $5x + 3y = 17$

11 $2x + 3y = 5$
  $5x - 4y = 2$

12 $x + 7y = 15$
  $2x + 9y = 20$

13 $3x + 5y = 7$
  $7x - y = 29$

14 $x + y = 4$
  $2x + 3y = 7$

15 $7x - 2y = 39$
  $5x = 21 - 2y$

16 $6(x + y) = 12$
  $x = 6y - 6$

17 $7x - 2y = 2$
  $3x + 4y = 30$

18 $3x - 2y = -5$
  $5x + 2y = -19$

19 $4x + y = 12$
  $2x - \dfrac{1}{2}y = 2$

20 $x + y = 1,500$
  $0.04x + 0.06y = 74$

Exercises 21–30: In the following problems, (a) write a system of two first-degree equations involving the variables x and y that represent the conditions stated. (b) Solve the system algebraically, and check.

21 George invested $2,000 at two different rates, 5% and 6%. If his total interest income was $106, how much did he invest at each rate?

22 Pauline invested $10,000 at two different rates, 4% and 6%. If her total interest income was $470, how much did she invest at each rate?

23 Amanda made two different investments that totaled $6,000. The rate for one investment was 4.5%, while the other was 7.5%. If the total return on these investments came to $366, how much was invested at each rate?

24 If two angles are complementary and the measure of one is 36° more than the measure of the other, what is the measure of each angle?

25 Two angles are supplementary. If the measure of the first angle is twice the measure of the second, what is the measure of each angle?

26 The perimeter of a rectangular garden is 320 yards. If the length is 8 yards less than 3 times the width, what are the dimensions of the garden?

27 To raise money, a high school musical sold adult and student tickets. The cost of an adult ticket was $6.20 and the cost of a student ticket was $3.00. The number of student tickets sold was 50 more than twice the number of adult tickets sold. If the total income was $4,237, how many of each type of ticket was sold?

28 Two angles are supplementary. If the degree measure of the larger angle is 60 less than twice the measure of the smaller angle, what is the degree measure of each angle?

29 Derek invested some money at 5% interest and another amount at 8.25% interest. The amount invested at 5% was $1,000 more than the amount invested at 8.25%. If the total interest income at the end of one year from these two investments was $315, how much was invested at each rate?

30 Kate deposited x dollars in a bank paying 8.5% interest and y dollars at a second bank paying 10.75% interest. If the x amount was $4,000 less than twice the y amount, and the total interest income for one year was $1,880, how much money did she invest at each rate?

Using Substitution to Solve Systems of Linear Equations

To Solve Systems of Equations With the Substitution Method

- Solve one of the equations for one of the variables.
- Substitute the resulting algebraic expression in the second equation.
- Solve the second equation for the second variable.
- Substitute the resulting value in either original equation.
- Solve for the first variable.
- Check by substituting both values in the equation not used in step 4.

 MODEL PROBLEMS

1 Solve this system of equations: $3x - 4y = 2$ and $x = 14 - 2y$

SOLUTION

Since the solutions are the same for each equation, $x = 14 - 2y$ is true in both equations.

Write the first equation.	$3x - 4y = 2$
Substitute $14 - 2y$ for x.	$3(14 - 2y) - 4y = 2$
Distribute the 3.	$42 - 6y - 4y = 2$
Combine like terms.	$42 - 10y = 2$
Add $10y$ to both sides.	$42 = 10y + 2$
Subtract 2 from both sides.	$40 = 10y$
Solve.	$4 = y$

Substitute 4 for y in either equation.
$$x = 14 - 2y$$
$$x = 14 - 2(4)$$
$$x = 14 - 8 = 6$$

Check by substituting 6 for x and 4 for y in both original equations.

$3x - 4y = 2$	$x = 14 - 2y$
$3(6) - 4(4) = 2$	$6 = 14 - 2(4)$
$18 - 16 = 2$ ✓	$6 = 14 - 8$ ✓

Answer: $(x, y) = (6, 4)$

2 Henrietta has seven bills, all tens and twenties, that total $100 in value. How many of each bill does she have?

SOLUTION

Let x represent the number of tens and y represent the number of twenties.

Henrietta's number of bills can be shown by $x + y = 7$.

The cash value of the bills can be shown by $10x + 20y = 100$.

Now we have the system $x + y = 7$ and $10x + 20y = 100$.

Write the first equation. $\quad x + y = 7$

Solve for x.
$$\frac{-y = \quad -y}{x \quad = 7 - y}$$

Write the second equation.
Substitute $(7 - y)$ for x.

Solve.

$$10x + 20y = 100$$
$$10(7 - y) + 20y = 100$$
$$70 - 10y + 20y = 100$$
$$70 \qquad + 10y = 100$$
$$\frac{-70 \qquad\qquad = -70}{10y = 30}$$
$$y = 3$$

Substitute 3 for y in one of the original equations and solve for x.

$$x + y = \quad 7$$
$$x + (3) = \quad 7$$
$$\frac{-3 = -3}{x = \quad 4}$$

To check, substitute 3 for y and 4 for x in each equation.

$$10x + 20y = 100 \qquad\qquad x + y = 7$$
$$10(4) + 20(3) = 100 \qquad\qquad 3 + 4 = 7 \checkmark$$
$$40 + 60 = 100 \checkmark$$

Check the original problem.

4 bills + 3 bills = 7 bills

$(4 \times 10) + (3 \times 20) = 40 + 60 = 100$

Answer: Henrietta has 4 ten-dollar bills and 3 twenty-dollar bills.

Note: When you are solving word problems, be sure that your answer fits the problem, not just your equations.

 Practice

Exercises 1–16: Solve each system of equations by substitution, and check.

1 $y = 2x$
$x + y = 9$

2 $y = -3x$
$5x - y = 8$

3 $y = 2x$
$3x + 2y = 28$

4 $y = x - 3$
$2x + 3y = 16$

5 $x = y - 4$
$4y - 3x = 14$

6 $x + 2y = 10$
$2x - y = 5$

7 $x - 5y = 4$
$2x + 14 = y$

8 $x + y = 6$
$3x - 4y = 4$

9 $8x = 2y$
$2x + 3y = 42$

10 $y = -4x$
$x - 2y = 27$

11 $x = 2y + 14$
$y - 4x = 0$

12 $x = 2y - 13$
$3x + y = 3$

13 $x = 2 - 2y$
$2x - 3y = 25$

14 $x + 3y = 0$
$2x + 5y = 3$

15 $x + 3y = 9$
$4x + 5y = 22$

16 $4y - 3 = x$
$4x + 1 = 6y$

Exercises 17–28: Use x and y to identify clearly the unknowns in each problem. Set up a system of linear equations and solve each system algebraically. Check your answers.

17 The sum of two numbers is 78. Their difference is 18. Find the numbers.

18 The sum of two numbers is 24. If 4 less than 6 times the smaller number equals 5 more than 3 times the larger number, what are the numbers?

19 The sum of John and Harry's ages is 19 years. If the difference of their ages is 5 years, what are their ages?

20 The Gateway Arch in St. Louis is 86 feet taller than the Washington Monument. If the height of the Gateway Arch is 369 feet more than one-half the height of the Washington Monument, how tall is each structure?

21 At an amusement park, the cost of 3 adult tickets and 4 children's tickets is $126.50. Another customer paid $120.50 for 2 adult tickets and 5 children's tickets. What is the price of each kind of ticket?

22 In the vote for school president, 476 seniors voted for one or the other of the two candidates. The candidate who won had a majority of 94. How many seniors voted for the winner?

23 The factory foreman makes $9 more per hour than Janet, the most senior worker. If one dollar is subtracted from the foreman's rate of pay, the resulting amount is $\dfrac{3}{2}$ of what Janet makes. Find the rate of pay for Janet and the foreman.

24 Thomas has a collection of 25 coins; some are dimes and some are quarters. If the total value of all the coins is $5.05, how many of each kind of coin are there?

25 Carlos and Sam together unpacked cartons for 3 hours at a rate of 8 cartons per hour. During that time, Carlos unpacked twice as many cartons as Sam. How many cartons did each of them unpack?

26 In a vegetable store, a customer paid $8.80 for 3 pounds of tomatoes and 5 pounds of potatoes. A second customer paid $15.15 for 7 pounds of tomatoes and 6 pounds of potatoes. What is the *positive difference* in the price per pound of tomatoes and potatoes?

27 A motorist paid $26.50 for 10 gallons of gas and 2 quarts of oil. Another customer paid $23.58 for 8 gallons of gas and 3 quarts of oil. Find the cost of 1 gallon of gas and 1 quart of oil.

28 Marie went out with $10.75 to cover the exact cost of a certain number of 25-cent stamps and 10-cent stamps. However, by mistake, she interchanged the number of 25-cent stamps and the 10-cent stamps and came back home with $3.30 in change. How many stamps of each kind was she supposed to buy?

29 A student was given the following two equations and asked to determine if they were equivalent: $n + \dfrac{m}{9} = \dfrac{1}{4}$ and $9n + m - \dfrac{1}{4} = 2$. Show how they are or are not equivalent. Explain your answer clearly.

30 Temperatures measured in degrees Celsius and degrees Fahrenheit are related by the formula $F = 1.8C + 32$ where F represents degrees Fahrenheit and C represents degrees Celsius. Jacques has a quick approximation: "Double the Celsius temperature and add 30 degrees." For what Celsius and Fahrenheit temperatures is his method exact?

Graph of the Solution Set of a System of Inequalities

The graph of the solution of a system of linear inequalities is the shaded region of the plane containing all the points that are common solutions of all the inequalities given.

To Find the Solution Set of a System of Linear Inequalities

- Solve each inequality for y.
- Identify slope and y-intercept and graph the boundary lines for each inequality.
- Shade the correct region for each graph.
- Label the common region shaded by both graphs with a capital letter, such as S for *solution*.
- If the two regions do not overlap, indicate that there is no solution.

 MODEL PROBLEM

Graph the following system of inequalities and label the solution set S:

$$y > x + 4$$

$$x + y \leq 0$$

SOLUTION

The first graph is a dashed line, with y-intercept or $b = 4$ and a slope of $m = 1$. The shading is above the line. The second inequality must be rewritten as $y \leq -x$. The second graph is a solid line, with y-intercept at the origin or $b = 0$ and a slope of $m = -1$. The shading is below the line. The solution to the system is the common region, marked S.

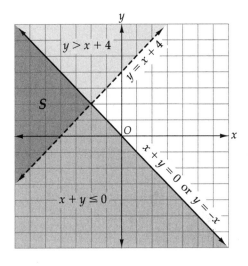

The keystrokes for the inequalities $y > x + 4$ and $x + y \leq 0$ (which converts to $y \leq -x$) are as follows:

Before entering each equation, tab back to the ⸪ sign using the left arrow key and press **ENTER** until the sign changes to ⸬ (a greater than sign) or ⸬ (a less than sign). To get a better view of the intersection, fix the WINDOW menu to approximately $-10 \leq x \leq 5$. Now enter and graph the equations:

Y= **X, T, θ, n** **+** **4** **ENTER** **(-)** **X, T, θ, n** **GRAPH**

It should be clear that the region of intersection is in Quadrants II and III. If a solid line is needed, as in $y \leq -x$, you must keep that in mind.

1 Which graph shows the solution to the system $y \geq -3x + 2$ and $x < 0$?

(1)

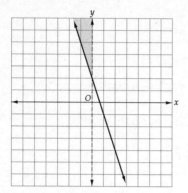

(2)

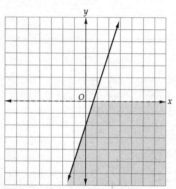

(3)

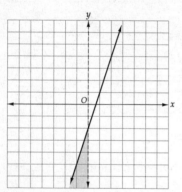

(4)

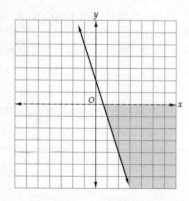

2 Which graph shows the solution set of $y \leq 1$ and $x + y \geq 2$?

(1)

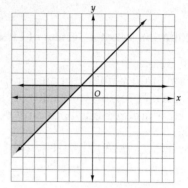

(2)

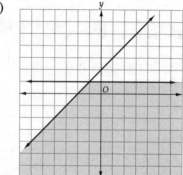

(3)

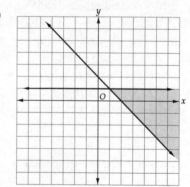

(4)

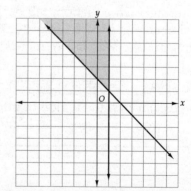

3 Which set of inequalities describes the shaded area of the graph?

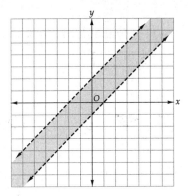

(1) $y > x - 1$ and $y < x + 2$
(2) $y < x - 1$ and $y > x + 2$
(3) $y < x - 1$ or $y > x + 2$
(4) $y > -1$ and $y < 2$

4 Which set of inequalities describes the shaded area of the graph?

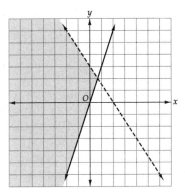

(1) $y < 3x$ and $y \geq -2x + 3$

(2) $y > \frac{1}{3}x$ and $y \geq -2x - 3$

(3) $y \leq 3x$ and $y < -2x + 3$
(4) $y \geq 3x$ and $y < -2x + 3$

Exercises 5–21: Graph each system of inequalities and label the solution set S. Pick a point in the solution set, if any, and verify that it satisfies both inequalities.

5 $y > x - 3$
   $y < x + 5$

6 $y > -2x - 8$
   $x - y > 1$

7 $y < x$
   $y > 0$

8 $y \geq x + 5$
   $x > -5$

9 $x + y < 7$
   $x - y > 3$

10 $y > -x$
   $x + 2y < 4$

11 $x + y \geq -2$
   $3x + 2y > 1$

12 $y > 2x + 1$
   $y < x - 2$

13 $x + y > 3$
   $x - y > 5$

14 $2x + 3y > 6$
   $x - y < 2$

15 $x \geq 2$
   $y \leq x$

16 $2y - 4x > -6$
   $3y - x \leq -9$

17 $x \geq 4$
   $y \geq 4$

18 $-2x - y \leq 1$
   $y \leq -3$

19 $y < \frac{3}{2}x - 2$
   $y < -x + 3$

20 $3x - 3 \leq y \leq \frac{1}{2}x - 3$

21 $y \geq -2x + 5$
   $x \leq 5$
   $y \leq 4$

1 You want to solve the system below by eliminating y. You multiply the first equation by 7. By what number should you multiply the second equation?

$$2x - 5y = 1$$
$$-3x + 7y = -3$$

   (1) -7
   (2) -5
   (3) 5
   (4) 7

2 What is the solution to this system of equations?

$$2x + y = 7$$
$$3x - y = 3$$

   (1) $(4, 1)$
   (2) $(2, -1)$
   (3) $(2, 3)$
   (4) $(3, 2)$

3 Prestige Parking charges $5 for the first hour or any part of that hour and $3 per hour for each additional hour or part of an hour. Paradise Parking charges $8 for the first hour or any part of that hour and $1.50 per hour for each additional hour or part of an hour. For how many hours of parking will the charge be the same in both garages?

   (1) From 1 hour and 1 minute to 2 hours
   (2) From 2 hours and 1 minute to 3 hours
   (3) From 3 hours and 1 minute to 4 hours
   (4) From 4 hours and 1 minute to 5 hours

4 A circus act has 3 times as many elephants as acrobats. Jorge noticed that all together, there were 56 legs in the circus ring. How many elephants were in the show?

   (1) 14 elephants
   (2) 12 elephants
   (3) 9 elephants
   (4) 4 elephants

5 Write the point-slope form of a line where m is the slope and the point is (x_1, y_1).

6 Graph the linear function f defined by $y = f(x) = 3x - 1$ by using the slope and y-intercept.

7 Describe the graph of a constant function. Give two different examples.

8 Use the x- and y-intercepts to graph the line $3x - 2y = 6$.

Exercises 9–11: Identify the slope and y-intercept.

9 $y = \dfrac{3}{5}x - 7$

10 $y + x - 8 = 0$

11 $x = -4$

Exercises 12–15: Write an equation of the line that satisfies the given conditions.

12 $m = \dfrac{2}{3}$, and y-intercept $(0, -2)$

13 slope $= -\dfrac{1}{3}$, and passing through $(9, 2)$

14 Passing through the points $(3, -2)$ and $(1, 6)$

15 Perpendicular to $3x + y - 1 = 0$ and passing through $(3, -1)$

16 Write an equation of the line passing through the point $(2, -3)$ and
   a parallel to the x-axis
   b parallel to the y-axis

17 Write an equation in point-slope form of a line with $m = 5$ and that passes through the point $(-1, 1)$. Verify that $(-2, -4)$ is on that line.

Exercises 18 and 19: Select the equation whose graph would not be parallel to the other two.

18 $2x - y = 9$; $2y - x = 7$; $2x - y = 2$

19 $x + 3y = 7$; $3x + y = 7$; $y = 7 - 3x$

20 Write an equation of the line passing through the points $(2, -3)$ and $(3, -1)$ in
   a point-slope form
   b slope-intercept form
   c general linear form $Ax + By = C$

21 The x- and y-intercepts of a line are $(-5, 0)$ and $(0, -2)$. Write a linear equation for the line in the form $y = mx + b$.

22 Find the x- and y-intercepts of the equation $5x - y - 5 = 0$.

Exercises 23–25: Solve the systems of equations graphically, and check.

23 $y = -2x$
$3x - y = 5$

24 $x - y = 5$
$y = -2x + 4$

25 $3x + 2y = -5$
$2x + 4y = 2$

Exercises 26–30: Find the ordered pair (x, y) that satisfies each system (if possible) and check. Identify the system of linear equations as consistent, inconsistent, or dependent.

26 $x + y = 10$
$y = -3x$

*(handwritten) *(2.5, 7.5) (1,9)(1,-3)
inconsistent
$x - 3x = 10$ (-5, 15)
$-2x = 10$
$x = -5$
$y = 15$*

27 $5x + 3y = 12$
$x + 2y = 8$

28 $2y = 2x + 2$
$-x + y = 1$

29 $x + 2y = 0$
$3x - 2y = 16$

30 $3x + 12 = y$
$8x - 2y = 40$

31 On the same coordinate axes, graph the system of inequalities. Pick a point in the solution set, if any, and verify that it satisfies both inequalities.

$x - y > 3$
$x - y < -2$

32 Graph the following inequalities on the same coordinate plane.

$x - y \leq 2$
$2x + 3y \geq 9$

Find the following points:

a a point *not* in either solution set

b a point that lies in only $x - y \leq 2$

c a point that lies in only $2x + 3y \geq 9$

d a point in the solution set that satisfies both inequalities

33 If Josh has 8 quarters and dimes with a combined value of $1.25, how many quarters and dimes does he have?

34 Three times Simon's age is 58 more than Max's age. One-third the sum of their ages is 10 less than Simon's age. What are their ages?

35 The difference between two numbers is 2. When the sum of the smaller number plus 3 is multiplied by 3, the result is equal to two times the sum of the larger number and 2. Find the numbers.

36 Valerie stayed at a working farm for 30 days. She received $25 for each day she worked, but she had to pay $3 for each day she did not work. At the end of her stay, she was $498 richer than when she started. For how many days did she work?

Now turn to page 440 and take the Cumulative Review test for Chapters 1–10. This will help you monitor your progress and keep all your skills sharp.

CHAPTER 11

Special Products and Factoring

Factoring

In working with algebraic fractions, fractional equations, formulas, and quadratic equations, we often need to find two or more **factors** whose product is a given expression. This process is called **factoring**. Factoring is the reverse of multiplication:

- In multiplication, the factors are given and we must find the product. For example, the product of $4m(r + 5)$ is $4mr + 20m$, and the product of $(x + 3)(x - 2)$ is $x^2 + x - 6$.
- In factoring, the product is given and we must find the factors. For example, factoring $3x + 6$ gives $3(x + 2)$, and factoring $x^2 + x - 6$ gives $(x + 3)(x - 2)$.

In algebra, factoring means breaking a polynomial into two or more parts, its factors. When these factors are multiplied, the product is the original polynomial. Three **types of factoring** in algebra are:

Type 1: Factoring out the greatest common monomial
Type 2: Factoring a binomial that is the difference of two squares
Type 3: Factoring trinomials

We will use two **special products** of polynomials (see Chapter 5) as shortcuts in factoring:

If a polynomial cannot be factored, it is called prime. For example, $a^2 + b^2$ is prime.

Special Product 1	Special Product 2
$(x + y)(x - y) = x^2 - y^2$	$(x + y)(x + y) = x^2 + 2xy + y^2$
	$(x - y)(x - y) = x^2 - 2xy + y^2$

Common Monomial Factors

To factor out the **greatest common monomial factor** (GCF), follow the steps in these model problems.

MODEL PROBLEMS

1 Factor: $2x^2 + 2x$

SOLUTION

Step 1. Examine the polynomial to find like factors that appear in each term. Look for the largest number and the variable with the highest exponent that will divide evenly into each term of the polynomial:

   $2, x$

Step 2. Expressed as a product, $2x$, this is the greatest common monomial factor (GCF). Write the GCF outside a pair of parentheses:

   $2x(\quad)$

Step 3. Divide each term by the GCF:

$2x^2 \div 2x = x$ $\dfrac{2x^{2^{x}}}{2x}$ $\dfrac{2x^1}{2x^1}$

$2x \div 2x = 1$

Step 4. Write the results as a polynomial inside the parentheses:

   $2x(x + 1)$

Check: Multiply.

$2x(x + 1)$
$= (2x \bullet x) + (2x \bullet 1)$
$= 2x^2 + 2x$ ✓

Column method:

$$
\begin{array}{r}
x + 1 \\
\times \quad 2x \\
\hline
2x^2 + 2x \checkmark
\end{array}
$$

2 Factor: $12abc^2 - 24a^2c$

SOLUTION

Step 1. Find like factors: $12, a, c$

Step 2. Set up parentheses: $12ac(\quad)$

Step 3. Divide:

$12abc^2 \div 12ac = bc$
$-24a^2c \div 12ac = -2a$

Step 4. Fill in the parentheses: $12ac(bc - 2a)$

Check: Multiply.

$12ac(bc - 2a)$
$= (12ac \bullet bc) + [12ac \bullet (-2a)]$
$= 12abc^2 + (-24a^2c)$
$= 12abc^2 - 24a^2c$ ✓

Column method:

$$
\begin{array}{r}
bc - \quad 2a \\
\times \quad\quad 12ac \\
\hline
12abc^2 - 24a^2c
\end{array}
$$

To check factors, multiply. The product should be the given expression.

Here are some more examples:

Expression	Factors
$x^3y + 4xy^2$	$xy(x^2 + 4y)$
$6a^3 + 12a^2 + 3a$	$3a(2a^2 + 4a + 1)$
$15a^2x - 3x$	$3x(5a^2 - 1)$
$6cy - 6cx^2$	$6c(y - x^2)$
$3x(4x - 1) + 5(4x - 1)$	$(4x - 1)(3x + 5)$

1 Which expression is prime?

(1) $x^2 + 2x$
(2) $3x^2 + 9$
(3) $x + 1$
(4) $2x^2 + 6x - 10$

Exercises 2 and 3: In which case is the greatest common monomial factored out correctly?

2 $6x^3 - 9x^2 - 12x$

(1) $3x^2(6x - 9 - 12)$
(2) $3x(2x^2 - 3x - 4)$
(3) $x(6x^2 - 9x - 12)$
(4) $3(2x^3 - 3x - 4x)$

3 $5a^2bc - 5ab^2c - 5abc$

(1) $5abc(abc)$
(2) $5abc(a - b - 5)$
(3) $5abc(a - b - 1)$
(4) $5abc(a - b - c)$

4 In which case is the greatest common monomial factored out *incorrectly*?

(1) $27x^3 - 6x^2 + 15x = x(27x^2 - 6x + 15)$
(2) $x^2(a - 3b) + x^2(a - 3b) = 2x^2(a - 3b)$
(3) $21xyz - 35axy = 7xy(3z - 5a)$
(4) $2g^2 + 2g = 2g(g + 1)$

Exercises 5–15: Factor each expression.

5 $5a - 5b$

6 $2x + 6y$

7 $ax + ab$

8 $gd - gr$

9 $ar^2 + 5a$

10 $10x^2y + 15xy^2$

11 $a(a - 7) + 9(a - 7)$

12 $x^2(x + 2) + 7(x + 2)$

13 $30x^5y^5 - 20x^3y^9 + 10x^3y^5$

14 $y(y - 1) + 2(y - 1)$

15 $8rta - 6rtb + 10rtc$

Factoring the Difference of Two Squares

Next we will learn how to factor a binomial of the form $x^2 - y^2$. We use special product 1 (see page 272), the product of binomials that are the sum and the difference of the same terms:

$$(x + y)(x - y) = x^2 - y^2 \quad (x + 6)(x - 6) = x^2 - 36 \quad (4 + x)(4 - x) = 16 - x^2$$

Certain products occur so often that you should recognize them at sight, and this product is one of them. It can be calculated using the distributive property or the FOIL method (see Chapter 5).

Special product 1 gives us an important rule:

- Two binomials of the form $(x + y)(x - y)$ produce the difference of two squares, $(x^2 - y^2)$.
- Therefore, to factor this special product, the difference of two squares, write two binomials that are the sum and difference of the square roots of the two terms.

MODEL PROBLEMS

Multiply:

SOLUTIONS

1 $(m + n)(m - n)$ $(m + n)(m - n) = m^2 - n^2$

2 $(2j + k)(2j - k)$ $(2j + k)(2j - k) = (2j)^2 - k^2 = 4j^2 - k^2$

3 $\left(\dfrac{x^3}{2} + \dfrac{y}{3}\right)\left(\dfrac{x^3}{2} - \dfrac{y}{3}\right)$ $\left(\dfrac{x^3}{2} + \dfrac{y}{3}\right)\left(\dfrac{x^3}{2} - \dfrac{y}{3}\right) = \left(\dfrac{x^3}{2}\right)^2 - \left(\dfrac{y}{3}\right)^2 = \dfrac{x^6}{4} - \dfrac{y^2}{9}$

Factor the following: **SOLUTIONS**

4 $a^2 - b^2$ $(\sqrt{a^2} + \sqrt{b^2})(\sqrt{a^2} - \sqrt{b^2}) = (a + b)(a - b)$

5 $16x^2 - 25$ $(\sqrt{16x^2} + \sqrt{25})(\sqrt{16x^2} - \sqrt{25}) = (4x + 5)(4x - 5)$

6 $4y^2 - 25x^2$ $(\sqrt{4y^2} + \sqrt{25x^2})(\sqrt{4y^2} - \sqrt{25x^2}) = (2y + 5x)(2y - 5x)$

7 $\dfrac{1}{4}a^2b^2 - x^4$ $\left(\sqrt{\dfrac{1}{4}a^2b^2} + \sqrt{x^4}\right)\left(\sqrt{\dfrac{1}{4}a^2b^2} - \sqrt{x^4}\right) = \left(\dfrac{1}{2}ab + x^2\right)\left(\dfrac{1}{2}ab - x^2\right)$

8 $x^4 - 16$ $(\sqrt{x^4} - \sqrt{16})(\sqrt{x^4} + \sqrt{16}) = (x^2 - 4)(x^2 + 4) = (x - 2)(x + 2)(x^2 + 4)$

 Practice

Exercises 1 and 2: Factor the binomial.

1 $x^2y^2 - 100 =$

   (1) $10xy(-10xy)$
   (2) $(x + y + 10)(x + y - 10)$
   (3) $(xy - 10)(xy - 10)$
   (4) $(xy + 10)(xy - 10)$

2 $\dfrac{9}{16}y^2 - 36 =$

   (1) $\left(\dfrac{9}{4}y + 4\right)\left(\dfrac{9}{4}y - 4\right)$
   (2) $\left(6y + \dfrac{3}{4}\right)\left(6y - \dfrac{3}{4}\right)$
   (3) $\left(\dfrac{3}{4}y + 6\right)\left(\dfrac{3}{4}y - 6\right)$
   (4) $\left(\dfrac{3}{4}y + 9\right)\left(\dfrac{3}{4}y - 9\right)$

3 Which binomial is factored correctly?

   (1) $\dfrac{x^2}{4} - \dfrac{y^2}{9} = \left(\dfrac{x}{2} + \dfrac{y}{3}\right)\left(\dfrac{y}{3} - \dfrac{x}{2}\right)$
   (2) $b^2 - 0.01 = (b - 0.1)(b - 0.1)$
   (3) $49 - 0.81x^2y^2 = (7 + 0.09xy)(7 - 0.09xy)$
   (4) $4a^6 - 9b^{10} = (2a^3 + 3b^5)(2a^3 - 3b^5)$

4 Which binomial is factored *incorrectly*?

   (1) $y^2 - 1 = (y + 1)(y - 1)$
   (2) $\dfrac{4}{9}a^2 - \dfrac{9}{25}y^2 = \left(\dfrac{2}{3}a + \dfrac{3}{5}y\right)\left(\dfrac{2}{3}a - \dfrac{3}{5}y\right)$
   (3) $9y^2 - 16 = (3y + 4)(3y - 4)$
   (4) $x^2y^2 - z^2 = (x^2y + 1)(x^2y - 1)$

Exercises 5–14: Find each product.

5   $(2m + 2n)(2m - 2n)$

6   $(0.2x + y)(0.2x - y)$

7   $(x^2 + y^2)(x^2 - y^2)$

8   $(a^2 + b^3)(a^2 - b^3)$

9   $(k + 5)(k - 5)$

10   $(4h + 3)(4h - 3)$

11   $\left(\dfrac{3}{4}p + \dfrac{2}{3}q\right)\left(\dfrac{3}{4}p - \dfrac{2}{3}q\right)$

12   $(12 + 3d)(12 - 3d)$

13   $(5f - 2g)(5f + 2g)$

14   $\left(\dfrac{3s^4}{t^2} - 6\right)\left(\dfrac{3s^4}{t^2} + 6\right)$

Exercises 15–30: Factor each binomial.

15   $a^2 - 49$ $(a + 7)(a - 7)$

16   $m^2 - 64$

17   $49x^2 - y^2$

18   $36 - x^2$ $(-x + 6)(+x - 6)$ $(6 + x)(6 - x)$

19   $16x^2 - 1$

20   $r^2 - s^2$

21   $x^2 - y^4$ $(x + y^2)(x - y^2)$

22   $a^2 - 4b^2$

23   $9a^2 - 16y^2$

24   $81x^4 - 16y^8$

25   $49 - 4m^2$

26   $25a^2 - 81b^2$

27   $y^2 - c^2d^2$

28   $s^2t^2 - k^2n^2$

29   $x^4 - 0.0016$

30   $81 - x^4$

Multiplying Binomials

The fastest way to multiply two general binomial expressions is to use the FOIL method, introduced in Chapter 5.

To Use the FOIL method for multiplying binomials

F   Multiply the first terms.
O   Multiply the outer terms.
I   Multiply the inner terms.
L   Multiply the last terms.

FOIL means First, Outer, Inner, Last—the order for multiplying the terms of two binomials.

Some binomials are especially easy to multiply because patterns are formed. The product of two identical binomials results in a pattern.

$(x + y)(x + y) = x^2 + 2xy + y^2$

Square the first term, *add* twice the product of the terms, and add the square of the second term.

$(x - y)(x - y) = x^2 - 2xy + y^2$

Square the first term, *subtract* twice the product of the terms, and add the square of the second term.

MODEL PROBLEMS

1 Find the product: $(3x + 2y)(3x + 2y)$

SOLUTION

Remember the pattern:

$(3x + 2y)(3x + 2y) = (3x)^2 + 2(3x \cdot 2y) + (2y)^2 = 9x^2 + 12xy + 4y^2$

2 Find the product: $\left(\dfrac{c}{2} - \dfrac{d}{3}\right)\left(\dfrac{c}{2} - \dfrac{d}{3}\right)$

SOLUTION

Remember the pattern:

$\left(\dfrac{c}{2} - \dfrac{d}{3}\right)\left(\dfrac{c}{2} - \dfrac{d}{3}\right) = \left(\dfrac{c}{2}\right)^2 - 2\left(\dfrac{c}{2}\right)\left(\dfrac{d}{3}\right) + \left(\dfrac{d}{3}\right)^2 = \dfrac{c^2}{4} - \dfrac{cd}{3} + \dfrac{d^2}{9}$

3 Find the product: $(x + 6)(x - 3)$

SOLUTION

Use FOIL.

Product of the FIRST terms: $x \cdot x = x^2$

Product of the OUTER terms: $-3 \cdot x = -3x$

Product of the INNER terms: $6 \cdot x = 6x$

Product of the LAST terms: $(6)(-3) = -18$

$x^2 - 3x + 6x - 18$ can be simplified to $x^2 + 3x - 18$.

 Practice

Find each product.

1 $(x + 3)(x + 3)$ $x^2 + 3x + 3x + 9 / x^2 + 6x + 9$

2 $(a + 5)(a + 3)$ $a^2 + 3a + 5a + 15 / a^2 + 8a + 15$

3 $(t + 1)(t + 1)$ $T^2 + T + T + 1 / T^2 + 2T + 1$

4 $(k + 9)(k + 7)$ $k^2 + 7k + 9x + 63 / k^2 + 16k + 63$

5 $(z + 8)(z + 8)$

6 $(n - 4)(n - 1)$

7 $(y - 7)(y - 2)$

8 $(j - 3)(j - 3)$

9 $(h - 8)(h - 8)$

10 $(b - 9)(b - 8)$

11 $(q + 5)(q - 2)$

12 $(w + 6)(w - 7)$

13 $(r + 10)(r - 2)$

14 $(d + 3)(d - 8)$

15 $(g + 5)(g - 6)$

16 $(k - 6)(k + 4)$

17 $(v - 1)(2v - 3)$

18 $(2m + 2)(3m + 9)$

19 $(4x + 1)(5x + 3)$

20 $(7n - 3)(7n + 3)$

21 $(8d - 2)(3d + 1)$

22 $(2y + 8)(7y - 3)$

23 $(w + 2z)(w + 3z)$

24 $(s - 3t)(2s - 9t)$

25 $(3q + 2r)(5q - 3r)$

Factoring Trinomials

A third type of factoring involves trinomials. Two cases of factoring trinomials are:

- Perfect trinomal squares
- General quadratic trinomials

Perfect Trinomial Squares   In factoring a perfect trinomial square, we use special product 2 (see page 272), the square of a binomial:

$$(x + y)^2 = (x + y)(x + y) = x^2 + 2xy + y^2$$
$$(x - y)^2 = (x - y)(x - y) = x^2 - 2xy + y^2$$

Methods of squaring a binomial are reviewed in Chapter 5. One method is FOIL. Special product 2 lets us identify a perfect trinomial square:

- The first and last terms must be perfect squares and must be positive (+).
- The middle term must be twice the product of the square roots of the first and last terms.
- The middle term can be positive (+) or negative (−). The sign of the middle term (+ or −) is the same as the sign between the terms of the binomials.

Special product 2 also gives us a rule for factoring a perfect trinomial square:

- If the middle term is positive, the factors will be of the form $(x + y)(x + y)$.
- If the middle term is negative, the factors will be of the form $(x - y)(x - y)$.
- The x term in the factors is the square root of the first term in the given trinomial.
- The y term in the factors is the square root of the last term in the given trinomial.

 MODEL PROBLEMS

Factor these perfect-square trinomials:

1 $x^2 + 6x + 9$

SOLUTION

The middle term is positive, so the factors will have the form $(x + y)(x + y)$.

The x term in the factors is $\sqrt{x^2} = x$.

The y term in the factors is $\sqrt{9} = 3$.

Answer: $(x + 3)(x + 3)$ or $(x + 3)^2$

2 $x^2 - 10x + 25$

SOLUTION

The middle term is negative, so the factors will have the form $(x - y)(x - y)$.

The x term in the factors is $\sqrt{x^2} = x$.

The y term in the factors is $\sqrt{25} = 5$.

Answer: $(x - 5)(x - 5)$ or $(x - 5)^2$

3 $4x^2 + 12x + 9$

SOLUTION

The middle term is positive, so the factors will have the form $(x + y)(x + y)$.

The x term in the factors is $\sqrt{4x^2} = 2x$.

The y term in the factors is $\sqrt{9} = 3$.

Answer: $(2x + 3)(2x + 3)$ or $(2x + 3)^2$

General Quadratic Trinomials A general quadratic trinomial has the form:

$$ax^2 + bx + c$$

It may be the product of two different binomials or the same binomials. (When it is the product of the same binomials, it is a perfect trinomial square, reviewed above.)

To factor a general quadratic trinomial, we use trial and error, testing all pairs of possible binomial factors until the product is the given trinomial. However, we can shorten this process by applying FOIL, the factoring method, and certain rules:

- If all three terms in the given trinomial are positive (+), both factors have the form $(x + y)$.
- If only the middle term of the trinomial is negative (−), both factors have the form $(x - y)$.
- If the last term is negative (−), one factor has the form $(x + y)$ and the other $(x - y)$. (In this case the middle term can be positive or negative.)
- When the coefficient of the first term is 1, we need to test only the factors of the last term. In this case, the sum of the factors of the last term must equal the coefficient of the middle term.

 MODEL PROBLEMS

Factor each quadratic trinomial.

1 $x^2 + 7x + 12$

SOLUTION

Since all the signs of the given trinomial are positive, both factors will have the form $(x + y)$.

Here the coefficient of the first term is 1, so we try only factors of 12: 1 • 12, 2 • 6, and 3 • 4:

   Try $(x + 1)(x + 12) = x^2 + 13x + 12$ (wrong)

   Try $(x + 2)(x + 6) = x^2 + 8x + 12$ (wrong)

   Try $(x + 3)(x + 4) = x^2 + 7x + 12$ ✓

Shortcut: The sum of the factors of 12 must be 7. Only one pair meets this condition: 3, 4.

2 $x^2 - 10x + 24$

SOLUTION

Only the middle term is negative, so both factors will have the form $(x - y)$.

Since the coefficient of the first term is 1, test just the factors of 24. In this case, at least one of these factors must be negative, since their sum must be −10. Because their product is +24, *both* must be negative. Thus the possible factors are: −1 • (−24), −2 • (−12), −3 • (−8), and −4 • (−6).

Only one pair (−4 and −6) gives a sum of −10.

Answer: Therefore, the factors must be $(x - 4)(x - 6)$.

3 $m^2 - m - 2$

SOLUTION

Here, the last term is negative, so the factors will have the form $(x + y)(x - y)$.

The coefficient of the first term is 1, so test only the factors of the last term. Since the last term is -2, one factor must be negative and the other positive: $1 \cdot (-2)$ or $-1 \cdot 2$.

The coefficient of the middle term is -1, and only the pair $1, -2$ will add up to -1.

Answer: The factors are $(m + 1)(m - 2)$.

4 $x^2 + 3x - 18$

SOLUTION

The factors will have the form $(x + y)(x - y)$.

We need to test only the factors of the last term. One must be positive and the other negative. The possible factors are $1 \cdot (-18)$, $-1 \cdot 18$, $2 \cdot (-9)$, $-2 \cdot 9$, $3 \cdot (-6)$, and $-3 \cdot 6$.

Of these, only the pair $-3, 6$ will add up to the middle coefficient, 3.

Answer: The factors are $(x + 6)(x - 3)$.

5 $2x^2 + 9x - 35$

SOLUTION

The factors will have the form $(x + y)(x - y)$.

Here the coefficient of first term is 2. Therefore, we must consider the factors of both 2 and -35. Factors of 2: $1 \cdot 2$ and $2 \cdot 1$

Factors of -35: $1 \cdot (-35)$, $-1 \cdot 35$, $5 \cdot (-7)$, and $-5 \cdot 7$

We can eliminate $1 \cdot (-35)$ and $-1 \cdot 35$, since these would yield sums that are too great.

Use trial and error with the remaining choices, applying FOIL to check. For example:

Try $(x - 5)(2x + 7) = 2x^2 + 7x - 10x - 35 = 2x^2 - 3x - 35$ (wrong)

Try $(2x - 7)(x + 5) = 2x^2 + 10x - 7x - 35 = 2x^2 - 3x - 35$ (wrong)

Try $(2x - 5)(x + 7) = 2x^2 + 14x - 5x - 35 = 2x^2 + 9x - 35$ ✓

Answer: $(2x - 5)(x + 7)$

With experience, you will get better and better at guessing and testing.

1 Which expression is a perfect trinomial square?

(1) $x^2 - 5x + 4$

(2) $x^2 + \frac{1}{2}x + \frac{1}{4}$

(3) $4x^2 - 4x + 1$

(4) $x^2 + 7x + \frac{4}{49}$

2 Factor: $7x^2 + 9x - 10$

(1) $(7x + 10)(x - 1)$
(2) $(7x - 5)(x + 2)$
(3) $(7x + 2)(x - 5)$
(4) $(7x - 1)(x + 10)$

3 Factor: $2x^2 - x - 3$

(1) $(2x + 1)(x + 3)$
(2) $(2x + 3)(x - 1)$
(3) $(2x - 3)(x + 1)$
(4) $(2x - 3)(x - 1)$

4 Which expression is prime?

(1) $x^2 + 4x + 3$
(2) $x^2 + 5x + 6$
(3) $x^2 + 6x + 8$
(4) none of the above

Exercises 5–20: Factor each trinomial if possible.

5 $x^2 - 10x + 25$ $(x-5)(x-5)$

6 $x^2 - 7x + 12$ $(x-4)(x-3)$

7 $x^2 + 2x - 8$ $(x+4)(x+2)$

8 $x^2 - 8x - 20$

9 $11x^2 + 12x + 1$

10 $11x^2 - 12x + 1$

11 $x^2 - 5x + \frac{25}{4}$

12 $3y^2 - 4y - 4$ $(3y-1)(y+4)$ $(3y+2)(y-2)$

13 $x^2 + 2x + 1$

14 $x^2 + 3x + 2$

15 $4x^2 - 20x + 25$

16 $2x^2 + 5x + 6$

17 $16x^2 + 40x + 25$

18 $a^4 + 2a^2b^2 + b^4$

19 $6x^2 - 11x + 5$

20 $4x^2 - 39x + 81$

Factoring Completely

In general, to factor a polynomial completely:

- Find any common monomial factors.
- If possible, find the binomial factors of the remaining terms, and continue until there are no more possible factors.
- Last, write all the factors as a product.

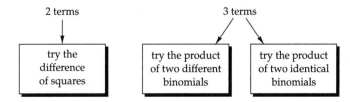

Flowchart for Factoring Completely

First: Remove common monomial factors.

Second: If the items that remain are

2 terms

3 terms

| try the difference of squares | try the product of two different binomials | try the product of two identical binomials |

MODEL PROBLEMS

Factor completely:

SOLUTIONS

1 $ax^2 - a$

$a(x^2 - 1)$
$a(x - 1)(x + 1)$

2 $9a^4 - 36b^4$

$9(a^4 - 4b^4)$
$9(a^2 - 2b^2)(a^2 + 2b^2)$

3 $x^4 - 3x^3 - 40x^2$

$x^2(x^2 - 3x - 40)$
$x^2(x - 8)(x + 5)$

4 $ax^5 - a^5x^5$

$ax^5(1 - a^4)$
$ax^5(1 - a^2)(1 + a^2)$
$ax^5(1 - a)(1 + a)(1 + a^2)$

Practice

1 In factoring completely, the first step is:

   (1) Write the factors as a product.
   (2) Find common monomial factors.
   (3) Use the FOIL method.
   (4) Find the bionomial factors.

Exercises 2–4: Factor the given expression completely.

2 $2x^2 - 72y^2$

   (1) $2(x + 6y)(x - 6y)$
   (2) $(\sqrt{2}x + 6\sqrt{2}y)(\sqrt{2}x - 6\sqrt{2}y)$
   (3) $2x(x - 6y)^2$
   (4) $2(x - 6y)^2$

3 $2x^2 - 8x - 10$

   (1) $2(x - 5)(x - 1)$
   (2) $2(x - 5)(x + 1)$
   (3) $(2x - 10)(x + 1)$
   (4) $(x - 10)(2x + 1)$

4 $x^3 - 8x^2 + 16x$

   (1) $(x^2 - 8)^2$
   (2) $(x - 8)(x^2 + 2)$
   (3) $x(x - 4)^2$
   (4) $x(x - 8)(x + 2)$

Exercises 5–20: Factor each expression completely.

5 $5x^2 - 20$ $5(x^2-4)\ 5(x+2)(x-2)$

6 $ab^4 - ax^4$ $a(b^4-x^4)\ a(b^2-x^2)^2$

7 $3x^2 + 12x + 12$ $3(x^2+4x+4)\ 3(x+2)(x+2)$

8 $9x^3 - 9x$ $9x(x^2-1)\ 9x(x+1)(x-1)$

9 $3x^2 - 75$

10 $6a^2 - 6a^4$

11 $x^3 - x^2 - 2x$

12 $a^3 - a$

13 $x - 25x^3$

14 $ax^3 - 36ax$

15 $25x^2 - 100y^2$

16 $2a^4 - 32b^4$

17 $9x^2 + 18xy + 9y^2$

18 $5x^2 - 25x + 30$ $5(x^2-5x+6)$
$5(x-3)(x-2)$

19 $a - ar^2$

20 $x^2(x + 2) - 9(x + 2)$

$x\ 8x \quad x^2-8x+16$

$(x$

1 Which expression is prime?

   (1) $3x + 9y$
   (2) $x - 4$
   (3) $x^2 - 16$
   (4) $x^2 - 5x + 6$

Exercises 2–15: Find each product.

2 $3x(x - 4)$ $3x^2 + 12x$

3 $-4j(2j - 5)$ $8j^2 + 20j$

4 $(3 + d)(3 - d)$ $9 - d^2$

5 $(m + 8)(m - 8)$ $m^2 - 64$

6 $(g + 4)(g + 2)(g - 2)$

7 $(x + 7)^2$

8 $(s - 1)(s - 1)$

9 $(y + 3)(y + 2)$

10 $(t + 8)(t - 7)$

11 $(j + 4)(2j + 1)$

12 $(3r - 5)(2r + 5)$

13 $4x^2(3 - 2x)$

14 $(4 - x)(x + 1)$

15 $(7 + m)(m + 8)$

Exercises 16–30: Factor each expression completely if possible.

16 $3x^2 - 9x$ $3x(x - 3)$

17 $2ab^2c^3 - 8abc^2$

18 $s^2 - 9$ $(s - 3)(s + 3)$

19 $v^2 - 16c^2$

20 $a^2 + b^2$ to Done

21 $d^2 - 81$

22 $k^2 + 5k + 6$ $(k + 2)(k + 3)$

23 $m^2 - 14m + 40$

24 $15 - 2x - x^2$

25 $x^2 - 14x + 9$

26 $2x^2 + 24x + 70$

27 $3ax^2 - 30ax + 48a$ $3a(2 + x)(8 + x)$

28 $-x^2 + 3x + 28$

29 $a^4 - b^4$

30 $3r^2 - 12s^2$ $3(r + 2s)(r + -2s)$

$(s - 3)(s + 3)$ $(a + b)(a + b)$
$s^2 + 3s - 3s - 9$ $a^2 + ab - ab - b^2$

Now turn to page 443 and take the Cumulative Review test for Chapters 1–11. This will help you monitor your progress and keep all your skills sharp.

x^2

$(x$

$(k + 2)(k + 3)$
$k^2 + 3k + 2k + 6$

$(ax -)(ax +)$

$3(r^2 - 4s^2)$ $3(r + 2s)(r + 2s)$

48
24·2
16·3
6·8
12·4

1, 2–5, 16, 18, 20, 22, 27, 30

CHAPTER 12

Operations With Radicals

Powers and Roots

Square Roots

To find the **square** of a number means to multiply the number by itself. To denote the square of any number n, we write n^2. Thus, the square of 3 is written 3^2 and is equal to 3×3 or 9. To find the square of any number n on the calculator, enter the number, press $\boxed{x^2}$, and press $\boxed{\text{ENTER}}$.

To find the **square root** of a number means to find one of two equal factors of a number. Every positive number has two different square roots. They are positive and negative numbers with the same absolute value. The positive value is called the **principal square root**. The principal square root of 9 is 3 since $3 \times 3 = 9$. Likewise, the negative square root of 9 is -3. Written in mathematical notation, $\sqrt{9} = 3$ means the principal square root of 9 is 3. The symbol $\sqrt{}$ is called the **radical sign**. The quantity under the radical sign is called the **radicand**. In the example just discussed, 9 is the radicand and the expression is referred to as the **radical**. To find the principal square root of any number n on the calculator, press $\boxed{\text{2nd}}\boxed{\sqrt{}}$, enter the number, and press $\boxed{\text{ENTER}}$. For our example, the calculator screen will display the following:

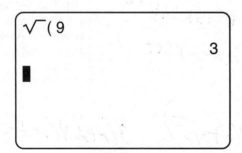

You certainly may close the parenthesis by pressing $\boxed{)}$, but it is not necessary.

A number by which a square root is multiplied is called the **coefficient**. Thus, the product of 4 and $\sqrt{5}$ is written $4\sqrt{5}$. The number 4 is the coefficient and the number 5 is the radicand.

- $\sqrt{b} = x$ *if and only if* $x \geq 0$ *and* $x^2 = b$.

The expression $\pm\sqrt{n}$ refers to both the principal square root of n and the negative square root of n. Thus, the values of $\pm\sqrt{9}$ are 3 and -3.

A negative number does not have a real-number square root.

Remember that **rational** numbers are the set composed of integers, fractions, terminating decimals, and repeating decimals. A number that is the square of a rational number is called a **perfect square**.

$11^2 = 121$	$\sqrt{121} = 11$	121 is a perfect square
$1.6^2 = 2.56$	$\sqrt{2.56} = 1.6$	2.56 is a perfect square
$\left(\dfrac{2}{3}\right)^2 = \dfrac{4}{9}$	$\sqrt{\dfrac{4}{9}} = \dfrac{2}{3}$	$\dfrac{4}{9}$ is a perfect square

Points to Remember

- The square root of every perfect square is rational.
- The square root of every number that is not a perfect square is irrational.
- For every real number n: $\left(\sqrt{n}\right)^2 = \sqrt{(n)^2} = n$.
- The square root of a negative number does not exist in the set of real numbers.

Cube Roots and Other Roots

The nth root of a number is one of n equal factors of the number. Just as $n = 2$ results in a special name (square root), when $n = 3$, we refer to the root as the **cube root**. For example, the cube root of 27 is 3 because $3 \times 3 \times 3 = 27$.

When written in mathematical notation, $\sqrt[3]{27} = 3$ means *the cube root of 27 is 3*. Using the calculator, press [MATH] [4] (for choice 4: $\sqrt[3]{}$) [2] [7] [ENTER].

The symbol $\sqrt[x]{b}$ means the *xth root of b*. Now b is the **radicand** and x is called the **index**. To find the xth root of any number b on the calculator, press x (the number that corresponds to the index) [MATH] [5] (for choice 5: $\sqrt[x]{}$), b (the number that corresponds to the radicand) [ENTER]. To find the fourth root of 16, or $\sqrt[4]{16}$, press [4] [MATH] [5] [1] [6] [ENTER]. For our example, the calculator screen will display the following:

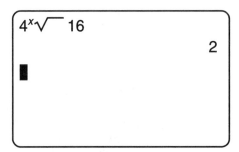

Points to Remember

- Finding the nth root of a number is the inverse operation of raising a number to the power n. In general, the nth root of b is x (written as $\sqrt[n]{b} = x$) if and only if $x^n = b$.
- When no index appears, the index is 2 and the operation is square root.
- If the index n is even, the operation is closed in the real numbers for nonnegative radicands only. When we multiply an even number of identical values together, the product is always nonnegative.
- If the index n is odd, the operation is closed regardless of the sign of the radicand. The root has the same sign as the radicand.

Radicals and the Irrational Numbers

If n is not a perfect square, $\sqrt{n}$ is irrational and the calculator display for the solution of $\sqrt{n}$ is an approximation based on the setting of the calculator. Unless otherwise specified, the full power of the calculator should be used. If a specific form is not required for an answer, the answer can be left in any equivalent form, such as $\sqrt{10}$ or 3.162277660.

MODEL PROBLEMS

1 Find the principal square root of 529.

SOLUTION

Using the calculator, enter [2nd] [√] [5] [2] [9] [ENTER]. The display shows that the answer is 23.

Answer: 23

2 Find the value of $-\sqrt{0.09}$.

SOLUTION

Using the calculator, press [(-)] [√] [0] [.] [0] [9] [ENTER]. The display shows that the answer is -0.3.

Answer: -0.3

3 Solve for x: $x^2 = 49$.

SOLUTION

If $x^2 = 49$, then $x = \pm\sqrt{49}$. Then $x = 7$ or $x = -7$.

Answer: $\{7, -7\}$

4 If the two legs of a triangle measure 4 cm and 6 cm, find the hypotenuse.

SOLUTION

Using the Pythagorean theorem:
$$c^2 = a^2 + b^2$$
$$c^2 = 2^2 + 3^2$$
$$c^2 = 4 + 9$$
$$c^2 = 13$$
$$c = \sqrt{13}$$

Answer: Since the form of the answer is not specified, the answer is $\sqrt{13}$ or 3.605551275.

Practice

Exercises 1–20: Evaluate each expression.

1 $\sqrt{121}$

2 $\sqrt{\dfrac{9}{16}}$ $\frac{3}{4}$

3 $\sqrt{0.0081}$

4 $\pm\sqrt{1}$ ±1

5 $-\sqrt{441}$ -21

6 $\pm\sqrt{289}$

7 $\pm\sqrt{\dfrac{25}{49}}$ $\pm\frac{5}{7}$

8 $\sqrt{1.21}$

9 $-\sqrt{\dfrac{1}{81}}$

10 $\sqrt[3]{729}$ 9

11 $\sqrt[3]{-1,728}$ -12

12 $\sqrt[3]{2.744}$

13 $-\sqrt[3]{29.791}$

14 $\sqrt[3]{\left(\dfrac{27}{64}\right)}$ $\frac{3}{4}$

15 $-\sqrt[3]{-343}$

16 $(\sqrt{20})^2$

17 $\left(\sqrt{\dfrac{1}{3}}\right)^2$

18 $\left(\sqrt[3]{12}\right)^3$

19 $\sqrt{\left(\dfrac{5}{6}\right)^2}$

20 $\sqrt[3]{5^3}$

Exercises 21–25: Replace each ? with >, <, or = to make a true statement.

21 $\dfrac{2}{3}$? $\left(\dfrac{2}{3}\right)^2$

22 $\dfrac{3}{7}$? $\sqrt{\dfrac{3}{7}}$

23 $\sqrt{\dfrac{24}{17}}$? $\dfrac{24}{17}$

24 $\left(\dfrac{8}{3}\right)^2$? $\dfrac{8}{3}$

25 k ? k^2, $0 < k < 1$

Exercises 26–30: Solve each equation for the variable when the replacement set is the set of real numbers.

26 $x^2 = 36$ $x = 6 \; -6$

27 $x^2 = \dfrac{25}{36}$

28 $y^2 - 81 = 0$

29 $n^2 + 4 = 53$

30 $2g^3 = 250$

Exercises 31–35: Evaluate each expression, rounded as indicated.

31 $\sqrt{24}$, rounded to the nearest hundredth

32 $\sqrt{11}$, rounded to the nearest tenth

33 $\sqrt[3]{-151}$, rounded to the nearest integer

34 $\sqrt{12}$, rounded to the nearest thousandth

35 $-\sqrt{18}$, rounded to the nearest tenth

Finding the Principal Square Root of a Monomial

Just as some rational numbers are perfect square numbers because they are the product of two identical factors, a monomial that is the product of two identical factors is a perfect square monomial.

Since $(x)(x) = x^2$, then x^2 is a perfect square monomial and $\sqrt{x^2} = x$.

Since $(4n)(4n) = 16n^2$, then $16n^2$ is a perfect square monomial and $\sqrt{16n^2} = 4n$.

When the square root contains both numerical and variable factors, we can determine the square root by multiplying the square roots of its factors. In the last example above, $\sqrt{16n^2} = \sqrt{16} \cdot \sqrt{n^2} = 4 \cdot n = 4n$.

 Practice

Find the principal square root of each monomial. Assume that all variables represent positive numbers.

1 $9j^2$

2 $\dfrac{9}{16}c^2$

3 $0.64m^2$

4 $16d^4$

5 $0.81d^6$

6 $1.21t^2$

7 y^2z^2

8 $4c^2r^2$

9 $64p^4q^6$

10 $0.49x^2y^8z^{12}$

Simplifying Square Root Radicals

Most often, radical expressions will not contain perfect square monomials and we will be asked to simplify the radical. A radical is simplified when the integer remaining in the radical has no perfect square factor other than 1. The final expression has no radical in the denominator. In order to simplify radical expressions, the following property must be applied.

In general, if a and b are nonnegative integers or nonnegative valued variables:

- $\sqrt{a \cdot b} = \sqrt{a} \cdot \sqrt{b}$

- $\sqrt{\dfrac{a}{b}} = \dfrac{\sqrt{a}}{\sqrt{b}}$

 MODEL PROBLEMS

1 Simplify $\sqrt{32}$.

SOLUTION

Factor using 16, the greatest perfect square factor of 32.

$$\sqrt{32} = \sqrt{16 \cdot 2} = \sqrt{16} \cdot \sqrt{2} = 4\sqrt{2}$$

Note that if we factored using 4, which is also a perfect square factor of 32, the process would require an additional step.

$\sqrt{32} = \sqrt{4 \cdot 8} = \sqrt{4} \cdot \sqrt{8} = 2\sqrt{8}$. Since 8 has a perfect square factor, the process is repeated, simplifying $2\sqrt{8}$.

$$2\sqrt{8} = 2\sqrt{4 \cdot 2} = 2\sqrt{4} \cdot \sqrt{2} = 2 \cdot 2\sqrt{2} = 4\sqrt{2}$$

Answer: $4\sqrt{2}$

2 Simplify $\sqrt{50x^3y^2}$.

SOLUTION

Simplify using $25x^2y^2$, the greatest square factor of $50x^3y^2$.

$$\sqrt{50x^3y^2} = \sqrt{25x^2y^2 \cdot 2x} = \sqrt{25x^2y^2} \cdot \sqrt{2x} = 5xy\sqrt{2x}$$

Answer: $5xy\sqrt{2x}$

3 Simplify $\sqrt{\dfrac{2}{3}}$.

SOLUTION

Remember that the denominator must not contain a radical. Multiply the numerator and denominator by the radical in the denominator you want to eliminate.

$$\sqrt{\dfrac{2}{3}} = \dfrac{\sqrt{2}}{\sqrt{3}}$$

Multiply the numerator and denominator by $\sqrt{3}$, which is the same as multiplying by 1.

$$\dfrac{\sqrt{2}}{\sqrt{3}} \cdot \dfrac{\sqrt{3}}{\sqrt{3}} = \dfrac{\sqrt{2} \cdot \sqrt{3}}{\sqrt{3} \cdot \sqrt{3}} = \dfrac{\sqrt{2 \cdot 3}}{\sqrt{3 \cdot 3}} = \dfrac{\sqrt{6}}{\sqrt{9}} = \dfrac{\sqrt{6}}{3}$$

Since the radicand in the numerator has no perfect square factors other than 1 and the denominator has no radical, the expression is simplified.

Answer: $\dfrac{\sqrt{6}}{3}$

Practice

1   The principal square root of 64 is

   (1)   8
   (2)   −8
   (3)   8 and −8
   (4)   not a real number

2   Simplify: $\sqrt{1{,}176}$

   (1)   42
   (2) $7\sqrt{24}$
   (3) $14\sqrt{3}$
   (4) $14\sqrt{6}$

3   Simplify: $\dfrac{3^2}{\sqrt{80}}$

   (1) $\dfrac{\sqrt{80}}{3^{-2}}$

   (2) $\dfrac{4}{9}\sqrt{5}$

   (3) $\dfrac{5}{4}\sqrt{5}$

   (4) $\dfrac{9}{20}\sqrt{5}$

4   $\dfrac{7}{\sqrt{45}} =$

   (1) $\dfrac{7}{9}$

   (2) $\dfrac{3}{7}$

   (3) $\dfrac{7\sqrt{3}}{9}$

   (4) $\dfrac{7\sqrt{5}}{15}$

Exercises 5–20: Simplify.

5   $\sqrt{25}$

6   $\sqrt{864}$

7   $\sqrt{162}$

8   $\dfrac{7}{\sqrt{11}}$

9   $\dfrac{6}{\sqrt{18}}$

10   $\dfrac{19}{\sqrt{19}}$

11   $\dfrac{1}{2}\sqrt{32}$

12   $\dfrac{4}{5}\sqrt{50}$

13   $\sqrt{\dfrac{1}{4}}$

14   $\sqrt{\dfrac{2}{5}}$

15   $\sqrt{\dfrac{4}{7}}$

16   $6\sqrt{\dfrac{5}{6}}$

17   $\sqrt{24x^2y}$

18   $\sqrt{72a^2b^4c^3}$

19   $\sqrt{\dfrac{4}{5xy}}$

20   $\dfrac{2}{3}\sqrt{\dfrac{2c^2d}{3a^2b}}$

Operations With Radicals

Rules for Adding and Subtracting Square Root Radicals

- **Like radicals** have the same index and the same radicand. Only like radicals can be added or subtracted.
- If the indices are different, the radicals cannot be added or subtracted.
- If the radicands are different, try to simplify by factoring to see if the radicands are then the same.
- Then add or subtract the coefficients.

MODEL PROBLEMS

1 Add: $5\sqrt{7} + 2\sqrt{112}$

SOLUTION

Simplify $2\sqrt{112}$: $\qquad 2\sqrt{112} = 2\sqrt{16 \times 7} = 2 \times 4\sqrt{7} = 8\sqrt{7}$

Add the coefficients: $\qquad 5\sqrt{7} + 8\sqrt{7} = 13\sqrt{7}$

2 Subtract: $3\sqrt{48} - \sqrt{27}$

SOLUTION

Simplify $3\sqrt{48}$: $\qquad 3\sqrt{48} = 3\sqrt{16 \times 3} = 12\sqrt{3}$

Simplify $\sqrt{27}$: $\qquad \sqrt{27} = \sqrt{9 \times 3} = 3\sqrt{3}$

Subtract the coefficients: $\quad 12\sqrt{3} - 3\sqrt{3} = 9\sqrt{3}$

Rules for Multiplying Square Roots

- The radicands do *not* need to be the same.
- Write the factors under one radical sign.
- Multiply.
- If possible, simplify the product.

 MODEL PROBLEMS

Multiply:	Solutions
1 $\sqrt{3} \cdot \sqrt{6} =$	$\sqrt{3 \cdot 6} = \sqrt{18} = \sqrt{9} \cdot \sqrt{2} = 3\sqrt{2}$
2 $\sqrt{10} \cdot \sqrt{15} =$	$\sqrt{10 \cdot 15} = \sqrt{150} = \sqrt{25 \cdot 6} = 5\sqrt{6}$

Rules for Dividing Square Roots

- The radicands do *not* need to be the same.
- Write the divisor and the dividend as a fraction under one radical sign.
- Simplify the denominator and numerator by factoring.
- If the denominator of the answer contains a radical, rationalize.

 MODEL PROBLEM

Divide: $\dfrac{\sqrt{10}}{\sqrt{15}}$

SOLUTION

Rewrite under one radical: $\qquad \dfrac{\sqrt{10}}{\sqrt{15}} = \sqrt{\dfrac{10}{15}}$

Simplify: $\qquad \sqrt{\dfrac{10}{15}} = \sqrt{\dfrac{2 \times 5}{3 \times 5}} = \sqrt{\dfrac{2}{3}}$

Rationalize: $\qquad \sqrt{\dfrac{2}{3}} = \dfrac{\sqrt{2}}{\sqrt{3}} \cdot \dfrac{\sqrt{3}}{\sqrt{3}} = \sqrt{\dfrac{6}{9}} = \dfrac{\sqrt{6}}{3}$

1 $3\sqrt{48} + 11\sqrt{75} =$

$3\sqrt{48} = \sqrt{16}\sqrt{3} = 12\sqrt{3} +$
$11\sqrt{75} = \sqrt{25}\sqrt{3} = 55\sqrt{3}$

  (1) $33\sqrt{48}$

  (2) $67\sqrt{3}$

  (3) $72\sqrt{5}$

  (4) $81\sqrt{2}$

2 $\sqrt{14} \div \sqrt{6} =$ $\dfrac{\sqrt{84}}{6}$ $\dfrac{\sqrt{4}\sqrt{21}}{6}$ $\dfrac{2\sqrt{21}}{6}$

  (1) $\dfrac{2}{3}$

  (2) $\dfrac{21}{\sqrt{3}}$

  (3) $\dfrac{3}{\sqrt{21}}$

  (4) $\dfrac{\sqrt{21}}{3}$

3 $\sqrt{54} - \sqrt{96} =$

  (1) $-\sqrt{6}$

  (2) $2\sqrt{3}$

  (3) $\sqrt{6}$

  (4) $7\sqrt{6}$

4 $3\sqrt{125} + 6\sqrt{80} =$

  (1) $-29\sqrt{5}$

  (2) $-9\sqrt{5}$

  (3) $39\sqrt{5}$

  (4) 145

5 $\sqrt{8}(\sqrt{13} - \sqrt{117}) =$ $\sqrt{104} - \sqrt{936}$

$\sqrt{4}\sqrt{26} \quad \sqrt{36}\sqrt{26}$
$2\sqrt{26} \quad -6\sqrt{26}$

  (1) $-4\sqrt{26}$

  (2) $4\sqrt{2}$

  (3) $2\sqrt{13}$

  (4) $2\sqrt{26}$

6 In simplest form, $5\sqrt{12} + 7\sqrt{108} =$

  (1) $12\sqrt{120}$

  (2) $52\sqrt{6}$

  (3) $52\sqrt{3}$

  (4) $20\sqrt{3}$

Exercises 7–20: Perform the indicated operations. Give your answers in simplified radical form.

7 $8\sqrt{12x} + \sqrt{27x}$

8 $4\sqrt{3} - 3\sqrt{3} + 3\sqrt{2}$

9 $3\sqrt{8} - 4\sqrt{3} + \sqrt{18}$

10 $\sqrt{4} + \sqrt{50} - \sqrt{32}$

11 $3\sqrt{6x^2} - 4\sqrt{24x^2} + 2\sqrt{x^2}$

12 $\sqrt{0.5} \cdot \sqrt{32}$

13 $\sqrt{m^2n} \cdot \sqrt{mn^2}$

14 $2\sqrt{5x} \cdot 4\sqrt{3x}$ $8\sqrt{15x}^2$ $8x\sqrt{15}$

15 $3\sqrt{7} \cdot 7\sqrt{6}$ $21\sqrt{42}$

16 $\sqrt{2x^3} \cdot 4\sqrt{10x}$

17 $\sqrt{2} \cdot \sqrt{0.02x}$

18 $\dfrac{\sqrt{x^7}}{\sqrt{x^3}}$

19 $\sqrt{\dfrac{x}{4}}$

20 $\dfrac{\sqrt{8x^3}}{\sqrt{2x}}$

Exercises 1–5: Evaluate each expression.

1 $\pm\sqrt{\dfrac{16}{81}}$ *(handwritten: 8·9·12·4 / 27·3−9)*

2 $\sqrt{1.69}$ = 1.3

3 $-\sqrt{\dfrac{1}{49}}$ *(handwritten: −1/7)*

4 $\sqrt[3]{1{,}331}$ 11

5 $\sqrt[3]{-3{,}375}$ = −15

Exercises 6–10: Solve each equation for the variable when the replacement set is the set of real numbers.

6 $x^2 = 100$ X = ±10

7 $x^2 = \dfrac{81}{121}$ X = ±9/11

8 $y^2 - 4 = 0$ Y = ±2

9 $n^2 + 10 = 74$ n = ±8

10 $2g^3 = 1{,}024$ g = ±8

Exercises 11 and 12: Find the principal square root of each monomial.

11 $64x^2y^2$ 8xy

12 $4c^4d^6$ 2c²d³

Exercises 13–20: Simplify the expression.

13 $\dfrac{1}{3}\sqrt{50}$

14 $\dfrac{4}{9}\sqrt{48}$ Wrong $\dfrac{16}{9}\sqrt{3}$

15 $\sqrt{\dfrac{1}{9}}$

16 $\sqrt{\dfrac{4}{3}}$

17 $6\sqrt{12x^4y}$ 24x²$\sqrt{3xy}$

18 $\sqrt{8ab^3c^8}$ 4b²c⁴$\sqrt{2abc^2}$

19 $\sqrt{\dfrac{5}{3x}}$

20 $\dfrac{1}{6}\sqrt{\dfrac{5c^2}{3d}}$

Exercises 21–30: Perform the indicated operations. Give your answer in simplest radical form.

21 $3\sqrt{20m} + 2\sqrt{45m}$ 12$\sqrt{5m}$

22 $4\sqrt{12} - 3\sqrt{2} + \sqrt{3} + \sqrt{18}$ 9$\sqrt{3}$

23 $3\sqrt{12x^3} + 2\sqrt{27x^3}$

24 $\sqrt{a^2b} \cdot \sqrt{ab^3}$

25 $3\sqrt{2c^3} \cdot 2\sqrt{8c^5}$ 12$\sqrt{4c^4}$ 24c⁴

26 $\dfrac{\sqrt{s^3}}{\sqrt{s^5}}$

27 $\sqrt{\dfrac{c^3}{2}}$ $\sqrt{\dfrac{c^3}{2}} \cdot \dfrac{\sqrt{2}}{\sqrt{2}}$ $\dfrac{\sqrt{2c^3}}{2}$ $\dfrac{c\sqrt{2c}}{2}$

28 $\dfrac{2\sqrt{x^6}}{3\sqrt{x^3}}$

29 $\dfrac{\sqrt{3b} \cdot \sqrt{2b}}{\sqrt{4b^2}}$

30 $\dfrac{2\sqrt{3x^3}}{3x^3}$

Now turn to page 446 and take the Cumulative Review test for Chapters 1–12. This will help you monitor your progress and keep all your skills sharp.

(handwritten: 1-12 14, 17, 18, 21, 22, 25, 27)

(handwritten: Test 10-12)

CHAPTER 13

Quadratic Relations and Functions

Solving Quadratic Equations

A **second-degree polynomial equation in one variable,** such as $x^2 + 2x - 15 = 0$, is called a **quadratic equation.**

Standard Form

The **standard form of a quadratic equation** is:

$ax^2 + bx + c = 0$

where a, b, and c are real numbers and $a \neq 0$.

    When a quadratic equation is written in standard form, all of the terms on one side are arranged in descending order of exponents, and the other side is zero. For example:

$x^2 + x - 6 = 0 \qquad x^2 - 5 = 0$

 MODEL PROBLEMS

Write in standard form:

SOLUTIONS

1   $x^2 + 3x = 4$ $x^2 + 3x - 4 = 0$

2   $2x + x^2 + 1 = 0$ $x^2 + 2x + 1 = 0$

3   $10 - 13x + 3x^2 = 0$ $3x^2 - 13x + 10 = 0$

4   $9 + 6x + x^2 = 0$ $x^2 + 6x + 9 = 0$

5   $x^2 + x + x + 1 = 0$ $x^2 + 2x + 1 = 0$

6   $3x + 4 = x^2$ $-x^2 + 3x + 4 = 0$ (Or: $x^2 - 3x - 4 = 0$)

Practice

1 If $n \neq 0$, which quadratic equation is written in standard form?

 (1) $x + x^2 = n$
 (2) $-x^2 - x - n = 0$
 (3) $x + x^2 + n = 0$
 (4) $x^2 - x = n$

2 If these quadratic equations are written in standard form, in which is it true that $a = 1$, $b = 2$, and $c = 3$?

 (1) $2x + x^2 = 3$
 (2) $3 + 2x = -x^2$
 (3) $2x = 3 + x^2$
 (4) $1 + 2x + 3x^2 = 0$

3 Which sentence represents a quadratic equation that can be expressed in standard form?

 (1) A number squared is equal to the sum of zero and the same number squared.
 (2) There are three consecutive even integers such that one-third the sum of the greater two is equal to the least of the three.
 (3) The square of the difference between a number and one is thirty-six.
 (4) One divided by a number is equal to one divided by the sum of twice the number and one.

4 Which of the following can be written as a quadratic equation in standard form?

 (1) $x^2 + 3x - 5 = x^2 + x + 7$
 (2) $x(x + 3) = 5x(1 - x^2)$
 (3) $x^2 - 9 = \dfrac{1}{x}$
 (4) $3(x^2 + 1) = (x + 5)(x - 5)$

Exercises 5–9: Write each quadratic equation in standard form.

5 $x(x + 2) = 8$

6 $x^2 = 35 - x - 15$

7 $x(x - 5) = 24$

8 $x^2 - 7x = -2x + 6$

9 $x(2x - 7) = 3x^2 - 8$

10 The following examples can *not* be written as quadratic equations in standard form. For each, explain why not.

 a $(x + 1)(x - 1) = x^2$
 b $x(x + 1)(x - 1) = 0$
 c $x + 1 = 5x - 5$

Solving Quadratic Equations Algebraically

Second-degree polynomial expressions can often be factored to get two **first-degree**, or **linear**, expressions—that is, expressions in which the highest power of x is 1. This gives us a strategy for solving quadratic equations.

Suppose that the product of two expressions is 0. Using the zero product property of multiplication, we know that *at least one* of these expressions equals zero:

If a and b are real numbers, then $ab = 0$ if and only if $a = 0$ or $b = 0$.

Similarly, to solve a quadratic equation, such as $x^2 + 2x - 15 = 0$, we can factor the quadratic trinomial to get a product of two linear binomials. Using the rules for factoring we get $(x + 5)(x - 3) = 0$. Set each factor equal to 0, such that $x + 5 = 0$ and $x - 3 = 0$. Solve each linear equation, so that, $x = -5$ or $x = 3$. Check each solution or root by replacing x in the original quadratic with -5 and then 3. Each result should equal zero.

The rules for factoring are reviewed in Chapter 11.

General Procedure

(1) Write the quadratic equation in standard form.
(2) Factor the quadratic expression.
(3) Set each factor equal to 0 (by the zero product property).
(4) Solve each equation to find the solution set, or **roots**.
(5) Check each **root** in the original quadratic equation.

 MODEL PROBLEMS

Solve each quadratic equation and check your solution.

1 $x^2 + 5x + 4 = 0$

SOLUTION

Factor the left side of the equation:

$x^2 + 5x + 4 = (x + 1)(x + 4)$

Solve the equation:

$x^2 + 5x + 4 = (x + 1)(x + 4) = 0$

At least one factor must equal zero: $x + 4 = 0$ or $x + 1 = 0$.

Set each factor equal to zero and solve each equation:

$x + 4 = 0 \qquad x + 1 = 0$
$ x = -4 \qquad x = -1$

Check:

$x = -4$	$x = -1$
$x^2 + 5x + 4 = 0$	$x^2 + 5x + 4 = 0$
$(-4)^2 + 5(-4) + 4 = 0$	$(-1)^2 + 5(-1) + 4 = 0$
$16 - 20 + 4 = 0$	$1 - 5 + 4 = 0$
$0 = 0 \checkmark$	$0 = 0 \checkmark$

Answer: $x = -4$ or $x = -1$. The solution set is $\{-4, -1\}$.

2 $x^2 - 8x + 16 = 0$

SOLUTION

Factor the left side of the equation:

$x^2 - 8x + 16 = (x - 4)(x - 4) = 0$

Set each factor equal to zero and solve:

$x - 4 = 0 \quad \text{and} \quad x - 4 = 0$
$ x = 4 \quad \text{and} \quad x = 4$

While every quadratic has two roots, in this case, both roots are the same. So the **double root** is written only once.

Check:

$x = 4$
$x^2 - 8x + 16 = 0$
$(4)^2 - 8(4) + 16 = 0$
$16 - 32 + 16 = 0$
$0 = 0$

Answer: $x = 4$. The solution set is $\{4\}$.

3 $x^2 + 2x = 15$

SOLUTION

Rewrite the equation in standard form:

$x^2 + 2x - 15 = 0$

Factor the left side of this equation. (Look for two numbers whose product is -15 and whose sum is 2.)

$x^2 + 2x - 15 = (x + 5)(x - 3) = 0$

At least one factor must equal zero, so $x + 5 = 0$ or $x - 3 = 0$. Solve both equations:

$x + 5 = 0 \qquad x - 3 = 0$

$\qquad x = -5 \qquad\quad x = 3$

Check:

$x = -5$	$x = 3$
$x^2 + 2x = 15$	$x^2 + 2x = 15$
$(-5)^2 + 2(-5) = 15$	$(3^2) + 2(3) = 15$
$25 - 10 = 15$	$9 + 6 = 15$
$15 = 15\ \checkmark$	$15 = 15\ \checkmark$

Answer: $x = -5$ or $x = 3$. The solution set is $\{-5, 3\}$.

4 $3x^2 + 8x + 4 = 0$

SOLUTION

Factor the left side of the equation:

$3x^2 + 8x + 4 = (3x + 2)(x + 2) = 0$

At least one factor must equal zero, so $3x + 2 = 0$ or $x + 2 = 0$. Solve both equations:

$3x + 2 = 0 \qquad x + 2 = 0$

$\qquad x = -\dfrac{2}{3} \qquad\quad x = -2$

Check:

$x = -\dfrac{2}{3}$	$x = -2$
$3x^2 + 8x + 4 = 0$	$3x^2 + 8x + 4 = 0$
$3\left(-\dfrac{2}{3}\right)^2 + 8\left(-\dfrac{2}{3}\right) + 4 = 0$	$3(-2)^2 + 8(-2) + 4 = 0$
	$3(4) - 16 + 4 = 0$
$3\left(\dfrac{4}{9}\right) - \dfrac{16}{3} + 4 = 0$	$12 - 16 + 4 = 0$
	$-4 + 4 = 0$
$\dfrac{4}{3} - \dfrac{16}{3} + 4 = 0$	$0 = 0\ \checkmark$
$-\dfrac{12}{3} + 4 = 0$	
$-4 + 4 = 0$	
$0 = 0\ \checkmark$	

Answer: $x = -\dfrac{2}{3}$ or $x = -2$. The solution set is $\left\{-\dfrac{2}{3}, -2\right\}$.

5 Jose throws a ball into the air with an initial velocity of 48 feet per second, from a height of 5 feet above the ground. If the equations $h(t) = -16t^2 + 48t + 5$ represents the distance, $h(t)$, in feet, that the ball is above the ground at any time, t, after how many seconds is the ball at a height of 37 feet?

SOLUTION

Since the height $h(t)$ is 37 feet, then

Subtract 37 and rewrite the equation in standard form:

Multiply every term of the trinomial by -1:

Divide every term by 16:

Factor the trinomial:

$$37 = -16t^2 + 48t + 5$$
$$0 = -16t^2 + 48t - 32$$
$$0 = 16t^2 - 48t + 32$$
$$0 = t^2 - 3t + 2$$
$$0 = (t - 1)(t - 2)$$
$$t - 1 = 0 \qquad t - 2 = 0$$
$$t = 1 \qquad\qquad t = 2$$

Check:

$t = 1$	$t = 2$
$37 = -16(1)^2 + 48(1) = 5$	$37 = -16(2)^2 + 48(2) + 5$
$37 = -16 + 48 + 5$	$37 = -16(4) + 96 + 5$
$37 = 37 ✓$	$37 = -64 + 96 + 5$
	$37 = 37 ✓$

ALTERNATIVE SOLUTION (Calculator)

Set the WINDOW to $-5 \le x \le 10$ and $-5 \le y \le 50$ (scale 2) or anything similar.

Press $\boxed{\text{Y=}}$ $\boxed{\text{(-)}}$ $\boxed{1}$ $\boxed{6}$ $\boxed{\text{X, T, θ, n}}$ $\boxed{x^2}$ $\boxed{+}$ $\boxed{4}$ $\boxed{8}$ $\boxed{\text{X, T, θ, n}}$ $\boxed{+}$ $\boxed{5}$ $\boxed{\text{ENTER}}$ $\boxed{3}$ $\boxed{7}$ $\boxed{\text{GRAPH}}$

To find the coordinates of intersection press $\boxed{\text{TRACE}}$ and the curser to the first intersection then press $\boxed{\text{2nd}}$ $\boxed{\text{CALC}}$ $\boxed{5}$ $\boxed{\text{ENTER}}$ $\boxed{\text{ENTER}}$ $\boxed{\text{ENTER}}$

Press $\boxed{\text{TRACE}}$ again to find the second coordinate, repeat the same process as above.

The two answers will be (1 sec, 37 feet) and (2 sec, 37 feet).

Answer: The ball is at a height of 37 feet after 1 second as it rises and after 2 seconds as it falls.

In some cases, factoring can be used to solve a higher-order equation by expressing it as a factor and a quadratic expression. If there is a common monomial factor that contains a variable, that factor may be zero and give you a root. Do *not* eliminate it by division.

The next model problem is a typical example. It involves a **cubic equation**, an equation of the form:

$$ax^3 + bx^2 + cx + d = 0$$

where a, b, c, and d are real numbers and $a \ne 0$. A factorable cubic equation has three real roots.

MODEL PROBLEM

Solve, and check your solution: $a^3 = 4a^2 + 5a$

SOLUTION

Write the cubic equation in standard form:

$a^3 - 4a^2 - 5a = 0$

Factor the left side to get a monomial and a quadratic expression:

$a(a^2 - 4a - 5) = 0$

Then factor completely:

$a(a - 5)(a + 1) = 0$

Set each factor equal to zero and solve the resulting equations:

$a = 0$	$a - 5 = 0$	$a + 1 = 0$
$a = 0$	$a = 5$	$a = -1$

Check:

$a = 0$	$a = 5$	$a = -1$
$a^3 = 4a^2 + 5a$	$a^3 = 4a^2 + 5a$	$a^3 = 4a^2 + 5a$
$0^3 = 4(0^2) + 5(0)$	$5^3 = 4(5^2) + 5(5)$	$(-1)^3 = 4(-1)^2 + 5(-1)$
$0 = 0 + 0$ ✓	$125 = 4(25) + 25$	$-1 = 4(1) + (-5)$
	$125 = 100 + 25 = 125$ ✓	$-1 = 4 - 5 = -1$ ✓

Answer: $a = 0$, $a = 5$, or $a = -1$. The solution set is $\{0, 5, -1\}$.

"Solve the equation"—as in the model problems above—is a typical problem situation. But problems involving quadratic equations may take other forms and therefore may call for different strategies. Look at the next model problems.

 MODEL PROBLEMS

1 One root of the equation $x^2 + 3x + k = 0$ is -1.
   a Find the value of k.
   b Find the second root.

SOLUTION

a The value $x = -1$ makes the equation true, so substitute -1 for x:

$(-1)^2 + 3(-1) + k = 0$

$1 - 3 + k = 0$

$-2 + k = 0$

$k = 2$

Answer: The value of k is 2.

b Substitute 2 for k in the given equation:

$x^2 + 3x + 2 = 0$

Factor:

$(x + 2)(x + 1) = 0$

Set each factor equal to zero and solve the resulting equations:

$x + 2 = 0 \qquad x + 1 = 0$

$\qquad x = -2 \qquad\quad x = -1$

Check the second root:

$$x^2 + 3x + 2 = 0$$
$$(-2)^2 + 3(-2) + 2 = 0$$
$$4 + (-6) + 2 = 0$$
$$-2 + 2 = 0$$
$$0 = 0 \checkmark$$

Answer: The second root is -2.

2 Write an equation of the form $ax^2 + bx + c = 0$ such that the roots (the solution set) will be $\{-2, 7\}$.

SOLUTION METHOD 1

Work backward: Let $x = -2$ and $x = 7$

Rewrite the equations: $x + 2 = 0$ and $x - 7 = 0$

Write the expressions on the left as factors, in parentheses, and set the product equal to 0:

$(x + 2)(x - 7) = 0$

Multiply, using FOIL: $x^2 - 5x - 14 = 0$

Check:

$x = -2$	$x = 7$
$x^2 - 5x - 14 = 0$	$x^2 - 5x - 14 = 0$
$(-2)^2 - 5(-2) - 14 = 0$	$7^2 - 5(7) - 14 = 0$
$4 + 10 - 14 = 0$	$49 - 35 - 14 = 0$
$0 = 0 \checkmark$	$0 = 0 \checkmark$

ALTERNATIVE SOLUTION METHOD 2 (Sum and Product of the Roots)

If we divide each term of $ax^2 + bx + c = 0$ by a, then $\dfrac{ax^2}{a} + \dfrac{bx}{a} + \dfrac{c}{a} = 0$ and $x^2 + \dfrac{b}{a}x + \dfrac{c}{a} = 0$.

By definition, the **sum of the roots**, $r_1 + r_2 = -\dfrac{b}{a}$.

Thus, $-2 + 7 = 5 = -\dfrac{b}{a}$, so that $-5 = \dfrac{b}{a}$.

By definition, the **product of the roots**, $r_1 \times r_2 = \dfrac{c}{a}$.

Thus, $(-2)(7) = -14 = \dfrac{c}{a}$.

By substitution, $x^2 + \dfrac{b}{a}x + \dfrac{c}{a} = x^2 + (-5)x + -14 = x^2 - 5x - 14 = 0$.

Note: In Model Problem 2, the answer could also be any equivalent equation.

Practice

1 Solve: $x^2 - 13x - 30 = 0$

  (1) $\{-15, -2\}$

  (2) $\{-15, 2\}$

  (3) $\{15, -2\}$

  (4) $\{15, 2\}$

2 Solve: $x^2 + 5x = 6$

  (1) $\{-1, 6\}$

  (2) $\{1, -6\}$

  (3) $\{2, -3\}$

  (4) $\{2, 3\}$

3 For which equation is the solution set $\{3, 4\}$?

  (1) $x^2 + 3x + 4 = 0$

  (2) $x^2 - 7x + 12 = 0$

  (3) $x^2 + 12x + 7 = 0$

  (4) $x^2 - 9x = 16$

4 For which equation is the solution set $\{-8, 2\}$?

  (1) $x^2 + 6x - 16 = 0$

  (2) $x^2 - 6x - 10 = 0$

  (3) $x^2 - 12x - 64 = 0$

  (4) $x^2 - 16x + 6 = 0$

Exercises 5–13: Solve each equation and check your solution.

5 $x^2 - 10x + 25 = 0$

6 $x^2 + 22x + 57 = 0$

7 $x^2 + 14x + 40 = 0$

8 $x^2 - 11x + 18 = 0$

9 $2x^2 + 9x + 7 = 0$

10 $5x^2 - 26x + 5 = 0$

11 $3x^2 + 8x + 5 = 0$

12 $2x^2 + 32x - 114 = 0$

13 $3x^2 + 14x + 8 = 0$

Exercises 14–17: In these problems, solution sets are given. For each solution set, write an equation of the form $ax^2 + bx + c = 0$.

14 $\{4, -2\}$

15 $\{5, 8\}$

16 $\{-3\}$

17 $\{-11, 3\}$

Items 18–20: In each of these problems, an equation and one of its roots are given. Find:

  a the value of k

  b the second root

18 5 is a root of $x^2 - 7x + k = 0$

19 5 is a root of $x^2 - 3x + k = 0$

20 7 is a root of $x^2 - 3x = -k$

21 A ball is thrown into the air with an initial velocity of 24 feet per second from a height of 6 feet above the ground. The equation that models that event is $h(t) = -16t^2 + 24t + 6$, where t is the time, in seconds, that the ball has been in the air. After how many seconds is the ball at height of 14 feet?

22 Three positive consecutive odd integers are represented by $x, x + 2$, and $x + 4$. If 19 is subtracted from twice the square of the smallest number, the result is equal to the product of the other two integers. Find the three positive consecutive odd integers.

23 At 4:20 in the afternoon, a baseball is tossed in the air. If the height of the ball is modeled by the equation $y = -2t^2 + 38t + 10$, where t is the time, in seconds, and y is the height, in feet, at what time is the ball exactly 150 feet above the ground?

24 In the figure below, the area of rectangle *LAND* is 154 square inches, and the side of square *S* is x. Using the information in the figure below, what is the length of side x?

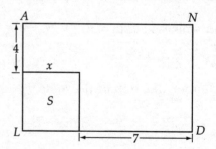

25 A ball is thrown upward at an initial speed of 72 feet per second from a platform 50 feet high. If the height in feet is given by the equation $h(t) = -16t^2 + 72t + 50$, where t is time in seconds, how long will it take the ball to reach a maximum height of 131 feet?

Incomplete Quadratic Equations

Recall that a quadratic equation is an equation of the form $ax^2 + bx + c = 0$ where a, b, and c are real numbers and $a \neq 0$.

An **incomplete quadratic equation** is a quadratic equation in which $b = 0$ or $c = 0$ or both $b = 0$ and $c = 0$. In general, the following three forms represent incomplete quadratic equations.

- Constant is missing: $ax^2 + bx = 0$
- Linear term is missing: $ax^2 + c = 0$
- Constant and linear term are missing: $ax^2 = 0$

Note that each type can be written in standard ("complete") form:

Incomplete Form	Standard Form
$ax^2 + bx = 0$	$ax^2 + bx + 0 = 0$
$ax^2 + c = 0$	$ax^2 + 0x + c = 0$
$ax^2 = 0$	$ax^2 + 0x + 0 = 0$

Solving Quadratic Equations When the Constant Is Missing   To solve an incomplete quadratic of the form $ax^2 + bx = 0$:

- Rewrite the equation, if necessary, so that all terms with the unknown are on one side of the equals sign, leaving zero on the other side.

  If the equation is fractional, first multiply by the LCD to clear the equation of all fractions, and then rewrite.

  If there are parentheses, remove them, and then rewrite.

- Combine like terms, if any.
- Factor completely.
- Set each factor equal to zero and solve the resulting equations.
- Check both solutions.

 MODEL PROBLEMS

1 Solve and check your solution: $x^2 = 6x$

SOLUTION

Step 1. Rewrite: $x^2 - 6x = 0$

We omit step 2, since there are no like terms to combine.

Step 3. Factor: $x(x - 6) = 0$

Step 4. Set each factor equal to zero and solve:

$$x = 0 \qquad x - 6 = 0$$
$$x = 0 \qquad\qquad x = 6$$

Step 5. Check:

$x = 0$	$x = 6$
$x^2 = 6x$	$x^2 = 6x$
$0^2 = 6(0)$	$6^2 = 6(6)$
$0 = 0$ ✓	$36 = 36$ ✓

Answer: $x = 0$ or $x = 6$. The solution set is $\{0, 6\}$.

2 Solve for x and check: $ax^2 + bx = 0$

SOLUTION

We do not need to rewrite (step 1), and there are no like terms to combine (step 2), so we go on to steps 3, 4, and 5.

Step 3. Factor: $x(ax + b) = 0$

Step 4. Set each factor equal to zero and solve:

$$x = 0 \qquad ax + b = 0$$
$$ax = -b$$
$$x = \frac{-b}{a} \text{ or } -\frac{b}{a}$$

Step 5. Check:

$x = 0$	$x = -\dfrac{b}{a}$
$ax^2 + bx = 0$	$ax^2 + bx = 0$
$a(0^2) + b(0) = 0$	$a\left(-\dfrac{b}{a}\right)^2 + b\left(-\dfrac{b}{a}\right) = 0$
$0 + 0 = 0$	$a\left(\dfrac{b^2}{a^2}\right) + b\left(-\dfrac{b}{a}\right) = 0$
$0 = 0$ ✓	$\dfrac{b^2}{a} + \left(-\dfrac{b^2}{a}\right) = 0$
	$0 = 0$ ✓

Answer: $x = 0$ or $x = -\dfrac{b}{a}$.

The solution set is $\left\{0, -\dfrac{b}{a}\right\}$.

Solving Quadratic Equations When the Linear Term Is Missing To solve incomplete quadratics of the form $ax^2 + c = 0$:

- Rewrite, if necessary, so that all terms with the unknown are on one side of the equation and a constant is on the other side.

  If necessary, before rewriting, multiply by the LCD to clear the equation of all fractions; also, remove any parentheses.

- Combine like terms, if any.
- Divide both sides of the equation by the coefficient of the x^2 term.
- Extract the square root of both sides of the equation, writing the symbol $\pm$ before the square root of the known quantity. If possible, simplify.
- Check each root.

Remember:
Square roots of
equals are equal.

MODEL PROBLEMS

1 Solve and check your solution: $4x^2 - 27 = x^2$

SOLUTION

Step 1. Rewrite: $4x^2 - x^2 = 27$

Step 2. Combine like terms: $3x^2 = 27$

Step 3. Divide both sides by 3: $x^2 = 9$

Step 4. Take the square root of both sides and simplify:

$$\sqrt{x^2} = \pm\sqrt{9}$$
$$x = \pm 3$$

Step 5. Check:

$x = 3$	$x = -3$
$4x^2 - 27 = x^2$	$4x^2 - 27 = x^2$
$4(3)^2 - 27 = (3)^2$	$4(-3)^2 - 27 = (-3)^2$
$4(9) - 27 = 9$	$4(9) - 27 = 9$
$36 - 27 = 9$	$36 - 27 = 9$
$9 = 9$ ✓	$9 = 9$ ✓

ALTERNATIVE SOLUTION

Sometimes, as with $4x^2 - 27 = x^2$, an equation can be solved by factoring.

Rewrite so that all terms are on one side:
$$4x^2 - x^2 - 27 = 0$$

Combine: $3x^2 - 27 = 0$

Divide by 3: $x^2 - 9 = 0$

Factor: $(x + 3)(x - 3) = 0$

Set each factor equal to zero:
$$x + 3 = 0 \text{ or } x - 3 = 0$$

Solve: $x = -3$ and $x = 3$

Answer: $x = 3$ or $x = -3$.

The solution set is $\{3, -3\}$.

2 Solve and check: $4x^2 = 49$

SOLUTION

Divide both sides by 4: $x^2 = \dfrac{49}{4}$

Take the square root of both sides and simplify:

$x = \pm\sqrt{\dfrac{49}{4}} = \pm\dfrac{7}{2}$

Check:

$x = \dfrac{7}{2}$	$x = -\dfrac{7}{2}$
$4x^2 = 49$	$4x^2 = 49$
$4\left(\dfrac{7}{2}\right)^2 = 49$	$4\left(-\dfrac{7}{2}\right)^2 = 49$
$4\left(\dfrac{49}{4}\right) = 49$	$4\left(\dfrac{49}{4}\right) = 49$
$49 = 49$ ✓	$49 = 49$ ✓

Answer: $x = \dfrac{7}{2}$ or $x = -\dfrac{7}{2}$.

The solution set is $\left\{\dfrac{7}{2}, -\dfrac{7}{2}\right\}$.

3 Solve for x and check: $9x^2 - m^2 = 0$

SOLUTION

Rewrite: $9x^2 = m^2$

Divide by 9: $x^2 = \dfrac{m^2}{9}$

Take the square root of both sides and simplify:

$x = \pm\sqrt{\dfrac{m^2}{9}} = \pm\dfrac{m}{3}$

Check:

$x = \dfrac{m}{3}$	$x = -\dfrac{m}{3}$
$9x^2 - m^2 = 0$	$9x^2 - m^2 = 0$
$9\left(\dfrac{m}{3}\right)^2 - m^2 = 0$	$9\left(-\dfrac{m}{3}\right)^2 - m^2 = 0$
$9\left(\dfrac{m^2}{9}\right) - m^2 = 0$	$9\left(\dfrac{m^2}{9}\right) - m^2 = 0$
$m^2 - m^2 = 0$	$m^2 - m^2 = 0$
$0 = 0$ ✓	$0 = 0$ ✓

Answer: $x = \dfrac{m}{3}$ or $x = -\dfrac{m}{3}$. The solution set is $\left\{\dfrac{m}{3}, -\dfrac{m}{3}\right\}$.

Solving Quadratic Equations When the Constant and Linear Term Are Missing

To solve a quadratic equation of the form $ax^2 = 0$, follow this simple rule:

If $ax^2 = 0$, then $x = 0$.

 MODEL PROBLEM

Solve: $5x^2 = 0$

SOLUTION

Divide both sides by 5: $x^2 = 0$

Solve: $\sqrt{0} = 0$, so x must equal 0.

Answer: $x = 0$

 Practice

1 Solve: $x^2 - 4x = 5x$

   (1) $\{-5, 0, 1\}$
   (2) $\{-5, 1\}$
   (3) $\{0, 9\}$
   (4) $\{-9, 0, 9\}$

2 Solve: $\dfrac{x}{2} = \dfrac{2}{x}$

   (1) $\{2\}$
   (2) $\{0, 2\}$
   (3) $\{-2, 2\}$
   (4) $\{-2, 0, 2\}$

3 For which equation is the solution set {0, 1}?

(1) $x^2 - x = 0$
(2) $x^3 - x = 0$
(3) $x^2 - 1 = 0$
(4) $x - 1 = 0$

4 For which equation is the solution set $\left\{-\dfrac{6}{5}, \dfrac{6}{5}\right\}$?

(1) $\dfrac{12}{5x} = \dfrac{x}{60}$

(2) $\dfrac{6 - x}{4} = \dfrac{5}{6 + x}$

(3) $\dfrac{6}{x} = \dfrac{25x}{6}$

(4) $5x^2 + 6x = 0$

Exercises 5–19: Solve and check your solution.

5 $x^2 + 2x = 0$

6 $x^2 = 5x$

7 $4x^2 = 28x$

8 $3x^2 = -5x$

9 $8a^2 = 2a$

10 $3x^2 - 4x = 5x$

11 $\dfrac{x^2}{5} = \dfrac{x}{15}$

12 $5x(x - 6) - 8x = 2x$

13 $3x^2 + 25 = 25 - 15x$

14 $3x^2 = 6ax$ for x

15 $\dfrac{2x^2}{25} = 18$

16 $16x^2 - 400 = 0$

17 $x^2 - 16 = 48$

18 $(x - 6)(x + 6) = 28$

19 $a^2x^2 = 49$ for x

20 Solve each formula for the variable indicated.

a $A = \pi r^2$ for r

b $S = at^2$ for t

c $A = 4\pi r^2$ for r

d $E = mc^2$ for c

e $K = \dfrac{1}{2}mv^2$ for v

f $F = \dfrac{mv^2}{r}$ for v

g $s = \dfrac{1}{2}gt^2$ for t

h $V = \pi r^2 h$ for r

Fractional Quadratic Equations

Recall that to solve a fractional equation such as $\dfrac{4x}{9} = \dfrac{2(x + 4)}{3}$, we cross multiply and solve for x:

. $18(x + 4) = 12x$

$18x + 72 = 12x$

$18x - 12x = -72$

$6x = -72$

$x = -12$

Sometimes cross multiplying results in a quadratic equation. To solve a fractional quadratic equation:

- Cross multiply only if there is just one fraction on each side of the equal sign.
- For any other fractional equation, clear the fractions by multiplying each term by the lowest common denominator (LCD).
- Rewrite the equation in standard form, with all terms on one side of the equal sign: $ax^2 + bx + c = 0$.
- Factor and solve.
- Check your solution set.

 MODEL PROBLEMS

1   Solve and check your solution:

$$\frac{x + 5}{3} = \frac{10}{x - 8}$$

SOLUTION

Cross multiply: $(x + 5)(x - 8) = 30$

Use FOIL: $x^2 - 8x + 5x - 40 = 30$

Combine terms and write the equation in standard form: $x^2 - 3x - 70 = 0$

Factor: $(x + 7)(x - 10) = 0$

Solve:

$$\begin{array}{cc} x + 7 = 0 & x - 10 = 0 \\ x = -7 & x = 10 \end{array}$$

Check: The check must be done with the *original* equation.

$x = -7$	$x = 10$
$\dfrac{x + 5}{3} = \dfrac{10}{x - 8}$	$\dfrac{x + 5}{3} = \dfrac{10}{x - 8}$
$\dfrac{-7 + 5}{3} = \dfrac{10}{-7 - 8}$	$\dfrac{10 + 5}{3} = \dfrac{10}{10 - 8}$
$\dfrac{-2}{3} = \dfrac{10}{-15}$ or $-\dfrac{2}{3} = -\dfrac{10}{15}$	$\dfrac{15}{3} = \dfrac{10}{2}$
$-\dfrac{2}{3} = -\dfrac{2}{3}$ ✓	$5 = 5$ ✓

Answer: $x = -7$ or $x = 10$. The solution set is $\{-7, 10\}$.

2 Solve and check your solution: $2 + \dfrac{5}{n} = \dfrac{12}{n^2}$

SOLUTION

Multiply each term by the LCD, n^2:

$$2(n^2) + \frac{5}{n}(n^2) = \frac{12}{n^2}(n^2)$$

Simplify: $2n^2 + 5n = 12$

Write in standard form: $2n^2 + 5n - 12 = 0$

Factor: $(2n - 3)(n + 4) = 0$

Solve:

$$2n - 3 = 0 \qquad n + 4 = 0$$
$$n = \frac{3}{2} \qquad\quad n = -4$$

Check:

$n = \dfrac{3}{2}$	$n = -4$
$2 + \dfrac{5}{n} = \dfrac{12}{n^2}$	$2 + \dfrac{5}{n} = \dfrac{12}{n^2}$
$2 + \left(5 \div \dfrac{3}{2}\right) = 12 \div \left(\dfrac{3}{2}\right)^2$	$2 + \dfrac{5}{-4} = \dfrac{12}{(-4)^2}$
$2 + \dfrac{10}{3} = \dfrac{48}{9}$	$\dfrac{8}{4} - \dfrac{5}{4} = \dfrac{12}{16}$
$\dfrac{16}{3} = \dfrac{16}{3}$ ✓	$\dfrac{3}{4} = \dfrac{3}{4}$ ✓

Answer: $n = \dfrac{3}{2}$ or $n = -4$. The solution set is $\left\{\dfrac{3}{2}, -4\right\}$.

Note: In checking, decimal equivalents can also be used.

 Practice

1 In which case will cross multiplying result in a quadratic equation?

(1) $\dfrac{x}{7} = \dfrac{4}{x - 3}$

(2) $\dfrac{x}{7} = \dfrac{x - 3}{4}$

(3) $\dfrac{x}{x - 3} = \dfrac{4}{7}$

(4) $\dfrac{7}{x} = \dfrac{4}{x - 3}$

2 In which case do we need to use the LCD?

(1) $\dfrac{2x}{3} = \dfrac{6}{x}$

(2) $\dfrac{x}{2} - 2 = \dfrac{6}{x}$

(3) $\dfrac{x}{2} - \dfrac{8}{x} = 0$

(4) each of the above

3 Find the solution set: $\dfrac{2x+3}{6x+1} = \dfrac{1}{2x}$

    (1) $\left\{\dfrac{1}{2}, -\dfrac{1}{2}\right\}$

    (2) $\{2, -2\}$

    (3) $\{1, -1\}$

    (4) $\left\{\dfrac{1}{3}, -\dfrac{1}{3}\right\}$

4. Find the solution set: $\dfrac{2}{x} = \dfrac{3}{x^2-1}$

    (1) $\left\{-\dfrac{1}{2}, 2\right\}$

    (2) $\left\{\dfrac{1}{2}, -2\right\}$

    (3) $\left\{\dfrac{1}{2}, -\dfrac{1}{2}\right\}$

    (4) $\{1, -1\}$

Exercises 5–20: Solve each equation and check your solution.

5 $\dfrac{x}{5} = \dfrac{3}{x+2}$

6 $\dfrac{8}{x} = \dfrac{x+2}{3}$

7 $\dfrac{3x}{4} = \dfrac{x^2}{8}$

8 $\dfrac{7x}{3} = \dfrac{x^2}{6}$

9 $\dfrac{x+2}{2} = \dfrac{1}{x+3}$

10 $\dfrac{x+4}{3} = \dfrac{3}{x+4}$

11 $\dfrac{x-2}{2} = \dfrac{3}{x+3}$

12 $\dfrac{x-1}{4} = \dfrac{12}{x+1}$

13 $\dfrac{x+2}{3} = \dfrac{4}{x-2}$

14 $\dfrac{3x+4}{3} = \dfrac{3}{3x-4}$

15 $\dfrac{5x+2}{8} = \dfrac{4}{5x-2}$

16 $\dfrac{2x^2-3}{2} = \dfrac{x^2-3}{3}$

17 $\dfrac{x+3}{2} = \dfrac{8}{x-3}$

18 $\dfrac{4+x}{2x} = \dfrac{x}{4-x}$

19 $\dfrac{4x^2-5}{3} = \dfrac{2x^2-3}{2}$

20 $\dfrac{3x-2}{x} = \dfrac{3x+3}{x+2}$

Graphing Quadratic Functions: Finding the Turning Point and Roots of Parabolas*

Graphing a Parabola

At the beginning of this chapter, we learned to factor and solve quadratic equations of the form $ax^2 + bx + c =$, where $a \neq 0$. The graph of a quadratic equation in the form $y = ax^2 + bx + c$, where $a \neq 0$, is a special curve called a **parabola**.

To Graph a Parabola, Given a Domain

- Express the equation in the form $y = ax^2 + bx + c$.
- Create a table of coordinates by using values from the given domain.
- Plot the points from the table of values and join them to make a smooth curve.

———
*8th Grade May–June Topic

MODEL PROBLEM

Graph $y = x^2 + 4x + 3$ using integral values from -5 to 1.

SOLUTION

Make a table of values.

x	$x^2 + 4x + 3$	y
-5	$(-5)^2 + 4(-5) + 3$	8
-4	$(-4)^2 + 4(-4) + 3$	3
-3	$(-3)^2 + 4(-3) + 3$	0
-2	$(-2)^2 + 4(-2) + 3$	-1
-1	$(-1)^2 + 4(-1) + 3$	0
0	$(0)^2 + 4(0) + 3$	3
1	$(1)^2 + 4(1) + 3$	8

You can use the graphing calculator to find this table of values quickly. See the appendix.

When you plot the ordered pairs (x, y), you get the smooth curve shown.

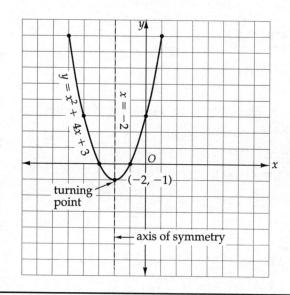

The graph of this parabola has certain interesting features. The graph is symmetric with respect to the line $x = -2$. That line has a special name, the **axis of symmetry**. Every parabola $y = ax^2 + bx + c$ has an axis of symmetry. The equation for the axis of symmetry is $x = \dfrac{-b}{2a}$. For the parabola $y = x^2 + 4x + 3$, $a = 1$ and $b = 4$. The equation of the axis of symmetry can be found by using the formula:

$x = \dfrac{-b}{2a}$.

$x = \dfrac{-4}{2(1)}$ so $x = -2$

The turning point is also called the vertex.

The curve of this parabola has a lowest point on the graph where it crosses the axis of symmetry. This minimum point is called the **turning point** of the parabola. The turning point is on the axis of symmetry. Therefore, its abscissa, or x-value, is $\dfrac{-b}{2a}$. In this example, the abscissa is -2. The ordinate, or y-value, is found by substituting the x-value (-2) back into the quadratic equation. In the table, when $x = -2$, $y = -1$, so the turning point is $(-2, -1)$.

This parabola happens to turn upward, like a bowl, but not all parabolas must point that way. The direction of the parabola can be determined by the value of the coefficient a. If a is positive, then the graph of the equation $y = ax^2 + bx + c$ opens upward and the turning point is a **minimum point**. If a is negative, then the graph of the equation $y = ax^2 + bx + c$ opens downward and the turning point is a **maximum point**.

By applying the vertical line test, we find that this parabola is a function. In fact, *every parabola of the form $y = ax^2 + bx + c$ is a function.*

To Graph a Parabola, Not Given a Domain

• Express the equation in the form $y = ax^2 + bx + c$.

• Obtain a table of values by finding the axis of symmetry, $x = \dfrac{-b}{2a}$, and then choose integer values of x both greater and smaller than $\dfrac{-b}{2a}$.

• Plot the points from the table of values and join them to make a smooth curve.

Note: (1) The turning point of the parabola must occur on the axis of symmetry. (2) The axis of symmetry is always an equation. It is never just a number.

 MODEL PROBLEM

Graph $y = -x^2 + 6x - 5$ and label the turning point.

SOLUTION

Substitute -1 for a and 6 for b in the equation for the axis of symmetry.

$$x = \frac{-b}{2a} = \frac{-6}{2(-1)} = \frac{6}{2} = 3$$

The equation of the axis of symmetry is $x = 3$, so choose values for x near 3 from the domain, $\{0, 1, 2, 3, 4, 5, 6\}$.

Make a table of values.

x	$-x^2 + 6x - 5$	y
0	$-(0)^2 + 6(0) - 5$	-5
1	$-(1)^2 + 6(1) - 5$	0
2	$-(2)^2 + 6(2) - 5$	3
3	$-(3)^2 + 6(3) - 5$	4
4	$-(4)^2 + 6(4) - 5$	3
5	$-(5)^2 + 6(5) - 5$	0
6	$-(6)^2 + 6(6) - 5$	-5

Plot and graph the ordered pairs.

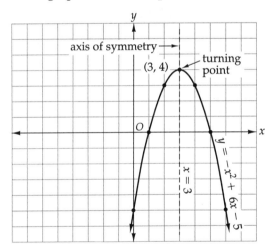

The turning point of the parabola is on the axis of symmetry where the x-value is 3. The ordinate, or y-value, is found by substituting 3 for x in the quadratic equation. Looking at our table, when $x = 3$, $y = 4$. The turning point is $(3, 4)$.

1 What is the equation of the axis of symmetry for $y = x^2 - 4x$?

(1) $x = 2$

(2) $x = -\dfrac{1}{8}$

(3) $y = \dfrac{1}{8}$

(4) $y = -2$

2 Identify the turning point of $y = -x^2 - 2x$.

(1) $(4, 8)$

(2) $(1, -3)$

(3) $(-1, 1)$

(4) $(-4, -8)$

3 Which equation does the parabola in the graph represent?

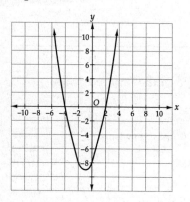

(1) $y = x^2 + 2x + 8$
(2) $y = x^2 + 2x - 8$
(3) $y = x^2 - 2x - 8$
(4) $y = x^2 - 2x + 8$

4 Which parabola is the graph of the equation $y = -x^2 + 4x - 3$?

(1)

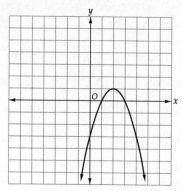

(2)

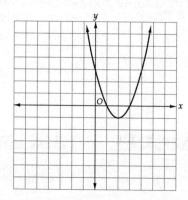

(3)

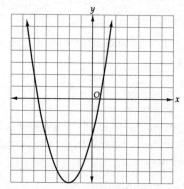

(4)

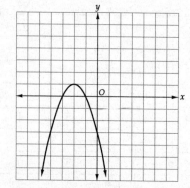

Exercises 5–9: What are the coordinates of the vertex or turning point of each of the following? Identify the turning point as a maximum or a minimum.

5   $y = -x^2 + 6x + 10$

6   $y = x^2 - 10x - 14$

7   $y = 4x^2 + 8x - 11$

8   $y = -x^2 - 6$

9   $y = 2x^2 - 7x$

Exercises 10–15: Using the domain indicated in the parentheses, prepare a table of values and graph the quadratic equation. Find the equation of the axis of symmetry and the turning point. Identify the turning point as a maximum or a minimum.

10   $y = x^2 - 6x - 7$ $(0 \le x \le 6)$

11   $y = -2x^2$ $(-3 \le x \le 3)$

12   $y = x^2 + 2$ $(-3 \le x \le 3)$

13   $y = x^2 - 3x - 4$ $(-1 \le x \le 5)$

14   $y = 2(x^2 - 1)$ $(-3 \le x \le 3)$

15   $y = -x^2 + 4x - 1$ $(1 \le x \le 5)$

Exercises 16–20:

   a   Find the axis of symmetry and turning point.

   b   Create a table to get 7 points for the graph, centered on the turning point.

   c   Graph the equation.

   d   Identify the turning point as a maximum or a minimum.

16   $y = x^2 + 2x + 1$

17   $y = -2x^2 + 1$

18   $y = 2x^2 + 4x + 1$

19   $y = -2x^2 + 8x$

20   $y = x^2 - 6x$

Solving Quadratic Equations Graphically

Earlier in this chapter, we found solutions for quadratic equations by factoring and setting each factored term equal to 0. The solutions, or **roots**, of a quadratic equation can also be found by graphing the equation and looking at the x-intercepts of the graph.

To Solve a Quadratic Equation Graphically

- Express the equation in the form $y = ax^2 + bx + c$.
- Graph the parabola $y = ax^2 + bx + c$ using a suitable table of values.
- Identify where the parabola crosses the x-axis (where $y = 0$). These are the roots or solutions to the quadratic equation.

A quadratic equation can have two, one, or zero solutions.

Using a graphing calculator, we can find noninteger roots to a specified degree of accuracy. See the appendix.

Case I: Parabola intersects the x-Axis at Two Distinct Points   An example is the graph of $y = x^2 - 4$. We can solve this equation algebraically by setting the quadratic $x^2 - 4 = 0$, then factoring and solving each linear equation.

$$x^2 - 4 = 0$$

$$(x + 2)(x - 2) = 0$$

$$x + 2 = 0 \qquad\qquad x - 2 = 0$$

$$x = -2 \qquad\qquad x = 2 \quad \text{The solution set is } \{2, -2\}.$$

Now we solve the equation graphically.

Find the axis of symmetry, $x = \dfrac{-b}{2a} = \dfrac{0}{2} = 0.$

Make a table of values.

x	$x^2 - 4$	y
-3	$(-3)^2 - 4$	5
-2	$(-2)^2 - 4$	0
-1	$(-1)^2 - 4$	-3
0	$(0)^2 - 4$	-4
1	$(1)^2 - 4$	-3
2	$(2)^2 - 4$	0
3	$(3)^2 - 4$	5

Using the table, graph $y = x^2 - 4$.

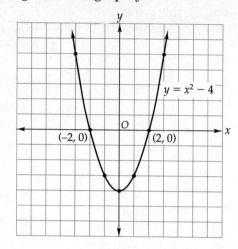

The x-intercepts of the graph are $(-2, 0)$ and $(2, 0)$. The roots of the equation are -2 and 2. *If the graph crosses the x-axis at two distinct points, the roots are real and un-equal.*

Case II: Parabola Intersects the *x*-Axis at Exactly One Point An example is the graph of $y = x^2 + 4x + 4$. We can solve this equation algebraically by setting the quadratic equation equal to zero.

$$x^2 + 4x + 4 = 0$$
$$(x + 2)(x + 2) = 0$$
$$x + 2 = 0 \quad x + 2 = 0$$
$$x = -2 \quad\quad x = -2 \quad \text{The roots of the equation are } both -2.$$

Now we solve the equation graphically.

Find the axis of symmetry, $x = \dfrac{-b}{2a} = \dfrac{-4}{2} = -2$.

Make a table of values.

x	$x^2 + 4x + 4$	y
-5	$(-5)^2 + 4(-5) + 4$	9
-4	$(-4)^2 + 4(-4) + 4$	4
-3	$(-3)^2 + 4(-3) + 4$	1
-2	$(-2)^2 + 4(-2) + 4$	0
-1	$(-1)^2 + 4(-1) + 4$	1
0	$(0)^2 + 4(0) + 4$	4
1	$(1)^2 + 4(1) + 4$	9

Using the table, graph $y = x^2 + 4x + 4$ around the axis of symmetry.

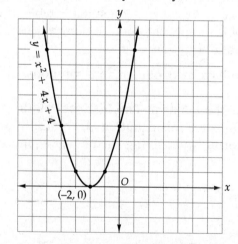

The x-intercept of the graph is the point $(-2, 0)$, which is also the turning point of the parabola. The solution set is $\{-2\}$. *Since the graph crosses the x-axis at exactly one point, the roots are real and equal.*

Case III: Parabola Does Not Intersect the *x*-Axis An example is the graph of $y = x^2 - 2x + 2$.

x	$x^2 - 2x + 2$	y
-2	$(-2)^2 - 2(-2) + 2$	10
-1	$(-1)^2 - 2(-1) + 2$	5
0	$(0)^2 - 2(0) + 2$	2
1	$(1)^2 - 2(1) + 2$	1
2	$(2)^2 - 2(2) + 2$	2
3	$(3)^2 - 2(3) + 2$	5
4	$(4)^2 - 2(4) + 2$	10

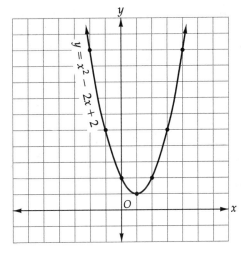

Since the graph does not intersect the x-axis, the equation has no real roots.

Parabolas as Graphs of Real Situations

The parabolic shape appears often in real situations. When answering questions about parabolas, remember:

- Questions that involve minimum or maximum vales of the dependent variable will usually require you to find the coordinates of the turning point.
- Questions that provide a value for the dependent value and ask for the corresponding value of the independent variable may have more than one answer.

📋 MODEL PROBLEM

At exactly 6 P.M. a football is kicked upward from ground level with an initial velocity of 32 feet per second. The formula $h(t) = -16t^2 + 32t$ gives the height of the ball in feet after t seconds.

a What is the maximum height reached by the football? (What is the turning point?)

b After how many seconds does the ball touch the ground?

c Exactly what time does the ball touch the ground?

SOLUTION

Axis of symmetry of $y = -16t^2 + 32t$ is $t = \dfrac{-b}{2a} = \dfrac{-32}{2(-16)} = \dfrac{-32}{-32} = 1$.

Substitute 1 for t and solve for y.
$y = -16t^2 + 32t = -16(1)^2 + 32(1) = -16 + 32 = 16$. The turning point is (1, 16).

a Therefore, in 1 second, the football reached a maximum height of 16 feet.

b Since the ball touches the ground at 0 feet, set $-16t^2 + 32t = 0$ and solve for t.

Factor: $t(-16t + 32) = 0$

Set each factor to 0. $t = 0$ sec (before it was kicked) and $-16t + 32 = 0$, so that $-16t = -32$ and $t = 2$, which means 2 seconds (after it was kicked).

c The time is exactly 2 seconds after 6 P.M.

1 How many x-intercepts does the graph of $x^2 + x + 5 = 0$ have?

   (1) 0
   (2) 1
   (3) 2
   (4) an infinite number of intercepts

2 What is the largest root of $x^2 + 5x - 6 = 0$?

   (1) 6   (3) 3
   (2) 5   (4) 1

3

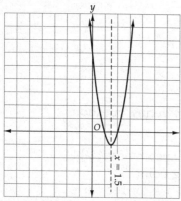

From this graph of $3x^2 - 9x + 6 = 0$, we can conclude that the equation has

   (1) no roots
   (2) one root at 6
   (3) one root at 1.5
   (4) two roots, one at 1 and one at 2

4 The single solution of $x^2 + 7x + 12.25 = 0$ lies between what two integer values of x?

   (1) -6 and -5
   (2) -4 and -3
   (3) 3 and 4
   (4) 5 and 6

Exercises 5–20: Solve the quadratic equations by graphing and labeling the roots. Identify whether the roots are real and unequal, real and the same (double roots), or no real roots.

5 $x^2 - x - 6 = 0$

6 $x^2 + 2x = 0$

7 $x^2 - 1 = 0$

8 $x^2 - 6x + 9 = 0$

9 $x^2 + 8x + 16 = 0$

10 $-x^2 + 6x - 27 = 0$

11 $x^2 + 3x = 0$

12 $x^2 - 4x - 21 = 0$

13 $f(x) = x^2 - 2x - 3$

14 $y = x^2 - 12x + 36$

15 $h(x) = -x^2 + 4x + 12$

16 $y = x^2 + 2x + 5$

17 $x^2 - 10x = -25$

18 $x^2 - x + 4 = 0$

19 $x^2 + 9 = 0$

20 $2x^2 - 18 = 0$

Exercises 21–25: Answer *yes* or *no* and explain your answer without graphing.

21 If the coordinates of the vertex (or turning point) of the parabola $y = x^2 + 4x + 1$ are $(-2, -3)$, does the quadratic equation $x^2 + 4x + 1 = 0$ have two different real roots?

22 If the coordinates of the vertex (or turning point) of the parabola $y = x^2 - 4x + 4$ are $(2, 0)$, does the quadratic equation $x^2 - 4x + 4 = 0$ have two different real roots?

23 If the coordinates of the vertex (or turning point) of the parabola $y = -2x^2 + x + 3$ are $\left(\dfrac{1}{4}, 3\dfrac{1}{8}\right)$, does the quadratic equation $-2x^2 + x + 3 = 0$ have two different real roots?

24 If the coordinates of the vertex (or turning point) of the parabola $y = -x^2 + 3x$ are $\left(1\dfrac{1}{2}, 2\dfrac{1}{4}\right)$, does the quadratic equation $-x^2 + 3x = 0$ have two different real roots?

25 If the coordinates of the vertex (or turning point) of the parabola $y = x^2 - 4x + 5$ are $(2, 1)$, does the quadratic equation $x^2 - 4x + 5 = 0$ have two different real roots?

26 Alice tosses a volleyball in the air. The function $h(t) = -16t^2 + 8t + 8$ represents the distance, in feet, that the ball is from the ground at any time t.

  a What is the maximum height of the ball?

  b After how many seconds is the ball at maximum height?

  c After how many seconds does the ball touch the ground?

27 Lee has 40 feet of fencing material with which to enclose a rectangular garden that has a brick wall on one side. If the width of the garden is x, then we can represent the length of the garden as $40 - 2x$. What is the maximum area of the garden that can be enclosed by the 40 feet of fencing? (Hint: Find the turning point.)

28 Robert plans to build a deck against his house. He decides to fence in the three other sides first with 120 feet of wooden fencing. What is the maximum area of the deck he can build based on the amount of fencing he has?

29 Karen is on the beach and throws a seashell straight up. The equation that models that flight is $h(t) = -16t^2 + 96t$, where t is the time in seconds, and $h(t)$ is the height.

  a What is the maximum height of the seashell?

  b How many seconds does it take for the seashell to reach maximum height?

  c For how many seconds is the seashell in the air? (Hint: When is the height equal to zero again?)

30 The height of a baseball $h(t)$ at time t, where $t \geq 0$ and where the ball is struck initially at 4 feet above ground, is modeled by the equation $h(t) = -16t^2 + 64t + 4$.

  a After how many seconds is the ball at maximum height?

  b What is the maximum height of the baseball?

  c After how many seconds is the ball at a height of *exactly* 52 feet?

Graphic Solutions to Quadratic-Linear Systems

The graph of a quadratic-linear system consists of the graph of a quadratic equation (a parabola) and a linear equation (a line). As before, the intersections of the graphs reveal the solutions common to both equations.

To Solve Quadratic-Linear Systems Graphically

- Draw the graphs of both equations on the same coordinate plane.
- Find the common solutions by reading the points of intersection of the two graphs.
- Write the solutions as ordered pairs.
- Check the solutions in both original equations.

The solution set to a quadratic-linear pair may consist of two points, one point, or no points. Some possibilities for these systems are illustrated below.

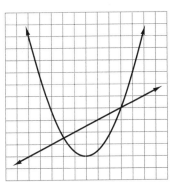
Two Solutions

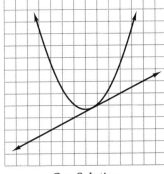
One Solution

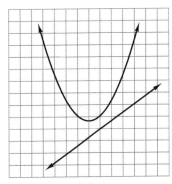
No Solution

The following model problems, all using the same quadratic equation, demonstrate each case.

 MODEL PROBLEMS

1 Find the solution set for

$y = x^2 - 2x + 1$

$y = -x + 3$

SOLUTION

For $y = x^2 - 2x + 1$, the equation of the axis of symmetry is $x = \dfrac{-b}{2a} = \dfrac{-(-2)}{2(1)} = 1$.

Create a table centered on $x = 1$.

x	$x^2 - 2x + 1$	y
-2	$(-2)^2 - 2(-2) + 1$	9
-1	$(-1)^2 - 2(-1) + 1$	4
0	$(0)^2 - 2(0) + 1$	1
1	$(1)^2 - 2(1) + 1$	0
2	$(2)^2 - 2(2) + 1$	1
3	$(3)^2 - 2(3) + 1$	4
4	$(4)^2 - 2(4) + 1$	9

Plot the points and draw the parabola. The line $y = -x + 3$ is already in slope-intercept form. The y-intercept is 3 and the slope is -1. Graph the line.

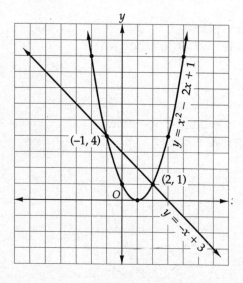

The graphs intersect at the two points $(-1, 4)$ and $(2, 1)$. The solution set is $\{(-1, 4), (2, 1)\}$.

Check for $(-1, 4)$:

$y = x^2 - 2x + 1$	$y = -x + 3$
$4 = (-1)^2 - 2(-1) + 1$	$4 = -(-1) + 3$
$4 = 1 + 2 + 1$	$4 = 1 + 3$
$4 = 4$ ✓	$4 = 4$ ✓

Check for $(2, 1)$:

$y = x^2 - 2x + 1$	$y = -x + 3$
$1 = (2)^2 - 2(2) + 1$	$1 = -(2) + 3$
$1 = 4 - 4 + 1$	$1 = 1$ ✓
$1 = 1$ ✓	

2 Find the solution set for

$y = x^2 - 2x + 1$

$y = -2x + 1$

SOLUTION

The parabola is copied from the example above. For the line $y = -2x + 1$, the slope is -2 and the y-intercept is 1.

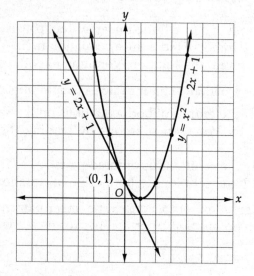

The graphs intersect at only one point $(0, 1)$. The solution set is $\{(0, 1)\}$.

Check for $(0, 1)$:

$y = x^2 - 2x + 1$	$y = -2x + 1$
$1 = (0)^2 - 2(0) + 1$	$1 = -(0) + 1$
$1 = 1$ ✓	$1 = 1$ ✓

3 Find the solution set for

$$y = x^2 - 2x + 1$$
$$y = -x - 3$$

SOLUTION

Again, the parabola is copied from the example above. For the line $y = -x - 3$, the slope is -1 and the y-intercept is -3.

The graphs do not intersect. The solution is the empty set, $\varnothing$.

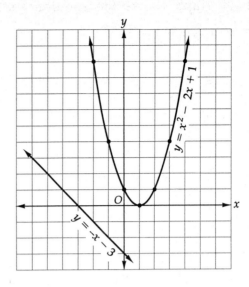

Practice

1 Which graph shows the solution to the system $y = x - 2$ and $y = x^2 - 6x + 4$?

(1)

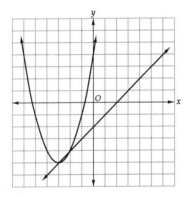

(3)

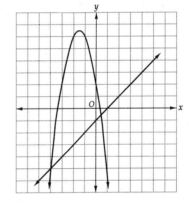

(2)

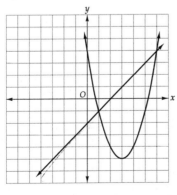

(4)

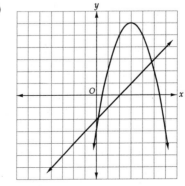

2 Which graph shows the solution set of $y = -\frac{1}{2}x - 4$ and $y = x^2 - 4$?

(1)
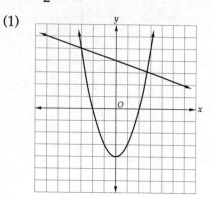

(2)
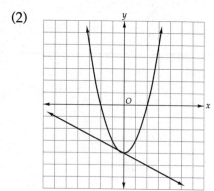

(3)
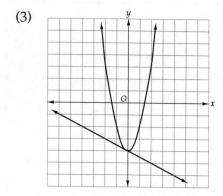

(4)
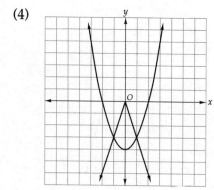

3 Which set of equations describes the graph?

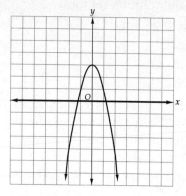

(1) $x = 0$ and $y = -2x^2 + 3$
(2) $x = 0$ and $y = 2x^2 + 3$
(3) $y = 0$ and $y = 2x^2 + 3$
(4) $y = 0$ and $y = -2x^2 + 3$

4 Which set of equations describes the graph?

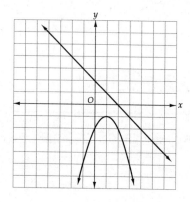

(1) $y = x + 2$ and $(x - 1)^2 + (y - 1) = 0$
(2) $y = x + 2$ and $(x - 1)^2 - (y - 1) = 0$
(3) $x + y = 2$ and $-(x - 1)^2 + (y - 1) = 0$
(4) $x + y = 2$ and $(x - 1)^2 + (y - 1) = 0$

Exercises 5–20: Solve each system of equations graphically and check. If there is no solution, write "no solution."

5 $y = x - 6$
$\quad y = x^2 - 6$

6 $y = x^2 - 2x$
$\quad y = x + 4$

7 $y = -x^2 + 4x + 1$
$\quad y = x - 3$

8 $(x - 3)^2 + (y + 2) = 4$
$\quad y = -2$

9 $y = x^2 + 2$
$\quad y = x + 4$

10 $y = x^2 + 4x + 4$
$y = -2x - 5$

11 $y = -x^2 + 6x - 4$
$y = 2x$

12 $y = 2x^2$
$y = -2x + 4$

13 $2x^2 + 2y = 18$
$x = 3$

14 $y = x^2$
$y = -3$

15 $y = x^2 - 4x + 9$
$y = 2x + 1$

16 $y = x^2 - 5x + 4$
$y = -2$

17 $y = x^2 + x - 6$
$y = 6$

18 $y = 2x^2 + 4x - 2$
$x = 3$

19 $2y = x^2 - 16$
$y = -2x + 8$

20 $y = x^2 - 5x + 8$
$y - 3x = 1$

Solving Quadratic-Linear Pairs Algebraically

A **quadratic-linear pair** is a system of one quadratic equation and one linear equation with the same two variables x and y. In such a system the quadratic equation has the form:

$$y = ax^2 + bx + c$$

where a, b, and c are real numbers and $a \neq 0$.

The solutions to a quadratic-linear system are the ordered pairs of values (x, y) that satisfy both equations. As reviewed in Chapter 10, a system of two linear equations can be solved algebraically by the **substitution method** or the **addition method** (also called the **elimination method**). These methods can be adapted to solve a quadratic-linear pair.

Substitution Method

- Solve the linear equation for one of the variables, x or y. (Solving for either variable will work. Common sense will usually indicate which is better.)
- Substitute this expression for the appropriate variable in the quadratic equation.
- Solve the quadratic equation.
- Substitute the solutions found in step 3 in the linear equation and solve.
- Check by substituting the ordered pairs in both given equations.

Solve by the substitution method:

$$y = x^2 - 4x + 4$$
$$2y = x + 4$$

SOLUTION

Since the x term is squared in the quadratic equation, we solve the linear equation for y:

$$2y = x + 4$$
$$y = \frac{1}{2}x + 2$$

Substitute this expression for y in the quadratic equation:

$$y = x^2 - 4x + 4$$
$$\frac{1}{2}x + 2 = x^2 - 4x + 4$$

To clear the fraction, multiply each term by 2. Then write in standard form.

$$x + 4 = 2x^2 - 8x + 8$$
$$0 = 2x^2 - 9x + 4$$

Or:

$$2x^2 - 9x + 4 = 0$$

Solve by factoring: $2x^2 - 9x + 4 = (2x - 1)(x - 4) = 0$. Then:

$$2x - 1 = 0 \qquad x - 4 = 0$$
$$x = \frac{1}{2} \qquad x = 4$$

Substitute both x values in the linear equation to find the corresponding y values.

$x = \dfrac{1}{2}$	$x = 4$
$2y = x + 4$	$2y = x + 4$
$2y = \dfrac{1}{2} + 4 = 4\dfrac{1}{2} = \dfrac{9}{2}$	$2y = 4 + 4$
	$2y = 8$
$y = \dfrac{9}{2} \div 2 = \dfrac{9}{4}$	$y = 4$

Check: Substitute both ordered pairs in both given equations.

$(x, y) = \left(\dfrac{1}{2}, \dfrac{9}{4}\right)$		$(x, y) = (4, 4)$	
$y = x^2 - 4x + 4$	$2y = x + 4$	$y = x^2 - 4x + 4$	$2y = x + 4$
$\dfrac{9}{4} = \left(\dfrac{1}{2}\right)^2 - 4\left(\dfrac{1}{2}\right) + 4$	$2\left(\dfrac{9}{4}\right) = \dfrac{1}{2} + 4$	$4 = 4^2 - (4 \bullet 4) + 4$	$2(4) = 4 + 4$
$\dfrac{9}{4} = \dfrac{1}{4} - 2 + 4$	$\dfrac{18}{4} = 4\dfrac{1}{2}$	$4 = 16 - 16 + 4$	$8 = 8 \checkmark$
$2\dfrac{1}{4} = 2\dfrac{1}{4} \checkmark$	$4\dfrac{1}{2} = 4\dfrac{1}{2} \checkmark$	$4 = 4 \checkmark$	

Answer: $(x, y) = \left(\dfrac{1}{2}, \dfrac{9}{4}\right)$ or $(4, 4)$

Addition (or Elimination) Method

- Add the two equations to eliminate one variable, y. You may need to add an opposite (subtract). If necessary, first write an equivalent equation for one or both of the original equations.
- The sum will be a quadratic equation in one variable, x. Solve it.
- Substitute the solutions in the original linear equation and solve.
- Check by substituting the ordered pairs in the given equations.

 MODEL PROBLEM

Solve by the addition (elimination) method:

$$y = x^2 - 4x + 4$$
$$2y = x + 4$$

SOLUTION

To eliminate y, multiply all terms in the quadratic equation by 2. Multiply the linear equation by -1 and add:

$$
\begin{array}{lll}
y = x^2 - 4x + 4 & \rightarrow & 2y = 2x^2 - 8x + 8 \\
2y = x + 4 & \rightarrow & \underline{-2y = \quad\quad - x - 4} \\
& & 0 = 2x^2 - 9x + 4
\end{array}
$$

Now proceed as in the Model Problem on the previous page: Solve this quadratic equation, substitute the values of x in the linear equation to solve it, and check the ordered pairs by substitution in the given equations.

Shortcut: When the y term is the same or equivalent in both equations, set the two expressions equal to each other, simplify (write in standard form), and solve.

 Practice

---

1 Solve:

$$y = 3 - x^2$$
$$y = -x - 3$$

(1) $(x, y) = (-3, 0)$ or $(2, -5)$
(2) $(x, y) = (-1, 4)$ or $(6, -9)$
(3) $(x, y) = (-2, -1)$ or $(3, -6)$
(4) $(x, y) = (0, -3)$ or $(1, -4)$

2 Solve:

$$y = x^2 - 8x + 7$$
$$y = -x - 3$$

(1) $(x, y) = (-5, -2)$ or $(-2, 1)$
(2) $(x, y) = (-2, 1)$ or $(4, -7)$
(3) $(x, y) = (1, -4)$ or $(7, 10)$
(4) $(x, y) = (2, -5)$ or $(5, -8)$

3 If $7x - y = 10$ and $y = x^2 + 3x - 10$, which is a possible value for x?

(1) $x = \dfrac{10}{7}$
(2) $x = 2$
(3) $x = 4$
(4) $x = 5$

4 If $x^2 - y = 15$ and $x + y = 15$, which is a possible value for x?

(1) $x = 0$
(2) $x = 5$
(3) $x = 10$
(4) $x = 15$

5 When Alice and Valerie tried to solve the following system of equations, Alice said there were an infinite number of real solutions and Valerie said there were no real solutions. Which student, if either, is correct? Explain.

$$y = 2x^2 - 2x + 3$$
$$y = -2x - 3$$

Exercises 6–25: Solve each system and check your solution.

6 $y = 4x^2$
$y = 8x$

7 $x^2 + 3 = y$
$x + y = 5$

8 $y = x^2$
$y = -2x + 8$

9 $y = x^2 - 4$
$y = x + 2$

10 $y^2 = 4x$
$x - y = -4$

11 $x^2 - 4x - 5 = y$
$y = 3x - 11$

12 $2y = x - 10$
$y = x^2 + 2x - 15$

13 $y = -x^2 - 4x + 1$
$y = 2x + 10$

14 $y = -\dfrac{1}{2}x^2 + 3x$
$2y - x = 0$

15 $y = -x^2 + 6x - 1$
$y = x + 3$

16 $y = \dfrac{1}{2}x^2 + 3x - 2$
$2y = 8x - 1$

17 $y = -\dfrac{1}{2}x^2 + 3x - \dfrac{1}{2}$
$y = \dfrac{5}{4}x - 6$

18 $y = \dfrac{1}{2}x^2 - 5x + 2$
$x - 2y = 24$

19 $x^2 + y^2 = 10$
$x + y = 4$

20 $x^2 + y^2 = 20$
$3x + y = 2$

21 $x^2 + y^2 = 16$
$y^2 - 2x = -8$

22 $x^2 + y^2 = 25$
$x + 2y = 10$

23 $2x^2 - y^2 = 14$
$x - y = 1$

24 $x^2 + 1 = 4y$
$3x - 2y = 2$

25 $y - 2x = 1$
$x^2 - 3xy + y^2 = -1$

Verbal Problems Involving Quadratics

Factoring polynomial equations is a tool for solving word problems. In this section, quadratics are applied in number problems and then in real-world problems.

Number Problems

A common problem situation involves finding the value of a described number or numbers. The next model problems, solved alegbraically, are typical.

Remember:
$n, n + 1, n + 2, \ldots$ are consecutive integers
$n, n + 2, n + 4, \ldots$ are consecutive even or consecutive odd integers

MODEL PROBLEMS

1 Find two consecutive integers whose product is 72.

SOLUTION

Let n and $n + 1$ = the two integers

Then $n(n + 1) = 72$

Solve:

Simplify.	$n^2 + n = 72$
Write in standard form.	$n^2 + n - 72 = 0$
Factor.	$(n + 9)(n - 8) = 0$
Set each factor equal to 0.	$n + 9 = 0$ or $n - 8 = 0$
Find n.	$n = -9$ or $n = 8$
Find $n + 1$.	$n + 1 = -8$ or $n + 1 = 9$

Check:

$n = -9$	$n = 8$
$n(n + 1) = 72$	$n(n + 1) = 72$
$-9(-9 + 1) = 72$	$8(8 + 1) = 72$
$-9(-8) = 72$	$8(9) = 72$
$72 = 72$ ✓	$72 = 72$ ✓

Answer: The integers are -9 and -8 or 8 and 9.

2 The sum of two numbers is 13. The sum of their squares is 89. Find the numbers.

SOLUTION

Let x = one number

$13 - x$ = the other number

Then $x^2 + (13 - x)^2 = 89$

Solve:

Simplify and write in standard form.	$x^2 + 169 - 26x + x^2 = 89$
	$2x^2 - 26x + 169 - 89 = 0$
	$2x^2 - 26x + 80 = 0$
Divide by 2.	$x^2 - 13x + 40 = 0$
Factor.	$(x - 8)(x - 5) = 0$
Find x.	$x - 8 = 0$ so $x = 8$
	$x - 5 = 0$ so $x = 5$
Find $13 - x$.	$13 - x = 5$ or $13 - x = 8$

Answer: Both factors yield the solution 5 and 8.

1   Twice the square of an integer is 3 less than 7 times the integer. Find the integer.

   (1) -3
   (2) -1
   (3) 1
   (4) 3

2   The square of a number increased by 3 times the number equals 4. Find all possible solutions.

   (1) $\{1, -4\}$
   (2) $\{-1, -5\}$
   (3) $\{1\}$
   (4) $\{0, -3\}$

3   The sum of the squares of two consecutive odd integers is 202. Find the integers.

   (1) $\{11, 9\}$ or $\{-9, -11\}$
   (2) $\{11, 9\}$
   (3) $\{5, 7\}$ or $\{-7, -5\}$
   (4) $\{-11, -13\}$ or $\{9, 11\}$

4   When a number is decreased by its reciprocal, the result is $2\frac{1}{10}$. Find the number.

   (1) $2\frac{1}{2}$

   (2) $\frac{2}{5}$

   (3) $2\frac{1}{2}$ or $-\frac{2}{5}$

   (4) $2\frac{1}{2}$ or $-2\frac{1}{2}$

5   Six times the square of a number decreased by 5 times the number equals 1. Find the negative solution.

6   Find two pairs of consecutive odd integers whose product is 63.

7   The sum of the squares of two consecutive even integers is 164. Find the integers.

8   The square of a number is 12 more than the number. Find the number.

9   The square of a number decreased by 3 times the number is 18. Find the number.

10   The product of a number and 5 less than the number is 24. Find the number.

11   The product of two consecutive integers is 42. Find the integers.

12   The square of 1 more than a number is equal to 4 more than 4 times the number. Find the number.

13   The sum of two numbers is 14 and their product is 48. Find the numbers.

14   One number is 3 less than another number. Their product is 40. Find the numbers.

15   The sum of 3 times the square of a number and 6 times the number is equal to twice the square of that number, decreased by 8. Find the number.

16   If the square of a number is increased by 4 times the number, the result is 12. Find the number.

17   The difference of the squares of a number and one-half the number is 27. Find the number.

18   Two numbers are consecutive integers. The square of the lesser added to twice the greater is 37. Find the numbers.

19   The sum of a number and its reciprocal is $2\frac{1}{6}$. Find all solutions.

20   If 4 is added to 7 times a number, the result is twice the square of the number. Find the number.

Real-World Applications

In a real-world problem, not all values that satisfy a given equation are necessarily the answer. We need to consider the conditions of the problem and reject answers that are not reasonable. Some typical problems, like the models below, involve geometry. See Chapter 7 for a review of geometric concepts.

1 The length of a rectangle is twice the width. The area is 32 square units. Find the length and width. (Area = length × width.)

SOLUTION

Let w = width

$2w$ = length

Then:

$A = lw$

$32 = (2w)(w) = 2w^2$

$w^2 = 16$

Here, the value of w is obvious by inspection, but when that is not the case, we can solve by taking a square root or by factoring.

Method 1: Take the square root of both sides of the equation.

$\sqrt{w^2} = \sqrt{16}$

$w = 4$ or -4

We reject -4, since a length cannot be negative. The solution is the principal square root.

Answer: The width is 4 units. Therefore, the length is $2 \cdot 4 = 8$ units.

Method 2: Factor. First write the equation in standard form.

$$w^2 = 16$$

$$w^2 - 16 = 0$$

$$(w - 4)(w + 4) = 0$$

Then:

$w - 4 = 0 \qquad w + 4 = 0$

$w = 4 \qquad\qquad w = -4$

Reject the negative root, since a length must be positive.

$w = 4$

$l = 2w = 2(4) = 8$

Answer: As above, width is 4 units and length is 8 units.

2 The area of Mr. Lamb's rectangular garden is 100 square feet. One side is a stone wall. He encloses the other 3 sides with 30 feet of fencing. What are the dimensions of his garden? Perimeter = (2 × length) + (2 × width). Area = length × width.

SOLUTION

Let w = width in feet

Now use $P = 2l + 2w$. For 3 sides, $l + 2w = 30$. Therefore:

$l = 30 - 2w$

Then:

$A = lw$

$100 = w(30 - 2w)$

$100 = 30w - 2w^2$

$2w^2 - 30w + 100 = 0$

$w^2 - 15w + 50 = 0$

Factor:

$(w - 10)(w - 5) = 0$

Solve:

$w - 10 = 0 \qquad w - 5 = 0$

$w = 10 \qquad\qquad w = 5$

Both solutions are postive, so both are possible.

Answers: If $w = 10$ feet, then length = $30 - 2w = 30 - 20 = 10$ feet.

If $w = 5$ feet, then length = $30 - 2w = 30 - 10 = 20$ feet.

ALTERNATIVE SOLUTION

Assume that the wall is width w.

Then for 3 sides, $2l + w = 30$, so $w = 30 - 2l$.

Therefore, $100 = l(30 - 2l) = 30l - 2l^2$.

Proceed as above, solving for l.

Answer: If $l = 10$ feet, then $w = 10$ feet. If $l = 5$ feet, then $w = 20$ feet.

Linear dimensions are units. Areas are square units. Formulas to use are:

Perimeter of rectangle	Perimeter = (2 • length) + (2 • width) $P = 2l + 2w$
Area of rectangle	Area = length • width $A = lw$
Area of triangle	Area = $\frac{1}{2}$ • base • height $A = \frac{1}{2}bh$

1 The length l of a rectangle is twice the width w. The area is 18. Find the width.

(1) $w = 9$
(2) $w = 8$
(3) $w = 4$
(4) $w = 3$

2 The width w of a rectangle is 7 less than the length l. The area is 60. Find the length.

(1) $l = 10$
(2) $l = 11$
(3) $l = 12$
(4) $l = 15$

3 The length l of a rectangle is 3 more than twice the width w. The area is 90. Find the length.

(1) $w = 3$
(2) $w = 6$
(3) $w = 7.5$
(4) $w = 9$

4 Base b and height h of a triangle have the same measure. The area of the triangle is 8. Find the base.

(1) $b = 8$
(2) $b = 4$
(3) $b = 2\sqrt{2}$
(4) $b = 2$

5 The area of a rectangle is 99 square inches. The length is is 2 feet longer than the width. Find the dimensions.

6 The length of a rectangle is 8 feet longer than the width. The area is 105 square feet. Find the dimensions of the rectangle.

7 A pool is in the shape of a triangle. The sum of the base and height is 19 yards. The area is 42 square yards. What are the dimensions of the pool?

8 The altitude (height) of a triangle is 8 feet more than twice its base. The area is 45 square feet. Find base and altitude.

9 A rectangle is 10 feet longer than it is wide. Its area is 39 square feet. Find the dimensions.

10 The length of a rectangle is 3 inches less than twice the width. The area is 65 square inches. Find length and width.

11 The length of a rectangular garage is 2 yards more than its width. The area is 80 square yards. What are the dimensions of the garage?

12 The area of Janina's rectangular garden is 45 square meters. The length of the garden is 4 meters more than the width. What are the dimensions of the garden?

13 The area of a rectangle is 70 square inches. The width is 3 inches less than the length. What are the dimensions?

14 A rectangular minipark is 16 yards long and 40 yards wide. The town adds the same amount to the length and the width, increasing the area by 305 square yards. How much is added to each dimension?

15 Two opposite sides of a square are each increased by 6 inches. The other two opposite sides are each decreased by 1 inch. The result is a rectangle that is twice the area of the square. What is the length of a side of the square?

16 The perimeter of a rectangle is 22 feet, and the area is 24 feet. Find length and width.

17 The perimeter of a rectangular walk-in closet is 26 feet. If the length is increased by 4 feet and the width is increased by 3 feet, the area of the new closet will be 96 square feet. Find the dimensions of the new closet.

18 One side of a rectangular garden plot is the bank of a stream. The other 3 sides are enclosed by 12 yards of fencing. The area is 16 square yards. Find the possible dimensions of the garden.

19 A rectangle is 3 times as long as it is wide. If the width is increased by 6 feet and the length is decreased by 3 feet, the area is doubled. Find the dimensions of the original rectangle.

20 The length of a rectangle exceeds its width by 7 inches. The length of the rectangle is decreased by 2 inches, and the width is increased by 3 inches. The resulting new rectangle has an area 1 square inch less than twice the area of the original rectangle. Find the dimensions of the original rectangle.

 # CHAPTER REVIEW

1 Solve for x: $64x^2 = 9m^2$

(1) $\{24m, -24m\}$

$\sqrt{8}x = 3m$

$x = \frac{3}{8}m$

(2) $\left\{2\frac{2}{3}m\right\}$

(3) $\left\{\frac{3}{8}m\right\}$

(4) $\left\{-\frac{3}{8}m, \frac{3}{8}m\right\}$

2 One root of $x^2 - 10x + k = 0$ is 5. Find k and the other root.

(1) $k = 25$ and the other root is 5
(2) $k = -25$ and the other root is 5
(3) $k = 25$ and the other root is -5
(4) $k = -25$ and the other root is -5

3 Solve: $\dfrac{x+7}{9} = \dfrac{3}{x+1}$

(1) $\{-2, 10\}$
(2) $\{-10, 2\}$
(3) $\{2, 10\}$
(4) $\{10, 2\}$

4 Three numbers are consecutive integers. The square of the second number is 8 more than the sum of the other two numbers. Which of the following is a solution?

(1) 0, 1, 2
(2) 1, 2, 3
(3) 2, 3, 4
(4) 3, 4, 5

5 Which of the following states the vertex and axis of symmetry for the quadratic equation $y = x^2 + 2x - 3$?

(1) $(1, 0); x = 1$
(2) $(-1, -4); x = -1$
(3) $(-1, -6); x = -1$
(4) $(2, 5); x = 2$

6 A small rectangular garden 6 feet by 10 feet has a brick path of uniform width, x, placed around it. If the entire area of both the garden and the walkway equals 140 square feet, which of the following equations can be used to find the uniform width, x?

(1) $x^2 + 16x - 20 = 0$
(2) $x^2 + 16x - 80 = 0$
(3) $x^2 + 8x - 20 = 0$
(4) $x^2 + 8x - 80 = 0$

Exercises 7–20: Solve each quadratic equation algebraically and check your solutions.

7 $x(x - 1) = 56$

8 $x^2 + 15x + 44 = 0$

9 $x^2 - 13x + 22 = 0$

10 $25x^2 - 4 = 32$

11 $x^2 - 12 = 11x$

12 $4x^2 + 28x = 0$

13 $5x^2 + 4x - 1 = 0$

14 $2x^2 - 7x - 15 = 0$

15 $(x + 8)^2 = 25$

1-3, 5,8,9,21,25,27 graph

16 $\dfrac{x+3}{5} = \dfrac{6}{x+4}$

17 $2a^2 + 5a = 3$

18 $x^2 + 16 = 8x$

19 $(2x - 1)^2 = 9$

20 $(x + 1)^2 - 5x = 71$

Exercises 21–24: Use the roots given below to write a quadratic equation.

21 $\{2, 7\}$

22 $\{-2, -5\}$

23 $\{-1, 9\}$

24 $\{-6, -6\}$

25 If one root of $x^2 - 8x + k = 0$ is -3, what is

    a the other root?

    b the value of k?

Exercises 26–30: For each of the given functions,

    a write the equation of the axis of symmetry

    b find the coordinates of the turning point and identify it as the a maximum or minimum

    c graph the quadratic equation and determine the roots of the equation

    d check the solution set by solving algebraically

26 $y = x^2 - 7x + 10$

27 $y = x^2 - 12x + 35$

28 $y = -2x^2 - 4x + 1$

29 $y = 2x^2 - 4x$

30 $y = x^2 - 2x + 1$

Exercises 31 and 32: In the following systems of quadratic-linear pairs, use both algebraic and graphic methods to find the solution sets. Check your answers.

31 $y = x^2 - 6x + 5$
$y = 2x - 10$

32 $3x - y = 9$
$x^2 = 2y + 10$

33 Solve the following systems of equations algebraically.
$xy = 6$
$x + y = 5$

34 The perimeter of a rectangle is 42 inches and the area is 98 square inches. Find the dimensions of the rectangle.

35 A rectangular sheet of copper is twice as long as it is wide. From each corner a 3-inch square is cut out and the ends are then turned up to form a tray. If the volume of the tray is 324 cubic inches, what were the original dimensions of the sheet of copper?

36 A cement walkway of uniform width has been built around an in-ground rectangular pool. The area of the walkway is 1,344 square feet. The pool itself is 80 feet long by 20 feet wide. What is the width of the walkway?

37 An artist drew a rainbow mural on a school wall. The mural is 8 feet wide at the base. Its shape can be represented by a parabola with equation $y = -\dfrac{1}{2}x^2 + 4x$, where y is the height of the rainbow.

    a Graph the parabola from $x = 0$ to $x = 8$.

    b Determine the height y of the rainbow.

38 The height (in feet) of a golf ball hit into the air is given by $h = 64t - 16t^2$, where t is the number of seconds elapsed since the ball was hit.

    a Graph the height of the ball versus time for the first 4 seconds.

    b What is the maximum height of the ball during the first 4 seconds?

    c How long will it take for the ball to reach its maximum height?

39 During a tropical storm, an antenna broke loose from the roof of a building 144 feet high. Its height h above the ground after t seconds is given by $h = -16t^2 + 144$. Graph the height of the antenna with respect to time until it hits the ground.

40 When an arrow is shot into the air, its height h (in feet) above the ground is given by $h = -16t^2 + 32t + 5$, where t is the time elapsed in seconds. If the arrow hit a target after 0.75 second, what was the maximum height of the arrow?

Now turn to page 448 and take the Cumulative Review test for Chapters 1–13. This will help you monitor your progress and keep all your skills sharp.

Algebraic Fractions and Equations, and Inequalities Involving Fractions

The Meaning of an Algebraic Fraction

The principles used in the study of fractions in arithmetic can be generalized in working with algebraic fractions.

A fraction indicates division, for example, $\dfrac{a}{d}$ means a divided by d, where division by zero is excluded. Thus, a rational number in arithmetic is a number that can be written in the form $\dfrac{a}{d}$, where a and d are integers and $d \neq 0$. A **rational expression** (or **algebraic fraction**) is the quotient of two polynomials.

For example, $\dfrac{m}{3}, \dfrac{3}{x}, \dfrac{5xy}{m}, \dfrac{3a}{x+y}, \dfrac{2x+3}{x^2-4}, \dfrac{a^2+5a+4}{a+4}$ are all rational expressions. In none of the fractions can the denominator equal 0. For any numbers that make the denominator equal to 0, the fraction is said to be **undefined**.

 MODEL PROBLEM

When is the algebraic expression $\dfrac{x+3}{x^2+5x-14}$ undefined?

SOLUTION

Factor the denominator. $\dfrac{x+3}{x^2+5x-14} = \dfrac{x+3}{(x+7)(x-2)}$

Set each factor in the denominator equal to 0 and solve. $x+7=0$ and $x-2=0$

$x=-7$ and $x=2$. The rational expression $\dfrac{x+3}{x^2+5x-14}$ is *undefined* when $x \in \{-7, 2\}$.

Exercises 1–15: Identify the real values, if any that cannot be members of the domain of each of the following rational expressions.

1 $\dfrac{5}{x}$

2 $\dfrac{4}{a + 2}$

3 $\dfrac{9}{xy}$

4 $\dfrac{4}{x^2 - 1}$

5 $\dfrac{8}{2x - 4}$

6 $\dfrac{a - 5}{a - 5}$

7 $\dfrac{6}{x^2 + 1}$

8 $\dfrac{7}{2x - 1}$

9 $\dfrac{x - 2}{3x + 6}$

10 $\dfrac{x - 3}{(x - 2)(x + 11)}$

11 $\dfrac{3}{x^2 + 3x + 2}$

12 $\dfrac{3x + 1}{3x - 1}$

13 $\dfrac{n - 2}{n^2 + 3n}$

14 $\dfrac{2a}{4a^2 - 2a}$

15 $\dfrac{x}{x - 2y}$

Reducing Fractions to Lowest Terms

It is important to remember that dividing or multiplying the numerator and denominator of a fraction by the same nonzero number and/or variable produces a fraction that is equivalent to the given fraction.

Examples:

$$-\frac{24}{32} = -\frac{24 \div 8}{32 \div 8} = -\frac{3}{4} \text{ and } \frac{5}{6x} = \frac{5}{6x} \cdot \frac{2x^2}{2x^2} = \frac{10x^2}{12x^3} \text{ if } x \neq 0$$

Of course, we say that $-\dfrac{3}{4}$ and $\dfrac{5}{6x}$ are fractions in **lowest terms** or **simplest form** if the greatest common factor of the numerator and denominator is 1.

To Reduce Fractions to Lowest Terms

• Find the largest common factor of both the numerator and denominator.

   Note: If the numerator, denominator, or both are polynomials, factor them, if possible.

• Divide the numerator and denominator by their largest common factor (cancellation).

Examples: $\dfrac{4\not{x}}{5\not{x}} = \dfrac{4}{5}, \ \dfrac{c\not{y}}{d\not{y}} = \dfrac{c}{d}, \text{ and } \dfrac{2(x\not{+}6)}{3(x\not{+}6)} = \dfrac{2}{3}$

MODEL PROBLEMS

1 Reduce to lowest terms: $\dfrac{8x^3y^4}{12x^5y^3}$

SOLUTION

$$\dfrac{8x^3y^4}{12x^5y^3} = \dfrac{4x^3y^3 \cdot 2y}{4x^3y^3 \cdot 3x^2} = \dfrac{2y}{3x^2}$$

2 Reduce to lowest terms: $\dfrac{2g + 6}{g^2 - 9}$

SOLUTION

$$\dfrac{2g + 6}{g^2 - 9} = \dfrac{2(g + 3)}{(g + 3)(g - 3)} = \dfrac{2}{g - 3}$$

3 Reduce to lowest terms: $\dfrac{x^2 + 6x + 9}{x^2 - 9}$

SOLUTION

$$\dfrac{x^2 + 6x + 9}{x^2 - 9} = \dfrac{(x + 3)(x + 3)}{(x + 3)(x - 3)} = \dfrac{x + 3}{x - 3}$$

Practice

Reduce each fraction to lowest terms.

1 $\dfrac{bx}{by}$

2 $\dfrac{g}{g^3}$

3 $\dfrac{ab}{a^2b^2}$

4 $\dfrac{a^4x^3}{ax}$

5 $\dfrac{x^8y^3z^6}{x^9y^4z^4}$

6 $\dfrac{18a^3b}{30ab^3}$

7 $\dfrac{10a^2d^3}{ad^4}$

8 $\dfrac{-32a^3b^3}{48a^3b^4}$

9 $\dfrac{5a^2(x + y)}{15a(x + y)}$

10 $\dfrac{2x(a + b)}{14x^3}$

11 $\dfrac{9x - 18}{4x - 8}$

12 $\dfrac{(x + 5)^2}{x + 5}$

13 $\dfrac{ax - ay}{rx - ry}$

14 $\dfrac{5x - 5}{x^2 - 1}$

15 $\dfrac{64 - x^2}{16 + 2x}$

16 $\dfrac{x^2 - 4}{(x - 2)^2}$

17 $\dfrac{2ab^2x}{2ab + 4ax}$

18 $\dfrac{x}{x^2 + x}$

19 $\dfrac{3a}{6a - 9a^2}$

20 $\dfrac{5x^2 - 20}{(x - 2)^2}$

21 $\dfrac{3x^2 - 3y^2}{(x - y)^2}$

22 $\dfrac{a^2 + a}{2a^3 + 2a^2}$

23 $\dfrac{75 - 12x}{15 - 6x}$

24 $\dfrac{x^2 - 16}{x^2 - 8x + 16}$

25 $\dfrac{2a^2 + 2ay}{a^2 - y^2}$

26 $\dfrac{a^3 - ab^2}{ab(a - b)^2}$

27 $\dfrac{2x^2 - 50}{x^2 + 8x + 15}$

28 $\dfrac{x^2 + 4x - 5}{x^2 + 8x + 15}$

29 $\dfrac{ax - a^2x^2}{bx - abx^2}$

30 $\dfrac{x^2 - 2x + 1}{x^2 + 3x - 4}$

A Special Case: Factoring Out −1

When the numerator and denominator of a fraction are the same, we divide and get 1 as the quotient. When they are opposites, we get −1.

$\dfrac{n}{n} = 1$	$\dfrac{-n}{-n} = 1$	$\dfrac{n}{-n} = -1$	$\dfrac{-n}{n} = -1$
$\dfrac{3}{3} = 1$	$\dfrac{-7}{-7} = 1$	$\dfrac{4}{-4} = -1$	$\dfrac{-6}{6} = -1$

The examples above are obvious, but something like $\dfrac{x - 7}{7 - x} = -1$ is not so obvious. To get a clearer picture, factor out −1 from either the numerator or the denominator so that $x - 7$ is the same as $-1(7 - x)$.

$$\frac{x - 7}{7 - x} = \frac{-1(7 \diagup x)}{(7 \diagup x)} = -1$$

 MODEL PROBLEMS

In each problem, factor out −1 and then simplify.

1 Factor −1 out of the denominator: $\dfrac{2x - 5}{5 - 2x}$

SOLUTION

$$\frac{2x - 5}{5 - 2x} = \frac{(2x \diagup 5)}{-1(2x \diagup 5)} = \frac{1}{-1} = -1$$

In general, if the fraction is of the form $\dfrac{K - N}{N - K}$, the result is −1.

2 Factor -1 out of the numerator: $\dfrac{7-x}{x^2-49}$

SOLUTION

$$\frac{7-x}{x^2-49}=\frac{-1(x-7)}{(x+7)(x-7)}=\frac{-1}{x+7}$$

3 Factor -1 out of the denominator: $\dfrac{6xy-2x^2}{x-3y}$

SOLUTION

$$\frac{6xy-2x^2}{x-3y}=\frac{2x(3y-x)}{x-3y}=\frac{2x(3y-x)}{-1(3y-x)}=\frac{2x}{-1}=-2x$$

4 Factor -1 out of the numerator: $\dfrac{3-6x}{2x^2+5x-3}$

SOLUTION

$$\frac{3-6x}{2x^2+5x-3}=\frac{-(6x-3)}{(2x-1)(x+3)}=\frac{-1(3)(2x-1)}{(2x-1)(x+3)}=\frac{-3}{x+3}$$

 ## Practice

1 Which is equivalent to -1?

   (1) $\dfrac{x^2-4}{(2-x)^2}$ (3) $\dfrac{4x-6y}{6y-4x}$

   (2) $\dfrac{x^2-xy}{y-x}$ (4) $\dfrac{2x-y}{2y-x}$

Exercises 2–4: For each given expression, factor out -1 and simplify.

2 $\dfrac{x^2-xy}{y^2-xy}$

   (1) $-\dfrac{x}{y}$ (3) $-\dfrac{y-x}{x-y}$

   (2) $\dfrac{xy-x^2}{y^2-xy}$ (4) $\dfrac{2x}{y}$

3 $\dfrac{8-2x}{x^2-16}$

   (1) $\dfrac{-2}{x+4}$ (3) $\dfrac{2}{4-x}$

   (2) $\dfrac{4-x}{x-8}$ (4) $\dfrac{-1}{x-2}$

4 $\dfrac{x^2+x-56}{64-x^2}$

   (1) $\dfrac{7-x}{x+8}$ (3) $\dfrac{7-x}{8-x}$

   (2) $-\dfrac{x-7}{x-8}$ (4) $-\dfrac{x+7}{x+8}$

Exercises 5–18: Simplify each fraction.

5 $\dfrac{5-z}{z-5}$

6 $\dfrac{a-b}{b-a}$

7 $\dfrac{x-6y}{6y-x}$

8 $\dfrac{x-y}{2y-2x}$

9 $\dfrac{x^2-9}{3-x}$

10 $\dfrac{2x-6}{9-3x}$

11 $\dfrac{7-a}{3a-21}$

12 $\dfrac{x-7}{49-x^2}$

13 $\dfrac{x^2-4x}{16-x^2}$

14 $\dfrac{a^2+2a-15}{3-a}$

15 $\dfrac{3-2x}{2x^2+3x-9}$

16 $\dfrac{4-x}{x^2-8x+16}$

17 $\dfrac{9-a^2}{a^2-4a+3}$

18 $\dfrac{8-x}{x^2+x-72}$

Exercises 19 and 20: Factor each trinomial by first factoring out -1.

19 $\dfrac{x+3}{6-x-x^2}$

20 $\dfrac{a-b}{b^2-a^2}$

Multiplying Fractions

The product of two or more fractions is the product of their numerators divided by the product of their denominators. For example, $\dfrac{3}{n} \times \dfrac{2}{5n} = \dfrac{6}{5n^2}$ and $\dfrac{a}{b} \bullet \dfrac{x}{y} = \dfrac{ax}{by}$.

To Multiply Rational Expressions

- Factor the numerators and denominators, if possible.
- Divide the numerators and denominators by common factors (cancellation).
- Multiply the remaining factors: numerator by numerator, denominator by denominator, and simplify.

 MODEL PROBLEMS

1 Multiply: $\dfrac{25x^2}{7y} \bullet \dfrac{42y^2}{15x^3}$

SOLUTION

Cancel common factors.

$$\dfrac{25x^2}{7y} \bullet \dfrac{42y^2}{15x^3} = \dfrac{\overset{5}{\cancel{25x^2}}}{\cancel{7y}} \bullet \dfrac{\overset{6y}{\cancel{42y^2}}}{\underset{3x}{\cancel{15x^3}}}$$

Multiply the remaining factors of the numerator and the denominator and then simplify.

$$\dfrac{5 \bullet 6y}{1 \bullet 3x} = \dfrac{\overset{10}{\cancel{30}}y}{\underset{1}{\cancel{3}}x} = \dfrac{10y}{x}$$

Answer: $\dfrac{10y}{x}, x \neq 0$

2 Multiply: $\dfrac{x^2-9}{10x^3} \bullet \dfrac{5x^2}{2x+6}$

SOLUTION

Factor and cancel common factors.

$$\dfrac{x^2-9}{10x^3} \bullet \dfrac{5x^2}{2x+6} = \dfrac{(x-3)(\overset{1}{\cancel{x+3}})}{\underset{2x}{\cancel{10x^3}}} \bullet \dfrac{\overset{1}{\cancel{5x^2}}}{2(\underset{1}{\cancel{x+3}})}$$

Multiply the remaining factors in numerator and denominator.

$$\dfrac{(x-3) \bullet 1 \bullet 1}{2x \bullet 1} = \dfrac{x-3}{2x}$$

Answer: $\dfrac{x-3}{2x}, x \neq 0$

Multiply and simplify.

1 $\dfrac{x^2}{36} \cdot 20$

2 $ab \cdot \dfrac{8}{a^2b^2}$

3 $\dfrac{18}{x^2} \cdot 3x$

4 $\dfrac{24a}{35y} \cdot \dfrac{14y}{8a}$

5 $\dfrac{7x^2}{4yz} \cdot \dfrac{8yz^2}{21x^3z}$

6 $\dfrac{2a^2}{(3ab)^3} \cdot \dfrac{9a^2}{4y}$

7 $\dfrac{14a^2}{5b} \cdot \dfrac{b^3}{a^3} \cdot \dfrac{15a}{4b^2}$

8 $\dfrac{x^2-1}{16} \cdot \dfrac{2}{x+1}$

9 $\dfrac{3x}{x^2-16} \cdot \dfrac{4-x}{9}$

10 $\dfrac{3x-15}{7} \cdot \dfrac{5+x}{25-x^2}$

11 $\dfrac{x+y}{10xy} \cdot \dfrac{5x^3y}{(x+y)^2}$

12 $\dfrac{(a+3)^3}{x^2} \cdot \dfrac{5x^2}{5a+15}$

13 $\dfrac{7x-7y}{x^2y} \cdot \dfrac{xy^2}{x^2-y^2}$

14 $\dfrac{x^2-9}{3x} \cdot \dfrac{6x}{5x-15}$

15 $\dfrac{x^2-4}{10x^3} \cdot \dfrac{5x^2}{2x+4}$

16 $\dfrac{x^2-7x-8}{2x+2} \cdot \dfrac{5}{x-8}$

17 $\dfrac{6x^5}{(a-b)^2} \cdot \dfrac{a^2-b^2}{9x}$

18 $\dfrac{a^2-4a+4}{4b} \cdot \dfrac{16b^2}{a^2-4}$

19 $\dfrac{x^2+6x+5}{9m^2} \cdot \dfrac{3m}{x+1}$

20 $\dfrac{(a+b)^2}{a^2-b^2} \cdot \dfrac{a^2-2ab+b^2}{ak-kb}$

21 $\dfrac{a(a-b)^2}{6b} \cdot \dfrac{18b}{a^3-ab^2}$

22 $\dfrac{x-y}{x+y} \cdot \dfrac{x^2-y^2}{x^2-2xy+y^2}$

23 $\dfrac{a^2+2ab+b^2}{a^2-b^2} \cdot \dfrac{ax-bx}{ay+by}$

24 $\dfrac{4x-4}{a^2-b^2} \cdot \dfrac{a^3b^2-a^2b^3}{abx-ab}$

25 $\dfrac{x^2-8x+16}{x^2+3x-10} \cdot \dfrac{x^2+2x-8}{x^2-16}$

Dividing Fractions

To Divide Two Rational Expressions

- Multiply the dividend (the first term) by the reciprocal of the divisor (the second term).
- Proceed as in the multiplication of fractions.

For example:

Arithmetic

$$\dfrac{5}{8} \div \dfrac{3}{4} = \dfrac{5}{\overset{}{\underset{2}{8}}} \times \dfrac{\overset{1}{4}}{3} = \dfrac{5 \times 1}{2 \times 3} = \dfrac{5}{6}$$

Algebraically

$$\dfrac{4x}{7} \div \dfrac{3}{2x} = \dfrac{4x}{7} \cdot \dfrac{2x}{3} = \dfrac{8x^2}{21}$$

1 Simplify: $\dfrac{16x^3}{21m^2} \div \dfrac{24x^4}{14m^3}$, $(m \neq 0, x \neq 0)$

SOLUTION

Change division into multiplication by
using the reciprocal of the divisor.

$$\dfrac{16x^3}{21m^2} \div \dfrac{24x^4}{14m^3} = \dfrac{16x^3}{21m^2} \bullet \dfrac{14m^3}{24x^4}$$

Cancel common factors.

$$\dfrac{\overset{2}{\cancel{16x^3}}}{\underset{3}{\cancel{21m^2}}} \bullet \dfrac{\overset{2m}{\cancel{14m^3}}}{\underset{3x}{\cancel{24x^4}}} = \dfrac{2 \bullet 2m}{3 \bullet 3m} = \dfrac{4m}{9x}$$

Answer: $\dfrac{4m}{9x}$

2 Divide $\dfrac{8a^2}{a^2 - 25}$ by $\dfrac{4a}{3a + 15}$ $(a \neq 0, -5, 5)$.

SOLUTION

$$\dfrac{8a^2}{a^2 - 25} \div \dfrac{4a}{3a + 15} = \dfrac{8a^2}{a^2 - 25} \times \dfrac{3a + 15}{4a} = \dfrac{\overset{2a}{\cancel{8a^2}}}{(a \cancel{+} 5)(a - 5)} \times \dfrac{3(a \cancel{+} 5)}{\underset{1}{\cancel{4a}}} = \dfrac{6a}{a - 5}$$

Answer: $\dfrac{6a}{a - 5}$

3 Simplify $\dfrac{x^2 - 6x + 8}{x^2 - 8x + 16}$ divided by $\dfrac{x^2 + 2x - 8}{x^2 - 16}$.

SOLUTION

$$\dfrac{x^2 - 6x + 8}{x^2 - 8x + 16} \text{ divided by } \dfrac{x^2 + 2x - 8}{x^2 - 16} = \dfrac{x^2 - 6x + 8}{x^2 - 8x + 16} \times \dfrac{x^2 - 16}{x^2 + 2x - 8}$$

Factor and cancel.

$$\dfrac{(x \cancel{-} 2)(x \cancel{-} 4)}{(x \cancel{-} 4)(x \cancel{-} 4)} \times \dfrac{(x \cancel{-} 4)(x \cancel{+} 4)}{(x \cancel{-} 2)(x \cancel{+} 4)} = 1$$

Answer: 1 $(x \neq 2, -4, 4)$

4 Simplify $\dfrac{9 - a^2}{x^3 - x} \bullet \dfrac{x - 1}{a + 3} \div \dfrac{a - 3}{x^2}$.

SOLUTION

Factor the fractions, where possible, and change division
into multiplication by using the reciprocal of the divisor.

$$\dfrac{(3 - a)(3 + a)}{x(x - 1)(x + 1)} \bullet \dfrac{x - 1}{a + 3} \bullet \dfrac{x^2}{a - 3}$$

Factor out -1 from $(3 - a)$ in the numerator.

$$\dfrac{-1(a - 3)(3 + a)}{x(x - 1)(x + 1)} \bullet \dfrac{x - 1}{a + 3} \bullet \dfrac{x^2}{a - 3}$$

Cancel common factors and simplify.

$$\dfrac{-1(a \cancel{-} 3)(3 \cancel{+} a)}{\cancel{x}(x \cancel{-} 1)(x + 1)} \bullet \dfrac{x \cancel{-} 1}{a \cancel{+} 3} \bullet \dfrac{\overset{x}{\cancel{x^2}}}{a \cancel{-} 3}$$

$$= \dfrac{-1x}{x + 1} = \dfrac{-x}{x + 1}$$

Divide and express the result as a single fraction in lowest terms.

1 $\dfrac{12}{35} \div \dfrac{4}{7}$

2 $\dfrac{1}{a^2} \div \dfrac{1}{a^3}$

3 $\dfrac{2}{x^2} \div \dfrac{2}{x}$

4 $\dfrac{3x}{5y} \div \dfrac{24x}{25y}$

5 $8ab \div \dfrac{24a}{b}$

6 $\dfrac{6a^3b^3}{10c} \div 3ab$

7 $\dfrac{18a^2b^3}{4x^3} \div \dfrac{9ab}{16x^2}$

8 $\dfrac{9}{a^2 - 1} \div \dfrac{3}{a + 1}$

9 $\dfrac{x^2 - 25}{18} \div \dfrac{x - 5}{27}$

10 $\dfrac{3x - 3y}{xy^2} \div \dfrac{x^2 - y^2}{x^2y}$

11 $\dfrac{5}{x - y} \div \dfrac{10}{y - x}$

12 $\dfrac{8k^4}{(a - 7)^2} \div \dfrac{20k}{a^2 - 49}$

13 $\dfrac{a^2 - 3a - 10}{8a^2} \div \dfrac{2a - 10}{16a^2}$

14 $\dfrac{a^2 - 8a}{8 - a} \div \dfrac{a}{2 - a}$

15 $\dfrac{x^2 - 16}{9x^2 - 25} \div \dfrac{x - 4}{3x + 5}$

16 $\dfrac{x^2 - 4}{(x - 2)^2} \div \dfrac{4x + 8}{5x - 10}$

17 $\dfrac{x^2 - 49}{(y + 7)^2} \div \dfrac{3x - 21}{2y + 14}$

18 $\dfrac{(a - 2)^2}{4a^2 - 16} \div \dfrac{21a}{3a + 6}$

19 $\dfrac{x^2 - 4x}{x^2 - 2x} \div (x - 4)$

20 $\dfrac{x^2 - x - 6}{x^2 - 4} \div \dfrac{x^2 - x - 2}{x + 2}$

21 $\dfrac{x^2 - 7x + 12}{x - 1} \div \dfrac{x^2 - 16}{x^2 - 1}$

22 $\dfrac{ab^2 - a^2b}{ab^2 - ab} \div \dfrac{b^2 - a^2}{ab}$

23 $\dfrac{a^2 - ab}{na^2 - nb^2} \div \dfrac{a^3 - a^2}{na^2 - na}$

24 $\dfrac{(2x + y)^2}{8x - 4y} \div \dfrac{4x^3 - xy^2}{8xy - 4y^2}$

25 $\dfrac{x^2 - 4x + 3}{x^2 + 5x - 6} \div \dfrac{x^2 - 2x - 3}{x^2 - x - 2}$

26 $\dfrac{2a^2 - 5a - 3}{4a^2 - 1} \div \dfrac{a^2 - 6a + 9}{6a^2 - 3a}$

27 $\dfrac{x^2 - 16}{x^2 + 2x + 1} \div \dfrac{16 - x^2}{3 + 2x - x^2}$

28 $\dfrac{6x^2 - 5x - 4}{2x^2 - x - 1} \div \dfrac{12x^2 - 7x - 12}{4x^2 - x - 3}$

29 $\dfrac{x^2 - 64}{x^2 - 10x + 25} \div \dfrac{64 - x^2}{5 - x}$

30 $\dfrac{16x - 4}{5x + 5} \cdot \dfrac{20x + 5}{6x + 6} \div \dfrac{16x^2 - 1}{x^2 + 2x + 1}$

Adding and Subtracting Algebraic Fractions

When adding and subtracting rational expressions with the *same denominator* follow the general procedure listed below.

- Add and subtract the numerators as indicated by their signs.
- Write the result over the common denominator.
- Reduce the fraction to lowest terms.

Examples:

$$\frac{2}{8} + \frac{1}{8} + \frac{3}{8} = \frac{2 + 1 + 3}{8} = \frac{6}{8} = \frac{3}{4}$$

$$\frac{3a}{x} + \frac{b}{x} - \frac{2b}{x} = \frac{3a + b - 2b}{x} = \frac{3a - b}{x}$$

$$\frac{3}{x - 3} + \frac{1}{x - 3} - \frac{19 - 5x}{x - 3} =$$

$$\frac{3 + 1 - (19 - 5x)}{x - 3} = \frac{3 + 1 - 19 + 5x}{x - 3} = \frac{5x - 15}{x - 3} = \frac{5(\overset{1}{\cancel{x - 3}})}{\underset{1}{\cancel{x - 3}}} = 5$$

Note: In the third example above, since the fraction bar is a grouping symbol, we enclose the numerator $(19 - 5x)$ in parentheses to indicate that all the signs within them will be changed by the subtraction sign on the outside.

To add or subtract fractions with *unlike denominators*, the fractions must be changed to equivalent fractions with a common denominator. To accomplish this, we must use the special **fundamental theorem of fractions**; that is, the value of the fraction does not change if the numerator and denominator are each multiplied by the same quantity. For example, $\frac{3}{5} = \frac{3}{5} \times \frac{2}{2} = \frac{6}{10}$. When we multiply by $\frac{2}{2}$, we are really multiplying by the number 1. Similarly, $\frac{4a}{7b} = \frac{4a}{7b} \bullet \frac{5x}{5x} = \frac{20ax}{35bx}$, where $b \neq 0$ and $x \neq 0$.

To Add and Subtract Rational Expressions With Unlike Denominators

- Factor denominators where possible.
- Find the *lowest common denominator* (LCD).
  Note: Remember that the LCD is the term into which all the denominators will divide evenly. Also, the LCD contains all the *different* factors present in the given denominators. Lastly, a factor is never repeated in the LCD unless it is repeated in a given denominator.

- Divide *each given denominator* into the LCD and multiply the numerator and denominator by the result. This will give equivalent fractions with the same LCD.
- Add the numerators and place the sum over the LCD.
- Reduce the fraction wherever possible.

MODEL PROBLEMS

1 Combine $\dfrac{x}{3} + \dfrac{3x - 2}{4} - \dfrac{1}{6}$.

SOLUTION

The least common denominator (LCD) is 12. Three into 12 is 4; multiply both the numerator and denominator of the first fraction by 4. Four into 12 is 3; multiply both the numerator and denominator of the second fraction by 3. Six into 12 is 2; multiply both the numerator and denominator of the third fraction by 2.

$$\dfrac{x}{3} + \dfrac{3x - 2}{4} - \dfrac{1}{6} = \dfrac{4 \bullet x}{4 \bullet 3} + \dfrac{3(3x - 2)}{3 \bullet 4} - \dfrac{2 \bullet 1}{2 \bullet 6} = \dfrac{4x}{12} + \dfrac{9x - 6}{12} - \dfrac{2}{12} = \dfrac{4x + 9x - 6 - 2}{12} = \dfrac{13x - 8}{12}$$

2 Combine $\dfrac{3}{4x} - \dfrac{6}{5x^2} - \dfrac{7}{10x}$.

SOLUTION

The LCD for $\dfrac{3}{4x} - \dfrac{6}{5x^2} - \dfrac{7}{10x}$ is $20x^2$.

$$\dfrac{5x \bullet 3}{5x \bullet 4x} - \dfrac{4 \bullet 6}{4 \bullet 5x^2} - \dfrac{2x \bullet 7}{2x \bullet 10x} = \dfrac{15x}{20x^2} - \dfrac{24}{20x^2} - \dfrac{14x}{20x^2} = \dfrac{x - 24}{20x^2}$$

Note: We assume in Model Problem 2 that $x \neq 0$. Whenever we are working with rational expressions, the denominator cannot equal zero. For example, $\dfrac{x + 7}{x + 7}$ will always equal 1 except when $x = -7$. If $x = -7$, then the fraction $\dfrac{x + 7}{x + 7}$ is undefined.

There is a simple method for adding and subtracting rational expressions. From now on we will be using this method.

Simple Method for Adding and Subtracting Rational Expressions

- Find the LCD and write it in the denominator.
- Divide each given denominator into the LCD and multiply the result by the numerator of the fraction. Place the products in the numerator with the proper sign between them.
- Simplify the result.

 MODEL PROBLEMS

1 Combine $\dfrac{a + 3}{3} - \dfrac{a + 2}{5}$.

SOLUTION

The LCD is 15.

$$\dfrac{a + 3}{3} - \dfrac{a + 2}{5} = \dfrac{5(a + 3) - 3(a + 2)}{15} = \dfrac{5a + 15 - 3a - 6}{15} = \dfrac{2a + 9}{15}$$

2 Combine $\dfrac{3}{2a^2x} - \dfrac{5x}{3ax^2} + \dfrac{2}{a^3}$, $(a \neq 0, x \neq 0)$

SOLUTION

The LCD is $6a^3x^2$.

$$\frac{3}{2a^2x} - \frac{5x}{3ax^2} + \frac{2}{a^3} = \frac{3(3ax) - 5x(2a^2) + 2(6x^2)}{6a^3x^2}$$

$$= \frac{9ax - 10xa^2 + 12x^2}{6a^3x^2} = \frac{\cancel{x}(9a - 10a^2 + 12x)}{6a^3\cancel{x^2}} = \frac{9a - 10a^2 + 12x}{6a^3x}$$

3 Combine $\dfrac{4}{x} - \dfrac{3}{x+3}$, $(x \neq 0, -3)$

SOLUTION

The LCD is $x(x+3)$.

$$\frac{4}{x} - \frac{3}{x+3} = \frac{4(x+3) - 3(x)}{x(x+3)} = \frac{4x + 12 - 3x}{x(x+3)} = \frac{x+12}{x(x+3)}$$

4 Combine $\dfrac{5}{a-3} - \dfrac{2}{a-2}$, $(a \neq 3, 2)$

SOLUTION

The LCD is $(a-3)(a-2)$.

$$\frac{5}{a-3} - \frac{2}{a-2} = \frac{5(a-2) - 2(a-3)}{(a-3)(a-2)} = \frac{5a - 10 - 2a + 6}{(a-3)(a-2)} = \frac{3a-4}{(a-3)(a-2)}$$

5 Combine $\dfrac{2}{x+1} + \dfrac{2}{x^2+x}$, $(x \neq -1, 0)$

Since $\dfrac{2}{x+1} + \dfrac{2}{x^2+x}$ can be written as $\dfrac{2}{x+1} + \dfrac{2}{x(x+1)}$, the LCD is $x(x+1)$.

Thus, $\dfrac{2}{x+1} + \dfrac{2}{x(x+1)} = \dfrac{2x+2}{x(x+1)} = \dfrac{2\overset{1}{\cancel{(x+1)}}}{x\underset{1}{\cancel{(x+1)}}} = \dfrac{2}{x}$.

The following table of examples shows the LCD for the denominators of various pairs of algebraic fractions.

Denominators	LCD
$x + 5$ and $x + 2$	$(x+5)(x+2)$
ab and $a + b$	$ab(a+b)$
$(x+4)(x+3)$ and $(x+3)(x-7)$	$(x+4)(x+3)(x-7)$
$x^2 - 3x$ and $x^2 - 9$	$x(x-3)(x+3)$
$x^2 - 6x + 9$ and $x^2 + 4x - 21$	$(x-3)(x-3)(x+7)$
$(x-3)$ and $(3-x)$ **Note:** $(3-x)$ is equivalent to $-1(x-3)$.	$-1(x-3)$

![Practice]

Exercises 1–10: Add or subtract fractions with like denominators.

1 $\dfrac{5}{4x} + \dfrac{9}{4x} - \dfrac{8}{4x}$

2 $\dfrac{x}{x+1} + \dfrac{1}{x+1}$

3 $\dfrac{a}{a^2-4} - \dfrac{2}{a^2-4}$

4 $\dfrac{4x+12}{16} - \dfrac{8x+4}{16}$

5 $\dfrac{12x-15}{12} - \dfrac{9x-6}{12}$

6 $\dfrac{x+3}{7x+3} - \dfrac{x-4}{7x+3}$

7 $\dfrac{x}{x^2-y^2} - \dfrac{y}{x^2-y^2}$

8 $\dfrac{x}{x^2-x-2} - \dfrac{2}{x^2-x-2}$

9 $\dfrac{2x}{2x^2+15x-12} - \dfrac{3}{2x^2+15x-12}$

10 $\dfrac{4x}{4x^2-3x-10} - \dfrac{5}{4x^2-3x-10}$

Exercises 11–20: Add or subtract fractions with unlike monomial denominators.

11 $\dfrac{5x}{6} - \dfrac{3x}{8}$

12 $\dfrac{3a}{2} + \dfrac{7a}{4} - \dfrac{a}{6}$

13 $\dfrac{a}{2} + \dfrac{b}{3} + \dfrac{c}{4}$

14 $\dfrac{1}{2x} - \dfrac{1}{x} + \dfrac{3}{8x}$

15 $\dfrac{2}{x^3} - \dfrac{3}{x^2} + \dfrac{7}{x}$

16 $\dfrac{5}{a^3b^2} + \dfrac{9}{2ab^4}$

17 $\dfrac{3a-4}{5a} - \dfrac{2a-3}{20a}$

18 $\dfrac{3a-b}{c} - \dfrac{3b+a}{b}$

19 $\dfrac{2x+5}{4x^2} - \dfrac{3}{2x}$

20 $\dfrac{3x-2}{7} + \dfrac{x+1}{14}$

Exercises 21–35: Add or subtract fractions with unlike binomial and trinomial denominators.

21 $\dfrac{2}{x-1} - \dfrac{1}{x}$

22 $\dfrac{2x+y}{x-y} + \dfrac{x}{y}$

23 $\dfrac{11a}{8a-8} - \dfrac{3a}{4a-4}$

24 $\dfrac{9}{x^2-y^2} - \dfrac{3}{x-y}$

25 $\dfrac{x+2}{3x} + \dfrac{3x-1}{x-2}$

26 $\dfrac{1}{a^2-3a} + \dfrac{1}{a^2-9}$

27 $\dfrac{9}{x+8} - \dfrac{2}{x}$

28 $\dfrac{2}{3x-1} + \dfrac{7}{15x-5}$

29 $\dfrac{1}{x-4} + \dfrac{1}{x+4}$

30 $\dfrac{9}{a^2-ab} + \dfrac{3}{ab-b^2}$

31 $\dfrac{4}{x^2-49} - \dfrac{3}{7-x}$

32 $\dfrac{2}{x+3} + \dfrac{4}{3-x} + \dfrac{3x+15}{x^2-9}$

33 $\dfrac{x-2}{x+4} - \dfrac{x^2-3x-18}{x^2+7x+12}$

34 $\dfrac{x}{x^2-6x+9} - \dfrac{1}{x^2+4x-21}$

35 $\dfrac{5x}{x^2-5x+6} + \dfrac{2}{x-3} - \dfrac{6}{x-2}$

Mixed Expressions and Complex Fractions

A **complex fraction** has one or more fractions in its numerator or denominator or both. There are two methods for simplifying complex fractions.

Method 1
Multiply the numerator and denominator of the complex fraction by the LCD of all the denominators that appear in both the numerator and denominator.

Method 2
Invert the divisor, multiply, and cancel common factors.

To Simplify Complex Fractions

- If there is addition or subtraction of fractions to be done, simplify those first, and then apply Method 1 or Method 2 (see above).
- Reduce to simplest terms.

Examples

$$1 \quad \frac{\dfrac{3}{4}}{\dfrac{15}{16}}$$

SOLUTION

METHOD 1   Multiply each fraction by the LCD, which is 16.

$$\frac{\dfrac{3}{4}(16)}{\dfrac{15}{16}(16)} = \frac{3 \cdot 4}{15 \cdot 1} = \frac{12}{15} = \frac{4}{5}$$

METHOD 2   Invert the divisor, multiply, and cancel common factors.

$$\frac{\dfrac{3}{4}}{\dfrac{15}{16}} = \frac{3}{4} \div \frac{15}{16} = \frac{\overset{1}{\cancel{3}}}{\underset{1}{\cancel{4}}} \cdot \frac{\overset{4}{\cancel{16}}}{\underset{5}{\cancel{15}}} = \frac{4}{5}$$

$$2 \quad \frac{\dfrac{a}{b}}{\dfrac{c}{d}}$$

SOLUTION

Use Method 1 to simplify the fraction. It's easier.

$$\frac{\dfrac{a}{\cancel{b}}(\cancel{b}d)}{\dfrac{c}{\cancel{d}}(b\cancel{d})} = \frac{ad}{cb}$$

1 Simplify $\dfrac{\dfrac{x}{y} + 3}{\dfrac{x^2}{y^2} - 9}$.

SOLUTION

METHOD 1

The LCD is y^2. Multiply every term in both the numerator and the denominator by y^2. Then factor and cancel.

$$\dfrac{\dfrac{x}{y} + 3}{\dfrac{x^2}{y^2} - 9} = \dfrac{y^2 \bullet \dfrac{x}{y} + 3 \bullet y^2}{y^2 \bullet \dfrac{x^2}{y^2} - 9 \bullet y^2} = \dfrac{yx + 3y^2}{x^2 - 9y^2} = \dfrac{y(x + 3y)}{(x - 3y)(x + 3y)} = \dfrac{y}{x - 3y}$$

METHOD 2

Rewrite the problem using the division sign. Simplify each fraction in the parentheses, then invert, factor, and cancel.

$$\left(\dfrac{x}{y} + 3\right) \div \left(\dfrac{x^2}{y^2} - 9\right) = \left(\dfrac{x + 3y}{y}\right) \div \left(\dfrac{x^2 - 9y^2}{y^2}\right) = \left(\dfrac{x + 3y}{y}\right)\left(\dfrac{y^2}{x^2 - 9y^2}\right)$$

$$= \left(\dfrac{x + 3y}{y}\right)\left(\dfrac{y^2}{(x + 3y)(x - 3y)}\right) = \dfrac{y}{x - 3y}$$

2 Simplify $\dfrac{\dfrac{x^2 - y^2}{a + b}}{\dfrac{x - y}{a^2 - b^2}}$.

SOLUTION

Method 2 is easier here. Invert the second fraction, factor, cancel, and simplify.

$$\dfrac{\dfrac{x^2 - y^2}{a + b}}{\dfrac{x - y}{a^2 - b^2}} = \dfrac{x^2 - y^2}{a + b} \div \dfrac{x - y}{a^2 - b^2} = \dfrac{x^2 - y^2}{a + b} \bullet \dfrac{a^2 - b^2}{x - y} = \dfrac{(x - y)(x + y)}{a + b} \bullet \dfrac{(a - b)(a + b)}{x - y} = (x + y)(a - b)$$

3 Simplify $\dfrac{\dfrac{x}{y} - \dfrac{y}{x}}{\dfrac{x^2}{y} - y}$.

SOLUTION

METHOD 1

The LCD is xy. Multiply every term by the LCD. Cancel, simplify, and cancel again.

$$\frac{\dfrac{x}{y} - \dfrac{y}{x}}{\dfrac{x^2}{y} - y} = \frac{xy \bullet \dfrac{x}{y} - \dfrac{y}{x} \bullet xy}{xy \bullet \dfrac{x^2}{y} - y \bullet xy} = \frac{x \bullet x - y \bullet y}{x \bullet x^2 - xy^2} = \frac{x^2 - y^2}{x(x^2 - y^2)} = \frac{1}{x}$$

METHOD 2

First add the fractions in the numerator and the fractions in the denominator. Rewrite using the division sign. Invert the second fraction cancel, where possible, and simplify.

$$\frac{\dfrac{x}{y} - \dfrac{y}{x}}{\dfrac{x^2}{y} - y} = \frac{\dfrac{x^2 - y^2}{xy}}{\dfrac{x^2 - y^2}{y}} = \frac{x^2 - y^2}{xy} \div \frac{x^2 - y^2}{y} = \frac{x^2 - y^2}{xy} \bullet \frac{y}{x^2 - y^2} = \frac{1}{x}$$

4 Simplify $\dfrac{x + \dfrac{x}{x + 2}}{x - \dfrac{x}{x + 2}}$.

SOLUTION

Use Method 1. Multiply each term by the LCD, $(x + 2)$.

$$\frac{x + \dfrac{x}{x + 2}}{x - \dfrac{x}{x + 2}} = \frac{x(x + 2) + \dfrac{x}{x + 2}(x + 2)}{x(x + 2) - \dfrac{x}{x + 2}(x + 2)} = \frac{x(x + 2) + x}{x(x + 2) - x}$$

> With enough practice, selecting the easier method to simplify a complex fraction will soon be obvious.

Remove parentheses, simplify, factor, and cancel.

$$\frac{x^2 + 2x + x}{x^2 + 2x - x} = \frac{x^2 + 3x}{x^2 + x} = \frac{x(x + 3)}{x(x + 1)} = \frac{x + 3}{x + 1}$$

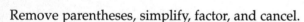
Practice

1 $\left(\dfrac{a}{b} + 3\right)\left(\dfrac{a}{b} + 2\right)$

2 $\left(\dfrac{a}{b} - 1\right)\left(1 + \dfrac{b}{a}\right)$

3 $\left(1 + \dfrac{x}{x + y}\right)\left(1 - \dfrac{y^2}{x^2}\right)$

4 $\left(3 + \dfrac{6}{a + 1}\right)\left(2 - \dfrac{1}{a + 3}\right)$

5 $\dfrac{1}{1 - \dfrac{x}{y}}$

6 $\dfrac{\dfrac{x^2}{2} - 2}{\dfrac{x}{2} - 1}$

7 $\dfrac{x}{x - \dfrac{x}{3}}$

8 $\dfrac{\dfrac{1}{x} + \dfrac{1}{y}}{\dfrac{1}{xy}}$

9 $\left(4 + \dfrac{1}{a}\right) \div \left(4 - \dfrac{1}{a}\right)$

10 $\left(1 - \dfrac{c}{d}\right) \div \left(d - \dfrac{c^2}{d}\right)$

11 $\dfrac{6 + \dfrac{3}{2a}}{\dfrac{1}{16a} - a}$

12 $\dfrac{\dfrac{a}{b} - \dfrac{b}{a}}{\dfrac{a}{b} + \dfrac{b}{a}}$

13 $\dfrac{x - \dfrac{a^2}{x}}{\dfrac{x}{a} - \dfrac{a}{x}}$

14 $\dfrac{\dfrac{3}{x^2} - \dfrac{3}{x}}{\dfrac{3}{x^2} + \dfrac{3}{x}}$

15 $\left(\dfrac{a - b}{a} - \dfrac{a - b}{a}\right) \div \left(\dfrac{a}{b} - \dfrac{b}{a}\right)$

16 $\left(\dfrac{x^2}{4} - 4a^2\right) \div \left(\dfrac{x}{2} + 2a\right)$

17 $\dfrac{a - \dfrac{ab}{a + b}}{a + \dfrac{ab}{a - b}}$

18 $\dfrac{\dfrac{16}{a} - a}{\dfrac{8}{a^2} + \dfrac{10}{a} - 3}$

19 $\dfrac{1 - \dfrac{7}{m} + \dfrac{12}{m}}{\dfrac{2m}{5} + 2}$

20 $\dfrac{\dfrac{x - y}{x} + \dfrac{x - y}{y}}{\dfrac{x - y}{y} - \dfrac{x - y}{x}}$

Solving Equations That Have Fractional Coefficients

When algebraic equations have coefficients that are fractions, the most convenient method for solving is to use the *Multiplication Property of Equality*, which will clear the equation of fractions. The method is simple and direct.

To Solve Equations With Fractional Coefficients

- Find the lowest common denominator (LCD).
- Multiply every term (whole number and fraction) on both sides of the equation by the LCD. This will clear out all the fractions.
- Remove any parentheses, collect like terms, and solve in the usual manner.

- Check by substituting the root into the given equation.

Note: If we are working with proportions, we can use the *Rule for Proportions*; the product of the means equals the product of the extremes (or cross multiplication). Hence a quick *alternative method* is to simply:

- Cross multiply.
- Set the first product equal to the second product.
- Solve the resulting equation.
- Check by substituting the root in the given equation.

 MODEL PROBLEMS

1 Solve for m in $\dfrac{m}{3} - \dfrac{3m}{4} = 5 - \dfrac{5m}{6}$.

SOLUTION

Multiply each term by the LCD, 12. Then cancel the common factors and combine.

$$12\left(\frac{m}{3}\right) - 12\left(\frac{3m}{4}\right) = 12(5) - 12\left(\frac{5m}{6}\right)$$

Cancel common factors and combine.

$$4m - 9m = 60 - 10m$$
$$-5m = 60 - 10m$$
$$5m = 60$$
$$m = 12$$

Check:

$$\frac{m}{3} - \frac{3m}{4} = 5 - \frac{5m}{6}$$

$$\frac{12}{3} - \frac{3 \cdot 12}{4} = 5 - \frac{5 \cdot 12}{6}$$

$$4 - 9 = 5 - 10$$

$$-5 = -5$$

2 Solve for a in $\dfrac{6a - 5}{6} - \dfrac{2a - 3}{4} = \dfrac{2}{3}$.

SOLUTION

The LCD is 12. Multiply each term by 12 and cancel common factors.

$$\overset{2}{\cancel{12}} \times \left(\frac{6a - 5}{\underset{1}{\cancel{6}}}\right) - \overset{3}{\cancel{12}} \times \left(\frac{2a - 3}{\underset{1}{\cancel{4}}}\right) = \overset{4}{\cancel{12}} \times \frac{2}{\underset{1}{\cancel{3}}}$$

Simplify and solve.

$$2(6a - 5) - 3(2a - 3) = 8$$
$$12a - 10 - 6a + 9 = 8$$
$$6a - 1 = 8$$
$$6a = 9$$
$$a = \frac{9}{6} \text{ or } \frac{3}{2}$$

346 Chapter 14: Algebraic Fractions and Equations, and Inequalities Involving Fractions

Check:

$$\frac{6\left(\frac{3}{2}\right) - 5}{6} - \frac{2\left(\frac{3}{2}\right) - 3}{4} = \frac{2}{3}$$

$$\frac{9 - 5}{6} - \frac{3 - 3}{4} = \frac{2}{3}$$

$$\frac{4}{6} - \frac{0}{4} = \frac{2}{3}$$

$$\frac{2}{3} = \frac{2}{3}$$

3 Solve for x in $\dfrac{x}{3} = \dfrac{x-1}{2}$.

SOLUTION

The LCD is 6. However, the more direct method is to cross multiply.

Cross multiplying. $\qquad\qquad\qquad 2(x) = 3(x - 1)$

Remove the parentheses and solve. $\qquad 2x = 3x - 3$

$$3 = x$$

Check:

$$\frac{x}{3} = \frac{x-1}{2}$$

$$\frac{3}{3} = \frac{3-1}{2}$$

$$1 = 1$$

4 Solve for x in $0.7x + 0.6 = 0.2x + 2.1$.

SOLUTION

Since $0.7x + 0.6 = 0.2x + 2.1$ is the same as $\dfrac{7}{10}x + \dfrac{6}{10} = \dfrac{2}{10}x + \dfrac{21}{10}$, the rule in decimal equations is to multiply all the terms by some multiple of 10 (in this case, just 10), in order to clear the equation of decimals.

$$10 \cdot \frac{7}{10}x + 10 \cdot \frac{6}{10} = 10 \cdot \frac{2}{10}x + 10 \cdot \frac{21}{10}$$

$$7x + 6 = 2x + 21$$

$$5x = 15$$

$$x = 3$$

Check:

$$\frac{7}{10}x + \frac{6}{10} = \frac{2}{10}x + \frac{21}{10}$$

$$\frac{7}{10}(3) + \frac{6}{10} = \frac{2}{10}(3) + \frac{21}{10}$$

$$\frac{21}{10} + \frac{6}{10} = \frac{6}{10} + \frac{21}{10}$$

$$\frac{27}{10} = \frac{27}{10}$$

Practice

Exercises 1–5: Solve for the indicated variable in the following proportions.

1 $\dfrac{4x + 2}{3} = \dfrac{x + 3}{2}$

2 $\dfrac{4m + 3}{3} = \dfrac{7m - 1}{4}$

3 $\dfrac{5x - 2}{3} = \dfrac{8 - 3x}{5}$

4 $\dfrac{2x - 5}{15} = \dfrac{3x - 20}{10}$

5 $\dfrac{4k - 3}{5} = \dfrac{7k - 9}{8}$

Exercises 6–25: Solve for the indicated variable.

6 $\dfrac{3x}{8} - \dfrac{3}{4} = \dfrac{x}{2}$

7 $x - \dfrac{x}{2} + \dfrac{x}{4} = 6$

8 $\dfrac{2}{3}a - \dfrac{1}{6}a = 15$

9 $a + \dfrac{a}{2} + \dfrac{a}{3} = 22$

10 $x - \dfrac{x}{3} + \dfrac{x}{5} = 26$

11 $m = 1 + \dfrac{m}{2} + \dfrac{m}{4} + \dfrac{m}{8} + \dfrac{m}{16}$

12 $\dfrac{2x - 7}{5} + 3 = 2x$

13 $\dfrac{4a - 5}{3} - 3a = 10$

14 $\dfrac{a - 1}{3} + \dfrac{a + 5}{5} = 6$

15 $\dfrac{x - 2}{6} + \dfrac{x - 4}{8} = \dfrac{3}{2}$

16 $\dfrac{x + 4}{3} - \dfrac{x - 5}{6} = 4$

17 $\dfrac{4x}{3} - \dfrac{2x - 1}{5} = \dfrac{x + 3}{2}$

18 $\dfrac{x - 5}{2} - \dfrac{x - 3}{4} = \dfrac{x - 7}{10}$

19 $\dfrac{x + 1}{3} + \dfrac{x + 3}{4} = \dfrac{x + 3}{2}$

20 $\dfrac{a + 9}{4} + \dfrac{a + 1}{2} = \dfrac{a - 11}{5}$

21 $\dfrac{m + 2}{2} - \dfrac{m - 6}{8} = \dfrac{m + 11}{4}$

22 $\dfrac{x + 10}{4} - \dfrac{x - 10}{6} = \dfrac{x + 10}{2}$

23 $\dfrac{5a - 1}{2} - \dfrac{3a + 5}{5} = \dfrac{7a + 13}{6}$

24 $\dfrac{4 - 8k}{8} + 2 = \dfrac{k - 5}{4} - k$

25 $\dfrac{3x}{4} - \dfrac{2x}{3} - 4 = \dfrac{x}{6} - 7$

Exercises 26–35: Solve for the indicated variable in the following decimal equations.

26 $c + 0.4 = 0.6c + 2$

27 $0.05x = 0.04(x + 200)$

28 $0.03(x - 10) = 0.07(x - 50)$

29 $x + 0.05x + 0.02x = 321$

30 $y - 0.25y = 0.35y + 24$

31 $1.2m - 0.5m = 0.15m + 5.5$

32 $0.06n + 0.04(1{,}500 - n) = 72$

33 $0.04x - 0.03(5{,}000 + x) = 170$

34 $0.05a = 0.02(3{,}200 - a) + 62$

35 $2.4x + 3.5(7 - x) = 17.9$

Solving Inequalities Containing Fractional Coefficients

The method for solving inequalities that contain fractional coefficients is the same as that used for equations with fractional coefficients. However, when working with inequalities, we need to keep in mind the special *Multiplicative Properties of Inequalities*:

- If $a > b$ and $c > 0$, then $ac > bc$; conversely, if $a < b$ and $c < 0$, then $ac > bc$.

Simply put, when each member of an inequality is multiplied by a negative number, the order of the inequality is *reversed*.

Keep in mind the following translations of words into symbols of inequality.

Words	Symbols
x is greater than y	$x > y$
x is less than y	$x < y$
x is at least y x is no less than y x is greater than or equal to y	$x \geq y$
x is at most y x is no greater than y x is less than or equal to y	$x \leq y$

 MODEL PROBLEMS

1 Solve for k in $\dfrac{k}{4} - k < \dfrac{1}{2}$.

SOLUTION

Multiply every term by the LCD, 4, and cancel where possible.

$$4 \cdot \frac{k}{4} - 4 \cdot k < 4 \cdot \frac{1}{2}$$

$$k - 4k < 2$$

$$-3k < 2$$

Divide by -3. $k > -\dfrac{2}{3}$

2 Solve for n. $\dfrac{n-3}{8} - \dfrac{n+2}{3} > \dfrac{5}{12}$

SOLUTION

Multiply each term by the LCD, 24, and cancel where possible.

$$24\left(\frac{n-3}{8}\right) - 24\left(\frac{n+2}{3}\right) > 24\left(\frac{5}{12}\right)$$

$$3(n-3) - 8(n+2) > 2 \cdot 5$$

$$3n - 9 - 8n - 16 > 10$$

$$-5n - 25 > 10$$

$$-5n > 35 \quad \text{(Divide by } -5 \text{ and reverse the inequality.)}$$

$$n < -7$$

When dividing by a negative number, the inequality will be reversed.

3 In order to go to the movies, Connie and Stan need to put all their money together. Connie has one-third as much money as Stan. Together they have more than $17. Assuming they have no pennies, what is the *least* amount of money each of them can have?

SOLUTION

Let Stan's money be represented by x.

Then Connie's money can be represented as $\frac{1}{3}x$ or $\frac{x}{3}$.

The equation is $x + \frac{x}{3} > 17$.

Multiply by the LCD, 3.

$$3 \bullet x + 3 \bullet \frac{x}{3} > 3(17)$$

$$3x + x > 51$$

$$4x > 51$$

$x > 12.75$ and $\frac{1}{3}x > 4.25$

Answer: Since Connie has more than $4.25, the least she can have is $4.30. Since Stan has more than $12.75, the least he can have is $12.80.

4 Kate has *no more than* $10 in nickels, dimes, and quarters in her purse. If the number of dimes is three more than the number nickels, and the number of quarters is four times the number of dimes, what is the *greatest* number of nickels she can have in her purse?

SOLUTION

Identify the unknowns.

Let n = the number of nickels, with a total value of $0.05n$.

Let $n + 3$ = the number of dimes, with a total value of $0.10(n + 3)$.

Let $4(n + 3)$ = the number of quarters, with a total value of $0.25[4(n + 3)]$.

Since "*no more than*" means the same as *less than or equal to*, the equation is
$0.05n + 0.10(n + 3) + 0.25[4(n + 3)] \leq 10$.

Multiply each term by the LCD, 100. This will move the decimal two places to the right for each term.

$$5n + 10(n + 3) + 25[4(n + 3)] \leq 1{,}000$$

$$5n + 10n + 30 + 25(4n + 12) \leq 1{,}000$$

$$15n + 30 + 100n + 300 \leq 1{,}000$$

$$115n + 330 \leq 1{,}000$$

$$115n \leq 670$$

$$n \leq 5.82$$

Answer: $n = 5$

5 Peggy is two-thirds as old as her sister Susan. Six years from now, the sum of their ages will be less than 68. What is the *largest possible integer value* for each sister's present age?

SOLUTION

Let S = Susan's present age, and $S + 6$ = Susan's age 6 years from now.

Let $\frac{2}{3}S$ = Peggy's present age, and let $\frac{2}{3}S + 6$ = Peggy's age 6 years from now.

The equation is

$S + 6 + \frac{2}{3}S + 6 < 68$

Multiply each term by the LCD, 3.

$3S + 18 + 2S + 18 < 3 \cdot 68$

$\qquad\quad 5S + 36 < 204$

$\qquad\qquad\quad 5S < 168$

$\qquad\qquad\quad\; S < 33.6$

Answer: Susan's present age is 33 and Peggy's present age is 22.

 Practice

Exercises 1–15: Find the solution set for each inequality.

1 $\dfrac{a}{6} - \dfrac{a}{3} > \dfrac{1}{2}$

2 $\dfrac{5a}{6} + \dfrac{a}{2} > \dfrac{1}{3}$

3 $\dfrac{5m}{6} - \dfrac{m}{2} > \dfrac{4}{3}$

4 $\dfrac{b}{3} - \dfrac{b + 2}{2} < 9$

5 $\dfrac{2x}{5} - \dfrac{5}{6} > \dfrac{x}{3} + \dfrac{1}{2}$

6 $\dfrac{2m}{3} - 4 < \dfrac{m + 1}{2}$

7 $\dfrac{r + 2}{3} - \dfrac{r - 1}{6} \geq 1$

8 $\dfrac{x + 3}{2} \geq \dfrac{x - 8}{5} + 1$

9 $\dfrac{x + 8}{4} - \dfrac{x + 5}{9} \leq 2$

10 $\dfrac{x + 5}{6} - \dfrac{7 - x}{4} < 4$

11 $\dfrac{x + 1}{3} + \dfrac{x + 3}{4} \geq \dfrac{x + 3}{2}$

12 $\dfrac{2n - 3}{4} + \dfrac{n - 7}{2} \geq 12$

13 $\dfrac{a + 2}{2} - \dfrac{a - 2}{6} < \dfrac{2a + 1}{3}$

14 $x - \dfrac{2x}{3} + \dfrac{x - 3}{5} > 5$

15 $\dfrac{a}{2} + \dfrac{a + 2}{3} - \dfrac{a + 3}{4} \leq 4$

16 The width of a rectangle is three more than one-half the length. If the perimeter is greater than 36 meters, what is the smallest integer length possible?

17 The base of a triangle is 18 inches and the height is $x + 4$ inches. If the area of the triangle is less than 90 in.^{2}, what is the maximum integral height of the triangle?

18 The length of a rectangle is three inches less than the one-eighth the width. If the perimeter of the rectangle is less than 75 inches, what could be the maximum width of the rectangle expressed as an integer?

19 Dr. Kesten invested a total of $12,000 in two local industries and received yearly dividends of 8% and 5%. If his dividends totaled at least $840, what is the *greatest* sum he could have invested in the industry paying 5%?

20 An empty book crate weighs 25 pounds. What is the *greatest* number of art books weighing 1.6 pounds each that can be packed in the crate, if the filled crate can weigh *no more than* 60 pounds?

21 The owner of an electronics store buys CD players that cost him $60 each, and he wants to sell them at a price that would of profit *at least* 20% of the selling price. What is the *least* price he can sell a CD player? (Hint: selling price − cost = profit).

22 Four times the difference between half a number, n, and 6 is less than or equal to six times the sum of that number, n, and $\frac{2}{3}$. Find the smallest number that would satisfy the inequality.

23 The sum of one-half of an integer and one-fourth of that integer is less than 40. What is the greatest possible integer for which this is true?

24 Twice the sum of a number and one-third of that number is greater than seven less than four times half the number. What is the smallest integer that will satisfy this inequality?

25 What is the *largest* possible integer for which the following is true? The smaller of two integers is three-fourths of the larger, and the sum of the integers is less than 50.

26 A small box of coins contains nickels, dimes, and quarters. The number of dimes is eight more than the number of nickels, and the number of quarters is twice the number of dimes. The total value of the coins is no greater than $8.85. What is the greatest possible number of nickels in the box?

27 During one week, Janet spent one-third of her after-school earnings on books and one-half of her earnings on clothes. If she had less than $35 left, what (in dollars) is the most she could have earned?

28 Reese is at least two and one-half times her cousin Melina's age. Five years ago, the difference between their ages was greater than 5. What is the *smallest* possible integer value of each cousin's present age?

Solving Fractional Equations

Generally, if both sides of fractional equations are multiplied by the same non-zero quantity (the LCD), an equivalent equation will result that does not contain any fractions.

To Solve Fractional Equations

- Find the LCD of all the fractions involved.
- Multiply every term by the LCD
- Cancel common factors and remove parentheses (if any).
- Solve in the usual manner.

Examples

1 $\dfrac{1}{4} + \dfrac{2}{x} = \dfrac{1}{8}$

Multiply by the LCD, $8x$, and cancel common factors.

$$8x \bullet \dfrac{1}{4} + 8x \bullet \dfrac{2}{x} = \dfrac{1}{8} \bullet 8x$$

$$2x + 16 = x$$

$$x = -16$$

Note: (1) Whenever you multiply both sides of an equation by a polynomial containing a variable, the solution set of the resulting equation always contains all the roots of the equation. But sometimes it also contains numbers that are *not* roots of the original equation. Therefore, we must always test each root in the original equation. (2) Similarly, solutions derived by cross multiplying are not always solutions of the original equation. The roots that do not work are called **extraneous solutions**. Consider the following two examples, which include extraneous solutions.

2 $\dfrac{6x + 18}{x + 3} = 5$

$6x + 18 = 5(x + 3)$ Cross multiply, simplify, and solve.

$6x + 18 = 5x + 15$

$\qquad\quad x = -3$ However, since this solution makes the equation meaning-less, -3 is an *extraneous solution*.

3 $\dfrac{1}{x + 2} = \dfrac{2}{x^2 - 4}$

Cross multiply.	$2x + 4 = x^2 - 4$
Form a quadratic equation equal to 0.	$0 = x^2 - 2x - 8$
Factor.	$0 = (x - 4)(x + 2)$
Set each factor equal to 0 and solve.	$x - 4 = 0 \qquad x + 2 = 0$
	$\qquad x = 4 \qquad\qquad x = -2$

Answer: {4}. -2 is an *extraneous solution* since it makes the value for both denominators 0.

1 Solve for x and check: $3 - \dfrac{7}{x} = -\dfrac{2}{x^2}$

SOLUTION

Multiply each term by the LCD, x^2. $\quad 3(x^2) - \dfrac{7}{x}(x^2) = -\dfrac{2}{x^2}(x^2)$

Simplify. $\quad\quad\quad\quad\quad\quad\quad\quad 3x^2 - 7x = -2$

Write in standard from. $\quad\quad\quad 3x^2 - 7x + 2 = 0$

Factor and solve. $\quad\quad\quad\quad (3x - 1)(x - 2) = 0$

$$3x - 1 = 0 \quad\quad x - 2 = 0$$

$$x = \dfrac{1}{3} \quad\quad\quad x = 2$$

Check:

$x = \dfrac{1}{3}$ $\quad\quad\quad\quad\quad\quad\quad\quad x = 2$

$3 - \left(7 \div \dfrac{1}{3}\right) = -2 \div \left(\dfrac{1}{3}\right)^2$ $\quad\quad 3 - \dfrac{7}{2} = -\dfrac{2}{2^2}$

$\quad\quad 3 - 21 = -2 \times 9$ $\quad\quad\quad\quad\quad -\dfrac{1}{2} = -\dfrac{2}{4}$

$\quad\quad\quad\quad -18 = -18$ $\quad\quad\quad\quad\quad -\dfrac{1}{2} = -\dfrac{1}{2}$

Answer: The solution set is $\left\{\dfrac{1}{3}, 2\right\}$.

2 Solve for a: $\dfrac{a}{a + 2} - \dfrac{4}{a^2 + 2a} = \dfrac{2}{a}$

SOLUTION

Factor the denominators. $\quad\quad\quad\quad\quad \dfrac{a}{a + 2} - \dfrac{4}{a(a + 2)} = \dfrac{2}{a}$

Multiply each term by the LCD, $a(a + 2)$, and simplify by cancellation.

$$a(a + 2)\left(\dfrac{a}{a + 2}\right) - a(a + 2)\left(\dfrac{4}{a(a + 2)}\right) = a(a + 2)\left(\dfrac{2}{a}\right)$$

$\quad\quad a \bullet a - 4 = (a + 2) \bullet 2$

$\quad\quad\quad a^2 - 4 = 2(a + 2)$ $\quad\quad\quad$ Remove parentheses and rearrange terms.

$\quad\quad\quad a^2 - 4 = 2a + 4$

$\quad a^2 - 2a - 8 = 0$ $\quad\quad\quad\quad\quad$ Factor and solve.

$(a - 4)(a + 2) = 0$

$a = 4$ or $a = -2$

Since the denominator $a + 2 = 0$ when the root -2 is substituted for a, then -2 is an extraneous solution. But $a = 4$ works.

Check:

$$\frac{4}{4 + 2} - \frac{4}{4^2 + 2 \cdot 4} = \frac{2}{4}$$

$$\frac{4}{6} - \frac{4}{24} = \frac{1}{2}$$

$$\frac{4}{6} - \frac{1}{6} = \frac{1}{2}$$

$$\frac{3}{6} = \frac{1}{2}$$

$$\frac{1}{2} = \frac{1}{2}$$

3 Solve for x in $\dfrac{a + mx}{x} = g$.

SOLUTION

Cross multiply

$$a + mx = gx$$

$$a = gx - mx$$

$$a = x(g - m)$$

$$x = \frac{a}{g - m}$$

 Practice

Exercises 1–25: Solve each equation and check your solution. Identify any extraneous solutions.

1 $\dfrac{1}{2} = \dfrac{3}{3 + x}$

2 $\dfrac{N + 3}{N - 4} = \dfrac{3}{4}$

3 $\dfrac{4}{x - 1} = \dfrac{7}{x - 5}$

4 $\dfrac{6}{x - 2} = \dfrac{8}{x + 1}$

5 $\dfrac{1}{4x - 5} = \dfrac{4}{2x - 7}$

6 $\dfrac{x + 2}{2} = \dfrac{1}{x + 3}$

7 $\dfrac{x + 4}{3} = \dfrac{3}{x + 4}$

8 $\dfrac{x - 2}{2} = \dfrac{3}{x + 3}$

9 $\dfrac{4}{x + 5} = \dfrac{x}{x + 3}$

10 $\dfrac{m+3}{m-3} = \dfrac{m+15}{m}$

11 $\dfrac{a+1}{a-1} = \dfrac{1}{3a-1}$

12 $\dfrac{a+1}{a-2} = \dfrac{a+2}{a+1}$

13 $\dfrac{3m+1}{8} = \dfrac{-m}{m-3}$

14 $\dfrac{4}{x^2-9} = \dfrac{1}{x-3}$

15 $\dfrac{2x^2-x-2}{3x^2+2x-4} = \dfrac{2}{3}$

16 $\dfrac{4}{m} + \dfrac{15}{2m} = \dfrac{23}{4}$

17 $\dfrac{4}{y} + 2 = \dfrac{14}{y} - 3$

18 $\dfrac{1}{2} - \dfrac{3}{2h} = \dfrac{4}{h} - \dfrac{5}{12}$

19 $\dfrac{2}{x} + 4 = x - \dfrac{3}{x}$

20 $\dfrac{x-2}{x+4} = \dfrac{x+1}{x+10}$

21 $\dfrac{5}{x+7} - \dfrac{3}{x-5} = \dfrac{2}{x}$

22 $\dfrac{1}{a-1} - \dfrac{2}{a+1} = \dfrac{1}{a(a-1)}$

23 $\dfrac{5}{x-1} - \dfrac{4}{x+1} = \dfrac{-9}{x+3}$

24 $\dfrac{2}{d+4} + \dfrac{1}{d+2} + \dfrac{d^2+3}{d^2+6d+8} = 1$

25 $\dfrac{5a-7}{2a-3} + \dfrac{a+2}{2a+3} - \dfrac{6}{4x^2-9} = 3$

Exercises 26–38: Solve for x or y.

26 $\dfrac{a}{x} = \dfrac{b}{c}$

27 $\dfrac{6a}{x-a} = 3$

28 $\dfrac{a}{x} - 1 = \dfrac{b}{x} - 9$

29 $\dfrac{4}{x-2k} = \dfrac{2}{x-6k}$

30 $\dfrac{x}{a} + \dfrac{x}{b} = c$

31 $\dfrac{x+1}{1-x} = \dfrac{a}{b}$

32 $\dfrac{1}{x} = \dfrac{1}{a} + \dfrac{1}{b}$

33 $\dfrac{a-bx}{c} + b = \dfrac{bc-x}{c}$

34 $\dfrac{y}{r} - s = r - \dfrac{y}{s}$

35 $\dfrac{x+1}{x-1} = \dfrac{m+n}{m-n}$

36 $\dfrac{x-a}{bx} = \dfrac{1}{a} - \dfrac{b}{ax}$

37 $\dfrac{a^2}{x} - a = \dfrac{b^2}{a} - a$

38 $\dfrac{am}{x} = a^2m^2 - am + \dfrac{1}{x}$

39 Solve for a: $\dfrac{1+a}{1-a} = \dfrac{b}{c}$

40 Solve for r, then solve for p: $A = p + prt$

356 Chapter 14: Algebraic Fractions and Equations, and Inequalities Involving Fractions

Word Problems With Fractional Coefficients and Fractional Equations

Number Problems

MODEL PROBLEMS

1 The numerator of a fraction is six less than twice the denominator. If the denominator is doubled and the numerator is increased by one, the value of the fraction is now $\frac{1}{2}$. Find the value of the original fraction.

SOLUTION

Let x = the denominator.

Let $2x - 6$ = the numerator.

The original fraction is $\dfrac{2x - 6}{x}$ and the new fraction is $\dfrac{2x - 6 + 1}{2(x)}$.

The equation is $\dfrac{2x - 6 + 1}{2x} = \dfrac{1}{2}$ or $\dfrac{2x - 5}{2x} = \dfrac{1}{2}$.

Cross multiply and solve.

$$4x - 10 = 2x$$
$$2x = 10$$
$$x = 5$$

The original fraction $\dfrac{2x - 6}{x}$ is now $\dfrac{2 \cdot 5 - 6}{5} = \dfrac{10 - 6}{5} = \dfrac{4}{5}$.

Answer: $\dfrac{4}{5}$

Check:

$$\frac{4 + 1}{2 \cdot 5} = \frac{5}{10} = \frac{1}{2}$$

2 The sum of two numbers is 49. If the larger is divided by the smaller, the quotient is 7 and the remainder is 1. Find the numbers.

SOLUTION

Let x = the smaller number.

Let $49 - x$ = the larger number.

$$\frac{49 - x}{x} = 7 + \frac{1}{x}$$

Multiply by the LCD, x.

$$x \bullet \frac{49 - x}{x} = 7 \bullet x + \frac{1}{x} \bullet x$$
$$49 - x = 7x + 1$$
$$48 = 8x$$
$$x = 6, \text{ the smaller number}$$
$$49 - 6 = 43, \text{ the larger number}$$

Answer: 6 and 43

Check

$6 + 43 = 49$ $\dfrac{49 - 6}{6} = 7 + \dfrac{1}{6}$ $\dfrac{43}{6} = \dfrac{43}{6}$

1 The sum of one-fourth of a number and three-eighths of the same number is 20. Find the number.

2 The sum of 21 divided by a number and 12 divided by the same number is 11. Find the number.

3 When the reciprocal of a number is decreased by three, the result is eight. Find the number.

4 The numerator of a fraction is 19 less than the denominator. If the value of the fraction is $\frac{3}{8}$, what is the original fraction?

5 What number must be added to both the numerator and the denominator of the fraction $\frac{5}{11}$ to make the result equal $\frac{5}{9}$?

6 One number is five less than another. If twice the larger is divided by the smaller, the quotient is 3 and the remainder is 4. If none of the numbers is equal to zero, what are the two numbers?

7 If one-third of a number plus three-fourths of the number is five greater than the number itself, what is the number?

8 One number is 37 larger than another. If the larger is divided by the smaller, the quotient is 5 and the remainder is 5. What are the two numbers?

9 Divide 54 into two parts of so that one-third of the larger plus four-thirds of the smaller equals the larger. What are the two parts?

10 If one-third of a number plus three-fifths of a number is ten greater than the number itself, what is the number?

11 If the value of a fraction is one-half and the denominator is four more than the numerator, what is the fraction?

12 The numerator of a fraction is seven less than the denominator. If the numerator is doubled and the denominator is increased by four, the new fraction is $\frac{2}{3}$. Find the original fraction.

13 The denominator is one more than twice the numerator. If the numerator is increased by 1, the resulting fraction is $\frac{2}{3}$, what is the original fraction?

14 The denominator of a fraction is the same as the numerator plus the numerator squared. If the numerator and denominator are each increased by two, the resulting fraction is $\frac{1}{2}$. What is the original fraction?

15 Divide 60 into two parts so that the quotient obtained by dividing one part by the other will be $\frac{9}{11}$.

16 A and B are two consecutive integers. If four times the smaller is divided by the larger, the quotient is 3 and the remainder is 4. Find A and B.

17 Separate 78 into two parts. If one part is divided by the other, the quotient is 7 and the remainder is 6. Find the two parts.

18 The larger of two numbers is 13 more than three times the smaller. If the larger is divided by the smaller, the quotient is 6 and the remainder is 1. Find the two numbers.

19 If four times the largest of three consecutive even integers is divided by the smallest, the quotient is 9 and the remainder is 6. Find the three integers.

20 The denominator of a fraction is two less than twice the numerator. If the numerator is doubled and the denominator is increased by 12, the resulting fraction is equal to $\frac{3}{4}$. Find the original fraction.

Ratio Problems

Remember that in Chapter 6 we learned that any ratio, a to b, can be represented by an equivalent fraction $\frac{a}{b}$.

MODEL PROBLEMS

1 Two numbers are in the ratio 5:6. If eight is added to each of them, they form a new ratio of 7 to 8. What are the original two numbers?

SOLUTION

Let x = common factor.

Let $5x$ = one number and $6x$ the other number.

The original ratio 5:6 can be represented as the fraction $\frac{5x}{6x}$.

So $\dfrac{5x + 8}{6x + 8} = \dfrac{7}{8}$

Cross multiply and solve.
$$42x + 56 = 40x + 64$$
$$2x = 8$$
$$x = 4$$

The original two numbers are $5x = 20$ and $6x = 24$.

Check:

$$\frac{20 + 8}{24 + 8} = \frac{28}{32} = \frac{7}{8}$$

Answer: 20 and 24

---

2 Cecilia's Accessories for Ladies sold handbags that were either red or black. On Saturday, the ratio of red bags to black bags sold was 2 to 3. If Cecilia's store had sold 4 more red bags, the ratio of red to black bags would have been 3 to 4. How many red bags were sold on Saturday?

SOLUTION

Let x = the common factor.

Let $2x$ = the number of red bags sold and $3x$ = the number of black bags sold.

Therefore, the original ratio was $\frac{2x}{3x}$.

Add 4 to the number of red bags sold in the numerator so that $\dfrac{2x + 4}{3x} = \dfrac{3}{4}$ is the new stated ratio. Cross multiply and solve.

$$4(2x + 2) = 3(3x)$$
$$8x + 16 = 9x$$
$$x = 16 \text{ (the common factor)}$$

The number of red bags sold was $2x = 2(16) = 32$.

Check:

$\dfrac{2x}{3x} = \dfrac{2 \bullet 16}{3 \bullet 16} = \dfrac{32}{48} = \dfrac{2}{3}$, which is the original ratio of red bags to black bags.

Add 4 to the numerator. $\qquad \dfrac{32 + 4}{48} = \dfrac{36}{48} = \dfrac{3}{4}$.

Answer: 32 red bags were sold on Saturday.

1 Two numbers are in the ratio 4:5. If six is added to each number, they will be in the ratio 6:7. Find the numbers.

2 Two numbers are in the ratio 7:10. If nine is subtracted from each of them, the new ratio is 2:3. What are the numbers?

3 Find the number that must be added to both 9 and 29 so that the result will produce the ratio 3:4.

4 Find the number that must be subtracted from both 31 and 71 in order to produce the ratio 3:8.

5 The numerator and denominator are in a ratio of 5:6. When the numerator is decreased by five and the denominator is increased by six, the value of the new fraction is $\frac{1}{2}$. Find the original fraction.

6 Two numbers are in the ratio 4:7. If the smaller number is doubled and 11 is added to the larger, they will then be in the ratio 3:4. What are the numbers?

7 The larger of two numbers is three more than three times the smaller. If four is added to the smaller number and one is added to the larger number, they will then be in the ratio 3:7. Find the original numbers.

8 The numerator and denominator of a fraction are in the ratio 2:5. If 2 is subtracted from both the numerator and denominator, the resulting fraction will be equal to one-third. What is the original fraction?

9 Fred and Dorothy have sums of money in the ratio 3:8. If Dorothy gives Fred $12, their sums of money will be in the ratio 2:5. How much money did they each have to begin with?

10 The ratio of boys to girls in the Unknown X Fan Club is 4:7. The ratio of boys to girls will become 1:2 after 3 boys leave and one girl joins the club. How many members were originally in the club?

Money and Investment Problems

 MODEL PROBLEMS

1 Mr. Brescia invests $4,200, part at 6% and the rest at 4% annual interest. If his total annual interest income from both investments is $216, how much did he invest at each rate?

SOLUTION

Let x = the amount invested at 6%.

Let $0.06x$ = the interest income from the 6% investment.

Let $4,200 - x$ = the amount invested at 4%.

Let $0.04(4,200 - x)$ = the interest income from the 4% investment.

$0.06x + 0.04(4,200 - x) = 216$. Multiply by 100.

$6x + 4(4,200 - x) = 21,600$

$6x + 16,800 - 4x = 21,600$

$\qquad\qquad 2x = 4,800$

$\qquad\qquad\quad x = 2,400$

Answer: $2,400 is invested at 6% and $1,800, $(4,200 - 2,400)$, is invested at 4%.

2 Mr. Brown has one-half of his money invested at 4%, one-third at $3\frac{1}{2}$%, and the remainder at 5%. How much money has he invested at each rate if his annual interest income is $12,000?

SOLUTION

Let x = all of the money invested.

Let $\frac{1}{2}x$ = the money invested at 4%.

Let $\frac{1}{3}x$ = the money invested at $3\frac{1}{2}$%.

Let $x - \left(\frac{1}{2}x + \frac{1}{3}x\right)$ or $x - \left(\frac{3}{6}x + \frac{2}{6}x\right) = x - \left(\frac{5}{6}x\right) = \frac{1}{6}x$, which is the remainder of his money to be invested at 5%.

The equation for his annual interest income is:

$$0.04\left(\frac{1}{2}x\right) + 0.035\left(\frac{1}{3}x\right) + 0.05\left(\frac{1}{6}x\right) = 12{,}000$$

To clear out the decimals, multiply each term by 1,000.

$$\frac{40x}{2} + \frac{35x}{3} + \frac{50x}{6} = 12{,}000{,}000$$

Multiply by the LCD, 6 and cancel common factors.

$$6 \cdot \frac{40x}{2} + 6 \cdot \frac{35x}{3} + 6 \cdot \frac{50x}{6} = 6 \cdot 12{,}000{,}000$$

$$3(40x) + 2(35x) + 50x = 72{,}000{,}000$$

$$120x + 70x + 50x = 72{,}000{,}000$$

$$240x = 72{,}000{,}000$$

$$x = \$300{,}000$$

Answer: The total amount invested is $300,000. The investments are $150,000 at 4%, $100,000 at 3.5%, and $50,000 at 5%.

 Practice

---

1 Evelyn invests $15,000 more at 4% than she does at 5%. If the total annual income from both investments is $2,310, how much does she invest at each rate?

2 Dr. Clarkin invests $28,000, some of it at 6% and the rest at 8%. How much does he invest at each rate if he receives the same amount of annual interest on each investment?

3 Mr. Diaz invests twice as much money at 6% as he does at 4.25%. If his total annual income from both investments is $2,600, how much does he invest at each rate?

4 Andrew borrowed a total of $12,000 from his friends, Brad and Charlie. If Andrew paid Brad interest at the rate of 6.5% and Charlie at the rate of 4.5%, and Andrew paid a total of $690 interest, how much did Andrew borrow from each his friends?

5 If Nancy invests $5,000 at 8%, how much should John, her husband, invest at 10% so that together they have an annual income of $825?

6 Dr. Serdna gave three-fourths of his land to his son, one-fifth of the remaining land to his daughter, and the rest which was 30 acres, to his nephew. How many acres of land did Dr. Serdna have?

7 Mrs. Meier invests $\frac{1}{4}$ of her savings at 4% annual interest, $\frac{2}{3}$ at $5\frac{1}{2}$% interest, and the rest at 6%. The total annual interest income from these investments is $5,580.

 a What is the amount invested at each rate?

 b What is the total amount of her investments?

8 Janet decided to share her lotto winnings with her two sons and two daughters. She gave one-half to her first son, Douglas, and two-fifths of the remainder to her second son, Robert. She gave $20,000 to each of her daughters, Lauren and Joanne, and she kept the rest, $50,000, for herself. What was the original sum of her lotto winnings?

9 Bob gave one-fifth of his lotto prize windings to his wife, Anne, and one-fourth of the remaining money to his eldest son, Jay. He then gave one-third of the remaining money to his youngest son, Robert, and he gave one-half of what was left to his daughter, Kathy. He kept $300,000 for himself.

 a What was the total value of the prize?

 b How much did Anne, Jay, Robert, and Kathy receive?

10 Mr. Hernandez owns an appliance store and pays $560 each for refrigerators. If he wants to make a 25% profit on the selling price after allowing for a 20% discount, how much should he charge for each refrigerator?

Work Problems

Two basic principles are involved in solving work problems.

Principle 1 The rate at which work is done is the reciprocal of the time it takes to do the entire job. If Maria takes 3 hours to do a job, she works at rate of $\frac{1}{3}$ of the job per hour.

Principle 2 The portion of the job that is done is the product of the rate at which it is being done and the amount of time worked. Since Maria works at the rate of $\frac{1}{3}$ of the job per hour, in 2 hours she does $2\left(\frac{1}{3}\right)$ or $\frac{2}{3}$ of the job. At the rate of $\frac{1}{3}$ of the job per hour, after 3 hours she will have done $3\left(\frac{1}{3}\right)$ of the job, or 1, the whole job. We sum up the fractional parts of the job being done by one or more people and set them equal to 1 to indicate that the job is completed.

 MODEL PROBLEMS

1 Jen and Liz are both paralegals. Jen can produce a legal manuscript in 40 minutes, while Liz requires 60 minutes to do the same job. If Jen and Liz pool their skills and work together, how long will it take to produce the manuscript?

SOLUTION

Let $\frac{1}{40}$ = the fraction of the job done in 1 minute by Jen.

Let $\frac{1}{60}$ = the fraction of the job done in 1 minute by Liz.

Let x = the time (in minutes) it takes for the two of them to do the job.

Therefore, $\dfrac{x}{40}$ and $\dfrac{x}{60}$ are the fractions of the job done by each of them working together. Using a table, work problems generally look like this:

	Part of the job done in 1 minute	×	Amount of time working together	=	Part of the job completed
Jen	$\dfrac{1}{40}$	×	x	=	$\dfrac{x}{40}$
Liz	$\dfrac{1}{60}$	×	x	=	$\dfrac{x}{60}$

The sum of the two fractions should equal the whole job completed, or the number 1. $\dfrac{x}{40} + \dfrac{x}{60} = 1$.

Multiply by the LCD, 120, and cancel common factors.

$$120\left(\dfrac{x}{40}\right) + 120\left(\dfrac{x}{60}\right) = 1 \cdot 120$$

$$3x + 2x = 120$$
$$5x = 120$$
$$x = 24$$

Answer: Working together, it will take Jen and Liz 24 minutes to produce one legal manuscript.

2   William figures it will take him 15 hours to dig out a circular garden, and his father, Darren, 10 hours to do the same job. If William works for 3 hours alone, and then his father joins him,

 a what is the time they will take together to complete the job?

 b what is the total time for the whole job?

 c what would have been the total time if they had started and finished the job together?

SOLUTION

After 3 hours, William has done $\dfrac{3}{15}$ or $\dfrac{1}{5}$ of the job.

Therefore, $\dfrac{x}{15} + \dfrac{x}{10} = \dfrac{4}{5}$ of the job is left

Multiply each term by LCD, 30, and solve.

$2x + 3x = 24$

$\qquad 5x = 24$

$\qquad\quad x = 4\dfrac{4}{5}$

 a It will take $4\dfrac{4}{5}$ hours or 4 hours and 48 minutes to complete the job working together.

 b 3 hours for William alone *plus* the 4 hours and 48 minutes, of the two working together equals 7 hours and 48 minutes.

 c To find the total time for William and Darren working together from the beginning, set up and solve the following fractional equation:

$\dfrac{x}{15} + \dfrac{x}{10} = 1$ Multiply each term by the LCD, 30.

$\quad 2x + 3x = 30$

$\qquad\quad 5x = 30$

$\qquad\quad\; x = 6$ hours working together

1 Simon can cut the lawn in 4 hours and Max can do the same job in 2 hours. How long will it take them to do the job if they work together?

2 James can unpack a house-moving van in 8 hours, while Patrick usually takes 12 hours to do the same job. How long would it take them to the job together?

3 Chris can clean the house in 4 hours and Sara can clean the house in 6 hours. How long would it take them if they worked together?

4 Larry can pack a car for vacation in 5 hours while Betsy takes 3 hours to do the same job. How long would it take them to do the job working together?

5 Together, Brian and Scott can paint the exterior of a house in 10 days. Working alone, Brian can paint the house in 30 days. How long would it take Scott to paint the house alone?

6 It takes Andrew 1 hour to straighten out the bookshelves in a store, while Tom can do the job in 2.5 hours. How long would it take them if they worked together?

7 A 16-page document can be printed by machines A and B working together in 150 seconds. If machine A prints a single page in 15 seconds, how many seconds does it take machine B to print a page?

8 George and Ken can put up an 81-square-foot gazebo in 22 hours. Working alone, it would take George twice the time it takes Ken. How long would it take each of them working alone?

9 A small pool has two input pipes and one drain. The pool can be filled with one input pipe in 3 hours and from the other pipe in 4 hours. The drain can empty pool in 2 hours. If both input pipes and the drain were all open at the same time, how long would it take to fill the pool?

10 Working together, Sophie, Taylor, and Tommy can rake all the leaves on the lawn in 6 hours. Alone, it takes Sophie twice the time it takes Tommy, and Taylor can do the job all by himself in 12 hours. Find the time it would take Sophie and Tommy to each do the job alone.

Age, Mixture, and Geometry Problems

Age Problems

The key to age problems is to identify the *now* and to build on that algebraic identity for the past and/or the future. Then substitute those algebraic time descriptions in the verbal statement of the given equation.

MODEL PROBLEM

Ben is one-third as old as his sister, Emma. In 6 years he will be one-half as old as Emma. What are their ages now?

SOLUTION

We can set up a table.

	Present age	Future age (in 6 years)
Ben	$\frac{1}{3}x$	$\frac{1}{3}x + 6$
Emma	x	$x + 6$

$\frac{1}{3}x + 6 = \frac{1}{2}(x + 6)$

$\frac{1}{3}x + 6 = \frac{1}{2}x + 3$ Multiply by the LCD, 6, and solve.

$2x + 36 = 3x + 18$

$\quad\quad x = 18$

Answer: Emma is 18 years old and Ben is $\frac{1}{3}(18)$ or 6 years old.

Mixture Problems

There are two types of simple mixture problems:

The solution is strengthened.
The solution is weakened.

To Solve Mixture Problems:

- Set up a proportion.
- Use an equivalent fraction or decimal for the percent given.
- Solve the proportion and check the word problem, not the equation.

 MODEL PROBLEMS

1 A certain liquid mixture contains 45 pounds of chemical Z and 3 pounds of salt. How much salt must be added to the mixture to produce a 10% salt solution? (strengthened mixture problem)

SOLUTION

The present salt solution is $\frac{3}{45 + 3}$ or $\frac{3}{48}$.

Let x = the additional amount of salt needed to produce a 10% salt solution.

$\dfrac{3 + x}{45 + 3 + x} = 10\%$ Change 10% to a fraction.

$\dfrac{3 + x}{48 + x} = \dfrac{1}{10}$ Cross multiply.

$30 + 10x = 48 + x$

$\quad\quad 9x = 18$

$\quad\quad\; x = 2$

Answer: 2 pounds of salt

2 How many ounces of water must be added to 20 ounces of a 25% nitric acid solution to make a 10% solution? (weakened mixture problem)

SOLUTION

25% of 20 or $\frac{1}{4}$ of 20 = 5 ounces of nitric acid is now present in the solution

Note: The 5 ounces of nitric acid will not change.

$\frac{5}{20}$ is the present fraction of the solution that is nitric acid.

Let x = the amount of water to be added.

$$\frac{5}{20 + x} = 10\%$$

$$\frac{5}{20 + x} = \frac{1}{10} \quad \text{Cross multiply and solve.}$$

$$20 + x = 50$$

$$x = 30$$

Answer: 30 ounces of water must be added.

 # Practice

1 Jessie is one-fourth her grandfather Ed's age. In 9 years she will be one-third his age. How old are they now?

2 Chuck is one-fourth as old as his dad. Eight years ago he was one-tenth as old. What are their ages now?

3 Alex is twice as old as Peter. In 6 years Peter will be three-fourths Alex's age. How old are they now?

4 Eleven years ago, Maria was three-fifths of what her age will be three years from now. How old is she now?

5 Steve's age 6 years ago was two-thirds of what his age will be two years from now. How old is he now?

6 Maggie says that, according to her figures, 8 years ago she was three-sevenths of what her age will be 8 years from now. How old is she now? If she has a daughter who is 29 years old, were her figures correct?

7 How many pounds of sugar must be added to 240 pounds of water to make a 25% sugar solution?

8 How many ounces of vinegar must be added to 6 ounces of a 10% solution to make a 15% solution?

9 How many quarts of alcohol must be added to 48 quarts of a 25% solution to make a $33\frac{1}{3}\%$ solution?

10 How many ounces of water must be added to 20 ounces of a 30% sulfuric acid solution to make a 10% solution?

11 A dairy farmer has 400 quarts of milk containing 6% butter fat. How many quarts of milk containing no butter fat must be added to produce milk containing 4% butter fat?

12 There are 10 quarts of a 30% antifreeze solution in the radiator of a car. How many quarts of antifreeze must be added to make a 50% antifreeze solution?

13 If the base of a triangle is 4 more than its height, and the area is 30, what is the measure of the height?

14 The length of Robert's rectangular putting green is 6 feet greater than its width. The width of Kristi's rectangular garden is equal to the length of Robert's putting green and its length is 32 feet. Since the two plots of grounds are similar rectangles, the ratio of the length to the width of Kristi's garden equals the ratio to the length of the width of Robert's putting green. Find the possible dimensions of each rectangle. Since there are two possible answers, which one makes more sense?

15 The dimensions of a garden are 17.5 feet by 31 feet. If a cement walkway of uniform width is to be built around the garden so that the outside dimensions will be in the ratio 5:8, what should the width of the walkway be?

16 The design of the width to the length of a house deck showed the ratio to be 3:5. However, zoning laws required that a 2-foot-wide strip had to be cut from the length, shortening it. The ratio of the width to the length is now 7:11. What were the original dimensions of the deck?

 CHAPTER REVIEW

1 For the algebraic expression $\dfrac{x+2}{(x^2-4)}$, what are the restrictions?

   (1) $x = 2, x = -2$
   (2) $x > 2$
   (3) $x < 2$
   (4) $x \neq 2, x \neq -2$

2 For what values, if any, are the following fractions undefined?

  a $\dfrac{x}{x-8}$

  b $\dfrac{9x}{3x-1}$

  c $\dfrac{x-4}{x^2+6x+5}$

  d $\dfrac{x-4}{x^2-3x-4}$

  e $\dfrac{n}{n^2-7n}$

  f $\dfrac{6}{x^2-9}$

3 Reduce the following to simplest form.

  a $\dfrac{2x+y}{y+2x}$

  b $\dfrac{2x+4}{x^2-4}$

  c $\dfrac{5a-5b}{15(a-b)^2}$

  d $\dfrac{(x-2y)^2}{3x-6y}$

  e $\dfrac{a^2-49}{a^2+6a-7}$

  f $\dfrac{3x-y}{y-3x}$

  g $\dfrac{x^2+2x}{x^2-3x-10}$

  h $\dfrac{2a-2b}{b-a}$

  i $\dfrac{b^2-c^2}{c^2-2bc+b^2}$

4 Multiply or divide as indicated. Assume that no denominators equal zero.

  a $\dfrac{b^3c^7}{a^3d^4} \cdot \dfrac{a^2d^3}{abc^4}$

  b $\dfrac{4x^3y^2}{-9r^4c^2} \div \dfrac{x^2}{-3rc}$

  c $\dfrac{7a^2b^2}{8m^3n^2} \div 21ab^4$

  d $\dfrac{x^2-36}{7y^3} \div \dfrac{x-6}{14y^4}$

  e $\dfrac{3x+6}{9y-27} \cdot \dfrac{6y-18}{2x+4}$

  f $\dfrac{a^2-b^2}{9x^3} \cdot \dfrac{27x^3}{a^2-2ab+b^2}$

  g $\dfrac{x^2-2x-15}{25-x^2} \div \dfrac{x^2-9}{x+5}$

  h $\dfrac{x^2-4}{x^2+4x+4} \cdot \dfrac{2x+4}{x^2+x-6}$

  i $\dfrac{a^2+a-2}{a^2-7a} \cdot \dfrac{a^2-13a+42}{a^2+2a}$

5 If the sides of a triangle are $\dfrac{x}{3}, \dfrac{5x}{8},$ and $\dfrac{3x}{4}$, express the perimeter in simplest form.

6 Add or subtract as indicated. Assume that no denominators equal zero.

a $\dfrac{x+4}{2} + \dfrac{x+5}{3}$

b $\dfrac{x+y}{2} + \dfrac{y-x}{3}$

c $\dfrac{x+2}{2x} + \dfrac{x-3}{3x}$

d $\dfrac{a+b}{2} - \dfrac{2a-b}{6}$

e $\dfrac{3x-4}{5} - \dfrac{x-2}{4}$

f $\dfrac{x-y}{y-x} + 1$

g $\dfrac{8x}{3-x} + \dfrac{3x}{x+3}$

h $\dfrac{2}{x-1} + \dfrac{2}{x+1}$

i $\dfrac{3x}{x+6} + \dfrac{x-1}{2x+12}$

j $\dfrac{7x}{x^2-y^2} - \dfrac{7}{x+y}$

k $\dfrac{a-5}{a+5} - \dfrac{a+1}{a-2}$

l $\dfrac{4x}{xy-y^2} - \dfrac{4y}{x^2-xy}$

m $\dfrac{5a+2}{6a-3} - \dfrac{3a-5}{8a-4}$

n $\dfrac{a+3}{a-1} + \dfrac{2}{1-a}$

7 Simplify: $7 - 5(x+2)^{-1}$

8 Simplify the following complex fractions.

a $\dfrac{2 + \dfrac{1}{x}}{\dfrac{1}{x} - 3}$

b $\dfrac{a}{\dfrac{1}{x} + \dfrac{1}{y}}$

c $\dfrac{3 - \dfrac{1}{a}}{9 - \dfrac{1}{a^2}}$

d $\dfrac{\dfrac{x}{x+y}}{1 + \dfrac{y}{x+y}}$

e $\dfrac{7 - \dfrac{3}{a+2}}{5 - \dfrac{2}{a+2}}$

f $\dfrac{\dfrac{1}{a} + \dfrac{1}{b}}{\dfrac{1}{a^2} - \dfrac{1}{b^2}}$

g $\dfrac{a + 2 - \dfrac{3}{a}}{1 - \dfrac{3}{a} + \dfrac{2}{a^2}}$

h $\dfrac{m - 4 + \dfrac{3}{m+4}}{m + 4 + \dfrac{3}{m+4}}$

9 Solve and check the following equations with fractional coefficients.

a $\dfrac{x}{3} + \dfrac{x}{5} = 8$

b $\dfrac{x}{8} = \dfrac{x}{12} + \dfrac{1}{3}$

c $\dfrac{2}{3}m - \dfrac{3}{5}m = \dfrac{1}{15}$

d $\dfrac{m+3}{2} - \dfrac{m-1}{3} = 0$

e $\dfrac{2x-1}{7} - \dfrac{3x+5}{3} = \dfrac{1}{3}$

f $0.3a + 1.2a = 4.5$

g $0.04a + 0.05(500 - a) = 23$

10 Solve the following inequalities.

a $\dfrac{x}{2} - 4 > \dfrac{x}{3}$

b $\dfrac{3x - 3}{2} < x + 1$

c $\dfrac{2x + 1}{7} \geq \dfrac{x + 5}{5}$

d $\dfrac{x}{3} - \dfrac{x}{5} \leq \dfrac{2}{3}$

e $\dfrac{n - 1}{2} - \dfrac{1 - n}{10} \leq \dfrac{n + 1}{5}$

f $3.5x - 1.7x > 5$

11 Solve the following fractional and literal equations.

a $\dfrac{1}{x} + \dfrac{1}{6} = \dfrac{1}{2}$

b $\dfrac{6}{x - 1} = \dfrac{x}{2}$

c $\dfrac{4}{x} = \dfrac{5}{x} - 1$

d $\dfrac{2}{x} + 4 = x - \dfrac{3}{x}$

e $\dfrac{1}{x - 1} = \dfrac{x - 1}{4}$

f $\dfrac{1}{x} + \dfrac{1}{x + 3} = 2$

g $R = \dfrac{v^2 PL}{a}$ (solve for P)

h $k(h - 1) = R$ (solve for h)

i $A = x + xyz$ (solve for x)

12 If three times an integer is increased by 9 the result is at most 20. What is the largest possible integer?

13 If three-fifths of an integer is decreased by 7, the result is at least 4. Find the smallest possible integer.

14 Pat invested a sum of money at $8\frac{1}{2}$%, while Buster invested his money at 8%, which was $20,000 less than the amount Pat invested. If the total annual interest for these two investments is at least $1,800, what is the smallest amount of money (to the nearest thousand) that Pat could have invested?

15 One-fifth of the sum of 8 and a certain number equals one-third of the result obtained when 6 is subtracted from that number. Find the number.

16 Two numbers differ by 9, and one-tenth of the greater is equal to one-seventh of the smaller. Find the numbers.

17 Find the sum of three consecutive numbers such that one-half of the first number, plus one-third of the second, plus one-fourth of the third equals 16.

18 Devon's basketball team scored a record number of points. They scored one-fourth of their points in the first quarter, one-fifth of their points in the second quarter, 26 points in the third quarter, and one-third of their points in the fourth quarter. How many points did his team score all together?

19 In a pre-election survey, 5 out of 8 voters said they would vote in a special city election. At this rate, how many people would be expected to vote in a city with the population of 280,000?

20 A U.S. postal warehouse has 20 packers. Each packer can load $\dfrac{1}{8}$ of a truck in 9 minutes. How many trucks can be loaded in $1\frac{1}{2}$ hours by all 20 packers?

21 Randy invested $4,200 at 6%. How much additional money must he invest at 3% in order to have his total annual income equal 4% of the entire investment?

22 Sara invested some money at 5% and twice that amount at 4%. If the sum invested at 4% produces 350 more interest than the one invested at 5%, how much money is invested at each rate?

23 If Adrian can plan a birthday party in 2 days and Vickie can do the same job in 4 days, how many days would it take to do the job if they were working together?

24 One printer can print all the restaurant menus in 60 minutes, while a second printer can print the same number of menus in 90 minutes. How long would it take to print the menus with both printers operating at the same time?

25 An experienced roofer can tile a garage roof twice as fast as an apprentice. Working together, the two roofers can tile the roof in 4 hours. How long would it take the apprentice working alone to do the job?

26 The sum of the ages of Tom and his son, Jim, is 36. In 10 years, Jim will be two-fifths of his father's age. Find their ages.

27 Karen has twin daughters. Each girl is one-fourth her mother's age. In 5 years, the sum of the twin's ages will be two-thirds their mother's age. What are the present ages of Karen and her children?

28 How many ounces of vinegar must be added to 40 ounces of a 15% solution to make it a $33\frac{1}{3}\%$ solution?

29 A biochemist has 10 cubic centimeters of a 10% solution of acid. He wishes to dilute the solution to 8% acid by adding water. How many cubic centimeters of water must he add?

30 A post has one-third of its length in the ground, one-fourth in the water, and 14 feet above the water. What is the length of the post?

31 The length of a rectangle exceeds the width by 5.5 feet. If the length was decreased by 3 feet and the width increased by 1.5 feet, the area would not change. What are the dimensions of the original rectangle?

32 Meghan drove 240 miles at r miles per hour and the next 300 miles at $r + 10$ miles per hour. If the time she drove the first 240 miles equals the time she drove the next 300 miles, how fast was she driving during each part of the trip? (Hint: Use the formula $\textbf{time} = \dfrac{\text{distance}}{\text{rate}}$.)

Now turn to page 450 and take the Cumulative Review test for Chapters 1–14. This will help you monitor your progress and keep all your skills sharp.

Probability

CHAPTER 15

Probability is a branch of mathematics in which a numerical value is used to express the likelihood of an event, or outcome. Probability has to do with certainty, uncertainty, and prediction—that is, with chance. The probability of an event is the chance that it will occur, expressed as a ratio of a specific event to all possible events:

$$\text{Probability} = \frac{\text{number of actual events}}{\text{number of possible events}}$$

This ratio can be written as a fraction (such as $\frac{1}{2}$), as a percent (50%), or as a decimal (.5). In probability it is customary to omit the zero before a decimal point.

Principles of Probability

Theoretical and Empirical Probability

In real life, outcomes are often *not* equally likely. For instance, if you toss a paper cup, it can land faceup, facedown, or on its side. You might predict that it is most likely to land on its side, but to determine the probability of each of the three possible outcomes, you would need to experiment and observe the results. You would need to run a large number of trials to obtain a useful *estimate* of the probabilities of each possibility. Our cup, for which the possible results of tossing it are not equally likely, is called **biased object**. **Empirical probability** deals with sets of possibilities based on experimentation with biased objects. Remember that the greater the number of trials, the more likely the results are to be useful for predicting results of future trials.

Coins, standard dice, and equally sectioned spinners are examples of **fair and unbiased objects**. An object is fair when all of the different possible results are equally likely to occur. **Theoretical probability** deals with results involving fair or unbiased objects or events.

Rules of Probability

The following definitions and rules are generally applicable to situations involving probability, but we will refer to a specific example of theoretical probability: rolling a single fair die, or number cube, one time.

- **Outcome.** The result of some activity. For the die, the possible outcomes are:

  1, 2, 3, 4, 5, 6

- **Sample space.** Set of all possible outcomes. For the die:

  sample space $S = \{1, 2, 3, 4, 5, 6\}$

- **Event.** Any subset of the sample space. The event of rolling a 6 is:

  $E = \{6\}$

- A **formula for probability** P of a single event E is:

  $$P(E) = \frac{n(E)}{n(S)}$$

  where $n(E)$ is the number of ways E can occur, and $n(S)$ is the number of elements in sample space S. For example, the probability of rolling a 6 is:

  $$P(6) = \frac{n(6)}{n(S)} = \frac{1}{6} \text{ or } 16.\overline{6}\% \text{ or } .1\overline{6}$$

- The **probability of an impossible event is 0**, because $n(E) = 0$. For example, the probability of rolling a 7 is:

  $$P(7) = \frac{n(7)}{n(S)} = \frac{0}{6} = 0$$

- The **probability of a certain event is 1**. For example, the probability of rolling a positive number is:

  $$P(+) = \frac{n(+)}{n(S)} = \frac{6}{6} = 1$$

- For any event E, the range of probabilities is from 0 to 1:

  $0 \le P(E) \le 1$

- **Dependent probability**, the probability of a single event with two conditions, is the number of ways both conditions can be satisfied, divided by $n(S)$. For example, to find the probability $P(A$ and $B)$ of (A) rolling an even number and (B) rolling a number greater than 3, we first find $n(A$ and $B)$, in this case $n(\text{even}, >3)$:

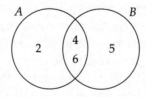

There are two elements, 4 and 6, in the intersection, so $n(\text{even}, >3) = 2$. Then:

$$P(\text{even}, >3) = \frac{2}{n(S)} = \frac{2}{6} = \frac{1}{3}$$

- **Independent probability**, the probability that two different events will both occur, simultaneously or in succession, is the product of their individual probabilities:

$P(A \text{ and } B) = P(A) \times P(B)$

For example, if you roll the die twice, the probability of getting a 5 both times is:

$P(5 \text{ and } 5) = \dfrac{1}{6} \times \dfrac{1}{6} = \dfrac{1}{36}$

- **Conditional probability**, the probability that a second event B will occur *given* that a first event A has already occurred, requires us to introduce new notation: **$P(B|A)$** denotes the probability of event B occurring, given that event A has occurred:

$P(B|A) = \dfrac{P(A \text{ and } B)}{P(A)}$

For example, at the Wheatley School, the probability that a student takes Math 8 and Technology is .12. The probability that a student takes Math 8 is .16. The probability that a student takes Technology (B) given that he is taking Math 8 (A) is $P(B|A) = \dfrac{P(A \text{ and } B)}{P(A)} = \dfrac{.12}{.16} = .75$ or 75%.

- The **probability of a single event that must satisfy one condition *or* another** is found with this formula:

$P(A \text{ or } B) = P(A) + P(B) - P(A \text{ and } B)$

For example, to find the probability of rolling (A) an odd number *or* (B) a number greater than 2, we find the set that satisfies A: {1, 3, 5}. Then we find the set that satisfies B: {3, 4, 5, 6}. Two numbers, 3 and 5, are members of both sets, so $n(A \text{ and } B) = 2$. Therefore:

$P(A \text{ or } B) = \dfrac{3}{6} + \dfrac{4}{6} - \dfrac{2}{6} = \dfrac{5}{6}$

- Two events are **mutually exclusive** if they cannot occur at the same time. Thus, $P(A \text{ and } B) = 0$ and the **probability of two mutually exclusive events** is:

$P(A \text{ or } B) = P(A) + P(B) - 0 = P(A) + P(B)$

For example, you cannot roll a 2 and a 6 at the same time, so the probability of rolling (A) a 2 *or* (B) a 6 is:

$P(2 \text{ or } 6) = \dfrac{1}{6} + \dfrac{1}{6} = \dfrac{2}{6} = \dfrac{1}{3}$

- The condition "not A" is called the **complement** of A and can be written $\overline{A}$ or $\sim A$. The probability of this condition is:

$P(\text{not } A) = 1 - P(A)$ or $P(\overline{A}) = 1 - P(A)$ or $P(\sim A) = 1 - P(A)$

For example, the probability of rolling any number that is not 3 is:

$P(\text{not } 3) = 1 - P(3) = 1 - \dfrac{1}{6} = \dfrac{5}{6}$

- In calculating an **empirical probability**, $n(S)$ is the total number of past occurrences, such as observations or trials, and $n(E)$ is the number of times the particular event occurred:

$$P(E) = \frac{\text{number of occurrences of } E}{\text{total number of observations}}$$

For instance, if we toss a cup 25 times and observe that it lands up 3 times, down 2 times, and sideways 20 times, the empirical probabilities are:

$$P(\text{up}) = \frac{3}{25} \qquad P(\text{down}) = \frac{2}{25} \qquad P(\text{side}) = \frac{20}{25} = \frac{4}{5}$$

Random Variables and Probability Distributions

Often each outcome of a probability experiment can be represented by a real number. If x represents the different numbers corresponding to the possible outcomes of some probability situation, then x is called a **random variable**.

For example, suppose a travel agent knows that $\frac{1}{5}$ of her customers book 2-day trips, $\frac{1}{4}$ book 3-day trips, $\frac{2}{5}$ book 4-day trips, and $\frac{3}{20}$ book 5-day trips. If x represents number of days, then x is a random variable that takes the value 2 with probability $\frac{1}{5}$, the value 3 with probability $\frac{1}{4}$, the value 4 with probability $\frac{2}{5}$, and the value 5 with probability $\frac{3}{20}$.

A **probability distribution** for a random variable is a list or formula that gives the probability for each value of the random variable. The sum of the probabilities must equal 1:

x	$P(x)$
2	$\frac{1}{5}$
3	$\frac{1}{4}$
4	$\frac{2}{5}$
5	$\frac{3}{20}$

$$\frac{1}{5} + \frac{1}{4} + \frac{2}{5} + \frac{3}{20} = \frac{4}{20} + \frac{5}{20} + \frac{8}{20} + \frac{3}{20} = \frac{20}{20} = 1$$

MODEL PROBLEMS

1 Two dice are rolled. Find P(dice show the same number).

SOLUTION

We need to determine how many outcomes are possible (sample space). We can list the possible outcomes in a table as ordered pairs.

		\multicolumn{6}{c}{Second Die}					
		1	**2**	**3**	**4**	**5**	**6**
First Die	**1**	(1, 1)	(1, 2)	(1, 3)	(1, 4)	(1, 5)	(1, 6)
	2	(2, 1)	(2, 2)	(2, 3)	(2, 4)	(2, 5)	(2, 6)
	3	(3, 1)	(3, 2)	(3, 3)	(3, 4)	(3, 5)	(3, 6)
	4	(4, 1)	(4, 2)	(4, 3)	(4, 4)	(4, 5)	(4, 6)
	5	(5, 1)	(5, 2)	(5, 3)	(5, 4)	(5, 5)	(5, 6)
	6	(6, 1)	(6, 2)	(6, 3)	(6, 4)	(6, 5)	(6, 6)

There are 36 possible outcomes in the sample space. Of these, there are 6 outcomes where the dice show the same number. So:

$$P\text{(dice show the same number)} = \frac{n(E)}{n(S)} = \frac{6}{36} = \frac{1}{6}$$

Answer: $\frac{1}{6}$

2 Two dice are rolled. Find P(sum of 11).

SOLUTION

To get a sum of 11, one die must show 5 and the other die must show 6. Referring to the table, we find 2 possible outcomes with a sum of 11. So:

$$P\text{(sum of 11)} = \frac{n(E)}{n(S)} = \frac{2}{36} = \frac{1}{18}$$

Answer: $\frac{1}{18}$

3 In Ms. Macrina's class there are five more boys than girls. Ms. Macrina asked one student to explain a homework problem to the class. She is equally likely to ask any student. The probability that she asks a boy is .6. How many boys and how many girls are in the class?

SOLUTION

Let $x =$ the number of girls

Let $x + 5 =$ the number of boys

So let $2x + 5 =$ the number of students in the class

$$P\text{(boy)} = \frac{\text{number of boys}}{\text{number of students}} = \frac{x + 5}{2x + 5} = .6 \qquad \text{Cross multiply and solve for } x.$$

$$.6(2x + 5) = x + 5$$
$$1.2x + 3 = x + 5$$
$$.2x = 2$$
$$x = 10$$
$$x + 5 = 15$$

Answer: 15

1 The probability that the Talbot Agency will win a new advertising contract is .3. What is the probability that it will *not* win the contract?

(1) .5
(2) .7
(3) .9
(4) 1.3

2 Dana, Ed, and Laurie are the only candidates for class president. Their respective probabilities of winning are $\frac{1}{2}, \frac{3}{10},$ and $\frac{1}{5}$. What is the probability that the winner will be either Dana or Laurie?

(1) $\frac{2}{5}$

(2) $\frac{1}{2}$

(3) $\frac{7}{10}$

(4) $\frac{4}{5}$

3 A die was tossed 100 times. The outcomes are shown below:

Number	Frequency
1	14
2	18
3	20
4	4
5	22
6	22

On the basis of this experiment, $P(4 \text{ or } 5)$ is

(1) $\frac{1}{25}$

(2) $\frac{1}{3}$

(3) $\frac{7}{10}$

(4) $\frac{13}{50}$

4 Which of the following could NOT represent a probability distribution for the random variable x?

(1)

x	$P(x)$
1	.2
2	.2
3	.3
4	.4

(2)

x	$P(x)$
0	$\frac{1}{8}$
2	$\frac{3}{8}$
5	$\frac{3}{8}$
8	$\frac{1}{8}$

(3)

x	$P(x)$
1	$\frac{1}{6}$
2	$\frac{1}{6}$
3	$\frac{1}{6}$
4	$\frac{1}{6}$
5	$\frac{1}{6}$
6	$\frac{1}{6}$

(4)

x	$P(x)$
10	.1
11	.2
12	.1
13	.55
14	.05

5 Two dice are rolled. What is P(sum is at least 2)?

(1) 0   (3) $\dfrac{3}{4}$

(2) $\dfrac{1}{6}$ (4) 1

6 The table shows the number of juices sold in the cafeteria one morning.

Juice	Number
apple	13
orange	21
grapefruit	11
tomato	5
cranberry	6
mango	4

On the basis of these data, P(orange or grapefruit) is

(1) $\dfrac{8}{15}$ (3) $\dfrac{16}{25}$

(2) $\dfrac{11}{21}$ (4) $\dfrac{7}{20}$

Exercises 7–12: A spinner with eight equal sectors numbered 1 to 8 is spun. Find each probability.

7 P(even)

8 P(greater than 2 or less than 7)

9 P(less than 1)

10 P(less than 10)

11 P(multiple of 3 and odd)

12 P(not a multiple of 4)

Exercises 13–18: Two dice are rolled. Find the probability of each outcome

13 At least one die shows a 5.

14 Neither die shows a 2.

15 The dice show different numbers.

16 Exactly one die shows a 1.

17 The sum of the numbers shown is 7 *or* 11.

18 The sum of the numbers shown is greater than 9.

19 There are 5 flashlights in a box. Each flashlight can be either good or defective. Define a random variable x to represent the number of defective flashlights. What are the possible values of x?

20 Of 500 sweaters examined, 6 have irregular sleeves, 19 are discolored, and 133 have other flaws. The rest have no defects.

  a What is the probability of getting a sweater with other flaws?

  b What is the probability of getting a sweater with no defects?

  c Which kind of probability does this situation involve: theoretical or empirical? Why?

21 The probability that it is Saturday and the community pool parking lot is full is 12%. Find the probability that the parking lot is full given that it is Saturday. (Remember that there are seven days in a week.)

22 A jar contains colored lollipops. The probability of selecting a green lollipop followed by selecting a red lollipop without replacement is .4. The probability of selecting a green lollipop as the first selection is .8. What is the probability of selecting a red lollipop on the second draw given that a green lollipop was selected on the first draw?

23 In the Wheatley School Orchestra, 5% of the students play both violin and cello while 75% of the students play violin. What is the probability that a student plays the cello given that he plays the violin? Round your answer to the nearest tenth of a percent.

24 Mr. Meyers has six more calculus books than statistics books on his shelf. One of his students selected a book at random to look for a research assignment topic. The probability that she chose a statistics book is 40%. Find the number of statistics books on the shelf.

25 Mr. Fina coaches baseball. Among his regular players he has 15 more right-handed batters than left-handed batters. Twenty percent of his batters are left-handed.

  a How many players are left-handed?

  b How many players are right-handed?

Calculating Sample Spaces

As reviewed above, the **sample space** S is the number of ways an event can occur.

In some cases, the sample space is obvious: for instance, if a spinner has four equal sectors, $n(S) = 4$ for a single spin. And in some cases the sample space is a familiar array, such as the table of possible outcomes of rolling two dice. However, in many problems involving a series of possibilities, it is necessary to calculate the sample space. This section reviews several calculation methods.

Tree Diagrams

Using a **tree diagram** is one way to show a sample space and count the number of possible outcomes.

 MODEL PROBLEM

If a family has 2 children, how many different arrangements of male (M) and female (F) are there? Make a tree diagram to show the sample space.

SOLUTION

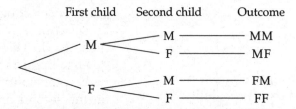

The tree diagram shows that there are 4 possible outcomes.

Answer: Four different arrangements are possible.

The Counting Principle

The **counting principle** states that:

- For a sequence of possibilities, the total number of possible outcomes is the product of the number of outcomes for each part of the sequence.

Thus if there are m choices for event A and n choices for event B, then there are mn choices for event A followed by event B.

In this situation, two concepts are important:

- **With replacement** means that an outcome can be included more than once. That is, the first event does *not* affect the possibilities for the second event. We call such events **independent**.

- **Without replacement** means that an outcome *cannot* be included more than once. In this case, the first event *does* affect the possibilities for the second event. These events are **dependent**.

For instance, consider a bag containing 2 apples and 2 oranges. Suppose that:

(1) We take out one piece of fruit at random. It is an apple. We replace it. Then we draw another piece at random.

Or:

(2) We take out one piece at random. It is an apple. We do *not* replace it. Then we draw another piece at random.

The events in situation 1—with *replacement*—are *independent*. Since the first apple drawn is replaced, the probability of getting an apple on the second draw does not change. In contrast, the events in situation 2—*without* replacement—are *dependent*. Since the first apple drawn is *not* replaced, there are fewer apples left for the second draw, and so the probability of drawing an apple changes.

To take another case, tossing a coin is a situation involving independent events, since the outcome of one toss does not affect the outcome of the next.

 MODEL PROBLEMS

1   A pizza can be ordered in 3 sizes: small (S), medium (M), or large (L). One of 3 extra toppings can be ordered: pepperoni (P), vegetables (V), or cheese (C). How many different ways can a pizza be ordered?

SOLUTION

Use a tree diagram:

```
     Size        Topping        Outcome
                    P ——————— SP
            S  <    V ——————— SV
                    C ——————— SC

                    P ——————— MP
     ———— M  <      V ——————— MV
                    C ——————— MC

                    P ——————— LP
            L  <    V ——————— LV
                    C ——————— LC
```

Use the counting principle:

Choice of sizes is event A, with $m = 3$ possibilities.

Choice of toppings is event B, with $n = 3$ possibilities.

Then:

   total possible outcomes = $mn = 3 \times 3 = 9$

Answer: A pizza can be ordered 9 different ways.

2   A department store has 6 entrances. There are 3 ways of getting from floor to floor: stairs, elevator, or escalator. How many ways are there to enter the store and go from the first floor to the second floor? Use the counting principle.

SOLUTION

6 entrances $\times$ 3 ways to the second floor = 18 different ways

3   How many ways can a red flag, a white flag, and a blue flag be lined up in a row?

SOLUTION

This is a problem *without replacement*, since the same flag cannot appear twice. There are 3 choices for the first flag. After the choice is made, there are 2 choices left for the second flag. After that choice is made, there is 1 choice for the third flag:

   $3 \times 2 \times 1 = 6$

Answer: 6 arrangements

4 How many different 3-digit numbers can be made from the 10 digits if each digit may be used only once and the 3-digit number must be greater than 600?

SOLUTION

Since each digit is used only once, this is a problem *without replacement*. The number could have any of these forms:

6_ _   7_ _   8_ _   9_ _

There are 4 choices for the hundreds digit: 6, 7, 8, or 9.

After the hundreds digit is chosen, 9 choices are left for the tens digit. After the tens digit is chosen, 8 choices are left for the units digit.

Then:

$4 \times 9 \times 8 = 288$

Answer: 288 numbers

Sets of Ordered Pairs

Another way to count a sample space is to write **sets of ordered pairs**. For example, in a toss of two coins, the possible outcomes are the ordered pairs:

{(H, H), (H, T), (T, H), (T, T)}

Note: We can also write **sets of ordered triples**. For example, the outcomes of tossing 3 coins would be:

{(H, H, H), (H, H, T), (H, T, T), (T, T, T), (T, T, H), (T, H, H), (H, T, H), (T, H, T)}

 MODEL PROBLEM

Pairs of black (B), white (W), and red (R) socks are in a drawer. You take out 1 sock at random and then take out another sock. Use ordered pairs to find the number of possible outcomes.

SOLUTION

The set of possible outcomes is:

{(B, B), (B, W), (B, R), (W, B), (W, W), (W, R), (R, B), (R, W), (R, R)}

Answer: There are 9 possible outcomes.

1 Three children are born in a family. How many of the possible outcomes include exactly 2 females?

(1) 2   (3) 4
(2) 3   (4) 5

2 For his vacation, Leon will travel to New York City and then to Paris. He can travel to New York by bus, train, car, or plane. He can travel from New York to Paris by plane or ship. How many different ways can Leon plan his trip?

(1) 4   (3) 7
(2) 6   (4) 8

3 How many different ways can the letters in the word MONEY be arranged?

(1) 10   (3) 3,125
(2) 120   (4) 1,953,125

4 How many different 3-digit numbers are possible if the first digit cannot be 0 and the second digit must be 0 or 1?

(1) 90   (3) 180
(2) 162   (4) 729

5 A true-false test has 4 questions. How many different sets of answers are possible?

(1) 4   (3) 16
(2) 8   (4) 256

6 Ellen has 4 pairs of slacks, 3 shirts, and 3 scarves that all match. How many outfits that include slacks, a shirt, and a scarf can she put together? Make a tree diagram.

7 A delicatessen serves sandwiches on rye bread, white bread, or rolls. There are eight different sandwich fillings. Customers have a choice of lettuce or no lettuce on the sandwich. How many different sandwiches can be assembled?

8 A spinner is divided into 4 equal sectors, each a different color. If the spinner is spun twice, how many different results can occur?

9 There are 4 entrances to a building, 3 escalators up, and 2 escalators down. How many ways can a person enter from outside, go to the second floor, return to the first floor, and then leave the building?

10 A six-sided die and a fair coin are tossed together. How many outcomes are in the sample space?

11 A six-sided die and a fair coin are tossed together. How many outcomes that do NOT include both an even number and tails are in the sample space?

12 How many 7-digit telephone numbers can be created if the first digit cannot be 0?

Permutations

In some situations, the order of outcomes, or events, is important. In other situations, the order of outcomes is *not* important. This difference can affect the size of a sample space. A **permutation** (reviewed here) is an ordered arrangement of events. A **combination** (reviewed next) is a selection of events in which the order does not matter.

Two kinds of sample spaces involving permutations are:

• Number of permutations of a set taken as a whole.

• Number of permutations when we select from a set.

To illustrate **permutations of a set taken as a whole**, consider the earlier example of finding how many arrangements can be made if 3 different flags are lined up. Using the counting principle, we found that the number of arrangements is $3 \times 2 \times 1 = 6$. Two standard ways to write $3 \times 2 \times 1$ are 3! (3 **factorial**) and $_3P_3$ (the permutation of 3 items taken 3 at a time.)

In general, $n! = {_nP_n} = n \times (n - 1) \times (n - 2) \times \ldots \times 1$.

0! is defined as 1.
1! is also defined as 1.

 MODEL PROBLEM

How many different ways can 5 students be seated in a row of 5 chairs?

SOLUTION

$_5P_5 = 5! = 5(5 - 1)(5 - 2)(5 - 3)(5 - 4) = 5 \times 4 \times 3 \times 2 \times 1 = 120$

Answer: 120 ways

To illustrate **permutations of selected members of a set**, consider the model problem on page 383, which involves 3 items out of a set of 10. In a situation like this, the arrangement involves some number r that is less than the number n of all the items. The number of arrangements is $10 \times 9 \times 8$ or $_{10}P_3$ (the permutation of 10 items taken 3 at a time.)

In general, $_nP_r = \dfrac{n!}{(n - r)!} = n \times (n - 1) \times (n - 2) \times \ldots \times (n - r + 1)$.

Most of the time, we will use the calculator to compute $n!$ and $_nP_r$. To find $n!$, press the number that corresponds to n, press (MATH), ▶ to PRB (Probability), and 4 (ENTER).

For example, to find 8!, press 8 (MATH), ▶ to PRB, and 4 (ENTER). The screen will display the following:

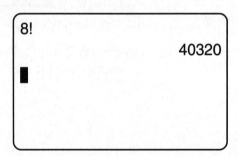

8!
40320

To find $_nP_r$, press the number that corresponds to n, press (MATH), ▶ to PRB (Probability), 2, the number that corresponds to r, and (ENTER).

For example, to find $_7P_5$, press 7 (MATH), ▶ to PRB (Probability), and 2 5 (ENTER). The screen will display the following:

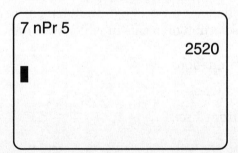

7 nPr 5
2520

MODEL PROBLEM

How many signals can be made by lining up 3 flags selected from 10 different colored flags?

SOLUTION

Here, $n = 10$ and $r = 3$.

There are 10 choices for the first spot, 9 choices for the second spot, and 8 choices for the third spot. Then:

$$_{10}P_3 = 10 \times 9 \times 8 = 720$$

Answer: 720 ways

When we find $n!$ or $_nP_n$ each item must be unique. For example, think of the letters BOB and suppose we treated the two B's as different items, B_1 and B_2. Then B_1OB_2 and B_2OB_1 would appear, misleadingly, as different arrangements.

Thus, if a set includes repetition, there are fewer than $n!$ arrangements of n items. This is a **special case of permutation**:

- Number of permutations of n items taken n at a time with r items identical $= \dfrac{n!}{r!}$

If there is more than one set of identical items, the denominator shows each of these sets as a factorial product.

 MODEL PROBLEM

How many different arrangements can be made from the letters in MISSISSIPPI?

SOLUTION

MISSISSIPPI has 11 letters, with 3 sets the same: 4 I's, 4 S's, and 2 P's.

Use the special case formula $\dfrac{n!}{r!}$ with $n = 11$. Show each of the repeated sets as a factorial in the denominator:

$$\frac{11!}{4! \bullet 4! \bullet 2!} = \frac{39,916,800}{24 \bullet 24 \bullet 2} = \frac{39,916,800}{1,152} = 34,650$$

Answer: 34,650 arrangements

In summary, here are the **formulas** for numbers of permutations.

- For a set of n **events taken n at a time**: $_nP_n = n!$

- For a set of n **events taken r events at a time**: $_nP_r = \dfrac{n!}{(n-r)!}$

- For n **events taken n at a time with r items identical**, permutations $= \dfrac{n!}{r!}$

1 The expression $_8P_4$ is equal to

(1) 12
(2) 32
(3) 1,680
(4) 4,096

2 How many different ways can 7 runners be assigned to 7 lanes at the start of a race?

(1) 14
(2) 49
(3) 210
(4) 5,040

3 Steve has 6 coins in his pocket: 1 penny, 1 nickel, 1 dime, and 3 quarters. In how many different orders can Steve take the 6 coins out of his pocket?

(1) 36
(2) 120
(3) 720
(4) 46,656

4 There are 12 students in a club. In how many different ways can a president, vice president, treasurer, and secretary be elected from the club members?

(1) 16
(2) 48
(3) 1,320
(4) 11,880

5 The expression $_{10}P_1$ is equal to

(1) 1
(2) 10
(3) 11
(4) 100

6 How many ways can all of 6 different flags be lined up?

7 How many ways can 4 of 10 flags be lined up?

8 How many ways can a 3-digit number be created if the digits are all different and the number is at least 500?

9 How many 4-digit numbers can be created if all the digits are odd?

10 How many different ways can you arrange the letters in BUFFALO?

11 How many different ways can you arrange the letters in BUFFALO if the F's must remain together?

12 How many ways can you arrange the letters in BUFFALO if the first letter must be B?

13 How many different ways can you arrange the letters in MAMARONECK?

14 How many different ways can you arrange the letters in MINISINK?

15 How many different ways can you arrange 2 of 6 minivans, followed by 4 of 5 convertibles?

Combinations (Optional Topic)

A selection of events in which order does *not* matter is called a **combination**. For example, if a committee of 3 students is being chosen from a group of 10, the order of the students does not matter. The committee {Bob, Carol, Sam} is the same as {Carol, Bob, Sam} or {Sam, Carol, Bob}, and so on.

Two kinds of sample spaces involving combinations are:

• Number of **combinations of a set of n events taken n events at a time**. This number is always 1. In other words, a set of n events taken as a whole, $_nC_n$, has only one combination:

$$_nC_n = 1$$

- Number of **combinations of a set of n events taken r events at a time**. This situation can be written as $_nC_r$. The **formula** is:

$$_nC_r = \frac{_nP_r}{r!} \qquad \text{or} \qquad _nC_r = \frac{n!}{r! \bullet (n-r)!}$$

To find $_nC_r$ with a calculator, press the number that corresponds to n, press MATH, then ▶ to PRB (Probability), 3, the number that corresponds to r, and ENTER.

Remember the standard expressions:

Notation	Meaning
$_nC_n$	Combinations of a set of n events taken n events at a time (always = 1)
$_nC_r$	Combinations of a set of n events taken r events at a time

Here are some more facts about combinations.

 MODEL PROBLEMS

1 Ms. Simpson is faculty adviser to the school's National Honor Society chapter. There are 50 members. How many ways can she choose 5 members to attend a conference?

SOLUTION

This situation does *not* involve a permutation: order does *not* matter. Therefore, we want the number of *combinations* of 50 items taken 5 at a time. Find $_{50}C_5$ on your calculator:

$$_{50}C_5 = 2{,}118{,}760$$

As a check, find $\frac{_{50}P_5}{5!}$ on your calculator. You should get the same result:

$$\frac{_{50}P_5}{5!} = \frac{254{,}251{,}200}{120} = 2{,}118{,}760$$

Answer: 2,118,760 ways

2 Ms. Leonardi is forming a committee of students to work on a school project. If 3 freshmen, 2 sophomores, 4 juniors, and 4 seniors volunteer, how many ways can Ms. Leonardi choose a committee of 8 students, with 2 from each grade level?

SOLUTION

Ms. Leonardi needs 2 freshmen out of 3, 2 sophomores out of 2, 2 juniors out of 4, and 2 seniors out of 4.

Calculate:

$$_3C_2 \bullet {_2C_2} \bullet {_4C_2} \bullet {_4C_2} = 3 \bullet 1 \bullet 6 \bullet 6 = 108$$

Answer: 108 ways

Note: For the $_nC_r$'s in this problem, the sum of the n's is the number of elements in the sample space, and the sum of the r's is the total number of elements being chosen.

- Just as there is only 1 combination of a set as a whole, or only 1 way to choose all the items ($_nC_n = 1$), there is only 1 way to choose *none* of the items:

$$_nC_0 = 1$$

- Choosing (including) r out of n items is the same as *not* choosing (excluding) $n - r$ items. This is reasonable, since selecting 2 of 5 is the same as excluding or leaving out 3 of 5. Thus if $r \le n$, then:

$$_nC_r = {_nC_{n-r}}$$

Note: Here are some guidelines for determining whether a problem involves permutations or combinations.

• Ask whether *order* is important (a permutation) or unimportant (a combination).

• Look for *key words*:

Words associated with permutations include *order*, *ordering*, *arrange*, and *arrangement*.

Words associated with combinations include *group*, *gather*, and *assemble*.

• Recognize *typical situations*. For example:

A problem that involves choosing people to fill specific roles—such as club president, secretary, and treasurer—is a permutation problem.

A problem that involves choosing people for a group with no specific roles—such as members of a committee—is a combination problem.

 Practice

---

1 $_8C_3 =$

   (1) 24
   (2) 56
   (3) 336
   (4) 1,680

2 $_{14}C_{14} =$

   (1) 0
   (2) 1
   (3) 14
   (4) 196

3 If $_nC_6 = {_nC_4}$, then $n =$

   (1) 2
   (2) 8
   (3) 10
   (4) 24

4 $_{15}C_8 =$

   (1) $_8C_7$
   (2) $_{15}C_7$
   (3) $_7C_{15}$
   (4) $_{23}C_{15}$

5 Acme Company wants to open accounts at 3 different local banks. If 10 banks are available, how many ways can Acme choose the 3 banks?

   (1) 30
   (2) 120
   (3) 720
   (4) 1,000

6 Leslie bought 5 flavors of ice cream and 3 toppings. She will choose 2 flavors and 1 topping for a sundae. How many different sundaes can she make?

7 If 4 Jets, 4 Giants, and 4 Bills volunteer for a Big Brother project, how many ways can 2 men from each team be chosen?

8 A family of 5 received 3 free tickets to a concert. The baby will not go. How many ways can the tickets be distributed?

Exercises 9–12: Kyle goes to a video rental store with enough money to rent 3 videos. He finds 3 mysteries, 4 dramas, and 2 comedies that he wants to see.

9 How many selections of 3 videos would be all mysteries?

10 How many selections of 3 videos would be all dramas?

11 How many selections of 3 videos would be all comedies?

12 How many selections of 3 videos would be one of each kind?

Exercises 13–16: Ten girls and 8 boys are interested in visiting a job fair off campus. The school district has a minibus that can hold 14 students. Susan and Peter must go to the job fair.

13 How many ways can students be chosen for the bus?

14 How many ways can students be chosen if all of the girls must go?

15 How many ways can the students be chosen if the same number of girls and boys must go?

16 How many ways can the students be chosen if Marta must go?

17 How many ways can a committee of 4 juniors and 4 seniors be selected from 10 juniors and 12 seniors?

18 A box of 12 cell phones has 3 defective ones. How many ways can 4 phones be selected so that 2 are good and 2 are defective?

Probability Problems Involving Permutations and Combinations

Probability problems, including real-world situations, often involve permutations and combinations. The model problems below are typical examples.

 MODEL PROBLEMS

1 From a standard 52-card deck, you draw 1 card and put it aside. Then you draw another card. What is the probability that the first card is an ace (A) and the second is a king (K)?

SOLUTION

Since order is important, this is a permutation problem. Note that the events are dependent, and that there are 4 aces and 4 kings in a standard deck. Three solution methods are shown.

Method 1: Counting Principle	Method 2: $P(A \text{ and } B) = P(A) \cdot P(B)$	Method 3: $_nP_r$
Possibilities for 1st card: 4 out of $52 = \dfrac{4}{52}$ Possibilities for 2nd card: 4 out of $51 = \dfrac{4}{51}$ Multiply: $\dfrac{4}{52} \cdot \dfrac{4}{51} =$ $\dfrac{16}{2,652} = \dfrac{4}{633} \approx .006$	Event A is an ace (A) and event B is a king (K). For 1st card: $P(A) = \dfrac{n(E)}{n(S)} = \dfrac{n(A)}{52} = \dfrac{4}{52}$ For 2nd card: $P(K) = \dfrac{n(E)}{n(S)} = \dfrac{n(K)}{51} = \dfrac{4}{51}$ Then: $P(A \text{ and } K) = P(A) \cdot P(K)$ $= \dfrac{4}{52} \cdot \dfrac{4}{51} = \dfrac{16}{2,652} \approx .006$	Ways to get 1 ace of $4 = {_4P_1}$ Ways to get 1 king of $4 = {_4P_1}$ So for ace followed by king: $n(E) = {_4P_1} \cdot {_4P_1}$ Ways to draw 2 cards in order from $52 = {_{52}P_2}$, so: $n(S) = {_{52}P_2}$ Calculate: $\dfrac{n(E)}{n(S)} = \dfrac{{_4P_1} \cdot {_4P_1}}{{_{52}P_2}}$ $= \dfrac{4 \cdot 4}{52 \cdot 51} = \dfrac{16}{2,652} \approx .006$

Answer: The probability is approximately .006.

2 At the Pet of the Month awards ceremony, 9 collies and 6 poodles are available for a news photo. The photographer chooses 3 dogs at random. What is the probability that 2 collies and 1 poodle will be chosen?

SOLUTION

Order is not important, so this is a combination problem. The events are dependent, since any dog can be chosen only once. Here is one solution method.

Calculate:

$n(E) = {}_9C_2 \bullet {}_6C_1 = 36 \bullet 6 = 216$

$n(S) = {}_{15}C_3 = 455$

$P = \dfrac{n(E)}{n(S)} = \dfrac{{}_9C_2 \bullet {}_6C_1}{{}_{15}C_3} = \dfrac{216}{455} \approx .47$

Answer: The probability is approximately .47.

 Practice

Note: Combination problems have been grouped at the end so they can easily be eliminated to match certain curriculum models.

1 Two cards are drawn without replacement from a standard 52-card deck. The probability that both cards are diamonds is

(1) $\dfrac{1}{17}$

(2) $\dfrac{169}{2,652}$

(3) $\dfrac{1}{221}$

(4) $\dfrac{1}{4}$

2 A box contains 3 red pens, 2 green pens, and 5 blacks pens. Two pens are picked at random (without replacement of the first pen before the second is picked). What is the probability of getting a red pen, then a green pen?

(1) $\dfrac{3}{50}$ (3) $\dfrac{1}{6}$

(2) $\dfrac{1}{15}$ (4) $\dfrac{2}{27}$

3 Cindy has forgotten her friend's phone number. She knows it starts with 555 and the other four numbers consist of one 3, one 7, and two 9's. If she picks a combination and dials, what is the chance she will dial the correct number?

(1) 1 in 4
(2) 1 in 12
(3) 1 in 24
(4) 1 in 420

4 A coin bank contains 9 nickels, 4 dimes, and 5 quarters. If you shake out 3 coins from the bank, without replacement, what is the probability that you will get a nickel, a quarter, and a nickel in that order?

(1) $\dfrac{1}{6}$

(2) $\dfrac{3}{34}$

(3) $\dfrac{5}{68}$

(4) $\dfrac{5}{136}$

5 A box of 12 batteries has 3 defective ones. If 2 batteries are taken from the box without replacement, what is the probability that 1 battery is defective?

(1) $\dfrac{1}{22}$

(2) $\dfrac{1}{16}$

(3) $\dfrac{9}{44}$

(4) $\dfrac{9}{22}$

6 Asa, Bill, Cathy, Dino, and Eve are randomly seated in a row of 5 seats. Find the probability that Asa will sit next to Bill.

(1) $\dfrac{1}{60}$

(2) $\dfrac{2}{5}$

(3) $\dfrac{1}{10}$

(4) $\dfrac{4}{15}$

7 If the letters of the word MATHEMATICS are arranged at random, find the probability that the first letter is

a M

b a vowel

8 From a deck of 52 cards, you draw 4 cards without replacement. What is the probability that the cards are ace, king, queen, and jack in that order?

9 From a deck of 52 cards, you draw 4 cards without replacement. What is the probability that the cards are different prime numbers?

10 If the letters in the word ALGEBRA are arranged at random, find the probability that the first letter is a vowel.

Combination Problems

11 Denzel picked 6 numbers out of 20 to play on an Internet lottery. Which expression is equal to the probability that his 6 numbers will match the 6 winning numbers? (The order of the numbers does not matter.)

(1) $\dfrac{14!}{20! \times 6!}$　(3) $\dfrac{20!}{14!}$

(2) $\dfrac{14! \times 6!}{20!}$　(4) $\dfrac{6!}{20!}$

12 A librarian is arranging a display of new books. She has room for 8 books. She has 3 mysteries, 4 computer books, 3 biographies, and 2 books on family health. If her choices are random, what is the probability that the display will contain 2 of each type of book?

13 Ten students are applying for 3 positions on a team. The students include 4 boys (Adam, Alex, Anthony, and Arnold) and 6 girls (Abbey, Aurora, Agnes, Alice, Amanda, and Anna). All the students have an equal chance of being selected. Find the probability that the students selected will include

a 3 girls

b 1 boy and 2 girls

c at most 1 girl

d Adam, Anthony, and Alice

e Agnes and 2 other students

14 Three cards are drawn at random from a standard 52-card deck, without replacement. Find the probability of selecting

a any 3 hearts

b any 3 black cards

c any 3 red picture cards

15 A box of identically shaped candies contains 3 chocolate, 4 butterscotch, and 2 berry. Claire closes her eyes and picks 3 candies. Find the probability that she will get

a 3 of the same kind

b 1 of each kind

c 2 butterscotch and 1 chocolate

Note: Combination problems have been grouped at the end so they can easily be eliminated to match certain curriculum models.

1 A store has 3 entrances. Shoppers can go between the first floor and the second floor by a stairway, an elevator, or an escalator. How many ways can a shopper enter from outside, go to the second floor, return to the first floor, and leave the building?

   (1) 12
   (2) 27
   (3) 81
   (4) 243

2 A travel club has 200 members. If 50 members are picked at random each year to go on a trip, what is the probability that a member is picked 3 years in a row?

   (1) $\frac{1}{4}$

   (2) $\frac{1}{50}$

   (3) $\frac{1}{64}$

   (4) $\frac{1}{150}$

3 Meg buys 2 kinds of lettuce, 2 kinds of tomatoes, and 3 kinds of dressing. To make a salad, she will use 1 kind of lettuce, 1 kind of tomato, and 1 kind of dressing. How many salads can she make?

   (1) 3
   (2) 6
   (3) 7
   (4) 12

4 A spinner has 8 sectors, each a different color. If it is spun twice, how many different results are possible?

   (1) 8
   (2) 16
   (3) 32
   (4) 64

5 A 6-sided die is rolled and a coin is tossed. (Both are fair.) How many outcomes that include an even number on the die are in the sample space?

   (1) 2
   (2) 4
   (3) 6
   (4) 8

6 Mr. Goldman has 3 posters, 1 calculator chart, and 3 banners. If he arranges them all from left to right across a bulletin board, how many different arrangements can he make?

7 How many ways can a 3-digit number be created if the digits are all different and odd?

8 How many 3-digit numbers can be created if each number is a multiple of 10?

9 How many ways can you arrange the letters in MASSAPEQUA if the first letter is M?

10 How many ways can you arrange 2 marching bands out of 4, followed by 4 kick lines out of 6?

11 A school has 3 stairways between the first floor and the second floor, 2 stairways between the second floor and the third floor, and 2 stairways between the third and the fourth floors. If a student wants to avoid using the same stairway twice, how many ways can she go from the first floor to the fourth floor and then return to the first floor?

12 A school district's 9-digit identification number is determined as follows:

1st and 2nd numbers	represent the month of birth (01 to 12)
3rd and 4th numbers	represent the day of the month of birth (01 to 31)
5th, 6th, 7th, and 8th numbers	represent the year of the birth
9th number	0–9, separating students with the same birthdate

How many identification numbers are possible given that every student is born in the twentieth or twenty-first century?

13 The probability of a ninth-grade student participating in junior varsity soccer is 10%. The probability of a ninth-grade student participating in both junior varsity soccer and junior varsity tennis is 4%. What is the probability that Rob, a ninth-grade student, a junior varsity soccer player, also plays tennis?

14 A cheerleader supply box contains red, white, and blue pom-poms. There are twice as many white pom-poms as red and four more blue pom-poms than red. The probability of randomly selecting a blue pom-pom is $\frac{1}{3}$. Find the number of blue pom-poms.

15 Ms. Kandybowicz seats the chorus in a single row from left to right. She seats boys on the left side of the row and girls on the right side. There are 5 boys and 8 girls. How many ways can she arrange the chorus?

16 Ms. Bixhorn attended a county workshop on school improvement. There were six sessions to choose from at 9 o'clock, four sessions at 11 o'clock, and six sessions at 2 o'clock. How many ways could Ms. Bixhorn choose to attend three sessions?

17 The numbers 1, 2, 3, 4, 5, 6, 7, 8, 9, and 10 were placed on separate cards in a deck. If one card was selected at random, what is the probability that the number on the card was prime also a divisor of 30?

Exercises 18 and 19: A spinner has 6 equal sectors numbered 1 to 6. It is spun once. Find

18 P(not greater than 1)

19 P(less than 3)

Combination Problems:

Exercises 20 and 21: Two dice are rolled. Find **each** probability:

20 Both dice show 1.

21 The sum is 3 or 10.

22 Mr. Gadamowitz selected 2 lightbulbs out of a pack of 12. One bulb in the box is defective. What is the probability that Mr. Gadamowitz will select the defective bulb?

23 A home economics class is creating a cookbook. There is room for 6 more recipes, but 10 more are excellent enough to be entered. If Irene's key lime pie recipe is selected, how many ways can the remaining recipes by selected?

24 Five Republicans and five Democrats are available for four seats on a Senate committee. What is the probability that an equal number of Republicans and Democrats will be selected?

25 If $_nC_3$ is equivalent to $_nC_8$, what is the value of n?

26 A box of pastel chalk contains 3 lemon yellow, 4 peachy orange, 2 sky blue, and 1 leaf green. If 4 chalks are drawn at random, find the probability that one of each color will be chosen.

Now turn to page 452 and take the Cumulative Review test for Chapters 1–15. This will help you monitor your progress and keep all your skills sharp.

CHAPTER 16

Statistics

Statistics is the study of numerical **data**. These data are collections of related numerical information, such as sports scores and records, election results, real estate sales, and grades on Regents Examinations.

Once data are collected, they must be organized in a meaningful way so that conclusions can be drawn from them.

Sampling and Collecting Data

If a study requires information about every member of a population—such as the birthplace of every student in a particular high school—a **census** is conducted. A census includes every person or every situation. However, a census is often impractical or even impossible. For instance, to determine the life of 40-watt bulbs produced in a certain factory, only a small **sample**, or number, of the bulbs would be tested, because the owners of the factory would not want to burn out all of their inventory. An election poll does not include all voters; it counts only a sample of voters. Samples must be chosen carefully to avoid bias. **Bias** is a tendency to favor the selection of certain members of a population.

Selecting a Sample

- *A sample must fairly represent the entire population being studied.* The sample for a study of residents' satisfaction with a local park should represent all people in the neighborhood, not just those who use the park or come on weekends. People dissatisfied with the park may not visit it at all, and their opinions should also be included.

- *The number of data values must be significant.* The study of statistics includes determining the minimum amount of data needed to make a study meaningful.

- *The sample should be random or selected in an organized way that avoids bias.* Picking names out of a hat is an example of random selection. Studying every tenth person who enters a supermarket is an example of organized selection.

Practice

1   A survey that includes every member of a population is called a

(1)   poll
(2)   census
(3)   random sample
(4)   biased study

2   A well-chosen sample

(1)   represents an entire population
(2)   is large enough to provide meaningful data
(3)   is unbiased
(4)   all of the above

3   Statistics is the study of

(1)   lightbulbs
(2)   random samples
(3)   numerical data
(4)   election polls

4   Sampling is used to choose

(1)   an entire population
(2)   a fair representation of a group
(3)   a small number of people
(4)   sports statistics

Exercises 5–14: A sample must be selected to determine the favorite summer activities of people in a particular town. Is each of the following samples representative or not? Why?

5   tenth-grade students

6   women

7   people at a beach

8   residents of a nursing home

9   shoppers in a mall

10   people in the produce aisle of a supermarket

11   fans at a baseball game

12   every twentieth name in the town's telephone directory

13   concert musicians

14   millionaires

Organizing Data

Stem-and-Leaf Plots

A **stem-and-leaf plot** is a display that shows each data value.

 MODEL PROBLEM

In September, each of the 24 students in a math class reported the number of days he or she worked that summer:

25, 17, 15, 28, 24, 13, 16, 28, 19, 25, 24, 36, 33, 18, 24, 38, 28, 25, 27, 14, 37, 28, 35, 43

Represent these data in a stem-and-leaf plot, with the values in the *tens* place as the stem and the corresponding values in the *units* place as the leaves.

SOLUTION

Step 1.   Find the smallest and largest values in the data.

Step 2.   Draw a vertical line. To the left of the line, write each consecutive digit from the smallest stem value to the largest stem value.

Step 3:   Insert the leaves.

Step 4:   For each stem, reorder the leaves from smallest to largest.

Step 5:   Include a key.

For the data above, the smallest value is 13 and the largest value is 43. The smallest tens value is 1 and the largest tens value is 4. After step 3, the plot looks like this:

1	7	5	3	6	9	8	4				
2	5	8	4	8	5	4	4	8	5	7	8
3	6	3	8	7	5						
4	3										

After Step 4—ordering the leaves—the plot looks like this:

1	3	4	5	6	7	8	9				
2	4	4	4	5	5	5	7	8	8	8	8
3	3	5	6	7	8						
4	3										

The key (Step 5) can show any value, such as 2|4 = 24.

From this plot, we find that most students worked from 24 to 28 days.

A **back-to-back stem-and-leaf plot** can be used to compare two sets of data. The stem is drawn down the middle of the chart, and the leaves extend to the left for one data set and to the right for the other data set. The leaves are in increasing order moving away from the stems.

 MODEL PROBLEM

Two brands of soup are advertised as "low-fat." A study compares grams of fat per serving for 11 kinds of soup of each brand.

Brand A:

1.5, 1.6, 3.0, 4.2, 1.2, 3.1, 4.6, 2.4, 3.6, 2.4, 1.8

Brand B:

1.3, 3.5, 4.2, 3.3, 5.2, 4.1, 3.2, 5.1, 4.8, 4.1, 4.4

Display these results in a back-to-back stem-and-leaf plot.

SOLUTION

The stem for these data is the units digit. The leaves show the numbers in the tenths places.

Brand A						Brand B
8	6	5	2	1	3	
		4	4	2		
	6	1	0	3	2 3 5	
		6	2	4	1 1 2 4 8	
				5	1 2	

Key: 6|3 = 3.6   Key: 3|2 = 3.2

This plot shows that brand A soups generally have less fat than brand B soups.

Tally and Frequency Tables

Suppose you want to know how many hours members of your class spend on the Internet each week. You conduct a census and get these results: 0, 0, 7, 5, 0, 5, 0, 1, 5, 5, 3, 5, 0, 0, 5, 5, 7, 1, 0, 5.

Data presented in an unorganized format such as this are difficult to use. Questions like "What is the most common amount of time spent on the Internet?" and "How many students spend more than 4 hours a week on the Internet?" are answered more easily if the data are organized. A **tally** or **frequency table** is one form of organization.

 MODEL PROBLEM

Organize the above results in a tally or frequency table.

SOLUTION

Step 1. Label the columns: in this case "Hours on Internet," "Tally," and "Frequency."

Step 2. Start with the largest number in the data, in this case 7. Keep subtracting 1, entering the numbers down the first column. Stop at 0.

Step 3. For each piece of data, enter a mark (|) in the appropriate row under "Tally." Every fifth mark is a diagonal through the preceding four marks (||||).

Step 4. Under "Frequency," complete each row by counting the tally marks and recording the number.

Step 5. Add all the frequency values to get total frequency.

Sometimes, you need only tally marks or only frequencies, not both.

Hours on Internet	Tally	Frequency
7	||	2
6		0
5	|||| |||	8
4		0
3	|	1
2		0
1	||	2
0	|||| ||	7
Total frequency: 20		

We can see from the frequency table that 10 out of 20 or 50% of the students spent more than 4 hours weekly on the Internet.

In the model problem above, only a few pieces of data were reported. Sometimes, however, the number of values is so large that a table showing each value would be very long. In these cases, we group the data into equal-sized **intervals**. The resulting frequency chart looks the same except for the first column, which shows intervals.

For example, suppose that a guidance counselor wants to make a chart of the Math SAT scores for all her students. She groups scores into six intervals: 201–300, 301–400, 401–500, 501–600, 601–700, 701–800. (Each interval has a length of 100.) She then looks at each student's score and enters a tally mark in the appropriate interval. Then she enters the total for each interval in the frequency column.

Math SAT Scores

Interval	Tally	Frequency
701–800	ⅢⅠ ⅠⅠⅠ	8
601–700	ⅢⅠ ⅢⅠ ⅢⅠ ⅠⅠⅠⅠ	19
501–600	ⅢⅠ ⅢⅠ ⅢⅠ ⅢⅠ ⅢⅠ	25
401–500	ⅢⅠ ⅢⅠ ⅢⅠ ⅢⅠ ⅠⅠⅠ	23
301–400	ⅢⅠ ⅢⅠ ⅢⅠ Ⅰ	16
201–300	ⅠⅠⅠ	3
	Total frequency: 94	

To Group Data for a Tally or Frequency Table

- Make all your intervals equal in size. Try to use a length that will give a total of 5 to 10 intervals.

- Make sure that the intervals include the entire range of values in the data set.

- Construct the intervals from the bottom up. The highest value in each interval should be one less than the lowest value in the next interval. The intervals should not overlap.

Note: A grouped frequency table does not show individual data values.

Frequency Histograms

Often, it is useful to display grouped data in a **frequency histogram**, similar to a vertical bar graph. The widths of all the bars are equal and represent equal intervals. The frequency for each interval is represented by the height of its bar. Just as there are no gaps between intervals, there should be no gaps between bars.

To Construct a Frequency Histogram

- Construct a frequency table.

- Draw a horizontal axis and mark off the intervals. Label the horizontal axis. If the first interval does not start at 0, use a "break" symbol (-∿-) on the axis.

- Draw a vertical axis and identify a scale for the frequencies. Label the vertical axis. Often, the vertical axis is "Frequency."

- Draw bars with heights corresponding to the frequency values in the table.

- Give the graph an appropriate title.

MODEL PROBLEM

Construct a frequency histogram for these test grades: 100, 93, 71, 74, 85, 56, 62, 68, 70, 100, 99, 85, 77, 85, 48, 51, 79, 25, 86, 93, 67, 88, 70, 100, 26

SOLUTION

First construct the frequency table. Intervals of 10 are used here.

Test Scores	Frequency
91–100	6
81–90	5
71–80	4
61–70	5
51–60	2
41–50	1
31–40	0
21–30	2

Next draw the frequency histogram.

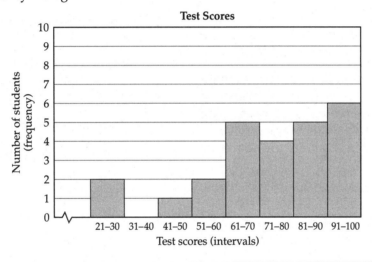

 Practice

1 The key for a stem-and-leaf plot is 4|7 = 47. The value 63 would be plotted as:

   (1) 3|6

   (2) 60|3

   (3) 6|3

   (4) 63

2 The frequency table shows favorite types of television programs for a group of 50 students. What percent of the students chose comedy or drama?

Favorite TV Programs

Program	Frequency
News	7
Sports	11
Drama	8
Talk	5
Comedy	14
Science	3
Cooking	2

   (1) 14%   (3) 28%

   (2) 22%   (4) 44%

3 The heights of a group of 36 people were measured to the nearest inch. The heights ranged from 47 inches to 76 inches. To construct a histogram showing 10 intervals, the length of each interval should be:

    (1) 2 inches
    (2) 3 inches
    (3) 4 inches
    (4) 5 inches

Exercises 4–7: A sample of community members is to be selected to determine the need to build a new swimming pool for the high school. Is each of the prospective samples fair or unfair? Why?

4 residents of the local senior citizen center

5 mothers at a Parent-Teacher Organization meeting

6 the high school swim team

7 random shoppers entering a large shopping mall located within the community

8 Sajan, a camp counselor, recorded the high temperature at camp each day. Construct a back-to-back stem-and-leaf plot comparing temperatures in July with temperatures in August. State one fact about the temperatures you are able to learn from the plot.

July (°F): 78, 79, 80, 86, 82, 90, 91, 91, 89, 94, 89, 95, 94, 91, 88, 86, 91, 87, 90, 88, 92, 90, 94, 93

August (°F): 92, 89, 89, 90, 86, 87, 90, 85, 84, 79, 90, 90, 89, 88, 90, 91, 98, 91, 87, 79, 82, 81, 86, 82

Exercises 9 and 10: Construct a frequency table for the data in each set.

9 Heights, in inches, of 30 students:

65, 66, 64, 70, 71, 68, 65, 70, 69, 67, 66, 65, 68, 67, 70, 64, 68, 67, 66, 70, 64, 65, 70, 65, 64, 71, 71, 65, 69, 68

10 Grades on a 10-point quiz for 25 students:

10, 5, 4, 8, 6, 3, 9, 10, 7, 8, 3, 7, 5, 5, 8, 8, 6, 7, 9, 10, 7, 5, 8, 3, 9

11 Following are test grades for 18 students:

72, 86, 95, 75, 100, 85, 87, 100, 81, 86, 78, 94, 96, 80, 100, 98, 96, 91

  a Complete the tally and frequency table.

Interval	Tally	Frequency
96–100		
91–95		
86–90		
81–85		
76–80		
71–75		
Total frequency:		

  b Draw a frequency histogram.
  c How many students had grades less than 81?

12 Following are weights, in pounds, of 30 students:

174, 126, 115, 150, 180, 185, 130, 105, 200, 176, 151, 194, 146, 180, 120, 118, 116, 131, 136, 190, 177, 149, 145, 165, 182, 156, 143, 199, 103, 130

  a Complete the tally and frequency table.

Interval	Tally	Frequency
191–200		
181–190		
171–180		
161–170		
151–160		
141–150		
131–140		
121–130		
111–120		
101–110		
Total frequency:		

  b Draw a frequency histogram.
  c Which intervals have the greatest number of students?

Measures of Central Tendency and Grouped Data

Measures of Central Tendency: Mean, Median, and Mode

Mean (average), median, and mode are **measures of central tendency**. They are selected values used to describe all the numbers in a set.

The **mean** (or average) of a set of numbers is found by adding the numbers and then dividing that total by the number of data items in the set. For example, if Matthew's grades are 80, 92, 85, 91, 95, and 88, the mean is:

$$\frac{80 + 92 + 85 + 91 + 95 + 88}{6} = \frac{531}{6} = 88.5$$

The **median** is the middle value when a set of numbers is arranged in order from least to greatest (or from greatest to least):

- If there is an odd number of items, the median is the middle number. For the numbers 2, 5, $\underline{7}$, 19, 20, the median is 7.

- If there is an even number of items, the median is the average of the two middle numbers. For the numbers 3, 4, $\underline{6}$, $\underline{7}$, 8, 9, the median is $\dfrac{6 + 7}{2} = \dfrac{13}{2} = 6.5$.

The **mode** is the value or values that appear most often in a set. A set of values may have **no mode** (if each value appears the same number of times), **one mode**, or **more than one mode**. For the numbers $\underline{3}$, 7, $\underline{5}$, $\underline{3}$, 2, $\underline{5}$, 8, the modes are 3 and 5. This set of numbers is said to be **bimodal** because it has two modes.

The median is not necessarily a number in the data set.

Using the Calculator to Find Mean, Median, and Mode

If the data set is large, you may wish to use the calculator to find the *mean* and *median*. Enter your data numbers in L_1 using the STAT-EDIT menu. Now press [STAT], [▶] to CALC, and select 1: 1-Var Stats. Your home screen will show 1-Var Stats, followed by the cursor. Press [2nd] [1] to insert L_1, and [ENTER]. The screen will display a list of information. $\bar{x}$ is the mean; press [▼] until you see Med, which is the median.

While you cannot find the *mode* directly from the calculator, you can sort the data (entered in L_1) and count the occurrences of each number more easily. Enter your data numbers in L_1 using the STAT-EDIT menu. Now press [STAT], select 2: Sort A(. Your home screen will show SortA(followed by the cursor. Press [2nd], [STAT], select 1: L_1, and press [ENTER]. The data values in L_1 will now be sorted in ascending order.

1 The average grade for the 26 students in Mr. Rottman's U.S. history class is 82. The average for the 24 students in Mr. Spence's U.S. history class is 86. What is the mean grade for all of the students in both classes?

SOLUTION

$$\text{Mean} = \frac{\text{sum}}{\text{number of items}}$$

$$82 = \frac{\text{sum of Mr. Rottman's grades}}{26}$$

Sum of Mr. Rottman's grades = $82 \times 26 = 2{,}132$

$$86 = \frac{\text{sum of Mr. Spence's grades}}{24}$$

Sum of Mr. Spence's grades = $86 \times 24 = 2{,}064$

$$\text{Average} = \frac{\text{sum of all scores}}{\text{total number of students}}$$

$$= \frac{2{,}064 + 2{,}132}{24 + 26} = \frac{4{,}196}{50} = 83.92$$

2 On Memorial Day, the Community Chest float had one student from each grade, 3 to 12, except grade 6. What was the median grade of the students on the float?

SOLUTION

Grades on the float were 3, 4, 5, 7, <u>8</u>, 9, 10, 11, 12. The middle grade is 8.

Answer: grade 8

3 Allan's test scores are 80, 90, 92, and 88. He needs a 90 average to make the principal's honor roll. What is the lowest score he can get on his next test to raise his average to at least 90?

SOLUTION

Let x = Allan's next test score

$$\frac{80 + 90 + 92 + 88 + x}{5} \geq 90$$

$$\frac{350 + x}{5} \geq 90$$

$$350 + x \geq 450$$

$$x \geq 100$$

Answer: To make the honor roll, Allan must get 100 on his next test. The answer actually comes out as ≥ 100, but since 100 is the highest possible score, we discard *greater than*.

4 The prices of beaded bracelets at a crafts fair were $8 for amethyst, $10 for jade, $10 for onyx, $9 for hematite, and $10 for topaz. What is the mode (in dollars) for these prices?

SOLUTION

8, 9, <u>10</u>, <u>10</u>, <u>10</u>
The most common price is $10.

Answer: $10

Sometimes it is necessary to find measures of central tendency for grouped data displayed in a frequency chart. Examine the table on the following page. We have frequencies for groups of data. For example, we know that 6 students scored in the 96–100 interval. We do *not* know the actual score for any student. Therefore, we cannot find the mean for data displayed in groups with intervals greater than 1. However, we can find the **modal interval** and the **interval containing the median**:

**Smalltown High School Living
Environment Regents Results**

Interval	Frequency
96–100	6
91–95	21
86–90	25
81–85	23
76–80	14
71–75	4
Total Frequency: 93	

In the table, the interval 86–90 is the *modal interval* because this interval has the greatest frequency.

To find the *interval containing the median*, we must find the interval containing the middle value. In our case, we want to find the interval containing the 47th value. Starting from the bottom of the table, count up:

71–75:	4	=	4	Keep going.
76–80:	4 + 14	=	18	Keep going.
81–85:	4 + 14 + 23	=	41	Keep going.
86–90:	4 + 14 + 23 +25	=	66	Stop.

The middle value, the 47th value, is in the 86–90 interval.

 Practice

---

1 What is the median of the set 80, 50, 67, 55, 70, 65, 75, 50?

(1) 50
(2) 64
(3) 66
(4) 67

2 The mean of a set of test scores is 83. If a score of 85 is added to the set and a new mean is calculated

(1) the new mean is greater than 83
(2) the new mean is less than 83
(3) the new mean is 83
(4) the effect on the new mean cannot be determined

3 Which *must* be a value in the data set?

(1) mean
(2) median
(3) mode
(4) none of the above

4 Find the mean of these shoe sizes.

Size	Frequency
5	2
6	4
7	5
8	6
9	3

(1) 7.0   (3) 7.8
(2) 7.2   (4) 8.4

5 Find the median of this stem-and-leaf plot.

```
3 | 3 5
4 | 4 4 6 8
5 | 0 1 3 7 9 9
6 | 2 2 5 8
```
Key: 3|3 = 33

(1) 50   (3) 52.25
(2) 52   (4) 59

6 The average of A and B is 6. The average of X, Y, and Z is 16. What is the average of A, B, X, Y, and Z?

7 The average grade on a test taken by 20 students was 75. When one more student took the test after school, the class average became 76. What score did that student receive?

8 Find the mean, median, and mode of this data set:

$$-2, 5, 10, -6, 7, 5, -2, 5, 10, -15, 14$$

9 On New Year's Day in Watertown, the following temperatures were recorded. What is their average (mean)?

Time	°F
6 A.M.	−10
10 A.M.	2
2 P.M.	8
6 P.M.	4

10 The average of four different positive integers is 9. What is the greatest value for one of the integers?

11 Five students took a makeup quiz for Mrs. Hald. Three students picked up their papers after school. Their grades were 75, 73, and 86. Mrs. Hald told them that the average of the five grades was 80. What was the average of the other two scores?

12 If $j > 0$, what is the average of $2j$, $4j - 3$, and 6?

13 If the sum of an odd number of consecutive integers is zero, what is the median?

14 Create a data set of seven integers in which the median is greater than the mode.

15 The average and the median of three fractions are each $\frac{1}{3}$. The largest fraction is $\frac{1}{2}$. What is the smallest fraction?

Exercises 16–18: Use the following frequency table.

Interval	Frequency
501–600	10
401–500	18
301–400	12
201–300	20
101–200	5

16 Find the modal interval.

17 Find the interval containing the median.

18 Why is it impossible to find the interval containing the mean?

Range, Quartiles, and Box-and-Whisker Plots

The **range** of a set of data is the difference between the greatest value and the least value. To find the range, it is often helpful to rank the members of the set from greatest to least (or vice versa). For example, when 84, 60, 89, 95, 63, and 74 are ranked in order, the range is obvious:

95, 89, 84, 74, 63, 60

Range = 95 − 60 = 35

The concept of range is important in quartiles and box-and-whisker plots.

The median of a data set divides the set into two equal parts—that is, two parts with the same number of members. **Quartiles** are values that separate a data set into four parts, each containing one-fourth or 25% of the members. For example:

$$\underbrace{53, 60, 61, 63, 64,}_{\boxed{64.5}} \quad \underbrace{65, 65, 65, 65, 66,}_{\boxed{66}} \quad \underbrace{66, 67, 67, 68, 69,}_{\boxed{69.5}} \quad \overbrace{70, 70, 71, 71, 73}$$

Median

First quartile   Second quartile   Third quartile

- The **first** or **lower quartile** is the center of the lower half.

- The **second quartile** is the median.

- The **third** or **upper quartile** is the center of the upper half.

- The **interquartile range** is the difference between the third quartile and the first quartile. In the example above, interquartile range = 69.5 − 64.5 = 5.

MODEL PROBLEM

Find the quartiles and the interquartile range:

  42, 25, 55, 58, 60, 75, 80, 85, 65, 55, 19, 72, 77, 50

SOLUTION

Step 1. Rank the members in order:
    19, 25, 42, 50, 55, 55, 58, 60, 65, 72, 75, 77, 80, 85

Step 2. Find the median. This is the second quartile:
    19, 25, 42, 50, 55, 55, <u>58, 60</u>, 65, 72, 75, 77, 80, 85
    Median = (58 + 60) ÷ 2 = 59

Step 3. First quartile is 50, the median of the seven values to the left of 59:
    19, 25, 42, <u>50</u>, 55, 55, 58

Step 4. Third quartile is 75, the median of the seven values to the right of 59:
    60, 65, 72, <u>75</u>, 77, 80, 85

Step 5. To find the interquartile range, subtract the first quartile from the third:
    75 − 50 = 25

Answer: The quartiles are 50, 59, and 75. The interquartile range is 25.

A **box-and-whisker** plot is a graph that describes data using the quartiles and the highest and lowest values (the **extreme** values) in the data. This plot is useful for comparing two or more data sets. Box-and-whisker plots show how the data for each set are distributed and what the extreme values are.

To Construct a Box-and-Whisker Plot

- Draw a number line to include the lowest value and the highest value in the data set.
- Above the number line, mark the quartiles and the extreme values.
- Draw a box above the number line, with vertical sides passing through the lower and upper quartiles. Draw a vertical line in the box through the median (second quartile).
- Draw the "whiskers," horizontal lines extending from the vertical sides of the rectangle to the extreme values.

Box-and-whisker plots can also be constructed with a graphing calculator. See the Appendix.

Note: **Outliers** are values much lower or much higher than most of the data. In a box-and-whisker plot, outliers are data that fall more than 1.5 times the interquartile range from the quartiles. Do *not* extend whiskers to any outliers.

MODEL PROBLEM

Draw a box-and-whisker plot for these data:

20 27 28 29 30 31 33 33 37 39 55

SOLUTION

Draw the box: The median is 31. The lower quartile is 28. The upper quartile is 37. Plot those values above a number line and draw the rectangle.

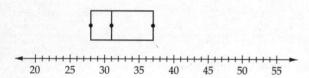

Draw the whiskers: The interquartile range is 37 − 28 = 9. Data more than 1.5(9) = 13.5 from the quartiles are outliers.

Left whisker:

28 − 13.5 = 14.5

No data are smaller than 14.5, so there are no low outliers. The left whisker will extend from the box to 20.

Right whisker:

37 + 13.5 = 50.5

One value, 55, is more than 50.5. The right whisker will therefore extend only to the next highest value, 39.

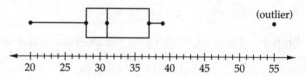

Practice

1 Identify the first quartile:

32, 24, 38, 26, 38, 36, 37, 39, 23, 40, 21, 31

(1) 21
(2) 25
(3) 32
(4) 34

2 The interquartile range of a data set is 18. The first quartile is 52. Which value could be the median?

(1) 25
(2) 34
(3) 61
(4) 97

3 This is a box-and-whisker plot for 60 test scores.

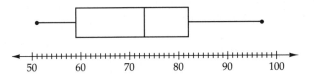

The upper quartile is

(1) 59
(2) 73
(3) 82
(4) 97

4 Find the interquartile range for this set of children's heights (in centimeters):

147, 130, 160, 150, 152, 120, 121, 125, 128, 121, 140, 142, 134, 126

(1) 7
(2) 22
(3) 33
(4) 40

5 These box-and-whisker plots show test scores for two classes:

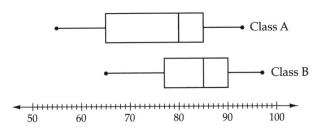

Which statement is FALSE?

(1) The interquartile range is greater for class A than for class B.
(2) The second quartile is higher for class B than for class A.
(3) The lowest score was in class A.
(4) Class A did better than class B.

Exercises 6 and 7: Use this data set:

60, 62, 62, 64, 68, 69, 71, 72, 74, 76, 78, 81, 83, 87

6 Find the quartiles and interquartile range.

7 Construct a box-and-whisker plot.

Exercises 8 and 9: use this data set:

30, 67, 67, 68, 68, 69, 71, 71, 71, 72, 73, 74, 74, 75, 80

8 Find the quartiles and interquartile range.

9 Construct a box-and-whisker plot.

10 In a box-and-whisker plot, what percentage of the scores are represented by the box?

11 In a box-and-whisker plot, what percentage of the scores are represented by each whisker?

12 In a box-and-whisker plot, what characteristic of the data would position the median in the middle of the box?

13 Is it possible to have a box-and-whisker plot with only one whisker? Explain your answer.

14 Two box-and-whisker plots for the same number of data points have the same extremes and the same median. However, the box is twice as long for the first plot as for the second. What differences would you expect to find if you compared the data?

15 A class decided to compare a supermarket-brand chocolate chip cookie with a famous name brand. The students broke apart nine cookies of each brand and recorded the number of chips. Make a box-and-whisker plot for each brand and compare the data, including quartiles, interquartile ranges, and the length of the whiskers.

Supermarket brand	Name brand
4	7
4	7
5	8
5	9
6	9
7	9
10	10
12	10
18	11

Percentiles and Cumulative Frequency Histograms

The **percentile** rank of a member of a data set tells us the percent of values in the set less than or equal to that member. If more than one value matches the member, include half of the matching values.

 MODEL PROBLEM

Find the percentile rank of 80 in the following 30-item data set:

63, 63, 63, 64, 65, 66, 66, 68, 70, 70, 74, 75, 80, 80, 80, 83, 83, 84, 87, 87, 88, 88, 89, 89, 89, 90, 90, 90, 91, 91

SOLUTION

12 numbers are less than 80

3 numbers are 80

$\frac{1}{2} \times 3 = 1.5$

$12 + 1.5 = 13.5$

$\frac{13.5}{30} = 0.45 = 45\%$

Answer: The number 80 is at the 45th percentile.

We have already reviewed frequency tables and frequency histograms for grouped data. Suppose we collected data on test scores and made this table:

Interval (Test Scores)	Frequency (Number)
91–100	50
81–90	60
71–80	60
61–70	20
51–60	10

By adding one more column to the table, **cumulative frequency**, we can record the number of scores that are:

100 or less

90 or less

80 or less

70 or less

60 or less

Starting with the top row, the cumulative frequency column is calculated by adding all the frequencies from that row down to the bottom of the table. Or, starting from the bottom, each new cumulative frequency would be found by adding the frequency of that row to the cumulative frequency recorded on the next lower row.

For this example, the cumulative frequency table is:

Interval (Test Scores)	Frequency (Number)	Cumulative Frequency
91–100	50	200
81–90	60	150
71–80	60	90
61–70	20	30
51–60	10	10

The graph of a cumulative frequency table is called a **cumulative frequency histogram**. It is constructed in exactly the same way as a frequency histogram. Notice that as we look at a cumulative frequency histogram from left to right, the bars increase in height.

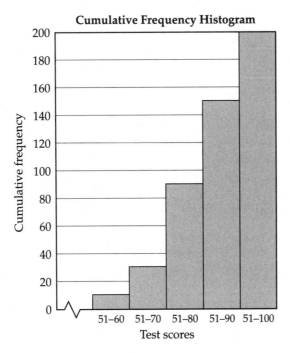

Cumulative Frequency Histogram

In the cumulative frequency histogram above, the frequency scale goes from 0 to 200. A different vertical scale, showing the cumulative frequency in percents, can also be used. We would write 0% instead of 0 and 100% in place of 200. The other markers usually indicate **quartiles** (0%, 25%, 50%, 75%, 100%) or **deciles** (multiples of 10%). For example, if we display quartiles:

0% is at 0

25% is at 25% of 200, or 50

50% is at 50% of 200, or 100

75% is at 75% of 200, or 150

100% is at 100% of 200, or 200

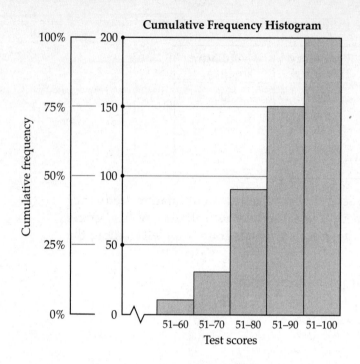

Cumulative Frequency Histogram

From this version of the cumulative frequency histogram, we can see that 75% of the students scored 90 or less. Thus, 90 is the value of the third quartile.

Often, we use a cumulative frequency histogram to find approximate quartile values. If we want to know the number of scores at or below an interval upper value, we can approximate from this chart. For instance, in this example, about 45% of the scores are at or below 80, and about 5% of the scores are at or below 60.

 Practice

1 If Bradley scored at the 90th percentile on a test, which statement *must* be true?

   (1) Bradley answered 90% of the questions correctly.
   (2) About 90% of the students who took the test had a score greater than or equal to Bradley's.
   (3) 90% of the students who took the test received the same score as Bradley.
   (4) About 90% of the students who took the test had a score less than or equal to Bradley's.

2 For a set of data consisting of basketball players' heights in inches, the 50th percentile is 76. Which statement could be *false*?

   (1) Fifty percent of the heights are 76 inches or less.
   (2) Half of the heights are 76 inches or more.
   (3) The mean height is 76 inches.
   (4) The median height is 76 inches.

3 For a set of data recording temperatures (degrees Fahrenheit) in Binghamton in July, the 25th percentile was 68° and the 75th percentile was 80°. Which statement *must* be true?

(1) Fifty percent of the temperatures were between 68 and 80 degrees.
(2) The median temperature was 74 degrees.
(3) Temperatures were recorded below 68 degrees.
(4) The mean temperature was 74 degrees.

4 What is the percentile rank of 90 in the following data set?

65 67 68 75 77 77 79 82 83 84 84 85 85 86 88 88 90 90 92 93 93 94 95 97 99

(1) 64
(2) 68
(3) 72
(4) 90

5 In the table below, what is the cumulative frequency for the salary range $25,000–$29,999?

Salary	Frequency	Cumulative Frequency
$40,000–44,999	6	60
$35,000–39,999	9	54
$30,000–34,999	18	45
$25,000–29,999	0	?
$20,000–24,999	12	27
$15,000–19,999	10	15
$10,000–14,999	5	5

(1) 0
(2) 12
(3) 27
(4) 39

Exercises 6–10: Refer to the table below.

Interval	Frequency	Cumulative Frequency
91–100	8	
81–90	10	
71–80	10	
61–70	8	
51–60	4	

6 Complete the table.

7 Draw a cumulative frequency histogram with a percent scale by quartile.

8 Find the interval that contains the median.

9 Find the interval that contains the 25th percentile.

10 Estimate what percent of the scores are 70 or less.

Exercises 11–15: Refer to the table below, which shows ungrouped data. The interval length is 1.

Score	Frequency	Cumulative Frequency
10	6	
9	7	
8	7	
7	6	
6	3	

11 Complete the table.

12 Draw a cumulative frequency histogram with a percent scale by decile.

13 Find the score that contains the median.

14 Find the score that contains the 10th percentile.

15 Estimate what percent of the scores are 6 or less.

Two-Valued Statistics

Often, we are asked to study relationships between two different data lists. We will investigate some basic ways of analyzing these relationships.

Scatter Plots

A **scatter plot** relates two sets of data. Both the vertical axes and the horizontal axes show numeric amounts.

To Construct a Scatter Plot

- Construct and label both axes, using reasonable scales for the values. (Use a "break" symbol if necessary.)

- Plot the data points.

- Give the scatter plot a title.

  For example, the graph below shows heights and shoe sizes for a group of males.

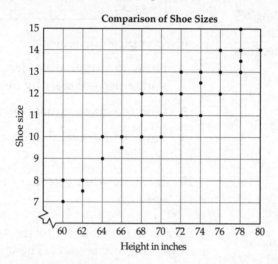

Here, the plotted points appear to cluster around a straight line. This graph is an example of **positive correlation**. The two sets of data increase together. The plotted points go from lower left to upper right.

By contrast, in a graph showing **negative correlation**, one data set increases while the other decreases. The graph would go from upper left to lower right.

Sometimes there is no obvious relationship between data sets. In such cases, we say that there is **no correlation**.

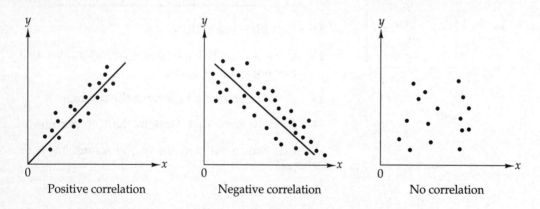

To construct a Scatter Plot on the Graphing Calculator

- Enter the data values for the independent variable in L_1.

- Enter the data values for the dependent variable in L_2.

- Check that there is the same number of values in both lists.

- Press 2nd Y= .

- Press 1 . The cursor should be over On. Press ENTER to turn STAT PLOT 1 on.

- Using the arrows and cursor, make sure the first graph type is selected, L_1 and L_2 are the lists to be graphed (unless your data is in other lists) and the mark is □.

- Adjust the window so all the values will appear on the graph. The best window is usually achieved by pressing [ZOOM] and selecting 9:ZoomStat.

Line of Best Fit

Data that appear to have a linear correlation can be approximated by a **line of best fit**. When we use the calculator to construct the line of best fit, the calculator can also be set to return a **correlation coefficient**, which is a measure of how well the data fit the line. Before using the calculator to construct the line, we set the calculator to show the *correlation coefficient* by turning Diagnostics On; follow the steps listed below.

- Press [2nd] [0] to get into the CATALOG menu.

- Press [▼] to DiagnosticsOn.

- Press [ENTER].

- Press [ENTER] again.

The slope of the line will depend on whether the correlation is positive or negative. The "goodness of fit" is determined by the strength of the correlation. Enter the data into the calculator as two lists. Press [STAT], [▶] to CALC, and [4] to select 4:LinReg(ax+b). The home screen shows LinReg(ax+b) and a blinking cursor. Press [2nd] [1] [,] [2nd] [2], to insert L_1 and L_2, then press [,] [VARS] [▶] to Y-VARS, press [1] to select 1:Function, press [1] for Y_1, and [ENTER].

The screen shows an equation for the line of best fit, displayed as $y = ax + b$. The value a is the slope. The value b is the y-intercept. The value r is the *correlation coefficient*, where $-1 \leq r \leq 1$. If r is positive, the correlation is positive. If r is negative, the correlation is negative.

- Strong positive or strong negative correlation: $|r| \geq 0.8$

- Moderate positive or moderate negative correlation: $0.5 > |r| < 0.8$

- Weak Correlation: $|r| \leq 0.5$

Press [Y=] and the formula for the line is assigned to Y_1 and can be graphed along with the scatter plot by pressing [GRAPH].

Correlation and Causation

We should be careful when we interpret scatter plots. In cases were we see strong correlation, we sometimes assume that the variable values in the X list cause the values in the Y list. Just because two variables are strongly correlated, we cannot assume that one causes the other. A correlation may be a mere coincidence. For example, if we find a high correlation between sales of a particular product and arrests for a particular crime, we cannot say that one causes the other. However, if we find that the frequency of a parent taking a child to the library is strongly correlated to the child's interest in books, we may be correct. If we are reasonably certain that the values in the X list cause the values in the Y list, we may safely interpolate within the range of values in the X list from the sample data to predict corresponding values in the Y list. However, it is much more dangerous to extrapolate. *Extrapolation* is making a prediction of a Y list value using an X list value outside the range of the sample data. For example, if a positive correlation was found between hours of studying and lines of poetry memorized, the line of best fit would probably fail to be an appropriate model for additional lines of poetry memorized after several additional hours of study.

 MODEL PROBLEMS

Copy the following data into L₁ and L₂. Make a scatter plot from the data. Looking at the scatter plot, describe the correlation, if any. Using the calculator, find the line of best fit. Find the value of r. Compare the correlation results to your estimate. Graph the line of best fit along with the scatter plot. Predict the L₂ value when L₁ is 210.

L_1	L_2
52	22
70	23
100	25
117	27
120	28
148	29
162	30
169	31
172	32
234	33
252	34
280	35

SOLUTION

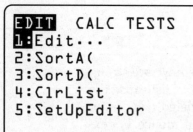

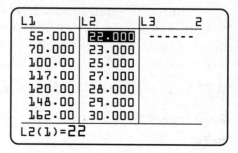

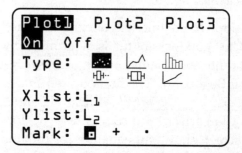

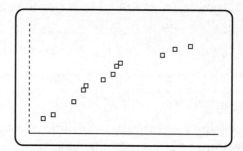

The points appear to have strong positive correlation. Use the calculator to find the line of best fit and the correlation coefficient. The calculator will display:

```
LinReg
 y=ax+b
 a=.057756451
 b=20.05407480
 r²=.937888508
 r=.968446440
LinReg(ax+b)
```

If you round your a and b values to the nearest hundredth and substitute them into the standard linear equation, the equation for the line of best fit is $y = 0.58x + 20.05$.

To graph the line of best fit, indicate the lists and the Y subscript for the line.

```
y=ax+b
a=.057756451
b=20.05407480
r²=.937888508
r=.968446440
LinReg(ax+b) L₁, L₂,
Y₁
```

The graph will show that the scatter plot points are close to the line.

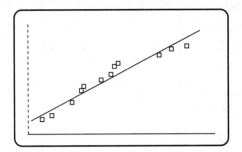

The value of r shown above, .968446440, verifies that there is a strong positive correlation between the two lists.

To find the value of L_2 when L_1 is 210, simply plug 210 into the equation of the line of best fit we found above; $y = 0.58x + 20.05$.

$$y = 0.58(210) + 20.05$$

$$y = 141.85$$

$$y \approx 142$$

 Practice

Exercises 1–4: Copy the data shown into L_1 and L_2. Make a scatter plot from the data. Looking at the scatter plot, describe the correlation, if any. Using the calculator, find the line of best fit. Find the value of r. Compare the correlation results to your estimate. Graph the line of best fit along with the scatter plot.

1 In a local community college, freshman mathematics marks were compared to physics marks, as shown in the table below. Copy the mathematics marks into L_1 and the physics marks into L_2.

2 At a family barbeque, the following amounts of burgers and soda were consumed. Copy the burger amounts into L_1 and the soda amounts into L_2.

	Burgers	Cans of Soda
Uncle Eric	5	8
Uncle Andrew	4	10
Aunt Wendy	3	4
Cousin Caryn	2	6
Aunt Courtney	1	2

Student number	1	2	3	4	5	6	7	8	9	10	11	12	13	14	15	16	17	18	19	20
Mathematics mark	45	67	93	45	56	67	68	34	54	89	59	60	43	90	41	30	56	76	89	65
Physics marks	56	69	89	39	52	61	69	43	59	94	60	52	41	84	41	39	60	73	92	62

3 A quiz was scaled from 0 to 6 points. The school psychologist measured the test anxiety of five students preparing for the test and recorded their test results. Copy the test anxiety scores into L_1 and the quiz scores into L_2.

	Anxiety Score	Quiz Score
Student 1	1	1
Student 2	2	4
Student 3	5	3
Student 4	4	4
Student 5	5	1

4 Student IQ scores were measured against their creativity scores. Copy the IQ scores into L_1 and the creativity scores into L_2.

	IQ Score	Creativity Score
Student 1	140	130
Student 2	130	125
Student 3	130	140
Student 4	125	125
Student 5	110	115

5 The heights and weights of several people waiting to board a bus in Trafalgar Square were recorded. Copy the heights (meters) into L_1 and the weights (kilograms) into L_2.

Height (m)	1.63	1.65	1.69	1.73	1.81	1.83	1.83	1.88
Weight (kg)	57	53	62	69	70	78	83	80

a Create a scatter plot that represents these data.

b Determine the line of best fit for the given data.

c What is the correlation coefficient?

d Predict the approximate weight of a person whose height is 1.75 meters.

6 The following study compares the amount of soda spending to candy spending for a small group of people in one week.

Soda Spending	Candy Spending
$4.03	$6.47
$3.76	$6.13
$3.77	$6.19
$3.34	$4.89
$3.47	$5.63
$2.92	$4.52
$3.20	$5.89
$2.71	$4.79
$3.53	$5.27
$4.51	$6.08
$4.56	$4.02

a Create a scatter plot that represents these data.

b Determine the line of best fit for the given data.

c What is the correlation coefficient?

d Predict how much one person spent on candy if he spent $2.45 on soda.

7 In recent years, physicians have used the so-called diving reflex to reduce abnormally rapid heartbeats in humans by submerging the patient's face in cold water. A research physician conducted an experiment to investigate the effects of various cold temperatures on the pulse rates of ten small children. The results are presented below. Create a scatter plot and determine and graph the line of best fit. What is the correlation coefficient?

Child	Temperature of Water x °F	Reduction in Pulse y beats/minute
1	68	2
2	65	5
3	70	1
4	62	10
5	60	9
6	55	13
7	58	10
8	65	3
9	69	4
10	63	6

8 The table shows the amount of study time, in hours, students spend before a test and the test grade. Create a scatter plot and determine and graph the line of best fit.

Study Time (in Hours)	Test Grade (in Percent)
10	90
5	80
4	72
12	94
3	68
6	87

9 A park ranger measured the diameter verses the height of trees in front of the Information Center. Create a scatter plot and determine and graph the line of best fit.

Diameter (ft)	Height (ft)
2.1	40
1.7	37
1.1	35
1.5	36
2.7	42

10 A comparison of high school student population (in thousands) and the dollar sales of pizza (in thousands) at ten schools is shown below.

number of students	2	6	8	8	12	16	20	20	22	26
pizza sales	58	105	88	118	117	137	157	169	149	202

a Create a scatter plot that represents these data.

b Determine the line of best fit for the given data.

c What is the correlation coefficient?

d Predict approximately how many pizzas would be sold if the population of a high school was 10,000.

 CHAPTER REVIEW

1 For a set of data showing the number of books read by Ms. Corson's AP English class, the median was 8 and the average was 12. Which statement *must* be true?

(1) Fifty percent of the students read 8 books.
(2) Fifty percent of the students read 12 books.
(3) At least one student read more than 12 books.
(4) Most students read 8 books.

2 This table shows the ages of 30 tennis players in a teen tournament. Which statement is true?

Age	Frequency
19	6
18	6
17	12
16	4
15	2

(1) median > mode
(2) median = mode
(3) median < mode
(4) median > mean

3 For seven weeks, the number of TVs Mark Stone sold were 2, 5, 0, 7, 4, 6, and 4. What is the minimum number of TVs Mark must sell next week to have a weekly sales average greater than 4?

(1) 3
(2) 4
(3) 5
(6) 6

4 What is the mean of the following data?

$3 + \sqrt{3}, \quad 4 + \sqrt{3}, \quad 5 + \sqrt{3}, \quad 6 + \sqrt{3}, \quad 7 + \sqrt{3}$

(1) 5
(2) 25
(3) $5 + \sqrt{3}$
(4) $5 + 5\sqrt{3}$

5 A box-and-whisker plot was constructed for a set of 100 test scores. Approximately how many scores are between the lower quartile and the highest score?

(1) 75
(2) 50
(3) 25
(4) cannot be determined

6 Which statements are true?

I The interquartile range is half the distance between the lower quartile and the upper quartile.

II The interquartile range is not affected by outliers.

III The median represents the 50th percentile.

(1) I and II
(2) II only
(3) II and III
(4) I and III

7 A recent study indicates that there is a positive correlation between women's skirt lengths and the composite value of stocks on the New York Stock Exchange. Do you believe one of these occurrences influences the other? Explain your reasoning.

8 Following are test grades of 18 students:

80, 80, 95, 90, 90, 85, 83, 97, 86, 86, 80, 94, 100, 80, 100, 98, 96, 91

a Complete the table.

Interval	Tally	Frequency
96–100		
91–95		
86–90		
81–85		
76–80		
71–75		
Total frequency:		

b Draw a frequency histogram.

c How many students received grades less than 81?

9 Following are weights in pounds of 30 students:

174, 126, 115, 150, 180, 185, 130, 105, 200, 176, 151, 194, 146, 180, 120, 118, 116, 131, 136, 190, 177, 149, 145, 165, 182, 156, 143, 199, 103, 130

a Complete the table.

Interval	Tally	Frequency
191–200		
181–190		
171–180		
161–170		
151–160		
141–150		
131–140		
121–130		
111–120		
101–110		
Total frequency:		

b Draw a frequency histogram.

Exercises 10 and 11: Refer to the following frequency table.

Grade Interval	Frequency
91–100	8
81–90	16
71–80	14
61–70	6
51–60	0
41–50	0
31–40	1
21–30	2

10 Find the modal interval.

11 Find the interval containing the median.

12 The following table shows the relationship between height and arm span, measured in centimeters, for a group of men. Create a scatter plot and determine the line of best fit. Using the correlation coefficient, r, describe the correlation in the data.

Person #	Arm Span	Height
1	156	162
2	157	160
3	159	162
4	160	155
5	161	160
6	161	162
7	162	170
8	165	166
9	170	170
10	170	167
11	173	185

13 The average grade on a test taken by 15 students was 70. When one more student took the test after school, the class average became 71. What score did that student receive?

14 If $k > 0$, what is the average of $3k - 1$, $4k - 3$, and $1 - 10k$?

15 Give an example of a data set for each of the following situations.
    a mean = median = mode
    b mean < median = mode
    c mean = median < mode

Exercises 16 and 17: Use this data set:

51, 75, 75, 77, 81, 82, 84, 86, 87, 90, 91, 92, 96, 99, 100

16 Find the quartiles and interquartile range.

17 Construct a box-and-whisker plot.

18 Find the percentile rank of 189 in the following set of heights (in centimeters):

148 162 166 167 168 175 175 177 179 180 182
182 183 188 189 189 189 189 190 190 191 191
191 193 194 197 198 200 200 202

19 A class average on a science test was 28.5 correct out of 40 questions. The 19 girls in the class scored 539 correct. How many correct did the 11 boys score?

20 Use this table:

Interval	Frequency	Cumulative Frequency
91–100	6	
81–90	12	
71–80	8	
61–70	8	
51–60	6	

    a Complete the table.
    b Draw a cumulative frequency histogram with a percent scale by quartile.
    c Find the interval that contains the median.
    d Find the interval that contains the 25th percentile.

Now turn to page 455 and take the Cumulative Review test for Chapters 1–16. This will help you monitor your progress and keep all your skills sharp.

APPENDIX

Using Your Graphing Calculator

by Kim E. Genzer and David Vintinner

The Integrated Algebra Regents Examination requires that you have access to a calculator for the duration of the test. These calculators have a multitude of functions to aid you in finding answers and checking your answers and checking your solutions.

Graphing calculators vary widely in format and capability. As their name implies, these calculators can graph equations and draw bar charts, scatter plots, and other statistical graphs. They have several rows of function keys like scientific calculators, but many of their special functions can be accessed only by selecting menu choices on the display screen. For example, to change from radians to degrees, you will need to press MODE to access a menu. Then you can highlight the word *Degree* (if it is not already highlighted) and press ENTER.

Calculators vary widely in the location of function keys and menu choices. We will show general guidelines for the procedures you are most likely to use on the Regents Exam, but there are many more powerful operations open to you. Take the time to explore your calculator's menus and find the functions *you* will need the most.

One important difference you should notice is that the graphing calculator does not have an equals = key. Instead, it has ENTER. Other types of calculators perform some operations as you go along. However, a graphing calculator does not calculate anything until you press ENTER. It then follows the rules for order of operations to find the answer. One nice feature is that the operation you put in is generally still visible on the screen above the answer that comes out. Then if you don't get the answer you expected, you can see what you entered to determine if you made an error.

Some other differences: it may not be necessary to press × in order to do multiplication. Some calculators let you type the same way you would write an expression. *Example*: 3(5 + 2) or 6 TAN 30 could be entered exactly as just shown, without having to insert a times sign. Also, the graphing calculator does not have an x^y key. Instead it has a $\wedge$ key. To use this key, enter the base, press $\wedge$, enter the exponent, and then press ENTER.

Note: Some graphing calculators can also solve linear and quadratic equations, draw lines of best fit, calculate with matrices, and perform various other high-level mathematical calculations. Since the procedures for such activities are not consistent from one calculator model to the next, we will not cover them here. You will need to experiment with your calculator, ask your teacher, or consult the calculator's manual.

△ ▽ ◁ ▷ Moving the Cursor

These four arrow keys allow you to move around in equations, menus, and graphs.

WINDOW Defining the Screen Layout

This key lets you access a menu that defines the area of a graph. The horizontal axis will extend from *Xmin* to *Xmax* with markings at an interval equal to *Xscl*. Similarly, the vertical axis will extend from *Ymin* to *Ymax* with markings at an interval of *Yscl*.

Graphing Equations

Y= This key lets you enter equations to be graphed. It is sometimes possible to enter more than one equation. The equation should be solved for *y* in terms of *x* (which must be entered with the special variable key X, T, θ, *n*). Use CLEAR to erase equations you no longer need.

To see a table of values for the equation(s) you enter in the Y= screen, press TABLE. To change the increment by which the *x*-value changes, or to enter the values individually, press TBLSET and adjust the settings as you wish.

GRAPH This key allows you to see the graph defined by the WINDOW menu with the equations from Y= graphed on it. To find the coordinates of specific points on the graph, such as *x*-intercepts, press TRACE and use the arrows to move the cursor to the point of interest. You may also be able to enter *x*-values with the keypad.

You can alter the type of line drawn on a graph or add shading to a graph by choosing one of several options. In the Y= screen, press the left arrow key until the cursor is on the diagonal slash to the left of the *Y* for the equation whose graph you wish to alter. Press ENTER several times to see the various options for shading and line weight and style. When you have chosen the one you want, press GRAPH to see the result.

Graphing Data

STAT Pressing this key allows you to access statistical data. Choosing EDIT allows you to enter lists of data you wish to graph. Choosing CALC allows you to calculate values (like the median of your data, $\bar{x}$) or find equations to approximate your data (like the linear regression and median-median lines of best fit).

STAT PLOT Pressing this key allows you to select and turn on different types of graphs of your data: broken-line graphs, histograms, scatter plots, and box-and-whisker plots are among the choices.

Depending on which graph you choose, options such as Xlist, Ylist, and Mark may appear to allow you to tell the calculator where the lists of data are stored (e.g., L1), and what type of point you would like the graph to display. Once you have entered this information, press GRAPH to see the display. You can use TRACE and the arrow keys to identify points on the graph.

Note: The WINDOW menu also controls the appearance of statistical graphs. The *Xscl* value controls the range of values for each bar in the histogram.

INTERSECT is an operation found under the CALC menu. This operation finds the coordinates of a point at which two or more functions intersect. Make sure that the cursor is on the graph of the first function by pressing ENTER. Press the up and down arrow keys to move the cursor closer to the point of intersection on the first function. Then press ENTER to select the second function and press the up and down arrow keys to move the cursor closer to the point intersection. Press ENTER. The location you found will be displayed as Guess? on the bottom of the screen. Press ENTER again. The coordinates of the intersection will be displayed and the cursor will be moved to the intersection.

ZERO is another operation found under the CALC menu. This operation finds the root of the function where it crosses the *x*-axis. Using the left and right arrow keys, select one point on either side of the root you wish to find. Press ENTER to record the left bound. Move the left and right arrows again to record the right bound and press ENTER again. The coordinates of the function where it intersects the *x*-axis are displayed.

SOLUTIONS

1   Graph the line $y = -0.068x + 0.34$ and use **ZERO** to find where it crosses the x-axis. You may need to change your window settings to zoom in on the solution.

1   It crosses at $x = 5$.

2   Graph the lines $y = 10x + 15$ and $y = \frac{1}{2}(x + 11)$ and use **INTERSECT** to find where they intersect.

2   They intersect at $(-1, 5)$.

3   Graph the parabola $y = x^2 + \frac{41}{18}x - 10$ and find where the graph crosses the x-axis. (Hint: One of the roots is a repeating decimal.)

3   The x-intercepts are -4.5 and $2.\overline{2}$.

4   Enter the following quiz grades into a [STAT] list:

60, 65, 67, 70, 70, 86, 86, 89, 89, 90, 90, 95, 97, 99, 100

a   Find the mean grade ($\bar{x}$) with the CALC menu.

b   Plot the grades as a histogram with settings $Xmin = 60$, $Xmax = 100$, and $Xscl = 4$ and use [TRACE] to find the bar with the most scores.

c   Plot the grades as a box-and-whisker diagram and use [TRACE] to find the median grade and the upper and lower quartiles.

4   a $\bar{x} = 83.5\overline{3}$

b   There are 4 quiz scores in the range 88 to 91.

c   The median score is 89. The lower and upper quartile scores are 70 and 95.

Cumulative Reviews

CUMULATIVE REVIEW
CHAPTERS 1–2

Part I

All questions in this part will receive 2 credits. No partial credit will be allowed.

1 Order these values from least to greatest.

   (a) $-|5|$ (b) $-|7|$ (c) $-3 - 3^2$

   (d) $|-8|$ (e) $-(-3)^2$

   (1) a, b, e, c, d   (3) c, e, d, b, a

   (2) b, c, a, d, e   (4) c, e, b, a, d

2 If $n - 1$ is an odd integer, what is the next largest even integer?

   (1) $n - 2$ (3) $n + 1$

   (2) n (4) $n + 2$

3 For what value of x is $x^3 < x < \dfrac{1}{x} < x^2$ true?

   (1) -2 (3) $-\dfrac{1}{2}$

   (2) -1 (4) $\dfrac{1}{2}$

4 The center of a line segment is at 5. If the line segment has length of 12, what is the sum of the endpoints of the line segment?

   (1) 7   (3) 11

   (2) 10   (4) 12

5 Which fraction represents $\dfrac{1}{8} \div \dfrac{1}{4}$?

   (1) $\dfrac{1}{32}$ (3) $\dfrac{1}{2}$

   (2) $\dfrac{1}{4}$ (4) $\dfrac{2}{1}$

6 If $\dfrac{2}{5} < \dfrac{x}{20} < \dfrac{1}{2}$, what is the integer value of x?

   (1) 10   (3) 8

   (2) 9   (4) 7

7 On Thursday at 8 A.M., the temperature is 25°F. By noon it rises 11 degrees, by 6 P.M. it drops 4 degrees, and by 8 A.M. on Friday it drops another 10 degrees. What is the change in temperature from 8 A.M. on Thursday to 8 A.M. on Friday?

   (1) −14 degrees   (3) 5 degrees

   (2) −3 degrees   (4) 22 degrees

8 $2 \times 3^3 \times 3^2 =$

   (1) $6^3 \times 3^2$ (3) 2×3^5

   (2) 2×9^5 (4) 2×3^6

9 $\left(4\dfrac{5}{8} - 2\dfrac{3}{4}\right) \div \dfrac{5}{4} =$

(1) $\dfrac{2}{3}$ (3) $2\dfrac{11}{32}$

(2) $1\dfrac{1}{2}$ (4) $5\dfrac{1}{5}$

10 If $\dfrac{4}{5} \cdot \dfrac{5}{6} \cdot \dfrac{6}{7} \cdot \dfrac{7}{8} \cdot \dfrac{8}{9} \cdot \dfrac{9}{10} \cdot \dfrac{10}{11} \cdot \dfrac{11}{12} = \dfrac{1}{n}$,
then $n =$

(1) 3   (3) 12

(2) 4   (4) 48

Part II

Each correct answer will receive 2 credits. Clearly indicate the necessary steps, including appropriate formula substitutions, diagrams, charts, etc. Correct numerical answers without work shown will receive only 1 credit.

11 Is the set of irrational numbers closed under multiplication? Explain why or why not, using at least one example.

12 List the numbers in the set {natural numbers between −4 and 8} and graph them on a number line.

13 Is the set of real numbers an infinite set? Explain your reasoning.

14 For the local minor league baseball team, the ratio of games won to games played is 8 : 11. Write the ratio of games lost to games played.

Part III

Each correct answer will receive 3 credits. Partial credit will be allowed. Clearly indicate the necessary steps, including appropriate formula substitutions, diagrams, charts, etc. Correct numerical answers without work shown will receive only 1 credit.

15 In each equation, find the value of k.

a $3^3 + 3^4 = k$

b $(a^k)^k = a^9$

c $2^k \cdot 2^4 = 2^7$

16 The product of two consecutive positive integers is always divisible by an integer greater than 1. What is that number? Why is this true?

17 Which number below is irrational? Why?

$$\dfrac{\sqrt{4}}{3} \qquad \sqrt{8} \qquad \sqrt{169}$$

Part IV

Each correct answer will receive 4 credits. Partial credit will be allowed. Clearly indicate the necessary steps, including appropriate formula substitutions, diagrams, charts, etc. Correct numerical answers without work shown will receive only 1 credit.

18 Match each item in Column I with one item in Column II.

Column I	Column II
1 ∅	(a) {Numbers that equal their own square}
2 {0, 1}	(b) {Squares of even numbers}
3 {0, 4, 16, 36, . . .}	(c) {Integers greater than 0 and less than 1}
4 {1, 9, 25, 49, . . .}	(d) {Squares of prime numbers}
5 {4, 9, 25, 49, 121, . . .}	(e) {Squares of odd numbers}

19 Neil and Jackie are describing the same number. Neil says, "The number is a negative integer greater than − 12." Jackie says, "The number is divisible by 3." If Neil's statement is true and Jackie's statement is false, what are all the possible numbers?

20 Of the 150 stores in the Hicksville mall, 100 stores have alarm systems and 75 have security guards. If 40 stores have neither alarm systems nor security guards, how many stores have *both* alarm systems and security guards? How many have just alarm systems? How many have just security guards?

CUMULATIVE REVIEW
CHAPTERS 1–3

Part I

All questions in this part will receive 2 credits. No partial credit will be allowed.

1 Order these real numbers from smallest to greatest: $0.5, \sqrt{0.5}, 0.\overline{5}$.

   (1) $0.5 < \sqrt{0.5} < 0.\overline{5}$

   (2) $\sqrt{0.5} < 0.\overline{5} < 0.5$

   (3) $0.5 < 0.\overline{5} < \sqrt{0.5}$

   (4) $\sqrt{0.5} < 0.5 < 0.\overline{5}$

2 The sum of the first three prime numbers is

   (1) 6

   (2) 9

   (3) 10

   (4) 15

3 A verbal description of the set $\{8, 12, 16, 20, \ldots\}$ is

   (1) the set of multiples of 8

   (2) the set of multiples of 4

   (3) the set of multiples of 4 greater than 4

   (4) the set of multiples of 4 greater than 4 and less than 24

4 If a, b, and c are real numbers, the commutative property of addition states that

   (1) $(a + b) + c = c + (a + b)$

   (2) $a(b + c) = ab + ac$

   (3) $a(bc) = (ab)c$

   (4) $(a + b) + c = a + (b + c)$

5 If the temperature was $-39.5°$ yesterday and $+6.7°$ today, by how much did the temperature rise?

   (1) 3.28°   (3) 32.8°

   (2) 4.62°   (4) 46.2°

6 Which number below is rational?

   (1) π (3) $\sqrt{0.09}$

   (2) $\sqrt{0.9}$ (4) $\sqrt{-9}$

7 Which number line is the proper representation of the set of all numbers with an absolute value less than 2?

   (1)

   (2)

   (3)

   (4)

8 Evaluate the following:
$10 - 2(2 - 5) - 5(-0.2)^2 \div 10$

   (1) 0.044

   (2) 0.398

   (3) 2.38

   (4) 15.98

9 If $m - 3 = n$, then what is the value of $(n - m)^3$?

   (1) -27 (3) 9

   (2) -9 (4) 27

10 What is the smallest number that has four different prime factors?

   (1) 16

   (2) 30

   (3) 210

   (4) 945

Part II

Each correct answer will receive 2 credits. Clearly indicate the necessary steps, including appropriate formula substitutions, diagrams, charts, etc. Correct numerical answers without work shown will receive only 1 credit.

11 What are the common elements of the set of even whole numbers less than 4 and the set of even integers less than 4 and greater than −4?

12 Simplify: $-\dfrac{7}{16} \div \left(-\dfrac{21}{32}\right)$

13 If $a = 3$, $b = 2$, and $c = -1$, find the value of $\dfrac{ab - abc}{bc - ab}$.

14 Maria exercised on her bicycle for 40 minutes. Michael exercised $\dfrac{3}{8}$ as long. How many more minutes did Maria exercise than Michael?

Part III

Each correct answer will receive 3 credits. Partial credit will be allowed. Clearly indicate the necessary steps, including appropriate formula substitutions, diagrams, charts, etc. Correct numerical answers without work shown will receive only 1 credit.

15 Do $(-1)^{27}$ and $(-1)^{28}$ represent the same number? Why or why not?

16 One hundred students were asked about two kinds of music; jazz and classical. Sixty students said they listened to jazz while 45 said they listened to classical, and 20 didn't listen to either. How many students listened to both styles?

17 If the domain for $x = \{0, 2, 4, 6\}$, identify and graph on a number line the solution set for $2x = x^2$.

Part IV

Each correct answer will receive 4 credits. Partial credit will be allowed. Clearly indicate the necessary steps, including appropriate formula substitutions, diagrams, charts, etc. Correct numerical answers without work shown will receive only 1 credit.

18 Two sodas cost the same as five coffees. One soda costs the same as one coffee and one doughnut. How many doughnuts cost the same as three coffees?

19 More than half of the members of the school glee club are boys. Despite the snowstorm, $\dfrac{4}{7}$ of the boys and $\dfrac{7}{11}$ of the girls in the club come to the January rehearsal. What is the smallest number of members the glee club could have?

20 A 1-hour driver's test has 100 questions. Mike spends an average of 30 seconds each on the first 60 questions. To finish the test on time, what is the average number of seconds he can spend on each of the remaining questions?

CUMULATIVE REVIEW
CHAPTERS 1–4

Part I

All questions in this part will receive 2 credits. No partial credit will be allowed.

1 Which radical represents a rational number?

(1) $\sqrt{10}$　　　　(3) $\sqrt{14}$

(2) $\sqrt{12}$　　　　(4) $\sqrt{16}$

2 Which of the following rational numbers is between -2.1 and -2.2?

(1) -2.25　　　　(3) -2.04

(2) -2.15　　　　(4) 2.14

3 Which expression represents the number of feet in x yards?

(1) $\dfrac{x}{12}$　　　　(3) $3x$

(2) $\dfrac{x}{3}$　　　　(4) $12x$

4 The inequality $\dfrac{1}{2}x + 5 < 2x - 10$ is equivalent to

(1) $x > -10$　　　　(3) $x < 10$

(2) $x < -10$　　　　(4) $x > 10$

5 If x is an odd integer, then which of the following is *not equal* to an even integer?

(1) $5x - 2$　　　　(3) $2x^2 - 2$

(2) $6(x - 1)$　　　　(4) $x^2 - 5$

6 If a is an odd integer and b is an even integer, which of the following is an even integer?

(1) $a + 2b$　　　　(3) $a^2 + b$

(2) $3a + 3$　　　　(4) $a^2 + 2b$

7 The smallest positive integer is

(1) 2　　　　(3) 0.0001

(2) 1　　　　(4) 0

8 If $A = \dfrac{1}{2}h(b + c)$, what is the value of b when $A = 50$, $h = 4$, and $c = 11$?

(1) 14　　　　(3) 36

(2) 24　　　　(4) 56

9 A salesperson earns a weekly salary of $550 plus 8% commission on every dollar of merchandise sold. Which equation represents salary, s, given dollars, d, of merchandise sold?

(1) $s = 555 + 8d$　　　　(3) $s = 550 + 0.8d$

(2) $s = 558d$　　　　(4) $s = 550 + 0.08d$

10 Parking charges at a public garage are $5 for the first hour and $1.20 for each additional 30 minutes. If Zack has $12.80, what is the maximum amount of time he will be able to park his car at the garage?

(1) $3\dfrac{1}{4}$ hours

(2) $4\dfrac{1}{4}$ hours

(3) 6.5 hours

(4) 7.5 hours

Part II

Each correct answer will receive 2 credits. Clearly indicate the necessary steps, including appropriate formula substitutions, diagrams, charts, etc. Correct numerical answers without work shown will receive only 1 credit.

11 Susan told Bill that every time an even number is divided by an even number, the result is an even number. Bill tried to think of an example to show Susan that she was incorrect. Find an example for Bill.

12 Solve for d. $g = a + (n - 1)d$

13 The formula for simple interest is $I = prt$.

a Solve for p.

b Find p if the interest is $45, the rate is 5%, and $t = \dfrac{1}{2}$ year.

14 Three times a number increased by 6 is at most 50 more than the number. Find the greatest integer value of the number.

Each correct answer will receive 3 credits. Partial credit will be allowed. Clearly indicate the necessary steps, including appropriate formula substitutions, diagrams, charts, etc. Correct numerical answers without work shown will receive only 1 credit.

15 State whether each of the following sets is closed or not closed under the given operation. If it is *not* closed, provide an illustration to support your answer.

    a {0, 1, 2} addition

    b {1, 3, 5} subtraction

    c {−1, 0, 1} multiplication

16 A home is to be built on a rectangular plot with a perimeter of 800 feet. If the length is 20 feet less than 3 times the width, what are the dimensions of the rectangular plot?

17 In the tenth grade, 52 students made phone calls on a blood drive and 16 helped register blood donors. If 120 of the 180 students in the tenth grade did not participate in the blood drive, how many students both phoned and registered?

Part IV

Each correct answer will receive 4 credits. Partial credit will be allowed. Clearly indicate the necessary steps, including appropriate formula substitutions, diagrams, charts, etc. Correct numerical answers without work shown will receive only 1 credit.

18 In a science lab, a lever positioned on a fulcrum is used to balance weights. The positions of the weights with respect to the fulcrum can be represented with a proportion: $\dfrac{F_1}{F_2} = \dfrac{D_2}{D_1}$, where F_1 and F_2 are the weights (forces) and D_1 and D_2 are the distances from the fulcrum.

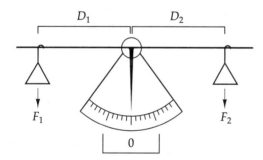

Solve each of the following.

    a A movable weight is 2 pounds and hangs 3 inches from the fulcrum. If a gold deposit weighs 0.5 pound, how far from the fulcrum must it hang to create a balance?

    b An 8-pound weight hangs 8 inches from the fulcrum. A quartz stone hanging 5 inches from the fulcrum balances the scale. How much does the stone weigh?

19 Popcorn is sold at a carnival for $2.50 per bag and candy apples are sold for $1.50 per apple. An inventory for last week showed that the number of bags of popcorn sold was four times the number of apples. The total amount collected for the two snacks was at least $500. What was the least possible number of bags of popcorn sold?

20 A garden is in the shape of an isosceles triangle. If the length of the third side of the triangle is 13 feet greater than the length of each of the equal sides and the perimeter of the garden is 196 feet, what is the length of each side of the garden?

CUMULATIVE REVIEW
CHAPTERS 1–5

Part I

All questions in this part will receive 2 credits. No partial credit will be allowed.

1 Which equation illustrates the additive inverse property?

(1) $a + (-a) = 0$ (3) $a + (-a) = 1$

(2) $a + 0 = a$ (4) $a + \dfrac{1}{a} = 1$

2 Which of the following numbers is not a rational number?

(1) $\dfrac{11}{7}$ (3) $1\dfrac{4}{7}$

(2) $1.\overline{7}$ (4) $\sqrt{7}$

3 The distance from Pluto to the sun is approximately 3,700,000,000 miles. Which of the following represents the distance in scientific notation?

(1) 3.7×10^9 (3) 0.37×10^{10}

(2) 3.7×10^{10} (4) 37×10^{10}

4 Which monomial is equivalent to $2x^5y^2 \bullet 5xy^3z^2 \bullet 2yz$?

(1) $10x^{15}y^6z^2$ (3) $20x^5y^6z^2$

(2) $20x^6y^6z^3$ (4) $20x^5y^3z^3$

5 The length of a rope is given exactly as 50.05 feet. The measure has how many significant digits?

(1) 1   (3) 3

(2) 2   (4) 4

6 If $3x - 5 = 2 + 14x$, then x equals

(1) $-\dfrac{7}{11}$ (3) $\dfrac{3}{17}$

(2) $-\dfrac{3}{17}$ (4) $\dfrac{7}{11}$

7 Which of the following is not correct?

(1) $2^8 = (2^4)^2$

(2) $2^4 \times 2^4 = 2^{16}$

(3) $2^4 \times 2^4 = 2^8$

(4) $2^{10} \div 2^5 = 2^5$

8 Which is the smallest number in the solution set of the inequality $5x + 7 \le 7x + 3$?

(1) $\{-2\}$ (3) $\{1\}$

(2) $\{0\}$ (4) $\{2\}$

9 What is the perimeter of a square whose area is 49 in.²?

(1) 7 in.   (3) 14 in.

(2) 12.25 in.   (4) 28 in.

10 A bowl contains n jelly beans, only one of which is red. After six green ones are added to the bowl, how many jelly beans in the bowl will not be red?

(1) $n + 6$ (3) $n + 4$

(2) $n + 5$ (4) $n + 1$

Part II

Each correct answer will receive 2 credits. Clearly indicate the necessary steps, including appropriate formula substitutions, diagrams, charts, etc. Correct numerical answers without work shown will receive only 1 credit.

11 Evaluate: $2^3 + 100\left(\dfrac{1}{5}\right)^2$

12 Simplify: $\dfrac{7a^2 + 14a}{7a}$

13 What polynomial is the result when $3x^2 + 15x - 7$ is subtracted from $x^2 - 5x - 7$?

14 Write an equation that describes y in terms of x in the table below.

x	2	3	4	5
y	\$3.50	\$5.25	\$7.00	\$8.75

Part III

Each correct answer will receive 3 credits. Partial credit will be allowed. Clearly indicate the necessary steps, including appropriate formula substitutions, diagrams, charts, etc. Correct numerical answers without work shown will receive only 1 credit.

15 Lunch at Washington High School costs $2 for the basic lunch, 25¢ extra for a king-size drink, and 40¢ extra for a bag of potato chips. Twelve members of the golf team ate lunch together. Ten members ordered a king-size drink. The total bill for lunch for the golf team was $29.30. How many bags of potato chips were purchased?

16 Using the distributive property, solve and graph:
$6(x + 3) - 2(x + 5) \geq 7(x + 1) - 2$.

17 C.J. has one less than twice the number of stamps that Parker has. Dennis has 53 more stamps than Parker has. If C.J. gives Parker 25 stamps, C.J. and Dennis will have the same number of stamps. How many stamps did each of the three boys have to begin with?

Part IV

Each correct answer will receive 4 credits. Partial credit will be allowed. Clearly indicate the necessary steps, including appropriate formula substitutions, diagrams, charts, etc. Correct numerical answers without work shown will receive only 1 credit.

18 Shelley and Michael are describing the same number. Shelley says, "The number is between 10 and 30 and is a multiple of 4." Michael says, "The number is between 10 and 30 and is a multiple of 3."

a If Shelley's statement is true and Michael's statement is true, what are all the possible numbers?

b If Shelley's statement is true and Michael's statement is false, what are all the possible numbers?

19 A gardener is paid $8 per hour for an eight-hour workday. His boss wants to give him a 10% raise in his hourly salary but will cut his time to 7 hours per day. What will be his change in weekly salary if he works 5 days each week?

20 The coordinates of a quadrilateral *ABCD* are *A*(0, 0), *B*(0, 5), *C*(6, 5), and *D*(6, 0). Plot the points on the coordinate plane, draw the quadrilateral, and find the area.

CUMULATIVE REVIEW
CHAPTERS 1–6

Part I

All questions in this part will receive 2 credits. No partial credit will be allowed.

1 If $\sqrt{k} > k > k^2$, then k could be

   (1) 0   (3) 1

   (2) $\dfrac{1}{9}$ (4) 9

2 Which choice represents the scientific notation for 0.0000801?

   (1) 8.01×10^4

   (2) 80.1×10^{-5}

   (3) 80.1×10^6

   (4) 8.01×10^{-5}

3 The product of $4x^2y^2$ and xy^3 is

   (1) $4x^2y^5$ (3) $4x^3y^5$

   (2) $4x^2y^6$ (4) $4x^3y^6$

4 The formula $S = 3F - 24$ can be used to find a man's shoe size (S) for a given foot length measured in inches (F). What is the foot length of a man who wears a size 9 shoe?

   (1) 3 inches   (3) 9 inches

   (2) 5 inches   (4) 11 inches

5 What is 40% of $10 + 5x$?

   (1) $0.4 + x$

   (2) $4 + 2x$

   (3) $4 + 15x$

   (4) $0.4 + 6x$

6 If a soccer team played 40 games in a season and won 24 of them, what percent of the games did the team win?

   (1) 16%   (3) 40%

   (2) 24%   (4) 60%

7 If y varies directly as x and $y = 2$ when $x = 3$, find y when $x = 18$.

   (1) $\dfrac{1}{3}$ (3) 12

   (2) 3   (4) 27

8 The ratio of x to y is 3 to 5. If $y = 2a$, what is the ratio of x to a?

   (1) 3 to 2

   (2) 3 to 5

   (3) 6 to 5

   (4) 5 to 10

9 The direct distance between the main entrance to a high school and the entrance to the football field is $\dfrac{1}{2}$ mile. The direct distance between the main entrance to a middle school and the entrance to the football field is $1\dfrac{1}{2}$ miles. Which could *not* be the direct distance between the main entrances of the high school and the middle school?

   (1) $\dfrac{3}{4}$ mile   (3) $1\dfrac{1}{4}$ miles

   (2) 1 mile   (4) $1\dfrac{1}{2}$ miles

10 If $x < -3$ or $x > 3$, which of the following must be true?

   I. $x^2 > 3$

   II. $|x| > 3$

   III. $x^3 > 3$

   (1) III only   (3) I & III only

   (2) I & II only   (4) I, II, & III

Each correct answer will receive 2 credits. Clearly indicate the necessary steps, including appropriate formula substitutions, diagrams, charts, etc. Correct numerical answers without work shown will receive only 1 credit.

11 Which number below is irrational? Why?

$0.\overline{77}$ $\sqrt{50}$ $\sqrt{\dfrac{81}{121}}$

12 Solve for x: $3(x - 2) = 2.4 - x$

13 The area of a trapezoid is $\dfrac{1}{2}h(b_1 + b_2)$. If the sum of the bases is 12 and the area is 18, find the height.

14 Maggie bought a picnic table on sale for 50% off the original price. The store charged her 10% tax and her final cost was $22.00. What was the original price of the picnic table?

Each correct answer will receive 3 credits. Partial credit will be allowed. Clearly indicate the necessary steps, including appropriate formula substitutions, diagrams, charts, etc. Correct numerical answers without work shown will receive only 1 credit.

15 A commission was divided among three salespeople so that the most experienced person, Brendan, received 50% of the money and the least experienced person, Chad, received $\dfrac{1}{3}$ the amount Brendan received. What fraction of the commission did the third salesperson, Donna, receive?

16 The original retail price for a pair of earrings was $30. Becky used a 15% off coupon to help pay for the earrings. If the tax on the sale price was 8%, what was her change from $30?

17 If y varies directly as x^2, and $y = 8$ when $x = 2$, what is the value of y when $x = 3$?

Each correct answer will receive 4 credits. Partial credit will be allowed. Clearly indicate the necessary steps, including appropriate formula substitutions, diagrams, charts, etc. Correct numerical answers without work shown will receive only 1 credit.

18 The profits of a family business are divided so that the father receives half of the profits and the three children receive profits in the ratio of 4 to 3 to 3. The profit for the year was $238,000. Determine the amount of profit each family member received.

19 At the ball game, hot dogs sell for $3.25 and hamburgers for $4.50. During the last game, a total of 900 hot dogs and hamburgers were sold for $3,395. How many of each were sold?

20 An antiques dealer paid $300 for a desk. She wants to put the price tag on it so that she can offer customers a discount of 10% of the price marked on the tag and yet still make a profit of 20% of the amount she paid. What price should she put on the tag?

CUMULATIVE REVIEW
CHAPTERS 1–7

Part I

All questions in this part will receive 2 credits. No partial credit will be allowed.

1 The statement "If x is divisible by 6 then x is divisible by 4" is false if x equals

(1) 0   (3) 18

(2) 12   (4) 24

2 The sum of $2x^2 - 4 + x^2 + x - 4$ can be expressed as

(1) $2x^2 - 8$ (3) $2x^2 + x - 8$

(2) $3x^2 + x - 8$ (4) $3x^2 + x$

3 If $a + b = 9a + b$, then a is equal to

(1) b (3) 0

(2) $\frac{1}{9}b$ (4) 8

4 Simplify: $(-3)^{-1} + (-1)^{-3}$

(1) $-\frac{4}{3}$ (3) $3\frac{1}{3}$

(2) $\frac{4}{3}$ (4) 4

5 If $x = 4$ and $y = -2$, which point on the graph represents $(x, -y)$?

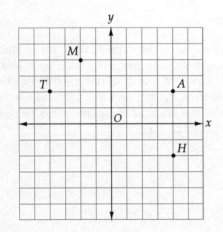

(1) M (3) T

(2) A (4) H

6 What is the greatest possible number of points of intersection of a triangle and a circle?

(1) 2   (3) 4

(2) 3   (4) 6

7 Two angles of a triangle measure 68° and 52°. Which is the measure of an exterior angle of the triangle?

(1) 28°   (3) 120°

(2) 60°   (4) 138°

8 In the given figure, the extended hypotenuse is a straight line. If angle C is a right angle, what is the sum of $x°$ and $y°$?

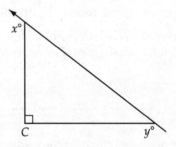

(1) 135°   (3) 180°

(2) 160°   (4) 270°

9 Which equation is an illustration of the commutative property of multiplication?

(1) $3 + 4 = 4 + 3$

(2) $\frac{3}{4} \cdot \frac{4}{3} = 1$

(3) $4 \cdot 3 = 3 \cdot 4$

(4) $\frac{4}{3} \cdot 1 = \frac{4}{3}$

10 In parallelogram $ABCD$, $m\angle A = 14x + 2$ and $m\angle B = 16x - 2$. Find $m\angle D$.

(1) 6   (3) 86

(2) 30   (4) 94

Each correct answer will receive 2 credits. Clearly indicate the necessary steps, including appropriate formula substitutions, diagrams, charts, etc. Correct numerical answers without work shown will receive only 1 credit.

11 Find three consecutive even integers such that the sum of 6 times the first number and 2 times the third number equals 200.

12 If $4^{x+1} = 64$, then what is the value of x^4?

13 Pat types 14 words every 20 seconds. At this rate, how many words does she type every 3 minutes?

14 If the sum of the measures of the interior angles of a polygon is 1,080°, name the polygon.

Each correct answer will receive 3 credits. Partial credit will be allowed. Clearly indicate the necessary steps, including appropriate formula substitutions, diagrams, charts, etc. Correct numerical answers without work shown will receive only 1 credit.

15 Members of a track team must run at least 25 laps each school week. Vinnie wants to build his endurance. He will increase the number of laps he runs by one every day for the five-day week. What is the least number of laps Vinnie must complete on Monday?

16 The 8% sales tax on a set of golf clubs was $29.70. What was the price of the golf clubs?

17 A flagpole casts a shadow of 42 feet while nearby a boy 5 feet tall casts a shadow of 7 feet. What is the height of the flagpole?

Each correct answer will receive 4 credits. Partial credit will be allowed. Clearly indicate the necessary steps, including appropriate formula substitutions, diagrams, charts, etc. Correct numerical answers without work shown will receive only 1 credit.

18 A sale of property is to be divided by three sisters in the ratio of 4 to 3 to 5. The selling price of the property was $600,132. Determine the number of dollars each sister is to receive.

19 Tula wants to tile a wall panel that is 8 feet high and 4.5 feet wide with square tiles that measure 4 inches on a side. The tiles cost $0.10 each. How much will she spend on tiling the panel?

20 In the two concentric circles, the radius of the small circle is 5 in. and the radius of the outer circle is 12 in. Find the area of the shaded region, rounded to the nearest hundredth of an inch.

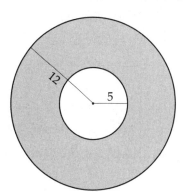

CUMULATIVE REVIEW
CHAPTERS 1–8

Part I

All questions in this part will receive 2 credits. No partial credit will be allowed.

1 The Eagle Scouts organized a party for the Cub Scouts. The heights of the Eagle Scouts ranged from 54 inches to 74 inches. The heights of the Cub Scouts ranged from 40 inches to 48 inches. Pictures of the scouts were taken in pairs, with one Eagle Scout and one Cub Scout. The difference between the heights of the boys in any picture was between

    (1) 13 inches and 27 inches

    (2) 5 inches and 27 inches

    (3) 5 inches and 35 inches

    (4) 13 inches and 35 inches

2 For which of the following values of radius, r, and height, h, will the volume of the cylinder shown below be the greatest?

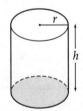

    (1) $r = 1, h = 5$ (3) $r = 3, h = 3$

    (2) $r = 5, h = 1$ (4) $r = 4, h = 2$

3 If $0.0038 = 3.8 \times 10^x$, then $x =$

    (1) -3 (3) 2

    (2) -2 (4) 3

4 In the given figure, if OB is 12 and $\angle AOB = 30°$, what are the coordinates of point B?

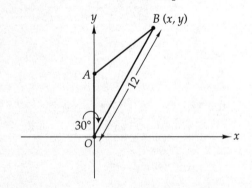

    (1) $(6, 12)$ (3) $(6, 6)$

    (2) $(6, \sqrt{2})$ (4) $(6, 6\sqrt{3})$

5 For which point in the given figure is it true that $|x| + |y| = 5$?

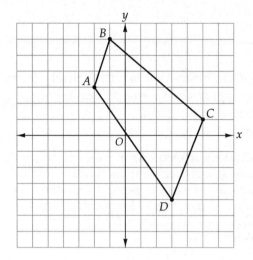

    (1) A (3) C

    (2) B (4) D

6 A road sign is shaped like a regular hexagon. If the length of one side is represented by $k + 8$, its perimeter would be represented by

    (1) $6k + 8$ (3) $6k + 48$

    (2) $8k + 8$ (4) $8k + 64$

7 In the accompanying diagram of triangle ABC, segment BC is extended through C to D. If $m\angle ABC = 4x - 6$, $m\angle BAC = 8x$, and $m\angle ACD = 10x + 10$, find $m\angle ACB$.

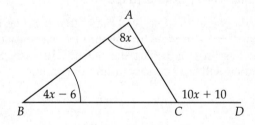

    (1) 26   (3) 90

    (2) 60   (4) 120

8 The statement "If x is a perfect square, then it is an even integer" is false if x is

    (1) 15   (3) 21

    (2) 16   (4) 25

9 In right triangle ABC, $\sin \angle A$ equals which of the following?

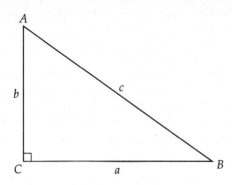

I. $\cos \angle B$

II. $\dfrac{a}{c}$

III. $\sin (90 - \angle B)$

(1) I only   (3) I & II only

(2) II only   (4) I, II, & III

10 What is the height of an equilateral triangle whose perimeter is 18?

(1) 3

(2) $3\sqrt{2}$

(3) $3\sqrt{3}$

(4) 4

Part II

Each correct answer will receive 2 credits. Clearly indicate the necessary steps, including appropriate formula substitutions, diagrams, charts, etc. Correct numerical answers without work shown will receive only 1 credit.

11 If $7 \times 10^2 + 3 \times 10^4 = N \times 10^4$, then what is the value of N?

12 Graph the solution set of $2(5 - x) < 16$ on a number line.

13 If the measure of an interior angle of a regular polygon is 135°, and a side of the polygon is 4 inches, find the perimeter of the polygon.

14 Falynn charges babysitting rates to the Brownes, who have triplets, as follows:

Before midnight: $6 per hour
After midnight: $8 per hour

If the Brownes came home at 2 A.M. and owed Falynn $40, what time did the job start?

Part III

Each correct answer will receive 3 credits. Partial credit will be allowed. Clearly indicate the necessary steps, including appropriate formula substitutions, diagrams, charts, etc. Correct numerical answers without work shown will receive only 1 credit.

15 The legs of a right triangle are represented by x and $x + 2$, and the hypotenuse is 10. Find the area of the triangle.

16 Natasha is a finalist in a spelling bee. She wants to learn at least 250 new words in time for the competition in 10 days. Each day, she will learn 2 more words than she learned the day before. What is the *least* number of words she must learn on the first day?

17 At a local high school football game, $1,350 was collected for hot dogs, hamburgers, tortillas, and soft drinks. Three times as many hot dogs were sold as hamburgers and twice as many tortillas were sold as hamburgers. As many soft drinks were sold as hot dogs, hamburgers, and tortillas combined. If each item sold for $1.50, how many soft drinks were sold?

Each correct answer will receive 4 credits. Partial credit will be allowed. Clearly indicate the necessary steps, including appropriate formula substitutions, diagrams, charts, etc. Correct numerical answers without work shown will receive only 1 credit.

18 When Justin received his weekly allowance, he decided to purchase candy bars for all his friends. Justin bought three Milk Chocolate bars and four Peanut Butter bars, which cost a total of $4.25. Then he realized this candy would not be enough for all his friends, so he returned to the store and bought an additional six Milk Chocolate bars and four Peanut Butter bars, which cost a total of $6.50. How much did each type of candy bar cost?

19 Samantha's homework is to determine the dimensions of her rectangular backyard. She knows that the length is 10 feet more than the width, and the total area is 144 square feet. Write an equation that Samantha could use to solve this problem. Then find the dimensions, in feet, of her backyard.

20 A ladder is leaning against a building as shown in the accompanying diagram. The ladder is 24 feet long and touches the building 8 feet from the roof. The angle of elevation to the point where the ladder touches the building is 64°. Find the height, *h*, of the building, to the *nearest foot*.

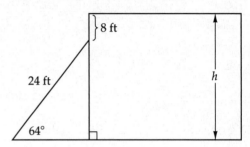

CUMULATIVE REVIEW
CHAPTERS 1–9

Part I

All questions in this part will receive 2 credits. No partial credit will be allowed.

1 How many integer values of x are there so that x, 6, and 10 could be sides of a triangle?

(1) 10

(2) 11

(3) 12

(4) 13

2 What is the distance between points $(-3, 2)$ and $(-2, 3)$?

(1) 1

(2) $\sqrt{2}$

(3) $\sqrt{5}$

(4) $\sqrt{10}$

3 In the accompanying diagram, $\overline{AB}$ is parallel to $\overline{CD}$. Transversal $\overline{EF}$ intersects $\overline{AB}$ and $\overline{CD}$ at G and H respectively. If $m\angle CHE = 4x - 4$ and $m\angle EGB = 3x + 2$, find $m\angle DHG$.

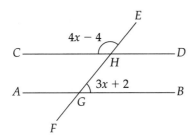

(1) 20

(2) 26

(3) 80

(4) 100

4 The distance between points A and B is 10 units. How many points are 5 units from A and 15 units from B?

(1) 0

(2) 1

(3) 2

(4) 4

5 The sum of all the integers in a certain list of consecutive integers is less than 25. If the least of these integers is -5, what is the greatest possible number of integers in the list?

(1) 9

(2) 13

(3) 14

(4) 21

6 The ratio of the surface areas of two cubes is 3 to 4. What is the ratio of the volume of the smaller cube to the volume of the larger cube?

(1) 3 to 8

(2) $\sqrt{3}$ to 2

(3) 3 to 4

(4) $3\sqrt{3}$ to 8

7 What is the equation of a line that has a y-intercept of -3 and is parallel to the line whose equation is $4y = 3x + 12$?

(1) $y = \dfrac{3}{4}x + 3$

(2) $y = \dfrac{4}{3}x - 3$

(3) $y = \dfrac{3}{4}x - 3$

(4) $y = -\dfrac{4}{3}x - 3$

8 What is the ratio of the number of males to the number of students if there are 45 males and 60 females?

(1) 105 : 45

(2) 45 : 65

(3) 3 : 7

(4) 3 : 4

9 Melissa saved money by working over the summer. Before school started, she spent 25% of the money on jewelry and then spent $\frac{2}{3}$ of the remaining money on a digital camera. She still had $213 left. How much money did Melissa have before she started shopping?

(1) $568 (3) $852

(2) $639 (4) $2,556

10 Which is true of the graph of $y = -3$?

(1) It is parallel to the y-axis.

(2) It contains point $(-3, 3)$.

(3) It has a slope of -3.

(4) Its slope is zero.

Part II

Each correct answer will receive 2 credits. Clearly indicate the necessary steps, including appropriate formula substitutions, diagrams, charts, etc. Correct numerical answers without work shown will receive only 1 credit.

11 Find the number of square units in the area of quadrilateral *ABCD*.

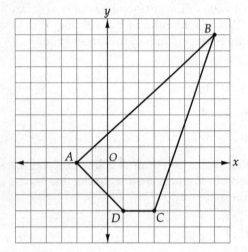

12 What is the slope of the line whose equation is $4x - 5y - 20 = 0$?

13 Solve this system of equations for the value of y:

$2x + y = 7$ and $x + y = 3$

14 If the lengths of two sides of an equilateral triangle are represented by $2x + 7$ and $3x - 5$, what is the perimeter of the triangle?

Part III

Each correct answer will receive 3 credits. Partial credit will be allowed. Clearly indicate the necessary steps, including appropriate formula substitutions, diagrams, charts, etc. Correct numerical answers without work shown will receive only 1 credit.

15 Mr. Fox bought a car for d dollars. After 5 years, the value of the car was half the original value. The following year, the value decreased another $1,500.

a Write an expression in terms of d to represent the value of the car after six years.

b If the price of the car when it was new was $24,000, find the value of the car when it was 6 years old.

16 A tree 15 feet tall casts a shadow 8 feet long. Find, to the *nearest degree*, the angle of elevation of the sun.

17 The angles in a triangle measure $7x - 1$, $18x + 2$, and $5x + 10$. Determine whether the triangle is acute, obtuse, or right. State your reason clearly.

Part IV

Each correct answer will receive 4 credits. Partial credit will be allowed. Clearly indicate the necessary steps, including appropriate formula substitutions, diagrams, charts, etc. Correct numerical answers without work shown will receive only 1 credit.

18 A survey showed that the ratio of Democrats to Republicans to Independents in Center City was 7 to 4 to 1. If 6,000 people were surveyed, determine how many identified with each political party.

19 The length of a rectangular garden is 3 feet more than 4 times the width. The perimeter is 66 feet.

   a What are the dimensions of the garden?

   b What is the area of the garden?

20 Sal wants to earn money by washing cars. Speedy Car Wash and Quick Car Wash offer different salary plans. The graph below represents the salary schedule for each car wash.

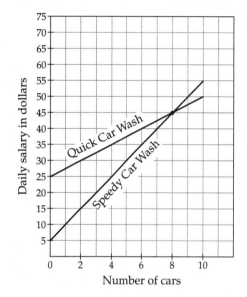

   a If the daily salary includes base pay and a commission based upon the number of cars washed, what is the difference in base pay between Speedy Car Wash and Quick Car Wash?

   b What is the rate of commission per car paid by Speedy Car Wash?

   c How many cars would Sal have to wash in order to make the same salary in both car washes?

   d How much salary would Sal earn where both salary plans pay the same?

CUMULATIVE REVIEW
CHAPTERS 1–10

Part I

All questions in this part will receive 2 credits. No partial credit will be allowed.

1 A package of chocolate is shown below:

The shape of the package is best described as a

(1) rectangular solid

(2) prism

(3) pyramid

(4) tetrahedron

2 The expression $\sqrt{48}$ can be simplified to

(1) $2\sqrt{12}$ (3) $4\sqrt{12}$

(2) $4\sqrt{3}$ (4) $16\sqrt{3}$

3 If the line $y = 6$ is graphed in the coordinate plane, which point would *not* be on the line?

(1) $(-6, 6)$ (3) $(0, 6)$

(2) $(6, 0)$ (4) $(6, 6)$

4 The shaded half plane in the accompanying figure is a graph of which inequality?

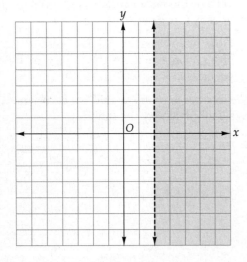

(1) $x > 2$ (3) $x < 2$

(2) $y > 2$ (4) $y \geq 2$

5 What is the slope of the line whose equation is $x + 2y - 4 = 0$?

(1) -2 (3) $\dfrac{1}{2}$

(2) $-\dfrac{1}{2}$ (4) 4

6 If two hamburgers and one soda cost \$6 and one hamburger and two sodas cost \$4.50, find the cost of one hamburger and one soda.

(1) \$2.50   (3) \$3.50

(2) \$3.00   (4) \$4.00

7 What is a solution for the system of equations $x + y = 0$ and $y = \dfrac{1}{2}x + 3$?

(1) $(-1, 1)$ (3) $(2, -2)$

(2) $(-2, 2)$ (4) $(-3, 3)$

8 Which of the following expressions could be used to show that integers are not closed under division?

(1) $0 \div 4$ (3) $-8 \div 4$

(2) $3 \div 4$ (4) $4.5 \div 1.5$

9 Which of the following inequalities is represented by the shaded region?

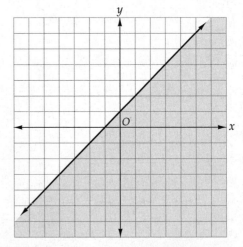

(1) $y \leq x + 1$ (3) $x + y \leq 1$

(2) $y \geq x + 1$ (4) $y + 1 \leq x$

10 If x and $2x$ have the same average as 11, 12, and 13, what is the value of x?

    (1) 3   (3) 8

    (2) 4   (4) 12

Part II

Each correct answer will receive 2 credits. Clearly indicate the necessary steps, including appropriate formula substitutions, diagrams, charts, etc. Correct numerical answers without work shown will receive only 1 credit.

11 Danielle's wallet had $2.65 in change: all quarters, dimes, and nickels. She had three times as many quarters as dimes and one more dime than nickels. How many of each coin did she have?

12 A highway rest area is planned so that the entry and exit paths form a right angle. The entry path is completed. It is 80 meters long and forms a 40-degree angle with the highway. How long will the exit path be to the nearest meter?

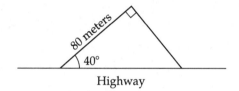

Highway

13 There are 28 students in a math class and 23 students in a chemistry class. If eight of these students take both math and chemistry, what is the ratio of the number of students taking only chemistry to those taking only math?

14 If the population of a certain American town in 1916 was 1,000 and seems to double every 12 years, what should its expected population be in the year 2012?

Part III

Each correct answer will receive 3 credits. Partial credit will be allowed. Clearly indicate the necessary steps, including appropriate formula substitutions, diagrams, charts, etc. Correct numerical answers without work shown will receive only 1 credit.

15 A student wrote the following four numbers in a table.

$\sqrt{\dfrac{4}{9}}$	$0.\overline{123}$
$0.\overline{3}$	$\sqrt{12}$

Which one of the above numbers is different from the others? Give a mathematical justification for your choice.

16 Jack and Susan participated in the New York City Marathon. They each maintained a constant pace for the first hour. Their times and distance for the first 40 minutes are shown in the accompany graph. Find, in miles per hour, how much faster Jack was running than Susan.

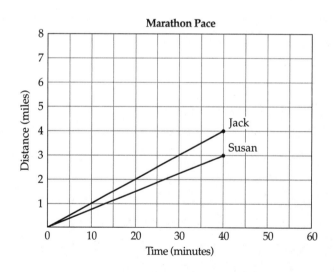

17 A cardboard square, 2 feet on each side, has 3 inches square cut out of each corner so that an open box can be constructed. Find the volume of the box in cubic inches.

Part IV

Each correct answer will receive 4 credits. Partial credit will be allowed. Clearly indicate the necessary steps, including appropriate formula substitutions, diagrams, charts, etc. Correct numerical answers without work shown will receive only 1 credit.

18 Line l contains the points $(0, -3)$ and $(1, 0)$. Show that the point $(-10, -27)$ does or does not lie on line l.

19 Lorna is playing a video game. In the game, she can drive through red gates or green gates. The first time she played, she drove through 3 red gates and 2 green gates and got three bonus points. The second time she played, she drove through 2 red gates and 4 green gates and got 10 bonus points.

    a How many points is a green gate worth?

    b How many points is a red gate worth?

20 A candy store sells 32-ounce bags of a mixture of chocolate and raisins. The price of the 32-ounce bag depends upon the amount of chocolate. If c ounces of chocolate are in the bag, the price p can be expressed as $p = 0.2c + 0.1(32 - c)$.

    a Find the price of a bag containing 24 ounces of chocolate.

    b Find the price of a bag containing 24 ounces of raisins.

    c Kate spent $4.20 on her purchase. Describe the mixture she bought.

CUMULATIVE REVIEW
CHAPTERS 1–11

Part I

All questions in this part will receive 2 credits. No partial credit will be allowed.

1 An expression equivalent to 7.003×10^{-3} is

(1) 0.7003

(2) 0.07003

(3) 0.007003

(4) 0.0007003

2 The statement "If x is divisible by 3, then it is divisible by 6" is false if x equals

(1) 12

(2) 15

(3) 25

(4) 30

3 The original price of a radio was $84. The sale ticket said "25% off original price." If Evan bought the radio on sale, what did he pay for it?

(1) $21

(2) $59

(3) $63

(4) $72

4 In right triangle PET, with $\angle T = 90°$, $\angle P = 44°$, and side $PT = 10$, what is the value, to the nearest hundredth, of side ET?

(1) 6.94

(2) 7.19

(3) 9.66

(4) 10.36

5 The ratio of the areas of two similar circles is 1 to 2. what is the ratio of the radii of the circles?

(1) $1 : \sqrt{2}$

(2) $1 : 2$

(3) $1 : 2\pi$

(4) $1 : 4$

6 The direct distance between Washington High School and Jefferson High School is 10 miles. The direct distance between Jefferson High School and Adams High School is 23 miles. Which could *not* be the direct distance between Washington High School and Adams High School?

(1) 10 miles

(2) 15 miles

(3) 20 miles

(4) 25 miles

7 What is the sum of $m^2n + 2mn + 7n$ and $3m^2n - 5mn + 2m$?

(1) $4m^4n^2 - 3m^2n^2 + 7n + 2m$

(2) $4m^2n - 3mn + 9mn$

(3) $2m^2n + 3mn + 2m + 7n$

(4) $4m^2n - 3mn + 7n + 2m$

8 Solve the following systems of equations. $x + 2y = 10$ and $3x - 2y = 6$

(1) $(4, 2)$ (3) $(4, 3)$

(2) $(1, -4.5)$ (4) $(1, 4.5)$

9 If two points on a line are $(-1, 4)$ and $(2, -2)$, what is the slope of the line?

(1) $-\dfrac{2}{3}$ (3) 2

(2) -2 (4) 6

10 If the value of a new car purchased for $46,000 in the year 2000 decreases at a steady rate of 10% a year, what is the total lost value, to the nearest dollar, of the car over the next 5 years?

(1) $8,326

(2) $18,837

(3) $23,000

(4) $27,163

Part II

Each correct answer will receive 2 credits. Clearly indicate the necessary steps, including appropriate formula substitutions, diagrams, charts, etc. Correct numerical answers without work shown will receive only 1 credit.

11 Factor $8x^2 - 24x + 18$ completely.

12 An emergency fuel container holds 6 quarts of gas. Jerry keeps the container in his trailer when he goes on wilderness hunting trips. If Jerry's trailer uses fuel at the rate of 12 miles per gallon, how far can Jerry travel using his reserve supply?

13 The numerator of a fraction is 6 less than the denominator of the fraction. The value of the fraction is $\frac{3}{5}$. Find the fraction.

14 The accompanying graph shows the closing price per share of a certain stock over a period of 7 days. (Note that a price such as $1\frac{1}{2}$ dollars is $1.50.)

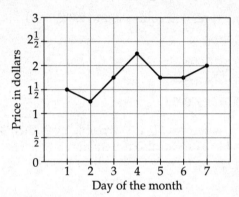

Between what two days did the price decrease most sharply? How much did the price decrease over those two days?

Part III

Each correct answer will receive 3 credits. Partial credit will be allowed. Clearly indicate the necessary steps, including appropriate formula substitutions, diagrams, charts, etc. Correct numerical answers without work shown will receive only 1 credit.

15 The grades on a 12-item quiz were scaled so that a perfect quiz received a grade of 100 by the following formula: $G = 8N + 4$, where G represents the final grade and N represents the number of correct answers.

  a Solve the grading formula for N.

  b For Abdul to receive a grade of 76, how many correct answers must he have?

16 The measures of the angles of a quadrilateral are in the ratio 3 to 4 to 5 to 6. Determine the number of degrees in each angle of the quadrilateral.

17 If the sum of four consecutive even integers is less than 250, what is the greatest possible value for one of these even integers?

Each correct answer will receive 4 credits. Partial credit will be allowed. Clearly indicate the necessary steps, including appropriate formula substitutions, diagrams, charts, etc. Correct numerical answers without work shown will receive only 1 credit.

18 In the 1850s, from a whaling ship's topmast, a sailor in the crow's nest is 155 feet above the deck. If he sights a whale, and the angle of depression to the sighting is 23°, what is the distance, to the nearest foot, from the ship to the whale?

19 Two tennis clubs offer different membership plans. The graph below represents the total cost of belonging to club A for one year.

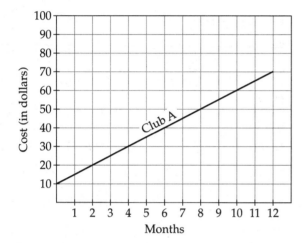

a On the same set of axes, draw the graph of the cost of belonging to club B for a year, if there is no initial membership fee and the monthly fee is $10.

b What is the initial membership fee for club A?

c In what month is the total cost the same for both clubs?

d What is the monthly charge for club A?

20 The length of a rectangle is 3 more than its width. The side of a square is equal to the width of the rectangle. The side of an equilateral triangle is equal to the length of the rectangle.

a If the width of the rectangle is represented by w, express, in terms of w:

  (1) the length of the rectangle

  (2) the perimeter of the square

  (3) the perimeter of the equilateral triangle

b If the perimeter of the square equals the perimeter of the equilateral triangle, what is the area of the rectangle?

Part I

All questions in this part will receive 2 credits. No partial credit will be allowed.

1 Before redistricting, a village in Westchester had 1,200 elementary school pupils. After redistricting, it had 300. What was the percent of decrease?

(1) 25%

(2) 30%

(3) $33\frac{1}{3}\%$

(4) 75%

2 Simplify: $\sqrt{18} + \sqrt{72} =$

(1) $\sqrt{90}$

(2) $3\sqrt{10}$

(3) $6\sqrt{3}$

(4) $9\sqrt{2}$

3 What is the equation of a line parallel to the y-axis and four units to the right of the y-axis?

(1) $y = -4$

(2) $y = 4$

(3) $x = -4$

(4) $x = 4$

4 If $0.4x - 8 = x + 1$, then x equals

(1) -0.15 (3) -15

(2) -9 (4) -90

5 The product of two consecutive even integers is 168. If x represents the smaller even integer, then which equation can be used to find the integers?

(1) $x + x + 2 = 168$

(2) $x + x + 1 = 168$

(3) $x(x + 1) = 168$

(4) $x(x + 2) = 168$

6 Factor the binomial $4xy^2 - 6xy^3$ completely.

(1) $2xy(2y - 3y^2)$

(2) $2xy^2(2 - 3y)$

(3) $xy^2(4 - 6y)$

(4) $2xy^2(2xy - 3y)$

7 An article of clothing costs m dollars to the store owner. Which of the following could *not* be used to find the selling price, SP, with a 20% profit?

(1) $m + 20\%m = SP$

(2) $m + 0.20 = SP$

(3) $1.2m = SP$

(4) $m(1 + 0.20) = SP$

8 The expression $\left(2x^2\right)^3$ is equal to

(1) $6x^5$ (3) $8x^5$

(2) $6x^6$ (4) $8x^6$

9 In the given figure, if the area is 16, then $x =$

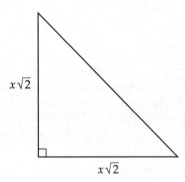

(1) 4   (3) $4\sqrt{3}$

(2) $4\sqrt{2}$ (4) 8

10 When x is divided by $x\%$ of x, the result is

(1) $\dfrac{100}{x}$

(2) $\dfrac{x}{100}$

(3) $\dfrac{x^2}{100}$

(4) $\dfrac{100}{x^2}$

Part II

Each correct answer will receive 2 credits. Clearly indicate the necessary steps, including the appropriate formula substitutions, diagrams, charts, etc. Correct numerical answers without work shown will receive only 1 credit.

11 Evaluate the following expression.

$$\left(\sqrt[3]{18}\right)^3 \div \sqrt{\left(\frac{3}{8}\right)^2} + \left(5\sqrt{2}\right)^2 + 1 \bullet x^0$$

12 Find the product. $(0.4x + z)(0.4x - z)$

13 If a varies directly as x and $a = 22$ when $x = 7$, find the value of a when $x = 21$.

14 Factor completely each of the following:

  a $p + prt$

  b $1 - 9a^2$

Part III

Each correct answer will receive 3 credits. Partial credit will be allowed. Clearly indicate the necessary steps, including appropriate formula substitutions, diagrams, charts, etc. Correct numerical answers without work shown will receive only 1 credit.

15 If a class has 25 students and 15 students have blond hair, 12 students have blue eyes, and 8 have both blond hair and blue eyes, how many students have neither blond hair nor blue eyes?

16 Solve the compound inequalities and graph the solution set on the number line.

$4x - 5 \geq 7$ or $4x - 4 < -8$

17 What is the product of the x- and y-intercepts of the linear equation $2x - 3y = 6$?

Part IV

Each correct answer will receive 4 credits. Partial credit will be allowed. Clearly indicate the necessary steps, including appropriate formula substitutions, diagrams, charts, etc. Correct numerical answers without work shown will receive only 1 credit.

18 The following is the compound interest formula:

$$P = A(1 + I)^n$$

where A is the original value of an investment, I is the interest rate per compounding period, n is the total number of compounding periods, and P is the value of the investment after n periods.

If an investor deposits $15,000 into an account that earns 8% interest compounded quarterly, what is the value of the investment, to the nearest dollar, after 7 years?

19 In triangle ABC, the measure of angle A is 20° more than twice the measure of angle B. If the measure of angle C is at least 2°,

  a find the largest possible integer measure of angle A

  b find the smallest integer measure of angle C

20 The Saturday evening gym rental for the faculty-alumni basketball game costs $60. Tickets for the game sell for $3 each. Write a linear equation to represent the relationship between the number of tickets sold and the profit from the game. Set up a table of values and graph your equation. How many tickets must be sold to

  a break even?

  b make $1,200?

  c make $1,800?

CUMULATIVE REVIEW
CHAPTERS 1–13

Part I

All questions in this part will receive 2 credits. No partial credit will be allowed.

1 Which is the correct factorization of $x^2 - 100$?

(1) $-(x + 10)^2$ (3) $(x + 10)(x - 10)$

(2) $(x + 10)^2$ (4) $(x - 10)^2$

2 What is the solution set of the equation $x^2 - 5x - 14 = 0$?

(1) $(-7, 2)$ (3) $(7, -2)$

(2) $(-7, -2)$ (4) $(2, 7)$

3 What is the integer root of the equation $2x^2 - x - 3$?

(1) -3 (3) 1

(2) -1 (4) 3

4 If $|x - 3| = 7$, what are the two possible values of x?

(1) -10 and 4 (3) -7 and 7

(2) -10 and 10 (4) -4 and 10

5 Which of the following equations represents a line that is perpendicular to the line $y = 4x - 10$?

(1) $y - \dfrac{1}{4}x = -7$ (3) $y - 4x = -5$

(2) $4y + x = -20$ (4) $y - 10 = 4x$

6 In triangle ABC, if $\angle A = 60°$, $AC = 1$, and $AB = 2$, then what is the value of $\cos \angle B$?

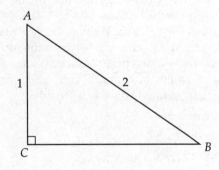

(1) $\dfrac{1}{2}$ (3) 2

(2) $\sqrt{3}$ (4) $\dfrac{\sqrt{3}}{2}$

7 If m is an odd integer, then $(-1)^{m-3}$ equals

(1) -3 (3) 0

(2) -1 (4) 1

8 In the coordinate plane, $(n, 0)$ is one of the points of intersection of the graphs of the equations $y = x^2 - 25$ and $y = -x^2 + 25$. If $n > 0$, then $n =$

(1) 5

(2) 10

(3) 25

(4) 50

9 If $x^N \neq 0$, $\dfrac{x^{N+R}}{x^N}$ equals

(1) x^{R+1}

(2) x^R

(3) x^{R+2N}

(4) $x^R + 1$

10 In the given figure, a half circle is drawn on the longest side of the rectangle whose length is $2x$ and width is x. Which expression represents the area of the whole figure?

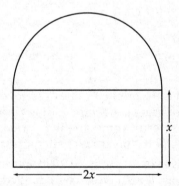

(1) $2x^2 + \dfrac{\pi x^2}{2}$

(2) $2\pi x^2$

(3) $3\pi x^2$

(4) $2x^2 + \pi x^2$

Part II

Each correct answer will receive 2 credits. Clearly indicate the necessary steps, including the appropriate formula substitutions, diagrams, charts, etc. Correct numerical answers without work shown will receive only 1 credit.

11 Simplify: $\frac{2}{3}\sqrt{24} \cdot 9\sqrt{3}$

12 On a coordinate plane, draw a line with slope $\frac{3}{2}$ that passes through point $(3, -2)$.

13 If $\frac{x + y}{4} = x$, what is the ratio of x to y?

14 If 12 men can lay a stretch of highway in 20 days, how many days would 15 men require to do the same job?

Part III

Each correct answer will receive 3 credits. Partial credit will be allowed. Clearly indicate the necessary steps, including appropriate formula substitutions, diagrams, charts, etc. Correct numerical answers without work shown will receive only 1 credit.

15 The Bank of Brescia offers a yearly CD rate of 3.6%. If $5,000 is deposited in this CD account, what is the total money available, to the nearest dollar, at the end of 6 years?

16 In the given figure, the circumference of circle O is 12π, and the degree measure of angle AOB is $45°$. In terms of π, what is the area of the shaded region XOY?

17 If A = {all numbers between -5.2 and 5.2, inclusive}, B = {all primes}, and C = {whole numbers}, then

    a the intersection of sets A, B, and C contains how many numbers?

    b Graph the solution set.

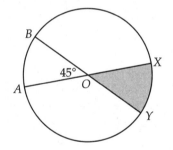

Part IV

Each correct answer will receive 4 credits. Partial credit will be allowed. Clearly indicate the necessary steps, including appropriate formula substitutions, diagrams, charts, etc. Correct numerical answers without work shown will receive only 1 credit.

18 Graph these inequalities on the set of axes.

    $y < 2x + 3$ and $2x + y < 1$

19 A rectangular garden 60 feet by 80 feet is surrounded by a walk of uniform width as indicated in the diagram. The area of the walk (the shaded region) is 7,200 square feet. Find the width, x, of the walk.

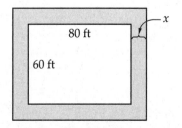

20 Solve the following system of quadratic-linear equations using an algebraic method.

    $y = -x^2 + 4x + 7$ and $y = -2x + 15$

Part I

All questions in this part will receive 2 credits. No partial credit will be allowed.

1 If n is a positive number and $n^{-3} = 8$, then what is the value of n^2?

(1) $\dfrac{1}{4}$

(2) $\dfrac{1}{2}$

(3) 2

(4) 4

2 In the given figure, the radius of circle O is 10. If the area of the shaded region is 80π, what is the area of the region not shaded?

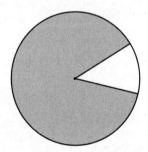

(1) 100π

(2) 80π

(3) 72π

(4) 20π

3 The roots of the equation $x^2 + 4x - 12 = 0$ are

(1) $\{2, -6\}$

(2) $\{4, -3\}$

(3) $\{3, -4\}$

(4) $\{6, -2\}$

4 Simplify: $\dfrac{1 + \dfrac{x}{y}}{1 + \dfrac{y}{x}}$

(1) $-\dfrac{x}{y}$

(2) 1

(3) $\dfrac{y}{x}$

(4) $\dfrac{x}{y}$

5 For what value or values of x is the fraction $\dfrac{x + 4}{x^2 + 3x - 4}$ undefined?

(1) $\{-4\}$

(2) $\{4\}$

(3) $\{1, -4\}$

(4) $\{-1, 4\}$

6 What is the equation of the axis of symmetry for the graph of the equation $y = \dfrac{1}{2}x^2 + 2x + 3$?

(1) $x = -4$ (3) $x = -1$

(2) $x = -2$ (4) $x = 4$

7 Simplify: $(2a + 3)(3a - 5) - (1 + 2a)(1 - 2a)$

(1) $2a^2 - a - 14$

(2) $2a^2 - 9a - 16$

(3) $10a^2 + 7a - 14$

(4) $10a^2 - a - 16$

8 The perimeter of a rectangle is at most 24 cm and the width is one-third the length. Find the greatest possible length of the rectangle.

(1) 3   (3) 9

(2) 6   (4) 12

9 Which expression is equivalent to $\dfrac{1}{a^2 - 1} + \dfrac{1}{a - 1}$?

(1) $\dfrac{a + 2}{a^2 - 1}$

(2) $\dfrac{a + 1}{a^2 - 1}$

(3) $\dfrac{2}{a^2 - 2}$

(4) $\dfrac{a + 2}{a^2 - 2}$

10 Which ordered pair (x, y) satisfies the given system of inequalities?

$y - 1 \le 2x$ and $3x - y < 4$

(1) $(5, 11)$ (3) $(3, -6)$

(2) $(2, 2)$ (4) $(-1, -1)$

Part II

Each correct answer will receive 2 credits. Clearly indicate the necessary steps, including the appropriate formula substitutions, diagrams, charts, etc. Correct numerical answers without work shown will receive only 1 credit.

11 Simplify: $\frac{1}{6}\sqrt{8} \cdot \frac{1}{2}\sqrt{18}$

12 A parabola whose equation is $y = x^2 - 2x + k$ has an x-intercept at $x = 5$. What is the other x-intercept?

13 Solve for the positive value of y: $\frac{2+y}{2y} = \frac{y-1}{y}$

14 Write the equation of a line that passes through the point $(4, -1)$ and is parallel to the line $y - 3x = -7$.

Part III

Each correct answer will receive 3 credits. Partial credit will be allowed. Clearly indicate the necessary steps, including appropriate formula substitutions, diagrams, charts, etc. Correct numerical answers without work shown will receive only 1 credit.

15 Solve for x: $\frac{x-5}{3} = 1 - \frac{5}{x}$

16 Bob and Vito collected 88 pounds of newspaper in a class paper drive. Bob announced that if he had collected 8 more pounds, he would have had twice the amount Vito collected. How many pounds did they each collect?

17 If 5 is a root of $x^2 - 3x + k = 0$, then
  a what is the value of k?
  b what is the other root?
  c what is the sum of the roots?

Part IV

Each correct answer will receive 4 credits. Partial credit will be allowed. Clearly indicate the necessary steps, including appropriate formula substitutions, diagrams, charts, etc. Correct numerical answers without work shown will receive only 1 credit.

18 Solve the following system of equations algebraically or graphically for x and y.
  $y = x^2 - 4x$ and $y = -x + 4$

19 A golf ball is hit off a tee with an initial velocity of 128 feet per second. If $h(t) = -16t^2 + 128t$ is the equation that models this event,
  a after how many seconds will the golf ball reach a height of exactly 112 feet?
  b after how many seconds will the ball reach its maximum height?
  c what is the maximum height of the golf ball?
  d after how many seconds will the ball touch the ground?

20 The base AB of isosceles triangle ABC is 40 inches. Each base angle measures $50°$.
  a Find the altitude drawn from vertex C to the base of the triangle (to the nearest tenth of an inch).
  b Find the area of the triangle, to the nearest square inch.

CUMULATIVE REVIEW

CHAPTERS 1–15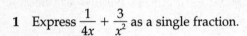

Part I

All questions in this part will receive 2 credits. No partial credit will be allowed.

1 Express $\dfrac{1}{4x} + \dfrac{3}{x^2}$ as a single fraction.

(1) $\dfrac{x + 12}{4x^2}$

(2) $\dfrac{x^2 + 12}{4x^3}$

(3) $\dfrac{13}{4x}$

(4) $\dfrac{1 + 12x}{4x^2}$

2 If two fair dice (with numbers 1 through 6) are rolled. What is the probability that the sum of the numbers on the top is less than 4?

(1) $\dfrac{2}{36}$

(2) $\dfrac{3}{36}$

(3) $\dfrac{33}{36}$

(4) $\dfrac{34}{36}$

3 For which of the following values of N is $\left(-\dfrac{1}{3}\right)^N$ the largest?

(1) 0

(2) 1

(3) 2

(4) 3

4 From a group of 8 senators, how many different committees of exactly 5 can be chosen?

(1) 40

(2) 56

(3) 336

(4) 6,720

5 The graph below is the solution set of which inequality?

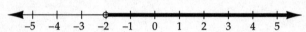

(1) $4x - 5 \le x - 11$

(2) $3(x + 1) > 1.5x$

(3) $\dfrac{x}{4} + \dfrac{3}{2} \le 2$

(4) $7 - (x + 2) < -7$

6 Simplify: $\dfrac{\left(xy^2\right)^2 (x^3 y)}{x^4 y^6}$

(1) xy

(2) $\dfrac{1}{y}$

(3) $\dfrac{x}{y}$

(4) $\dfrac{x^2}{y^2}$

7 For what value of x is the expression $\dfrac{4x - 8}{x - 4}$ undefined?

(1) 4

(2) 2

(3) 0

(4) −4

8 The sum of $\dfrac{n + 3}{n - 1}$ and $\dfrac{2}{1 - n}$ is

(1) 1

(2) $\dfrac{n + 1}{n - 1}$

(3) $\dfrac{n + 5}{n - 1}$

(4) $\dfrac{n + 5}{n^2 - 1}$

9 When $\dfrac{x-p}{x^2-p^2}$ is simplified, what is the denominator?

(1) 1

(2) $x - p$

(3) $x + p$

(4) $x^2 - p^2$

10 How many unique ways can the letters in the word DIAGRAM be arranged?

(1) 5,040

(2) 2,520

(3) 1,260

(4) 720

Part II

Each correct answer will receive 2 credits. Clearly indicate the necessary steps, including the appropriate formula substitutions, diagrams, charts, etc. Correct numerical answers without work shown will receive only 1 credit.

11 What is the slope of a line perpendicular to the line $6x + 3y = 15$?

12 Solve for x. $x - a = a + b - 3x$

13 If $|x| = |y|$ for all pairs of nonzero numbers x and y, then what are all the possible real values of $\dfrac{x}{y}$?

14 The perimeter of a rectangle is 16. If the length of the rectangle is greater than 7, what is one possible value for the width?

Part III

Each correct answer will receive 3 credits. Partial credit will be allowed. Clearly indicate the necessary steps, including appropriate formula substitutions, diagrams, charts, etc. Correct numerical answers without work shown will receive only 1 credit.

15 The ratio of numerator to denominator is 2 to 5. If the numerator is decreased by 2 and its denominator is increased by 1, the fraction is equal to $\dfrac{1}{3}$. Find the numerator and denominator of the original fraction.

16 If $d = 16t^2$ is the formula for the distance in feet that an object falls after t seconds, then how many seconds will it take an object to fall 400 feet?

17 The Stepinac H.S. basketball team had a record of 15 wins and 9 losses. What is the least number of the remaining 36 games the team must win in order to finish the season winning at least 55% of all the games played?

Each correct answer will receive 4 credits. Partial credit will be allowed. Clearly indicate the necessary steps, including appropriate formula substitutions, diagrams, charts, etc. Correct numerical answers without work shown will receive only 1 credit.

18 If a tank holds 729 gallons of oil and $\frac{1}{3}$ of the oil is released each time the valve is opened, how much oil will be left in the tank after the valve is opened for the sixth time?

19 Mr. Campion has ten more students in his Java class than he has in his Visual Basics class. Only one of his students is selected randomly each year to enter a computer science contest. The probability that a student studying Visual Basics is selected is $\frac{3}{8}$. Find the number of students in the Visual Basics class.

20 Eunice is sending a package to California on Saturday by Speedy Mail Service. When she asked when the package would arrive in California, the clerk showed her the circle graph below.

Delivery Dates for Saturday Packages

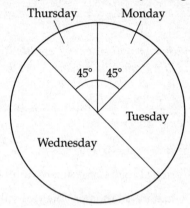

a What is the probability that her package will arrive on Tuesday?

b What is the probability that her package will arrive on or before Wednesday?

c Construct a cumulative frequency histogram to show the probability that the package will arrive on or before each weekday.

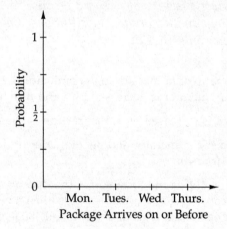

CUMULATIVE REVIEW
CHAPTERS 1–16

Part I

All questions in this part will receive 2 credits. No partial credit will be allowed.

1 If $x = m - 6$ and $y = m + 5$, then $x - y =$

(1) -11

(2) -1

(3) 1

(4) 11

2 The graph of the equation $y = x$ lies in which quadrants?

(1) I and II

(2) I and III

(3) II and III

(4) I and IV

3 A number N is selected at random from set $A = \{1, 2, 3, 4\}$ and a number K is selected from set $B = \{5, 6\}$. What is the probability that the sum of $N + K$ will be an even number?

(1) $\dfrac{1}{4}$

(2) $\dfrac{3}{8}$

(3) $\dfrac{1}{2}$

(4) $\dfrac{2}{3}$

4 Solve the compound inequality.

$$-5 \geq \frac{1}{2}x + 1 > -9$$

(1) $\{x: -20 < x \leq -12\}$

(2) $\{x: -10 < x \leq -8\}$

(3) $\{x: -19 < x \leq -11\}$

(4) $\{x: -17 < x \leq -9\}$

5 The sum of the squares of two consecutive integers is 31 more than their product. Find the integers.

(1) 6 and 7

(2) 4 and 5

(3) -6 and -5

(4) -7 and -6

6 Which of the following equations contains the points $(-2, -3)$ and $(-5, 3)$?

(1) $y = -x - 5$

(2) $y = -2x - 7$

(3) $y = -2x - 6$

(4) $y = -\dfrac{1}{2}x - 4$

7 The Hicksville golf team lost W matches, won twice as many matches as it lost, and tied X matches. The number of golf matches won was what fraction of the total number of matches played?

(1) $\dfrac{2W}{W + X}$

(2) $\dfrac{2W}{3W + X}$

(3) $\dfrac{2W}{WX}$

(4) $\dfrac{2W + X}{W}$

8 Which of the following equations is equivalent to $\dfrac{4}{(x + 1)^2} + \dfrac{3}{x + 1} = 1$?

(1) $x^2 + 2x + 3 = 0$

(2) $x^2 - 6x + 4 = 0$

(3) $x^2 + 2x - 3 = 0$

(4) $x^2 - x - 6 = 0$

9 The probability that it will rain on Monday is $\frac{3}{5}$ and, independently, the probability that it will rain on Wednesday is $\frac{4}{7}$. What is the probability that it will rain on Monday and that it will not rain on Wednesday?

(1) $\frac{6}{35}$ (3) $\frac{3}{7}$

(2) $\frac{9}{35}$ (4) $\frac{20}{21}$

10 When five integers are arranged from least to greatest, the median is 5. If the only mode for this set of numbers is 7, what is the greatest sum that these five integers can have?

(1) 26

(2) 27

(3) 28

(4) 33

Part II

Each correct answer will receive 2 credits. Clearly indicate the necessary steps, including the appropriate formula substitutions, diagrams, charts, etc. Correct numerical answers without work shown will receive only 1 credit.

11 If $x > 0$ and $4\sqrt{x} - 12 = 20$, what is the value of x?

12 If $7a = 3$ and $\frac{b}{4} = 7$, then what is the value of ab?

13 Find the roots for $4x^2 - 4x - 3 = 0$.

14 Battery life for two brands of batteries was tested under identical situations. The results were recorded in the box-and-whisker plots shown below.

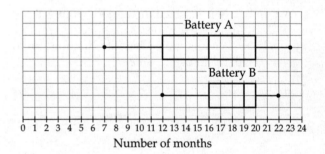

Number of months

If both batteries cost the same, which would you buy? Explain why.

Part III

Each correct answer will receive 3 credits. Clearly indicate the necessary steps, including the appropriate formula substitutions, diagrams, charts, etc. Correct numerical answers without work shown will receive only 1 credit.

15 The product of two consecutive positive integers is 19 more than their sum. Find the integers.

16 Sausage costs $\frac{5}{4}$ the price of eggs and cereal costs one-third as much as sausage. If eggs cost x dollars, then eggs cost what fraction of the cost of cereal?

17 Dante recorded the number of rainy days per month in a certain region in Oregon for five consecutive months: 17, 14, 9, 11, 9. Find the mean, median, and mode of his set of statistics, and determine which of the following statements is false.

I. The mean is greater than the mode.

II. The mean is greater than the median.

III. The median is equal to the mode.

Each correct answer will receive 4 credits. Partial credit will be allowed. Clearly indicate the necessary steps, including the appropriate formula substitutions, diagrams, charts, etc. Correct numerical answers without work shown will receive only 1 credit.

18 Solve the following system of equations algebraically or graphically.

$$y = x^2 - 6x - 7 \quad \text{and} \quad y = -x + 7$$

19 The sum of two numbers is 40. Four times the larger number decreased by 5 equals 11 more than eight times the smaller number. Write two equations to represent the previous sentence. Solve those two equations and clearly identify the solution set.

20 Copy the data shown in the table below into L_1 and L_2 of your graphing calculator. Make a scatter plot from the data. Looking at the scatter plot, describe the correlation, if any. Using the calculator, find the line of best fit. Find the value of r. Compare the correlation results to your estimate. Graph the line of best fit along with the scatter plot.

The following compares age in years to running distance, measured in kilometers, for a group of men who participated in a Thanksgiving Day charity event.

Age (years)	Distance (kilometers)
18	15
20	15
16	13
22	16
30	12
31	10
34	12
25	14
20	14
40	8
42	8
28	13
50	6
53	6
15	16
32	13
40	10
37	10
26	15
53	5

Reference Sheet

Area of a trapezoid $\qquad A = \frac{1}{2}h(b_1 + b_2)$

Volume of a cylinder $\qquad V = \pi r^2 h$

Surface Area

Rectangular Prism $\qquad SA = 2lw + 2hw + 2lh$

Cylinder $\qquad SA = 2\pi r^2 + 2\pi rh$

Trigonometric Ratios

$\sin A = \dfrac{\text{opposite}}{\text{hypotenuse}}$

$\cos A = \dfrac{\text{adjacent}}{\text{hypotenuse}}$

$\tan A = \dfrac{\text{opposite}}{\text{adjacent}}$

Formulas for Coordinate Geometry

$m = \dfrac{\Delta y}{\Delta x} = \dfrac{y_2 - y_1}{x_2 - x_1}$

Integrated Algebra Regents Examinations

Part I

Answer all 30 questions in this part. Each correct answer will receive 2 credits. No partial credit will be allowed. For each question, write on the separate answer sheet the numeral preceding the word or expression that best completes the statement or answers the question. [60]

1. The expression $x^2 - 36y^2$ is equivalent to
   (1) $(x - 6y)(x - 6y)$ (3) $(x + 6y)(x - 6y)$
   (2) $(x - 18y)(x - 18y)$ (4) $(x + 18y)(x - 18y)$

2. The legs of an isosceles right triangle each measure 10 inches. What is the length of the hypotenuse of this triangle, to the *nearest tenth of an inch*?
   (1) 6.3   (2) 7.1   (3) 14.1   (4) 17.1

3. The expression $\dfrac{12w^9y^3}{-3w^3y^3}$ is equivalent to

   (1) $-4w^6$ (2) $-4w^3y$ (3) $9w^6$ (4) $9w^3y$

4. The spinner shown in the diagram below is divided into six equal sections.

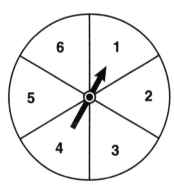

   Which outcome is *least* likely to occur on a single spin?
   (1) an odd number   (3) a perfect square
   (2) a prime number   (4) a number divisible by 2

5. What are the factors of the expression $x^2 + x - 20$?
   (1) $(x + 5)$ and $(x + 4)$ (3) $(x - 5)$ and $(x + 4)$
   (2) $(x + 5)$ and $(x - 4)$ (4) $(x - 5)$ and $(x - 4)$

6. What is $3\sqrt{250}$ expressed in simplest radical form?
   (1) $5\sqrt{10}$ (2) $8\sqrt{10}$ (3) $15\sqrt{10}$ (4) $75\sqrt{10}$

7. A survey is being conducted to determine which school board candidate would best serve the Yonkers community. Which group, when randomly surveyed, would likely produce the most bias?
   (1) 15 employees of the Yonkers school district
   (2) 25 people driving past Yonkers High School
   (3) 75 people who enter a Yonkers grocery store
   (4) 100 people who visit the local Yonkers shopping mall

8. An 8-foot rope is tied from the top of a pole to a stake in the ground, as shown in the diagram below.

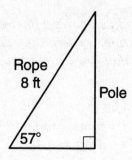

Rope
8 ft

Pole

57°

If the rope forms a 57° angle with the ground, what is the height of the pole, to the *nearest tenth of a foot*?
(1) 4.4   (2) 6.7   (3) 9.5   (4) 12.3

9. How many different ways can five books be arranged on a shelf?
(1) 5   (2) 15   (3) 25   (4) 120

10. What is the slope of the line passing through the points $(-2, 4)$ and $(3, 6)$?
(1) $-\dfrac{5}{2}$ (2) $-\dfrac{2}{5}$ (3) $\dfrac{2}{5}$ (4) $\dfrac{5}{2}$

11. Which type of function is represented by the graph shown below?

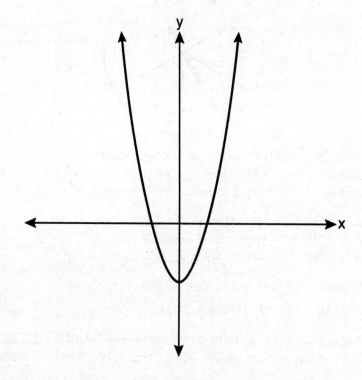

(1) absolute value   (2) exponential   (3) linear   (4) quadratic

12. Which equation represents a line parallel to the *y*-axis?
    (1) $y = x$ (2) $y = 3$ (3) $x = -y$ (4) $x = -4$

13. Melissa graphed the equation $y = x^2$ and Dave graphed the equation $y = -3x^2$ on the same coordinate grid. What is the relationship between the graphs that Melissa and Dave drew?
    (1) Dave's graph is wider and opens in the opposite direction from Melissa's graph.
    (2) Dave's graph is narrower and opens in the opposite direction from Melissa's graph.
    (3) Dave's graph is wider and is three units below Melissa's graph.
    (4) Dave's graph is narrower and is three units to the left of Melissa's graph.

14. In right triangle *ABC* shown below, $AB = 18.3$ and $BC = 11.2$.

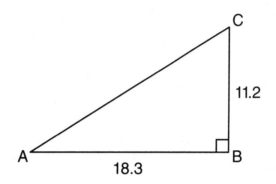

    What is the measure of $\angle A$, to the *nearest tenth of a degree*?
    (1) 31.5   (2) 37.7   (3) 52.3   (4) 58.5

15. The maximum height and speed of various roller coasters in North America are shown in the table below.

Maximum Speed, in mph, (x)	45	50	54	60	65	70
Maximum Height, in feet, (y)	63	80	105	118	141	107

Which graph represents a correct scatter plot of the data?

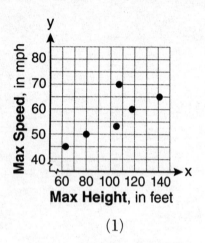

(1)

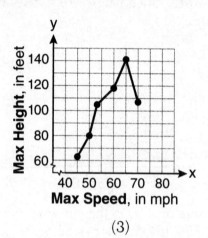

(3)

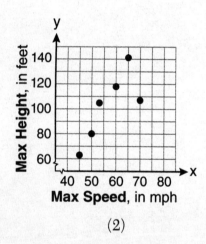

(2)

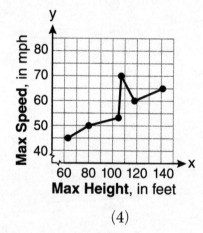

(4)

16. Which set of ordered pairs represents a function?
   (1) {(0, 4), (2, 4), (2, 5)}   (3) {(4, 1), (6, 2), (6, 3), (5, 0)}
   (2) {(6, 0), (5, 0), (4, 0)}   (4) {(0, 4), (1, 4), (0, 5), (1, 5)}

17. A hiker walked 12.8 miles from 9:00 a.m. to noon. He walked an additional 17.2 miles from 1:00 p.m. to 6:00 p.m. What is his average rate for the entire walk, in miles per hour?
   (1) 3.75   (2) 3.86   (3) 4.27   (4) 7.71

18. Which ordered pair is a solution of the system of equations $y = x + 3$ and $y = x^2 - x$?
    (1) (6, 9)   (2) (3, 6)   (3) (3, –1)   (4) (2, 5)

19. Which verbal expression can be represented by $2(x - 5)$?
    (1) 5 less than 2 times x
    (2) 2 multiplied by x less than 5
    (3) twice the difference of x and 5
    (4) the product of 2 and x, decreased by 5

20. The dimensions of a rectangle are measured to be 12.2 inches by 11.8 inches. The actual dimensions are 12.3 inches by 11.9 inches. What is the relative error, to the *nearest ten-thousandth*, in calculating the area of the rectangle?
    (1) 0.0168   (2) 0.0167   (3) 0.0165   (4) 0.0164

21. An example of an algebraic expression is
    (1) $y = mx + b$
    (2) $3x + 4y - 7$
    (3) $2x + 3y \leq 18$
    (4) $(x + y)(x - y) = 25$

22. A study showed that a decrease in the cost of carrots led to an increase in the number of carrots sold. Which statement best describes this relationship?
    (1) positive correlation and a causal relationship
    (2) negative correlation and a causal relationship
    (3) positive correlation and not a causal relationship
    (4) negative correlation and not a causal relationship

23. Given: $A = \{3, 6, 9, 12, 15\}$
              $B = \{2, 4, 6, 8, 10, 12\}$

    What is the union of sets A and B?
    (1) {6}
    (2) {6, 12}
    (3) {2, 3, 4, 8, 9, 10, 15}
    (4) {2, 3, 4, 6, 8, 9, 10, 12, 15}

24. The value of a car purchased for $20,000 decreases at a rate of 12% per year. What will be the value of the car after 3 years?
    (1) $12,800.00   (2) $13,629.44   (3) $17,600.00   (4) $28,098.56

25. For which set of values of x is the algebraic expression $\dfrac{x^2 - 16}{x^2 - 4x - 12}$ undefined?

    (1) {–6, 2}   (2) {–4, 3}   (3) {–4, 4}   (4) {–2, 6}

26. Michael is 25 years younger than his father. The sum of their ages is 53. What is Michael's age?
    (1) 14   (2) 25   (3) 28   (4) 39

27. What is the product of (6×10^3), (4.6×10^5), and (2×10^{-2}) expressed in scientific notation?
    (1) 55.2×10^6 (2) 5.52×10^7 (3) 55.2×10^7 (4) 5.52×10^{10}

28. Which notation describes $\{1, 2, 3\}$?

    (1) $\{x|1 \leq x < 3,$ where x is an integer$\}$

    (2) $\{x|0 < x \leq 3,$ where x is an integer$\}$

    (3) $\{x|1 < x < 3,$ where x is an integer$\}$

    (4) $\{x|0 \leq x \leq 3,$ where x is an integer$\}$

29. What is $\dfrac{7}{12x} - \dfrac{y}{6x^2}$ expressed in simplest form?

    (1) $\dfrac{7-y}{6x}$ (2) $\dfrac{7-y}{12x-6x^2}$ (3) $-\dfrac{7y}{12x^2}$ (4) $\dfrac{7x-2y}{12x^2}$

30. When $5x + 4y$ is subtracted from $5x - 4y$, the difference is

    (1) 0 (2) $10x$ (3) $8y$ (4) $-8y$

Part II

Answer all 3 questions in this part. Each correct answer will receive 2 credits. Clearly indicate the necessary steps, including appropriate formula substitutions, diagrams, graphs, charts, etc. For all questions in this part, a correct numerical answer with no work shown will receive only 1 credit. [6]

31. The area of a rectangle is represented by $x^2 - 5x - 24$. If the width of the rectangle is represented by $x - 8$, express the length of the rectangle as a binomial.

32. A method for solving $5(x - 2) - 2(x - 5) = 9$ is shown below. Identify the property used to obtain *each* of the two indicated steps.

      $5(x - 2) - 2(x - 5) = 9$

  (1) $5x - 10 - 2x + 10 = 9$ (1) _____

  (2) $5x - 2x - 10 + 10 = 9$ (2) _____

              $3x + 0 = 9$

               $3x = 9$

                 $x = 3$

33. State the equation of the axis of symmetry and the coordinates of the vertex of the parabola graphed below.

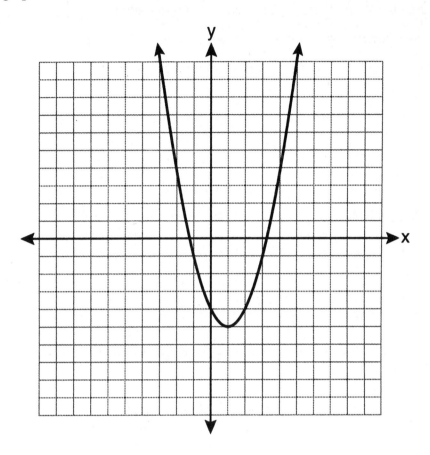

Part III

Answer all 3 questions in this part. Each correct answer will receive 3 credits. Clearly indicate the necessary steps, including appropriate formula substitutions, diagrams, graphs, charts, etc. For all questions in this part, a correct numerical answer with no work shown will receive only 1 credit. [9]

34. Given the following list of students' scores on a quiz: 5, 12, 7, 15, 20, 14, 7

    Determine the median of these scores.

    Determine the mode of these scores.

    The teacher decides to adjust these scores by adding three points to each score. Explain the effect, if any, this will have on the median and mode of these scores.

35. Chelsea has $45 to spend at the fair. She spends $20 on admission and $15 on snacks. She wants to play a game that costs $0.65 per game. Write an inequality to find the maximum number of times, x, Chelsea can play the game.

    Using this inequality, determine the maximum number of times she can play the game.

36. A plastic storage box in the shape of a rectangular prism has a length of $x + 3$, a width of $x - 4$, and a height of 5.

    Represent the surface area of the box as a trinomial in terms of x.

Part IV

Answer all 3 questions in this part. Each correct answer will receive 4 credits. Clearly indicate the necessary steps, including appropriate formula substitutions, diagrams, graphs, charts, etc. For all questions in this part, a correct numerical answer with no work shown will receive only 1 credit. [12]

37. Solve algebraically for x: $\dfrac{3}{4} = \dfrac{-(x + 11)}{4x} + \dfrac{1}{2x}$

38. An outfit Jennifer wears to school consists of a top, a bottom, and shoes. Possible choices are listed below.

    Tops: T-shirt, blouse, sweater
    Bottoms: jeans, skirt, capris
    Shoes: flip-flops, sneakers

    List the sample space or draw a tree diagram to represent all possible outfits consisting of one type of top, one type of bottom, and one pair of shoes.

    Determine how many different outfits contain jeans and flip-flops.

    Determine how many different outfits do *not* include a sweater.

39. Solve the following system of inequalities graphically on the set of axes below.

$$3x + y < 7$$

$$y \geq \frac{2}{3}x - 4$$

State the coordinates of a point in the solution set.

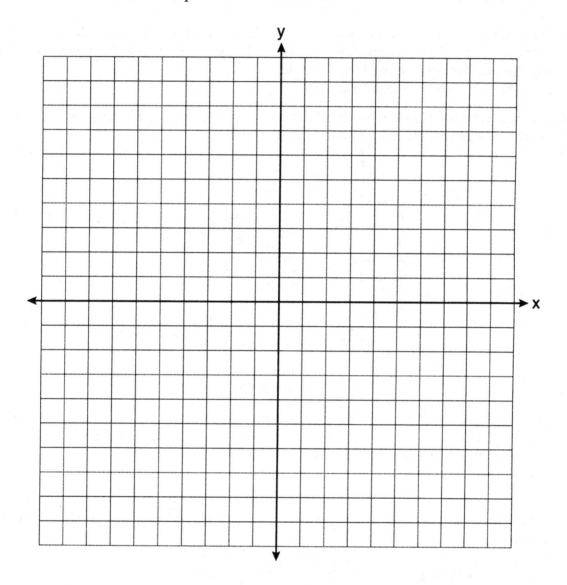

Part I

Answer all 30 questions in this part. Each correct answer will receive 2 credits. No partial credit will be allowed. For each question, write on the separate answer sheet the numeral preceding the word or expression that best completes the statement or answers the question. [60]

1. The number of calories burned while jogging varies directly with the number of minutes spent jogging. If George burns 150 calories by jogging for 20 minutes, how many calories does he burn by jogging for 30 minutes?
   (1) 100   (2) 180   (3) 200   (4) 225

2. The scatter plot below represents the relationship between the number of peanuts a student eats and the student's bowling score.

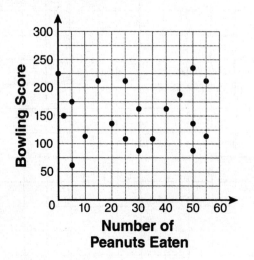

   Which conclusion about the scatter plot is valid?
   (1) There is almost no relationship between eating peanuts and bowling scores.
   (2) Students who eat more peanuts have higher bowling scores.
   (3) Students who eat more peanuts have lower bowling scores.
   (4) No bowlers eat peanuts.

3. If the universal set is {pennies, nickels, dimes, quarters}, what is the complement of the set {nickels}?
   (1) { }   (3) {pennies, dimes, quarters}
   (2) {pennies, quarters}   (4) {pennies, nickels, dimes, quarters}

4. Which situation does *not* describe a causal relationship?
   (1) The higher the volume on a radio, the louder the sound will be.
   (2) The faster a student types a research paper, the more pages the paper will have.
   (3) The shorter the distance driven, the less gasoline that will be used.
   (4) The slower the pace of a runner, the longer it will take the runner to finish the race.

5. A cylinder has a diameter of 10 inches and a height of 2.3 inches. What is the volume of this cylinder, to the *nearest tenth of a cubic inch*?
   (1) 72.3   (2) 83.1   (3) 180.6   94) 722.6

6. Based on the box-and-whisker plot below, which statement is *false*?

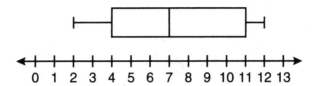

   (1) The median is 7.   (3) The first quartile is 4.
   (2) The range is 12.   (4) The third quartile is 11.

7. The ninth grade class at a local high school needs to purchase a park permit for $250.00 for their upcoming class picnic. Each ninth grader attending the picnic pays $0.75. Each guest pays $1.25. If 200 ninth graders attend the picnic, which inequality can be used to determine the number of guests, x, needed to cover the cost of the permit?
   (1) $0.75x - (1.25)(200) \geq 250.00$ (3) $(0.75)(200) - 1.25x \geq 250.00$
   (2) $0.75x + (1.25)(200) \geq 250.00$ (4) $(0.75)(200) + 1.25x \geq 250.00$

8. Which equation represents the line that passes through the point (1, 5) and has a slope of –2?
   (1) $y = -2x + 7$ (3) $y = 2x - 9$
   (2) $y = -2x + 11$ (4) $y = 2x + 3$

9. What is the solution of the system of equations $2x - 5y = 11$ and $-2x + 3y = -9$?
   (1) (–3, –1)   (2) (–1, 3)   (3) (3, –1)   (4) (3, 1)

10. Which algebraic expression represents 15 less than x divided by 9?
   (1) $\frac{x}{9} - 15$ (2) $9x - 15$ (3) $15 - \frac{x}{9}$ (4) $15 - 9x$

11. What are the vertex and the axis of symmetry of the parabola shown in the graph below?

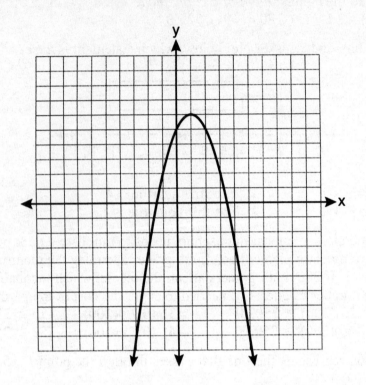

    (1) vertex: (1, 6); axis of symmetry: $y = 1$
    (2) vertex: (1, 6); axis of symmetry: $x = 1$
    (3) vertex: (6, 1); axis of symmetry: $y = 1$
    (4) vertex: (6, 1); axis of symmetry: $x = 1$

12. The diagram below shows right triangle *ABC*.

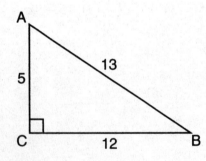

    Which ratio represents the tangent of $\angle ABC$?

    (1) $\dfrac{5}{13}$ (2) $\dfrac{5}{12}$ (3) $\dfrac{12}{13}$ (4) $\dfrac{12}{5}$

13 What is the value of the expression $-3x^2y + 4x$ when $x = -4$ and $y = 2$?
    (1) -112 (2) -80 (3) 80 (4) 272

14. Which expression is equivalent to $-3x(x-4) - 2x(x+3)$?
    (1) $-x^2 - 1$ (2) $-x^2 + 18x$ (3) $-5x^2 - 6x$ (4) $-5x^2 + 6x$

15. The data in the table below are graphed, and the slope is examined.

x	y
0.5	9.0
1	8.75
1.5	8.5
2	8.25
2.5	8.0

    The rate of change represented in this table can be described as
    (1) negative   (2) positive   (3) undefined   (4) zero

16. The length of a rectangle is 3 inches more than its width. The area of the rectangle is 40 square inches. What is the length, in inches, of the rectangle?
    (1) 5   (2) 8   (3) 8.5   (4) 11.5

17. In interval notation, the set of all real numbers greater than -6 and less than or equal to 14 is represented by
    (1) $(-6, 14)$ (2) $[-6, 14)$ (3) $(-6, 14]$ (4) $[-6, 14]$

18. Which equation represents a quadratic function?
    (1) $y = x + 2$ (2) $y = |x + 2|$ (3) $y = x^2$ (4) $y = 2^x$

19. Ben has four more than twice as many CDs as Jake. If they have a total of 31 CDs, how many CDs does Jake have?
    (1) 9   (2) 13   (3) 14   (4) 22

20. What are the roots of the equation $x^2 - 5x + 6 = 0$?
    (1) 1 and -6 (3) -1 and 6
    (2) 2 and 3   (4) -2 and -3

21. What is the solution of the inequality $-6x - 17 \geq 8x + 25$?
    (1) $x \geq 3$ (2) $x \leq 3$ (3) $x \geq -3$ (4) $x \leq -3$

22. Which set of data can be classified as qualitative?
    (1) scores of students in an algebra class
    (2) ages of students in a biology class
    (3) number of students in history classes
    (4) eye colors of students in an economics class

23. Jack wants to replace the flooring in his rectangular kitchen. He calculates the area of the floor to be 12.8 square meters. The actual area of the floor is 13.5 square meters. What is the relative error in calculating the area of the floor, to the *nearest thousandth*?
    (1) 0.051   (2) 0.052   (3) 0.054   (4) 0.055

24. The current student population of the Brentwood Student Center is 2,000. The enrollment at the center increases at a rate of 4% each year. To the *nearest whole number*, what will the student population be closest to in 3 years?
    (1) 2,240   (2) 2,250   (3) 5,488   (4) 6,240

25. Maria has a set of 10 index cards labeled with the digits 0 through 9. She puts them in a bag and selects one at random. The outcome that is most likely to occur is selecting
    (1) an odd number   (3) a number that is at most 5
    (2) a prime number   (4) a number that is divisible by 3

26. A right triangle contains a 38° angle whose adjacent side measures 10 centimeters. What is the length of the hypotenuse, to the *nearest hundredth of a centimeter*?
    (1) 7.88   (2) 12.69   (3) 12.80   (4) 16.24

27. Which ordered pair is in the solution set of the system of inequalities shown in the graph below?

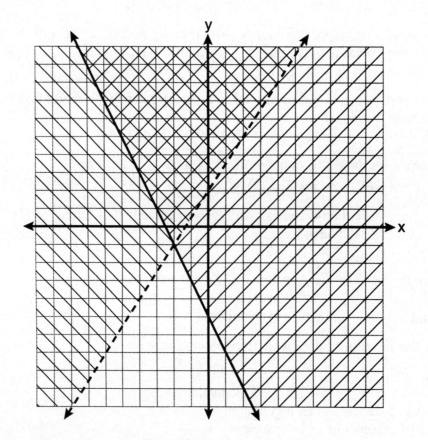

(1) (−2, −1)   (2) (−2, 2)   (3) (−2, −4)   (4) (2, −2)

28. A garden is in the shape of an isosceles trapezoid and a semicircle, as shown in the diagram below. A fence will be put around the perimeter of the entire garden.

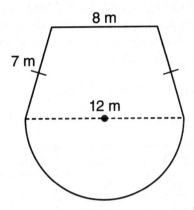

Which expression represents the length of fencing, in meters, that will be needed?
(1) $22 + 6\pi$　(2) $22 + 12\pi$　(3) $15 + 6\pi$　(4) $15 + 12\pi$

29. Which expression represents $36x^2 - 100y^6$ factored completely?
(1) $2(9x + 25y^3)(9x - 25y^3)$　　　　(3) $(6x + 10y^3)(6x - 10y^3)$
(2) $4(3x + 5y^3)(3x - 5y^3)$　　　　(4) $(18x + 50y^3)(18x - 50y^3)$

30. What is the quotient of $\dfrac{x}{x+4}$ divided by $\dfrac{2x}{x^2-16}$?

(1) $\dfrac{2}{x-4}$　(2) $\dfrac{2x^2}{x-4}$　(3) $\dfrac{2x^2}{x^2-16}$　(4) $\dfrac{x-4}{2}$

Part II

Answer all 3 questions in this part. Each correct answer will receive 2 credits. Clearly indicate the necessary steps, including appropriate formula substitutions, diagrams, graphs, charts, etc. For all questions in this part, a correct numerical answer with no work shown will receive only 1 credit. All answers should be written in pen, except for graphs and drawings, which should be done in pencil.   [6]

31. Solve for c in terms of a and b: $bc + ac = ab$

32. Ms. Hopkins recorded her students' final exam scores in the frequency table below.

Interval	Tally	Frequency
61–70	ﬀﬀ	5
71–80	IIII	4
81–90	ﬀﬀ IIII	9
91–100	ﬀﬀ I	6

On the grid below, construct a frequency histogram based on the table.

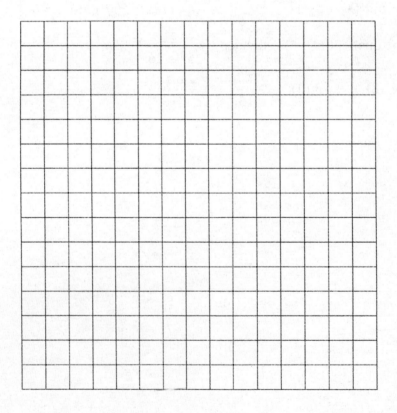

33. Mrs. Chen owns two pieces of property. The areas of the properties are 77,120 square feet and 33,500 square feet.

$$43{,}560 \text{ square feet} = 1 \text{ acre}$$

Find the total number of acres Mrs. Chen owns, to the *nearest hundredth of an acre.*

Part III

Answer all 3 questions in this part. Each correct answer will receive 3 credits. Clearly indicate the necessary steps, including appropriate formula substitutions, diagrams, graphs, charts, etc. For all questions in this part, a correct numerical answer with no work shown will receive only 1 credit. All answers should be written in pen, except for graphs and drawings, which should be done in pencil.   [9]

34. On the set of axes below, graph and label the equation $y = |x|$ and $y = 3|x|$ for the interval $-3 \le x \le 3$.

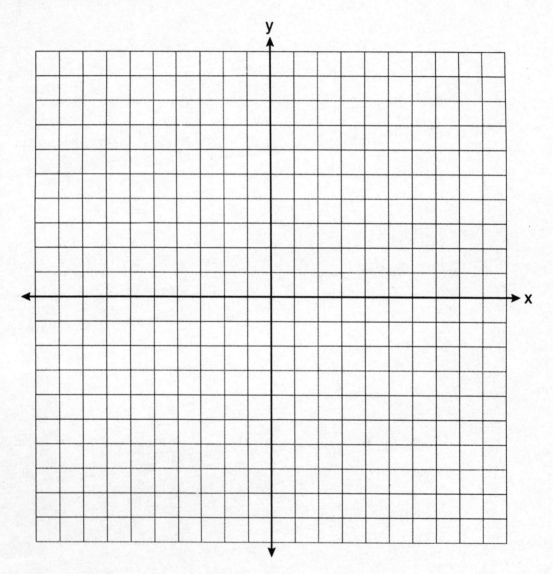

Explain how changing the coefficient of the absolute value from 1 to 3 affects the graph.

35. A trapezoid is shown below.

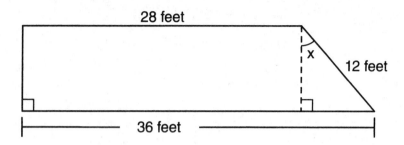

Calculate the measure of angle *x*, to the *nearest tenth of a degree.*

36. Express $\dfrac{16\sqrt{21}}{2\sqrt{7}} - 5\sqrt{12}$ in simplest radical form.

Part IV

Answer all 3 questions in this part. Each correct answer will receive 4 credits. Clearly indicate the necessary steps, including appropriate formula substitutions, diagrams, graphs, charts, etc. For all questions in this part, a correct numerical answer with no work shown will receive only 1 credit. All answers should be written in pen, except for graphs and drawings, which should be done in pencil. [12]

37. Vince buys a box of candy that consists of six chocolate pieces, four fruit-flavored pieces, and two mint pieces. He selects three pieces of candy at random, without replacement.

Calculate the probability that the first piece selected will be fruit flavored and the other two will be mint.

Calculate the probability that all three pieces selected will be the same type of candy.

38. On the set of axes below, solve the following system of equations graphically and state the coordinates of *all* points in the solution set.

$$y = -x^2 + 6x - 3$$

$$x + y = 7$$

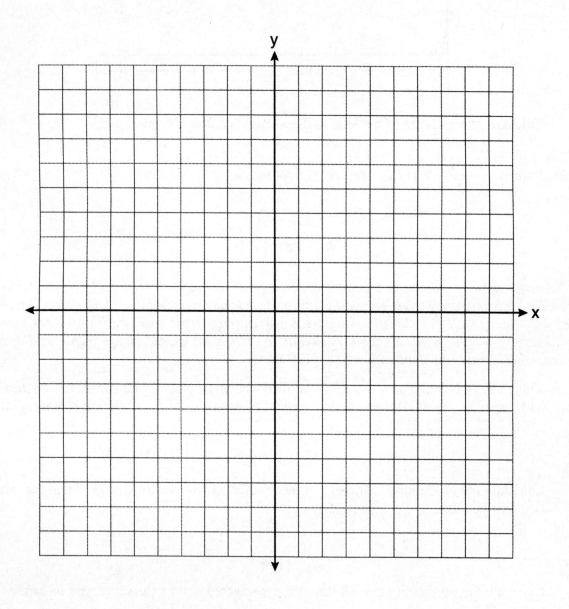

39. Solve for *m*: $\dfrac{m}{5} + \dfrac{3(m-1)}{2} = 2(m-3)$

Part I

Answer all 30 questions in this part. Each correct answer will receive 2 credits. No partial credit will be allowed. For each question, write on the separate answer sheet the numeral preceding the word or expression that best completes the statement or answers the question. [60]

1. Which expression is equivalent to $64 - x^2$?
   (1) $(8 - x)(8 - x)$ (3) $(x - 8)(x - 8)$
   (2) $(8 - x)(8 + x)$ (4) $(x - 8)(x + 8)$

2. Mr. Smith invested $2,500 in a savings account that earns 3% interest compounded annually. He made no additional deposits or withdrawals. Which expression can be used to determine the number of dollars in this account at the end of 4 years?
   (1) $2500(1 + 0.03)^4$ (3) $2500(1 + 0.04)^3$
   (2) $2500(1 + 0.3)^4$ (4) $2500(1 + 0.4)^3$

3. What is $2\sqrt{45}$ expressed in simplest radical form?

   (1) $3\sqrt{5}$ (2) $5\sqrt{5}$ (3) $6\sqrt{5}$ (4) $18\sqrt{5}$

4. Which graph does *not* represent a function?

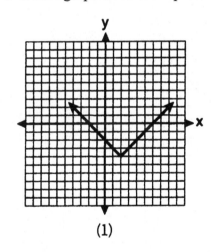

(1)

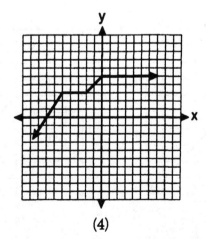

(3)

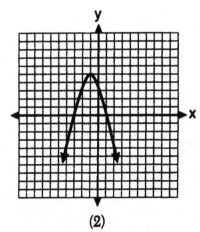

(2)

(4)

5. Timmy bought a skateboard and two helmets for a total of *d* dollars. If each helmet cost *h* dollars, the cost of the skateboard could be represented by

(1) $2dh$ (2) $\dfrac{dh}{2}$ (3) $d - 2h$ (4) $d - \dfrac{h}{2}$

6. The graph of $y = |x + 2|$ is shown below.

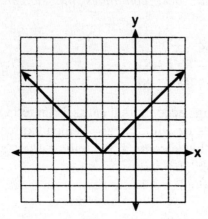

Which graph represents $y = -|x + 2|$?

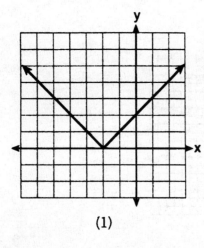

(1)

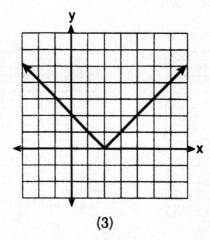

(3)

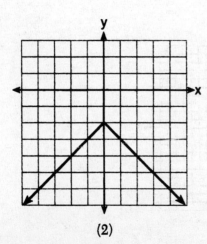

(2)

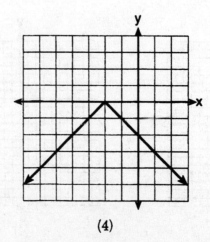

(4)

7. Two equations were graphed on the set of axes below.

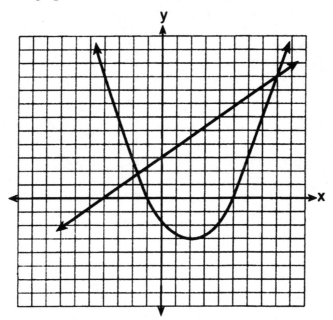

Which point is a solution of the system of equations shown on the graph?
(1) $(8, 9)$ (2) $(5, 0)$ (3) $(0, 3)$ (4) $(2, -3)$

8. Byron is 3 years older than Doug. The product of their ages is 40. How old is Doug?
(1) 10   (2) 8   (3) 5   (4) 4

9. The actual dimensions of a rectangle are 2.6 cm by 6.9 cm. Andy measures the sides as 2.5 cm by 6.8 cm. In calculating the area, what is the relative error, to the *nearest thousandth*?
(1) 0.055   (2) 0.052   (3) 0.022   (4) 0.021

10. Which graph represents the inequality $y > 3$?

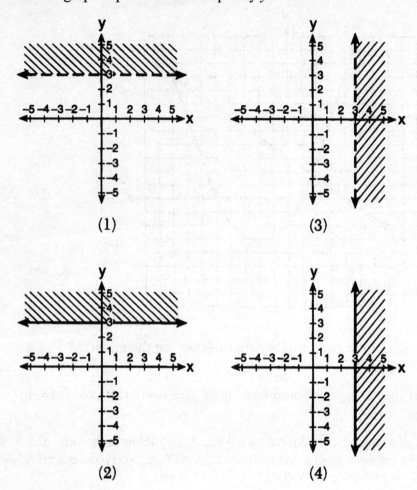

(1)   (3)

(2)   (4)

11. Which set of data can be classified as quantitative?
    (1) first names of students in a chess club
    (2) ages of students in a government class
    (3) hair colors of students in a debate club
    (4) favorite sports of students in a gym class

12. Three fair coins are tossed. What is the probability that two heads and one tail appear?

    (1) $\frac{1}{8}$ (2) $\frac{3}{8}$ (3) $\frac{3}{6}$ (4) $\frac{2}{3}$

13. What is the sum of $-3x^2 - 7x + 9$ and $-5x^2 + 6x - 4$?
    (1) $-8x^2 - x + 5$ (3) $-8x^2 - 13x + 13$
    (2) $-8x^4 - x + 5$ (4) $-8x^4 - 13x^2 + 13$

14. For which values of x is the fraction $\dfrac{x^2 + x - 6}{x^2 + 5x - 6}$ undefined?

    (1) 1 and -6 (2) 2 and -3 (3) 3 and -2 (4) 6 and -1

15. What is the slope of the line that passes through the points $(2, -3)$ and $(5, 1)$?

   (1) $-\dfrac{2}{3}$ (2) $\dfrac{2}{3}$ (3) $-\dfrac{4}{3}$ (4) $\dfrac{4}{3}$

16. The expression $\dfrac{(4x^3)^2}{2x}$ is equivalent to

   (1) $4x^4$ (2) $4x^5$ (3) $8x^4$ (4) $8x^5$

17. In the diagram below, circle O is inscribed in square $ABCD$. The square has an area of 36.

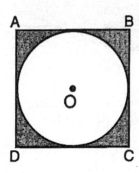

   What is the area of the circle?
   (1) 9π (2) 6π (3) 3π (4) 36π

18. Which point lies on the graph represented by the equation $3y + 2x = 8$?
   (1) $(-2, 7)$ (2) $(0, 4)$ (3) $(2, 4)$ (4) $(7, -2)$

19. The equation of the axis of symmetry of the graph of $y = 2x^2 - 3x + 7$ is

   (1) $x = \dfrac{3}{4}$ (2) $y = \dfrac{3}{4}$ (3) $x = \dfrac{3}{2}$ (4) $y = \dfrac{3}{2}$

20. The box-and-whisker plot below represents the ages of 12 people.

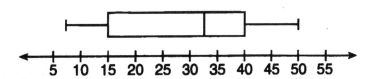

   What percentage of these people are age 15 or older?
   (1) 25   (2) 35   (3) 75   (4) 85

21. Campsite A and campsite B are located directly opposite each other on the shores of Lake Omega, as shown in the diagram below. The campsites form a right triangle with Sam's position, S. The distance from campsite B to Sam's position is 1,300 yards, and campsite A is 1,700 yards from his position.

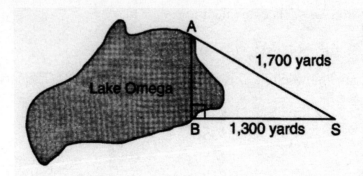

What is the distance from campsite A to campsite B, to the *nearest yard*?
(1) 1,095   (2) 1,096   (3) 2,140   (4) 2,141

22. Which set builder notation represents $\{-2, -1, 0, 1, 2, 3\}$?
(1) $\{x | -3 \leq x \leq 3,$ where x is an integer$\}$
(2) $\{x | -3 < x \leq 4,$ where x is an integer$\}$
(3) $\{x | -2 < x < 3,$ where x is an integer$\}$
(4) $\{x | -2 \leq x < 4,$ where x is an integer$\}$

23. The roots of the equation $3x^2 - 27x = 0$ are
(1) 0 and 9   (2) 0 and −9   (3) 0 and 3   (4) 0 and −3

24. Which equation is an example of the use of the associative property of addition?
(1) $x + 7 = 7 + x$ (3) $(x + y) + 3 = x + (y + 3)$
(2) $3(x + y) = 3x + 3y$ (4) $3 + (x + y) = (x + y) + 3$

25. Given:

$A = \{2, 4, 5, 7, 8\}$

$B = \{3, 5, 8, 9\}$

What is $A \cup B$?
(1) $\{5\}$ (2) $\{5, 8\}$ (3) $\{2, 3, 4, 7. 9\}$ (4) $\{2, 3, 4, 5, 7. 8. 9\}$

26. The diagram below shows right triangle *LMP*.

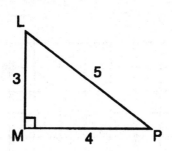

Which ratio represents the tangent of $\angle PLM$?

(1) $\dfrac{3}{4}$ (2) $\dfrac{3}{5}$ (3) $\dfrac{4}{3}$ (4) $\dfrac{5}{4}$

27. Mr. Stanton asked his students to write an algebraic expression on a piece of paper. He chose four students to go to the board and write their expression.

Robert wrote: $4(2x + 5) \geq 17$

Meredith wrote: $3y - 7 + 11z$

Steven wrote: $9w + 2 = 20$

Cynthia wrote: $8 + 10 - 4 = 14$

Which student wrote an algebraic expression?
(1) Robert   (2) Meredith   (3) Steven   (4) Cynthia

28. If $s = \dfrac{2x + t}{r}$, then x equals

(1) $\dfrac{rs - t}{2}$ (2) $\dfrac{rs + 1}{2}$ (3) $2rs - t$ (4) $rs - 2t$

29. A scatter plot was constructed on the graph below and a line of best fit was drawn.

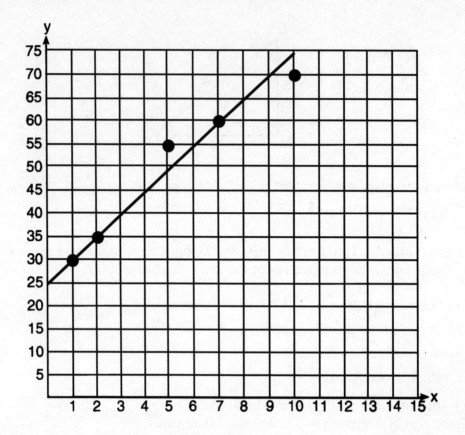

What is the equation of this line of best fit?

(1) $y = x + 5$ (2) $y = x + 25$ (3) $y = 5x + 5$ (4) $y = 5x + 25$

30. What is the sum of $\dfrac{2y}{y+5}$ and $\dfrac{10}{y+5}$ expressed in simplest form?

(1) 1   (2) 2   (3) $\dfrac{12y}{y+5}$ (4) $\dfrac{2y+10}{y+5}$

Part II

Answer all 3 questions in this part. Each correct answer will receive 2 credits. Clearly indicate the necessary steps, including appropriate formula substitutions, diagrams, graphs, charts, etc. For all questions in this part, a correct numerical answer with no work shown will receive only 1 credit. All answers should be written in pen, except for graphs and drawings, which should be done in pencil. [6]

31. The length and width of the base of a rectangular prism are 5.5 cm and 3 cm. The height of the prism is 6.75 cm. Find the *exact* value of the surface area of the prism, in square centimeters.

32. Casey purchased a pack of assorted flower seeds and planted them in her garden. When the first 25 flowers bloomed, 11 were white, 5 were red, 3 were blue, and the rest were yellow. Find the empirical probability that a flower that blooms will be yellow.

33. Express in simplest form: $\dfrac{x^2 - 1}{x^2 + 3x + 2}$

Part III

Answer all 3 questions in this part. Each correct answer will receive 3 credits. Clearly indicate the necessary steps, including appropriate formula substitutions, diagrams, graphs, charts, etc. For all questions in this part, a correct numerical answer with no work shown will receive only 1 credit. All answers should be written in pen, except for graphs and drawings, which should be done in pencil. [9]

34. Solve algebraically for x: $2(x - 4) \geq \frac{1}{2}(5 - 3x)$

35. On the set of axes below, solve the following system of equations graphically. State the coordinates of the solution.

$$y = 4x - 1$$
$$2x + y = 5$$

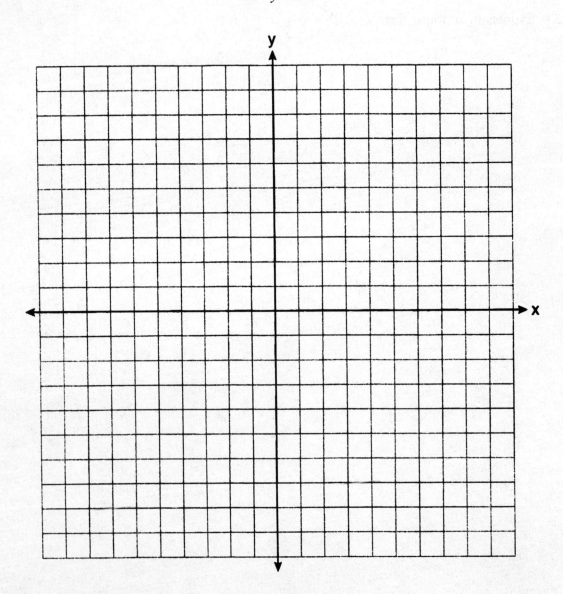

36. A turtle and a rabbit are in a race to see who is first to reach a point 100 feet away. The turtle travels at a constant speed of 20 feet per minute for the entire 100 feet. The rabbit travels at a constant speed of 40 feet per minute for the first 50 feet, stops for 3 minutes, and then continues at a constant speed of 40 feet per minute for the last 50 feet.

Determine which animal won the race and by how much time.

Part IV

Answer all 3 questions in this part. Each correct answer will receive 4 credits. Clearly indicate the necessary steps, including appropriate formula substitutions, diagrams, graphs, charts, etc. For all questions in this part, a correct numerical answer with no work shown will receive only 1 credit. All answers should be written in pen, except for graphs and drawings, which should be done in pencil. [12]

37. The sum of three consecutive odd integers is 18 less than five times the middle number. Find the three integers. [Only an algebraic solution can receive full credit.]

38. A sandwich consists of one type of bread, one type of meat, and one type of cheese. The possible choices are listed below.

        Bread: white, rye

        Meat: ham, turkey, beef

        Cheese: American, Swiss

Draw a tree diagram or list a sample space of all the possible different sandwiches consisting of one type of bread, one type of meat, and one type of cheese.

Determine the number of sandwiches that will *not* include turkey.

Determine the number of sandwiches that will include rye bread and Swiss cheese.

39. Shana wants to buy a new bicycle that has a retail price of $259.99. She knows that it will be on sale next week for 30% off the retail price. If the tax rate is 7%, find the total amount, to the *nearest cent*, that she will save by waiting until next week.

Part I

Answer all 30 questions in this part. Each correct answer will receive 2 credits. No partial credit will be allowed. For each question, write on the separate answer sheet the numeral preceding the word or expression that best completes the statement or answers the question. [60]

1. In a baseball game, the ball traveled 350.7 feet in 4.2 seconds. What was the average speed of the ball, in feet per second?
(1) 83.5   (2) 177.5   (3) 354.9   (4) 1,472.9

2. A survey is being conducted to determine if a cable company should add another sports channel to their schedule. Which random survey would be the *least* biased?
(1) surveying 30 men at a gym
(2) surveying 45 people at a mall
(3) surveying 50 fans at a football game
(4) surveying 20 members of a high school soccer team

3. The quotient of $\dfrac{8x^5 - 2x^4 + 4x^3 - 6x^2}{2x^2}$ is

(1) $16x^7 - 4x^6 + 8x^5 - 12x^4$ (3) $4x^3 - x^2 + 2x - 3x$
(2) $4x^7 - x^6 + 2x^5 - 3x^4$ (4) $4x^3 - x^2 + 2x - 3$

4. Marcy determined that her father's age is four less than three times her age. If x represents Marcy's age, which expression represents her father's age?
(1) $3x - 4$ (2) $3(x - 4)$ (3) $4x - 3$ (4) $4 - 3x$

5. A set of data is graphed on the scatter plot to the right.

This scatter plot shows
(1) no correlation
(2) positive correlation
(3) negative correlation
(4) undefined correlation

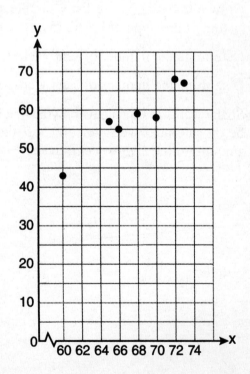

6. Which situation is an example of bivariate data?
   (1) the number of pizzas Tanya eats during her years in high school
   (2) the number times Ezra puts air in his bicycle tires during the summer
   (3) the number of home runs Elias hits per game and the number of hours he practices baseball
   (4) the number of hours Nellie studies for her mathematics tests during the first half of the school year

7. Brianna's score on a national math assessment exceeded the scores of 95,000 of the 125,000 students who took the assessment. What was her percentile rank?
   (1) 6 (2) 24 (3) 31 (4) 76

8. If $A = \{0, 1, 3, 4, 6, 7\}$, $B = \{0, 2, 3, 5, 6\}$, and $C = \{0, 1, 4, 6, 7\}$, then $A \cap B \cap C$ is
   (1) $\{0, 1, 2, 3, 4, 5, 6, 7\}$ (2) $\{0, 3, 6\}$ (3) $\{0, 6\}$ (4) $\{0\}$

9. Which graph represents a function?

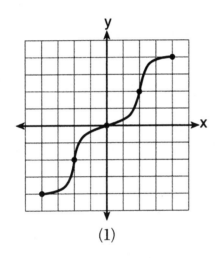

(1)

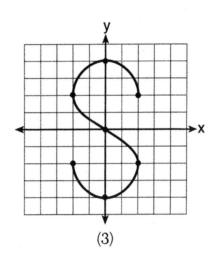

(3)

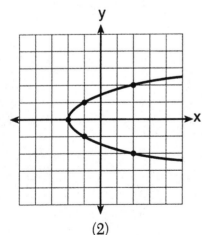

(2)

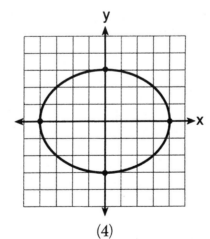

(4)

10. What is the product of $(3x + 2)$ and $(x - 7)$?
    (1) $3x^2 - 14$ (2) $3x^2 - 5x - 14$ (3) $3x^2 - 19x - 14$ (4) $3x^2 - 23x - 14$

11. If five times a number is less than 55, what is the greatest possible integer value of the number?
    (1) 12   (2) 11   (3) 10   (4) 9

12. The line represented by the equation $2y - 3x = 4$ has a slope of

    (1) $-\dfrac{3}{2}$ (2) 2   (3) 3   (4) $\dfrac{3}{2}$

13. What is the solution set of the system of equations $x + y = 5$ and $y = x^2 - 25$?
    (1) $\{(0, 5), (11, -6)\}$ (3) $\{(-5, 0), (6, 11)\}$
    (2) $\{(5, 0), (-6, 11)\}$ (4) $\{(-5, 10), (6, -1)\}$

14. What is the vertex of the parabola represented by the equation $y = -2x^2 + 24x - 100$?
    (1) $x = -6$ (2) $x = 6$ (3) $(6, -28)$ (4) $(-6, -316)$

15. If $k = am + 3mx$, the value of m in terms of a, k, and x can be expressed as

    (1) $\dfrac{k}{a + 3x}$ (2) $\dfrac{k - 3mx}{a}$ (3) $\dfrac{k - am}{3x}$ (4) $\dfrac{k - a}{3x}$

16. Which expression represents $\dfrac{x^2 - 3x - 10}{x^2 - 25}$ in simplest form?

    (1) $\dfrac{2}{5}$ (2) $\dfrac{x + 2}{x + 5}$ (3) $\dfrac{x - 2}{x - 5}$ (4) $\dfrac{-3x - 10}{-25}$

17. Which interval notation describes the set $S = \{x \mid 1 \le x < 10\}$?
    (1) $[1, 10]$ (2) $(1, 10]$ (3) $[1, 10)$ (4) $(1, 10)$

18. The bull's-eye of a dartboard has a radius of 2 inches and the entire board has a radius of 9 inches, as shown in the diagram at the right.

    If the dart is thrown and hits the board, what is the probability that the dart will land in the bull's-eye?

    (1) $\dfrac{2}{9}$ (2) $\dfrac{7}{9}$ (3) $\dfrac{4}{81}$ (4) $\dfrac{49}{81}$

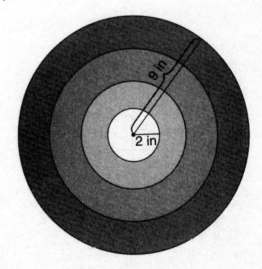

19. What is one-third of 3^6?
    (1) 1^2 (2) 3^2 (3) 3^5 (4) 9^6

20. The expression $\dfrac{2x + 13}{2x + 6} - \dfrac{3x - 6}{2x + 6}$ is equivalent to

    (1) $\dfrac{-x + 19}{2(x + 3)}$ (2) $\dfrac{-x + 7}{2(x + 3)}$ (3) $\dfrac{5x + 19}{2(x + 3)}$ (4) $\dfrac{5x + 7}{4x + 12}$

21. Which equation is represented by the graph below?

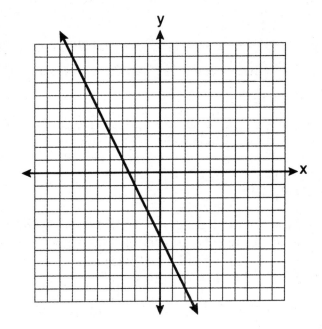

    (1) $2y + x = 10$ (2) $y - 2x = -5$ (3) $-2y = 10x - 4$ (4) $2y = -4x - 10$

22. Which coordinates represent a point in the solution set of the system of inequalities shown below?

$$y \le \frac{1}{2}x + 13$$

$$4x + 2y > 3$$

    (1) $(-4, 1)$ (2) $(-2, 2)$ (3) $(1, -4)$ (4) $(2, -2)$

23. The length of one side of a square is 13 feet. What is the length, to the *nearest foot*, of a diagonal of the square?
    (1) 13   (2) 18   (3) 19   (4) 26

24. In $\triangle ABC$, m$\angle C = 90$. If $AB = 5$ and $AC = 4$, which statement is *not* true?

    (1) $\cos A = \dfrac{4}{5}$ (3) $\sin B = \dfrac{4}{5}$

    (2) $\tan A = \dfrac{3}{4}$ (4) $\tan B = \dfrac{5}{3}$

25. If n is an odd integer, which equation can be used to find three consecutive odd integers whose sum is -3?
    (1) $n + (n + 1) + (n + 3) = -3$
    (3) $n + (n + 2) + (n + 4) = -3$
    (2) $n + (n + 1) + (n + 2) = -3$
    (4) $n + (n + 2) + (n + 3) = -3$

26. When $8x^2 + 3x + 2$ is subtracted from $9x^2 - 3x - 4$, the result is
    (1) $x^2 - 2$ (2) $17x^2 - 2$ (3) $-x^2 + 6x + 6$ (4) $x^2 - 6x - 6$

27. Factored completely, the expression $3x^3 - 33x^2 + 90x$ is equivalent to
    (1) $3x(x^2 - 33x + 90)$
    (3) $3x(x + 5)(x + 6)$
    (2) $3x(x^2 - 11x + 30)$
    (4) $3x(x - 5)(x - 6)$

28. Elizabeth is baking chocolate chip cookies. A single batch uses $\frac{3}{4}$ teaspoon of vanilla. If Elizabeth is mixing the ingredients for five batches at the same time, how many tablespoons of vanilla will she use?

$$\boxed{3 \text{ teaspoons} = 1 \text{ tablespoon}}$$

    (1) $1\frac{1}{4}$ (2) $1\frac{3}{4}$ (3) $3\frac{3}{4}$ (4) $5\frac{3}{4}$

29. A car depreciates (loses value) at a rate of 4.5% annually. Greg purchased a car for $12,500. Which equation can be used to determine the value of the car, V, after 5 years?
    (1) $V = 12{,}500(0.55)^5$
    (3) $V = 12{,}500(1.045)^5$
    (2) $V = 12{,}500(0.955)^5$
    (4) $V = 12{,}500(1.45)^5$

30. The cumulative frequency table below shows the length of time that 30 students spent text messaging on a weekend.

Minutes Used	Cumulative Frequency
31–40	2
31–50	5
31–60	10
31–70	19
31–80	30

    Which 10-minute interval contains the first quartile?
    (1) 31–40   (2) 41–50   (3) 51- 60   (4) 61–70

Part II

Answer all 3 questions in this part. Each correct answer will receive 2 credits. Clearly indicate the necessary steps, including appropriate formula substitutions, diagrams, graphs, charts, etc. For all questions in this part, a correct numerical answer with no work shown will receive only 1 credit. All answers should be written in pen, except for graphs and drawings, which should be done in pencil.   [6]

31. Solve the following system of equations algebraically for *y*:

$$2x + 2y = 9$$
$$2x - y = 3$$

32. Three storage bins contain colored blocks. Bin 1 contains 15 red and 14 blue blocks. Bin 2 contains 16 white and 15 blue blocks. Bin 3 contains 15 red and 15 white blocks. All of the blocks from the three bins are placed into one box.

    If one block is randomly selected from the box, which color block would most likely be picked? Justify your answer.

33. Students calculated the area of a playing field to be 8,100 square feet. The actual area of the field is 7,678.5 square feet. Find the relative error in the area, to the *nearest thousandth*.

Part III

Answer all 3 questions in this part. Each correct answer will receive 3 credits. Clearly indicate the necessary steps, including appropriate formula substitutions, diagrams, graphs, charts, etc. For all questions in this part, a correct numerical answer with no work shown will receive only 1 credit. All answers should be written in pen, except for graphs and drawings, which should be done in pencil. [9]

34. On the set of axes below, graph the equation $y = x^2 + 2x - 8$.

Using the graph, determine and state the roots of the equation $x^2 + 2x - 8 = 0$.

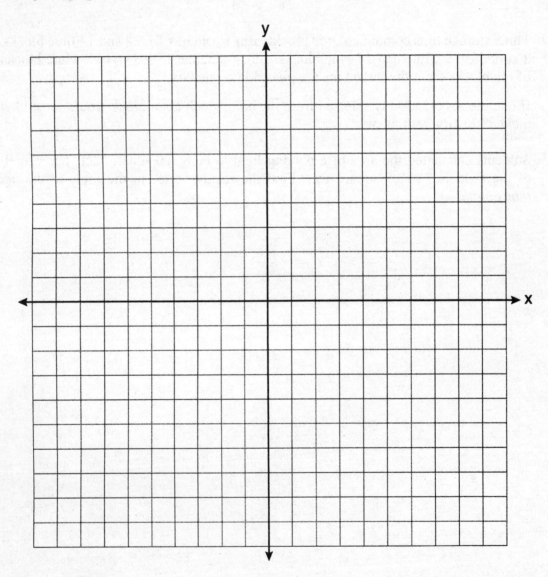

35. A 28-foot ladder is leaning against a house. The bottom of the ladder is 6 feet from the base of the house. Find the measure of the angle formed by the ladder and the ground, to the *nearest degree*.

36. Express $\dfrac{3\sqrt{75} + \sqrt{27}}{3}$ in simplest radical form.

Part IV

Answer all 3 questions in this part. Each correct answer will receive 4 credits. Clearly indicate the necessary steps, including appropriate formula substitutions, diagrams, graphs, charts, etc. For all questions in this part, a correct numerical answer with no work shown will receive only 1 credit. All answers should be written in pen, except for graphs and drawings, which should be done in pencil. [12]

37. Mike buys his ice cream packed in a rectangular prism-shaped carton, while Carol buys hers in a cylindrical-shaped carton. The dimensions of the prism are 5 inches by 3.5 inches by 7 inches. The cylinder has a diameter of 5 inches and a height of 7 inches.

    Which container holds more ice cream? Justify your answer.

    Determine, to the *nearest tenth of a cubic inch*, how much *more* ice cream the larger container holds.

38. Solve algebraically for x: $3(x + 1) - 5x = 12 - (6x - 7)$

39. A large company must chose between two types of passwords to log on to a computer. The first type is a four-letter password using any of the 26 letters of the alphabet, without repetition of letters. The second type is a six-digit password using the digits 0 through 9, with repetition of digits allowed.

    Determine the number of possible four-letter passwords.

    Determine the number of possible six-digit passwords.

    The company has 500,000 employees and needs a different password for each employee. State which type of password the company should choose. Explain your answer.

Index

Bisector, 150
  angle, 157
  perpendicular, 156–157
Boundary line, 231
Box-and-whisker plot, 403–404
  graphing calculator in constructing,
    404
Braces { }, 35, 39

C

Calculator. *See also* Graphing
    calculator
  in finding mean, median, and
    mode, 399–401
  in finding square root, 21
  in finding trigonometric functions,
    199
  in writing fractions as decimals,
    26
Cartesian coordinate system, 59, 206
Causation, interpreting, 411
Census, 392
Center of circle, 174
Central angle, 174
Certain event, probability of, 372
Checking solution, 75
Chord, 174
Circle(s), 174–175
  area of, 181
  center of, 174
  circumference of, 174, 177
  concentric, 174
  diameter of, 174
  radius of, 174
Circular cylinder
  right, 187
  surface area of, 186
Circumference, 174, 177
Closure, 35
Coefficients, 284
  correlation, 411
  fractional, 79
  numerical, 69
Collinear points, 146
Column method
  to find product of sum and
    difference, 110
  to find square of binomial, 110
  for multiplying polynomials, 108
Combinations, 381, 384–386
  probability problems involving,
    387–388
Common monomial factors, 272–273

Commutative property of addition or
    multiplication, 32, 100
Compass, 154
Complement, 373
  of set, 56
Complementary angles, 150
Complex fractions, simplifying,
    342
Composite number, 36
Compound inequalities, 90
Concentric circles, 174
Conditional equation, 74
Conditional probability, 373
Congruent angles, 148, 150
Congruent figures and angles,
    constructing, 155
Congruent line segment, 146
Consecutive angles, 169
Consecutive interior angles, 152
Constant, 69, 99
Constant function, 214
Constant of variation, 134
Constant ratio, 134
Construction
  of angle bisector, 157
  of box-and-whisker plot, 404
  of congruent figures and angles,
    155
  of perpendicular bisector, 156–157
  of scatter plot, 410
Continued ratio, 126
Contradiction, 74
Convex polygons, 160
Coordinates, 59, 206
Coplanar points, 146
Correlation, 411–412
  negative, 410
  no, 410
  positive, 410
Correlation coefficient, 411
Corresponding angles, 151
Cosine, 197, 198
Counting numbers, 20
Counting principle, 378–379
  with replacement, 378
  without replacement, 378
Cross multiplication, 129
Cross products, 129
Cube
  surface area of, 186
  volume of, 187
Cube roots, 285
Cubic equation, 297